AF653752

A Concise
TEXTBOOK OF BOTANY
(Cryptogams and Gymnosperms)

A Concise
TEXTBOOK OF BOTANY
(Cryptogams and Gymnosperms)

By

S.S. CHOUDHARY
University Professor & Head
Department of Botany
T.N.B. College, Bhagalpur-812007
T.M. Bhagalpur University, Bhagalpur-812007

Dr. (Mrs.) PRABHA CHOUDHARY
Reader in Botany
S.M. College, Bhagalpur-812001
T.M. Bhagalpur University, Bhagalpur-812001

CBS

CBS PUBLISHERS & DISTRIBUTORS
4596/1-A, 11 DARYAGANJ, NEW DELHI-110 002

ISBN 81-239-0494-0

First Edition 1997

© Author & Publishers

All rights reserved. No part of this publication may be reproduced, stored in a retrieval system, or transmitted in any form or by any means, electronic, mechanical, photocopying, recording or otherwise, without the prior permission of authors and publishers.

Published by:
Satish Kumar Jain
CBS Publishers and Distributors,
4596/1 A, 11 - Daryaganj, New Delhi-110002 (India).

Typeset at:
Phoenix Computer Centre, New Delhi-110002

Printed at:
Asia Printograph, Shahdara, Delhi-110 032

PREFACE

"*A Concise Textbook of Botany*" is among the few textbooks written on the various branches of cryptogams and gymnosperms together. Few other which are available, are prohibitive in cost as far as their accessibility to students is concerned. This book has been written from our experience of teaching undergraduate and post-graduate. classes for several decades. The vastness of the subject and continuing pace of development renders the choice of inclusions, a difficult one. We took all measures to include the syllabi of B.Sc. Part I (General and Honours) courses of Indian Universities. We sincerely hope that the chosen contents suffice the requirements of students.

This book is distinctly different from other such books because of the unique features as such:

1. It covers Algae, Fungi, Bryophyta and Pteridophyta under Cryptogams, Gymnosperms and some fossil plants have also been included in the text as these form a past of the syllabi of some universities at degree I stage.
2. A number of Indian examples and "practical" oriented concepts have been incorporated to suit Indian students in particular.
3. Separate chapters on Lichens, Schizomycetes and Viruses have been concisously written to facilitate learners.
4. Integration of various concepts, principles and ideas from different fields of classification have been mentioned.
5. Comprehensive treatment of widely scattered topics from various disciplines has been given.
6. Some general and special informations on the subject matters have been provided under appendix.
7. A comprehensive question bank has been inducted to provide ample materials for class discussion, home works, assignments and examinations.
8. The book contains 6 sections covering 35 chapters and 80 sub-chapters for maximum ease and flexibility in learning.

Finally, selected references for further readings, if desired, are also given.

As this edition comes out, revision begins for the next one. We, therefore, request the users of this book — both teachers and students to send us their suggestions for further improvement.

Authors

March, 1996

ACKNOWLEDGEMENTS

A project like this cannot be completed without help and advice from different sources. We have been fortunate in having the counsel of many scholars who have contributed comments and suggestions on the present text.

Our special thanks are due to Prof. K.S. Bilgrami, FNA; Ex-Head of the Post-graduate department of Botany; Emeritus scientist (C.S.I.R); Bhagalpur University and Prof. J.S. Dutta Munshi, FNA; Emeritus scientist (C.S.I.R), Ex-Head of Department , Bhagalpur University, for their valuable suggestions and encouragements for writing the book.

We also want to acknowledge the work on diagrams and illustrations of Shri N.K. Banerjee and manuscript typing of Shri Bansewan Singh. The talented staff of CBS Publishers & Distributors deserves praise for their role in shaping this book. Mr. V.K. Jain, CBS Publishers, offered excellent advice and co-operation for this edition.

We offer our thanks to all those people and others, whose efforts and contributions now escape our memory and who have been a constant source of inspiration and encouragement.

Finally, our thanks go to our Children, Praveen, Naveen and Rashmi, who have put up with us through the hectic times of book preparation. They provided the time, support and inspiration so necessary to complete a project of this nature.

Authors

June 1996

Contents

Preface v
Acknowledgements vi

SECTION I. ALGAE 1

1. Algae: General Features and Classification 3
2. Cyanophyta: Cyanophyceae or Myxophyceae 13
   - 2.1. *Gloeocapsa* 17
   - 2.2. *Oscillatoria* 18
   - 2.3. *Nostoc* 19
   - 2.4. *Scytonema* 20
   - 2.5. *Anabaena* 21
   - 2.6. *Rivularia* 22
3. Chlorophyta: Chlorophyceae 24
   - 3.1. *Chlamydomonas* 26
   - 3.2. *Volvox* 30
   - 3.3. *Cladophora* 32
   - 3.4. *Oedogonium* 35
   - 3.5. *Vaucheria* 39
   - 3.6. *Chara* 42
4. Chrysophyta: Xanthophyceae 47
   - 4.1. *Botrydium* 47
5. Bacillariophyceae 50
6. Phaeophyta: Phaeophyceae 54
   - 6.1. *Laminaria* 56
   - 6.2. *Fucus* 59
   - 6.3. *Ectocarpus* 63
   - 6.4. *Sargassum* 66
7. Rhodophyta: Rhodophyceae 69
   - 7.1. *Batrachospermum* 69
   - 7.2. *Polysiphonia* 73

SECTION II. FUNGI 77

1. General features and classification 79

2. Phycomycates 83
   2.1. *Synchytrium* 85
   2.2. *Saprolegnia* 87
   2.3. *Pythium* 91
   24. *Phytophthora* 94
   25. *Albugo (Cystopus)* 97

3. Ascomycetes 102
   3.1. *Asperqillus* (Eurotium) 105
   3.2. *Penicillium* 109
   3.3. *Erysiphe* 111
   3.4. *Claviceps* 114
   3.5. *Peziza* 116

4. Basidiomycetes 119
   4.1. *Ustilago* 121
   4.2. *Puccinia* 123

5. Deuteromycetes (Fungi imperfectii) 129
   5.1. *Alternaria* 130
   5.2. *Colletotrichum* 131

6. Lichens 133

7. Schizomycetes (Bacteria) 136

8. *Viruses* 143

SECTION III. BRYOPHYTA 149

1. General features and classification 151

2. Hepaticopsida 153
   2.1 *Riccia* 153
   2.2 *Marchantia* 159
   2.3 *Cyathodium* 165
   2.4 *Pellia* 167
   2.5 *Porella* 172

3. *Anthocerotopsida* 178
   3.1 *Anthoceros* 178
   3.2 *Notothylas* 183

4. *Bryopsida* 188
   4.1 *Sphagnum* 188
   4.2 *Pogonatum* 196
   4.3 *Funaria* 202

SECTION IV. PTERIODOPHYTA 207

1. General features and classification 209
2. Psilotopsida 214
   2.1. *Psilotum* 214
3. Lycopsida 219
   3.1. *Lycopdium* 219
   3.2. *Selaginella* 228
4. Sphenopsida 240
   4.1. *Equisetum* 240
5. Pteropsida 249
   5.1. *Ophioglossum* (Adder's tongue fern) 249
   5.2. *Marsilea* 255
   5.3. *Salvinia* 165
   5.4. *Azolla* 267

SECTION V. GYMNOSPERMS 271

1. General features and classification 273
2. *Cycas* 277
3. *Pinus and Taxus* 289
   3.1 *Pinus* 300
   3.2 *Taxus* 307
4. *Gnetum*

SECTION VI. FOSSILS AND PALAEOBOTANY 317

1. General features and classification 319
2. Fossil Pteridophytes : *Rhynia* 322
3. *Lepidodendron* 324
4. *Calamites* (Ancient Scouring Rushes) 327
5. Fossil Gymnosperms : *Bennettites* (*Cycadeoidea*) 333
6. *Lyginodendron* 338
7. *Williamsonia* 342
   Selected References 344
   Appendix 349
   Selected Questions 371
   Index 379

SECTION - I

ALGAE

1. General Features and Classification
2. Cyanophyceae / Myxophyceae
3. Chlorophyceae
4. Xanthophyceae
5. Bacillariophyceae
6. Phaeophyceae
7. Rhodophyceae

CHAPTER 1

ALGAE

GENERAL FEATURES AND CLASSIFICATION

Linnaeus (1754) used the word ''Cryptogamia'' for plants with concealed sex organs i.e., invisible sex organs from outside.

Stephan Endlicher (1836) introduced the term *Thallophyta* as the first division of the plant kingdom.

The division *Thallophyta* includes two sub-divisions (*i*) algae and (*ii*) fungi and have unicellular sex organs.

CHARACTERISTICS OF ALGAE

Algae are a group of chlorophyllous thalloid plants. Vegetative body is called thallus (Plural-thalli) and not differentiated into root, stem and leaves. The characteristics of the algae are as follows:

1. Plant body is thalloid
2. They are autophytes owing to the presence of chlorophyll as their primary photosynthetic pigment.
3. Majority of them are aquatic but semiaquatic and terrestrial forms are also found.
4. They possess unisexual sex organs without a jacket of sterile cells.
5. Embryo is not formed after fertilization.
6. They show distinct alternation of gametophytic and sporophytic generation.
7. Plant body is gametophyte.

OCCURRENCE

Algae are found in a variety of habitats such as aquatic, semiaquatic and terrestrial. Aquatic forms occur in running and stagnant, fresh and saline water of ponds, pools, river, ditches, lakes and sea. Algae may be attached to submerged substratum by means of organs of attachment called *holdfasts.* Free floating algae are known as *plankton*, while those that grow on the bottom of a body of water are called *benthos. Periphyton* forms may be *epizoic* (attached to the surface of animals), *epiphytic* (attached to the surface of plants), *epilethic* (attached to stones) and *epipelic* (living on surface of mud or sand). Some algae are terrestrial (*Vaucheria*) on the surface of the soil called *sapophytes* and some terrestrial forms may grow under the surface of the soil called *cryptophytes* (*Nostoc*). A few algae live at the interface of water and the atmosphere is called *neustonic.*

Some algae occur within the tissues of other plants and animals as *endophytes* or *endozoids* or as *symbionts* getting mutual benefits. Algae also grow on many animals and plants as *parasites* (e.g.

Cephaleuros virescens). Many cyanophycean forms like *Oscillatoria. Mastigoclades, Heterophormogonium* etc. are found in hot water springs (50°-70°C) and are called *thermophytes.*

PLANT BODY

The vegetative plant body of algae vary in size form microscopic (e.g. *Chlamydomonas*) to macroscopic (e.g. *Laminaria* — 30-50 meters). It may be unicellular or multicellular. Multicellular forms may be colonial (*Volvox*), filamentous (*Spirogyra*) siphonaceous (*Vaucheria*) or parenchymatous (*Ulva*).

Unicellular forms may be rhizopodial, flagellated, spiral, filamentous or non-motile. Similarly, colonial forms may be coenobial, palmelloid, dendroid or rhizopodial. Filamentous forms may also be simple, branched, heterotrichous and pseudoparenchymatous.

ALGAL CELL STRUCTURE

Algal cells may be prokaryotic and eukaryotic in nature. The prokaryotic cells are found in Cyanophyceae (blue-green algae) which lack membrane bound organelles including nucleus. The other groups of algae are eukaryotic. The eukaryotic cell has a cell wall composed of cellulose, pectin and mucilage. The cells are mostly uninucleate. Each cell has plastids. The chloroplastids contain pyrenoids which is proteinaceous body surrounded by starch plates. The reserve food material may be starch (in Chlorophyceae), cyanophycean starch (in Cyanophyceae), chrysolaminarin/diatomin (in Bacillariophyceae), laminarin, mannitol (in Phaeophyceae), floridean starch (in Rhodophyceae) in addition to paramylum, fats, oils, leucopin etc. in different algae.

FLAGELLA

Reproductive or vegetative motile cells are found in all classes of algae except Cyanophyceae and Rhodophyceae. Their locomotory organs are small, thread like protoplasmic appendages known as flagella. Flagella may be 1, 2 or 4 in number and are of following types:

1. **Pleuronematic or Tinsel flagella**: In this type the surface of the flagella is covered with fine filamentous structures known as *flimmers* or mastigonemes. This type of flagella has been further classified on the basis of arrangement of mastigonemes on the surface. They are: (i) Pantonemic (ii) Pantocrenemic and (iii) Stichonemic. In Pantonemic type mastigonemes are arranged in two opposite rows showing radial arrangement; in Pantocrenemic, flagellum has a terminal fibril and Stichonemic flagellum shows mastigonemes developed only on one side of the flagellum.

Transverse section of a flagellum shows nine peripheral and two central or axial fibrils. The peripheral fibrils are in pairs and the axial fibrils are singlet. All the fibrils are covered within a common envelop developed from the extension of the plasma membrane, whereas the two central fibrils have their own common covering.

2. **Acronematic or whiplash flagella**: This type of flagella have smooth surface.

Stigma or Eye spot: It is a pigmented spot in the reproductive cells and in the motile vegetative cells of algae. It is not found in Cyanophyceae, Bacillariophyceae and Rhodophyceae. It may be situated in the anterior, posterior or middle part of the cell. It directs the movement of swimming cells. It consists of osmophilic carotenoid lipid globules associated with a photoreceptive crystalline area near the axoneme of flagella. On the basis of location and structure, the eye spots were of following types:

Type A — Eye spot is not associated with flagella and it is situated in the Chloroplast as in Chlorophyceae.

Type B — Eye spot is located in the chloroplast and is associated with flagellum, e.g. Xanthophyceae, Phaeophyceae.

Type C — It is situated at anterior side of the cell and contains clusters of osmophilic granules, e.g. Euglenophyceae.

Type D — It is situated near the base of flagella and osmophilic granules are associated with membranous lamellae, as in Dinophyceae.

Type E — This type of eye spot is large, complex, made-up of lens, pigmented retinoid cup. They are found in some members of Dinophyceae.

PIGMENTS IN ALGAE

There are three types of pigments found in algae viz. (1) Chlorophylls, (2) Carotenoids and (3) Biloproteins. Prescott (1969) has mentioned 5 types of Chlorophylls (Chlorophyll a, b, c, d and e), 20 types of xanthophylls (Fucoxanthin found in Bacillariophyceae, Phaeophyceae; Peridivin found in Dinophyceae; Mycoxanthin and Mycoxanthophyll in Cyanophyceae; Taraxanthin in Rhodophyceae; Antheroxanthin in Euglenophyceae etc.), 5 types of carotenes (α, β, γ, Σ, and flavicene) and 7 types of phycobilins or billiproteins or biloproteins and they are present in the members of Cyanophyceae, Cryptophyceae and Rhodophyceae.

CHLOROPHYLL

Chlorophylls are of five types, viz. a, b, c, d and e. Chrlrophyll – a is present in all the groups of algae, Chlorophyll – b is present in Chlorophyceae and Euglenophyceae. Chlorophyll – c is found in Bacillariophyceae, Chrysophyceae and Phaeophyceae, Chlorophyll – d in some Rhodophycean members and Chlorophyll - e in some Xanthophyceae.

XANTHOPHYLL

It is found in the members of chlorophyceae and Phaeophyceae.

CAROTENES

There are five types of carotenes, viz., *a, b, g, d* and Flavicene. α - carotene is found in Chrlorophyceae, Rhodophyceae; β - carotene in all except Cryptophyceae, γ - carotene in Chlorophyceae, δ - carotene in Cyanophyceae, Bacillariophyceae, Cryptophyceae and Phaeophyceae and Flavicene is found in Cyanophyceae.

PHYCOBILINS

It is red pigment i.e. phycoerythrin and blue pigment i.e. phycocyanin which are found in Rhodophyceae and Cyanophyceae. Other organelles like Golgi bodies, Mitochondria, Endoplasmic reticulum etc. are found in almost all the groups of algae except Cyanophyceae.

REPRODUCTION

The reproduction in algae occurs by vegetative, asexual and sexual methods.

A. VEGETATIVE REPRODUCTION

It takes place in the following manners:

(*i*) **Cell division** — This method of propagation is found in unicellular algae like *Chlamydomonas*, diatom etc.

(*ii*) **Fragmentation** — This method is found in filamentous algae. The thallus breaks into fragments and each fragment develops into a new plant.

(*iii*) **Protonema** — It arises as adventitious branches formed on internodes of *Chara* or stolon of *Cladophora glomerata* which after detachment, develops into new plant.

(*iv*) **Tubers** — Some tuber like structures are formed on the rhizoids and lower node of *Chara* which on detachment forms a new plant.

(*v*) **Splitting of colonial forms** — Mature colony splits into two or many parts, each of them develops into new plant as in *Aphamothecene.*

B. ASEXUAL REPRODUCTION

It takes place by means of several types of motile and non-motile spores as follows:

(*i*) **Zoospores** — These are flagellate, naked structure with two (*Ectocarpus*), four (*Ulothrix*) or many (*Oedogonium*) flagella. They are formed in Zoosporangium, On liberation, it germinates into new plant.

(*ii*) **Aplanospores** — These are non-motile, without flagella, produced singly or more in aplanosporangium. It give rise new plants.

(*iii*) **Hypnospore** — It is thick walled aplanospore and germinates into new plant.

(*iv*) **Akinetes** — It is like aplanospre and non-motile. It develops additional wall layer and germinates into new plant.

(*v*) **Autospores** — These are resting spores, non-motle similar to parent cell in shape and structure as in Diatoms.

(*vi*) **Exospores** — These are thin walled, non-motile spores, cut off externally in some unicellular forms like *chamaesiphon.*

(*vii*) **Endospores** — These are formed internally within the cell. They are non-motile and thin walled. It germinates into new plant. e.g. *Dermocarpa* sp.

(*viii*) **Heterocyst** — These are thick walled, barrel shaped and pale yellow in appearance found in Cyanophyceae. The wall is differentiated into outer fibrous, middle homogenous and inner lamellar layer. Pores are present at one or both the ends. The pores are plugged with nodules (Polar granules). The heterocysts contain photosyntheic lamellae enclosing pigments. Any vegetative cell may become heterocyst. It is main site of nitrogen fixation. It helps in control of sporulation.

C. SEXUAL REPRODUCTION

Except Eustigmatophyceae and Cyanophyceae, all groups of algae reproduce sexually. During sexual reproduction, sex reproductive units i.e. gametes unite. On the basis of structure and physiological behaviour of uniting gametes, following types of sexual reproduction in algae are recognised.

(*i*) **Isogamy** — In this type two uniting gametes are morphologically and physiologically similar. They are usually motile and flagellate. e., *Ulothrix.*

(*ii*) **Anisogamy** — Here fusion takes place between morphologically and physiologically distinct gametes. The microgamete or male gamete is small where as macrogamete or female gamete is large e.g. *Chlamydomonas* spl. *Pandorina* etc.

(*iii*) **Oogamy** — In this type fusion take place between two gametes. Hence, it is a type of heterogamy or anisogamy. Here, male gametes are motile, active and flagellate where as female gametes are large, non-flagellate and passive and they are retained within the female gametangia or oogonia (Singular - oogonium). The male gametes or sperms or spermatozoids are produced in antheridium (Plural - antheridia) e.g. Rhodophyceae.

(*iv*) **Autogamy** — In this type two gametes of same mother cell fuse to form diploid nucleus e.g.

Diatoms.

(*v*) **Hologamy** — Here vegetative cells behave as gametes and they fuse to form a diploid zygote e.g. *Chlamydomonas.*

Classification

The basis of classification of algae are pigments, storage product of vegetative cells and morphology of reproductive cells.

F.E. Fritsch (1935) classified the algae into seven major divisions on the basis of the types of photosynthetic pigments and other features. They are:

Division 1. Chlorophyta : Photosynthetic pigments - chlorophyll a and b, carotens, xanthophylls, storage product - starch.
Class - 1. Chlorophyceae
Class - 2. Charophyceae

Division 2. Euglenophyta - Chlorophyll a and b, carotenes, xanthophylls are present, cell wall absent, paramylon is reserve food.
Class - 1. Englenophyceae.

Division 3. Chrysophyta (yellow green and golden algae) It has chlorophyll a and c, carotene, fucoxanthin, chrysolaminarin as reserve food.
Class - 1. Chrysophyceae
Class - 2. Xanthophyceae
Class - 3. Bacillariophyceae

Division 4. Pyrrophyta. Presence of chlorophyll a and c, carotene, xanthophylls, starch as reserve food etc.
Class - 1. Desmophyceae
Class - 2. Dinophyceae (Dinoflagellates).

Division 5. Phaeophyta - Chlorophyll a & c, carotenes, fucoxanthin and other xanthophyll present. Laminarin as storage food and alginic acid in cell wall present.
Class - 1. Isogeneratae
Class - 2. Hererogeneratae — Brown algae
Class - 3. Cyclosporae

Division 6. Rhodophyta - It has chlorophyll a & d, phycocyanin, phycoerythrin, carotene, xanthophylls and floridean starch as storage food. Cell wall contains cellulose, xylans, and galactans.
Class - 1. Rhodophyceae (Red Algae)

Division 7. Cyanophyta. It has phycocyanin and phycoerythrin in addition to chlorophyll. These pigments are not localised in plastids. Cyanophycean starch and protein granules are reserve food.

Several other phycolosists like G.M. Smith (1955), Christenson (1962), W.G. Prescott (1969), V.J. Chapman and D.J. Chapman (1973), Dodge (1974), Bold and Wynne (1978), Lee (1980), Parker (1982) etc. have classified algae in their own ways. Some of them are out-lined below. Chapman and Chapman (1973) have classified algae as follows: Algae has been divided into (A) Procaryotic and (B) Eucaryotic.

A. Procaryotic algae has only one division i.e. Cyanophyta having only one class Cyanophyceae.

B. Eucaryotic algae has 10 divisions as follows:

Division 1. Rhodophyta
Class 1 - Rhodophyceae

Division 2. Chlorophyta
Class 1 - Chlorophyceae
Class 2 - Prasinophyceae
Class 3 - Charophyceae
Division 3. Euglenophyta, Class - 1 Euglenophyceae
Division 4. Chloromonadophyta, Class - 1 Chloromonadophyceae
Division 5. Xanthophyta,
Class - 1 Xanthophyceae
Division 6. Bacillariophyta,
Class - 1 Bacillariophyceae
Division 7. Chrysophyta,
Class - 1 Chrysophyceae
Class - 2 Haptophyceae
Division 8. Phaeophyta,
Class - 1 Phaeophyceae
Division 9. Pyrrophyta,
Class - 1 Dinophyceae
Class - 2 Desmophyceae
Division 10. Cryptophyta,
Class - 1 Cryptophyceae

Parker's (1982) classification of algae is as follows:

Kingdom — Plantae
Division 1. Procaryota,
Class - 1 Cyanophycota
Class - 2 Prochlorophycota
Division 2. Eucaryota,
Class - 1 Rhodophyceae
Class - 2 Chrysophyceae
Class - 3 Prymnesiophyceae
Class - 4 Xanthophyceae
Class - 5 Eustigmatophyceae
Class - 6 Bacillariophyceae
Class - 7 Dinophyceae
Class - 8 Phaeophyceae
Class - 9 Raphidophyceae
Class - 10 Cryptophyceae
Class - 11 Euglenophyceae
Class - 12 Chrlorophyceae
Class - 13 Charophyceae
Class - 14 Prasinophyceae

Bold & Wynne (1978) have classified algae into 9 divisions as follows:

Division 1. *Cyanochloronta* (Blue-green algae): Plants of this division are fresh water, salt water and terrestrial in habitat. It contains chlorophyll a, c-phycocyanine, allophycocyanin, c-phycoerythrin, β-carotene and many xanthophylls. Reserved food occurs in the form of alanine and asparatic acid (cyanophycean granules) and glycogen like polyglucose.

It has further been divided into 3 Orders, viz., *Chroococcales, chaemosiphonales* and *Oscillatoriales.*

Division 2. *Chlorophycophyta* (Green algae): The habitat of plants belonging to this division is fresh water, saltwater and terrestrial. It contains chlorophyll a, b; carotenes (α, β and γ -) and xanthophylls. Reserved food is amylose, amylopectin (starch) and rarely oils. It has been divided into 15 Orders viz., *Volvocales, Tetrasporales, Chlorococcales, Chlorosarcinales, Chlorellales, Ulotrichales. Chaetophorales, Oedogoniales, Ulvales, Cladophorales, Acrosiphoniales, Caulerpales, Siphonocladales, Dasycladales* and *Zygnematales.*

Division 3. *Charophyta* (Stoneworts): It contain pigments similar to those of *Chlorophycophyta.* Reserved food is starch similar to land plants. They are fresh water and brackish water forms. It has a single class - *Charophyceae*, order *Charales.*

Division 4. *Euglenophyta*: They are fresh water, brackish water, salt water and terrestrial in habitat. Reserved foods are β, 1, 3-glucopyranoside (Paramylon) and oil. It contains chlorophyll a, b; β-carotene and xanthophylls. It has been divided into 3 orders viz. *Eutreptiales, Euglenales* and *Heteronematales.*

Division 5. *Phaeophycophyta* (Brown algae): They are characterised by the presence of chlorophyll a, c; β-carotene,fucoxanthin and xanthophylls. Reserved foods are mannitol and 1, 3-glucopyranoside (laminarin).

It has been divided into 13 orders viz., *Ectocarpales, Ralfsiales, Cordariales, Sporochnales, Desmarestiales, Cutleriales, Sphacelariales, Tilopteriales, Dictyotales, Dictyosiphonales, Scytosiphonales, Laminariales* and *Fucales.*

Division 6. *Crysophycophyta* (Diatoms, Golden and Yellow-green algae): They are adapted to fresh water, salt water and terrestrial habitat. It contains Chlorophyll a, c,; α, β and Σ carotenes and xanthophylls including fucoxanthin. Reserved foods are oil and chrysolaminarin. It has been divided into 6 classes and 14 orders viz.

Class - 1. *Chrysophyceae:* orders : *Ochromonadales, Phaeopthamniales, Chromulinales, Craspedomonadales, Dictyotales, Chrysophaerales* and *Thallochrysidales.*

Class - 2. *Prymnesiophyceae:* Order : *Isochrysidales* and *Prymnesiales.*

Class - 3. *Xanthophyceae :* Order : *Heterochloridales, Mischococcales, Tribonematales* and *Vaucheriales.*

Class - 4. *Eustigmatophyceae* : Without any Order.

Class - 5. *Chloromonadophyceae* : Order : *Chloromonadales*

Class - 6. *Bacillariophyceae* (Diatoms) : without any Order.

Division 7. *Pyrrhophycophyta* (Dinoflagellates): They are fresh water, brackish water and salt water in habitat.

Reserved foods are starch and oil. It contains chlorophyll a, c; β-carotene and xanthophylls.

It has been divided into 5 classes and 18 Orders viz.

Class - 1. *Ebriophyceae* : Order : *Ebriales*

Class - 2. *Ellobiophyceae* : Order : *Thalassomycetales*

Class - 3. *Syndiniophyceae* : Order : *Syndiniales*

Class - 4. *Dinophyceae* : Order : *Blastodiniales, Coccidiniales, Dinamoebales, Dinophysiales, Dinotrichales, Gloeodiniales, Gymnodiniales, Noctilucales, Peridiniales, Phytodiniales, Pyrocystales* and *Zooxanthellales.*

Class - 5. *Desmophyceae* : Orders : *Desmocapsales, Protocentrales* and *Protospidales.*

Table showing important features of various algal classes

Class	*Cell wall*	*Fllagella*	*Reserve food*	*Pigments*	*Reproduction*
1. *Cyanophyceae*	Murein & Peptidoglycon present	Absent	Phycocyanin granules with arginine & asparatic acid	Allophycocyanin C-Phycocyanin C-Phycoerythin β-Carotene chlorophyll	No Sexual reproduction.
2. *Rhodophyceae*	Polysaccharides, xylan	Absent	Floridean Starch	Chlorophyll a, Chlorophyll d, Phycocyanin & β Carotene	Specialised sexual Reproduction
3. *Chrysophyceae*	No cell wall, but membranous	Two unequal one smooth & other hairy	Chrysolaminarin	Chlorophyll a, Fucoxanthin, Diadinoxanthin	By the formation of statospores
4. *Prymnesiophyceae*	Covered with organic scales of one to many layers.	Two unequal and smooth	Crysolaminarin	Chlorophyll a, Chlorophyll C_1, C_2, β-carotene	Through hymenomonas & gloeothamion stage.
5. *Xanthophyceae*	Cellulose glucose and uronic acids	Two unequal hair & smooth	Glucan, fats & oils.	Chlorophyll a, Chlorophyll c, Carotene, Diatoxanthin Diadinoxanthin Heteroxanthin	Sexual, asexual & vegetative
6. *Eustigmatophyceae*	Naked cell wall	one and hairy	oils	Chlorophyll a Chlorophyll c, Violexanthin, Carotene	No sexual reproduction
7. *Bacillariophyceae*	Siliceous frustule	only male gametes with a hairy flagellum without a central microtubules	Chrysolaminarin, lipids	Chlorophyll a Chlorophyll c β-carotene, Fucoxanthin Diadinoxanthin Diatoxanthin	By Auxospore
8. *Dinophyceae*	Theca of cellulose body scales are rare	Usually two, one transverse, second longitudinal.	Starch	Chlorophyll a, Chlorophyll C_2, β-carotene, Peridinin Neoperidinin	After gametic union Plemozygote is formed
9. *Phaeophyceae*	Outer of fucoidan and alginic acid inner of cellulose	Usually two unequal, anterior longer & hairy, posterior smaller & smooth.	Mannitol, laminarin	Chlorophyll a Chlorophyll C_1, C_2, β-carotene Fucoxanthin	Oogamous

(*Contd.*)

10. *Raphidophyceae*	Naked	Usually two unequal		Chlorophyll a, Chlorophyll c Heteroxanthin Dinoxanthin Diadinoxanthin	
11. *Cryptophyceae*	Periplast	Two equal, hairy	Starch like substance	Chlorophyll d, Carotene Phycocyanin Phycoerythrin Diatoxanthin	Sexual reproduction not confirmed
12. *Prasinophyceae*	Naked usually scaly	One/two unequal or four equal	Mannitol, starch	Chlorophyll a, b β—carotene, Siphonoxanthin Siphonein	
13. Charophyceae	Cellulose and calcified	Only male gamete has two unequal flagella	Starch —1, 4 glucan	Chlorophyll a, b β— carotene, Xanthophylls	Oogamous
14. Chlorophyceae	Cellulose glycosides xylans mannans hydroxyproline some naked or calcified	Two, smooth sometimes four	Amylose amylopectin	Chlorophyll a, b, β—carotene, Lutein, Siphonein, Siphonoxanthin	Oogamous
15. Euglenophyceae	Proteinaceous pellicle	Usually two, unequal	paramylon, B-1, 3 glucan	Chlorophyll a, b β-carotene, Neoxanthin Astaxanthin, Antheraxanthin, Diadinoxanthin	Sexual reproduction not confirmed

Division 8. *Cryptophycophyta* : They are fresh water and salt water in habitat. Starch is the reserved food and the pigments are Chlorophyll a, c, α, β & Σ carotenes, alloxanthin, crocoxanthin, monadoxanthin and phycobilins. There is neither class nor order in this division.

Division 9. *Rhodophycophyta* (Red algae) : Majority of them are salt water and brackish water in habitat. Fresh water forms are a few. It contains chlorophyll a, d; phycocyanin r, c; allophycocyanin, r, b; phycoerythrin; α – β carotenes and many xanthophylls. Glycogen like floridean starch is the reserved food. It has a single class *Rhodophyceae* which has been divided into two sub classes, *Bangiophycidae* and *Florideophycidae*. The former has 4 orders: *Porphyridiales, Goniotrichales, Compsopogonales* and *Bangiales.* Sub class Florideophycidae has 5 orders : *Nemalionales, Cryptonemiales, Gigartinales, Rhodomeniales* and *Ceramiales.*

Parker (1982), South & Whittick (1987) have recognised the inclusion of **Cyanobacteria**, the blue-green algae (Cyanophycota) and Prochlorophycota - a term proposed by Lewin (1977), under the division *Procaryota* of the *Plantae* kingdom. The other division *Eucaryota* was divided into phyla and classes as follows:

1. Phyllum *Rhodophycota* : It includes only one class Rhodophyceae.
2. Phyllum *Chromophycota* : It has been divided into 9 classes, viz. (1) Chrysophyceae, (2) Prymnesiophyceae, (3) Xanthophyceae, (4) Eustigmatophyceae (5) Bacillariophyceae (6) Dinophyceae (7) Phaeophyceae (8) Raphidophyceae and (9) Cryptophyceae.
3. Phyllum *Euglenophycota* : It has only one class Euglenophyceae.
4. Phyllum *Chlorophycota* : It has been classified into 3 classes as such : (1) Chlorophyceae (2) Charophyceae and (3) Prasinophyceae.

However, Fritsch (1935) Classification has been followed in this text.

Diagnostic characters of different algal classes are given on next pages in a tabular form.

CHAPTER 2

CYANOPHYTA—CYANOPHYCEAE OR MYXOPHYCEAE

The members of Cyanophyceae show the following features —

1. Prokaryotic cellular organisation.
2. Plant body may be unicellular, colonial, multicellular filamentous or non-filamentous types.
3. Presence of phycocyanin (blue pigment), phycoerythrin (red pigment) myxoxanthin, myxoxanthophyll and chlorophyll-a are distributed in chromoplasm. Hence, its members are commonly known as blue-green algae.
4. Absence of nuclear membrane.
5. Genetic material DNA/RNA are present in the centroplasm.
6. Absence of endoplasmic reticulum, golgi bodies, mitochondria etc.
7. Presence of mucilaginous sheath around cell wall.
8. Cyanophycean starch and cyanophycin are present as reserve food materials.
9. Absence of motile reproductive organs.
10. Complete absence of sexual reproduction.
11. It reproduce by vegetative and asexual methods.

CLASSIFICATION

Class Myxophyceae has been divided into five orders by Fritsch (1942) and others. They are —

Orders 1. Chroococcales
2. Chamaesiphonales
3. Pleurocapsales
4. Nostocales
5. Stigonematales

However, Smith (1955) has classified the Class Myxophyceae into three orders as such —

Order 1. Chroococcales
2. Chamaesiphonales
3. Oscillatoriales or Hormogoniales.

GENERAL ACCOUNT OF CYANOPHYCEAE

The members of this class represent the primitive and simplest form of algae so far their morphological features and mode of reproduction are concerned. It is presumed that higher forms of algae have originated from this Cyanophycean group.

Occurrence

They are cosmopolitan in distribution. According to Smith (1955) there are about 150 genera and 1500 species in this class occurring in aquatic, terrestrial and aerial habitats. Some are as endophytes e.g. *Nostoc, Anabaena*, as epiphytes e.g. *chamaesiphon* and a few are marine also.

Plant body

The vegetative plant body may be unicellular (*Chroococcus, Gloeocapsa*), filamentous (*Oscillatoria, Rivularia*) or non-filamentous colonial form (*Polycystis*). Filamentous forms may be branched (*Nostocopsis*) or unbranched (*Nostoc, Anabaena*). A single row of cells in filament is known as *trichome* and a trichome with gelatinous sheath is called a filament.

Cell structure — A prokaryotic cell of blue green algae has a cell wall enclosing protoplast. The cell wall has an outer and an inner layer. The outer layer is covered by a gelatinous sheath, made up of cellulose fibrils. The inner layer contains glucosamine and muramic acid. This inner layer may be further divided into two layers. Plasma membrane is present beneath the cell wall. It contains two electron opaque layers separated by a translucent layer. The protoplast is distinguished into (i) central colourless region — called *centroplasm* and (ii) peripheral coloured region — known as *chromoplasm*.

The *chromoplasm* contains pigments, oil droplets, reserve food materials, lipids, granules, polyhedral bodies, 70S ribosomes etc. The chromoplasmic region is traversed by many lamellae. A lamella has two unit membranes, 70-80 Å thick. Several gas pockets or pseudovacuoles are distributed in the protoplast. These pseudovacuoles act as light screens against intense light and provide greater buoyancy in planktonic species. The colour of the pigmented region of the protoplast is directly complementary to the colour quality and light waves in which the plant grows. This type of adaptation is known as complementary chromatic adaptation or Gaidukov phenomenon after its discovery by Gaidukov (1902, 1903).

The central region i.e. centroplasm is considered as incipient nucleus or nucleoplasm. It contains several fine randomly organised fibrils with chromatin granules. this chromatin consists of DNA which is not associated with histones or protamines and therefore no chromosome like structure is present. Chromatin granules also contain RNA (Fig. 1).

MOVEMENT

Some filamentous forms like *Oscillatoria, Spirulina* etc. show spontaneous movement with a forward and backward gliding or creeping movement accompanied by rotation either in direction of clockwise or anticlockwise.

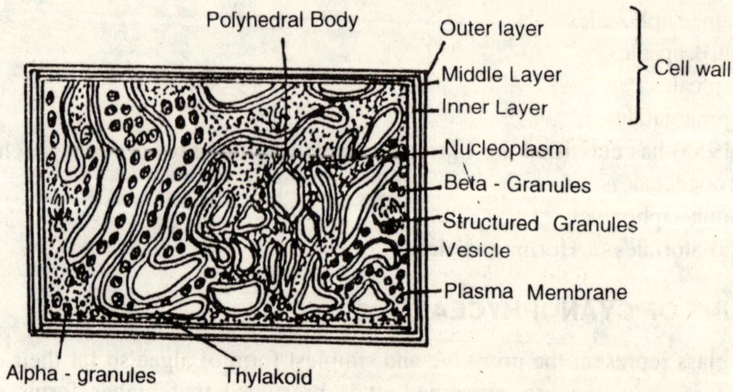

Fig. 1. Diaggramatic sketch of a Cyanophycean cell.

NUTRITION

Majority of its members are autophytes. They synthesize their own food materials like glycogen and granular proteinaceous substance known as cyanophycin. A special type of amino acid — i.e. diaminopimelic acid is also present. Many cyanophycean genera have been shown to fix atmospheric nitrogen. Heterocyst is the site for nitrogen fixation.

REPRODUCTION

There is no sexual reproduction in Cyanophyceae. It reproduces only by (i) vegetative and (ii) asexual methods.

(i) **Vegetative reproduction** — It occurs by fragmentation and simple cell division.

Fragmentation — In the filamentous forms, filaments break into two or more smaller parts, each part is called as hormogonium. Each hormogonium develops into a new filament by simple cell division. The filament breaks into hormogonium at certain points which is made up of thick walled cells known as *heterocysts* as in *Nostoc* or dead concave cells or discs of gelatinous substance known as separation disc, as in *Oscillatoria.*

Cell division — In this method a ring like outgrowth appears in the middle of the unicellular forms. It gradually deepens and finally divides the cell into two daughter cells within a common gelatinous sheath.

(ii) **Asexual reproduction** — It occurs by the formation of following non-motile spores.

1. *Hormospores* — It is multicellular spore like bodies developing from the tip of the hormogonium. It gives rise to new filament on germination.
2. *Akinetes* — In some filamentous forms, certain cells of the filament enlarge and secrete thick walls around itself and behave as reproductive cell called akinetes. These spores may be in chain or singly.
3. *Exospore* — In some epiphytic forms, the delicate cell wall ruptures and protoplast cuts off ex ternally into spore like bodies called exospores.
4. *Endospore* — In some unicellular forms, protoplast divides to form small, spherical, thin walled spores called endospores.
5. *Nannocysts* — It occurs in some filamentous types, much smaller abnormal cells are produced due to successive cell divisions - called *nannocysts.*
6. *Heterocysts* — Almost all filamentous forms, except members of oscillatoriaceae family, produce heterocysts. It looks as empty and double layered due to secretion and formation of another wall internal to the original cell wall. It may be terminal, or basal or intercalary in position. It has polar pores closed by polar nodules.

SEXUALITY

True sexuality represented by syngamy and meiosis is not found in Cyanophyceae. Kumar (1962), Singh & Sinha (1965) etc. have observed genetic recombination in *Anacystis nidulans* and others.

HETEROCYSTS AND NITROGEN FIXATION

Heterocysts are found in filamentous blue-green algae except in the members of oscillatoriaceae. These are cells having thick walls and may be intercalary or terminal in position. They may occur singly or in chains or sometimes in pair. Generally heterocysts are formed from newly divided vegetative cells by dissolution of the photosynthetic lamellae and storage granules.

Heterocyst has an envelop and photosynthetic lamellae alongwith cytoplasmic inclusions. Cell wall has three layers namely; outer, middle and inner. The outer layer is fibrous, middle is homogenous and inner wall is lamellated. There are one or two pores in the wall. Chemically, the envelops possess carbohydrates, lipid (glycolipid and acyl lipid) and amino compounds. It appears yellowish due to presence of carotenes. P700 form of chlorophyll pigments are present. Ribosomes and DNA fragments are present in the protoplasm of heterocyst. Heterocysts are unable to fix carbon dioxide, and it is a point from where filament breaks. According to Fogg (1951) it has relationship with nitrogen metabolism. Heterocyst induces the formation of akinetes and it has been termed as ''Botanical enigma'' by Fritsch (1951).

Presence of nitrogenase enzyme in heterocysts indicates that it is the sites of nitrogen fixation. Species like *Gloeocapsa* (unicellular) and *Plectonema boryanum* (filamentous) fix nitrogen in microaerobic environments and not in air. Nitrogen fixation ability is also found in blue green algae besides bacteria. Nitrogen fixation occurs in heterocysts under aerobic condition. The vegetative cells also fix nitrogen but under anaerobic situation.

The nitrogenase enzyme reduces nitrogen gas into (NH_3) ammonia. Ammonia is converted into glutamine under the influence of enzyme glutamine synthetase (GS) present in the heterocyst. The product glutamine is transported to the adjacent vegetative cell. Here glutamine is converted into glutamate. Glutamine and glutamate form other amino acids by various transamination processes as shown in the following scheme. Thus, the fixed nitrogen may be assimilated by blue green algae themselves. After liberation of soluble nitrogenous compounds from the living cells it is converted into ammonia. The ammonia is then converted into nitrate by nitrifying bacteria present in the soil. The blue green algae play an important role in increasing the fertility of rice fields by more than 20%.

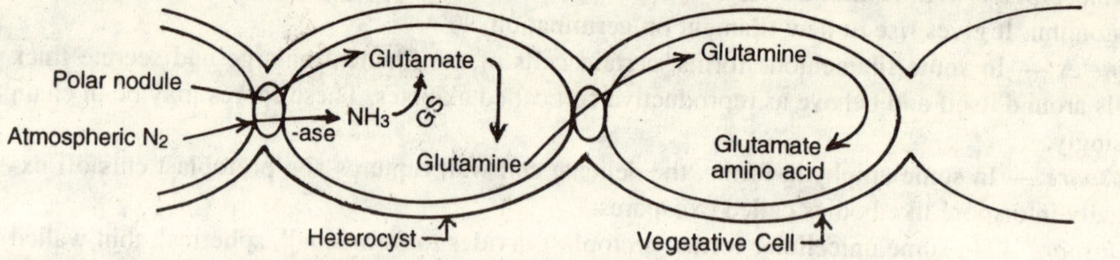

Schematic representation of Nitrogen fixation in heterocyst.

ECONOMIC IMPORTANCE

All the members of the family Cyanophyceae are capable of fixing atmospheric nitrogen there by increasing the soil fertility. It also serves as food for fish and other aquatic organisms. They act as primary colonisers in the establishments of soil flora.

It also cause foul odour in water reservoirs. Sometimes they form a dense growth on the surface of the pools called as ''Water bloom''. It has a role in the deposition of calcium carbonate.

RELATIONSHIP

The members of Cyanophyceae are primitive and simplest type of algae in having incipient (membraneless) nucleus, absence of plastids and in the mode of propagation. It resembles with red algae (Rhodophyceae) in the sense that both of them lack flagellated, motile reproductive spores and they have pit connections. Cytologically, Cyanophyceae are more primitive than any other organisms except bacteria. It resembles with bacteria also in absence of organised nucleus and method of reproduction. They also have similarities in cell wall composition. It is presumed that in course of evolution higher forms of algae originated from Cyanophyceae.

PHYLOGENY AND RELATIONSHIP OF CYANOPHYCEAE

The opponents of cyanophycean origin of Red algae (Rhodophyceae) refuse it on the ground that occurrence of sexual reproduction and presence of plastids (Chromatophore) in Red algae bifurcates the Cyanophyceae (blue-green algae) from Rhodophyceae.

However, Cyanophyceae shows great resemblances with bacteria as follows —

1. Both are equally simple and primitive.
2. Both have one celled members.
3. Presence of sheath and capsule of similar components.
4. Absence of true nucleus and plastids.
5. Both withstand extreme desication.
6. Both are saprophytes/parasites in absence of light.
7. Presence of diaminopimelic acid in cell wall.
8. Presence of DNA rich chromatin body.
9. Both fix atmospheric nitrogen
10. Cell divisions are of similar type.
11. Reproduction is by fission.
12. Both form resting cells.
13. Absence of motile spores in both of them.
14. Lack of sexual reproduction in both of them.

2.1 GLOEOCAPSA

It belongs to	Division	—	Cyanophyta
	Class	—	Cyanophyceae
	Order	—	Chroococcales
	Family	—	Chroococcaceae
	Genus	—	Gloeocapsa

HABITAT

It is found on damp rocks, moist flower pots, moist walls forming blue, violet, reddish, yellowish brown or olive coloured masses of mucilage.

SALIENT FEATURES

1. The plant body is unicellular surrounded by mucilaginous sheath.
2. They occur as single cell or group of cells in colony within mucillaginous sheath.
3. It reproduces by fission.

PLANT BODY

It consists of a single cell, spherical or oval in shape and surrounded by homogenous hyaline or coloured mucilaginous layers or stratified sheath. Each cell has an outer cell wall enclosing granular protoplast. The protoplast has centroplasm and chromoplasm. The contents of cell are of typical cyanophycean type.

MOVEMENT

It does not show any movement.

REPRODUCTION

It reproduces by simple cell division resulting in 2 - 4 cells. The divided cells secrete its own mucilaginous sheath. Several daughter cells may be together forming a colony, which are covered by mucilaginous substance. The common Indian species are *G. montana, G. atrata, G. geletinosa* etc. (Fig. 2).

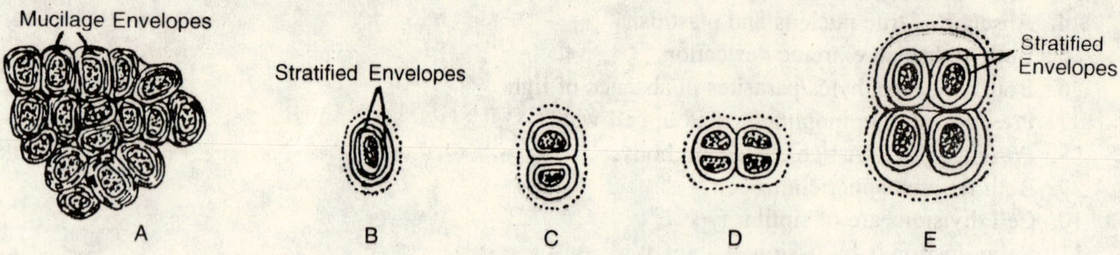

Fig. 2. A—*Gloeocapsa* sp., B–E staes in cell division.

2.2 OSCILLATORIA

It belongs to

Division	—	Cyanophyta
Class	—	Cyanophyceae
Order	—	Nostocales
Family	—	Oscillatoriaceae
Genus	—	*Oscillatoria*

SALIENT FEATURES

1. Plant body is filamentous and unbranched
2. Filaments or trichomes are made up of many simple and undifferentiated cells.
3. Generally cells are broader.
4. Trichomes are surrounded by mucilaginous substances.
5. It shows oscillating, gliding and bending movement.
6. It reproduces by fragmentation method only.

OCCURRENCE

The genus *Oscillatoria* is represented by more than 100 species found in streams, pools, drains and other polluted waters. They are free floating forms. Marine forms are also found. Some of the common Indian species are *O. nigra*, *O. chlorina*, *O. formosa*, *O. chilkensis* etc.

VEGETATIVE BODY

The plant is haploid and unbranched, trichome with mucilaginous sheath or without sheath. It shows various types of movement. The trichome has numerous simple cells whose breadth is more than the length. The apical cell is round and sometimes covered with a thick hood known as calyptra. The cells are a typical cynophycean type i.e. prokaryotic.

REPRODUCTION

They are the product of breaking up of the trichomes at separation disc. These hormogonia first move for sometime, then come to rest and finally divide to form a new species. There is no formation of resting spore or heterocyst in *Oscillatoria* (Fig. 3, 4).

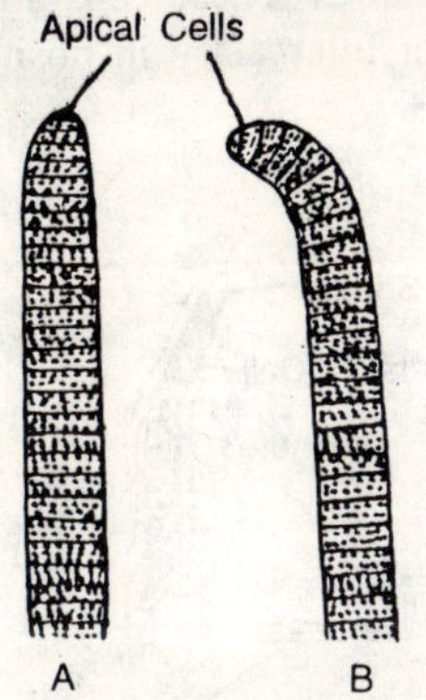

Fig. 3. *Oscillatoria* sp.

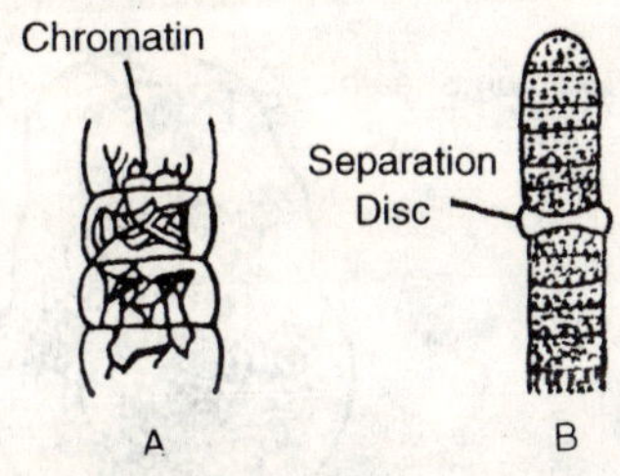

Fig. 4. A– *Oscillatoria* filament with new cells, B– formation of *hormogonium*.

2.3 NOSTOC

It belongs to			
	Division	—	Cyanophyta
	Class	—	Cyanophyceae or Myxophyceae
	Order	—	Nostocales
	Family	—	Nostocaceae
	Genus	—	*Nostoc*

The genus *Nostoc* is represented by more than 30 species. The most common species found in India are *N. muscorus*, *N. linkia* etc.

SALIENT FEATURES

1. Plant body is filamentous, unbranched and moniliform type.
2. Trichome is covered with gelatinous sheath and adjacent sheaths of other trichomes fuse together forming a common gelatinous matrix of *Nostoc* colony.
3. Cells are arrnaged like beads on a string.
4. Heterocysts are present, may be terminal or intercalary in position.
5. It reproduces by hormogonia and akinetes.

HABITAT

It is freshwater or terrestrial in habitat. Some terrestrial species grow on moist soils intermingles with mosses, while others occur as endophytes within the thallus of *Anthoceros*, roots of *Cycas*. Fresh water forms may be attached with substratum or may remain as free floating in the ponds forming bluish–green scum.

PLANT BODY

It is filamentous, unbranched and aggregated together within mucilage–envelop which appear ball–like gelatinous colony or *Nostoc* balls. The size of the *Nostoc* ball may be as big as hens egg and generally its size are like pin head. Each filament is made up of a row of oval rounded cells. In the filament some cells are larger, rounded and thick walled with two or one polar nodules. These cells are heterocysts. Akinetes are also formed in the filament which may be terminal or intercalary in position. The cell structure is a typical cyanophycean type (Fig. 5).

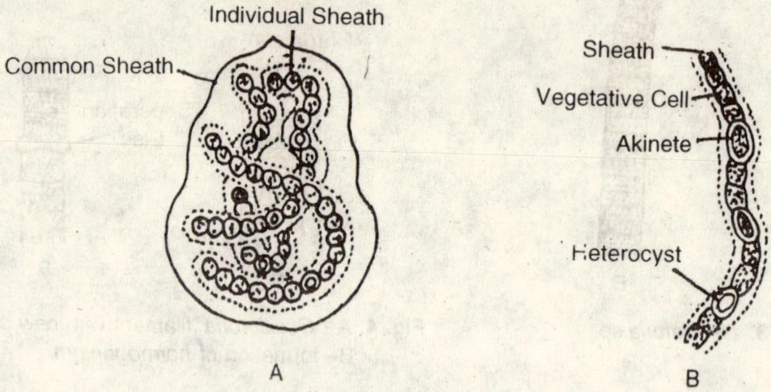

Fig. 5. A– *Nostoc* filaments in a ball, B–A filament of *Nostoc.*

REPRODUCTION

It takes place by fragmentation of the filament as a result of which hormogonia are formed. Each hormogone germinates into new filament. Filament breaks from heterocyst point. Asexaual reproduction occurs by akinetes which are oblong and spherical and larger than the vegetative cells. Akinete develops into a new filament under favourable condition. Sometimes heterocysts may act as spores which germinate to give new plants.

2.4 SCYTONEMA

It belongs to	Division	—	Cyanophyta
	Class	—	Cyanophyceae
	Order	—	Nostocales
	Family	—	Scytonemataceae
	Genus	—	*Scytonema*

The genus *Scytonema* are represented by more than 40 species and they may be aquatic (fresh and salt water), terrestrial or sub–aerial. It occurs on damp soil, wet rocks, grasslawns, tree barks etc. The most common Indian species are *S. iyengari*, *S. pascheri*, *S. amplum* etc.

SALIENT FEATURES

1. The plant body is filamentous and branched.
2. The trichome is covered with thick and stratified sheath.
3. Heterocysts are present.
4. The length and breadth of the cells are alike.
5. It reproduces by hormogonia.

PLANT BODY

The filamentous plant body often interwine to form a felty mass. Each filament has distinct base and apex. The branching is false which are formed laterally by the degeneration of an intercalary cell in between the two heterocysts. Each heterocyst is with two polar nodules. The length and breadth of the cells of the trichome are similar (Fig. 6).

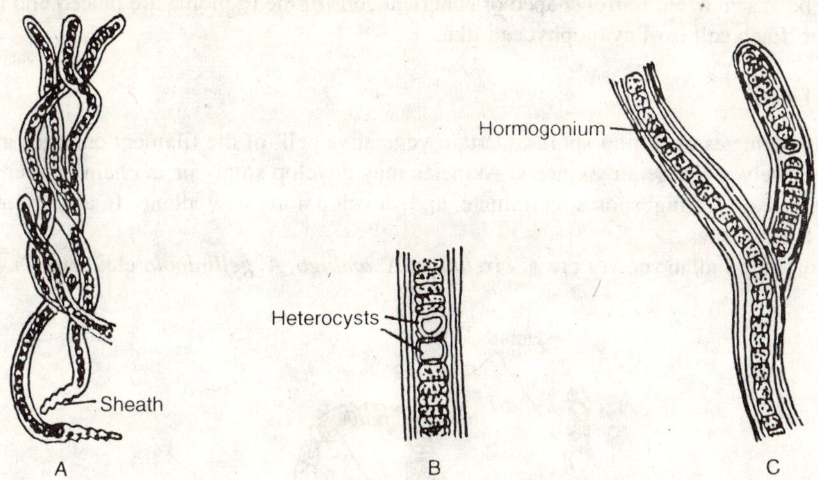

Fig. 6. A–filaments of *Scytonema*, B–Portion of trichome showing heterocysts, C–false branching.

REPRODUCTION

It reproduces by hormogonia and rarely by akinetes.

2.5 ANABAENA

It belongs to

Division	—	Cyanophyta
Class	—	Cyanophyceae
Order	—	Nostocales
Family	—	Nostocaceae
Genus	—	*Anabaena*

SALIENT FEATURES

1. Plant body is filamentous with or without mucilaginous sheath i.e. trichome is present.
2. Cells in the trichome are spherical or barrel shaped.
3. It reproduces by hormogonia.
4. Heterocysts are also found in the filament.

OCCURRENCE

They are freshwater forms found in pools, ponds. Some species are endophytes, they may be present in the coralloid root of *Cycas*, thallus of *Anthoceros* or leaves of *Azolla*.

PLANT BODY

The plant body is branched or falsely branched filamentous which may be covered by a hyaline sheath or sheath may be absent even. Barrel shaped or spherical cells of the trichome are placed end to end, one above the other. Each cell is of cyanophycean like.

REPRODUCTION

It reproduces by akinetes or resting spores. Certain vegetative cell of the filament enlarges and secretes wall around themselves. These are akinetes. Akinetes may develop singly or in chain. Under favourable condition akinetes or resting spores germinate and develop into new plant. It also reproduces by heterocysts or hormogones.

The most common Indian species are *A. circinalis*, *A. ambigo*, *A. geltinicola* etc. (Fig. 7).

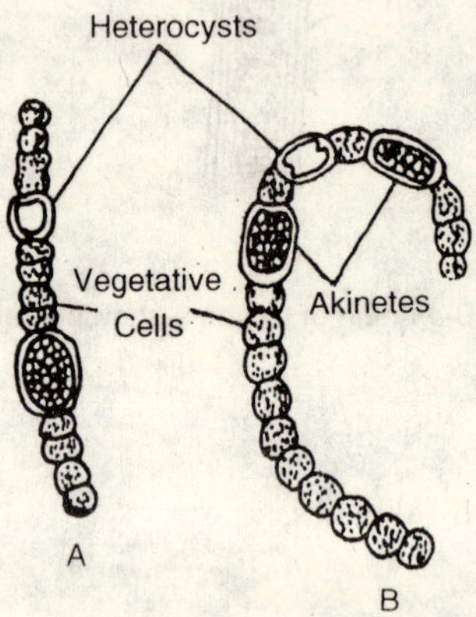

Fig. 7. A and B parts of the filaments of *Anabaena* sp. showing akinetes, heterocysts and vegetative cells.

2.6 RIVULARIA

It belongs to	Division	—	Cyanophyta
	Class	—	Cyanophyceae
	Order	—	Rivulariales
	Family	—	Rivulariaceae
	Genus	—	*Rivularia*

SALIENT FEATURES

1. It is found in fresh water or soil.
2. Marine form is also present e.g. *Rivularia bullata*.
3. They occur either in free floating condition or attached to substratum in sunny ponds, lakes etc.
4. They exhibit colonial form. The colony is of various shape and size and macroscopic.

5. Colony is of irregular shape, lobed and appear as gelatinous mass.
6. They are yellowish brown in colour.

PLANT BODY

Colony contains many trichomes which are unbranched or sometimes show false branching. The trichomes are whiplike in morphology. Each trichome is broad at the base and gradually tapers forming a long, colourless, multicellular long hair at its distal end. Meristematic zone is present below the hair. Trichome is covered with mucilaginous sheath forming filament. Cells of the trichome are barrel shaped, but hair zone is long and cylindrical.

REPRODUCTION

It occurs by hormogonia and heterocysts. Heterocyst is basal, single, spherical with a single pore. No sexual reproduction takes place (Fig. 8).

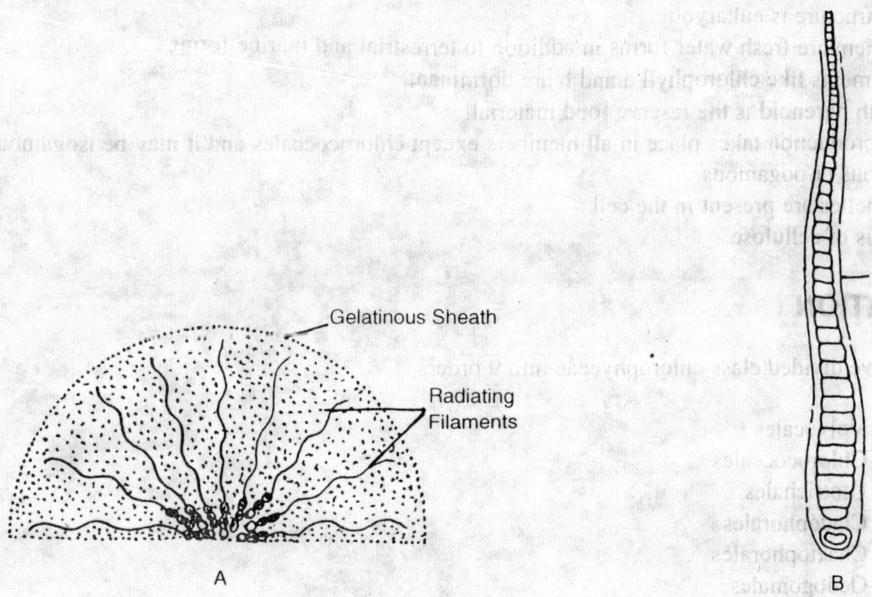

Fig. 8. *Ruvularia* sp. A– view of the colony, B– A filament,

CHAPTER 3

CHLOROPHYTA—CHLOROPHYCEA

The division chlorophyta has one class chlorophyceae. General accounts of the class chlorophyceae are as such —

1. It shows a wide range of thallus ranging from unicellular to multicellular heterotrichous habits.
2. The cell structure is eukaryotic.
3. Most of them are fresh water forms in addition to terrestrial and marine forms.
4. Green pigments like chlorophyll a and b are dorminant.
5. Starch with pyrenoid is the reserve food material.
6. Sexual reproduction takes place in all members except chlorococcales and it may be isogamous, anisogamous or oogamous.
7. Cell organelles are present in the cell.
8. Cell wall is of cellulose.

CLASSIFICATION

Fritsch (1935) have divided class chlorophyceae into 9 orders.

Order 1. Volvocales
2. Chlorococcales
3. Utotrichales
4. Cladophorales
5. Chaetophorales
6. Oedogoniales
7. Conjugales
8. Siphonales
9. Charales

Smith (1955) has divided chlorphyta into 2 classes viz. (1) Chlorophyceae and (2) Charophyceae. Class charophyceae has only one order charales. Class chlorophyceae has 12 orders as follows —

Order 1. Volvovales
2. Tetraporales
3. Ulotrichales
4. Ulvales
5. Cladophorales
6. Schizogonials
7. Siphonales

8. Siphonocladales
9. Oedogoniales
10. Zygnematales
11. Chlorococcales and
12. Dasycladales.

McClean and Cook (1956) placed the order charales in a separate division Charophyta. He divided class Chlorophyceae into 8 orders.

viz. order 1. Volvocales
2. Chaetophorales
3. Chlorococcales
4. Siphonales
5. Ulotrichales
6. Conjugales
7. Oedogoniales and
8. Siphonocladiales.

RANGE OF THALLUS STRUCTURE

A wide range of thallus organisations are found in the members of chlorophyceae as follows :

MOTILE FORMS

The primitive form of chlorophyceae like *Chlamydomonas* is unicellular and motile. In other members like *Volvox, Pandorina* etc. Several unicellular motile cells assemble within an envelop to form coenobium or colonial form which behave as a single unit.

NON–MOTILE COCCOID FORMS

Such member may be unicellular like *chlorella* or multicellular coenobial form like *Hydrodictyon*.

NON–MOTILE PALMELLATE FORMS

In this type of thallus structure, cells are loosely assembled embedded in a common gelatinous matrix secreted by the cells of the colony viz., *Tetraspora.*

FILAMENTOUS FORMS

In higher forms of Chlorophyceae, the plant body is filamentous and unbranched as in *Utothrix* or it may be branched filamentous e.g. *Cladophora*.

HETEROTRICHOUS FORM

In this type of thallus organisation plant body consists of creeping prostrate system and projecting erect system e.g. *Coleochaete.*

THALLOID FORM

This type develops from division of cells in more than one plane forming parenchymatous thalloid body as in *Ulva.*

SIPHONACEOUS FORM

It results from enlargement of the cells accompanied by nuclear divisions without septa formation in between them viz. *Vaucheria, Caulerpa* etc.

COMPLEX FORM

This type of thallus is shown by *Chara* in which plant body is differentiated unto corticated branched axis with rhizoids. Axis has nodes and internodes bearing leaves (Laterals) and complex sex organs, globule and nucule.

3.1 CHLAMYDOMONAS

It belongs to	Class	—	Chlorophyceae
	Order	—	Volvocales
	Family	—	Chlamydomonaceae
	Genus	—	*Chlamydomonas*

HABITAT AND HABIT

The genus *Chlamydomonas* has more than 500 species found in fresh water like ponds, pools, lakes and tanks rich in nitrogenous substance. Some species are terrestrial also occuring on moist soil.

Chlamydomonas is unicellular fresh water motile and microscopic alga. The common Indian species are *C. iyengari, C. engametose, C. granistigma* etc.

PLANT BODY

Unicellular plant is biflagellate, oval or pear shaped measuring 30 x 20 microns in length and breadth. The anterior end is papillate and posterior end is broader, but it is reversed in *C. candata*. The cell has a wall of cellulose. Within the cell. protoplasm is encircled by semipermeable plasma membrance. Each cell has a cup shaped chloroplast situated in the posterior broader part of the cell. One or two pyrenoids are found in the chloroplast. Pyrenoid has a protein core surrounded by starch. The cell has a nucleus and two contractile vacuoles responsible for osmoregulation activity of the cell. Near anterior end of the cell there is an eye spot or stigma. It is photoreceptive organ made up of colourless biconvex photosensitive lens and a curved pigmented plate. The whiplash type (smooth surfaced) flagella are situated near the papillate part of the cell. There is a blepharoplast — a granular structure at the base of flagella, a rhizoplast — soft & thin thread connecting bleoharoplast and centrosome of the nucleus and a paradesmose — transverse filament connecting the blepharoplast in the neuromotar apparatus associated with flagella. According to Roberts *et al* (1972) and Hill *et al* (1973) cell wall is multilayered made up pf cellulose fibrills. Plasma membrane is of lipoprotein and many ribosomes, mitochondria and endoplasmic reticulum are in the cytoplasm (Fig. 9).

NUTRITION

As *Chlamydomonas* possess pigments, it synthesises its own food material with the help of water and carbon dioxide in presence of sunlight.

REPRODUCTION

There are two types of reproduction in *Chlamydomonas* and these are (i) asexual and (ii) sexual.

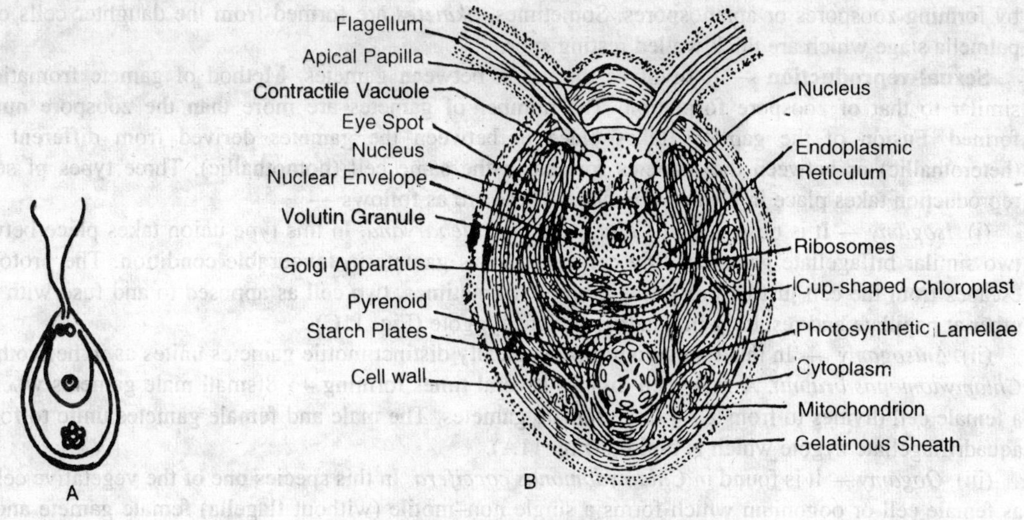

Fig. 9. A—Chlamydomonas sp. B—Enlarged view of the same.

Asexual Reproduction — It Takes Place By Following types of spores.

By zoospores — The protoplast of the vegetative cell divides and redivides to form 2 - 8 or more daughter protoplast during favourable condition. The flagella of the parent cell is withdrawn. Each part of the protoplast becomes associated with one of the mitotically divided nucleus and forms a swarmer identical to the parent cell. However, they are smaller in size. These new cells i.e. zoospores are liberated from the parent cell after dissolution of the parent cell wall. These swarmers behave as new *Chlamydomonas* plant (Fig. 10).

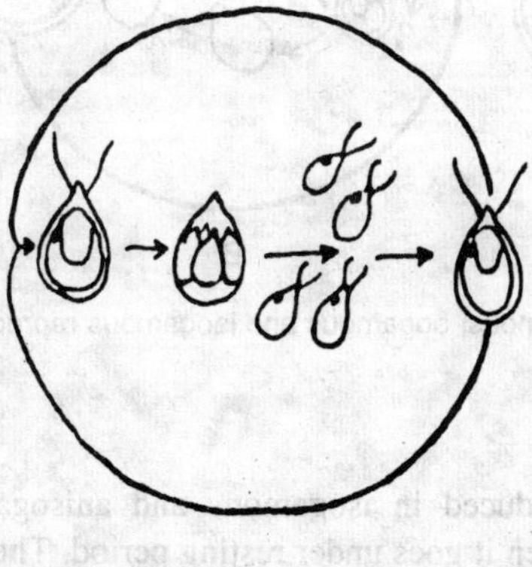

Fig. 10. Zoospores formation in *Chlamydomonas.*

By aplanospore — During unfavourable condition, the protoplast of the parent cell contracts from the cell wall, flagella are withdrawn and it is converted into thick walled, non–motile aplanospore. It germinates into new cell. Such non-motile spore is also called as *hypnospore.*

Palmella stage — Earlier, algologists considered this stage to be a species of a green algae — *Palmella.* In this stage the protoplast divides into many uninucleate parts. Each part becomes differentiated into non–flagellated small round cell and remain embedded within a gelatinous matrix formed by the parent cell wall. This stage is called palmella–stage. Later, when it is flooded with water, the cells develop flagella, become motile and escape from the matrix. Each cell develops into new plant by forming zoospores or aplanospores. Sometimes, *akinetes* are formed from the daughter cells of the palmella stage which are thick walled resting spore.

Sexual reproduction — It involves the union between gametes. Method of gamete fromation is similar to that of zoospore formation. The number of gametes are more than the zoospore number formed. Fusion of the gametes takes place in between the gametes derived from different cells (heterothallic) or between the gametes formed in the same cell (homothallic). Three types pf sexual reproduction takes place in *Chlamydomonas.* These are as follows —

(i). *Isogamy* — It is observed in *Chlamydomonas debaryana.* In this type union takes place between two similar biflagellate gametes. Any cell may act as gamete in favourable condition. The protoplast escapes from the cell just before gametic union. Sometimes, two cell as apposed to and fuse with each other at papillate end resulting in quadriflagellate zyggote (Fig. 11C).

(ii). *Anisogamy* — In this type two morphologically distinct motile gametes unites as in heterothallic *Chlamydomonas braunii.* A male cell divides several times forming 4 - 8 small male gametes whereas a female cell divides to from 2 - 4 large female gametes. The male and female gametes unite to form a aquadriflagellate zygote which is diploid (Fig. 11A).

(iii). *Oogamy* — It is found in *Chlamydomonas coccifera.* In this species one of the vegetative cell act as female cell or oogonium which forms a single non–motile (without flagella) female gamete and the other vegetative cell act as antheridium to give rise 8-32 small motile (with two flagella–biflagellate) male gametes or sperms. Fertilization takes place between male and female gamete to produce diploid zygote (Fig. 11B).

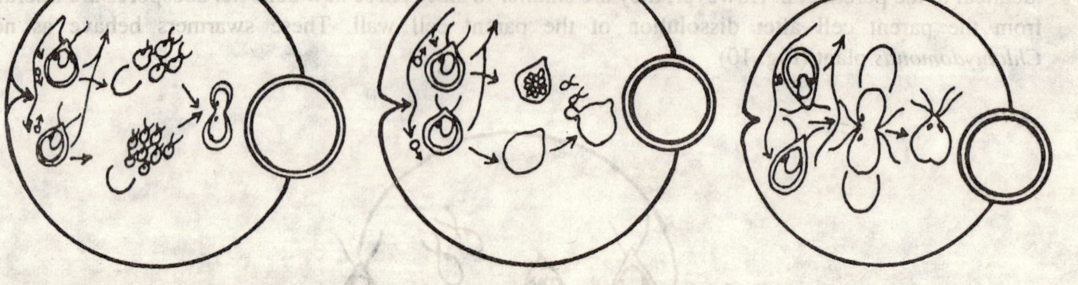

Fig. 11. A, B, C, showing Anisogamous, oogamous and isogamous reproduction respectively in Chalmydomanas.

GERMINATION OF ZYGOTE

The quadriflagellate zygote produced in isogamous and anisogamous type of sexual reproduction remains motile for sometime. Then it goes under resting period. The flagella are withdrawn followed by wall formation around the zygote. The diploid zygote nucleus divides meiotically into four haploid nuclei and each nucleus with some protoplast metamorphosed into haploid biflagellate zoospores. The zygote wall splits and the zoospores come out and swim in water and becomes a new plant. In some other species of *Chlamydomonas* the protoplast of the zygote divides into 8-16 or 32 parts and the nucleus also divides meiotically followed by mitotic division and each part (Protoplast with haploid necleus) metamorphosed into biflagellate zoospores.

PARTHENOGENESIS

Sometimes gametes fail to unite and germinate directly to give rise new plants. This process is called parthenogenesis.

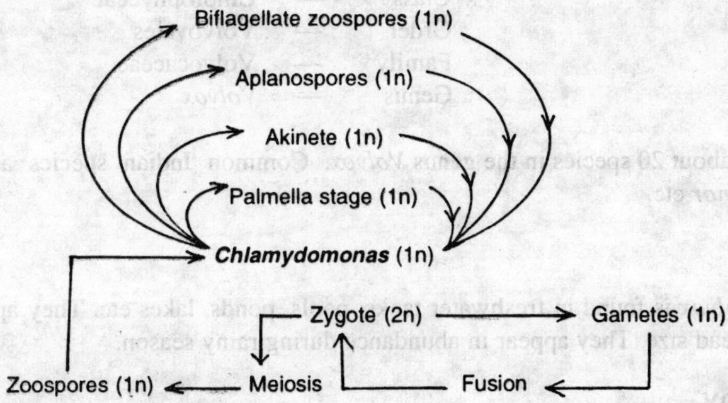

Graphic life cycle of *Chlamydomonas sp.*

ORIGIN AND EVOLUTION OF SEX IN *CHLAMYDOMANAS*

There are sets of events in sexual reproduction and these are (i) karyogamy and (ii) meiosis for segregation of chromosomes and genes.

The sexual reproduction in different species of *Chlamydomonas* varies. In isogamous species like *C. debaryana* the gametes are morphologically identical but physiologically different because union is possible only between pairs of clones. In anisogamous species like *C. braunii* both male and female gametes are biflagellate and motile, but differ in size only. In oogamous species like *C. coccifera* the large non–motile female gamete is passive and small, motile, flagellated male gamete is active representing a condition of egg and sperm of higher plants.

In *Chlamydomonas* the methods of formation of gametes and zoospores are similar. The gametes and zoospores are alike in their morphology except that the latter are larger. If the division of the protoplast of the parent cell stops at an early stage, zoospores are the result and if the division of the protoplast continues for longer period, gametes are produced. This can be explained by a theory known as *hunger theory of sex*. According to this theory gametes are undersized spores which were lacking food and energy required for the development of new individuals directly. That is why these undersized zoospores pool their resource by means of two by two fusion and in this way the zygote obtains sufficient food and energy essential for development.

The sexual behaviour is the basic mechanism of evolution because it provides the opportunity in the individuals for recombination of genes and their transmission to subsequent generation. After union, the diploidy makes physiologically advantageous because of increased production of enzymes.

Thus, sexual reproduction is an alternate method of reproduction which helps in tiding over un-favourable condition and recombination of genes which forms a basis for evolution. *In Chlamydomonas* isogamy, anisogamy and oogamy are successive advanced stages in sexual reproduction.

3.2 VOLVOX

It belongs to			
	Division	—	Chlorophyta
	Class	—	Chlorophyceae
	Order	—	Volvovales
	Family	—	Volvocaceae
	Genus	—	*Volvox*

There are about 20 species in the genus *Volvox*. Common Indian species are *Volvox globater*, *V. aureus*, *V. minor* etc.

HABITAT

The genus *Volvox* is found in freshwater tanks, pools, ponds, lakes etc. They appear as minute floating balls of pin head size. They appear in abundance during rainy season.

PLANT BODY

They are of colonial form and occur in colony or *coenobium*. A coenbium of *Volvox* contains several small pear shaped cells numbering from 500-50,000 or even more, arranged in one layer, joined with each other with the help of cytoplasmic strands within the gelatinous matrix. Each coenbium or colony consists of (i) vegetative cells, (ii) asexual reproductive cells and (iii) sexual reproductive cells. Each cell is covered by a gelatinous sheath of its own. Each oval or pear shaped cell has a nucleus, one cup shaped chloroplast with pyrenoids, an red coloured eye spot, two flagella at the anterior end of equal length and a vacuole in addition to reserve food and other cytoplasmic contents.

MOVEMENT

The entire colony of *Volvox* rolls over the surface of water.
The movement is by the action of flagella which in turn is controlled by eye spot.

REPRODUCTION

It takes place asexually and sexually.

Asexual reproduction — About 2-50 asexual reproductive cells known as *gonidia* are differentiated in the posterior half of the colony during summer. These cells loose their flagella, become rounded in outline and enlarges many times. They lie within a mucilaginous sac inside the colony. Each gonidium divides and redivides to produce spherical group of cells which are held together as a new daughter colony. When the gonidium divides and redivides to form 4 or 8 celled structure, they are quadrately or cruciately arranged having a tendency to form a curved plate known as *Plakea*. At 16 celled stage, the plakea becomes a hollow spherical body. When further cell division stops a pore is formed which is known as *phialopore*. Now the young daughter colony inverts through the phialopore. After inversion the individual cell of the daughter colony develops flagella and finally it (daughter colony) escapes out of the mother colony and grows into a new coenobium or colony of *Volvox* (Fig. 12).

Sexual Reproduction — The *Volvox* may be homothallic or heterothallic and it has oogamous type of sexual reproduction. The male sex organ–antheridium and female sex organ-oogonium develop from specialised large cells of coenobium.

A limited number of coenobial cells develop into oogonia. These cells loose their flagella and enlarge appearing young gonidia. The protoplast of each oogonium forms a spherical, large uninucleate egg.

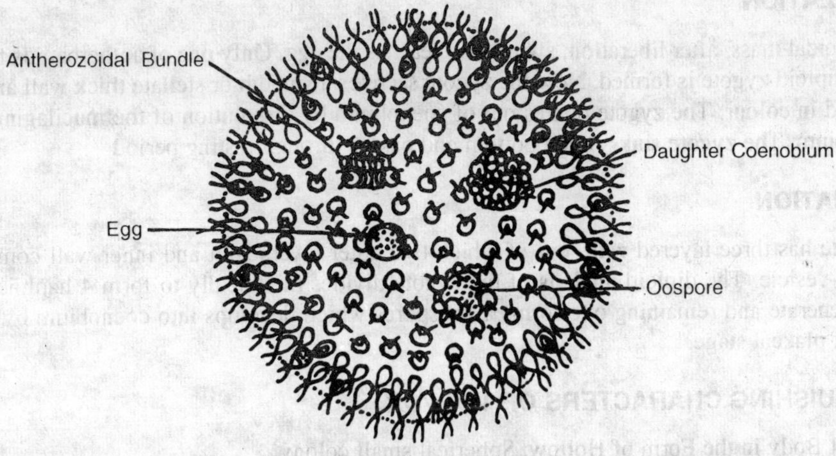

Fig. 12. A mature colony of *Volvox aureus.*

Some gonidia like specialised cell forms an antheridium. The contents of antheridium divides and redivides to give rise 16 to 128 small, yellowish, biflegellate spindle shaped antherozoids. The cell division is of plakea sequence and form a globose mass of antherozoids. The antheridial wall ruptures and mass of antherozoids are liberated (Fig. 13).

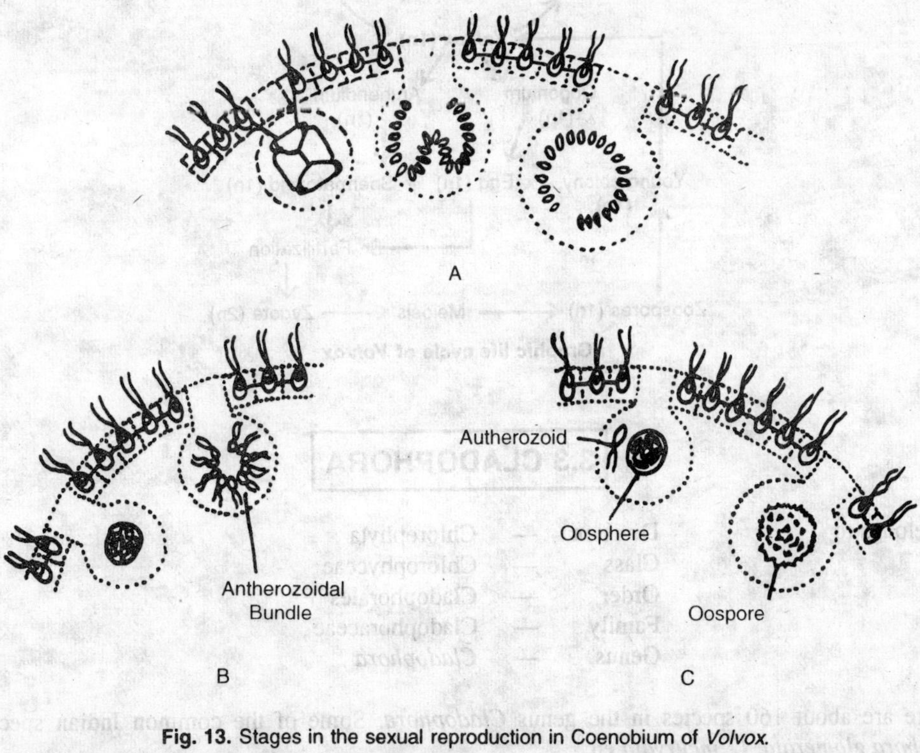

Fig. 13. Stages in the sexual reproduction in Coenobium of *Volvox.*

FERTILIZATION

Antherozoidal mass, after liberation, swims and reaches the egg. Only one of antherozoids fuses with the egg and diploid zygote is formed. Now the zygote secretes a smooth or stellate thick wall and it becomes orange red in colour. The zygote comes out of coenobium by dissolution of the mucilaginous matrix of the coenbium. The zygote sinks in the bottom and passes through resting period

GERMINATION

The zygote has three layered wall, out of which two outer layers split and inner wall comes out in the form of a vesicle. The diploid nucleus of the zygote divides meiotically to form 4 haploid nuclei, 3 of them degenerate and remaining one forms a zoospores which develops into coenobium by cell division process of plakeal stage.

DISTINGUISHING CHARACTERS OF *VOLVOX*

1. Plant Body in the Form of Hollow, Spherical small colony.
2. Each coenobium or colony is made up of many (500-50000) pear shaped cells connected to each other by protoplasmic strands.
3. Each cell of the coenobium has two flagella of equal length.
4. It reproduces asexually by gonidia which are specialised enlarged cells.
5. Oogamous type of sexual reproduction.
6. The diploid phase is represented by zygote.

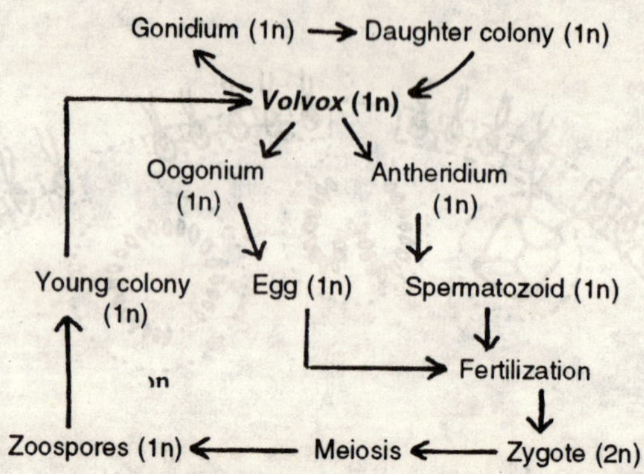

Graphic life cycle of *Volvox*

3.3 CLADOPHORA

It belongs to

Division	—	Chlorophyta
Class	—	Chlorophyceae
Order	—	Cladophorales
Family	—	Cladophoraceae
Genus	—	*Cladophora*

There are about 160 species in the genus *Cladophora.* Some of the common Indian species are *Cladophora glomerata, C. incurvata* etc.

DISTINGUISHING CHARACTERS

1. Plant body is, attached to the substratum, branched filamentous.
2. Branches develop from apical end of a cell below the septum.
3. Mode of branching is dichotomous or trichotomous.
4. Cell wall is three layered and thick.
5. Vegetative reproduction occurs by stolon like branches developing from rhizoid.
6. Asexual reproduction takes place by bi and quadriflagellate zoospores.
7. Isogamous type of sexual reproduction occurs.
8. It exhibits isomorphic alternation of generation.

HABITAT

Cladophora is cosmopolitan in distribution. They are found in fresh water and salt water both. They are observed in running water as well as stagnant water.

PLANT BODY

It is thalloid and profusely branched. They are attached to aquatic substrata by rhizoidal branches or rhizoids. The filament has row of elongated cells joined end to end one above the other. Branches develop and give appearance of a dichotomy or trichotomy. Cells are elongated and consists of walls of three layers. Outer layer is of chitin, middle layer is of pectin and inner layer is of cellulose. The cell wall is imprignated with calcium carbonate. Within the cell wall protoplasm has numerous nuclei, a central vacuole and reticulate chloroplast in addition to other cytoplasmic contents (Fig. 14).

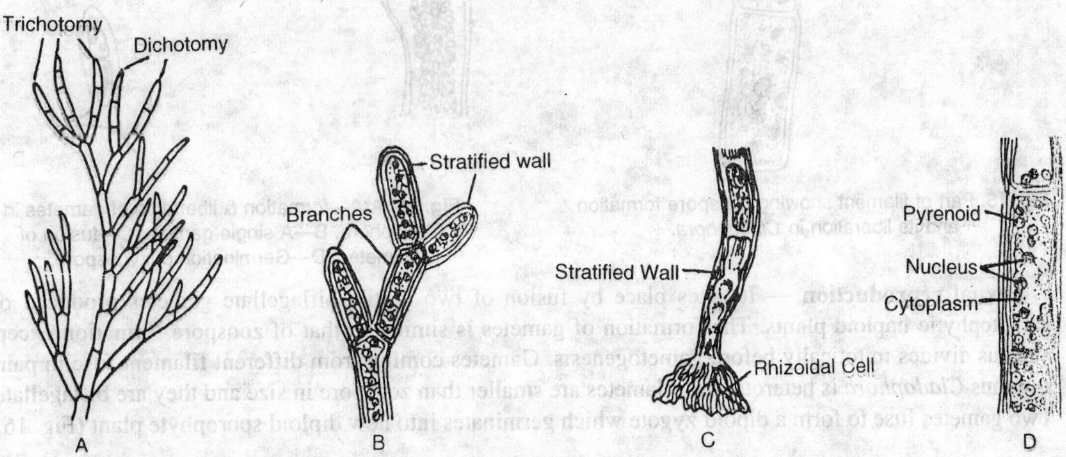

Fig. 14. A Cladophora thallus, B–A part of filament, C Basal part of filament, D — A Cel

REPRODUCTION

All the three types of reproduction i.e. vegetative, asexual and sexual occur in *Cladophora.*

Vegetative Reproduction — The upper erect portion of the thallus of some perennial species dies and the remaining prostrate rhizoidal portion becomes thick walled, pear shaped and swollen. This structure grows into new plant in the next season. In some fresh water species, akinetes are formed in the cells of the filament which give rise new plants. In some other species stolon like branches are formed from the rhizoid and develop into new plant.

Asexual reproduction — It takes place by biflagellate and quadriflagellate, pear shaped, small zoospores produced within zoosporangium near the tips of branches. Any vegetative cell except basal rhizoidal cell may act as zoosporangium. The nucleus divides meiotically and then mitotically several times. The protoplast cleaves into uninucleate structure which is metamorphosed into a quadriflellate haploid zoospore. Zoospores are liberated through a pore formed at the upper end of cell wall of zoosporangium or mother cell and swims for sometime. Then it rests and germinates into a new haploid plant. The resting zoospore is "germling" from which new haploid plant develops. The nucleus in germiling divides and redivides mitotically into multinucleate structure of cells of new gametophytic plant of haploid generation (Fig. 15).

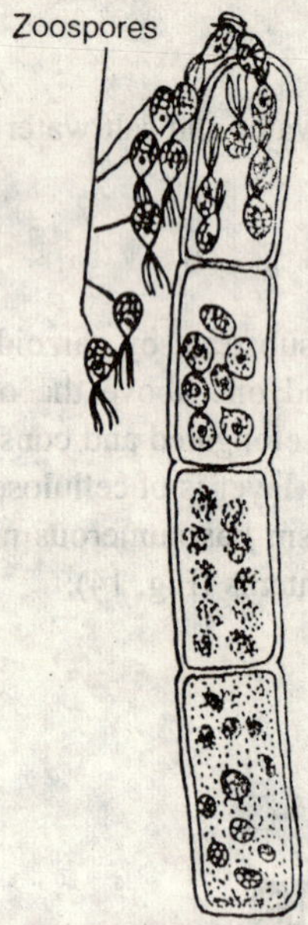

Fig. 15. Part of filament showing zoospore formation and its liberation in *Cladophora.*

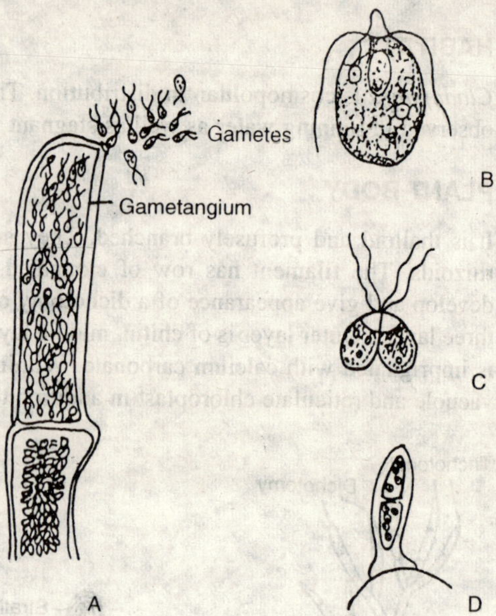

Fig. 16. A A—formation & liberation of gametes in Cladophora, B—A single gamete, C—fusion of gametes, D—Germination of zygospore.

Sexual reproduction — It takes place by fusion of two motile biflagellate gametes produced on gametophytic haploid plants. The formation of gametes is similar to that of zoospore formation except nucleus divides mitotically before gametogenesis. Gametes coming from different filament fuse in pairs and thus *Cladophora* is heterothallic. Gametes are smaller than zoospore in size and they are biflagellate. Two gametes fuse to form a dipoid zygote which germinates into new diploid sporophyte plant (Fig. 16).

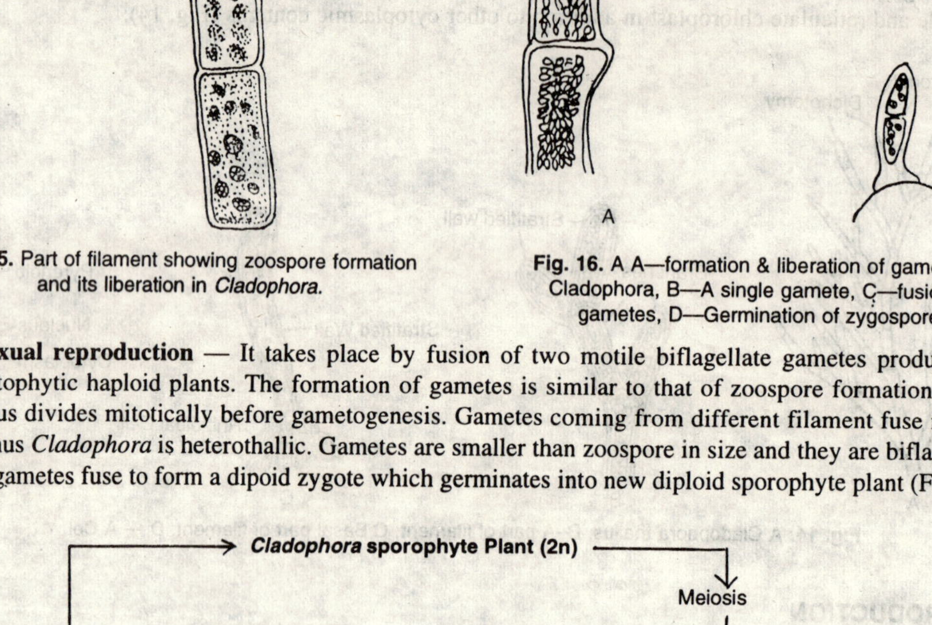

Graphic life cycle of *Cladophora sp.*

3.4 OEDOGONIUM

It belongs to	Division	—	Chlorophyta
	Class	—	Chlorophyceae
	Order	—	Oedogoniales
	Family	—	Oedogoniaceae
	Genus	—	*Oedogonium*

There are about 280 species in the genus *Oedogonium* and the common Indian species are *Oedogonium elegane*, *O. areolatum*, *O. cardiacum* etc.

DISTINGUISHING CHARACTERS

1. Plant body is unbranched filamentous
2. Presence of cap cells.
3. Cell has large single nucleus and reticulate plastid with numerous pyrenoids.
4. Asexual reproduction with the help of multiflagellate zoospores.
5. Oogamous type of sexual reproduction.
6. Antherozoids and zoospores both are multiflagellate but the formers are smaller in size.
7. Nannandrous forms develop antheridia on dwarf male filaments produced by androspore.
8. Each oogonium forms a single ovum or egg.

HABITAT AND VEGETATIVE PLANT BODY

The thallus is filamentous, made up of cylindrical cells joined end to end one above the other. Each mature filament is distinguished into base and apex. The basal cell is colourless and disc like known as hold fast. It acts as anchorage organ. Each cell has a thick cell wall. The other layer of the cell wall is made up of a chitin, middle layer of pectin and the inner most layer is of cellulose. Some cells of the filament has one or more ring like markings on lateral walls called cap-cells. Each cell has a nucleus and reticulate chloroplast with pyrenoids in addition to other cytoplasmic contents (Fig. 17). The plant is aquatic and fresh water form.

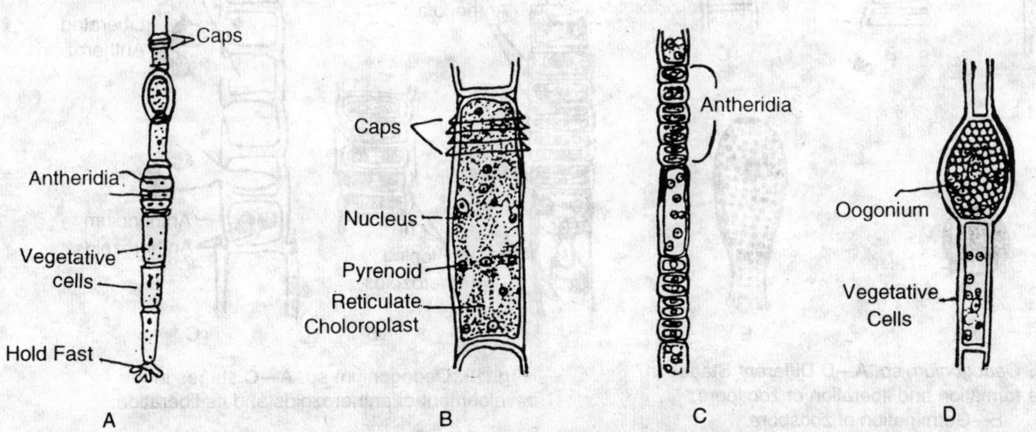

Fig. 17. *Oedogonium* sp. A–Habit of the Plant, B–A cell showing detail structure, C and D Macrandrous heterothallic forms.

GROWTH

It takes place by cell division in certain cell of the filament except basal and apical cell. During division, the nucleus elongates and then divides mitotically. At the same time a ring of wall materials appear which encircles the inner face of the lateral wall below the distal end of the cell. A septum is formed in between the two daughter nuclei. The ring gradually stretches to form a new wall. Some portion of the original wall remains at the upper end of the cell which forms the cap. This type of cell division may occur successively in any cell each forming a cap. The number of cap present will indicate the number of cell division has taken place.

REPRODUCTION

Oedogonium reproduces vegetatively, asexually and sexually.

Vegetative reproduction — It takes place by fragmentation of filaments into smaller pieces, each piece develops into new plant.

Asexual reproduction — It occurs by multiflagellate zoospores produced in zoosporangium. Any cell except apical and hold fast may behave like a zoosporangium. The protoplast of zoosporangium contracts and a lunar shaped hyaline area appears on one side of the protoplast. This hyaline area is known as receptive spot. At the base of receiptive spot, a ring of basal granule develops. One basal granule gives rise one flagellum. On maturation lateral wall of the zoosporangium breaks at the cap region and metamorphosed into multiflagellate zoospore surrounded by hyaline vesicle come out of the zoosporangium. The vesicle gelatinises and breaks. The zoospore is pyriform or oval, grey in colour with a crown of flagella. It swims freely in water for some time and then rests on suitable substratum under water. It withdraws flagella and germinates into new filament by repeated cell division (Fig. 18).

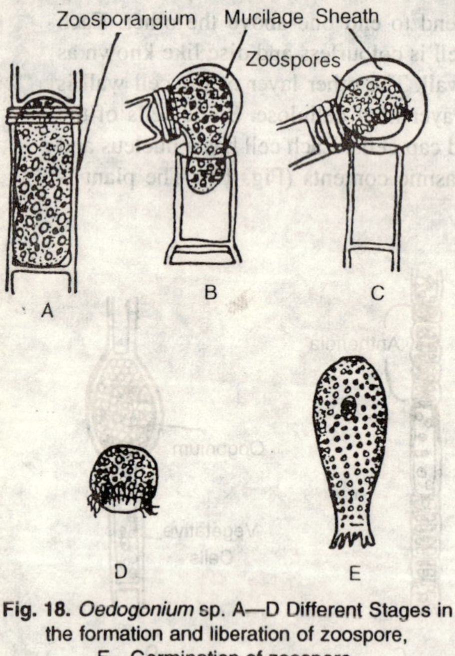

Fig. 18. *Oedogonium* sp. A—D Different Stages in the formation and liberation of zoospore, E—Germination of zoospore.

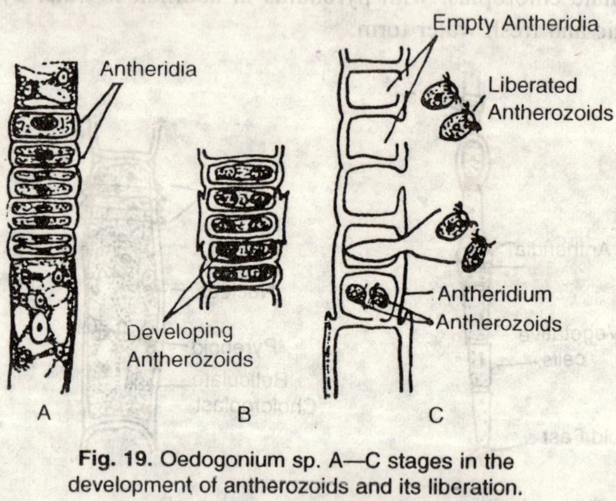

Fig. 19. Oedogonium sp. A—C stages in the development of antherozoids and its liberation.

During unfavourable condition, akinetes in chain of 10-40 in a filament are formed which are thick walled with reserve food. It directly germinates into new plant on the return of favourable condition.

Sexual reproduction — The plant may be monoecious or dioecious. The sexual reproduction is of oogamous type. Monoecious or homothallic species produces antheridia and oogonia on the same plant and they are *macrandrous forms*. Dioecious or heterothallic species produces male sex organ–antheridia and female sex organs–oogonia on different filaments (plants). In *nannandrous forms*, the oogonia are formed on normal sized filaments whereas, antheridia are formed on dwarf male or nannandrium which are small in size attached to oogonia or below oogonia. Thus nannandrous forms are always heterothallic (Fig. 19).

Macrandrous forms — Here antheridia are terminal or intercalary in position. Any cell except basal may act as antheridial mother cell which divides to form two daughter cells of unequal size. The smaller upper cell develops into an antheridium and the lower larger cell may act as an antheridial mother cell and thus a chain of 2-40 antheridia are formed. The protoplasmic content of each antheridium metamorphoses into one or two antherozoids. The antherozoids are similar in structure to that of zoospore except in size. The antherozoids are smaller than the zoospores and they are surrounded by a hyaline vesicle at the time of liberation. Intercalary cell of the filament act as oogonial mother cell which divides transversely into upper cap cell which act as oogonium and a lower supporting cell or *suffultory* cell. The suffultory cell may further divide into an oogonial mother cell and thus two or more oogonia are seen in a chain.

On maturity, a pore or transverse slit develops in the oogonial wall. The protoplasm of oogonium metamorphoses into an egg. The ovum or egg has a hyaline receptive spot (Fig. 20).

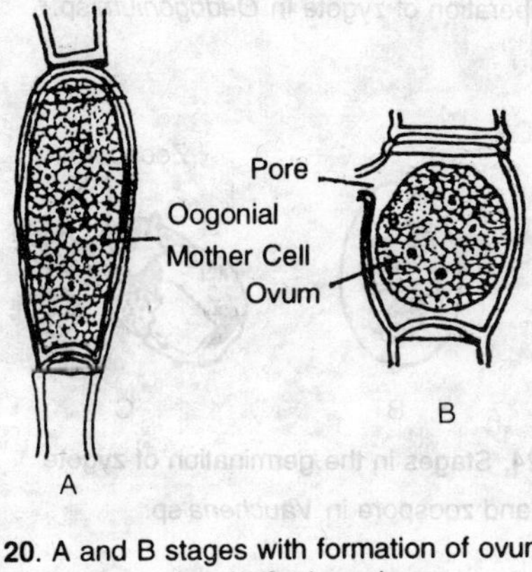

Fig. 20. A and B stages with formation of ovum in Oogonium in Oedogonium.

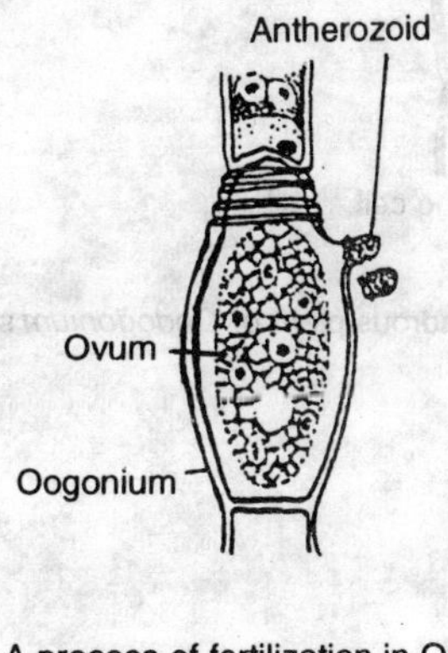

Fig. 21. A process of fertilization in Oedogonium.

Nannandrous forms — It is a few celled filament having a basal stalk cell and 2-3 antheridial cell. The nannandrous forms (dwarf male plants) are produced by androspores, formed singly within androsporangium like antherida of macrandrous form. It is produced from the vegetative cell in the similar fashion as that of antheridia produced in macrandrous form. The protoplasmic content of androsporangium is metamorphosed into a single androspore. On liberation, it swims in the surrounding water for sometime and settle on oogonial wall or suffultory cell. The androspore germinates in a dwarf male filament known as *nannandrium*. In dwarf male each antheridium produces two antherozoids. The mode of development and structure of oogonium are similar to those of macrandrous forms.

When both androsporangia and oogonia are born on the same filament of nannandrous form, it (plant) is termed as *gynandrosporous* and if these two are produced on different filament it is known as idioandrosporous (Fig. 21, 22).

FERTILIZATION

The swimming antherozoid enters the ovum through an opening in oogonial wall near receptive spot.

The nucleus of the antherozoid unites with the egg nucleus to form a diploid zygote. After fertilization the zygote secretes a thick wall and undergoes rest. Next, the zygote liberated on rupturing of the oogonial wall, falls to the bottom of the water body and finally germinates. During germination the diploid zygotic nucleus divides meiotically into 4 haploid nuclei. Each haploid nucleus in combination with cytoplasm forms a zoospore. These zoospores are liberated after rupturing of the zygote wall and swims freely in water. Then it settles and germinates into new haploid plant of Oedogonium (Fig. 23, 24).

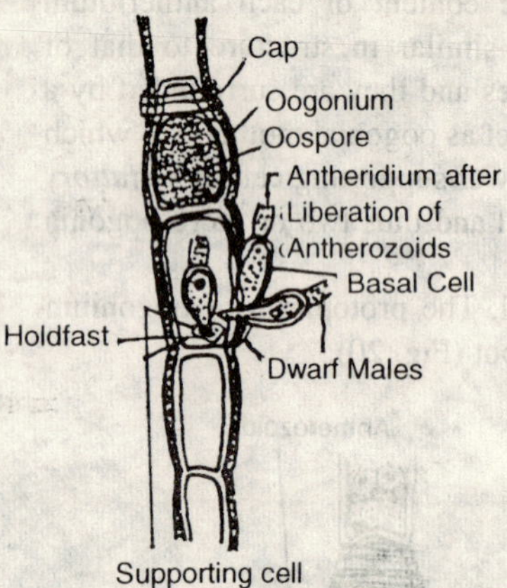

Fig. 22. A nannadrous plant of *Oedogonium* sp.

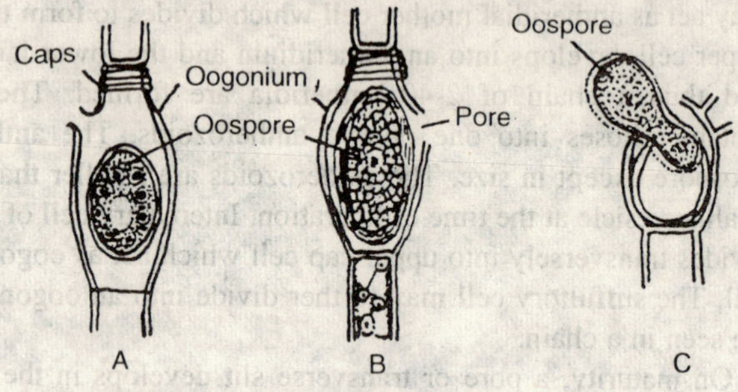

Fig. 23. A mature Oedogonium, B- the same, C–Liberation of zygote in *Oedogonium* sp.

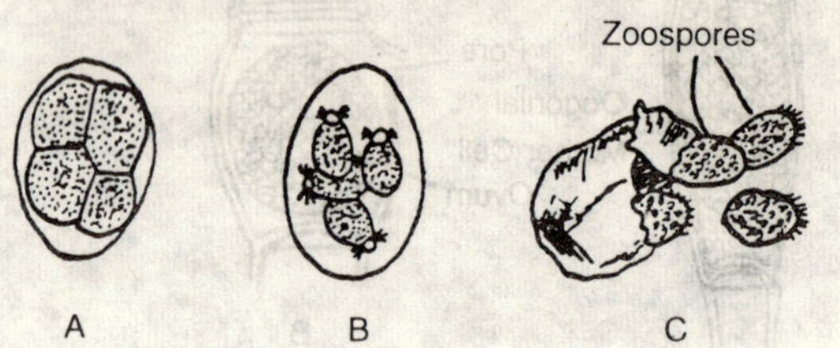

Fig. 24. Stages in the germination of zygote and zoospore in *Vaucheria* sp.

1.

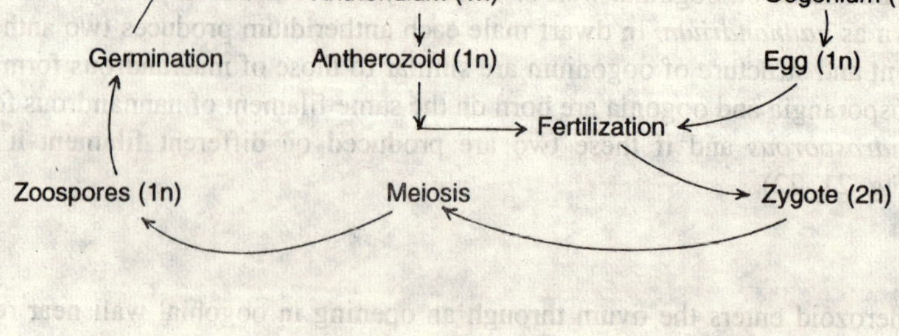

2.

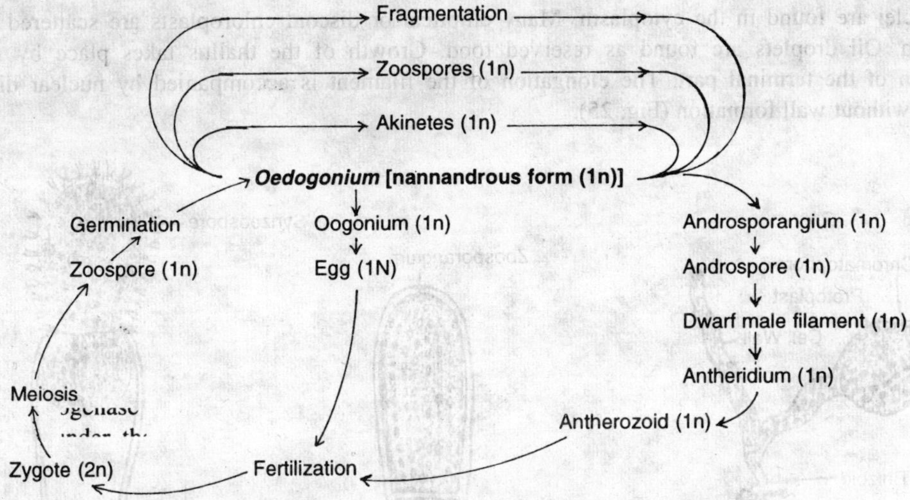

Graphic life cycle of Macrandrous & Nannandrous *Oedogonium sp.*

3.5 VAUCHERIA

It belongs to	Division	—	Chlorophyta
	Class	—	Chlorophyceae
	Order	—	Siphonales
	Family	—	Vaucheriaceae
	Genus	—	*Vaucheria*

The genus *Vaucheria* is represented by more than 40 species. The common Indian species are *Vaucheria clavata*, *V. terrestris*, *V. geminata*, *V. sessilis* etc.

DISTINGUISHING CHARACTERS

1. Thalloid plant body is branched filamentous and coenocytic.
2. Plant is attached to the substratum by rhizoids.
3. Fats and oils are reserve food in the cell.
4. It multiplies asexually by multiflagellate coenozoospores or synzoospores.
5. Sexual reproduction is of oogamous type.
6. Antheridium is cylindrical and hooked containing biflagellate sperms.

HABITAT

Vaucheria are aquatic as well as terrestrial found on moist soil, stagnant and flowing waters. Marine species are also found. Many species are amphibious also

PLANT BODY

It is branched, tabular and coenocytic filamentous without any septa except at the time of reproduction. It is several centimeters in length. The wall of the filament has two layers. Outer layer is made up of pectin and the inner of cellulose. A central vauole runs from one end of the cell to the other. Numerous small nuclei are found in the cytoplasm. Many elliptical or discoid chloroplasts are scattered in the cytoplasm. Oil droplets are found as reserved food. Growth of the thallus takes place by simple elongation of the terminal part. The elongation of the filament is accompanied by nuclear division (mitotic) without wall formation (Fig. 25).

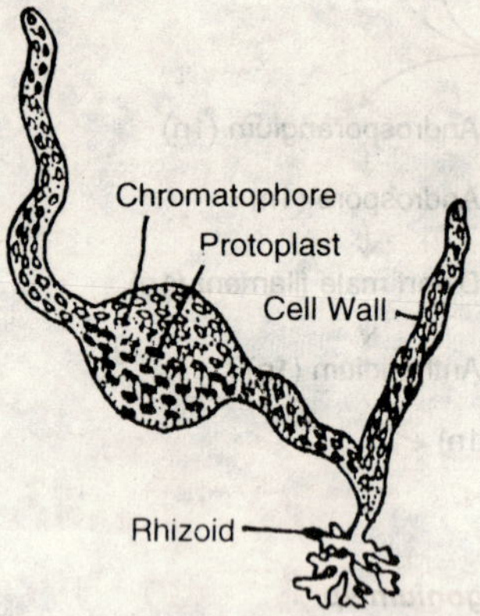

Fig. 25. A thallus of *Vaucheria* sp.

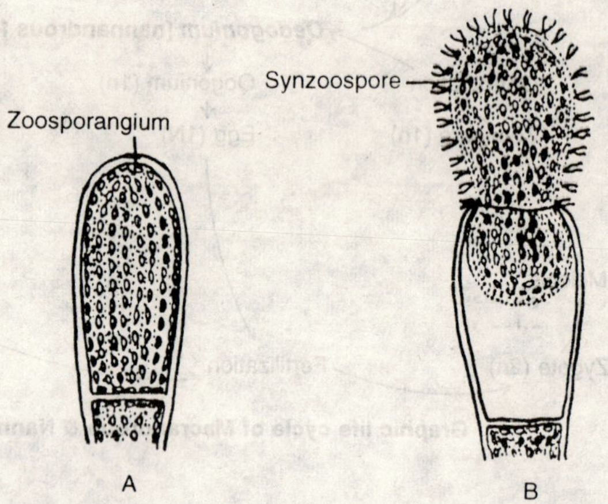

Fig. 26. A — A zoosporangium, B—Liberating zoospore in *Vaucheria* sp.

REPRODUCTION

Vaucheria has asexual and sexual reproduction.

Asexual reproduction — It takes place by large, multiflagellate *Zoospores.* At the time of zoospore formation, the apical part of the filament is delimited by wall formation which becomes club shaped zoosporangium. The whole zoosporangial protoplasm contracts to form an oval mass. A pair of flagella equal in size, develops opposite to each nucleus in the zoosporangium and thus a multiflagellate zoosporangium produces only one zoospore or synzoospore (Fig. 26).

(ii) By Aplanospore — In some terrestrial forms, the whole protoplast of zoosporangium develops into thin walled non-motile aplanospore or akinete in place of motile zoospore. Aplanospore is liberated by rupturing of the sporangial wall. It germinates into new thallus of *Vaucheria.*

(iii) Hypnospores or cysts — During dry season, entire protoplast of the filament of terrestrial form becomes segmented by transverse wall formation. Each protoplast rounds off and secrete a thick wall around itself. These are *hypnospores.* When wall is thin – it is cysts. During favourable condition hypnospores or cyasts germinate to give rise new plants.

Sexual reproduction — Fresh water and terrestrial forms are homothallic where as marine species are heterothallic. Sexual reproduction is of oogamous type.

In homothallic species the male sex organs — antheridia and the female sex organ — oogonia are born adjacent to one another either on adjoining branch or on a common lateral branch. A transverse septum is formed at the time of formation of sex organ.

A mature antheridium is a curved, hook like tubular and slender in structure. It is born on short lateral branch. The tip of the branch becomes densely filled with cytoplasm containing many nuclei and chlorplast. It is cut off by a wall formation. The protoplast of antheridium becomes divided into numerous uninucleate parts, each of which metamorphosed into a biflagellate antherozoid. The two flagella of antherozoid are of unequal length. The antherozoids are liberated in the surrounding water from a pore developed in antheridial wall at its apex.

The oogonium is formed by lateral out growth in the main branch (filament) near the base of an antheridial branch. Several nuclei and plastids migrate into the oogonial bulge which is separated from the main filament by a septum and thus oogonium is formed which is round, oval, sessile or short stalked body having a wall with a rounded beak which opens to receive the antherozoid on maturity. Mature oogonium has one uninucleate egg.

FERTILIZATION

When antherozoids are liberated it swim towards the oogonium. Only one of the antherozoids enters the oogonium through the pore and fertilizes the egg to produce a diploid zygote (Fig. 27).

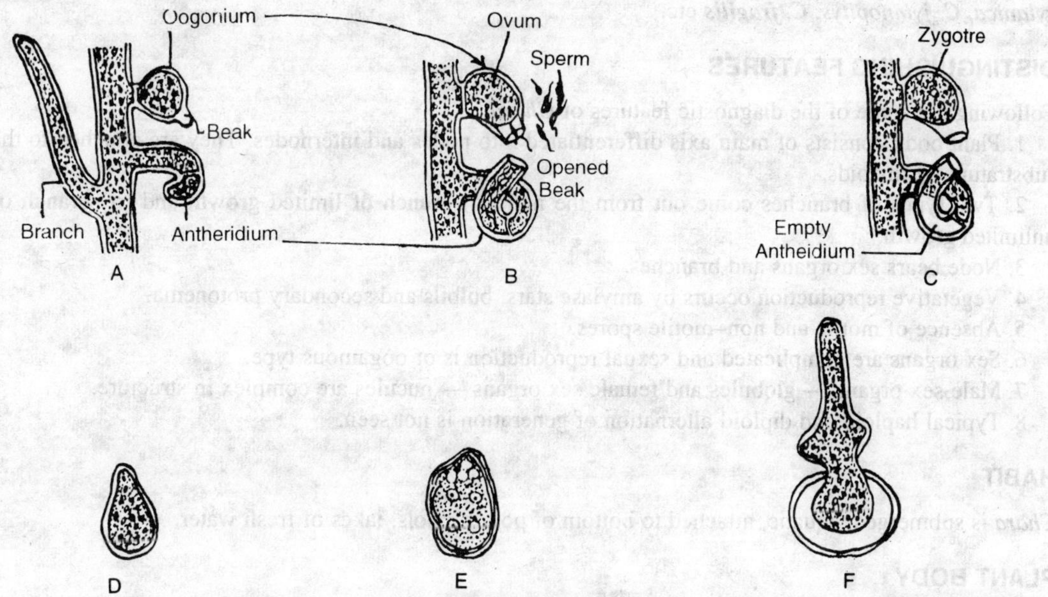

Fig. 27. Vaucheria sp. —Filament bearing antheridium and oogonium, B & C—stages in the fertilization, D, E and F—stages in the germination of zygote.

GERMINATION OF ZYGOTE

The zygote rests for several months. Meiosis occurs in zygotic nucleus during the germination of zygote into new haploid *Vaucheria.*

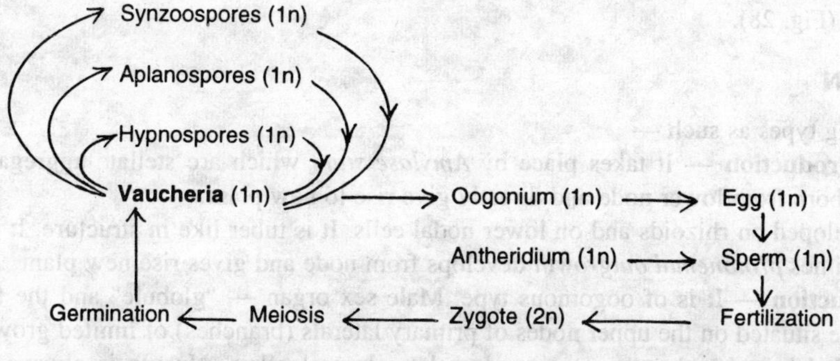

Graphic life cycle of *Vaucheria sp.*

3.6 CHARA

It belongs to	Division	—	Chlorophyta
	Class	—	Chlorophyceae
	Order	—	Charales
	Family	—	Characeae
	Genus	—	*Chara*

There are above 90 living species of the genus *Chara*. Some of the common Indian species are *Chara zylanica*, *C. jymnopitys*, *C. fragilis* etc.

DISTINGUISHING FEATURES

Following are some of the diagnostic features of *Chara*.

1. Plant body consists of main axis differentiated into nodes and internodes. They are attached to the substratum by rhizoids.
2. Two types of branches come out from the node (i) branch of limited growth and (ii) branch of unlimited growth.
3. Node bears sex organs and branches.
4. Vegetative reproduction occurs by amylase stars, bulbils and secondary protonema.
5. Absence of motile and non–motile spores.
6. Sex organs are complicated and sexual reproduction is of oogamous type.
7. Male sex organs — globules and female sex organs — nucules are complex in structure.
8. Typical haploid and diploid alternation of generation is not seen.

HABIT

Chara is submerged, aquatic, attached to bottom of ponds, pools, lakes of fresh water.

PLANT BODY

The vegetative plant body consists of erect, cylindrical branched main axis of 20-40 cm in length. Plant is attached to the muddy or sandy substratum by multicellular rhizoids developing from lower most nodes. The main axis and branches are differentiated into nodes and internodes. Branches are of limited growth and unlimited growth. At the node, central cell is surrounded by 6–20 peripheral cells. The internode is made up of a single cylindrical and elongated cell which are corticated. The corticating cells develop from upper and lower nodes. Cell contains elliptical or discoid plastids without pyrenoid, vacuoles and nucleus. Cell wall is made up of cellulose. In some species, cell wall is impregnated with calcium carbonate (Fig. 28).

REPRODUCTION

It is of following types as such —

Vegetative reproduction — It takes place by *Amylase stars* which are stellate aggregate of cells filled with starch, born from lower node and directly give rise to new plant.

Bulbils are developed on rhizoids and on lower nodal cells. It is tuber like in structure. It grows into new plants. Sometimes *protonemal outgrowth* develops from node and gives rise new plant.

Sexual reproduction — It is of oogomous type. Male sex organ — "globule" and the female sex organs "nucule" are situated on the upper nodes of primary laterals (branches) of limited growth, amidst whorls of one celled branches known as secondary laterals or leaflets. Nucule is always above the globule in chara while its relative position is reverse in the genus *Nitella* of the same family. The plant is homothallic or monoecious. It bears male and female sex organs on the same plant. (Fig. 29)

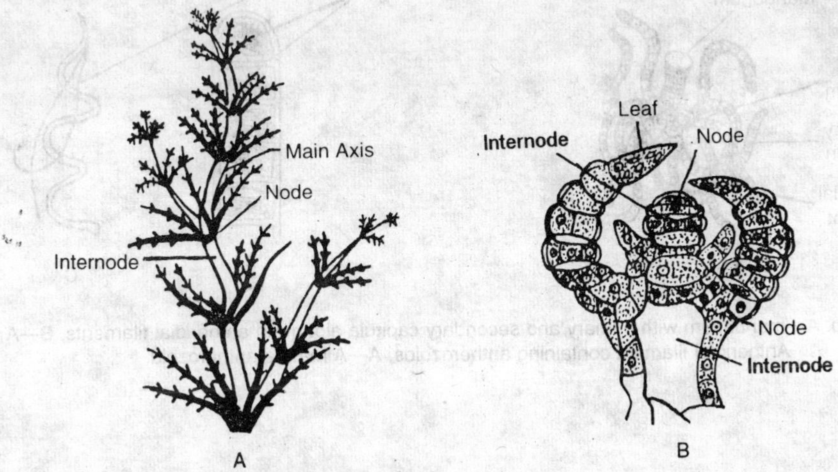

Fig. 28. A– portion of *Chara* thallus, B— vertical section of the apex of the main axis.

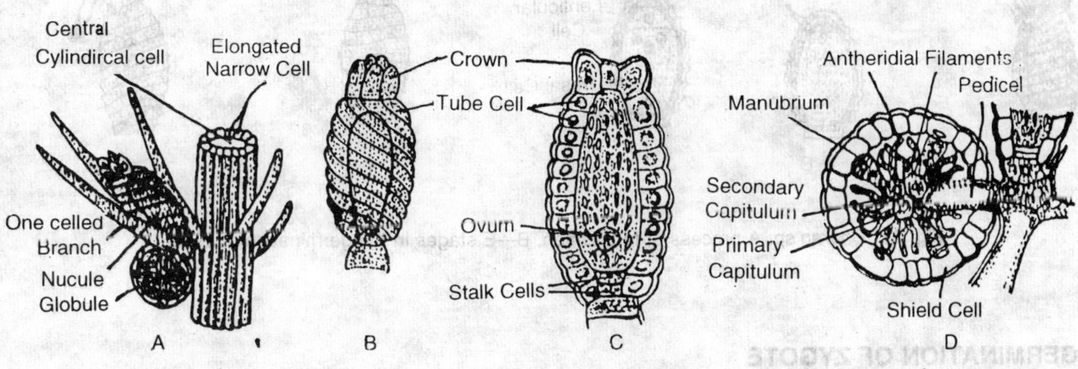

Fig. 29. A — part of *Chara* plant showing globule and nucule, B–A nucule, C— L.S. of nucule, D-T.S. of globule.

Globule is almost globular, stalked and of yellow or red colour. The wall of globule has 8 curved *Shield cells* forming a wall. Each shield cell has a rod shaped, *manubrium* cell. From the *manubrial* cell — one or more cells of *primary capitulum* comes out. Each primary capitulum gives rise six *secondary capitula* and each secondary capitulum develops two — long whip like threads or antheridial filaments. Each *antheridial filament* has 100-200 single row of cells, each of which produces one elongated, spirally coiled biflagellate *antherozoid* or sperm. On maturity, shield cells are separated from each other exposing the antheridial filaments and other cells below the shield cells. Antherozoids are liberated from upper cell of the antheridial filament (Fig. 30).

Nucule is stalked, elliptical or oval structure enveloped by five long tube cells spirally arranged side by side giving an appearance of a twisted structure. Each of the tube cells has a small cell at its apex known as *corona* or *crown*. The oogonium contains a single large uninucleate egg filled with starch and oil globules. On maturity the spirally twisted tube cells separate out below the corona and five openings are exposed through which liberated and swimming antherozoids enter and only one of them fuses with the egg to produce a diploid zygote (Fig. 31)

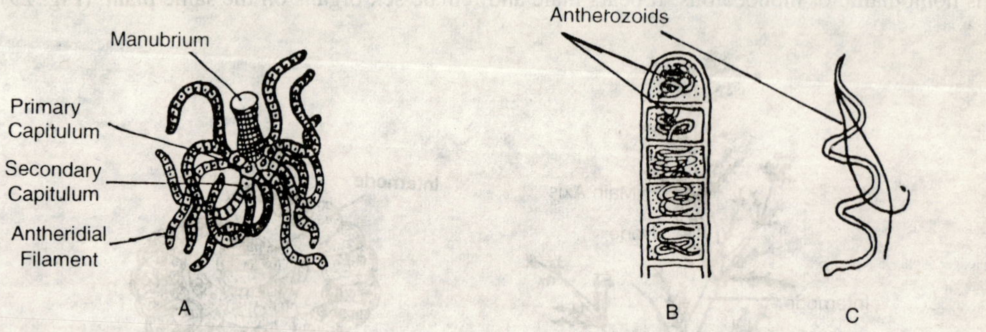

Fig. 30. *Chara sp.* A—manubrium with primary and secondary capitula alongwith antheridial filaments, B—A part of Antheridial filament containing antherozoids, A—A mature antherozoid.

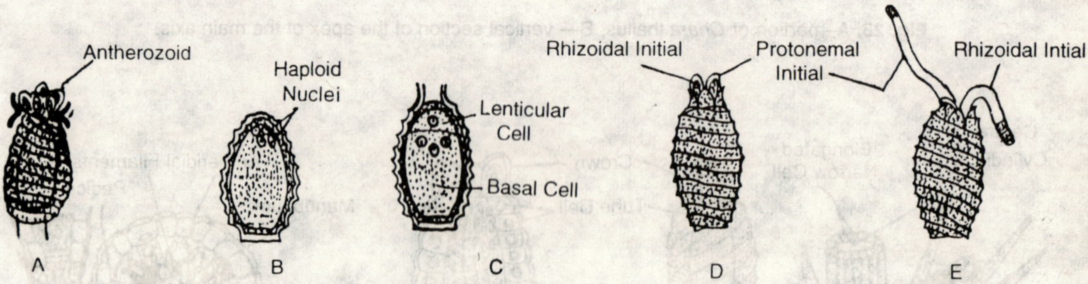

Fig. 31. *Charap* sp. A process of fertilization, B—E stages in the germination of zygote.

GERMINATION OF ZYGOTE

The zygote nucleus divides meiotically into 4 haploid nuclei. Then zygote divides into small apical lenticular cell and a large basal cell. The lenticular cell contain one haploid nucleus and the basal cell has 3 haploid nucleus. The uninucleate haploid lenticular cell divides vertically into two cells, one of which develops rhizoidal initial and the other develops protonemal initial. The basal three haploid nucleate cell does not divide and its nuclei degenerate. Primary protonema or pro–embryo is formed from protonemal initial and rhizoidal initial gives rise to colourless filamentous *rhizoid* which is differentiated into nodes and internodes. Primary protonema further develops into secondary protonema and ultimately new *Chara* plant is produced (Fig. 32).

ALTERNATION OF GENERATION

In *Chara* typical alternation of generation does not occur. The haploid gemetophyte plant is dominant and diploid structure is represented by zygote only.

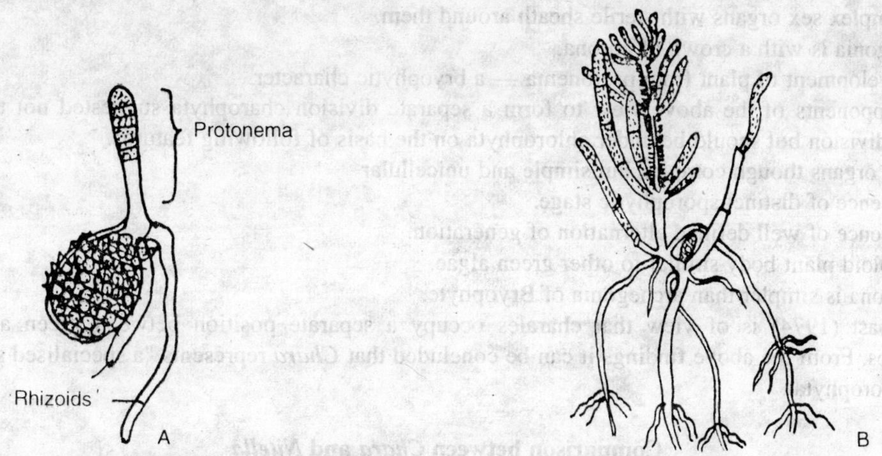

Fig. 32. *Chara* sp. A— germination of zygote B— young plant with protonema.

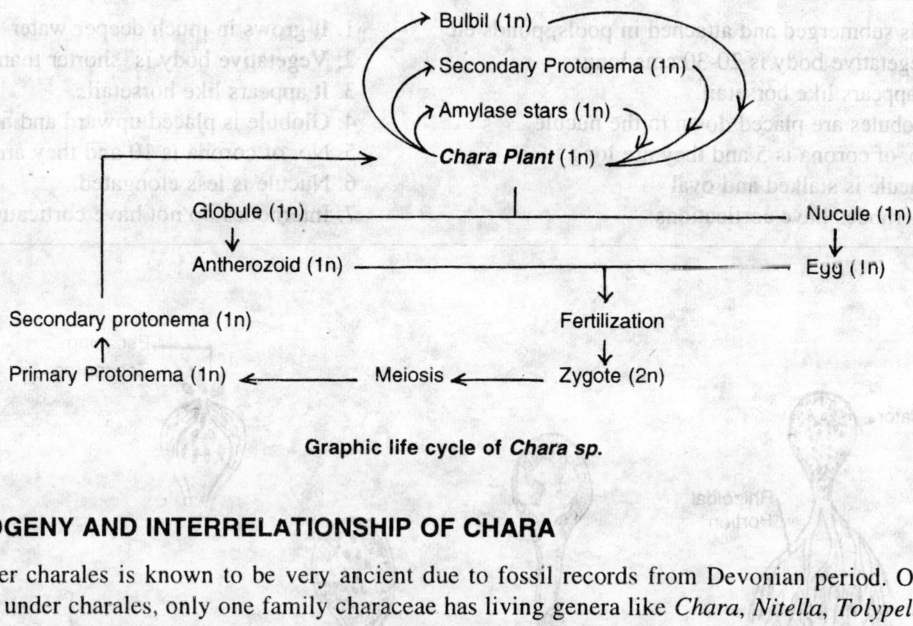

Graphic life cycle of *Chara sp.*

PHYLOGENY AND INTERRELATIONSHIP OF CHARA

The order charales is known to be very ancient due to fossil records from Devonian period. Out of 4 families under charales, only one family characeae has living genera like *Chara*, *Nitella*, *Tolypella* etc.

Charales are related to chlorophyceae. Previously it was thought to be a group of ferns.

Due to presence of chlorophyll and starch as reserve food charales were considered to be under class chlorophyceae. Therefore, Fritsch (1935) has placed as last order of chlorophyceae. The opponents did not consider the inclusion of charales under chlorophyceae due to complexity of sex organs and development of protonema from zygote.

Smith (1955) have given a separate rank of class charophyceae to the order charales. Prescott (1969) have divided division chlorophyta into two classes, viz. (i) chlorophyceae and (ii) charophyceae. Bold (1956), McLean & Cook (1956) hold that charales should be placed under a separate division Charophyta as they possess distinct features as such :

1. Highly organised and elaborate plant body.

2. Complex sex organs with sterile sheath around them.
3. Oogonia is with a crown of corona.
4. Development of plant from protonema — a bryophytic character.

The opponents of the above view to form a separate division charophyta suggested not to form a separate division but should be under chlorophyta on the basis of following features.

1. Sex organs though complex but simple and unicellular
2. Absence of distinct sporophytic stage.
3. Absence of well defined alternation of generation.
4. Haploid plant body similar to other green algae.
5. Corona is simpler than archegonia of Bryophyte.

Grambast (1974) is of view that charales occupy a separate position between green algae and bryophytes. From the above findings it can be concluded that *Chara* represents "a specialised side line" of the chlorophyta.

Comparison between *Chara* and *Nitella*

Chara	Nitella
1. It is submerged and attached in pools, ponds etc	1. It grows in much deeper water
2. Vegetative body is 20-30 cms long	2. Vegetative body is shorter than Chara.
3. It appears like horsetail.	3. It appears like horsetail.
4. Globules are placed down to the nucule	4. Globule is placed upward and nucule downward
5. No. of corona is 5 and they are long	5. No. of corona is 10 and they are short.
6. Nucule is stalked and oval	6. Nucule is less elongated.
7. Internodes have cortications.	7. Internodes do not have cortication.

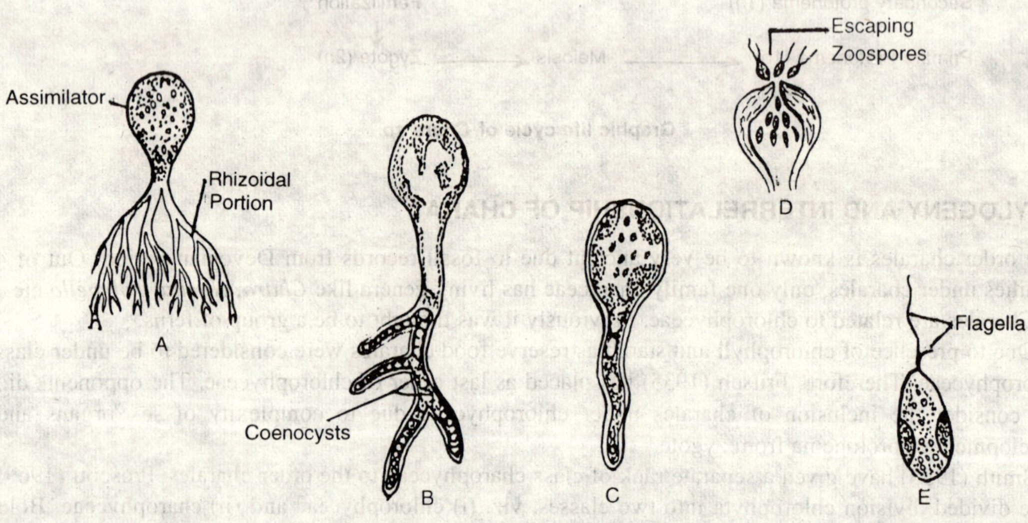

Fig. 33. *Botrydium* sp. A — A plant, B–Formation of coenocysts C–Germinating aplanospore, D–Liberation of zoospores, E — A single zoospore.

CHAPTER 4

CHRYSOPHYTA:XANTHOPHYCEAE

SALIENT FEATURES

1. The division chrysophyta has more than 2800 genera and 6000 species and most of them are fresh water forms, some forms are marine also.
2. The plant body ranges from unicellular to filamentous
3. The cell wall consists of two overlapping halves often impregnated with silica.
4. They contain yellowish green and golden brown pigments.
5. True pyrenoids are absent.
6. Reserve food materials are leucosin and oils.
7. It reproduces asexually by motile and non motile spores.
8. Isogamous type of sexual reproduction takes place. Motile reproductive cells have two flagella of unequal length.

CLASSIFICATION

According to Smith (1955) Chrysophyta has been divided into three classes as such

Class — 1. Xanthophyceae, 2. Chrysophyceae and 3. Bacillariophyceae.

Xanthophyceae

DISTINGUISHING FEATURES

1. Plant body unicellular or multicellular.
2. It contains chlorophyll a, e, Xanthophylls and β carotene.
3. No pyrenoids in the plastids.
4. Leucosin and oils are reserve food.
5. Vegetative and reproductive cells are biflagellate. Structure and life history of one member of this class has been described here.

4.1 BOTRYDIUM

It belongs to

Division	—	Chrysophyta
Class	—	Xanthophyceae
Order	—	Heterosiphonales
Family	—	Botrydiaceae
Genus	—	*Botrydium*

There are about six species in the genus *Botrydium.* The common Indian species are *B. granulatum, B. tuberosum* etc.

IMPORTANT CHARACTERS

1. Plant body is vesicular, coenocytic differentiated into baloon shaped or globose aerial part and under ground rhizoidal part is branched.
2. Aerial vesicle contains numerous nuclei scattered in the thin peripheral layer of cytoplasm.
3. Plastids are fusiform, leucosin and oildrops are reserve food.
4. The rhizoidal part is devoid of plastids with many nuclei.
5. During drought, the protoplasmic contents of the vesicle migrate to the rhizoidal part to form thick walled globose coenocysts or rhizocysts which germinate to produce zoospores.

HABITAT

Botrydium is a terrestrial alga growing on damp soil and drying muddy banks of streams or pools.

PLANT BODY

It is made up of coloured globose or vesicular aerial part known as assimilator and colourless, branched underground part. In fact, the whole plant body is unicellular thallus like with numberous nuclei and hence coenocytic and siphonaceous thallus. The aerial part is made up of hard wall of cellulose. The globose part is about 2 mm in diameter. Below the wall, there is cytoplasm containing nuclei, plastids, reserve food and other inclusions. The lower rhizoidal part is branched with many nuclei but devoid of plastids.

REPRODUCTION

There is no vegetative reproduction., It reproduces by means of asexual spores and sexual gametes.

Asexual reproduction — It takes place by biflagellate swarmers or zoospores, aplanospores and hypnospores.

Zoospore formation occurs in submerged condition of the plants. The vesicular protoplast divides into many uninucleate protoplast, each of them metamorphosed into pear shaped or pyriform biflagellate zoospores. The flagella are of unequal length. The zoospores are liberated by the gelatinization and disintegration of apical part of the wall of the vesicle. Each zoospore develops into new plant.

Aplanospores are formed during unfavourable condition when there is dry condition. The whole protoplast of the vesicle migrates to the rhizod and divides into several multinucleate or uninucleate segments. Each segment rounds up and secretes a wall around itself forming a spherical or eliipsoidal *aplanospore* or *coenocyst.* Thick walled aplanospore is called *hypnospores.* Sometimes hypnospores are also formed in the vesicular part or at the tip of rhizoid. Each such spore germinates into new plant.

Sexual reproduction — It is of isogamous or anisogamous type. The plant is homothallic or heterothallic. The gametes are produced in the vesicular part in the manner similar to that of zoospore formation. Each gamete is pear shaped with or without eye spot having two flagella of unequal length. Fusing gametes become apposed at their anterior ends and then fuse laterally to produce a globose zygote. The zygote germinates immediately after its formation and gives rise a new plant. Meiosis takes place in the zygote produced in heterothallic species resulting in the formation of 4 - 8 haploid biflagellate zoospores which germinate into new plant after its liberation from the zygote (Fig. 33)

Moewus (1940) has reported parthenogenesis in some species.

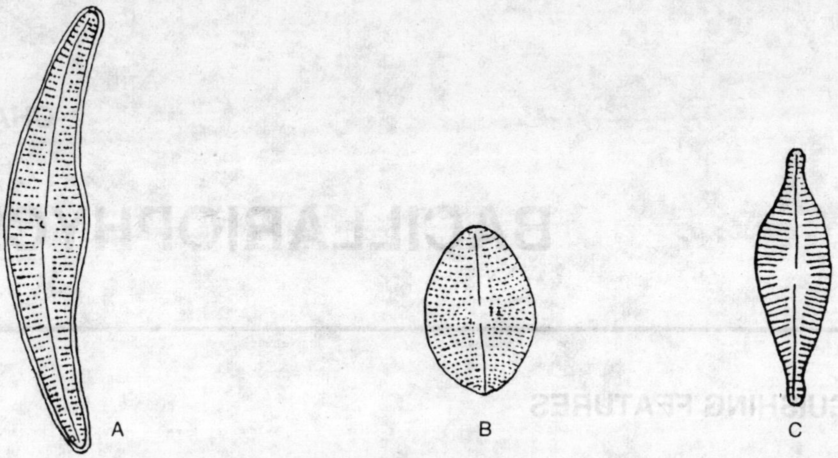

Fig. 34. Some of pinnate diatoms in valve view, A–*Cymbella* sp. B— *Cocconeis* sp., C– *Navicula* sp.

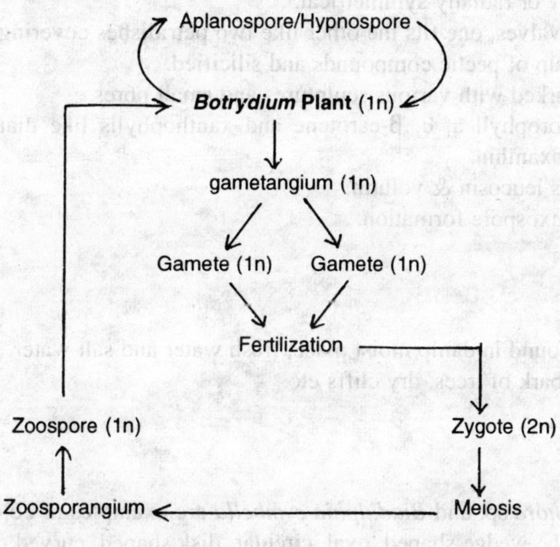

Graphic life cycle of *Botrydium sp.*

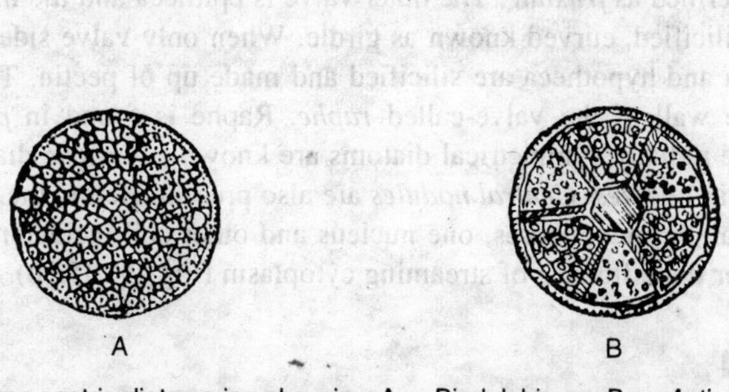

Fig. 35. Some centric diatoms in valve view A, – Biadulphia sp. B — *Actinoptychus* sp.

CHAPTER 5

BACILLARIOPHYCEAE

DISTINGUISHING FEATURES

1. Commonly it is known as diatoms.
2. They are of unicellular or colonial forms, occur in fresh or marine water.
3. Cells are bilaterally or radially symmetrical.
4. Cell wall has two valves, one fits the other like two petridishes covering each other.
5. Cell wall is made up of pectic compounds and silicified.
6. Wall surface is marked with various sculptures and small pores.
7. Cell contains chlorophyll a, c, β-carotene and xanthophylls like diatoxanthin, diadinoxanthin, fucoxanthin and neofucoxanthin.
8. The reserve food is leucosin & volutin.
9. It reproduces by auxospore formation.

HABITAT

The living diatoms are found in damp moist place, fresh water and salt water. Some species are aerial in habitat found on walls, bark of trees, dry cliffs etc.

PLANT BODY

It is unicellular. *Licmophora* sp. and *Biadulphia cymbella* are examples of colonial and chain like forms respectively. Cells may be wedge shaped, oval, circular, disk shaped, curved or rod shaped.

The cell wall is generally called as shell. It contains two overlapping valves. Both the valves or *shells* with its protoplast are termed as *frustule.* The outer valve is epitheca and the inner *hypotheca.* The edge of the two valves are silicified, curved known as girdle. When only valve side is seen it is called *valve view.* Both the epitheca and hypotheca are silicified and made up of pectin. There is furrow extending lengthwise through the wall of the valve-called *raphe*. Raphe is found in *pinnate* diatoms showing bilateral symmetry. The radially symmetrical diatoms are known as *centric* diatoms. The ends of raphe have nodules called polar *nodules. Central nodules* are also present. Below the cell wall — cytoplasm is found. There are several chromatophores, one nucleus and other cell inclusions. Some diatoms exhibit gliding movement under the influence of streaming cytoplasm (Fig. 34,35,36).

REPRODUCTION

It occurs by cell division and auxospore formation usually at night.

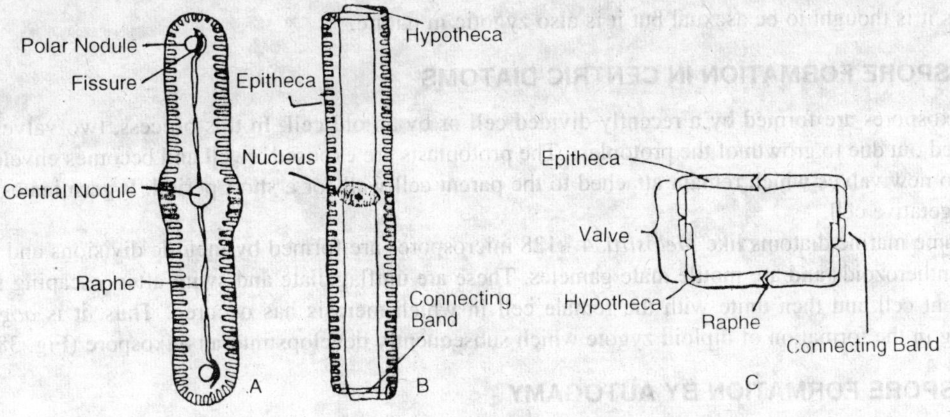

Fig. 36. *Pinnularia* sp. A valve view, B — Girdle view, C – T.S. showing parts of the body.

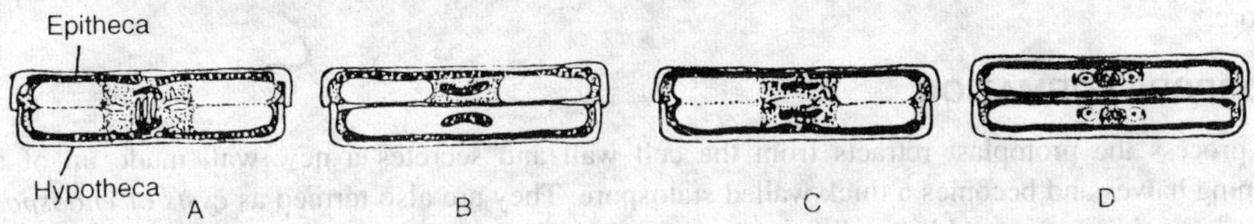

Fig. 37. A — D Different stages in the cell division of *Navicula* species.

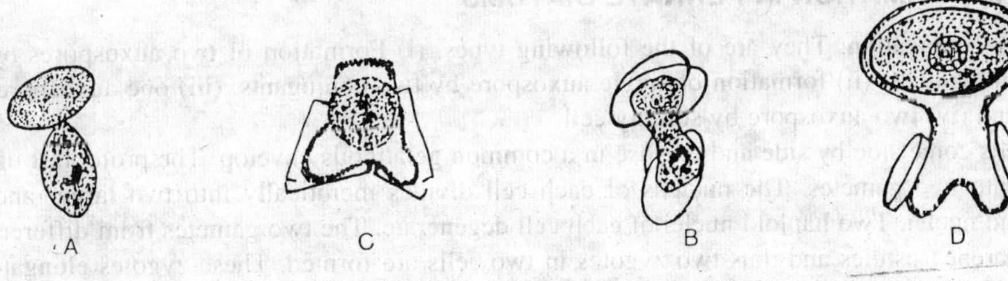

Fig. 38. Stages in the formation of one auxospore in pennate diatom A — D.

CELL DIVISION

In this process, the protoplast of the mother cell increase and pushed apart the two valves. Nucleus divides mitotically in a plane perpendicular to the long axis. Cytoplasm cleaves longitudinally resulting in the formation of two daughter protoplasts, each retained within the original valve or theca. Each daughter protoplast now secretes a new half wall on its naked side which fits into the old half wall. The newly formed half wall is hypotheca. Hence, the two valves of a new diatom cell are of different ages. Out of two cells formed after each cell division, one is of the same size as the parent cell and the other one is of smaller size. Thus, there is a progressive diminution in size of some cells which does not continue indefinitely. the reduced size cell develops a special type of rejuvenescent cell known as auxospores which reestablish their normal size (Fig. 37).

AUXOSPORE FORMATION

The auxospore formation in the members of order pennales and centrales are different. In pennales diatoms auxospore results from gametic union and thus, they are zygotic in nature where as in centric diatoms it is thought to be asexual but it is also zygotic in nature.

AUXOSPORE FORMATION IN CENTRIC DIATOMS

The auxospores are formed by a recently divided cell or by an old cell. In this process, two valves are separated out due to growth of the protoplast. The protoplasts are exposed, swell and becomes enveloped into two new valves which remain attached to the parent cell wall for a short period. It germinates into new vegetative cell.

In some marine diatoms like *Melosira*, 4 - 128 microspores are formed by meiotic divisions and they act as antherozoids and are motile male gametes. These are uniflagellate and swim after escaping from the parent cell and then unite with the female cell in which meiosis has occured. Thus, it is *oogamy* resulting in the formation of diploid zygote which subsequently develops into an auxospore (Fig. 38).

AUXOSPORE FORMATION BY AUTOGAMY

In centric diatoms like *Cyclotella*, the nucleus of a new forming auxospore divides meiotically. The two nuclei unite and the other two degenerate. The protoplast with fused diploid nucleus forms a diploid auxospore.

STATOSPORE FORMATION

In this process the protoplast retracts from the cell wall and secretes a new wall made up of two overlapping halves and becomes a thick walled statospore. They are also termed as *cysts* or *endospores*. They are formed in unfavourable condition.

AUXOSPORE FORMATION IN PENNATE DIATOMS

It occurs after conjugation. They are of the following types. (i) Formation of two auxospores by two conjugating individuals, (ii) formation of single auxospore by two conjugants, (iii) one auxospore by a solitary cell and (iv) two auxospore by solitary cell.

(*i*) Two cells come side by side and enclose in a common gelatinous envelop. The protoplast of each cell divides into two gametes. The nucleus of each cell divides meiotically into two larger and two smaller haploid nuclei. Two haploid nuclei of each cell degenerate. The two gametes from different cell unite in the parent frustules and thus two zygotes in two cells are formed. These zygotes elongate and form auxospore (Fig. 39).

(*ii*) Two cells are enclosed by a common gelatinous envelope and lie side by side. The nucleus of each cell divides meiotically into four, out of which three degenerate and one survives. The protoplast of each cell escapes out of wall and unites to form a zygote. The zygote then enlarges to form an auxospore.

(*iii*) Two individuals become enclose within a common gelatinous mass. The diploid nucleus divides mitotically. All but one degenerate. the remaining diploid nucleus in combination with protoplast comes out of the parent cell and form a diploid auxospore from each individual cell.

(*iv*) Sometimes two auxospores are formed from a single individual. The diploid nucleus divides meiotically into 4 haploid nuclei. Two unites into one diploid and another two into another diploid nucleus. These diploid nuclei in combination with cytoplasm form two zygotes and subsequently two auxospores are formed (Fig. 40).

ECONOMIC IMPORTANCE

Diatoms are economically important as such :-

1. It forms a basis of the food chain of aquatic animals.
2. It traps essential elements coming from the land water into the sea and keep them in circulation.

3. Deposits of diatom shells form diatomaceous earth or Fuller earth, and known as diatomite or kieselguh. Diatomite reduces the danger of explosions in mines.

4. It is used in tooth paste.

5. Diatomite is used in polishing the metal.

6 Diatomite is used as (i) insulating material in blast furnaces, (ii) bleaching powder (iii) absorbent for commercial fertilizers (iv) in paints (v) cleaning agent for fluids.

7. Some percentage of oil supply is of diatom origin.

8. According to Prescot (1969) there are about 190 genera of fossil diatoms of centrales nature. These fossil deposits occur as solid dunes may be hundreds of feet thick and many miles in length in Oregon and California. It helps in determining the ecological condition of the past.

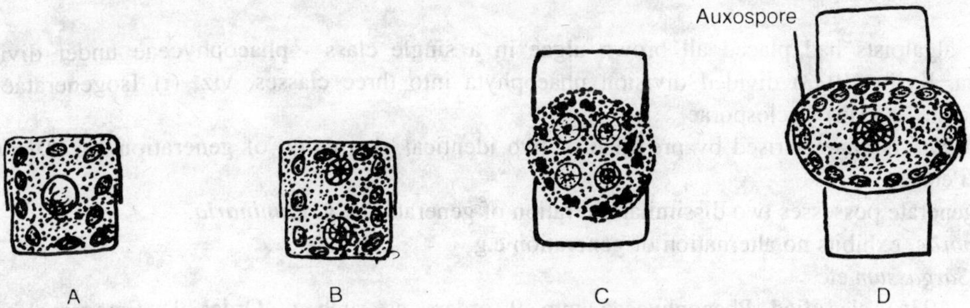

Fig. 39. Formation auxospore by autogamy in centric diatoms (A-D).

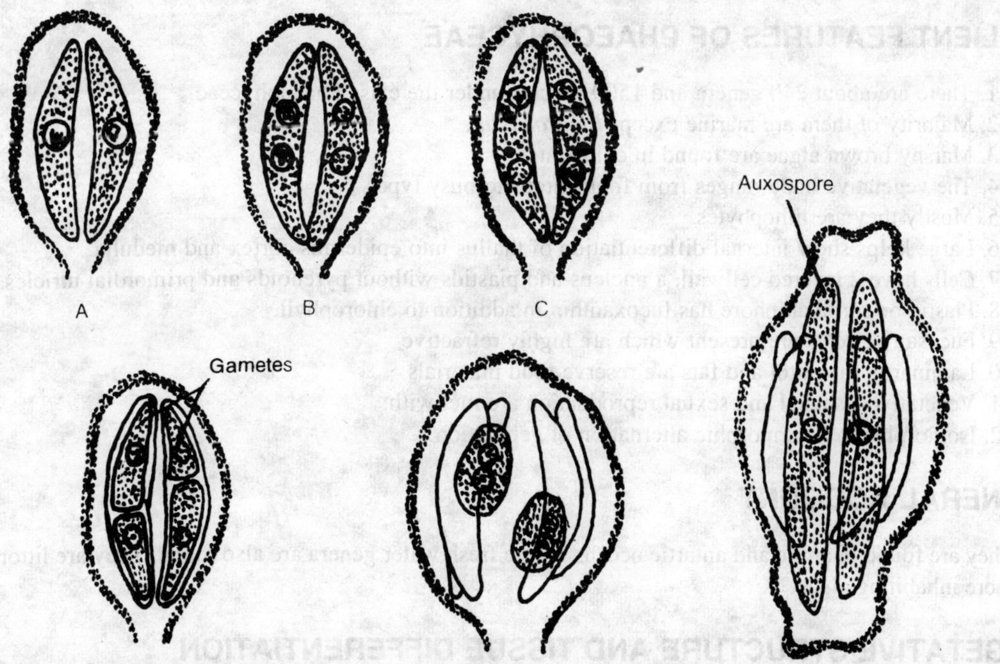

Fig. 40. Stages showing formation of two auxospores by two conjugating cell of pennate diatoms.

CHAPTER 6

PHAEOPHYTA—PHAEOPHYCEAE

The older algaloists had placed all brown algae in a single class - phaeophyceae under division Phaeophyta. Kylin (1933) divided division phaeophyta into three classes, viz. (i) Isogeneratae (ii) Heterogenerate and (iii) Cyclosporae.

Isogeneratae is characterised by presence of two identical alternation of generation e.g. *Dictyota*, *Ectocarpus* etc.

Heterogenerate possesses two dissimilar alteration of generation e.g. *Laminaria.*

Cyclosporae exhibits no alternation of generation e.g.

Fucus, *Sargassum* etc.

Fritsch (1935) classified Phaeophyceae into 9 orders as such :- Order 1. Ectocarpales, 2. Tilopteridales, 3. Cutleriales, 4. Sporochnales, 5. Desmarestiales, 6. Laminariales, 7. Sphacelariales, 8. Dictyotales and 9. Fucales

SALIENT FEATURES OF PHAEOPHYCEAE

1. There are about 240 genera and 1500 species under the class Phaeophyceae.
2. Majority of them are marine except *Pleurocladia.*
3. Marshy brown algae are found in cold water.
4. The vegetative body ranges from filamentous to busy types.
5. Mostly they are lithophytes.
6. Large kelps show internal differentiation of thallus into epidermis cortex and medulla.
7. Cells have 2 layered cellwall, a nucleus and plastids without pyrenoids and primordial utricles.
8. Plastid or chromatophore has fucoxanthin in addition to chlorophyll.
9. Fucosan vesicles are present which are highly refractive.
10. Laminarin, mannitol and fats are reserve food materials.
11. Vegetative, asexual and sexual reproduction are met with.
12. Isomorphic to hetermorphic alternation of generation.

GENERAL ACCOUNT

They are found in arctic and antartic oceans. Some fresh water genera are also found. They are littoral or shore inhabiting algae.

VEGETATIVE STRUCTURE AND TISSUE DIFFERENTIATION

They are most highly evolved type of algae. They display higher degree of body/tissue differentiation. Unicellular and colonial forms are not known. Simplest type of plant body is heterotrichous filament (*Ectocarpus*) Heterotrichy gradually disappears in higher forms like *Dictyota*, *Laminaria.* Higher members have differentiated body into lower hold fast and upper flattend part–frond. Thallus is differentiated into 3 layers in higher form while there is no differentiation into layers in the thallus of primitive form of Phaeophyceae.

Fucus has marked anatomical and morphological complexity. Vertical section (V.S.) of thallus reveals outer meristoderm layer, below this — cortical layers are present. Cortex may have outer palisade and inner parenchymatous layer. Central layer of medulla is present.

Still higher forms, viz. *Laminaria.* the sporophyte is differentiated into two main region i.e. stipe and lamina. Cross connections and trumpet hyphae in the cells are noticed. Sometimes perforation in the thallus equivalent to sieve tubes are found in certain pacific kelps.

Postelsia palmiformis a native of pacific shores of N. America resemble palm tree and hence commonly known as *Sea palm.* Trumphet hyphae are vertically elongated cells in medulla without plastid and discharge the function of water and nutrient conduction.

REPRODUCTION

It is of three types (i) Vegetative (ii) Asexual and (iii) Sexual. Vegetative reproduction is by fragmentation. In some brown algae like *Sphacelaria* — vegetative reproduction is by special branch called *propagule.*

Asexual reproduction occurs in all the members of brown algae except *Fucus.* Asexual spores may be biflagellate zoospores produced in unilocular or plurilocular sporangia.

Sexual reproduction may be isogamous, anisogamous or oogomous type. Fertilization may take place either when the egg is being discharged from the oogonium or when egg is retained within the oogonium.

Isomorphic or hetermorphic alternation of generations are of common occurrence. In the members of Fucales there is an alternation of multicellular diploid generation with unicellular haploid phase represented by gametes only. Various types of alternation of generation are found in the Phaeophyceae as follows —

1. Alternation of similar generation i.e. isomorphic e.g. *Dictyota*
2. Alternation of diploid and haploid isomorphic generation e.g. *Ectocarpus.*
3. Alternation of morphologically dissimilar generation (heteromorphic) e.g. *Cutleria*
4. Morphologically dissimilar alternation of generation having dominant (large) sporophyte and recessive (small) gametophyte e.g. *Chordariales.*
5. Heteromorphic alternation of dominant sporophyte generation with minute gametophytic generation e.g. Laminariales.
6. No true alternation of generation. Diploid sporophyte produces heterospores by meiosis and spores directly act as gametes e.g. Some members of Fucales

ECONOMIC IMPORTANCE

Phaeophyceae are of great economic importance as shown below.

1. As food — *Laminaria* and *Alaria* are used as a kind of food by Japanese. Algin obtained from *Macrocystis* is used in ice–cream making.
2. **Source of Iodine** — Iodine are obtained from *Fucus*, *Sargassum* etc.
3. As fodder — *Sargassum* is used as fodder.

ALTERNATION OF GENERATIONS IN PHAEOPHYTA

Following are the different types of alternation of generations observed among the members of Phaeophyta.

ISOMORPHIC TYPE OF ALTERNATION OF GENERATIONS

1. Here there is an alternation of diploid and haploid generations which are morphologically similar as in *Ectocarpus*.

2. Here there is an alternation of similar (morphologically) generation which produces heterogametes like egg and sperm e.g. *Dictyota*.

HETEROMORPHIC TYPE OF ALTERNATION OF GENERATIONS

1. In this type there is an alternation of morphologically dissimilar generations having small sporophyte and dominant gametophyte producing heterogametes as in *Cutleria*.

2. Here the sporophyte is dominant and the gametophyte is small forming isogametes e.g. members of Chordariales and Laminariales.

NO TRUE ALTERNATION

The members of Fucales are dominant diploid sporophyte which produce heterospores after meiosis. These spores metamorphose directly into egg and sperms.

On the basis of modes of alternation of generations Kylin (1933), Papenfues (1951) and Smith (1955) have classified Phaeophyta into three series as follows :

1. **Isogeneratae** : The members of this series show isomorphic alternation of generation. It has been divided into 5 orders viz. Ectocarpales, Sphacelariales, Tilopteridales, Cutleriales and Dictyotales.

2. **Heterogeneratae** : This shows heteromorphic alternation of generations. It has been further divided into 6 order viz. Chordariales, Sporochnales, Desmarestials (under sub class *Haplostichineae*), Punctariales Dictyosiphonales and Laminariales (under sub–class *Polystichineae*).

3. **Cyclosporae** : It shows only a diploid generation. It has only one order Fucales.

Bold and Wynne (1978) have divided Phaeophycophyta into thirteen orders (see classification of Algae).

LIFE HISTORY OF SELECTED GENERA OF PHAEOPHYCEAE

6.1 LAMINARIA

It belongs to

Division	—	Phaeophyta
Class	—	Phaeophyceae
Sub-class	—	Heterogeneratae
Orde r	—	Laminariales
Family	—	Laminariaceae
Genus	—	*Laminaria*

HABITAT

Laminaria occurs in lower or sub– littoral zone of the sea specially along the Atlantic and Pacific coasts of British Isles and U.S.A. Majority of them are rock loving and lithophytes and they are known as "*devils aprons*".

There are about 20 species and popularly called as "Kelps" for its uses in fertilizers, food and as source of iodine. Common species of *Laminaria* are *L. saccharina*, *L. digitata*, *L. ephemera* etc.

PLANT BODY

The sporophytic diploid plant body may be 6 or more meters in length, differentiated into simple or branched root like hold fast, stipe or stem and blade or leaf (Fig 41).

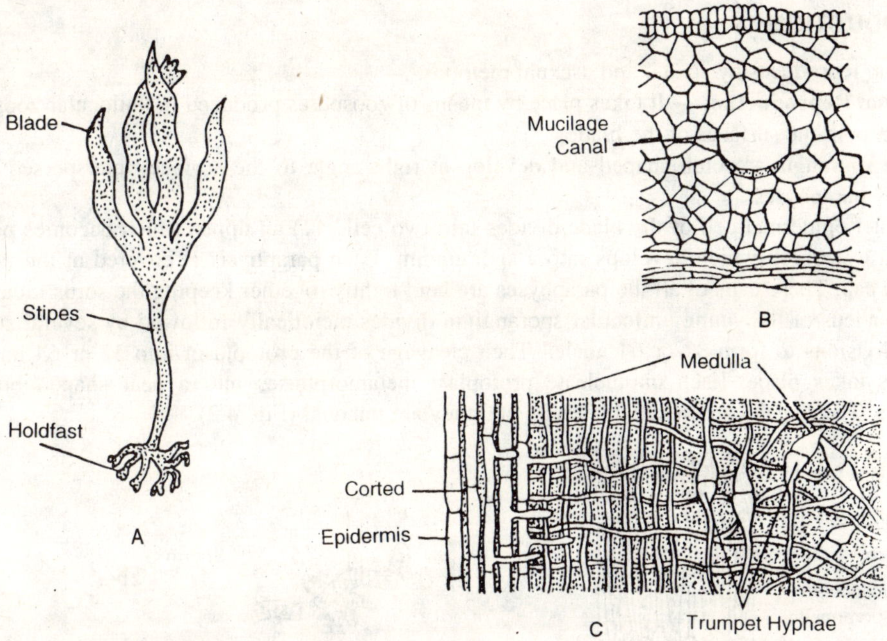

Fig. 41. *Laminaria* sp. A–Plant, B–T.S. of blade C–L.S. through medulla of stipe.

Hold fast may be simple (solid disc like structure) or complex (forked root like structure) called *haptera.* Stipe forms the main axis which is unbranched, cylindrical or flattered depending on the species. Blade may be entire or incised into several segments and appears terminating the stipe. The surface may be smooth or convoluted. It is leathery in texture.

GROWTH

It takes place by the activity of intercalary meristem located at the junction of the stipe and the blade.

ANATOMY OF STIPE / BLADE

Transverse section (T.S.) of both stipe and blade shows three distinct regions viz. (1) epidermis, (2) cortex and (3) medulla (Fig. 41).

Epidermis or meristoderm — It constitutes the outer most layer made up of single or more layers of similar small cubical cells containing chromatophores. The epidermis is covered externally by mucilage.

Cortex — It can be differentiated into outer and inner cortex. The outer cortex has vertically elongated and wider cell with tapering ends. Concentric zones of light and dark coloured cells are formed due to difference in the rate of cell division and hence it is termed as growth rings. Inner cortex has longer cells with square ends. Mucilage ducts are present in the cortex.

Medulla — It consists of unbranched filamentous cells which lie close to each other. Some filaments extend diagonally or transversely which provide mechanical strength. Some filaments elongate vertically and swell and widen near the crosswall to form *trumpet hyphae*. Trumpet hypha has several pores over its transverse walls through which cytoplasmic connections are established, in between adjoining cells. This can be compared with sieve cells of vascular plants. It acts as conducting cells, storage tissue or mechanical tissue.

REPRODUCTION

Laminaria reproduces by sexual and asexual methods.

Asexual Reproduction — It takes place by means of zoospores produced in unilocular zoosporangia in sori on both the surfaces of the blade.

These sporangia are club shaped and develop at right angle to the surface, interspersed and over topped by paraphyses.

An outer epidermal cell of the blade divides into two cells, (1) an upper which becomes paraphysis and (2) a lower cell which develops into a sporangium. Each paraphysis is covered at the top with a mucilage cap. These caps of all the paraphyses are held tightly together keeping the sorus intact.

The nucleus of the young unilocular sporangium divides meiotically followed by several successive mitotic divisions to form 32 or 64 nuclei. Then cleavage of the protoplasm into 32 or 64 uninucleate structures takes place. Each uninucleate protoplast metamorphoses into a pear shaped biflagellate zoospores. The flagella are inserted laterally and they are unequal (Fig. 4.2)

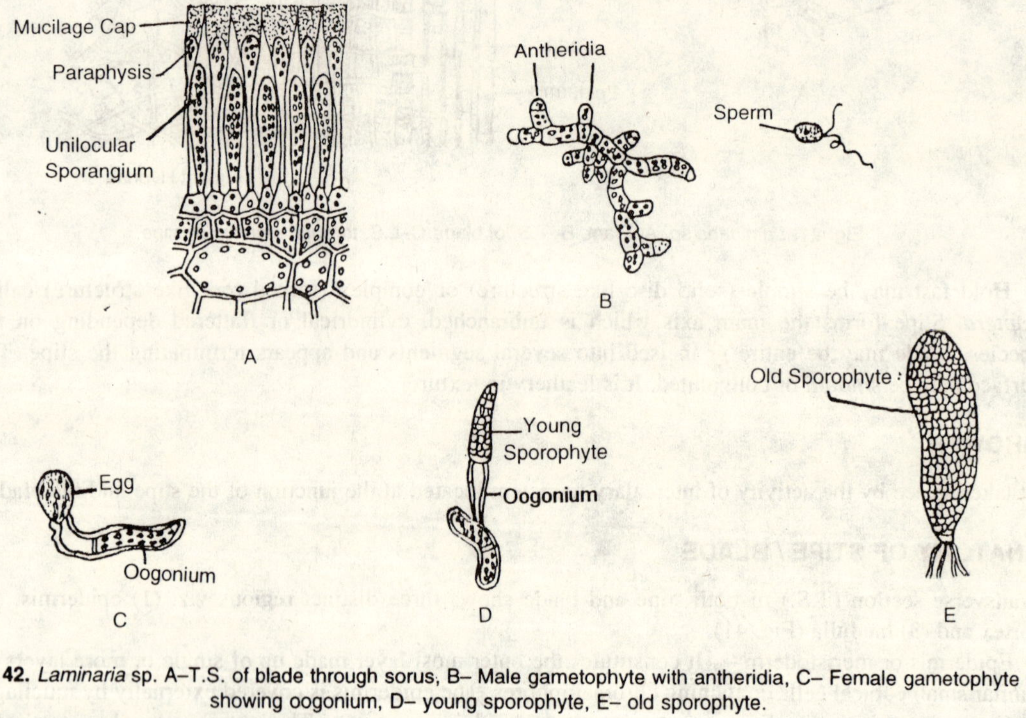

Fig. 42. *Laminaria* sp. A–T.S. of blade through sorus, B– Male gametophyte with antheridia, C– Female gametophyte showing oogonium, D– young sporophyte, E– old sporophyte.

On the dissolution of the tip of the zoosporangium mature zoospores in mass, enclosed within a gelatinous sheath, are liberated out. The sheath dissolves leaving the zoospores which swim freely in water. After some period of swimming the zoospore comes to rest, becomes round, secretes a wall around itself and germinates by giving a germ tube. Zoospores produce two types of gametophytic plants, one male gametophytic plant and the other female gametophytic plant.

Sexual Reproduction — It is of oogamous type. Gametes are produced by gametophytic plants, which are dioecious, few celled filamentous in structure.

The male gametes or antherozoids or sperms are produced in antheridium on male gametophytic plant. The antheridia develop singly or in groups at the terminal cells of the projecting filaments or as lateral outgrowths from the upperside of the creeping filament. Each antheridium is spherical, unicellular and small. The contents of the antheridium forms a simple, pear shaped antherozoid with two unequal flagella on lateral side. After the liberation of the antherozoid, the male plant disorganised. The female gametophytic plant is sparingly branched and develops oogonia from any cell. The cell producing oogonium elongates vertically and its contents metamorphose into an egg. The egg is escaped through a narrow aperture formed at the apex of the oogonial wall and remain attached to it till fertilization takes place.

After fertilization dipoid zygote is formed which secretes a thin wall around itself.

The zygote, without passing through any resting period, starts to grow into a new sporophytic plant.

ALTERNATION OF GENERATION

Laminaria exhibits distinct alternation of generations. The sporophytic plant is dominant and the gametophyte is small and recessive. The sporophyte produces diploid unilocular sporangia in sori. The sporangium forms haploid spores after meiosis. The spores germinate to form gametophyte male and female plants which differ structurally from sporophytic plants. The male plant produces antheridium which bears haploid antherozoid. The female plant produces oogonium which develops haploid egg. Fertilization takes place in between haploid motile antherozoid and haploid passive egg, thus it is of oogomous type. After the union, diploid zygote is produced and further development takes place to give rise new sporophytic diploid plant and thus life cycle is completed as shown in the following diagram.

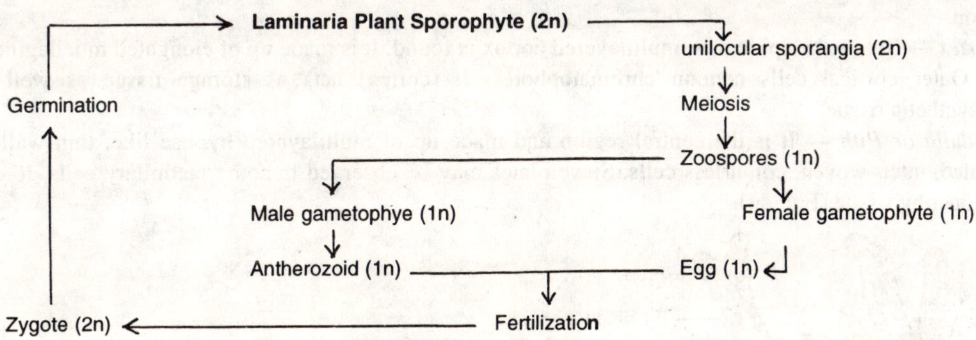

Graphic life cycle of *Laminaria* sp.

6.2 FUCUS

It belongs to

Division	—	Phaeophyta
Class	—	Phaeophyceae
Sub–class	—	Cyclosporae
Order	—	Fucales
Family	—	Fucaceae
Genus	—	*Fucus*

There are about 16 species under the genus *Fucus* and majority of them are marine, distributed along the sea coasts of temperate and arctic zones. They are commonly known as "rock weeds" as they remain attached to the rocks under cold water in between the low and high tide marks (intertidal zone) with the help of their discoid and flat hold fasts.

PLANT BODY

The vegetative plant body is thalloid, differentiated into hold fast, stipe and blade or frond. The plant is sporophyte. The Hold fast is the anchorage organ by which the plant is attached to the substratum under water.

The stipe is stem like part of the thallus and it is comparatively shorter. The blade is ribbon like, expanded, leathery, foliose like and dichotomously branched. The thallus is slimy in nature and appears dark brown in colour. The stipe is continued in the form of a mid rib in the blade and does not reach the apex of the blade. The margin of the blade is serrate or entire.

The thallus in several species like *F. vesiculosus* has several *bladder like*, hollow or air filled structures in pairs over the frond. It is known as *Air vesicles* or *Air bladders*. It provides buoyancy to the submerged thallus. The swollen tips of the fertile mature branches of the thallus are known as *receptacles*. The receptacle is devoid of mid rib and is covered with several small dot or pimple like outgrowths with minute apertures or ostioles. These Ostioles lead into flask shaped cavities, known as *conceptacle*. Sex organs (antheridia and oogonia) are found within the conceptacles. Sometimes wings like structures are formed lateral to the mid rib on the thallus. These structures may be provided with sterile conceptacles known as *Cryptostomata* or *Cryptoblasts*. (Fig. 43).

Transverse section of the thallus shows the following anatomical structures —

Epidermis — It is the outer most layer of thin walled small palisade like cells containing many chromatophores. This layer is also known as *meristoderm* or limiting layer which is photosynthetic in function.

Cortex — Below the epidermis, multilayered cortex is found. It is made up of elongated mucilaginous cells. Outer cortical cells contain chromatophores. It (cortex) acts as storage tissue as well as photosynthetic tissue.

Medulla or Pith — It is the central region and made up of multilayered hyphae like, thin walled, elongated, inter–woven, colourless cells. Sieve plates may be observed in some medullary cells. It acts as conducting tissue (Fig. 44).

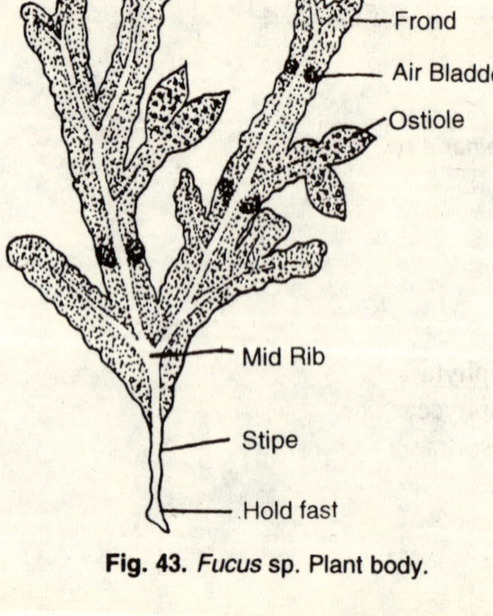

Fig. 43. *Fucus* sp. Plant body.

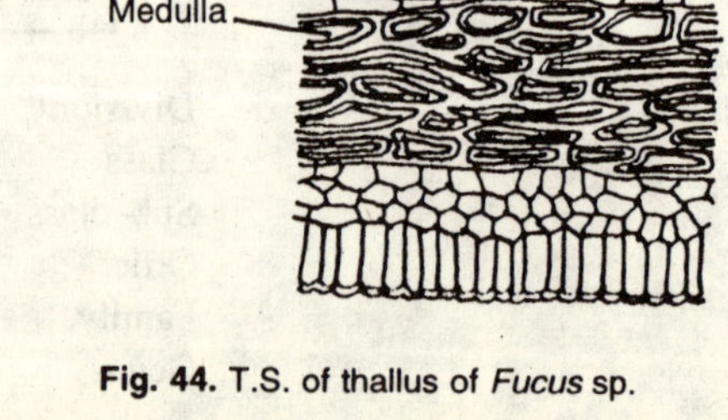

Fig. 44. T.S. of thallus of *Fucus* sp.

GROWTH

It takes place by an apical cell situated at the apex of the axis. The pyramid like apical cell has three cutting faces and it divides to provide vertical growth. Lateral growth is caused by divisions in the cells of meristoderm.

CELL STRUCTURE

Fucus has cells which are generally uninucleate, containing several disc shaped chromatophores which are devoid of pyrenoids. Fucoxanthin (brown pigments) are contained within the chromatophore.

REPRODUCTION

Fucus reproduces vegetatively as well as sexually. There is no means of asexual reproduction.

Vegetative reproduction — It is accomplished by fragmentation of the thallus. Each fragmented portion develops into a new thallus. Sometimes adventitious branches develope on the stipe which form new plants after detachment.

Sexual reproduction — It is of oogomous type. *Fucus* plant is diploid and sporophyte. Sex organs — antheridia and oogonia are produced within conceptacles. *F. vesiculosus* is heterothallic in which antheridia and oogonia are born in separate conceptacles on different plants. Some species like *F. spiralis* is homothallic in which both the sex organs i.e. antheridia and oogonia are produced in the same or in the different conceptacles on the same plant. The conceptacle opens outside by a small aperture known as ostiole. The inner wall of the conceptacle develops many multicellular, branched, sterile hairs like structures known as *paraphyses*. The upper region of the conceptacle may bear unbranched hairy structures known as *periphyses*.

Male sex organ — Antheridium — Antheridia are born in groups on paraphyses within the conceptacle. Each antheridium has two layered dilicate wall. Outer layer is *exochite* and inner layer is

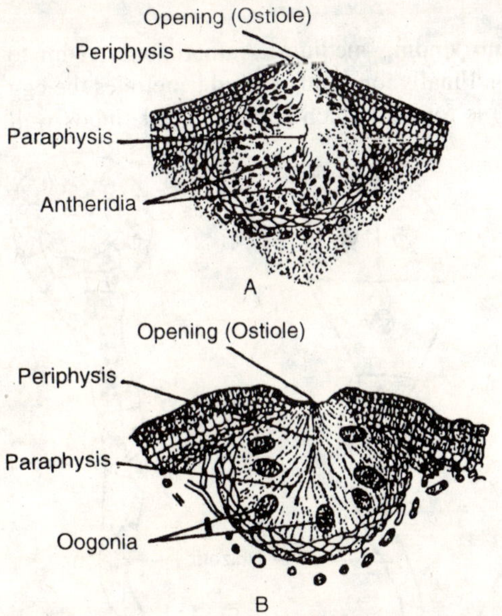

Fig. 45. A—T.S. of thallus of Fucus sp. through male conceptacle showing antheridia, B—T..S. of thallus through female conceptable showing oogonia.

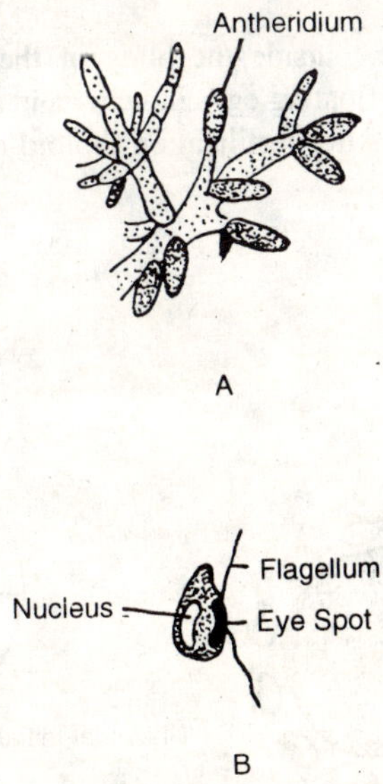

Fig. 46. *Fucus* sp. A—Antheridia, B—Antherozoid.

endochite. The diploid nucleus of the antheridium divides meiotically followed by mitotic divisions resulting into 64 daughter nuclei (haploid). The antheridal contents also cleaved into uninucleate protoplasts which metamorphoses into pear shaped antherozoid. The sperm or antherozoid has an eye spot and two unequal flagella inserted laterally (Fig. 45, 46).

At maturity the antheridial tip breaks and mass of antherozoids are liberated within the conceptacle and finally the sperms come out of conceptacle when the plant is reflooded by incoming tide.

Female sex organ–Oogonium — Oogonium is oval or ellipsoidal, one celled, stalked structure. They are born among the paraphyses within the conceptacle. Each conceptacle contains several oogonia. The oogonial wall is made up of 3 layers, exochite, mesochite and endochite. Its diploid nucleus divides meiotically into 4 haploid nuclei followed by mitotic divisions resulting into 8 haploid nuclei.

Then protoplast cleaves into 8 uninucleate eggs. Oogonial wall ruptures and mature eggs come out into the surrounding water (fig. 45,47).

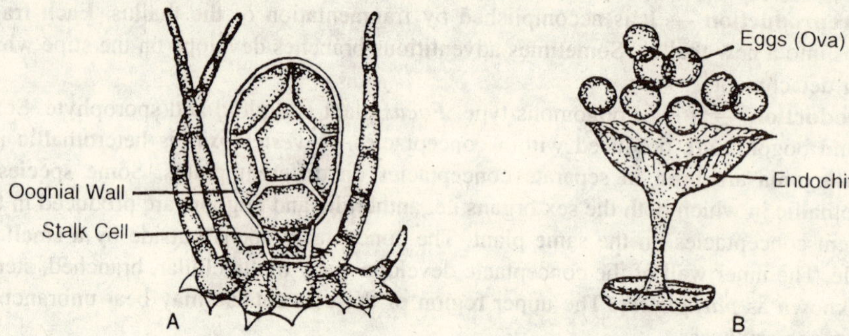

Fig. 47. *Fucus* sp. A– an oogonium, B–liberation of eggs.

FERTILIZATION

It is external i.e. outside the body of the plant in the surrounding medium. Antherozoids swim to non–motile free–floating eggs in water and assemble the egg. Finally, one antherozoid penetrates the egg and fertilizes it. After fertilization diploid oospore (zygote) is formed which secretes a gelatinous wall

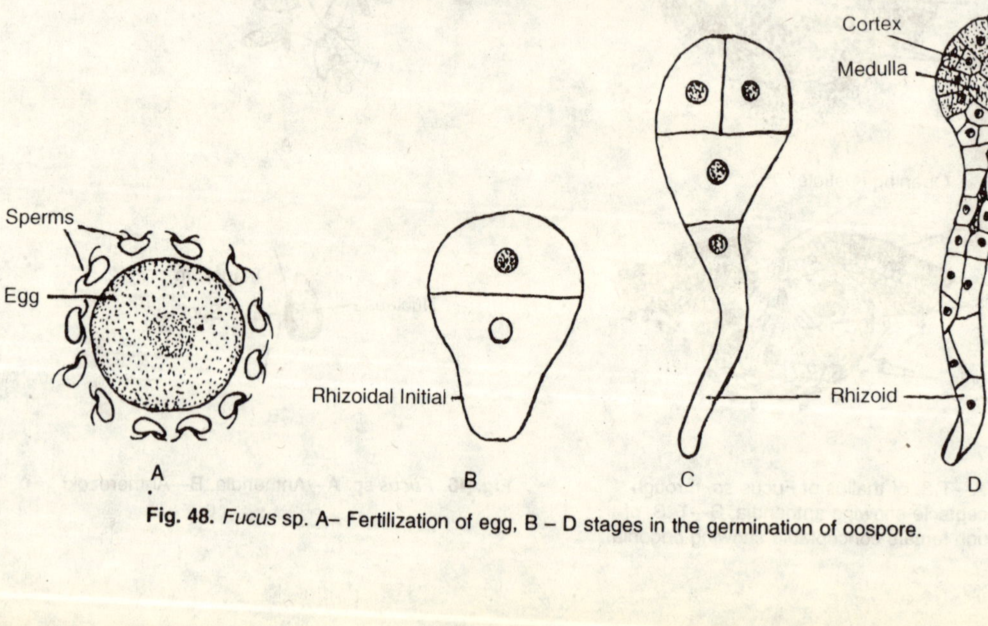

Fig. 48. *Fucus* sp. A– Fertilization of egg, B – D stages in the germination of oospore.

and then it affixes firmly to any substratum. It germinates immediately without passing any resting period, into a diploid new *Fucus* plant (Fig. 48)

ALTERNATION OF GENERATIONS

Fucus being sporophyte, bears sex organs unlike other member of phaeophyceae. The gametophytic generation is represented by gametes and so haploid phase is much reduced. After fertilization, diploid phase starts. Thus, there is no alternation of haploid gametophyte and diploid sporophyte. This factor can be compared with the higher animal body which is diploid and lacks a haploid phase except for the gametes. In this way in *Fucus* there is no morphological alternation of generation in its life cycle as has been shown in the following graphic cycle.

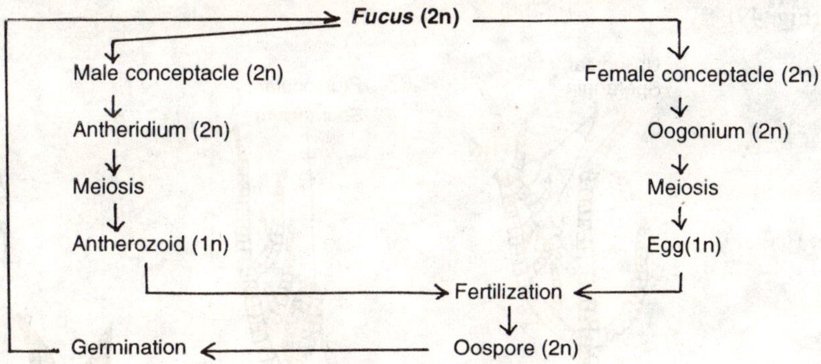

Graphic life cycle of *Fucus* sp.

6.3 ECTOCARPUS

It belongs to

Division	—	Phaeophyta
Class	—	Phaeophyceae
Order	—	Ectocarpales
Family	—	Ectocarpaceae
Genus	—	*Ectocarpus*

The genus *Ectocarpus* is represented by more than 12 species in India. Some of them are *Ectocarpus indicus*, *E. coniferus*, *E. enhali* etc.

DISTINGUISHING CHARACTERS

Following are the important features of *Ectocarpus.*

1. Vegetative body contains branched filaments.
2. Thallus is composed of prostrate and erect system.
3. Presence of unilocular and plurilocular sporangia which produce biflagellate zoospores meant for asexual reproduction.
4. Haploid zoospores produced in unilocular sporangia germinates into sex bearing gametophytes and the diploid zoospores developed in plurilocular sporangia give rise asexual sporophyte plants.
5. Isogamous and anisogamous types of sexual reproduction occur.
6. It exhibits distinct alternation of generation.
7. They grow in littoral and sublittoral zones of seas.

HABITAT

They are marıne forms. Epiphytic forms are also found e.g. *Ectocarpus coniferus*. Some species like *E. fasciculatus* grows on fishes and hence *epizoic*. In India they are found in western cost attached to the rocks or sea plants.

VEGETATIVE PLANT BODY

The thallus (sporophytic plant body) is differentiated into prostrate and erect branch system. The prostrate system is branched and creeping and the erect system consists of freely moving profusely branched filaments. These branches, in some species terminate into colourless mucilaginous hairs. Filaments are monosiphonous i.e. only one cell thick. Due to vertical division of the cells it becomes polysiphonous (Fig. 49)

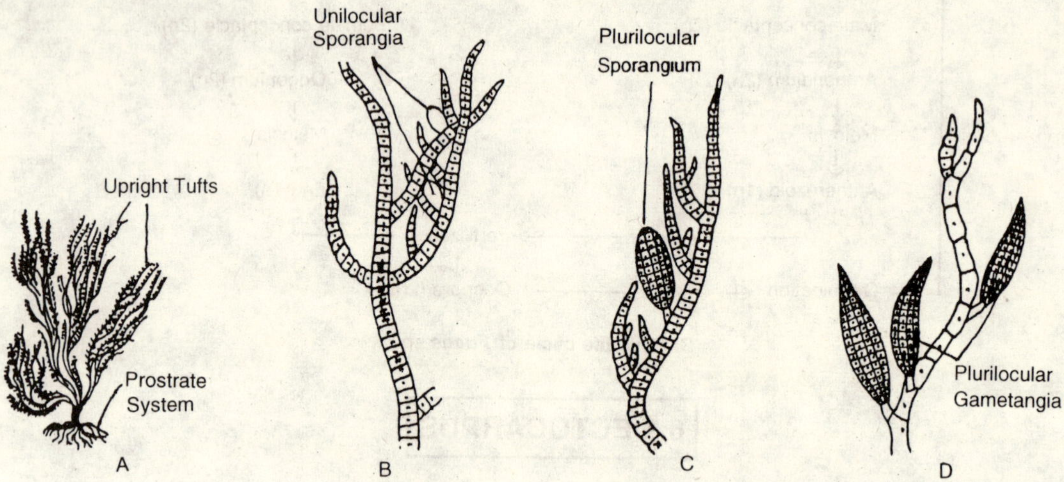

Fig.. 49. A—Habit of *Ectocarpus* sp. B—Thallus with Unilocular sporangia, C—thallus showing plurilocular sporangia, with plurilocular gemetangia.

CELL STRUCTURE

The filament of *Ectocarpus* is made up of semi–oval rectangular or cylindrical uninucleate cells. Cell wall is made up of cellulose and pectic substance. The outer mucilaginous wall layer contains algin and fucoiden. The cell has several plastids or chromatophores containing brown pigment fucoxanthin in addition to chlorophyll. Vacuoles and polyphenols are also present in the cytoplasm.

GROWTH

Prostrate system grows by apical meristems where as erect filaments grow by intercalary meristems. Intercalary meristem cuts off cells in both downward and upward direction. This type of growth is trichothallic growth and it is characteristics of *Ectocarpus*.

REPRODUCTION

Ectocarpus shows both sexual and asexual methods of reproduction.

Asexual Reproduction — It occurs by biflagellate, pyriform, uninucleate zoospores produced in unilocular or plurilocular sporangia. *Unilocular sporangia* develop singly at the tips of small branches. The terminal cell of lateral branchlet enlarges in size and behaves as sporangial initial. The diploid

nucleus divides meiotically followed by mitotic divisions to form 32 - 64 haploid nuclei. No wall formation takes place and hence sporangium remains unilocular. Each haploid nucleus in combination with cytoplasm is metamorphosed into pyriform, uninucleate, biflagellate zoospores. It has an eye spot and the two flagella of unequal length and inserted laterally. The zoospores are liberated through a small opening in the sporangial wall. They swim for a few minutes and germinates into new gametophyte plant. *Plurilocular sporangia* also develop from terminal diploid cell of the branchlet. The sporangial initial which is the enlarged terminal cell divides by transverse and vertical wall formation into more than 600 cubical cells. This multicellular structure is called as plurilocular sporangium. The nucleus of sporangial initial divides mitotically only and each diploid nucleus in combination with divided cytoplasm metamorphoses into a single biflagellate diploid zoospore. They are liberated through a pore in the plurilocular sporangial wall and after swiming for a short period, it germinates into sporophyte which is diploid.

The development of unilocular and plurilocular sporangia are temperature dependent as unilocular sporangia are produced at 13°C, plurilocular sporangia are formed at 19°C both unilocular and plurilocular at 16°C in *E.siliculosus* (Fig. 50).

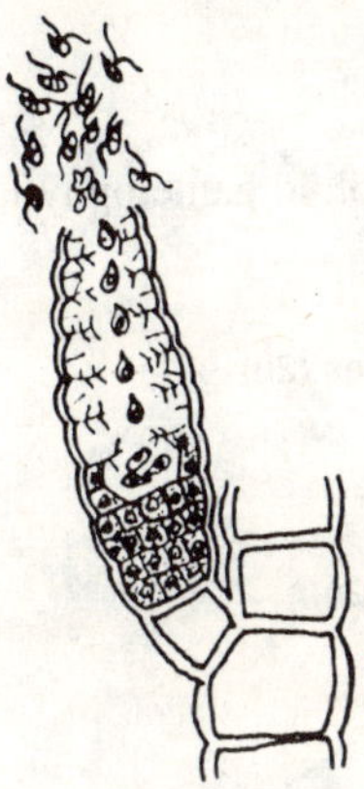

Ectocarpus sp

Fig. 50. Plurilocular sporangia in *Ectocarpus* sp. liberating zoospores.

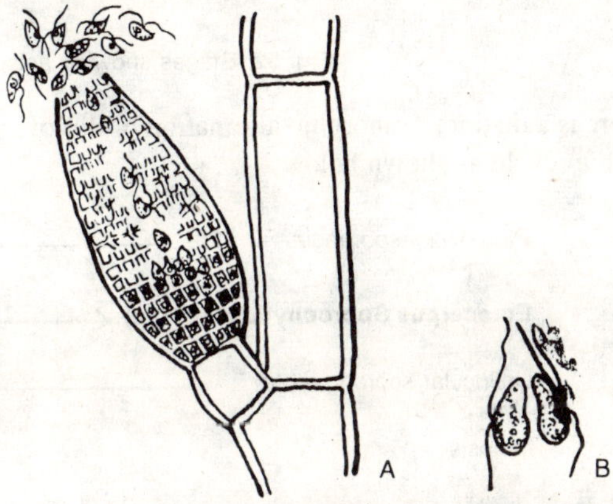

Ectocarpus sp

Fig. 51. A–Plurilocular gametangium liberating gametes, B–two uniting gametes in *Ectocarpus* sp.

Sexual reproduction — *Ectocarpus* are isogamous, anisogamous and sometimes oogomous also.

Formation of gametes within gametangium — The gametangia may be short stalked or sessile. It develops singly from the terminal cell of lateral branchlet of haploid gametophyte plant. The gametangial initial divides transversely into 6 - 12 cells followed by vertical division to produce hundreds of cubical cells. The nucleus also divides mitotically several times. Each nucleus in combination with cytoplasm is converted into a single pear shaped gamete with two lateral flagella of unequal length. The gametes are liberated through a terminal pore in the gametangial wall. The gametes coming from different plants fuse to form a diploid zygote. Thus, *Ectocarpus* is heterothallic. This has been observed in *E. siliculosus* (Fig. 51). *E. secundus* shows anisogamy. Two types of gametes are formed in macrogametangia and microgametangia. Micro and macro gametes pairs and fuse to form a diploid zygote. In physiologically anisogamous species the female gametes settles after a few minutes of swiming and secretes a chemical called sirenine which act as sexual attractant. The male gametes coming from different gametangia swims for more than 8 hours and are attracted towards the female passive gamete under the influence of *Sirenine.* One of the male gametes come in the contact of the female gamete and fuse to form diploid zygospore. During this process many male gametes cluster around female gamete and only one male gamete manages to fuse with the female gamete to form a diploid zygospore. This process is known as *clump formation*.

GERMINATION OF ZYGOSPORE

The diploid zygote or zygospore germinates directly to produce a new diploid sporophyte which resemble morphologically with gametophytic plant body. Sometimes gametes fail to unite and germinate parthenogenetically into new haploid gametophytic *Ectocarpus* plant (Fig. 52).

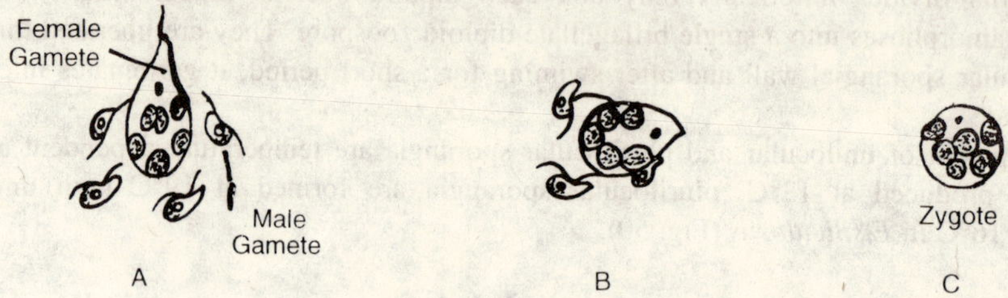

Fig. 52. Stages showing anisogamy in *Ectocarpus* sp.

There is a distinct isomorphic alternation of diploid sporophytic and haploid gametophytic generation in the life cycle as shown below —

Plurilocular sporangia (2n) → Zoospores (2n)
↑ ↓
Ectocarpus Sporophytic plant (2n) ← germination
↓ ↑
Unilocular sporangia (2n) Zygote (2n)
↓ ↑
Meiosis Fertilization
↓ ↗ ↖
Zoospores (1n) Gamete (1n) Gamete (1n)
↓ ↖ ↗
Gametophytic Plant (1n) → Plurilocular gametangium (1n)

Graphic Life Cycle of *Ectocarpus* sp.

6.4 SARGASSUM

It belongs to	Division	—	Phaeophyta
	Class	—	Phaeophyceae
	Order	—	Fucales
	Family	—	Sargassaceae
	Genus	—	*Sargassum*

There are about 150 species in the genus *Sargassum* found mainly in the tropical and subtropical seas of the southern hemisphere. About 16 species are reported from India, some of them are *Sargassum carpophyllum*, *S duplicatum*, *S. christifolium* etc.

DISTINGUISHING FEATURES

1. The plant body is sporophyte and diploid.
2. Thallus is differentiated into main axis, lateral branches and leaf like structure.
3. Air bladders are present.
4. Thallus has epidermis, medulla and cortex.
5. Devoid of asexual reproduction
6. Vegetative and oogamous sexual reproductions are noticed.
7. Oogonia and antheridia are born on conceptacles.
8. Meiosis occurs during gametogenesis.
9. Fertilized egg is liberated out in water but remains attached to the gelatinous wall of the conceptacle by a mucilaginous stalk.
10. It does not exhibit true alternation of generation.

HABITAT

They are aquatic and confined to warmer seas of tropical zone. Huge floating masses of *Sargassum* are seen in Sargasso sea and they are commonly known as "Gulf weed". In India, *Sargassum* is found on both eastern and western cost attached to the rocks below the low tide level.

PLANT BODY

The sporophytic diploid plant body appears busy consisting of stem like main axis or stipe and leafy frond like blades. It may reach several meters in height. The lateral branches are leaf like with or without mid rib depending on species. The margin of leaves are serrate. Air bladders are present on modified secondary stalk or branch. Fertile elongate, finger like branches are receptacles which bear *conceptacles*. In the beginning the plant is attached but later it becomes afloat and multiply by fragmentation. Vertical section of thallus shows (i) an outer epidermis of columnar cells containing plastids (ii) cortex multilayered and of isodimetric cells and (iii) medulla consists of elongated, narrow thin or thick walled cells, helps in conduction of food.

GROWTH

It occurs by a three sided uninucleate apical cell which divides and continue to grow.

REPRODUCTION

Asexual reproduction is absent. It reproduces by sexual and vegetative method.

Vegetative reproduction — It occurs by (i) progressive death and decay of the older parts and apical part grows and (ii) by fragmentation.

Sexual reproduction — Sexual reproduction is of oogamous type. The male and female organs are produced in flask shaped structure called conceptacle which in turn are found on receptacle of sporophytic thallus. *Sargassum* may be homothallic or heterothallic. In some species, conceptacles are sterile known as *crytoblast* without any sex organs but develops sterile hairs from the base.

Development of antheridium the male sex organ — Antheridia are produced in groups from the cells of the fertile layer of conceptacle. A young antheridium has a diploid nucleus which divides meiotically and mitotically resulting in 64 haploid nuclei. These haploid nuclei in combination with cytoplasm metamorphose into 64 pear shaped, biflagellate antherozoids. The flagella are laterally situated and of unequal length. The mature antherozoids are liberated in sea water through an opening in the conceptacle called ostiole.

Development of female sex organs (oogonia) — It also develops from basal fertile layer of conceptacle. The oogonial initial divides into small stalk cell and a large oogonial cell. The oogonial cell produces oogonium. Each oogonium is uninucleate and unicellular. The diploid oogonial nucleus divides meiotically and then mitotically into 8 haploid nuclei out of which only one survives and rest degenerate. The entire content with one nucleus rounds off and constitutes an egg or ovum. Each mature oogonium comes out of ostiole in the conceptacle and remains attached to the wall of conceptacle with the help of a mucilaginous stalk (Fig. 53).

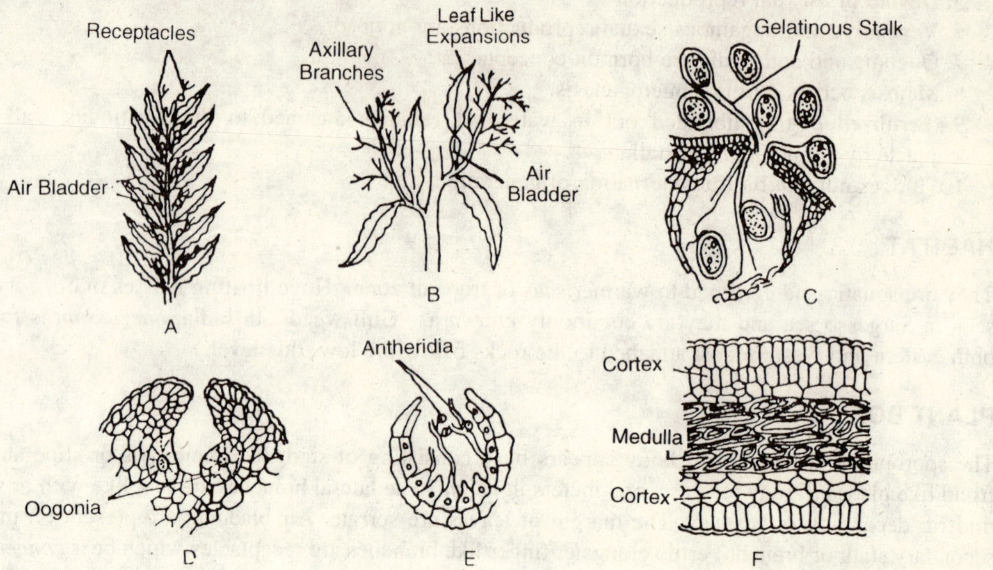

Fig. 53. *Sargassum* sp. A– Habit, B–A twig with air bladder and receptacle, C–female receptacle, E. Male receptacle in section, F-V.S. of thallus (A part).

FERTILIZATION

The liberated antherozoids surround the oogonium and become attached to the oogonial wall with the help of a flagella. One of the antherozoids are able to penetrate the oogonial wall and finally fuses with the egg to from a diploid zygote.

GERMINATION OF ZYGOTE

The germination of the zygote starts within the enclosed oogonium still attached to the wall of the conceptacle. After some time the oogonial wall breaks and the zygote is liberated out in water. Then it is attached to some substratum and germinates into new diploid sporophyte plant of *Sargassum*.

GRAPHIC LIFE CYCLE AND ALTERNATION OF GENERATION

It is shown in the following manner

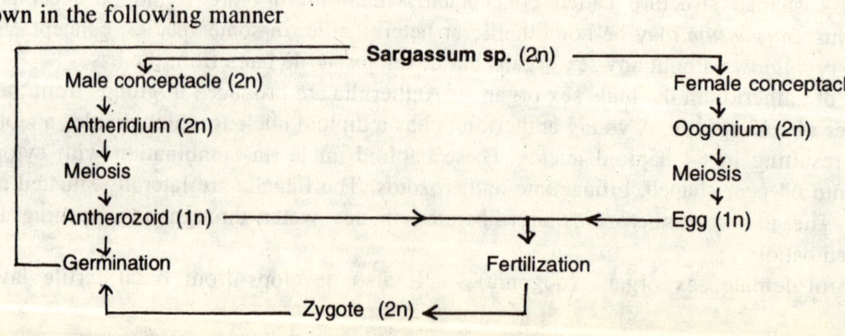

CHAPTER 7

RHODOPHYTA—RHODOPHYCEAE

SALIENT FEATURES

1. The members of the class Rhodophyceae are marine, epiphyte and endophyte.
2. Plant body i.e. thallus is multicellular, simple or branched, monosiphonous or polysiphonous.
3. Vegetative cell has single nucleus, sometimes — multinucleate.
4. Plastids contain Phycoerythrin red pigment, and hence red algae, in addition to chlorophyll.
5. Floridean starch is the reserve food, pyrenoid is absent or if present, it is naked.
6. No motile (flagellated) reproductive cell in the life history.
7. No vegetative reproduction by fragmentation
8. Asexual reproduction by monospore or tetraspore.
9. Male gametes are non–motile and known as *spermatia*
   During sexual reproduction spermatia are passively carried to the female sex organ called *carpogonium*
10. Sexual reproduction is of oogamous type.
11. Zygote germinates to produce carpospores.
12. There is alternation of generations and they exhibit three types of life cycle i.e. haplobiontic, diplobiontic and haplodiplobiontic.

CLASSIFICATION

Fritsch (1935,45) has divided the class Rhodophyceae into two sub classes, viz. (i) Bangioideae with only one order Bangiales and (ii) Florideae which has been divided into 6 orders as follows —

Order 1. Nemalionales, 2. Gelidiales, 3. Cryptonemiales, 4. Gigartinales, 5. Rhodomeniales and 6. Ceramiales.

Smith (1955) considered a class—Rhodophyceae under the division Rhodophyta. Further division and classification of Rhodophyceae are similar to that of Fritsch which has been followed in this text. The two representatives of the class Rhodophyceae i.e. *Batra chospermum* and *Polysiphonia* have been dealt.

7.1 BATRACHOSPERMUM

It belongs to	Class	—	Rhodophyceae
	Sub-class	—	Florideae
	Order	—	Nemalionales
	Family	—	Batrachospermaceae
	Genus	—	*Batrachospermum*

DISTINGUISHING CHARACTERS

1. Plant body is filamentous and branched. Branches are of limited and unlimited growth.
2. Two adjoining cells of the filament are connected by pits.
3. Devoid of flagellated cells.
4. Asexual reproduction takes place by monospore which is nonflagellated.
5. Female sex organ is complicated in structure.
6. Oogamous type of sexual reproduction.
7. Carposporangia bearing carpospores are produced after fertilization.
8. Presence of fruit body i.e. cystocarp.
9. Alternation of haploid and diplophasic generation.
10. Juvenile or chantransia stage is found in the life cycle.

HABITAT

It is fresh water forms growing in temperate and tropical regions. It is commonly known as "frog–spawn". It prefers to grow in cool shady and well aerated water of streams, lakes and ponds. The common Indian species are *Batrachospermum vagum* and *B. moniliforme*.

VEGETATIVE PLANT BODY

THE PLANT BODY OR THALLus of *Batrachospermum* reaches upto 15 cm in length, grey green or violet or dark red in colour depending on the intensity of light available where it grows.

The thallus has prostrate and erect system. The prostrate system are attached to the substratum and erect system floats freely in water. Thallus appears as an axial filament having whorls of dense branches enclosed in mucilaginous substance. Terminal cells may bear setae. Branches are of two types viz. (i) lateral branches of limited growth and (ii) vertical branches of unlimited growth. The primary or main axis is made up of uniseriate row of cylindrical cells. The cells are connected to the adjoining cells by protoplasm i.e., pit connections. Uninucleate cells contain parietal or discoid plastids. The main axis is differentiated into nodes and internodes. It grows by apical dome shaped cells. The whorl of filament of limited growth at nodal region is called as *glomerule* (Fig. 54).

Cortication — The basal cell of branches of limited growth develops elongated filamentous cells–called *cortical threads*. These grow downward upto the next node and envelop around the internode which constiture cortication.

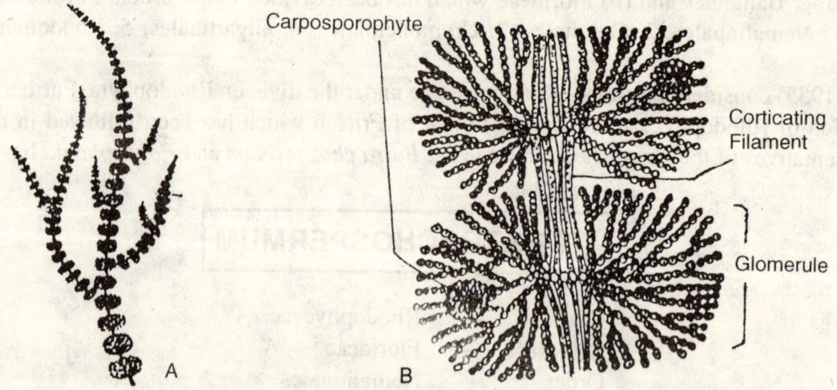

Fig. 54. A – A thallus (part) of *Batrachospermum* sp.. B – Magnified view of two nodes with branches.

REPRODUCTION

Batrachospermum shows asexual and sexual mode of reproduction as such —

Asexual reproduction — In young plant, uninucleate, non–flagellated *monospores* are produced in globose monosporangia. Monosporangia develop on young gametophytic plant–chantransia which is produced during post fertilization period of the sexual reproduction.

Sometimes, monospores are formed singly within monosporangia on short lateral branches of adult *Batrachospermum*. On liberation, the monospore secretes a wall around itself and germinates into new plant.

Sexual reproduction — The plants are heterothallic and homothallic both. The male sex organ antheridium or spermatangium is produced in pairs at the apex of the branches. Each spermatangium arises from spermatogonial cell. The protoplasmic content of spermatangium is metamorphosed into a nonflagellated spherical structure called spermatium or male gamete. The spermatium is liberated from the narrow apical slit in the spermatangial wall and floats in water and carried to trichogyne of the female sex organ — carpogonium. The female sex organ i.e. *Carpogonium* develops terminally on carpogonial filament of 3 - 5 cells developing near the base of a vegetative filament.

The mature carpogonium has a distal trichogyne and a basal swollen part containing nucleus and other cytoplasmic contents. The trichogyne receives the male gamete (Fig. 55).

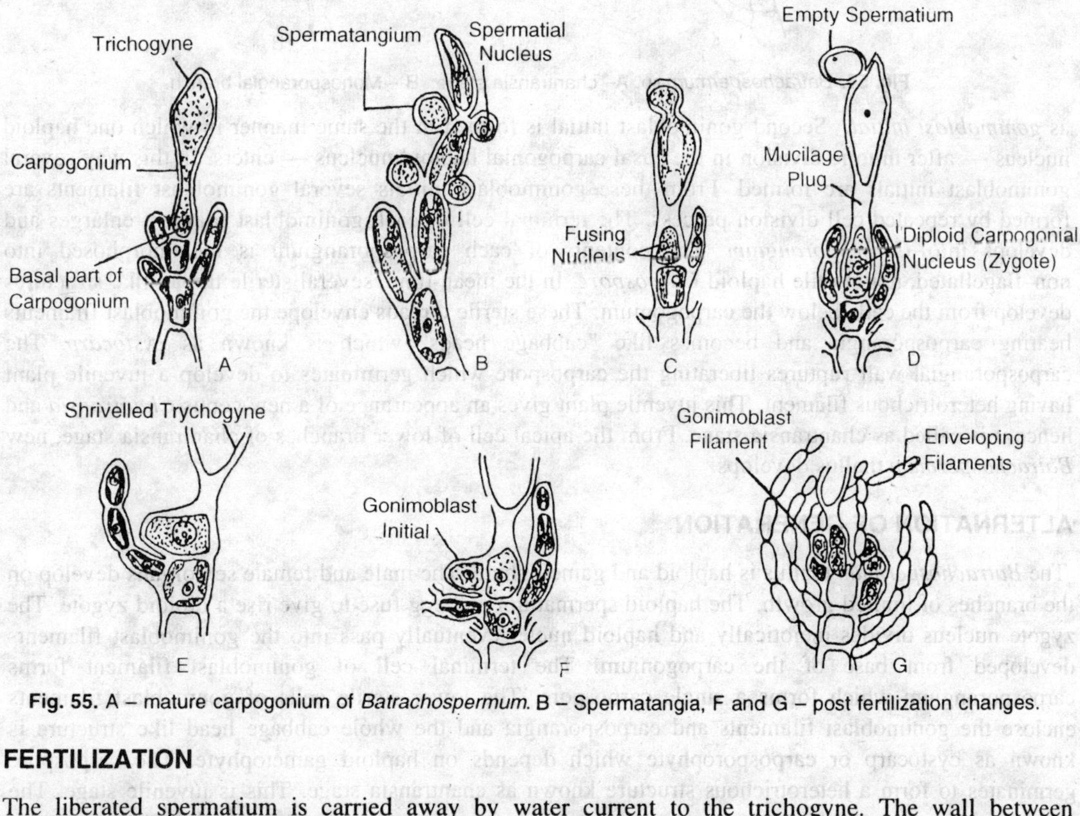

Fig. 55. A – mature carpogonium of *Batrachospermum.* B – Spermatangia, F and G – post fertilization changes.

FERTILIZATION

The liberated spermatium is carried away by water current to the trichogyne. The wall between trichogyne and spermatium dissolves at the point of their contact and nucleus of the spermatium moves into the trichogyne towards the base of the carpogonium where fertilization occurs with the egg nucleus of the carpogonium. The trichogyne is separated out from the carpogonial base just after fertilization (Fig. 56).

POST FERTILIZATION DEVELOPMENT

The diploid zygote nucleus divides meiotically into two haploid nucleus. A lateral protuberance develops from the carpogonial wall in which one of the two haploid nuclei migrates and the other remains within the base of the carpogonium. The protuberance is cut off by a wall and it is now called

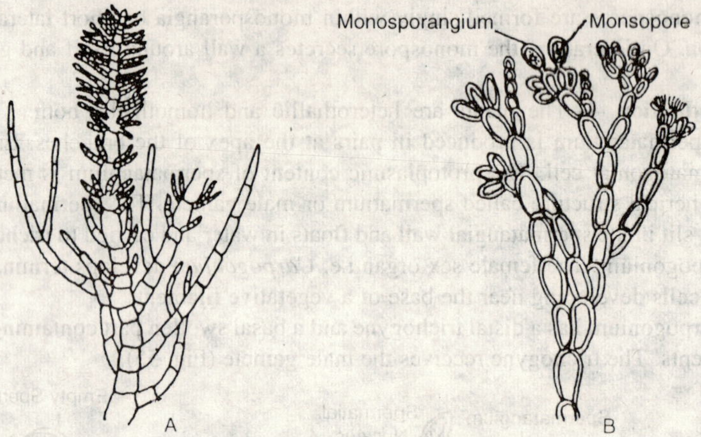

Fig. 56. *Batrachospermum* sp. A– chantransia stage. B – Monosporangial branch.

as *gonimoblast initial*. Second gonimoblast initial is formed in the same manner in which one haploid nucleus — after mitotic division in the basal carpogonial haploid nucleus — enters. In this way several gonimoblast initials are formed. From these gonimoblast initials several gonimoblast filaments are formed by repeated cell division process. The terminal cell of each gonimoblast filament enlarges and develops into *Carposporangium*. The contents of each carposporangium is metamorphosed into non–flagellated, non motile haploid *Carpospore*. In the mean time, several sterile thread like structures develop from the cells below the carpogonium. These sterile threads envelope the gonimoblast filaments bearing carposporangia and becomes like "cabbage heads" which is known as *cystocarp*. The carposporangial wall ruptures liberating the carpospore which germinates to develop a juvenile plant having heterotrichous filament. This juvenile plant gives an appearance of a new genus *Chantransia* and hence it is called as chantransia stage. From the apical cell of lower branches of chantransia stage, new *Batrachospermum* thallus develops.

ALTERNATION OF GENERATION

The *Batrachospermum* thallus is haploid and gametophyte. The male and female sex organs develop on the branches of limited growth. The haploid spermatium and egg fuse to give rise a diploid zygote. The zygote nucleus divides meiotically and haploid nuclei eventually pass into the gonimoblast filaments developed from base of the carpogonium. The terminal cell of gonimoblast filament forms carposporangium which forms a single carpospore. The lower sterile cells of gonmoblast filaments enclose the gonimoblast filaments and carposporangia and the whole cabbage head like structure is known as cystocarp or carposporophyte which depends on haploid gametophyte. The carpospore germinates to form a heterotrichous structure known as chantransia stage. This is juvenile stage. The chantrangia produces monospores — a means of asexual reproduction by which a haploid adult gametophyte plant of *Batrachospermum* is formed as shown in the graphic life cycle.

Here two haploid phases (i) gametophyte and (ii) carposporophyte alternate with the diploid zygote phase. This type of life cycle is known as haplophasic or haplobiontic or diphasic life cycle.

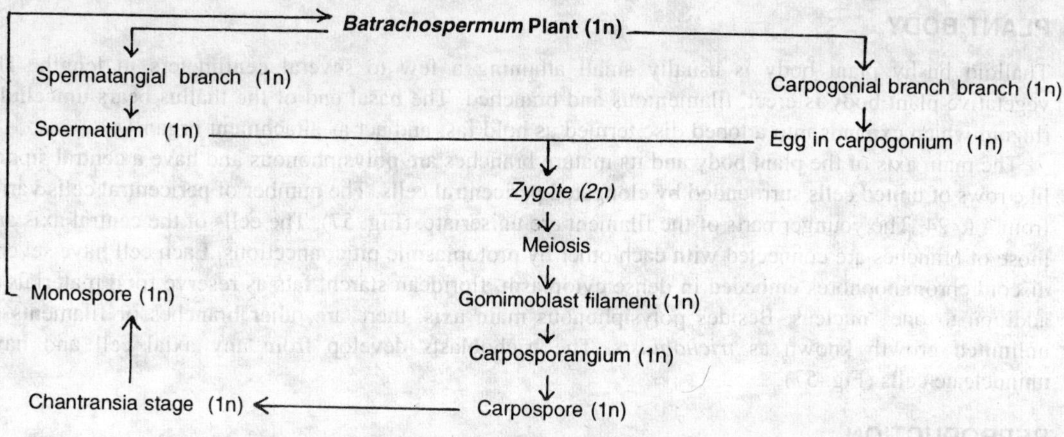

Graphic life cycle of *Batrachospermum* sp

7.2 POLYSIPHONIA

Polysiphonia belongs to

Class	—	Rhodophyceae
Sub-class		Floridac
Order		Ceramiales
Family	—	Rhodomelaceae
Genus	—	*Polysiphonia*

DISTINGUISHING CHARACTERS

1. The plant body is polysiphonous, filamentous and multicellular.
2. Pit connections are found between adjoining cells.
3. The haploid gametophytic male and female plants are morphologically similar to diploid plants bearing tetrasporangia.
4. Sporophyte occurs in two phases, viz. (i) Carposporophyte dependent upon gametophyte and (ii) independent tetrasporophyte.
5. It has triphasic isomorphic alternation of generation.
6. Sexual reproduction is oogamous type.
7. Cystocarps are produced after fertilization.

There are about 150 species in the genus *Polysiphonia* out of which more than 15 species are found in India. The common Indian species are *Polysiphonia variegata*, *P. angustissimum*, *P. platycarpa*, *P. ferulacea*, *P. tuticorensis* etc.

HABITAT

All the species grow in shallow and quiet water of *Pacific* and atlantic oceans. They are found in the sublittoral and tidal marshes along the coasts. Some of them also grow as epiphytes (*P. ferulacea*) on some other algae. In India, they are reported from west sea coast. *Polysiphonia* is marine. Some species grow as semiparasites e.g. *P. fastigiata*.

PLANT BODY

Thalloid bushy plant body is usually small attaining a few to several centimeters in length. The vegetative plant body is erect, filamentous and branched. The basal end of the thallus bears unicellular rhizoid which expands into a lobed disc termed as hold fast and act as attachment organ.

The main axis of the plant body and its mature branches are polysiphonous and have a central siphon like rows of united cells surrounded by elongated pericentral cells. The number of pericentral cells varies from 4 to 24. The younger parts of the filament are uniseriate. (Fig. 57). The cells of the central axis and those of branches are connected with each other by protoplasmic pit connections. Each cell have several discoid chromatophores embeded in dense cytoplasm, floridean starch, fats as reserve food materials in addition to one nucleus. Besides polysiphonous main axis, there are other branches or filaments of unlimited growth known as *trichoblasts.* The trichoblasts develop from any axial cell and have uninucleate cells (Fig. 57).

REPRODUCTION

Polysiphonia reproduces both asexually and sexually.

Sexual reproduction — The gametophytic plants of *Polysiphonia* are dioecious i.e. heterothallic. The male sex organs called as spermatangia are produced on fertile trichoblasts near the apex of male plant. This fertile trichloblast bearing spermatangia is known as *spermatangial branch.* Each spermatangium is a oval or spherical, short-stalked, one celled and colourless. The whole contents of each spermatangium is metamorphosed into a single male nucleus or *spermatium.* The spermatium is liberated out by rupturing of the spermatangial wall in the surrounding water. It swims and finally reaches to the carpogonium. Another new spermatangium may be proliferated within the old empty spermatangial wall (Fig. 57).

The female sex organs i.e. *carpogonia* are produced terminally on a fertile trichoblast of female plant. Carpogonia bearing branch is called carpogonial branch or filament. The carpogonial branch has a 4 celled curved structure developed from a specialised cell cut off from a vegetative branch known as supporting cell. The terminal cell of the carpogonial filament is metamorphosed into a flask shaped *carpogonium.* The carpogonium has a swollen base known as *carpogonial base* and a narrow extended part known as trichogyne which acts as a receptive organ for the spermatium. The uninucleate content of the basal part forms an egg or ovum (Fig. 58).

The formation of carpogonial filament is accompanied by the cutting off of basal sterile initial and lateral sterile initial. The lateral sterile initial divides to form 2 celled lateral sterile filament. At this stage fertilization occurs.

Asexual reproduction — The diploid tetrasporophytic plant produces asexual spores after meiosis. These haploid spores are termed as tetraspores. The tetraspores are produced in tetrasporangium. The tetrasporangia are produced in many successive tiers. Any pericentral cell of the branches of tetrasporophyte acts as a tetrasporangial initial. This initial increases in volume and its diploid nucleus divides meiotically into four haploid nuclei. These nuclei in combination with cytoplasm form four cruciately arranged tetraspores (1n). On rupturing of the tetrasporangial wall, the tetraspores are liberated. Out of four haploid tetraspores produced in a tetrasporangium, two of them germinate to give rise male gametophytic plants and the other two female plants (Fig. 60).

FERTILIZATION

The spermatia are carried by water current to the carpogonium. One of the spermatia attaches to the trichogyne, the common wall between the trichogyne and the spermatium dissolves and the contents of the spermatium migrate to the base of the carpogonium, where fertilization of male and female nuclei takes place to form a diploid zygote (Fig. 58).

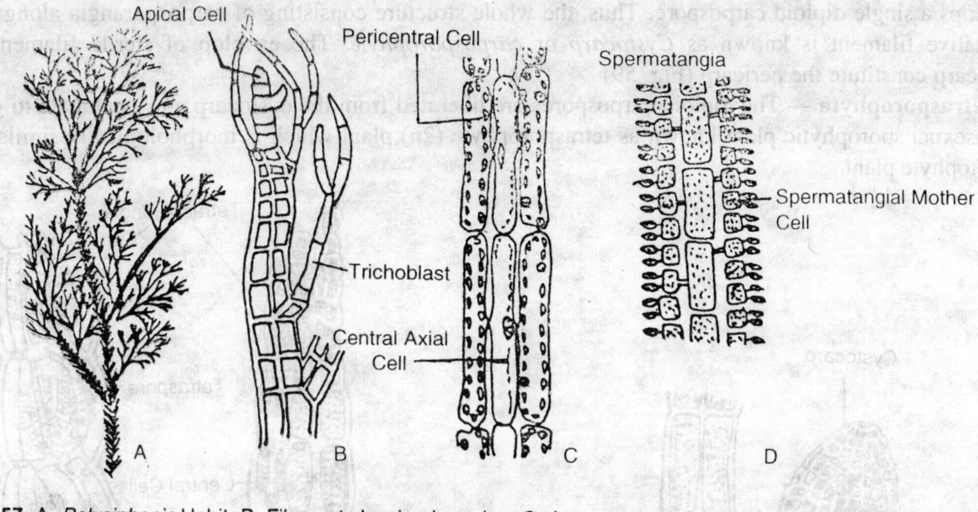

Fig. 57. A. *Polysiphonia* Habit, B. Filament showing branches C. Arrangement of central and pericentral cells. D. *Polysiphonia* – Central cells bearing spermatangia.

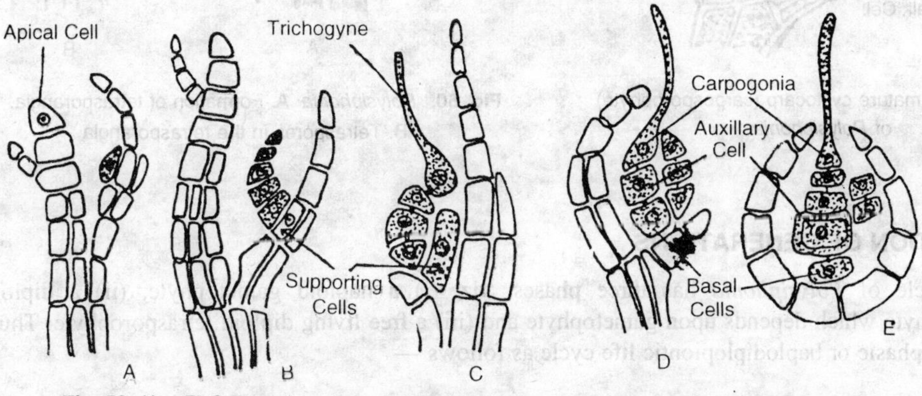

Fig. 58. (A – E) Successive stages in the development of carpogonium in *Polysiphonia.*

POST FERTILIZATION CHANGES AND FORMATION OF CYSTOCARP

After fertilization several changes takes place in the female reproductive structure and carposporophyte is formed. After zygote formation, the basal and lateral sterile initial/filament divide to form 2 - 4 and then 4 - 10 celled short filament. The supporting cell divides to form a auxillary cell which lies near base of the carpogonium and has one haploid nucleus. A tubular connection between the carpogonim and the auxillary cell is established.

The diploid zygote nucleus divides mitotically into two, one of which passes into the auxillary cells through the tubular connection and the other remains in the carpogonium proper. Now the trichogyne shrinks and fusion takes place between the carpogonium auxillary cell, supporting cell and sterile filaments. After fusion, a large irregularly shaped placentral cell is formed. The diploid nucleus of the auxillary cell divides mitotically into many diploid nuclei in the placentral cell. Several tubular outgrowths develop from the placentral cell and each outgrowth receives a diploid nucleus. This outgrowth with one diploid nucleus function as gonimoblast initials which divides and redivides to form small gonimoblast filaments. The terminal cell of gonimoblast filament becomes carporangium which develops a single diploid carpospore. Thus, the whole structure consisting of carposporangia alongwith vegetative filament is known as *Cystocarp* or *carposporophyte*. The envelop of sterile filament of cystocarp constitute the pericarp (Fig. 59)

Tetrasporophyte — The diploid carpospores are liberated from the cystocarp and germinate to give rise asexual sporophytic plant known as tetrasporophyte (2n) plant which is morphologically similar to gametophyte plant.

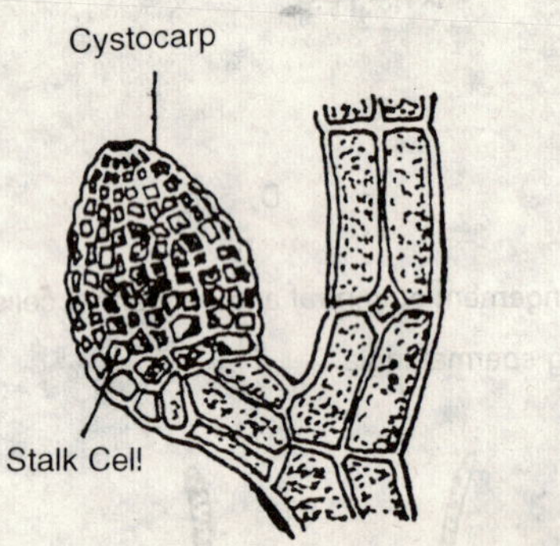

Fig. 59. A mature cystocarp (carposporophyte) of *Polysiphonia*.

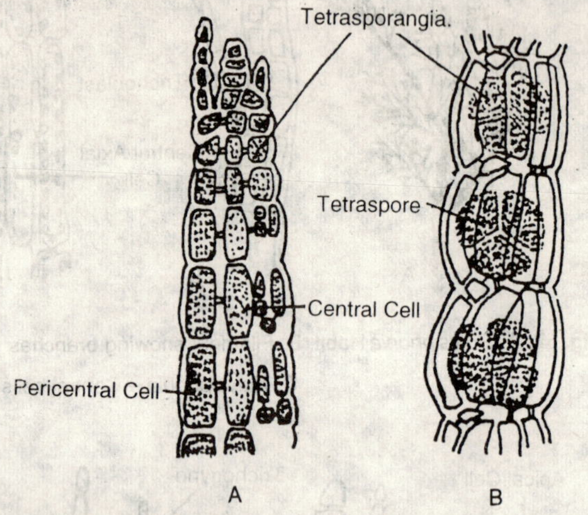

Fig. 60. *Polysiphonia* A. Formation of tetrasporangia. B. Tetraspores in the tetrasporangia

ALTERNATION OF GENERATIONS

The life cycle of *Polysiphonia* has three phases, viz. (i) a haploid gametophyte, (ii) a diploid carposporophyte which depends upon gametophyte and (iii) a free living diploid tetrasporophyte. Thus, it exhibits triphasic or haplodiplopiontic life cycle as follows —

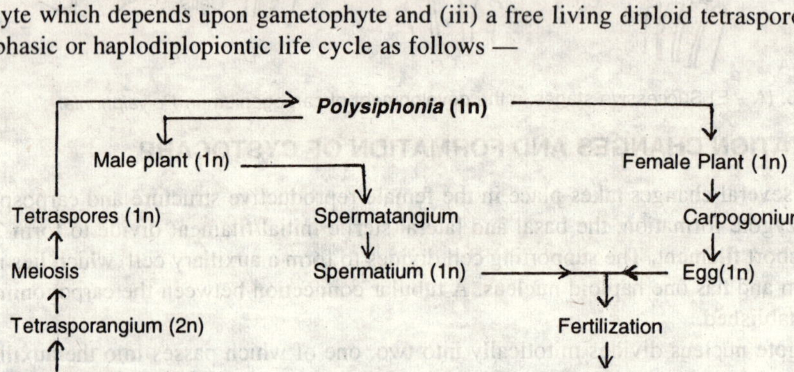

Graphic Life Cycle of Polysiphonia

SECTION - II

FUNGI

1. General Features and Classification
2. Phycomycetes
3. Ascomycetes
4. Basidiomycetes
5. Deuteromycetes (Fungi imperfectii)
6. Lichens
7. Schizomycetes (Bacteria)
8. Viruses

CHAPTER 1

FUNGI

GENERAL FEATURES & CLASSIFICATION

The word "fungus" (P. fungi) was derived from the Indian word "fungour" meaning to flourish and was applied to mushrooms.

The fungi are very large and an important group of Thallophyta characterized by unicellular sex organs and the absence of chlorophyll. They exhibit simplicity in structure and are unable to synthesize their own food meterial. They obtained their food either from living organisms or from dead organic matters behaving as parasites or saprophytes respectively. They are devoid of stem, root or leaves. Some fungi like *Cystopus*, *Puccinia* etc. cannot be grown artificially on a synthetic culture medium and they are called *obligate parasite*. On the other hand facultative parasite may also grow on dead organic substances, e.g. *Pestaltia.* Similarly, obligate saprophytes i.g. *Mucor*, *Rhizopus* live only on dead organic substance and facultative saprophyte may also infect a living organism e.g. *Botrytis*, *Ustilago* etc.

Sometimes fungi live in association with algae e.g. Lichens. This mode of life is called as symbiosis, in which both the organisms are mutually benefitted. Fungi sometimes live in close association with the roots of angiosperms and gymnosperms. Such association between roots of higher plants and fungal hyphae is called *mycorrhiza.*

VEGETATIVE STRUCTURE

Vegetative body of fungi may be unicellular as in yeast or may be made up of simple or branched filament known as hypha (plural-hyphae). Usually, hyphae branch freely and intertwine to form a web of hyphae called mycelium (Plural-mycelia). Hyphae may be coloured or hyaline, simple or branched, septate or aseptate. The wall of hypha when aseptate the hypha is more or less tubular having several nuclei scattered uniformly. Such a tubular hypha is known as a *coenocyte.*

The wall of the hypha is made up of chitin which is a polymer containing N–acetyl glucosamine units $(C_{22}\ H_{54}\ N_4\ O_{21})_n$. The fungal cell is an eukaryotic cell with one or more nuclei, mitochondria, endoplasmic reticulam, golgi bodies, ribosomes etc. The hyphal cell generally has glycogen as reserve food material. In some other fungi, oil drops, protein or mannitol are found as reserve food.

REPRODUCTION

In fungi, three general types of reproduction are known such as, (a) Vegetative, (b) Asexual and (c) Sexual.

A. VEGETATIVE REPRODUCTION

This types of reproduction occurs by following methods —

1. Budding — In this method, parent cell gives rise small outgrowths known as buds. Each bud grows into new individual on separation from the parent cell, e.g. Yeasts.
2. Fission — In this method, vegetative cell splits into two daughter cells by transverse wall or constriction.
3. Fragmentation — Hypha breaks into one or more pieces and each piece is capable of growing into a new individual.
4. Sclerotia (singular : Sclerotium) are resting bodies as in *Claviceps*. It also germinates in favourable conditions into a new vegetative body.

B. ASEXUAL REPRODUCTION

It occurs by asexual units known as spores. Spores may be unicellular or multicellular, motile or non–motile, exogenously or endogenously formed. Spores are of different types found in fungi as follows.

1. Oidium (plural-oidia) – It develops directly from hyphal fragments.
2. Conidium (Plural–conidia) — They are cut off externally either in chains (as in *Penicillium*) or singly (in *Phytophthora*) from the tip of specialised aerial hyphae known as phialids or conidiophores.
3. Chlamydospores — These are produced endogenously from terminal or intercalary hyphal cells. These are thick walled unicellular, non–motile, dark coloured resting spores e.g. *Mucor, Phytophthora* etc.
4. *Aplanospores* — These are formed within a sac like structure called sporangium developed at the tip of an erect hypha known as sporangiosphore as in *Mucor, Rhizopus* etc. Aplanospores are unicellular and non–motile.
5. *Zoospores* — Zoospores are motile with one or two flagella and unicellular. These are produced within a sac like structure called zoosporangium developed at the tip of zoosporangiophore as in *Phytophthora, Saprolegnia* etc.
6. *Basidiospores* — These are non motile, unicellular, exogenously produced after meiosis e.g. *Agaricus.*
7. Ascospores — These are non–motile, endogenously formed, 4 or 8 in number, after meiosis within ascus (e.g. *Peziza*).
8. *Zygospore* — These are diploid spores produced by the union of two morphologically undifferentiated gametes as in *Mucor*.
9. *Oospores* — These are products of the union between two morphologically distinct gametes an in the members of phycomycetes.

C. SEXUAL REPRODUCTION

There are several methods of sexual reproduction in fungi and they are as such.

1. *Gametangial contact* — In this method gametes are directly transferred from the gametangium into the other. Gametes are not liberated from the gametangium to the outside. Two gametangia of opposite sex i.e. male and female, come in contact with each other, followed by migration of one or more gametic nuclei from the male gametangium to the female gametangium either through fertilization tube developed from the male gametangium or through a pore produced by dissolution of the common wall of the two gametangia at the point of contact. e.g. *Pythium*.
2. *Gametangial copulation* — In this method entire contents of two copulating gametangia fuse

together into one cell e.g. *Mucor*. In some fungi, the entire contents of male gametangium is transferred into the female gametangium through a pore developed in the gametangial walls at the point of contact between two gametangia e.g. *Rhizophidium couchii*.

3. *Gametic copulation* — In this method fusion of two gametes takes place. The process may be isogamy, anisogamy depending on the nature of the fusing gametes e.g. *Monoblepharis*.
4. *Spermatization* — In this mode, small, unicellular uninucleate spore like structure called spermatium (Plural : spermatia) are transferred to the female gametangium or to a special receptive hypha. The contents of spermatium pass into the receptive hypha or female gametangium through a pore developed by the dissolution of walls at the point of contact. The spermatium act as male organ. e.g. *Puccinia*.
5. *Somatogamy* — In most of the higher fungi, where sex organs are absent as in *Agaricus*, somatic cells take over the sexual reproduction. In this process, compatible nucleus of one cell passes into the corresponding somatic cell by dissolving the walls between – a process known as, *anastomosis* which gives rise a dikaryotic condition.

CLASSIFICATION

The study of fungi is known as Mycology. According to Ainsworth and Bisby (1954) there are about 40,000 species of fungi known at present, though about one million species seem to be in existence. Fungi are found everywhere i.e. in soil, air, water even in the bodies of animals and plants. Persoon (1801) was the first to classify and describe the then known fungi of the world. He arranged the species into classes, order and families. Elias Fries (1821 – 29) gave a full account of all the then known fungi.

On the basis of septation of mycelium and characters of main spores, Gwynne–Vaughan and Barnes (1927) classified the fungi into three classes like *Phycomycetes*, *Ascomycetes* and *Basidiomycetes* and *Fungi imperfectii* was given the rank of fourth class. The outline of widely accepted classification of Gwynne–Vaughan and Barnes (1927) is as follows.

FUNGI

Class – 1. Phycomycetes
2. Ascomycetes
3. Basidiomycetes
4. Fungi imperfectii

1. *Phycomycetes* : Sub-Class
   - (i) Archimycetes: Mycelium absent. e.g. *Synchytrium*
   - (ii) Oomycetes: Mycelium well developed, anisogamy forming oospore. e.g. *Saprolegnia*
   - (iii) Zygomycetes: Isogamy forming zygospore. e.g. *Mucor*
2. Ascomycetes : Sub-Class
   - (i) Plectomycetes: Ascocarp rounded
   - (ii) Discomycetes: Ascocarp saucer shaped
   - (iii) Pyrenomycetes: Ascocarp flask shaped
3. Basidiomycetes: Sub-Class
   - (i) Hemibasidiomycetes : Indefinite number of basidiospores
   - (ii) Protobasidiomycetes: Septate basidium
   - (iii) Autobasidiomycetes: Non-septate basidium

According to Martin (1931, 1941) Fungi have been divided into three classes, viz. (1) Phycomycetes (2) Ascomycetes and (3) Basidiomycetes and two form classes like (i) Fungi imperfectii and (ii) Lichens. This classification is widely accepted which has been followed in the present text.

CHAPTER 2

PHYCOMYCETES

Phycomycetes (Phycos = sea–weeds, mycetes = fungi) are commonly known as "algae fungi" because it show similarity with some green algae in morphology and mode of reproduction.

OCCURRENCE

There are about 130 genera and 1500 species included in the class Phycomycetes. They are saprophytes as well as parasites. Majority of the genera are aquatic (fresh water as well as marine). Aquatic forms are generally known as water moulds. Some members are mycorhizative. They are formed in the roots of higher plants. Some genera are amphibious, occurring as saprophytes on damp soil and as parasites on plants or animals.

VEGETATIVE BODY

The vegetative body ranges from unicellular to profused branched, well developed filaments., aseptate coenocytic mycelial thalli spreading on and in the substratum. In some advanced members like *Rhizophidium* the vegetative body consists of weakly developed and branched rhizoids without a cell wall. Septate mycelium is also found as an exceptional case like *Allomyces, Entomophthora.* In other, septum formation may occur at the time of sexual reproduction. The primitive members have *holocarpic* thallus i.e. the entire thallus is used up in the formation of spores and gametes (e.g. *Synchytrium*). The advance members are eucarpic i.e. only part of the thallus is involved in the formation of reproductive structures.

REPRODUCTION

Both the types (Asexual & Sexual) of reproduction are found in the members of phycomycetes.

ASEXUAL REPRODUCTION

It takes place by sporangiospores, zoospores, apiam spores and conidia. In biflagellate zoospore flagella are of two types (1) Whiplash – whip like and (2) tinsel type – having lateral hairy mastigonemes in two rows along the flagellum. The shape, size and the number of spore in a sporangium vary from genus to genus. Zoospores may be monoplanetic, biplanetic or polyplanetic depending on the number of swarming period.

SEXUAL REPRODUCTION

The various members of the phycomycetes show different types of sexual reproduction mentioned below. These members may be homothallic–producing both the types of gametes on the same plant) or heterothallic producing only one type of gamete i.e. either male or female. The various types of sexual reproduction are gametic union, gametangial copulation and gametic copulation. After fertilization, normally the zygot is non motile, thick walled diploid structure. In primitive members the zygote may be planozygote i.e. motile which is formed by the fusion of planogametes. The diploid zygote or oospore, or zygospore divides meiotically before or at the time of its germination. The generalised life cycle in the phycomycetes can be observed as follows.

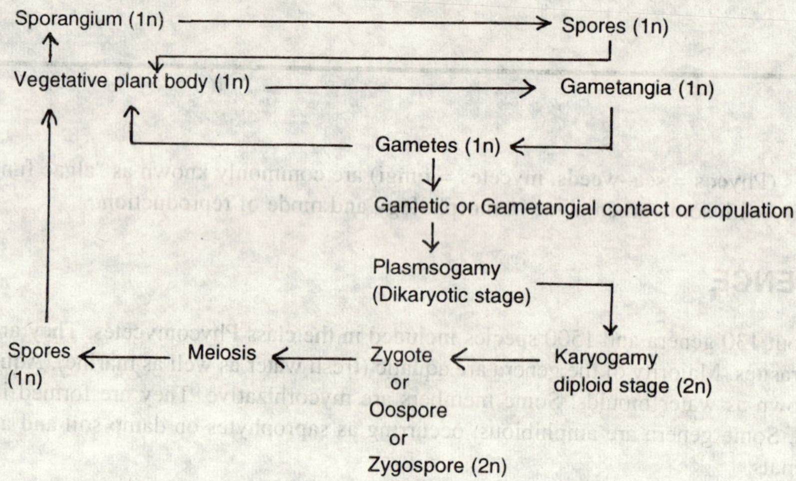

ECONOMIC IMPORTANCE

Phycomycetes, cause several diseases in plants, animals and in human beings. Some of them provide us citric acid, fumaric acid, alcohol etc.

CLASSIFICATION

Gwynne: Vaughan and Barnes (1927) classified the phycomycetes into following three sub classes, on the basis of structure of thallus and type of sexual reproduction.

CLASS — PHYCOMYCETES

Sub-class—	1. Archimycetes, (Unicellular Plant body)	2. Oomycetes, Well developed mycelium sexual reproduction by gametic *Union or gametic* contact.	3. Zygomycetes Sexual reproduction by gametic copulation
Order–	1. Chytridiales	1 Blastocladiales	1 Mucorales

2. Ancylistales	2. Monoblepharidales	2. Entomophthorales
3. Protomycetales	3. Leptomiales	
	4. Saprolegniales	
	5. Peronosporales	

2.1 SYNCHYTRIUM

Synchytrium belongs to

Class	—	Phycomycetes
Sub class	—	Archimycetes
Order	—	Chytridiales
Family	—	Synchytriaceae
Genus	—	*Synchytrium*

HABITAT AND HABIT

Synchytrium occurs as an holocarpic obligate endoparasite without rhizoids. It causes wart disease or black wart in potato. Potato tubers appear as warty due to hyperplasis and hypertrophy of surface cell caused by *Synchytrium* (Fig. 1). This pathogen also infects angiospermic plants like *Solanum nigrum*, *S. xanthocarpum*, *Sesamum indicum* besides algae, mosses and ferns.

On the basis of spore formation the genus *Synchytrium* has been divided into four sub genera viz. (1) *Eusynchytrium* (2) *Mesosychytrium* (3) Pycnosynchytrium and (4) *Woroninella. S. endobioticum*, well known representative of the subgenus mesosynchytrium is described below.

PLANT BODY

The somatic plant body consists of a naked, uninucleate, amoeboid protoplasmic mass which can be seen on infected epidermal cell of the host may be potato tuber. Thus, the fungus is endobiotic and has no mycelial body.

REPRODUCTION

There are two types of reproduction in *Synchytrium* as follows:

Asexual reproduction — The uninucleate amoeboid protoplasmic body of *Synchytrium* settles inside the epidermal cell of the host. It absorbs the food from the host cell and increase in size. It secretes a two layered chitinous wall which is golden brown in colour. This structure is called summer spore.

The host epidermal cell also enlarges and becomes pear shaped. This stimulates the surrounding epidermal and cortical cells to divide which form a gall or tumour or wart like structure. Therefore, the disease is commonly known as "wart disease". The infected host cell becomes surrounded by a rossette of epidermal cells.

The summer spore germinates in situ. The inner contents of the summer spore come out through a pore developed in the form of a vesicle surrounded by its hyaline layer wall. The protoplast migrates into the vesicle. The nucleus divides mitotically several times into 32 nuclei. This multinucleate structure is known as prosorus. The prosorus is cleaved into 4 – 9 multinucleate segments. The nuclei further divide until 200 – 300 nuclei are formed. Each multinucleate segment behave as summer sporangium or zoosporangium.

Many uniflagellate, uninucleate zoospores are formed within each zoosporangium.On maturity all the zoosporangium of the mature sorus, absorbs water and swell, which results in rupturing of the wall of the infected host cell. Thus, the zoosporangia come out on the surface of the potato tuber. The zoospores also come out through a slit in a film of water. The liberated zoospore, reaches a healthy host cell, withdraws its flagellum and penetrates the epidermal cell of the host (Potato tuber). The naked ameoeboid protoplast of the zoospore begins new infection and the asexual cycle goes on (Fig. 2).

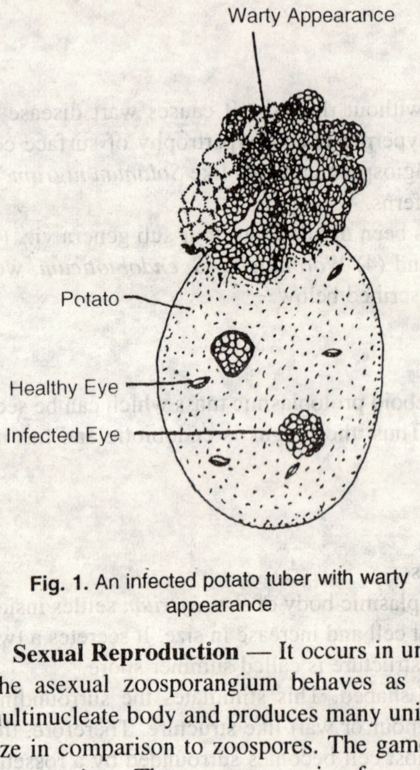

Fig. 1. An infected potato tuber with warty appearance

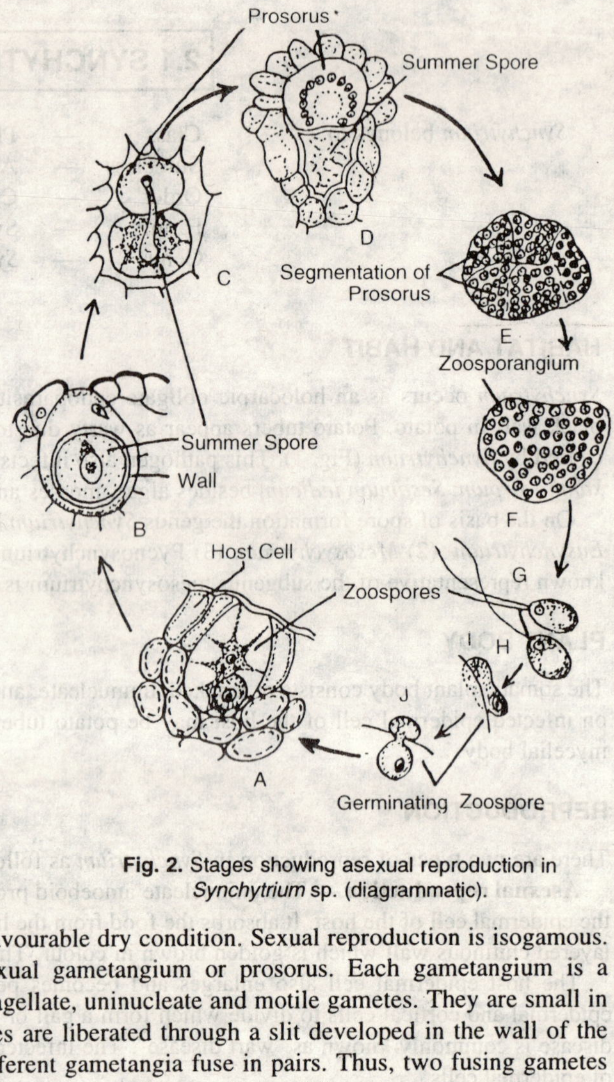

Fig. 2. Stages showing asexual reproduction in *Synchytrium* sp. (diagrammatic).

Sexual Reproduction — It occurs in unfavourable dry condition. Sexual reproduction is isogamous. The asexual zoosporangium behaves as sexual gametangium or prosorus. Each gametangium is a multinucleate body and produces many uniflagellate, uninucleate and motile gametes. They are small in size in comparison to zoospores. The gametes are liberated through a slit developed in the wall of the gametangium. The gametes coming from different gametangia fuse in pairs. Thus, two fusing gametes are morphologically similar but physiologically different. The copulation of the gametes occur in water., either on the surface of the host or in the soil. This is followed by karyogamy which results in a diploid biflagellate zygote (Fig. 3).

The zygote, after a short period of motility, comes to rest on the host, flagella are withdrawn and it penetrates in the epidermal cell of the host. The protoplast of the zygote settles at the bottom of the host cell. The host cell divides and surrounds the infected cell. The zygote protoplast secretes thick three layered wall forming a resting sporangium (Fig. 3) The resting sporangium tides over the unfavourable winter season.

In favourable period, the contents of the resting sporangium divide into a large number of haploid zoospores after meiosis. These haploid zoospores are large in size and oval in outline. The inner wall layer of the resting sporangium cracks and outer layer swells, facilitating the zoospores to come out. On liberation, the zoospores germinate to produce sori in the host. Each sorus becomes segmented. Each segment is multinucleate body which ultimately behave as zoosporangium in favourable condition and as gametangium in unfavourable dry season. The cycle goes on as illustrated in Fig. 3.

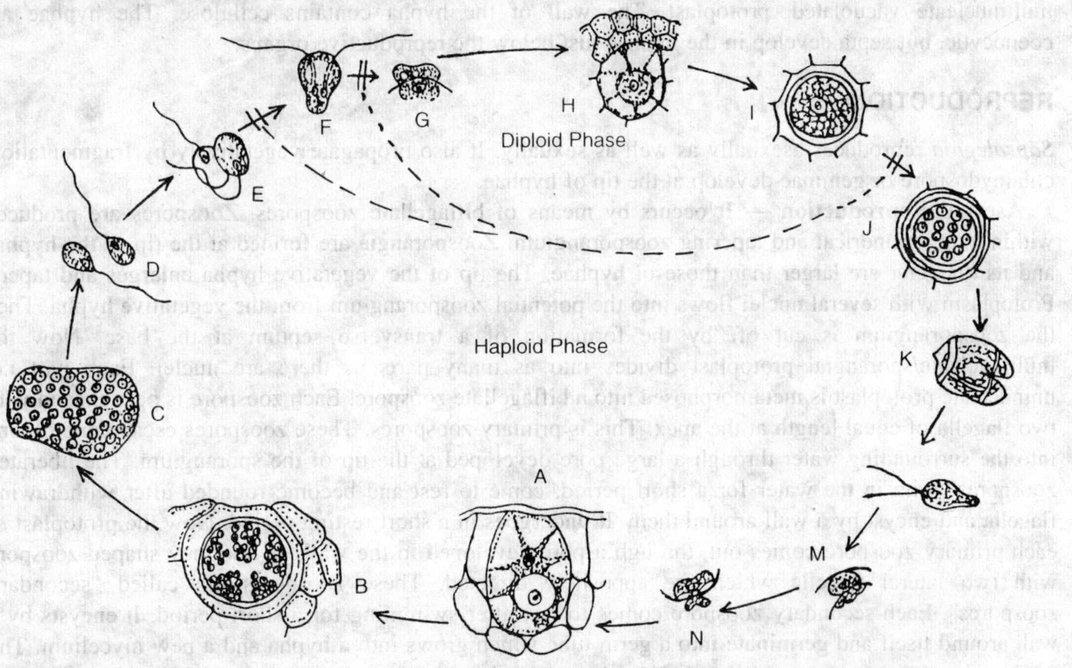

A—Summer Spore
B—Gametangium
C—Sngle Gametangium,
D—Uniflagellate Gametes
E—Copulation
F—Zygote
G—Germination of Zygote
H—Resting Sporangium
I—A Mature Resting Sporangium
J—Formation of Young Zoospore
K—Mature Resting Sporangium Liberating Zoospores
L—Zoospore
M—Germinating Zoospore
N—Penetration of Zoospore in the Host.

Fig. 3. Sequential stages showing sexual reproduction in *Synchytrium* sp. (diagrammatic).

2.2 SAPROLEGNIA

It belongs to

Class	—	Phycomycetes
Sub-class	—	Oomycetes
Order	—	Saprolegniales
Family	—	Saprolegniaceae
Genus	—	*Saprolegnia*

Saprolegnia is commonly known as "water mould". It is saprophyte — deriving their food from dead insects, animals, leaves, twigs, seeds etc. *S. parasitica* is parasite on fish causing serious disease.

PLANT BODY

The plant body consists of coenocytic mycelium made up of two types of hyphae, e.g. (i) the branched rhizoid hyphae— it penetrate the nutritive substratum for anchorage and absorption of nourishment and (ii) the slender, much branched hyphae–lying outside the substratum forming cottony mass at the tip of which reproductive organs are developed. The tips of hyphal branches are tapering. Hypha has multinucleate vacuolated, protoplast. The wall of the hypha contains cellulose. The hyphae are coenocytic, but septa develop in the hyphae just below the reproductive organs.

REPRODUCTION

Saprolegnia reproduces asexually as well as sexually. It also propagate vegetatively by fragmentation, chlamydospore or gemmae develop at the tip of hyphae.

Asexual Reproduction — It occurs by means of biflagellate zoospores. Zoospores are produced within long, cylindrical and tapering zoosporangium. Zoosporangia are formed at the tip of the hyphae and its diameter are larger than those of hyphae. The tip of the vegetative hypha enlarges and tapers. Protoplasm with several nuclei flows into the potential zoosporangium from the vegetative hypha. Then the zoosporangium is cut off by the formation of a transverse septum at the base. Now the multinucleate/sporangial protoplast divides into as many parts as there are nuclei. Each part i.e. uninucleate protoplast is metamorphosed into a biflagellate zoospore. Each zoospore is pear shaped with two flagella of equal length at the apex. This is primary zoospores. These zoospores escape one by one into the surrounding water through a large pore developed at the tip of the sporangium. The liberated zoospores swim in the water for a short period, come to rest and become rounded after withdrawing flagella and encyst by a wall around them. It undergoes in a short resting period. Now the protoplast of each primary zoospore comes out, through a pore developed in the wall, as a kidney shaped zoospore with two lateral flagella which are appositely directed. These zoospores are called "secondary zoospores". Each secondary zoospore comes to rest after swimming for a short period. It encysts by a wall around itself and germinate into a germ tube which grows into a hypha and a new mycelium. The production of two types of motile zoospore (one pear shaped primary zoospore and other kidney shaped secondary zoospore) is known as diplanetism which is found in *Saprolegnia.*

The formation of zoosporangia in successive manner, one – within the other, is known as sporangial proliferation. This is also found in *Saprolegnia.* After the liberation of primary zoospores, the basal septum of the primary zoosporangium may branch or proliferate forming another new secondary zoosporangium which also produces zoospores (Fig. 4).

Sexual reproduction — Sexual reproduction in *Saprolegnia* takes place by gemetangial contact. Male gametangia (antheridia) and female gametangia (oogonia) develop on the vegetative hyphae. Most of the species of *Saprolegnia* are homothallic.

Antheridia are borne terminally on different branches of the hyphae, located near the oogonial hyphae. This type of antheridia are called diclinous. Sometimes antheridia may develop on the same hypha which bears the oogonium and develop just below the oogonium. This type of antheridium is called androgynous. Antheridia are smaller than the oogonia. They are elongated and multinucleate. Antheridium develops by the enlargement of the terminal part of an antheridial branch and the enlarged part is cut off by the formation of a transverse septum. The free nuclei present within the protoplasm of an antheridium form male nuclei.

The oogonia may develop either singly or in chains. It may be terminal at the tips of main or lateral hypha or intercalary. Each oogonium is globose or oblong in shape, their walls are smooth or papillate and thicker. It has one to many oospheres or eggs. Each egg has a single nucleus. An oogonium develops on the tip of a hypha. The tip of the hypha swells and becomes oblong or globose. Within this swelling structure, many nuclei and cytoplasm flow. Now the structure is cut off by a transverse septum. The

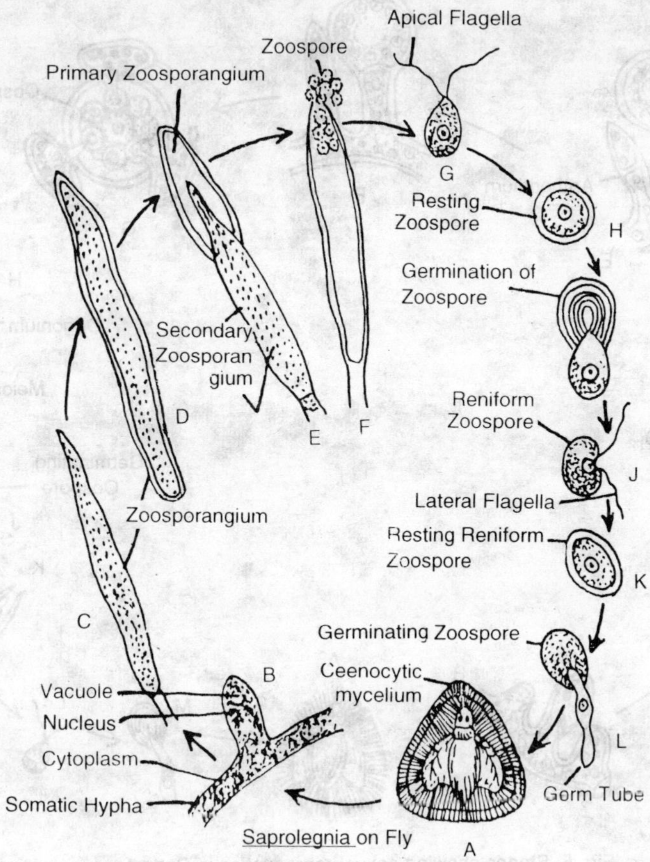

Fig. 4. stages showing asexual reproduction in *Saprolegnia sp.*

protoplasm undergoes progressive cleavage resulting in several uninucleate blocks which becomes eggs or oospheres.

Fully formed one or more antheridia get attached to the wall of the oogonium. A fertilization tube develops from each antheridium. It penetrates the oogonial wall and reaches to egg or oosphere. Several antheridia are attached to the oogonial wall. Each egg is approached by only one fertilization tube. Male nuclei migrate from the antheridium to the oosphere through the fertilization tube. Male nucleus fuses with the egg nucleus forming a diploid zygote. The diploid zygote develops a thick wall around it and formes an oospore (Fig. 5).

Each oospore has an outer thick epispore and an inner endospore. After a resting period, the oospore is liberated from the oogonium by the rupture of oogonial wall. The oospore germinates into a long germ tube which either invades the substratum and produces hypha of new plant. Sometimes the germ tube is germinated by a zoosporagium. Meiosis takes place during germination of the oospore.

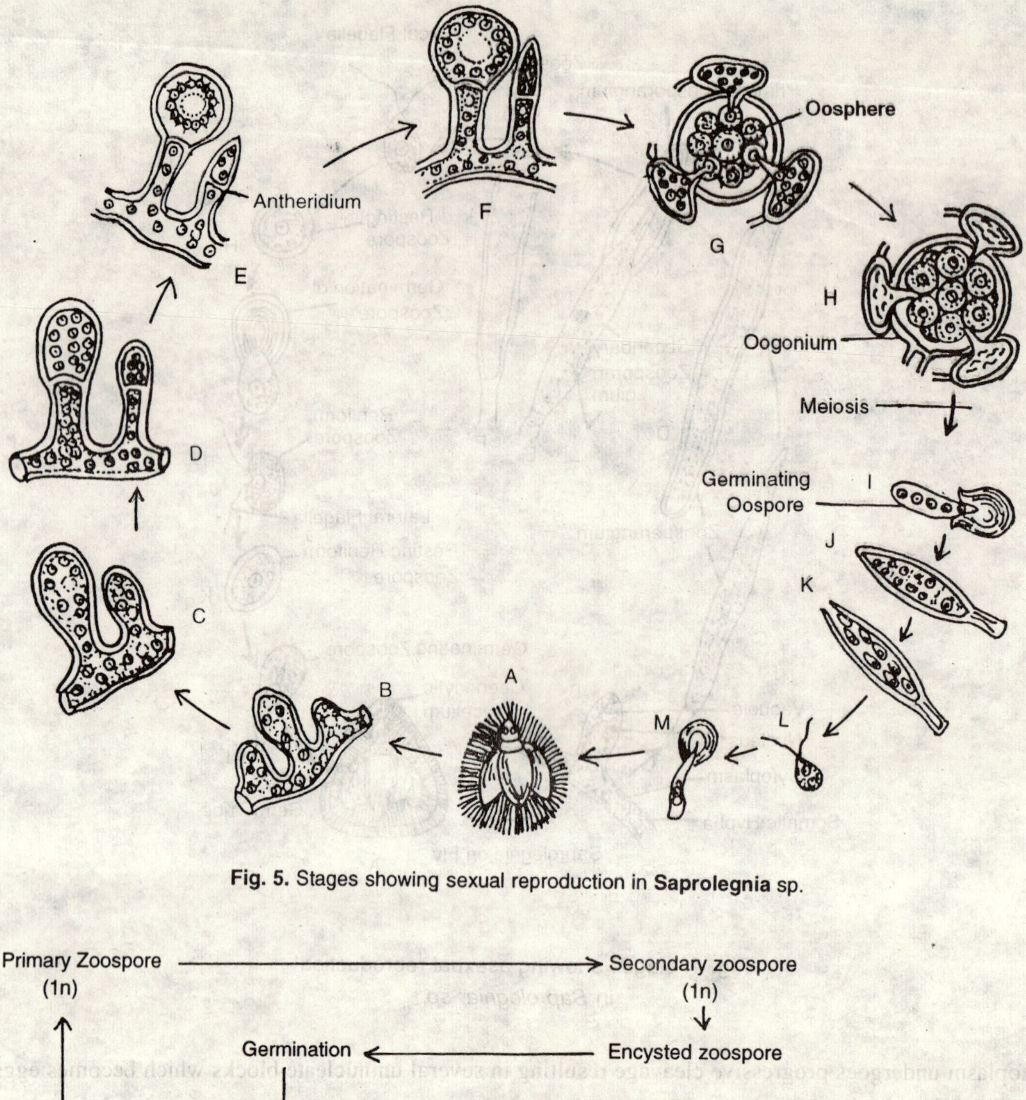

Fig. 5. Stages showing sexual reproduction in **Saprolegnia** sp.

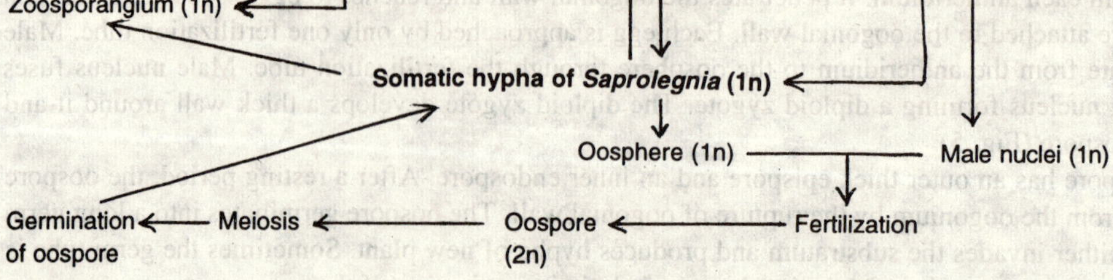

Graphic life cycle of Saprolegnia

2.3 PYTHIUM

Phythium belongs to

Class	—	Phycomycetes
Sub–class	—	Oomycetes
Order	—	Peronosporales
Family	—	Pythiaceae
Genus	—	*Pythium*

The genus *Pythium* is commonly known as "damping off" fungus. It has about 66 species. Butler (1907) has reported 17 species from India.

HABIT AND HABITAT

It is cosmopolitan in distribution. They live as amphibious saprophytes or aquatic parasites. They cause diseases of seedlings as "damping off", "soft rot", "foot rot", "collar rot" or "tuber rot". The disease appears in seedling stage. The infected seedling develops a girdle of brown colour decaying cortex in the hypocotyl extending downward and upward from the ground level and seedling becomes pale–green. This weakens the tissues and seedling collapses and fell over to the ground. The common species *P. debaryanum* causes damping off disease of the tobacco seedlings. The life history of this species is as follows.

PLANT BODY

The plant body consists of a hyaline branched multinucleate, coenocytic mycelium. The mycelium is protected by a cellulose wall enclosing many minute nuclei, vacuolated cytoplam, mitochondria, glycogen as reserve food. The mycelium enters the host tissue either through the stomatal aperture or by penetrating the epidermal wall of the host. The mycelium develops intercellularly as well as intracellulary in the cortex of the hypocotyl and kills the cortical tissue causing the seedlings to tumble down. The mycelium further enters into the vascular bundle from where it absorbs nourishment leaving some poisonous waste substances and ultimately the host dies. The hyphae comes out of the host and grow on the soil till they attack a new host. In this way *Pythium* shows distructive parasitic nature killing the host and lives on the dead host plant as *Saprophyte* (Fig 6).

REPRODUCTION

P. debaryanum reproduces sexually and asexually both.

Asexual reproduction — It occurs in favourable condition by the formation of zoospores within the zoosporangium and by conidia.

Zoospore Formation — In moist condition, aerial hypha becomes globose or oval at the tip. It is cut off from rest of the hyphae by means of a septum. This is called zoosporangium. It develops a beak like outgrowth at the apex known as papilla. This becomes a sac like swollen structure forming a thin walled vesicle. Within this vesicle the sporangium empties its contents.

The protoplasmic contents cleaved into twenty uninucleate parts. These parts metamorphosed into zoospores. Each zoospore is kidney shaped, biflagellate. The vesicle ruptures and the zoospores come out of it and swim in water. After some period of movement, flagella are withdrawn and the zoospore comes to rest. It secretes a wall around itself. The resting zoospore germinates by developing a new hypha. Sometimes zoosporangium proliferates as in *P. proliferum* (Fig. 7).

Conidia formation — In dry condition, zoosporangia fail to be cleaved into uninucleate pieces. Thus, a zoosporangium behave as a conidium. This is detached from the hyphal branches and germinates into a germ tube or hypha which may attack a new seedling in favourable conditions (Fig. 7).

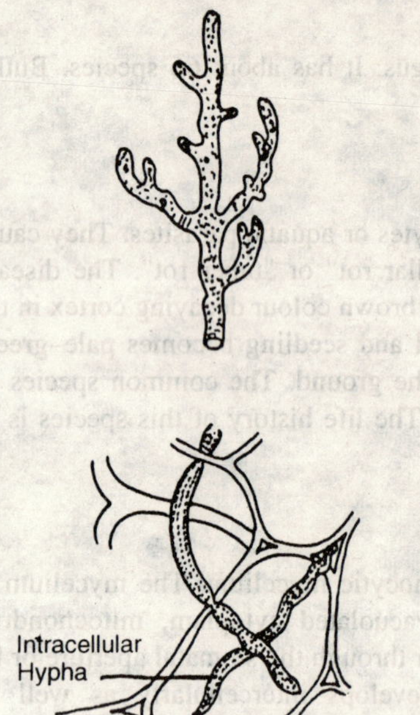

Fig. 6. Mycelial body of intercellular and intracellular hyphae of *Pythium* sp. (diagrammatic)

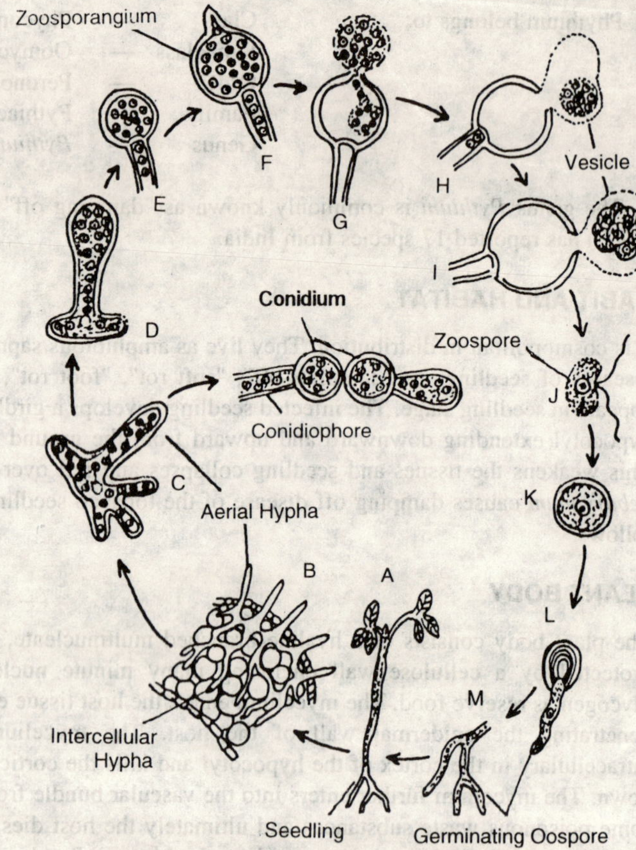

Fig. 7. Stages showing asexual reproduction in *Pythium* sp. (diagrammatic).

Sexual Reproduction — It is oogamous type. The male sex organs antheridia and the female sex organs — oogonia are produced in unfavourable condition. *Pythium* is homothallic i.e. both the sex organs develop on the same hypha.

Oogonium — The oogonium is globose in appearance and develops terminally on a lateral branch. It may be intercalary also. The oogonium is cut off by a septum from the oogonial branch and the protoplasm of the oogonium becomes differentiated into a central multinucleate ooplasm and a peripheral periplasm with few nuclei. The nuclei of the ooplasm migrate toward the periphery and divide. All the daughter nuclei–except one degenerate. This remaining single nucleus moves to the ooplasm and forms an egg or oosphere in the centre of the oosgonium. Generally one oosphere in the oogonium is found but in *P. polysporum*, it may be 2 – 6 (Fig. 8).

Antheridium — The antheridia appear as club shaped elongated and smaller in size. Antheridial branch arises from the stalk of the oogonium. An antheridium is cut off at the apex of this branch. Antheridia and oogonia may develop on different hyphal branch, they are called diclinous. Sometimes both the sex organs develope on the same hyphal branch – a condition known as androgynous.

Antheridial branch curves and comes in contact with oogonial wall. Each antheridium has many nuclei. They divide. All the nuclei except one degenerate. This remaining nucleus acts as a male nucleus.

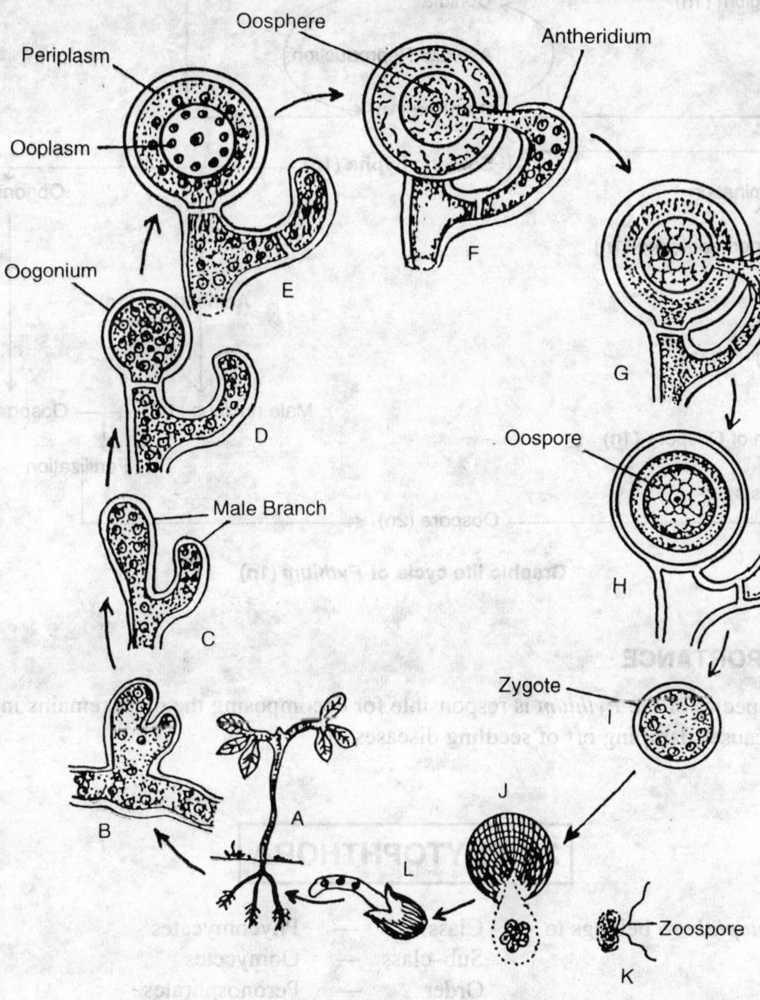

Fig. 8. Stages showing (diagrammatically) sexual reproduction in *Pythium* sp.

FERTILIZATION

On gametangial contact, a fertilization tube develops from the tip of the antheridium. The fertilization tube penetrates the wall of the oogonium and finally reaches the oosphere. The male nucleus goes to the oosphere through the fertilization tube and unites with the oosphere nucleus. After fusion a diploid,zygote or oospore is formed within the oogonium. A thick wall is secreted around the oospore and undergoes a resting period. At high temperature, the oospore germinates by germ tube which develops into new mycelium. At low temperature the further growth of the germ tube stops. The protoplast pushes out through the tip and develops a vesicle in which zoospores are formed. Meiosis occurs in the zygote nucleus followed by mitosis resulting in the multinucleate coenocytic hypha (Fig. 8)

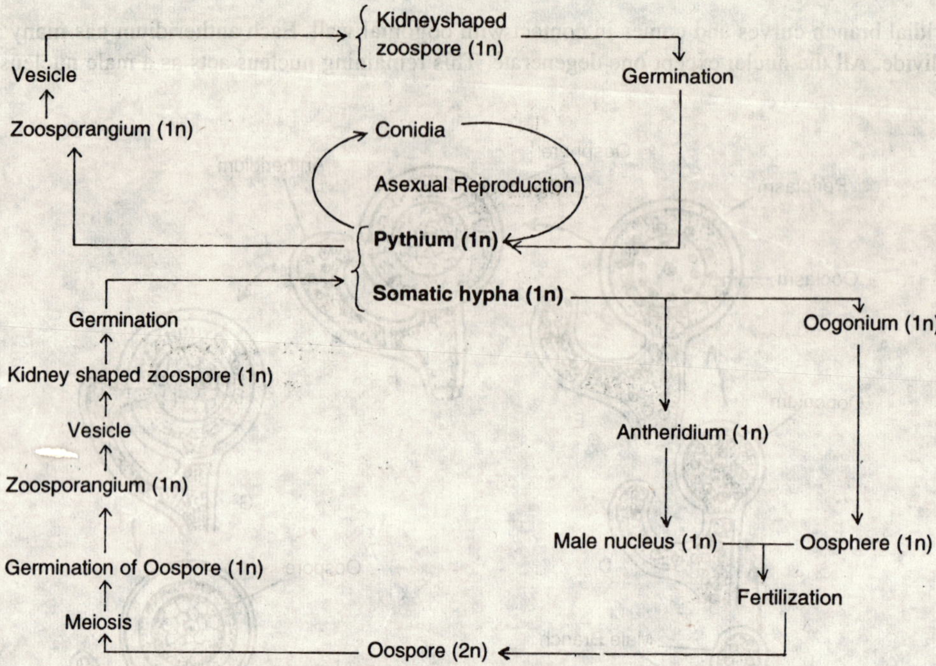

Graphic life cycle of *Pythium* (1n)

ECONOMIC IMPORTANCE

The saprophytic species of the *Pythium* is responsible for decomposing the plant remains in the soil. The parasitic species causes damping off of seedling diseases.

2.4 PHYTOPHTHORA

The genus *Phytophthora* belongs to

Class	—	Phycomycetes
Sub–class	—	Oomycetes
Order	—	Peronosporales
Family	—	Pythiaceae
Genus	—	*Phytophthora*

It has about 75 species and normally they live as parasites on angiospermic plants. They may be facultative saprophytes and facultative parasites also. It causes late blight and tuber rot disease in Potato plants. The most common species *Phytophythora infestans* (mont) de Bary has been described as follows.

PLANT BODY

It consists of typically tubular and coenocytic mycelium. The mycelium is profusely branched. Septum formation takes place at the time of sexual reproduction and also at older parts of hyphae to detain off.

The diameter of the mycelium ranges from 4 microns to 9 microns. The hyphae develop intercellulary as well as intracellularly and from haustoria by which they absorb nourishment from the adjacent living host cells. No haustoria has been reported in *P. parasitica* (Fig. 9).

REPRODUCTION

P. infestans reproduces vegetatively, asexually and sexually.

Vegetative propagation — On artificial culture medium thick walled chlamydospores are formed. Each chlamydospore is multinucleate and spherical which germinate to give rise 3 to 11 germ tubes. Each germ tube forms a sporangium at its tip. In *P. parasita* a secondary sporangium may be formed on germination by the first formed sporangium (Fig. 10).

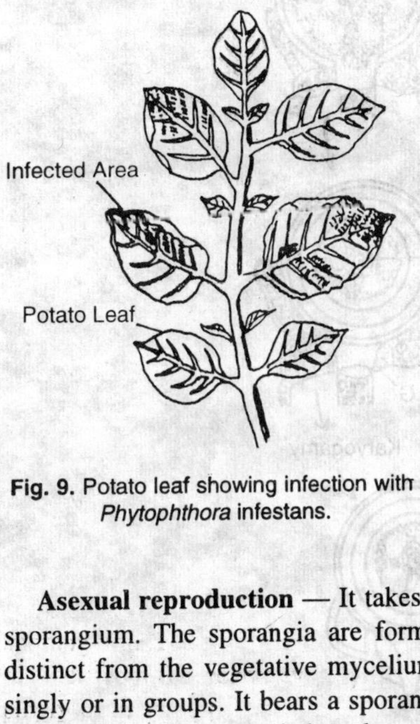

Fig. 9. Potato leaf showing infection with *Phytophthora* infestans.

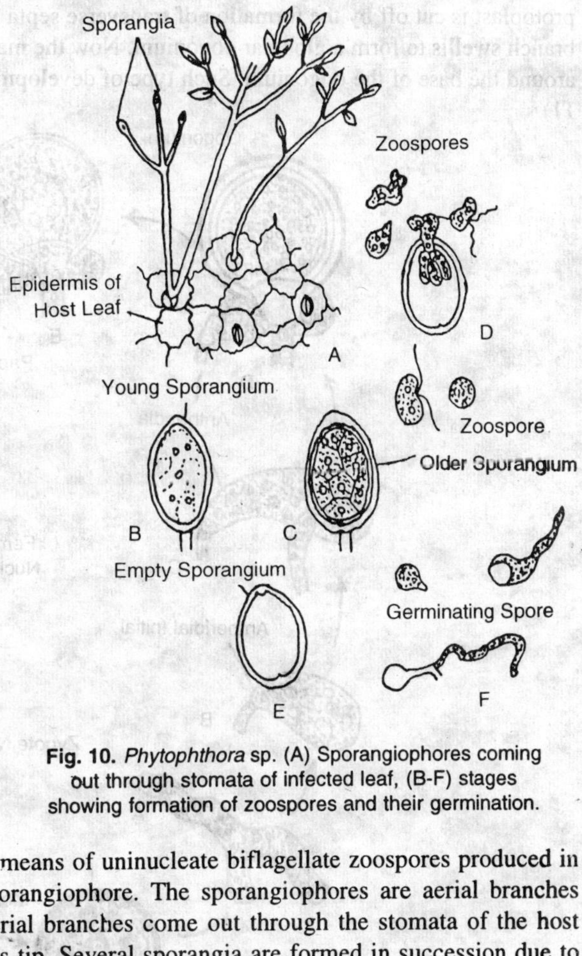

Fig. 10. *Phytophthora* sp. (A) Sporangiophores coming out through stomata of infected leaf, (B-F) stages showing formation of zoospores and their germination.

Asexual reproduction — It takes place by means of uninucleate biflagellate zoospores produced in sporangium. The sporangia are formed on sporangiophore. The sporangiophores are aerial branches distinct from the vegetative mycelium. The aerial branches come out through the stomata of the host singly or in groups. It bears a sporangium at its tip. Several sporangia are formed in succession due to the growth of the hypha below the primary sporangiophore.

Each sporangium is a hyaline or yellow in colour, papillate, ovoid or lemon shaped, measuring 22 – 32 microns in length and 16 – 24 microns in breadth. On maturity they are carried by showers of rain or wind, Bessey, Gaumann and others called it conidia. Further development of sporangia takes place in presence of moisture. The protoplast of the sporangium are divided into twenty uninucleate parts, which gradually metamorphosed into reniform, biflagellate zoospores. The papilla bursts and a pore is developed through which zoospores come out. The zoospores swim in dew or in rain water. Then it withdraws its cilia and encyst. The encysted zoospore germinate by sending out germ tubes which penetrate the host leaf through the stomatal apertures. (Fig. 10) In dry condition the sporangia (conidia of Bessey & Gaumann) germinate directly.

Sexual reproduction — It is of oogamous type. The male sex organs antheridia develop before the female sex organs oogonia. Sexual reproduction in *P. infestans* was reported by Clinton (1911)

P. infestans is heterothallic.

The antheridium develops at the tip of a specialised lateral hyphae.

The antheridial branch and the oogonial branch grow towards each other. The tip of oogonial branch penetrates the antheridial branch. The apical part of the antheridal branch containing dense multinucleate protoplast is cut off by the formation of transverse septa forming an antheridium. The tip of the oogonial branch swellls to form a globular oogonium. Now the mature antheridium forms a funnel–shapped collar around the base of the oogonium. Such type of development of sex organs are called *amphigynous*. (Fig. 11).

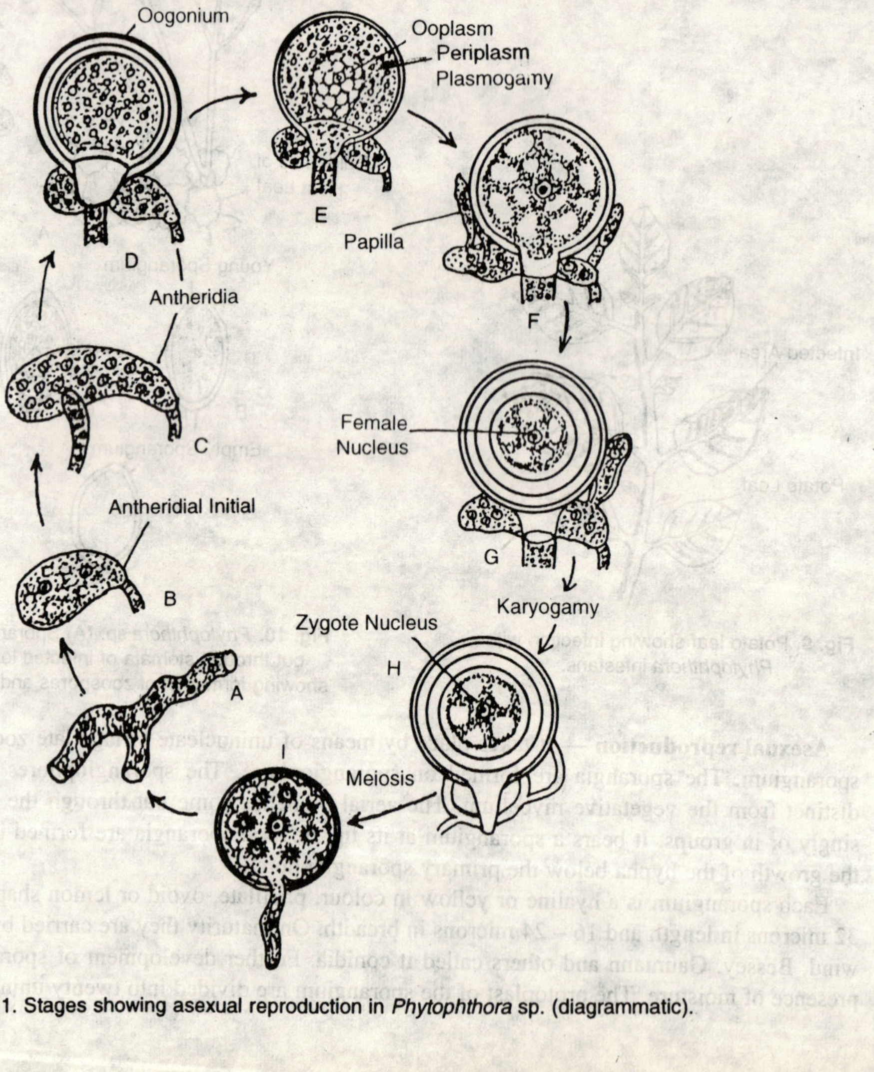

Fig. 11. Stages showing asexual reproduction in *Phytophthora* sp. (diagrammatic).

Out of many, only one nucleus in the mature antheridium survives to serve as the functional male nucleus. The multinucleate oogonium increases in size, its dense cytoplasm becomes vacuolated. The cytoplasm is differentiated into a central ooplasm and a peripheral hyaline periplasm. All the nuclei of the ooplasm except one, migrate to the periphery and disintegrate. The central nucleus divides mitotically into two, one of which dies and the remaining one functions as an egg nucleus. (Fig. 11).

FERTILIZATION

At the time of fertilization, 2 or 3 papillae are developed, out of which only one moves towards the oogonium. The swollen tip of the papilla gets close to the oogonial wall. The common wall dissolves making a passage for the male nucleus to the egg. In some cases fertilization tubes developing from antheridium have also been observed. First plasmogamy and then karyogamy takes place which results in the formation of a diploid zygote or oospore. The oospore undergoes a resting period within the oogonium and then germinates. During the germination of the oospore, meiosis takes place. On germination the inner wall of the oospore comes out in the form of a germ tube which develops a sporangium at the tip. The sporangium produces biflagellate haploid zoospores. Each zoospore produces vegetative hypha.

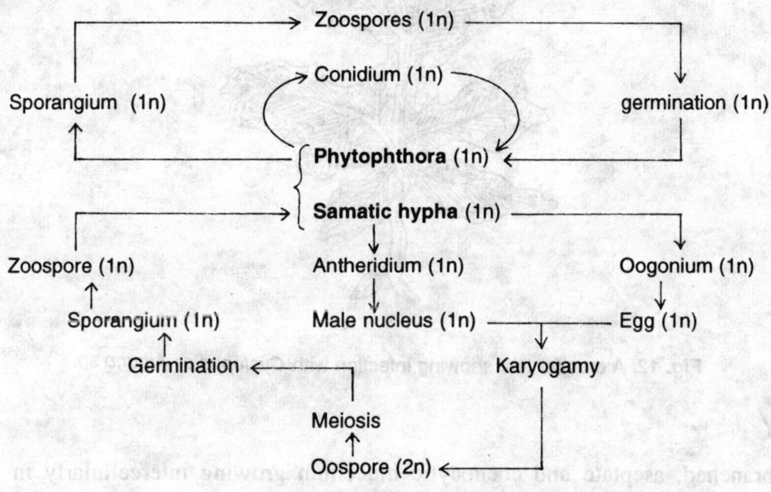

Graphic life cycle of *Phytophthora*

ECONOMIC IMPORTANCE

It causes colossal damage to crops like Potato, Castor, Toddy palms, Coconut palms, Pyrus, Prunus, *Chrysanthermum*, *Cinchona*, *Antirrhinum* etc.

2.5 ALBUGO (Cystopus)

It belongs to

Calss	—	Phycomycetes
Sub–class	—	Oomycetes
Order	—	Peronosporales
Family	—	Albuginaceae
Genus	—	*Albugo*.

There are about 25 species in the genus *Albugo*, out of which about 10 species are reported from India. This fungus occurs as an obligate endoparasites in higher plants causing "white rust" disease. It attacks the plants particularly the members of the family cruciferae like mustard, cabbage, cauliflower etc. The disecase appears on the aerial parts specially the leaves in the form of shining, white and irregualr patches or pustules. The leaves show dwarf appearance and become fleshy (Fig. 12). Stem and the floral parts are also attacked. The common species *A. candida* is described here.

Fig. 12. A crucifer leaf showing infection with *Cystopus* or *Albugo* sp.

PLANT BODY

It consists of branched, aseptate and coenocytic mucelium growing intercellularly in the host. The protoplasm has many minute nuclei in the cytoplasm besides glycogen and oil drops. The mycelium enter the host through the stomata causing some histological changes in the host as follows —

1. Intercellar spaces reduced.
2. No differentiation between palisade and parenchyma.
3. Cells of endodermis and pith multiply.
4. Sclerenchyma converted into parenchyma.
5. New cambium is formed.
6. Formation of starch in the pith and cambium cells.
7. Formation of violet pigment near the upper epidermis.
8. Leaves become dried.
9. Soft tissues disintegrate.

NUTRITION

Albugo exhibits heterophytic mode of nutrition. The mycelium/haustoria enter in the host cells to absorb food and it spreads within the host.

REPRODUCTION

Albugo reproduces both sexually and asexually without alternation of generations.

Asexual Reproduction — It is by means of conidia, or zoospores. The vegetative hyphae in the intercellular spaces of the host come out at several places. The tips of these hyphae become swollen and form a compact hypodermal tissue palisade like in appearance which are at right angles to the epidermis in T.S. of infected leaf (F. 13). These elevated hyphal tips are known as conidiophores or sporangiophores. A bud is produced from this swollen tip which possesses a few nuclei, food and cytoplasm. A transverse septum separates the bud from the conidiophore. This bud is now known as conidium or zoosporangium. The hyphal tip, just below the conidium or zoosporangium, elongates and a second conidium or bud is formed, below the first. This process in basipetal manner is repeated and a chain of conidia is formed from one condiophore. Between successive conidia, intercalary disc or disjunctor cell is present (Fig. 14). The pressure developed by the elongation of several parallel chains of conidia produced beneath the epidermis raises the epidermis and the epidermis ruptures exposing the white powdery mealy mass of conidia or zoosporangia. The conidia/zoosporangia are detached from one another and ultimately disseminated by wind (Fig.14). Each conidium, is spherical, multinucleate structure meassuring 12-18 microns in diameter. In moist condition the conidium/zoosporangium divides into 6 – 8 uninucleate parts. Each part organises into a biflagellate kidney shaped zoospores. The flagella are laterally inserted. On maturity the zoospores come out and spent a brief period of motility in water. Then it rests on the host tissue. Flagella are withdrawn and a wall is secreted. It germinates by a germ tube which enters the host tissue through the stomata. It grows and develops intercellularly within the host which after some time produces conidia or zoosporangia and the process goes on continuously.

On partially dried condition, conidia germinates into germ tube which enters into the host tissue through stomata.

Sexual reproduction — It is highly oogamous. The male sex organ antheridium and the demale sex organ–oogonium are formed on the same individual by swelling of intercellular mycelium. Some of the

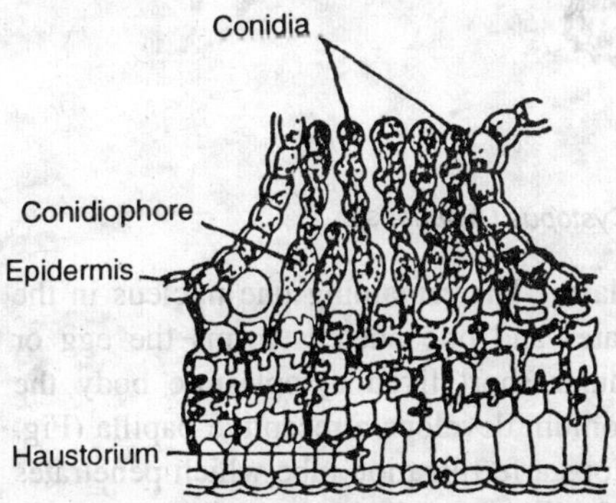

Fig. 13. T.S. of infected leaf showing conidia of *Cystopus/Albugo* sp.

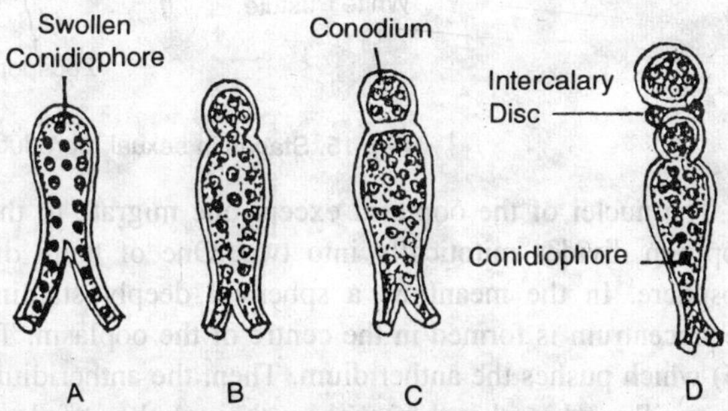

Fig. 14. Stages in the conidial development in *Cystopus* sp. (diagrammatically).

hyphae become erect, club shaped structure is antheridium and the globose structure is oogonium. These sex organs are terminal in position, multinucleate and are cut off from the rest of the hyphae by the formation of a septum.

In *Albugo candida*, both the oogonium and anteridium grow in close association. The oogonium has about one hundred nuclei and the antheridum contains 6 – 12 nuclei. The protoplasm of the oogonium differentiates into central ooplasm and peripheral periplasm.

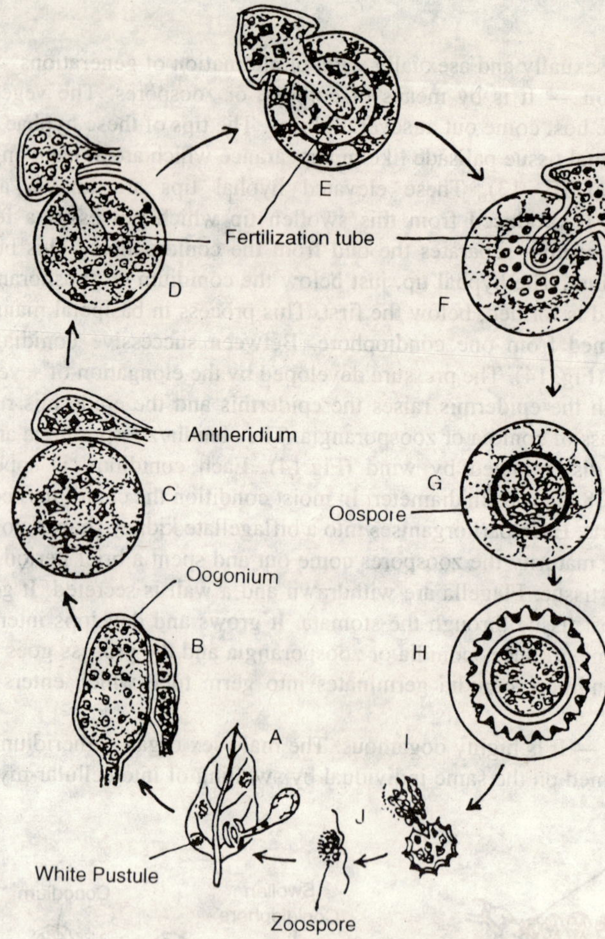

Fig. 15. Stages in sexual reproduction in *Cystopus* (*Albugo*) sp.

The nuclei of the ooplasm except one migrate to the periplasm. The remaining one nucleus in the ooplasm divides mitotically into two. One of them disintegrates and one nucleus forms the egg or oosphere. In the meantime a spherical deeply staining, granular short lived cytoplasmic body the coenocentrum is formed in the centre of the ooplasm. The oogonium develops a receptive papilla (Fig. 15) which pushes the antheridium. Then, the antheridium develops a fertilization tube which penetrates the papilla and reaches the oosphere through the periplasm. The fertilization tube bursts and the one male nucleus is discharged in the oosphere. The male and the egg nucleus fuses with each other forming a diploid oospore.

Germination of oospore — The oospore secretes three layers of wall around itself, the outer epispore, the middle exospore and the inner endospore. On the basis of the sculpturings on the surface of the epispore, identification of the species are done. The mature oospore undergoes seven divisions, the first being meiotic division to from 32 nuclei. Then it undergoes a period of rest. On return of favourable season the nuclei again divides into hundred of nuclei. Then protoplast of the oospore divides into uninucleate fragments and each fragment metamorphoses into a reniform biflagellate zoospore. The wall of the oospore breaks and a vesicle containing zoospores comes out. The vesicle disappear and the zoospores are escaped. They swim for a while then encyst after withdrawing flagella and finally germinates by germ tube and infects healthy plant.

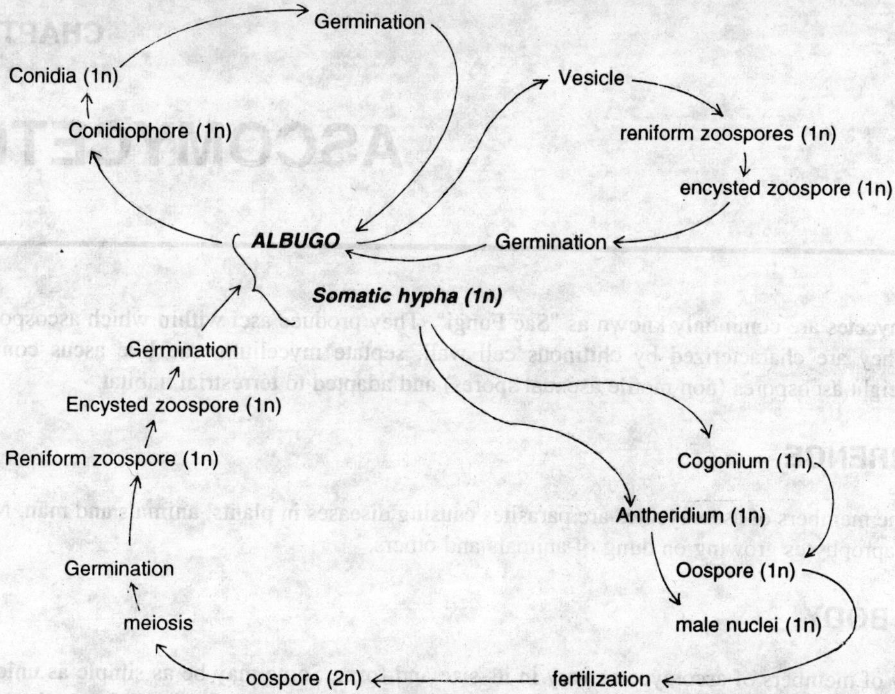

Graphic life cycle of *Albugo*

N.B. *Albugo* name given to the asexual stage and *Cystopus* to the sexual stage. But ICBON approved the name *Albugo*.

CHAPTER 3

ASCOMYCETES

The ascomycetes are commonly known as "Sac Fungi". They produce asci within which ascospores are formed. They are characterized by chitinous cell wall, septate mycelium, sac like ascus containing generally eight ascospores (non motile asexual spores) and adapted to terrestrial habitat.

OCCURRENCE

Many of the members of ascomycetes are parasites causing diseases in plants, animals and man. Most of them are saprophytes growing on dung of animals and others.

PLANT BODY

Plant body of members of ascomycetes vary in its size and form. Some may be as simple as unicellular form like yeasts while others may have complex branched septate inter or intracellular, endophytic or superficial mycelium with uninucleate or multinucleate cells. The mycelium may organise to become tissue like plectenchyma and pseudoparenchyma.

ASEXUAL REPRODUCTION

It occurs by means of non motile spores called conidia developed singly or in chains on simple or branched hyphae known as conidiophores. These are produced exogenously. Ascomycetes also exhibit asexual reproduction by means of fission, budding, fragmentation, chlamydospores or oidia.

SEXUAL REPRODUCTION

It takes place by several methods in different members. It may be by fusion of haploid vegetative cells functioning as gametes to from a diploid zygote as in yeasts. This method is termed as hologamy. The other method is "Gemetangial contact". The male copulation branch becomes antheridium and the female copulation branch as ascogonium. The male sex organs lies apposed to the female sex organ. The sex organs may be multinucleate as in *Ascobolus* or uninucleate as in *Erysiphe*. During gametangial contact the male nuclei from the antheridium migrate to the ascogonium through a pore or trichogyne developed in the oogonium. The male and female nuclei serve as male and female gametes respectively. They lie in pairs as dikaryon for a longer period. Due to sexual stimulus, the ascogonium develops several hyphal branches called ascogenous hyphae. The dikaryons divide conjugately and one or more dikaryon migrate in ascogenous hypha. Now the ascoganous hypha containing one or more a dikaryon is seperated by a septum forming one or more dikaryotic cells depending upon the number of dikaryons.

The terminal cell of the septate ascogenous hypha is generally binucleate having one male and one female nuclei. This terminal dikaryotic cell elongates and bends to form a *Crozier* or hook. The two nuclei divide mitotically into four and orientates in such a manner that a pair of male and female daughter nuclei remain near the bend of the Crozier while one (out of remaining two) remained at the tip and the second near the basal septum of the Crozier (Fig. 16). Now two transverse walls are formed dividing the crozier into three cells (i) terminal uninucleate cell (ii) basal uninucleate cell and (iii) binucleate penultimate or crook cell (Fig. 16).

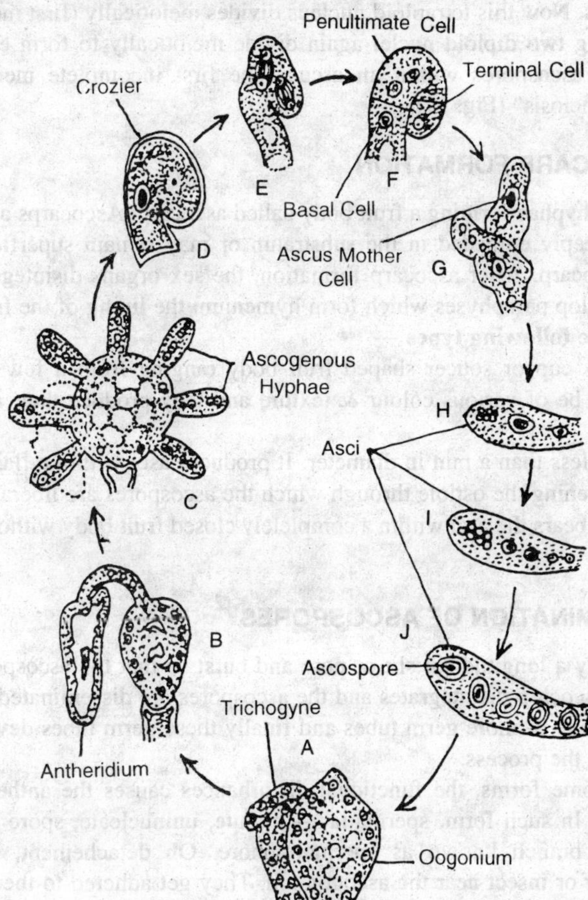

Fig. 16. Sequential stages in the development of an Ascus.

Now the male and female nuclei in dikaryotic penultimate cell fuse to form a diploid zygote nucleus. This is now ascus mother cell. The ascus mother cell elongates and the diploid zygote nucelus divides meiotically resulting into four haploid nuclei. These nuclei again divide mitotically forming eight haploid nuclei. These eight nuclei organise themselves into eight haploid ascospores. In some other members of ascomycetes, terminal and basal cell of the crozier fuse forming a new hook/crozier by the side of the first. This processes is repeated several times and a cluster of hook/crozier is formed. This method of asci formation was proposed by clausen (1906–1912), Dangeard (1907), Martin (1946), White house (1951) etc. There is another view regarding the development of asci proposed by Harper (1900),

Gwynne Vaughan and a Wilson (1931), Foster (1941) etc. According to them there are two reduction divisions preceded by two fusions.

First fusion takes place between uninucleate antheridium and uninucleate ascogonium producing a diploid zygote in the ascogonium. Now the ascogonium develops as ascogenous hypha in which diploid zygote nucleus migrates. There it divides mitotically twice to give rise four diploid nuclei. The ascogenous hypha bends forming a crozier and a subterminal crook cell with two diploid nuclei in them. The subterminal cell behaves as ascus mother cell. Both the diploid nuclei in ascus mother cell fuse forming a tetraploid nucleus. Now this tetraploid nucleus divides meiotically (first meiosis) forming two diploid nuclei. The resulting two diploid nuclei again divide meiotically to form eight haploid nuclei which organise into eight ascospores within an ascus. The first incomplete meiotic division (first meiosis) is called "brachy meiosis" (Fig. 17).

FRUIT BODY OR ASCOCARP FORMATION

The asci and the vegetative hyphae forming a fruit body called ascocarp. Ascocarps are formed singly or in groups. They may be deeply embeded in the substratun or may remain superficially. Usually one ascogonium forms one ascocarp. After ascocarp formation, the sex organs disintegrate and disappear. The vegetative hyphae develop paraphyses which form hymenium the lining of the fruit body.

Ascocarps may be of the following types —

1. Apothecium — It is cup or soucer shaped fruit body ranging from a few to several mm. in diameter. They may be of various colour & texture and they produce their asci in an open ascocarp (Fig. 18).
2. Perithecium — It is less than a mm in diameter. It produces asci within a flask shaped ascocarp having a terminal opening the ostiole through which the ascospores are liberated.
3. Cleistothecium — It bears the asci within a completely closed fruit body without any ostiole (Fig. 18)

LIBERATION AND GERMINATION OF ASCOSPORES

On maturity the asci open by a longitudinal slit or pore and burst so that the ascospores are forced out with a hissing sound. The ascocarp disintegrates and the ascospores are disseminated by wind, water or insects. They germinate by one or more germ tubes and finally these germ tubes develop into a septate mucelium which may repeat the process.

Spermatization — In some forms, the functional disturbances causes the antheridium to become superfluous and disappears. In such form, spermatia — minute, uninucleate, spore like bodies — are formed on special hyphal branch known as spermatiophore. On detachement, the spermatia are disseminated by wind, water or insect near the ascogonium. They get adhered to the trichogynes of the ascogonia and spermatial nuclei are transferred through the pore or trichogyne to the ascogonium where they lie with their counter parts i.e. female nuclei and form dikaryons.

Somatogamy — In this case, two somatic hyphae from different compatible mycelia fuse. The nucleus from one hypha migrates into the other through septal perforation. The cell i.e. hypha in which pairing of the male and female (+ and –) nuclei occurs, is considered as ascogonium. Thus, there is degeneration of trichogyne and ascogonium also. The further development in the ascogonium takes place as usual.

CLASSIFICATION

Gwynne – Vaughan and Barnes (1927) have subdivided class Ascomycetes on the basis of the structure of ascocarps as follows:-

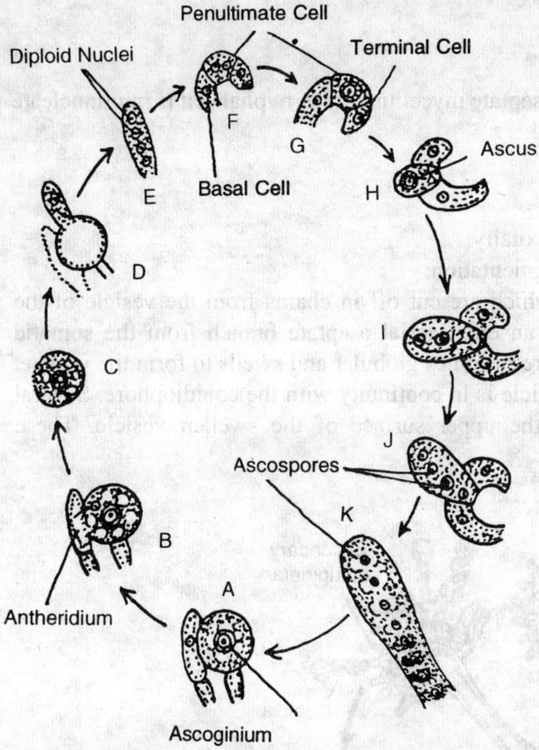

Fig. 17. Stages showing Harper's view of Brachy meiosis during ascus development

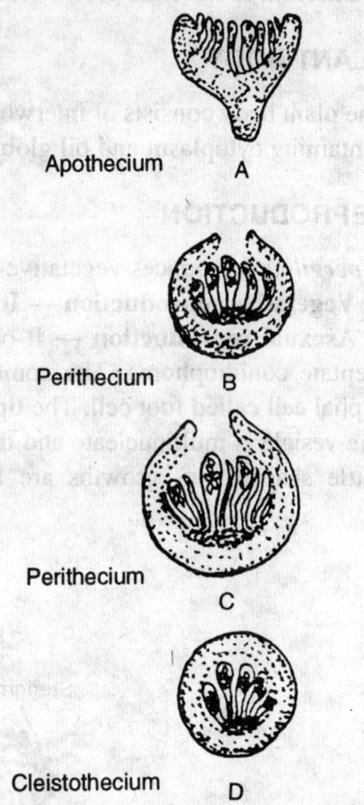

Fig. 18. Various kinds of Ascocarps In Ascomycetes (vertical section V.S.)

1. Subclass — Plectomycetes —ascocarp, cleistothecium type or absent.
2. Subclass — Discomycetes — ascocarp, apothecium type.
3. Subclass — Pyrenomycetes — ascocarp perithecium type

However, Martin (1948) subdivided class ascomycetes into two subclasses as follows —

1. Subclass — Hemiascomycetes — absence of ascocarp
2. Subclass — Euascomycetes — presence of ascocarp.

3.1 ASPERGILLUS (EUROTIUM)

It belongs to	Class	—	Ascomycetes
	Sub-class	—	Plectomycetes
	Order	—	Plectascales
	Family	—	Aspergillaceae
	Genus	—	*Aspergillus*

The genus *Aspergillus* is also known as *Eurotium*. It has about 80 species and they are cosmopolitan in distribution. They occurs as saprophytes on preserved fruits, syrup, cheese, jellies, jams, dung, wood, old leather on dried herbarium materials, tobacco etc. *A. flavus A. niger* live as parasite on man, animals and plants. They cause mycoses disease, disorders in skin, cornea, ears and lungs. The common colours of different species are green, blue, yellow and black.

PLANT BODY

The plant body consists of interwoven, branched and septate mycelium. Each hyphal cell is multinucleate containing cytoplasm and oil globules as reserve food.

REPRODUCTION

Aspergillus reproduces vegetatively, asexually and sexually.

Vegetative reproduction — It takes place by fragmentation.

Asexual reproduction — It occurs by conidia which are cut off in chains from the vesicle of the aseptate conidiophores. The conidiophore arises as an erect aerial aseptate branch from the somatic hyphal cell called foot cell. The tip of the conidiophore becomes globular and swells to form the vesicle. The vesicle is multinucleate and the cavity of the vesicle is in continuity with the conidiophore. Several bottle shaped out- growths are budded out from the upper surface of the swellen vesicle. These

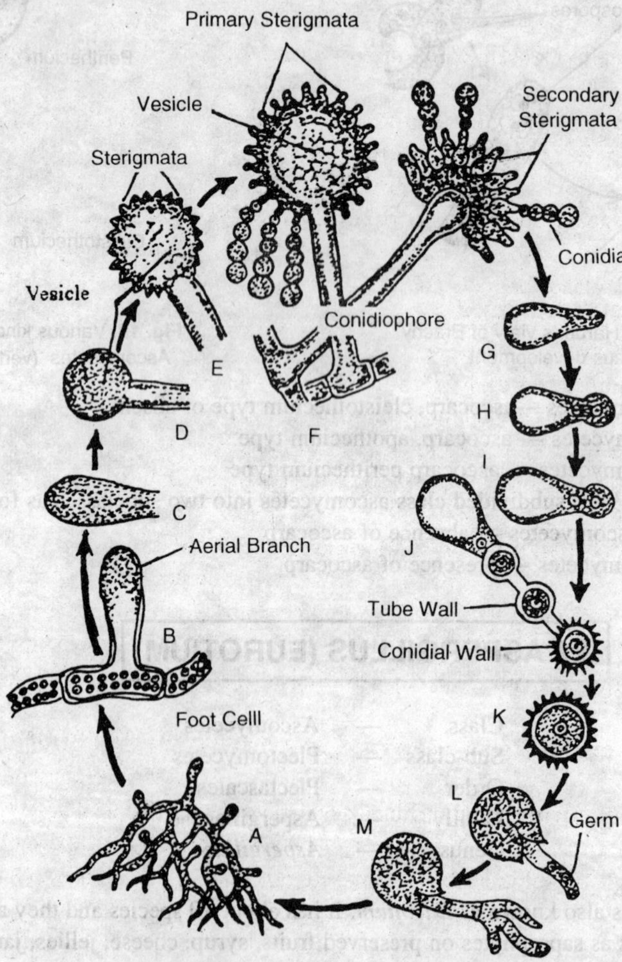

Fig. 19. Sequential stages showing asexual reproduction in *Aspergillus* sp. (diagrammatic).

outgrowths are known as 'sterigmata'. The sterigmata may be formed in one or two layers called as primary or secondary sterigmata. Only conidia bearing sterigmata are known as *phialids*. The nuclei from the vesicle migrate to the conidia. Each conidium is uninucleate, small, oval and 7 microns to 30 microns in diameter. On maturity they are dispersed by wind. They fall and germinate to produce a hypha on suitable organic medium. The hypha further develops a new mycelium and the process is repeated. (Fig. 19). This asexual stage has been named as *Aspergillus*.

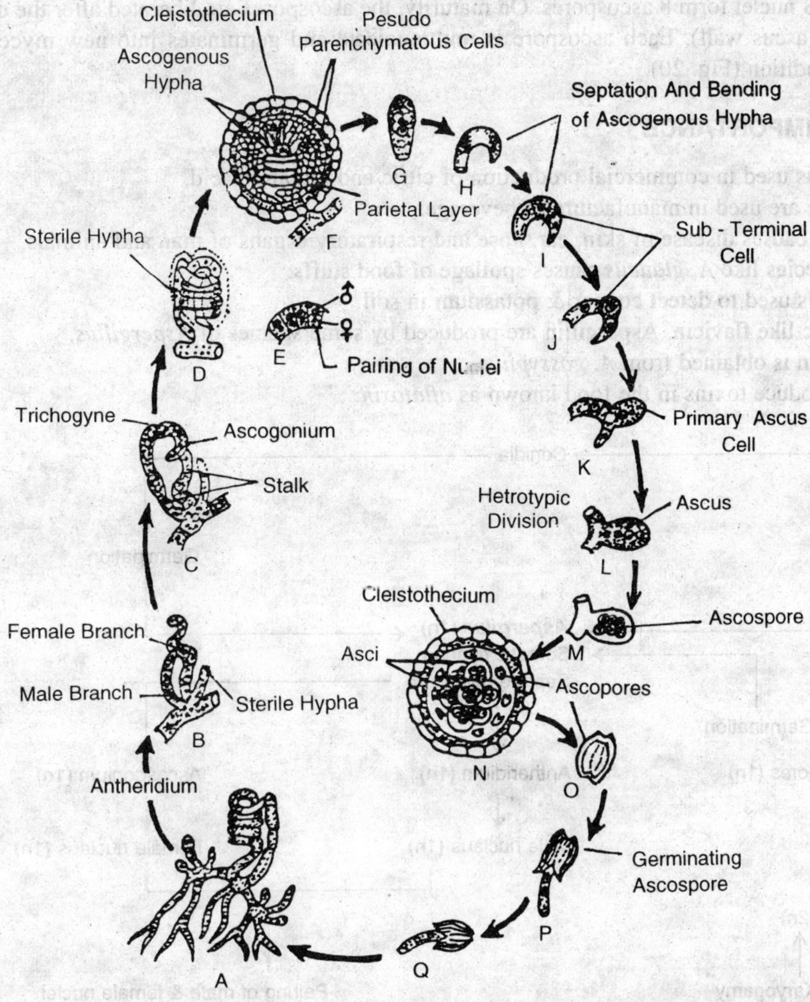

Fig. 20. Stages showing sexual reproduction in *Aspergillus* sp. (diagrammatic).

Sexual reproduction — G.R. Benjamin (1955) has given the name *Eurotium* for those *Aspergillus* species who possessed ascocarp. *Aspergillus herberiorum* produces sexually. The sex organ, both antheridia and ascognia are produced on the same somatic hyphae which produce conidia. The antheridial branch is septate, the tip is cut off into a unicellular, multinucleate antheridium proper. The ascogonium – a specialised hyphal branch is loosely coiled structure in the beginning but later it is differentiated into (1) a multicellular stalks (2) a unicellular ascogonium and (3) a unicellular trichogyne.

The antheridium bends and coils around the ascogonium, trichogyne and antheridial tip may or may not contact with each other. In any case, the nuclei in the ascogonium come to lie in pairs and septa formation in the ascogonium takes place resulting in the formation of cells with paired nuclei. In the mean time sterile hyphae develop from the stalks of the sex organ. The oogonium is covered by peridium or ascocarp wall and hence the ascocarp is *cleistothecium.*

Now, from the binucleate cell of ascogonium, ascogenous hyphae develop and from the terminal binucleate cell of each ascogenous hypha an ascus is formed. The young ascus is binucleate. The nuclei fuse to form a diploid nucleus which divides meiotically followed by mitosis resulting in 8 haploid nuclei. These 8 nuclei form 8 ascospores. On maturity, the ascospores are liberated after the decay of the peridium (the ascus wall). Each ascospore is multinucleate and germinates into new mycelium under favourable condition (Fig. 20).

ECONOMIC IMPORTANCE

1. *A. niger* is used in commercial production of citric and glutamic acid.
2. *A. oryzae* are used in manufacture of beverage.
3. *A. flavus* causes disease of skin, ear, nose and respiratory organs of man and animals.
4. Some species like *A. glaucus* causes spoilage of food stuffs.
5. *A. niger* is used to detect copper & potassium in soil.
6. Antibiotic like flavicin, Aspergillin are produced by some species of *Aspergillus.*
7. Riboflavin is obtained from *A. gossypii.*
8. It also produce toxins in the food known as *aflatoxin.*

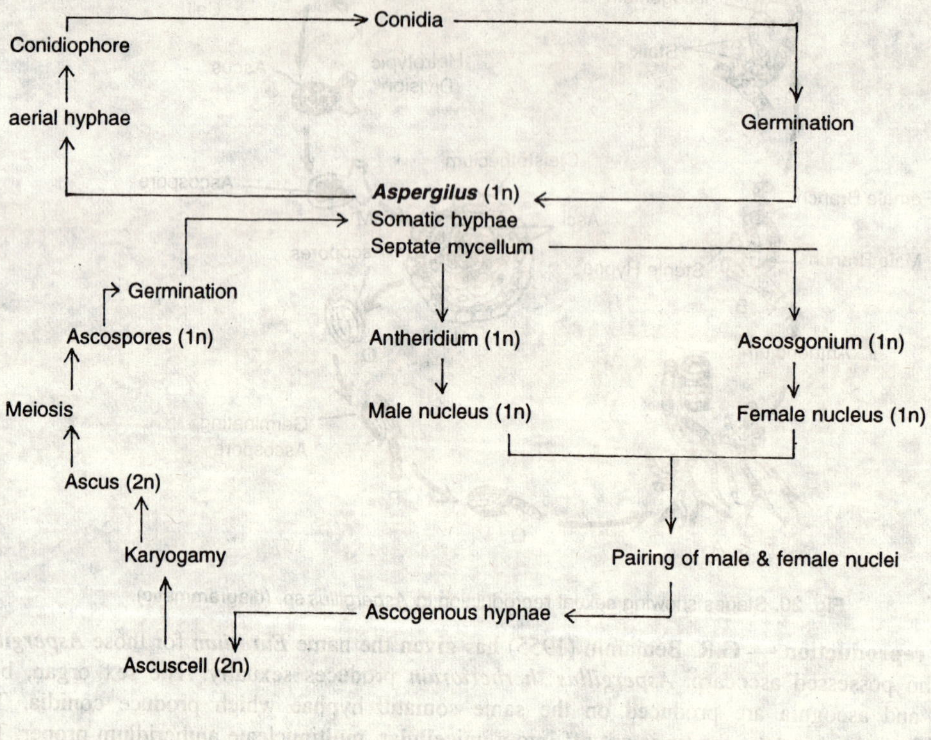

Graphic life cycle of *Aspergillus*

3.2 PENICILLIUM

It belongs to			
	Class	—	Ascomycetes
	Sub-class	—	Plectomycetes
	Order	—	Plectascales
	Family	—	Aspergillaceae
	Genus	—	*Penicillium*

There are about 140 species occuring as saprophytes on food stuffs and fruits causing green or blue coloured colonies and hence commonly known as green or blue moulds. They are cosmopolitan in distribution.

Penicillium digitatum causes blue green mould of citrus fruit.

PLANT BODY

Plant body is of mycelium made up of hyaline or coloured, septate, branched hyphae. The hyphae may be superficial or grow deep into the substratum forming a compact sclerotium. Hyphal cells may be uninucleate (apical hyphae in *P. notatum*) or multinucleate containing vacuolated and granulated cytoplasm with oil globules as food reserves. (Fig. 21).

REPRODUCTION

Penicillium Reproduces both sexually as well as asexually.

Asexual reproduction — It takes place by means of conidia formed on erect conidiophores. The conidiophores are usually branched in broom (brush) like fashion and hence its name *Penicillium* was given. In latin *Penicillium* stands for small brush. The conidiophore develops from ordinary hyphal cell. Each conidiophore may branches once or many times. These branches are known as metulae. Each metula gives rise a group of sterigmata or phialids. Each sterigma produces a chain of globose or oval conidia. The conidia may be bluish, greenish or yellow in colour. The upper most oldest conidia are detached from the chains usually by air currents. Each conidium germinates into a new mycelium. Sometimes, the conidia produce yeast like cells, if grown in a sugar solution (Fig., 22).

Sexual Reproduction — Sexual reproduction may be of gametangial contact type or somatogamy type and in some species functional antheridia and ascogonia may develop. In other species like *P. vermicularis* there is non functional antheridium. The ascogonium develops as an erect or elongated branch from the uninucleate mycelium. The nucleus of the ascognium divides & redivides to produce about 64 nuclei. By this time, the uninucleate branch as antheridium arises which coils round the ascogonium. At the point of contact between the antheridium and the ascogonium the wall dissolves and protoplasts come in contact. There is no migration of male nucleus to the ascogonium. The male nucleus remain in the antheridium and degenerate. Pairing of nuclei in the ascogonium takes place. Septation results into dikaryon cells. Each cell develops a lateral ascogenous hypha. The karyogamy takes place in the ascus mother cell. Sterile hyphae arise round the ascogonium and form a closed fruit body called cleistothecium (Fig. 23).

The ascospores are liberated after decay of the cleistothecium and germinate into a new branched septate mycelium.

ECONOMIC IMPORTANCE

Penicillium is useful in the cheese industry. Certain organic acids and many antibiotics are produced by different species of *Penicillium*, *P. notatum* is used in the production of gentisyle alcohol. Gallic acid is synthesized by *P. galcum*, *Penicillin* is synthesized from *P. notatum*. It causes spoilage of food and penicillosis disease in animals and man. *P. digitatum* spoils food. *P. divaricatum* causes yellow stain of hard wood.

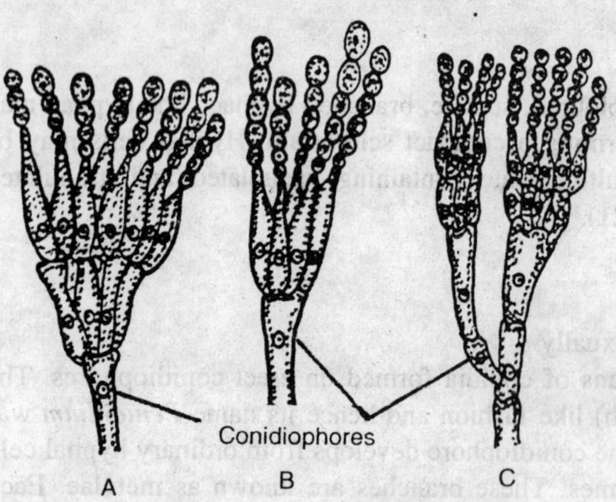

Fig. 21. Different types of conidiophores found in *Penicillium* sp. (diagrammatic).

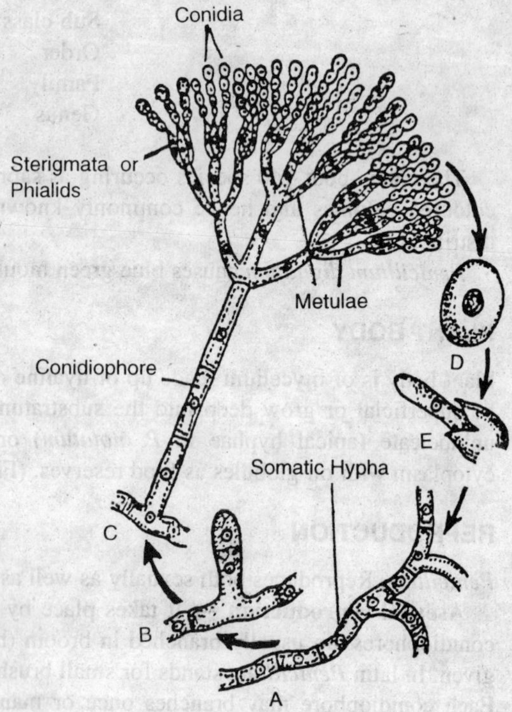

Fig. 22. Stages showing asexual reproduction in *Penicillium* sp. (diagrammatic).

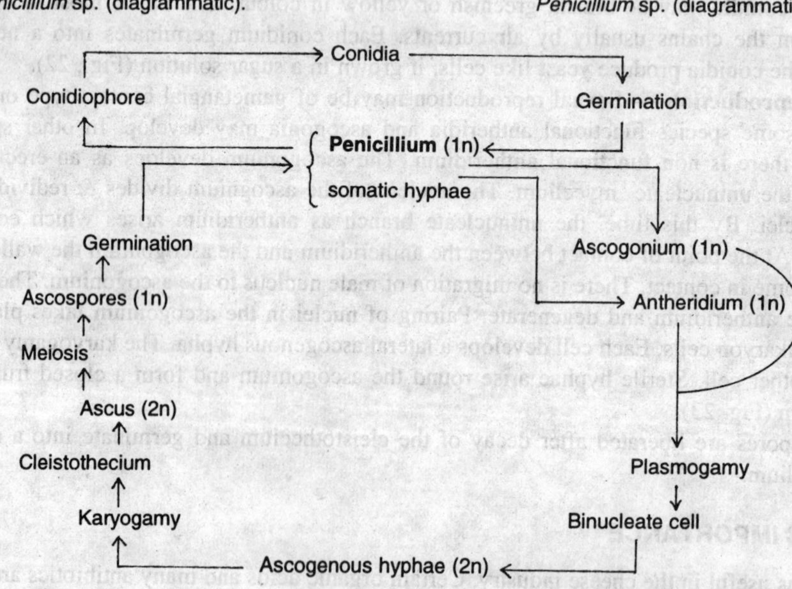

Graphic life cycle of *Penicillium*

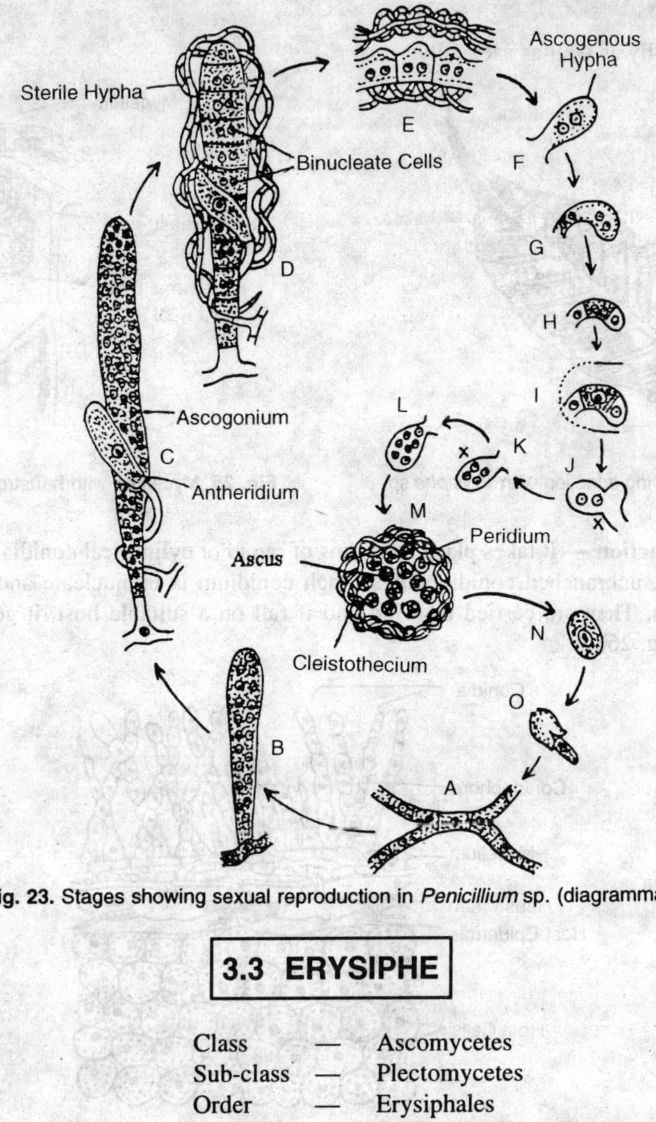

Fig. 23. Stages showing sexual reproduction in *Penicillium* sp. (diagrammatic).

3.3 ERYSIPHE

It belongs to

	Class	—	Ascomycetes
	Sub-class	—	Plectomycetes
	Order	—	Erysiphales
	Family	—	Erysiphaceae
	Genus	—	Erysiphe.

It is an obligate ectoparasite causing "Powdery mildews" disease in plants. Erysiphe first attacks leaves which spreads to leaf sheath, stem and glumes. The infected upper surface of leaf shows white, circular powdery spots (Fig. 24) The spots become brown later. The infected leaves get twisted and deformed.

PLANT BODY

It is colourless mycelial structure which sends finger like haustoria within the epidermal cells of the host and absorbs nourishment (Fig. 25).

REPRODUCTION

It reproduces sexually as well as asexually.

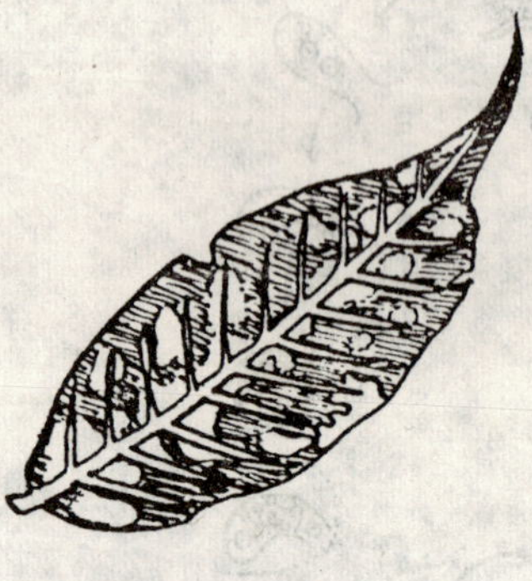

Fig. 24. A leaf showing infection with *Erysiphe* sp.

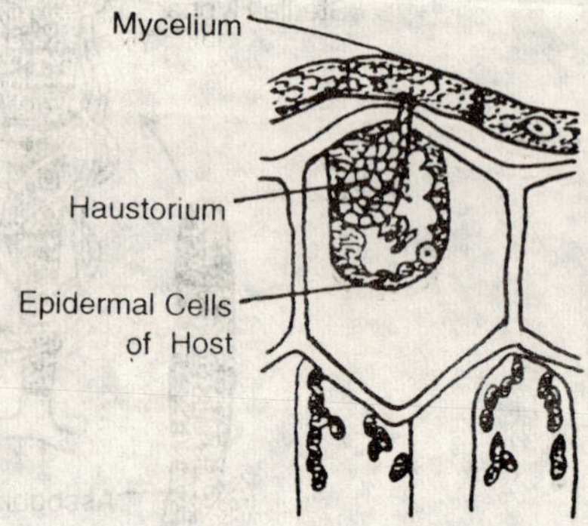

Fig. 25. Mycelium with haustronium of *erysiphe* sp.

Asexual reproduction — It takes place by means of ovoid or cylindrical conidia formed in chains on hyaline, erect, long, unbranched conidiophores. Each conidium is uninucleate and they are cut off in basipetal succession. They are carried by wind and if fall on a suitable host, it germinates and infect through stomata (Fig. 26).

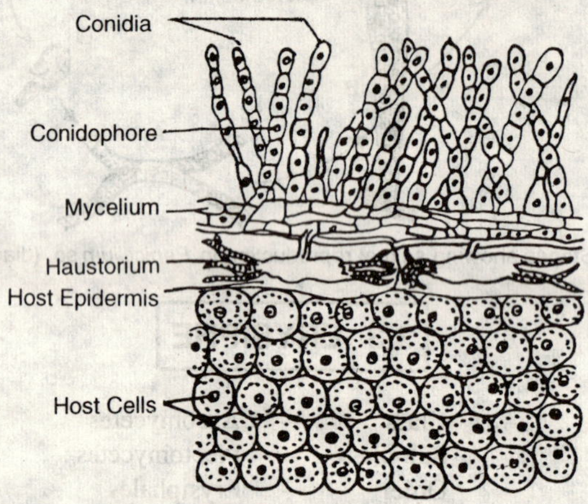

Fig. 26. Transverse section of infected leaf showing conidia of *Erysiphe* sp.

Sexual Reproduction — *Erysiphe* may be homothallic or heterothallic. The male and female sex organs are uninucleate. These sex organs i.e. antheridium and ascogonium are produced close to each other. The ascogonium develops from another hyphal branch near to the ascogonium. The terminal cell of the antheridial hypha divides to form upper antheridial cell and lower stalk cell. The point of contact between antheridium and ascogonium dissolves and a pore is formed. The male nucleus migrates into the ascogonium through this pore. Karyogamy followed by meiosis occurs in the ascogonium. The ascogonium divides to form a sub–terminal (penultimate) cell containing two nuclei and another uninucleate cell. The two nuclei of the penultimate cell, now known as ascus mother cell, fuse resulting into diploid zygote nucleus. Meiosis takes place forming four haploid nuclei which again divide mitotically to form 8 nuclei and subsequently 8 haploid ascospores are produced (Fig. 27). By this time vegetative hyphae grow around the sex organs enclosing the ascus to form –2 – 3 celled thick wall. The cleistothecium is formed which is a white spherical structure which becomes brown or black later. The cleistothecium develops mycelloid appendages from the outer wall of the peridium. Mechanical damage causes the cleistothecium to force out the asci in fan shaped manner. Ascospores are liberated after breakdown of the wall of the ascus. The liberated ascospores are carried by wind and reach to the host for germination and starting the life cycle (Fig. 27).

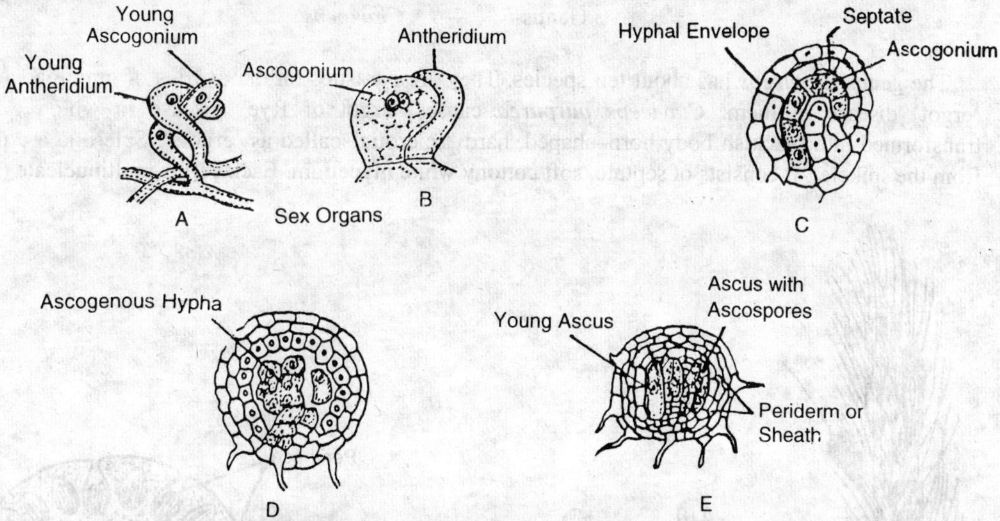

Fig. 27. Stages showing sexual reproduction/Ascus formation in *Erysiphe* sp.

The number of ascospores varies from two to six depending on the species.

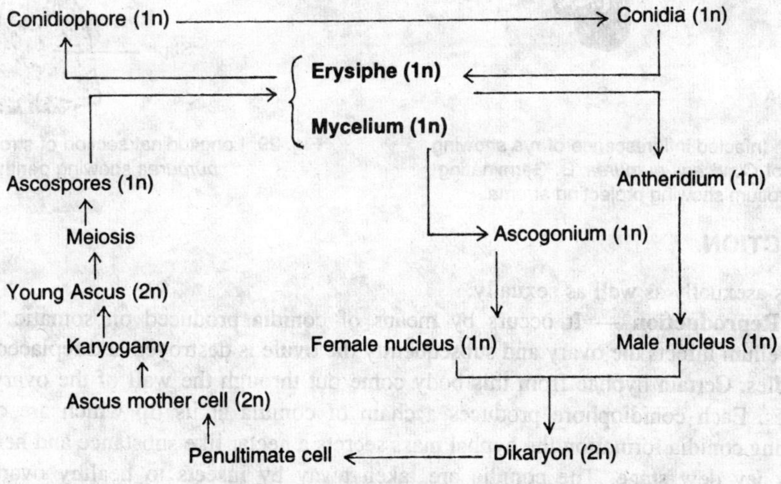

Graphic life cycle of *Erysiphe*

3.4 CLAVICEPS

It belongs to	Class	—	Ascomycetes
	Sub–class	—	Pyrenomycetes
	Order	—	Hypocreales
	Family	—	Hypocreaceae
	Genus	—	*Claviceps*

The genus *Claviceps* has about ten species. They are parasites on the ovaries of graminae and cause 'ergot' disease in them. *Claviceps purpurea* causes 'ergot of Rye' disease in which grains are transformed into blackish body horn–shaped, hard "sclerotia" called as 'ergots'. Sclerotia are projected from the spikelet. It consists of septate, soft cottony white mycelium. Each cell is multinucleate (Fig. 28).

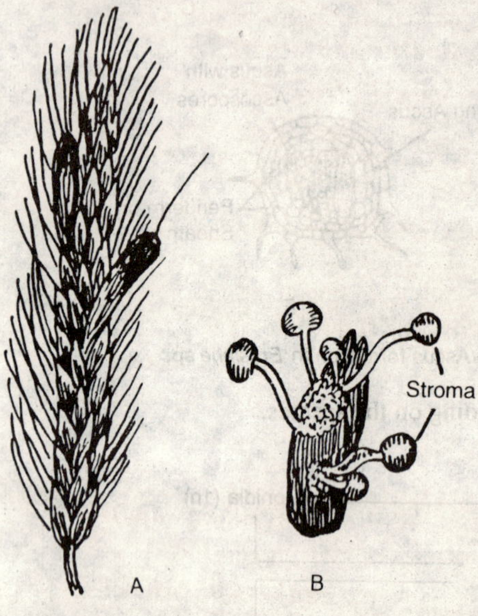

Fig. 28. A. Infected inflorescence of rye showing sclerotia of *Claviceps purpurea.* B. Germinating sclerotium showing projecting stroma.

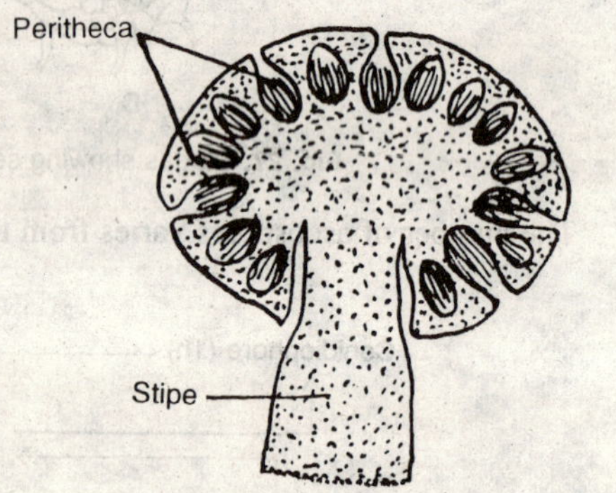

Fig. 29. Longitudinal section of stroma of *Claviceps purpurea* showing perithecia.

REPRODUCTION

It reproduces asexually as well as sexually.

Asexual Reproduction — It occurs by means of conidia produced on somatic mycelium. The somatic mycelium infects the ovary and subsequently the ovule is destroyed and replaced by soft, white, mycelial bodies. Certain hyphae from this body come out through the wall of the ovary which acts as conidiophores. Each conidiophore produces a chain of conidia at its tip which are oval, small and hyaline. During conidia formation the hyphal mass secrets a nectar like substance and hence this stage is known as honey dew stage. The conidia are taken away by insects to healthy ovaries where they germinate and cause fresh infection. Due to conidial infection, the ovary becomes enlarged and spongy in texture.

Sexual Reproduction — The soft mycelial mass in the ovary becomes compact and hard and it is gradually transformed into '*Sclerotium*' which is psendoparenchymatous mass of mycelia. Its outer covering is pink, purple or black while inner part is white. It is commonly known as Ergot. The sclerotium lies in between the glume of the rye spikelet. On maturity of ears of rye, the sclerotia fall on the ground and tides over the unfavourable period of winter. On the return of favourable condition, the sclerotia germinate to produce several mushroom like capitate outgrowths which are yellowish brown in colour. The length of these out growths varies from 10 to 20 mm. The upper globular head is called stroma. The stroma has several minute flask shaped cavities developed in the peripheral region. (Fig. 29) There is a single multinucleate ascogonium and many slender elongated antheridia within each cavity. A papilla is formed on the side of the ascogonium and nearer to the antheridium. The common wall between the ascognonium and the antheridium dissolves. Plasmogamy occurs and then the male nucleus passes into the tip of the ascognium resulting in the formation of dikaryons. It develops ascogenous hypha. The tip of the ascogenous hypha bends and forms a terminal cell. The subterminal cell behaves as the ascus mother cell and forms eight ascospores after meiosis. Each cavity has several asci and sterile paraphyses. The ascospores measures 0.6 to 0.7 microns in diameter and are long and filiform in appearance. The flask shaped cavities open by a minute pore called ostiole (Fig. 30). The cavity containing asci is known as perithecium. The perithecia are deeply situated in the stroma. The ascospores are liberated and carried by wind to healthy ovaries of graminae where they germinate to produce a septate, branched mycelium.

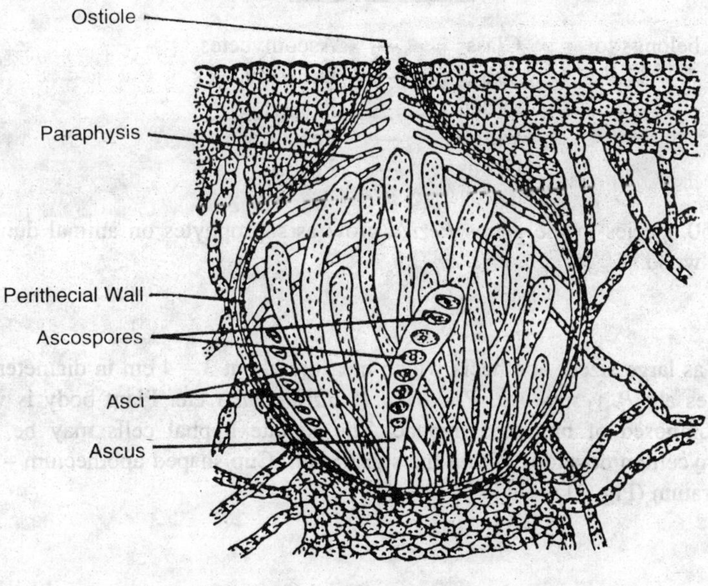

Fig. 30. Vertical section of sporocarp of *Claviceps purpurea* showing asci.

ECONOMIC IMPORTANCE

Sclerotia or Ergot causes loss of hair, teeth, nails and gangerine. Ergot causes ergot poisoning or ergotism. It also causes abortion in animals.

Ergotamine and ergotoxin present in ergot has medicinal values as it causes contraction of muscles of uterus during child birth. Prolonged use of ergot leads to paralysis.

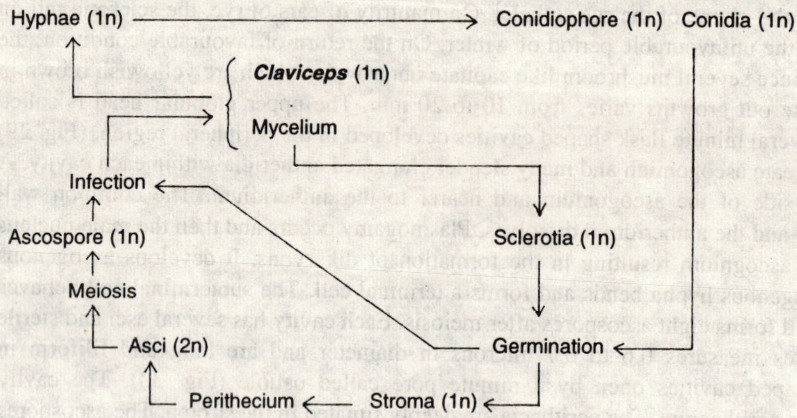

Graphic life cycle of *Claviceps* sp.

3.5 PEZIZA

The genus *Peziza* belongs to

Class	—	Ascomycetes
Sub-class	—	Discomycetes
Order	—	Pezizales
Family	—	Pezizaceae
Genus	—	*Peziza*

There are about 50 species in the genus *Peziza* grow as saprophytes on animal dungs, soil rich in humus and decaying wood.

PLANT BODY

It can be recognised as large sized apothecia which measure about 3 – 4 cm in diameters. Some of the common India species are *P. vesiculosa*, *P. citrina P. darjeelensis* etc. Plant body is well developed septate mycelium composed of branched hyphae. The septate hyphal cells may be uninucleate or multinucleate. The mycelium develops within the substratum. Cup shaped apothecium – a fruit body is seen above the substratum (Fig. 31).

REPRODUCTION

Peziza reproduces sexually and asexually both.

Asexual reproduction — It occurs by the formation of conidia or thick walled chlamydospores in *P. vesiculosa* and *P. repando*. Erect filaments develop from the mycelium which produce several ellipsoidal conidia. Chlamydospores are produced in groups or singly. On detachment, these conidia germinate to produce new mycelia. (Fig. 32).

Sexual reproduction — There is reduction in sexuality. In *P. confluens* the antheridia and the ascogonia develop closely. The terminal portion of the outer branch swell into vesicle known as archicarp. The archicarp has a curved trichogyne. The antheridium develops as a club shaped branch from cell below the archicarp. The antheridium and the ascogonium are unicellular and multinucleate.

The antheridial tip comes in contact with trichogyne. The common wall between them dissolves and a passage is formed through which male nuclei pass in the ascogonium to pair which the female nuclei. Now the ascogonium gives rise several ascogenous hyphae. In each ascogenous hypha a pair of nuclei enters from the ascogonium. The tip of ascogenous hypha bends to form a hook like structure called crozier, the penultimate or subterminal cell which acts as ascus mother cell having a diploid or tetraploid nucleus after fusion of dicaryon. It divides meiotically once or twice depending on diploid or tetraploid nature. The ultimate result is the formation of 8 haploid nuclei which metamorphoses into 8 ascospores obliquely arranged. The Asci are arranged in a concave disc known as hymenium which forms a red or orange layer. The hymenium is surrounded by peridium made up of vegetative hyphae developed around the rossette of sex organs. The hymenium, peridium and asci altogether form an open ascocarp or

Fig. 31. Apothecia of *Peziza* sp.

apothecium. The sex organs disintegrate and sterile hyphae arise from the apothecial cup in between the asci which are known as paraphyses (Fig. 32). The ascospores are liberated and are dispersed by wind which germinate to produce new mycelia. The colour of the apothecial cups may be white or pale yellow.

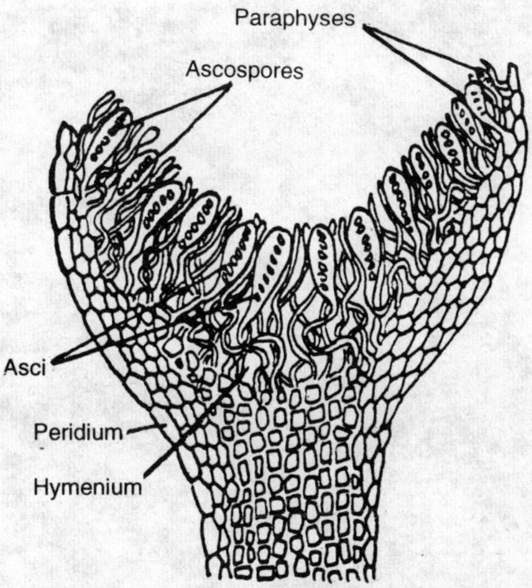

Fig. 32. Vertical section of Apothecium of *Peziza* sp. showing Asci.

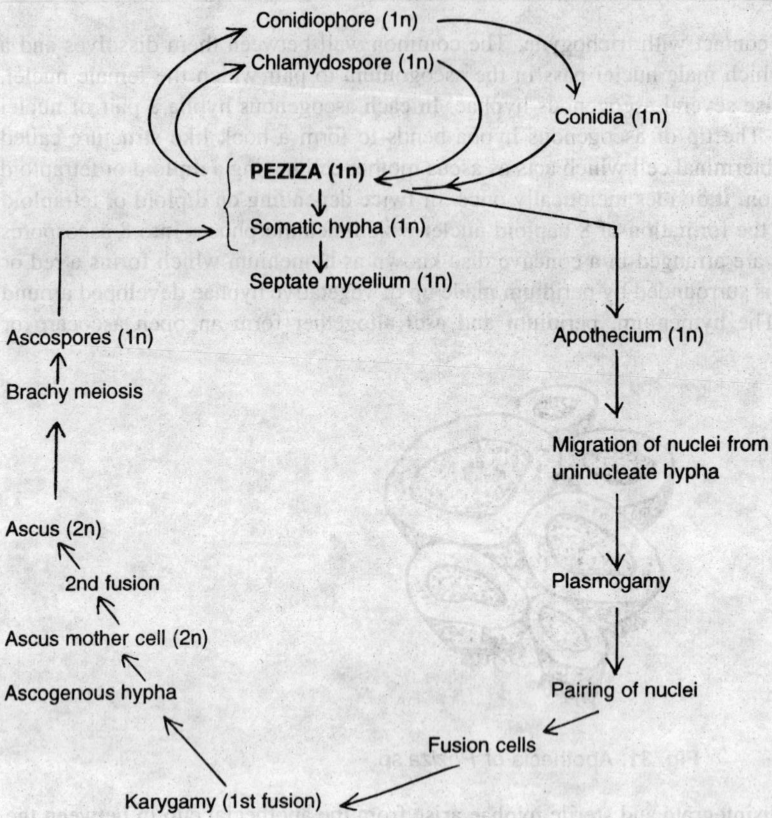

Graphic life cycle of *Peziza*

CHAPTER 4

BASIDOMYCETES

The class Basidiomycetes includes saprophytic and parasitic fungi with about 550 genera and 15,000 species distributed throughout the world. This class is of advanced group of fungi including smuts, rusts, mushrooms, puffs balls, gelly fungi, braket fungi, bird's nest fungi, stink horns etc. The class is characterised by a club shaped septate or aseptate basidium usually bearing four unicellular exogenously produced spores called basidiospores. The fruiting body of Basidiomycetes is known as basidiocarp which is fleshy or woody.

VEGETATIVE STRUCTURE

The plant body is made up of mycelium composed of branched septate hyphae. The hyphal cell wall is made up of chitin and the cell is binucleate. This dikaryotic cell gives rise basidium from which monokaryotic basidiospores are produced. The basidiospores on germination give rise uninucleate or monokaryotic mycelia. This uninucleate mycelium is known as primary mycelium and the dikaryotic mycelium is called secondary mycelium. The clamp connection usually occurs near the base of a basidium between adjacent cell of the dikaryotic mycelium (Fig. 33). The mycelium may be white, bright yellow, orange, deep brown or black in colour. The secondary mycelium gives rise tertiary mycelium. The cells of tertiary mycelium are binucleate. This type of mycelium forms the basidiocarps in advanced basidiomycetes.

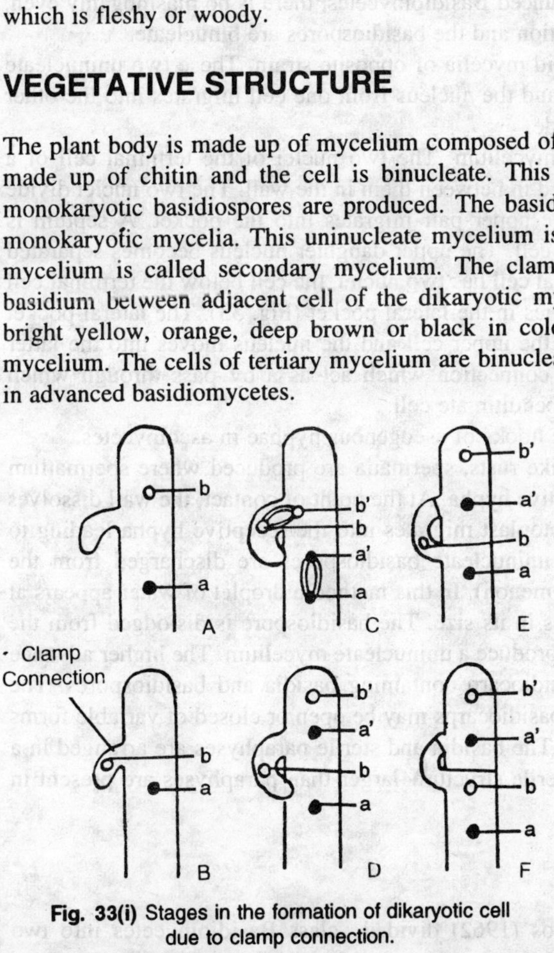

Fig. 33(i) Stages in the formation of dikaryotic cell due to clamp connection.

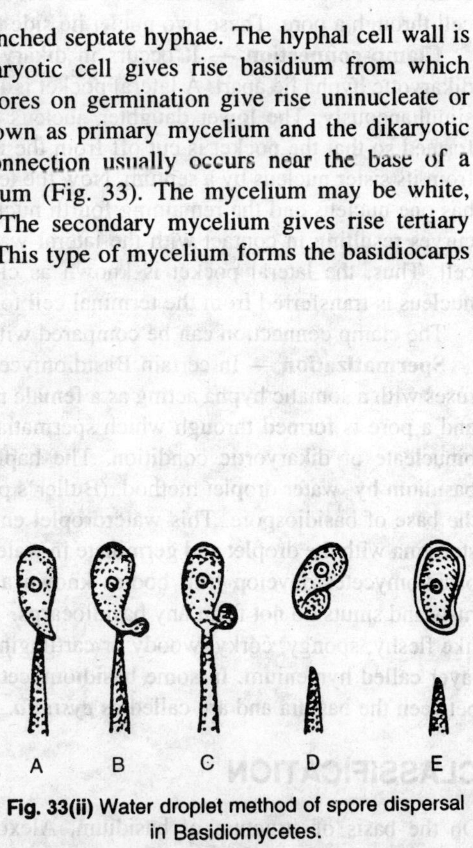

Fig. 33(ii) Water droplet method of spore dispersal in Basidiomycetes.

REPRODUCTION

The various members of the basidomycetes exhibit vegetative, asexual and sexual mode of reproduction.

VEGETATIVE REPRODUCTION

It takes place by fragmentation of the mycelium and by budding.

ASEXUAL REPRODUCTION

It occurs by means of oidia, conidia and arthrospores or chlamydospores.

SEXUAL REPRODUCTION

It is very much reduced and the sex organs like antheridia and ascognia are lacking in Basidiomycetes. Even then, there is a clear alternation of generations involving a change from monokaryotic mycelium (haplophase) to dikaryotic mycelium (diplophase). The monokaryotic mycelium and besidiospores are heterothallic either (+) or (–). Mycelium arising from a basidiospore comes in contact with the mycelium developing from a physiologically different basidiospores and hyphal fusion (plasmogamy) takes place leading to dikaryotisation. In some advanced Basidiomycetes, there is no plasmogamy even, but haplophase changes to diplophase by diplodization and the basidiospores are binucleate.

Diplodization takes place in between two haploid myçelia of opposite strain. These two uninucleate cells come in contact, the common wall dissolves and the nucleus from one cell migrates into the other cell through a pore. These two nuclei lie side by side.

Clamp connection — It occurs in dikaryotic mycelium. The two nuclei of the terminal cell of a dikaryotic hypha lie apart. A lateral pocket is formed in between them in the wall. The two nuclei divide simultaneously. The lower daughter nucleus of the upper pair migrates into the pocket. A septum is formed so that the pocket is cut off from the main cell. The upper daughter nucleus becomes separated from its sister nucleus by a septum. Now the terminal cell has two nuclei, the cell below the terminal cell has one nucleus and the remaining fourth nucleus lies in the lateral pocket (Fig. 33). The lateral pocket curves resulting in contact with the lateral wall of the upper cell and the nucleus moves into the latter cell. Thus, the lateral pocket is known as clamp connection which act as a by–pass through which nucleus is transferred from the terminal cell to the penultimate cell.

The clamp connection can be compared with the hooks of ascogenous hyphae in ascomycetes.

Spermatization — In certain Basidiomycetes like rusts, spermatia are produced where spermatium fuses with a somatic hypha acting as a female receptive hypha. At the point of contact, the wall dissolves and a pore is formed through which spermatial protoplast migrates into the receptive hypha leading to binucleate or dikaryortic condition. The haploid, uninucleate basidiospores are discharged from the basidium by water droplet method. (Buller's phenomenon). In this method a droplet of water appears at the base of basidiospore. This waterdroplet enlarges in its size. The basidiospore is dislodged from the sterigma with the droplet and germinate in water to produce a uninucleate mycelium. The higher advance basidiomycetes develop fruit bodies known as basidiocarp containing basidia and basidiospores. The rusts and smuts do not form any basidiocarps. The basidiocarps may be open or closed of variable forms like fleshy, spongy, corky, woody or cartilaginous. The basidia and sterile paraphyses are arranged in a layer called hymenium. In some basidiomycetes sterile structure–larger than paraphyses are present in between the basidia and are called as *cystidia*.

CLASSIFICATION

On the basis of structure of basidium, Alexopoulos (1962) divided class Basidiomycetes into two subclasses, (1) Heterobasidiomycetes and (2) Homobasidiomycetes. Sub class Heterobasidiomycetes has been further divided into three orders viz. (1) Tremellales (2) Uredinales and (3) Ustilaginales

Similarly, sub–class Homobasidiomycetes has been further divided into eight orders as follows.

1. Order — Exobasidiales
2. Order — Polyporales
3. Order — Agaricales
4. Order — Hymenogastrales
5. Order — Lycoperdales
6. Order — Sclerodermatales
7. Order — Phallales
8. Order — Nidulariales

This classification has been followed here.

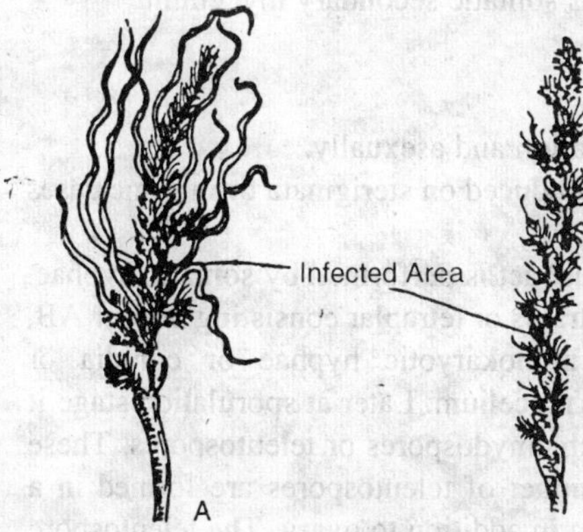

Fig. 34. Infected wheat ears (A, B) by *Ustilago tritici.*

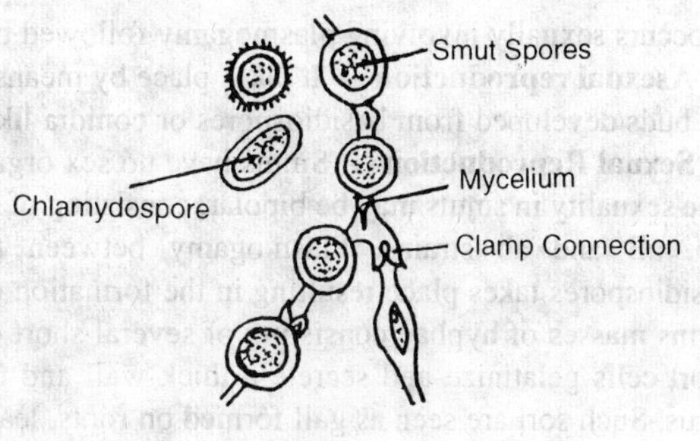

Fig. 35. Clamp connection and spore formation from mycelium of *Ustilago sp.*

4.1 USTILAGO

The genus *Ustilago* belongs to

Class	—	Basidiomycetes
Sub-class	—	Heterobasidiomycetes
Order	—	Ustilaginales
Family	—	Ustilaginaceae
Genus	—	*Ustilago*

It has about 300 species and they are commonly known as 'Smuts' or 'Smut fungi', as they produce black dusty spore masses on the host plant which resemble soot or smut. It infects various wild grasses in addition to wheat, barley, oats, maize, sugarcane etc and causes smut disease. It infects the host in the beginning but it makes its appearance after flowering period. Ear turns black and shrivelled. The grains in the ovary is completely replaced by sooty, black spores or chlamydospores (Fig. 34 & 35). Following are some of the Indian species of *Ustilago* causing diseases in crops.

1. *Ustilago tritici* causes loose smut of wheat (***Triticum aestivum***)
2. *Ustilago nuda* causes loose smut of Barley (*Hordeum vulgare*).
3. *U. hordei* causes covered smut of Barley (***Hordeum vulgare***)

4. *U. avenae* causes loose smut of Oat (*Avena sativa*)
5. *U. maydis* causes smut of maize (*Zea mays*)
6. *U. scitaminea* causes smut of sugarcance (*Saccharum officinarum*)

Smuts are of two types namely, (1) covered smut and (2) loose smut. In covered smut, the spores remain within the grain and they are liberated on breaking of the grain wall as in barley caused by *Ustilago hordei*. In loose smut the black powdery mass of spores is exposed during flowering time and the spores are blown by wind as in wheat caused by *Ustilago tritici*.

PLANT BODY

The vegetative plant body is parasite on flowering plants. It consists of septate mycelium which may be intracellular as in *U. maydis* or intercellular as in *U. sacchari*, Each septate cell has dikaryons. The haploid uninucleate basidiospores or conidia germinates to produce uninucleate primary mycelium. Dikaryotisation takes place in the cell of the primary mycelium which results in the formation of dikaryotic secondary mycelium. Sporulation takes place from this somatic secondary mycelium.

REPRODUCTION

It occurs sexually involving plasmogamy followed by dikaryotization and asexually.

Asexual reproduction — It takes place by means of conidia produced on sterigmata or in some cases by buds developed from basidiospores or conidia like yeast.

Sexual Reproduction — Smuts have no sex organs. The sexual act is performed by somatic hyphae. The sexuality in smuts may be bipolar, consisting of (+) and (–) strains or tetraplar consisting of four AB, Ab, aB and ab strains. Plasmogamy between two unlike monokaryotic hyphae or conidia or basidiospores takes place resulting in the formation of dikaryotic mycelium. Later at sporulation stage it forms masses of hyphae consisting of several short cells called chlamydospores or teleutospores. These short cells gelatinize and secrete a thick wall and thus large number of teleutospores are formed in a sorus. Such sori are seen as gall formed on roots, leaves, and stem in addition to ovary. The teleutospore may be pale, olive or brown in colour, globose or ellipsoidal in shape and 5-9 microns in diameter with a pair of nuclei (Fig. 36).

Fig. 36. Aa. Conidia formation from Basidiospore B. Conjugating basidiospores. C. Basidial cell forming dikaryotic cell. D. Conjugation between two basidia.

It also reproduce by thick walled spiny black chlamydospores formed from secondary dikaryotic mycelium. The teleutospores or chlamydospores are produced in large number and fill the ovary cavity fully and rupture it. Such sori, if produced on roots, leaves or stems, cause a gall formation.

During germination, two nuclei of chlamydospores, fuse to produce a diploid zygotic nucleus. The spore wall breaks open and a germ tube comes out known as promycelium or epibasidium. The diploid nucleus migrate into the promycelium and divides meiotically to form four haploid nuclei. Septa is formed dividing the promycelium or basidium into four uninucleate cells. This is called basidium. Each cell of the basidium cuts off externally a single basidiospore or sporidium at the side of each cell. The nucleus of each cell divides mitotically into two, one of them moves into a basidiospore and remaining one remains in the cell. Each basidiospore is thin walled, oval and uninucleate. The basidiospore repeatedly buds out new conidia or sprout cells or secondary basidiospores in *U. avenae*. These bring out new infection in the meristematic tissues of the host plants. (Fig. 37). Clamp connections are formed from dikaryotic mycelium. There is no basidiocarp formation in *Ustilago*.

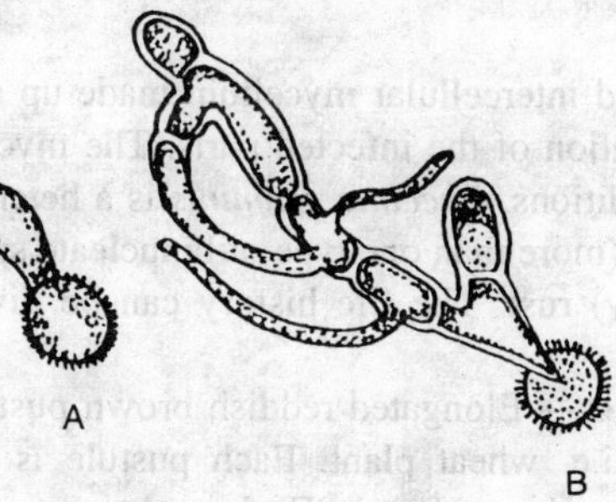

Fig. 37. Germination of Chlamydospore of *Ustilago tritici.*

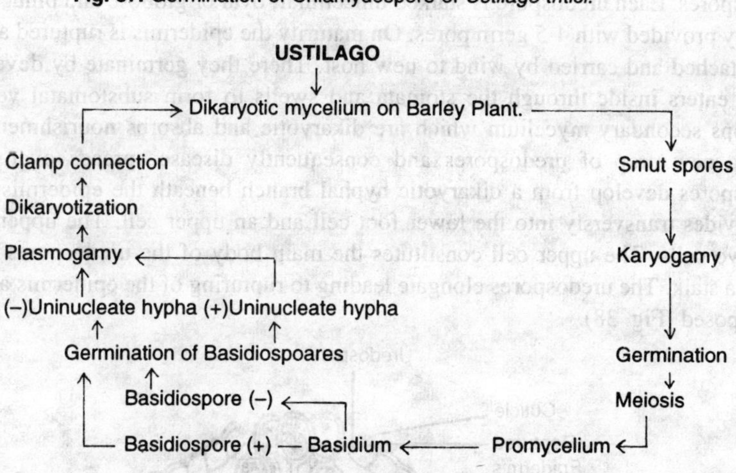

Graphic life cycle of *Ustilago*

4.2 PUCCINIA

The genus *Puccinia* belongs to

Class	—	Basidiomycetes
Sub-class	—	Protobasidiomycetes
Order	—	Uredinales
Family	—	Pucciniaceae
Genus	—	*Puccinia*

The genus *Puccinia* has more than 1800 species, cosmopolitan in distribution and occur as parasites on flowering plants specially Wheat, Oat, Barley etc. causing great loss to these crops. They are commonly known as 'rust fungi' as they produce rust like spores and appear as streaks on leaves, leafsheaths and stems of the host plants. The black rust of wheat caused by *Puccinia graminis tritici* occurs every year and is highly specialised and confined to a particular variety of host. This is called as physiological specialisation and hence a species has been divided into several sub–species which are called as physiological races and therefore, these are referred to in a trinomial nomenclature as mentioned below.

Puccinia graminis tritici is parasite on wheat i.e. *Triticum aestivum*, *P. graminis hordei* is parasite on Barley i.e. *Hordeum vulgare*. *P. graminis avena* is parasite on oat i.e. *Avena sativa*

PLANT BODY

It is in the form of well developed intercellular mycelium made up of branched and septate hyphae. It causes hypertrophy and malformation of the infected parts. The mycelium shows alternating phases of monokaryotic and dikaryotic conditions. *Puccinia graminis* is a heteroecious (two hosts are required to complete life cycle), macrocyclic (more than one type of binucleate spores) and polymorphic (more than one type of spores in life history) rust. The life history can be divided into five different stages as follows.

1. **Red Rust or uredial stage** — Elongated reddish brown pustules containing sori appear on the stem and leaves of host i.e. wheat plant. Each pustule is a sorus known as uredosorus or uredinium formed just below the epidermis. Each uredosorus contains many reddish spores called uredospores. Each uredospore is stalked unicellular, oval or globose and binucleate. Its outer wall is spiny provided with 4-5 germ pores. On maturity the epidermis is ruptured and the uredospores are detached and carried by wind to new host. There they germinate by developing germ tubes which enters inside through the stomata and swells to form substomatal vesicle. This vesicle develops secondary mycelium which are dikaryotic and absorbs nourishment from the host to form a new crop of uredospores and consequently disease spreads over a large area. The uredospores develop from a dikaryotic hyphal branch beneath the epidermis. The basal hyphal cell divides transversly into the lower foot cell and an upper cell. The upper cell again divides into two cells. The upper cell constitutes the main body of the uredospores and the lower cell forms a stalk. The uredospores elongate leading to rupturing of the epidermis and the uredospores are exposed (Fig. 38).

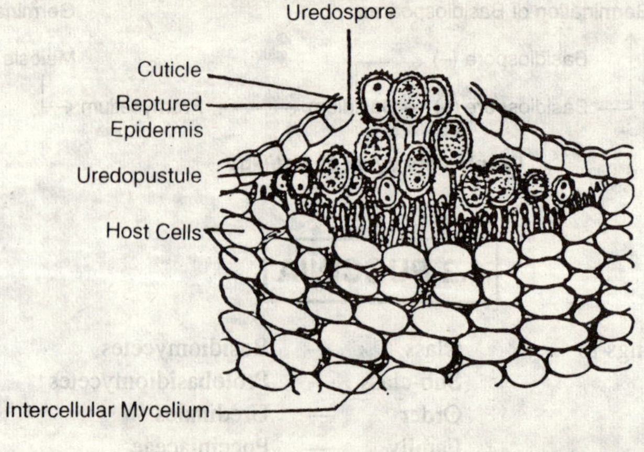

Fig. 38. T.S. of infected wheat leaf showing uredospores of *Puccinia graminis*.

2. **Black rust or telial stage** — Towards the end of growing season, oblong or elongated black pustules or streaks develop on the stem and leaves of the infected wheat plants. These pustules are telia or teleuto sori having teleutospores. The teleutospores are produced by the same mycelium which are producing uredospores. Sometimes, combination of uredospores and teleutospores are observed within the same pustule. Each teleutospore is bicelled, spindle shaped and stalked structure. It has an outer thick wall called exospore and inner delicate wall known as endospore. The apical portion has germ pore and the lower cell has a germ pore at the side below the septum (Fig. 39). Each cell of the teleuspore is binucleate. On maturity, the two nuclei of each cell fuse to form a diploid nucleus. The teleutospores either fall on the ground (soil) or may remain attached to the straw to tide over unfavourable season. The fungus completes its life cycle on wheat causing loss of chlorophyll leading to production of unhealthy grains and falling of stem to the ground.

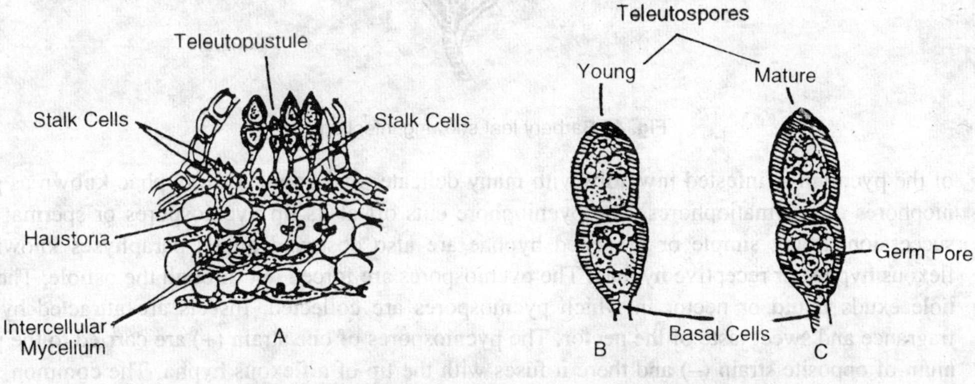

Fig. 39. A. T.S. of infected wheat stem showing teleutospores of *Puccinia graminis*, B and C Teleutospores.

3. **Basidial stage** — In the next favourable season i.e. spring, each cell of the teleutospore germinates independentally by an erect tubular outgrowth known as epibasidium or primary mycelium. The diploid nucleus migrates into the primary mycelium where it divides meiotically to form four haploid nuclei. Transverse walls are laid down separating the haploid nuclei into four uninucleate cells. This is called basidium. Each cell of the basidium develops short lateral outgrowth called sterigma. Each sterigma cuts off at its tip a single, uninucleate haploid basidiospore. At maturity, the basidiospores are violently ejected by water droplet method and are taken away by wind. The *Puccinia graminis* is heterotallic and hence, the four basidiospores produced on a basidium are of two different sexes or strains (+) or (–). These basidiospores are not capable to infect the wheat but it can germinate only when it comes in contact with the alternate secondary host the barbery (*Berberis vulgaris*) plant (Fig. 40).
4. **Spermogonial or Pycnial stage** — Basidiospore of (+) or (–) strain germinates by sending out a germ tube which penetrates the epidermis of leaf or young twig of a barbery plant. It divides into uninucleate cells and subsequently forms uninucleate\primary mycelium within the intercellular spaces of the host tissue. It obtains nourishment from the host cells through haustoria. Few days after infection, isolated dense mats of hyphae appears below the upper and lower epidermis of the host leaf. Later, the hyphal mats near the upper epidermis forms clusters of pycnia or spenmogonia and near the lower epidermis it forms the clusters of aecidia.

   The pycnium or spermogonium is a flask shaped structure opens towards the upper surface of the leaf by a small pore called ostiole guarded by several sterile hyphae called paraphyses. The cavity

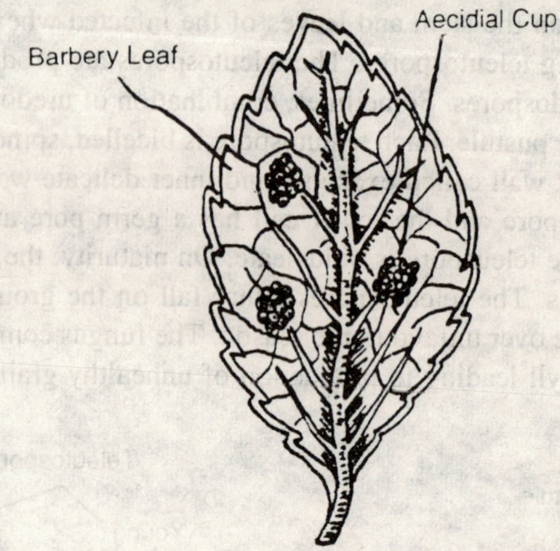

Fig. 40 Barbery leaf showing infection.

of the pycnium is infested inwardly with many delicate and uninucleate hyphae known as pycniophores or spermatiophores. The pycniophore cuts off at its tip pycniospores or spermat:- in succession. Many simple or branched hyphae are also observed amids paraphyses known as flexous hyphae or receptive hyphae. The pycniospores are forced out through the ostiole. The ostiole exuds liquid or nector in which pycniospores are collected. Insects are attracted by the fragrance and sweet taste of the nector. The pycniospores of one strain (+) are carried to the pycnium of opposite strain (–) and there it fuses with the tip of a flexous hypha. The common wall at the point of contact dissolves and the pycnial nucleus enters into the flexous hypha i.e. spermatization takes place. Development of aecidium and aecidiospores takes place only when pycniospore of one pycnium is transferred to the flexuous hypha or receptive hypha of opposite strain (Fig. 41).

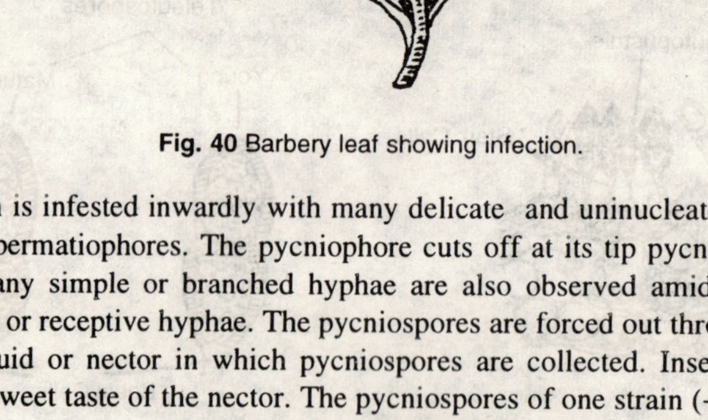

Fig. 41. A.T.S. of barbery leaf showing pycnidium and aecidial cups.

5. **Aecidial or aecial stage** — After spermatization, development of aecidium occurs. In the beginning a globose mass of hyphae are seen and its cells towards lower epidermis begins to differentiate into a layer of palisade like cells, known as basal cells. Remaining cells are called displacement cells (Fig. 42). During spermatization, the nucleus of pycniospore passes from the

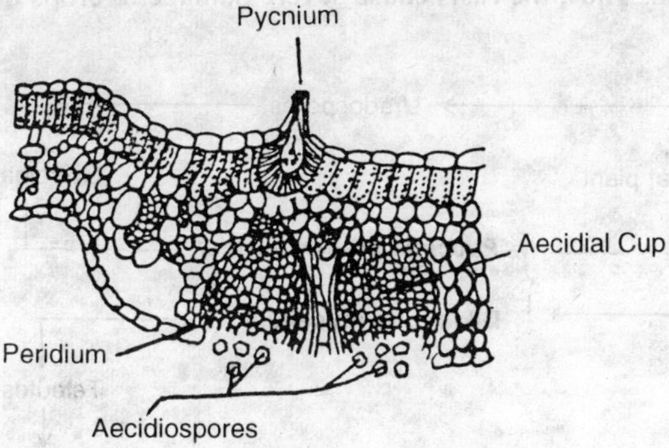

Fig. 41. B.T.S. of barbery leaf showing pycnidium, fusion of Pycniospore and receptive hypha and formation of dikaryotic mycelium.

pycniospore into the flexuous hypha and reaches the basal cell of the primordial structure of aecidium. This brings dikaryotic condition. Dikaryotization is followed by the formation of aecidium and subsequently aecidiosporesis. The binucleate basal cell cuts off binucleate cells in chain towards the lower epidermis into a cavity formed by the dissolution of displacement cells. The chain of the cells constitutes larger aeciospores and smaller sterile disjuncter cells or intercalary cells. Some basal cells near periphery of the aecidium form a protective layer known as peridium which is one cell thick. Thus, the entire structure is known as aecidium. It elongates and pushes through the lower epidermis of the barbery leaf and the aecidium looks as bell shaped body (Fig. 42). On maturity, the intercalary cells disintegrate separating the aeciospores free from each other which are carried by wind. Each acciospore has a germ pore through which germ tubes develop during germination.

Aeciospores are incapable to reinfect barbery plant and they infect wheat plant. The aeciospores germinate on the host (wheat) tissue forming dikaryotic mycelium which in term produces uredospores and the cycle goes on.

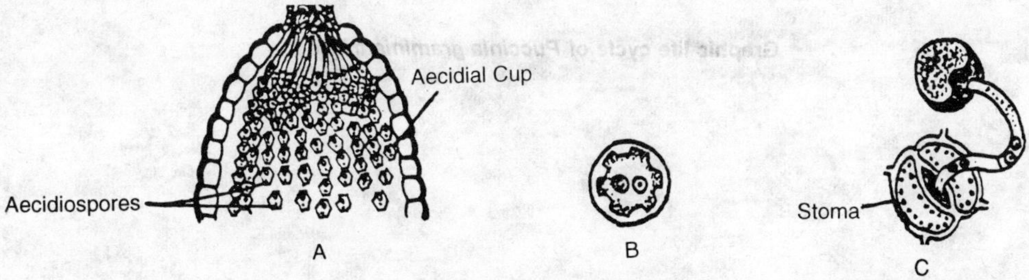

Fig. 42. A. Aecidial cup with aecidiosporees B–single aecidiospore and C–germinating aecidiospore.

ECONOMIC IMPORTANCE

Rusts are well known for their damaging effects on cereals, vegetable, linseed, coffee and other ornamental plants. Linseed rust, caused by *Melampsora*, plays a havoc in Maharastra, M.P., U.P. and Bihar. Black rust of wheat caused by *P. graminis* has a severe damage in peninsular India. The yellow rust and brown rust caused by *P. striiformis* and *P. recondita* respectively causes much damage to wheat in eastern and northern India. Thus, the rusts cause severe damage to crops of food and economic value.

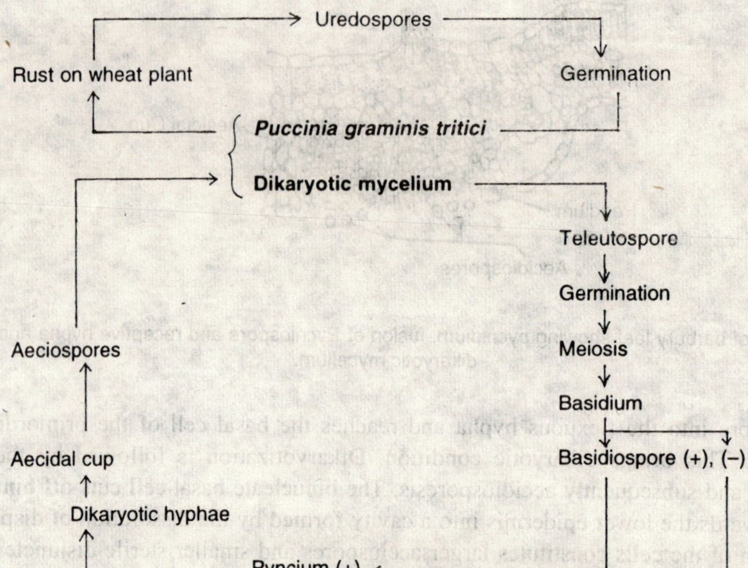

Graphic life cycle of *Puccinia graminis tritici*

CHAPTER 5

DEUTEROMYCETES (Fungi Imperfectii)

Deuteromytes include those fungi whose sexual stages are not known, either they have not been discovered or do not exist. Their life cycles are imperfectly known and hence fungi imperfectii.

HABIT & HABITAT

Members of fungi imperfectii are parasites or saprophytes. Vegetative plant body is thalloid consisting of mycelium of much branched, septate, long or short, coloured or hyaline hyphae. The hyphal cells are multinucleate. The septa are perforated through which migration of nuclei form one cell to the next takes place.

REPRODUCTION

There is no sexual stage in its life cycle. It exhibits only asexual reproduction mainly by means of conidia born on condiophores. Conidiophores may be inflated at the tips or inflated at intervals forming knee like structure on which group of conidia are formed. In some other form genera conidia are produced in flask shaped bodies called pycnidia. In *Collectotrichum* conidiophores develop from a somatic mass of hyphae forming acervulus.

Conidia vary in size, colour, shape, thickness of wall, number of septation etc. and its nomenclature are done on the basis of size, septation, shape etc. Conidia may be named as microconidia, macroconidia, pycnidiospores, porospores, phialospores (phialids) dictyospores (with vertical & horizontal septa). Scoleospores (wormlike), helicospores (coiled–like cork screw) and stautospores (with three or more arms–like star).

Other types of spores born on thallus are also produced. These are generally known as thallospore. The thallospores may be (1) Blastospore (produced by budding) (2) Chlamydospores (thick walled developed from somatic cells) and (3) arthrosopores or oidia. The members of deuteromycetes has no sexual stage and have parasexual cycle in which plasmogamy, karyogamy and haploidization (meiosis) takes place but not at a specific time and points in the life cycle.

CLASSIFICATION

Alexopoulos (1962) divided the fungi imperfectii into form–orders as follows —

1. Moniliales — Conidiophores are on a mycelium branch
2. Sphaeropsidales — Conidia born on pycnidia

3. Melanconiales — Conidia born in acervuli
4. Mycelia sterilia — Reproductive structure are not known.

The units of classification in fungi imperfectii are based on artificial resemblance and not phylogenetic relationship, therefore, these units are called form order, form–families, form–genera etc.

ECONOMIC IMPORTANCE

The members of the fungi imperfectii are responsible for diseases in plants and human beings. *Alternaria solani* causes early blight of potatoes, *Cercospora personata* causes tikka disease of ground nut, *Fusarium udam* causes wilt disease of pigeon pea, *Helminthosporium oryzae* causes brown spot disease in rise, *Collectotrichum falctum* causes red rot disease in sugar cane and so on.

The disease in human beings and animals like ring worm, Athlet's foot etc are also caused by *Epidermophyton flecossum*, *Blastomyces dermatitides* etc.

Some members of fungi imperfecti like *Arthrobotrys oligosporea*, *Dactyllela cinopaga* etc. develops sticky branch to which nematodes adhere. Other hyphae invade the body and digest the nematodes, thus they are helpful in controlling some of the soil born plant diseases caused by nematodes.

5.1 ALTERNARIA

It belongs to			
	Class	—	Deuteromycetes (Fungi imperfecti)
	Order	—	Moniliales
	Family	—	Dematiaceae
	Genus	—	*Alternaria*

HABITAT & HABIT

It is cosmopolitan in distribution. Majority of the species are saprophytes and are found in soil also. Some of the species are parasite on plants. Early blight of Potato disease is caused by *Alternaria solani*. It forms a round or pointed patch of yellow or brown colour of 3 mm to 6 mm diameter. Mycelial plant body is endophytic branched with intra or inter–cellular septa. Haustoria are not found (Fig. 43)

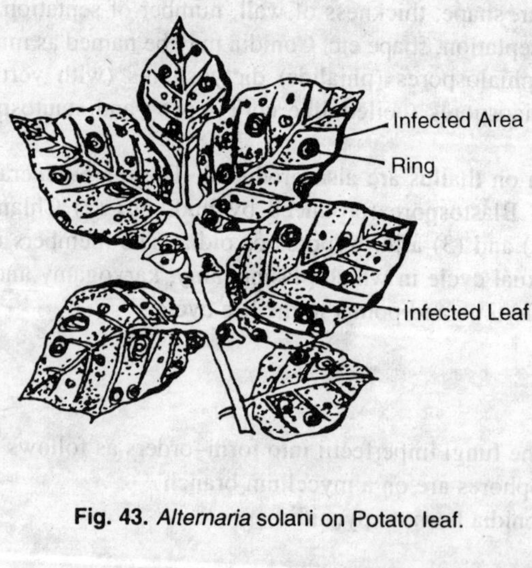

Fig. 43. *Alternaria* solani on Potato leaf.

REPRODUCTION

It multiplies by conidia produced on conidiophore singly or in chain. Conidiophores are small, erect and of deep colour. Conidia are multicellular and beaked. It has numerous transverse or longitudinal septa. Their size vary from 50 - 90 μ x 9 μ in *A. solani* and 15 – 70 x 14 – 18 μ in *A. brasicae*. (Fig. 44). μ = micron.

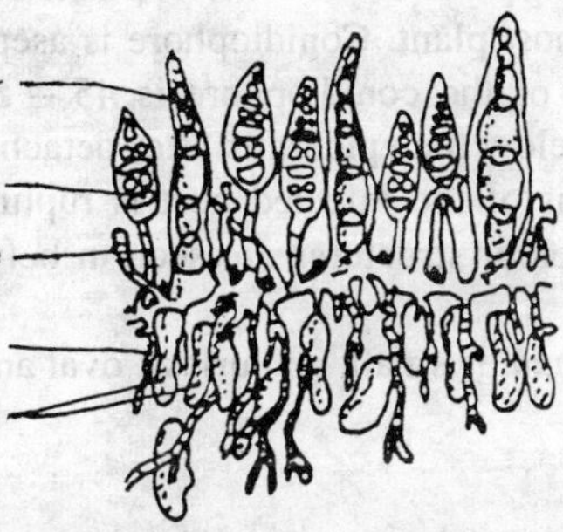

Fig. 44. T.S. of infected leaf showing conidiophore and conidia.

Conidia germinate immediately after falling which sends out 5 - 10 germ tubes which invade the leaf through stomata and cause disease. There is no sexual reproduction.

CONTROL OF THE DISEASE

The disease early blight of potato can be controlled by the following measures.

1. After harvesting the rotten debris should be burnt.
2. Spraying of Pesticides like Dithene M–45(0.2%), Zincle (0.32%) is recommended.
3. Resistant variety of Potato should be planted.
4. Crop rotation is also useful.
5. Appropriate irrigation help to control the disease.

5.2 COLLETOTRICHUM

It belongs to	Class	—	Deuteromycetes (Fungi imperfecti)
	Order	—	Melanconiales
	Family	—	Melanconiaceae
	Genus	—	*Collectotrichum*

HABITAT & HABIT

It is found as parasite on plants like Sugarcane, Jower, Bajra, Cotton, Onion etc. They produce several diseases in them which are commonly known as Anthracnose. Following are some of the diseases caused by it.

Red rot of sugarcane caused by *C. falcatum*
Anthracnose of water melon caused by *C. lagenarium*
Leaf spot of cotton caused by *C. indicum*
Die back of chillies caused by *C. capsici*
Anthrancose of cereals caused by *C. graminicolum*

PLANT BODY

The plant body is made up of uninucleate, hyaline, branched and septate mycelium. Its mycelia are found intercellularly or intra cellularly in the host tissue. It has glycogen and oil drops as reserve food.

REPRODUCTION

There is no sexual reproduction. It reproduces only by conidia. Conidia are produced on acervuls made up of mycelium below the epidermis of the host plant. These acervuli are seen as red or black spot on the infected surface of the host plant. Conidiophore is aseptate, elongated structure lying parallel to the palisade layer. The length of the conidiophore is 45 – 55 μ. The tip of the conidiophore forms conidium which accumulates below the epidermis after detachment. By the pressure of large number of conidia produced, the epidermis of the infected host is ruptured and the conidia are set free. Several septate, branched and brown colour structures are seen in between conidiophores. These structures are known as setae (Fig. 45).

The conidium of *Colletotrichum* is small, colourless, oval and unicellular. It has a nucleus and two oil drops.

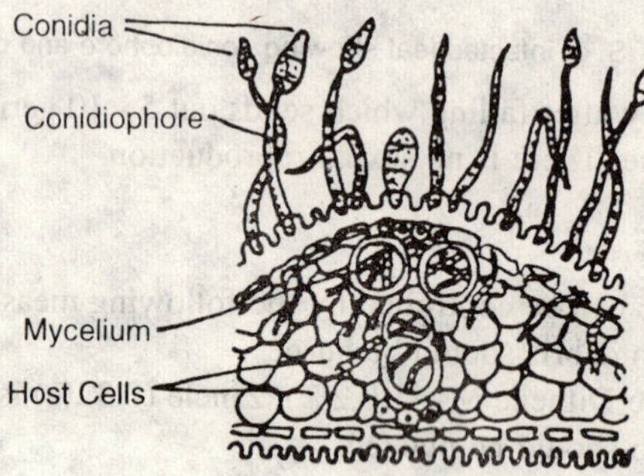

Fig. 45. Acervulus of *colletotrichum* sp.

It appears in group of pink colour. It is dispersed by rain drops. After liberation it reaches to the host surface where it germinates by sending a germ tube. The tip of the germ tube swells to form a structure known as appresorium. The appresorium forms a thread like structure which invades the host cuticle and enters inside the host tissue. Finally it forms a branched mycelium and subsequently conidia are produced.

SYMPTOMS OF THE DISEASE CAUSED BY *COLLETOTRICHUM*.

1. It appears on leaf, stem, branches and fruits.
2. It forms a red & brown coloured patch.
3. The infected parts get dry and leaves become yellow.
4. In sugar cane it produces red rot on stem & leaves.

Nodes become red and rotting of stem starts.

CONTROL OF DISEASES

It can be prevented by the following methods —

1. To cultivate resistant varieties of the crop.
2. Burn the infected plants.
3. Crop rotation helps in its control.
4. Fungicide may be sprayed. Bordeux mixture may be sprayed at an interval of 10 – 15 days.
5. Healthy and disease free seeds should be sown.

CHAPTER 6

LICHEN

The word 'lichen' was used by Theophrastus to indicate superfical growth on bark. A lichen is an association of two different plants one an alga and second a fungus in symbiotic relationship. Due to different evolutionary history of its two component partners – the alga and fungus, the systematic position of lichens has ever been a controversial problem. With this view, Bold (1959) has given the name mycophycophyta for lichens which indicates the dual algal fungal nature of the lichens.

On the basis of class of fungi present in lichens, the division mycophycophyta has been divided into two classes namely (1) Asco–lichens (having ascomycetous fungus) and (2) Basidio–lichens or Hymenolichens (having basidiomycetous fungus).

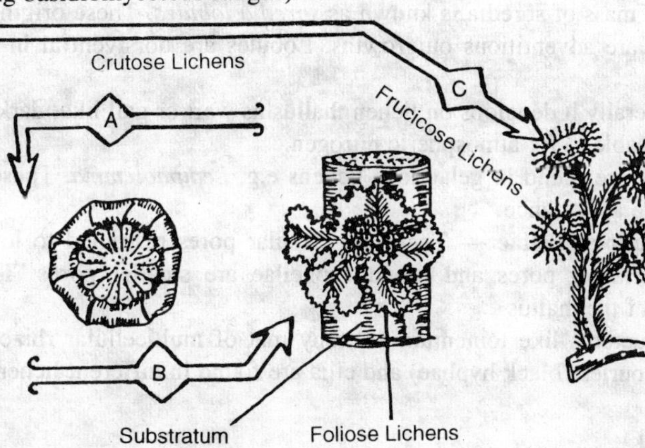

Fig. 46. Habit of crustose lichen (A), Foliose lichen (B) and fruticose lichen (C).

On the basis of size and form, the lichens have been divided into following types (Fig. 46)

1. Crustose lichens – e.g. *Graphis duplicate*
2. Foliose lichens – e.g. *Parmelia cirrhata*.
3. Fruticose lichens – e.g. *Usnea aspera*.

OCCURRENCE

There are about 16, 000 species covering 400 genera of lichens in the world. Generally they occur on the leaves, bark, rocks or soil. They are also reported from arctic and polar regions. The colour of the lichens are brown, green, yellow, orange or red. The size of the lichen thallus varies from 1 mm to several meters.

STRUCTURE

Vertical section of the lichen body shows an outer rind made up of hard layer of fungal hyphae on both the sides. This is called cortex. There are usnic acid, pulvic acid derivatives and certain pigments in the cortex. Central region is known as medulla. The peripheral part of the medulla has algal cells and it forms gonidial layer. In heteromerous thallus – algal components are arranged in a definite pattern, whereas in homomerous thallus, the algal components are scattered in the gonidial layer. Algal components may be *Chlorella, Gloeocapsa, Trentipohlia, Nostoc, Rivularia* etc. Fungal components may be ascomycetous or basidiomycetous. The medulla has a great water holding capacity and act as food storage organ.

VEGETATIVE STRUCTURE

Lichens have several vegetative structures such as soredia, isidia, lobules, cephalodia, hormocysts, cyphellae and pseudocyphellae.

Soredia — The diameter of soredia varies from 25 μ to 100 μ. It originates in the algal layer due to overgrowth of the algae. It comes out through pores in the cortex. These are non–corticated clumps of a few algal cells encircled by fungal hyphae. μ = micron.

Isidia — These are finger like, cylindrical outgrowths of the upper cortex in which algal and fungal tissues are associated. The diameter of the isidia varies from 0.01 to 0.3 mm and they are 0.5 to 3.00 mm in height. It helps in vegetative propagation and photosynthesis. Generally, foliose & fruticose lichens develop isidia.

Lobule— Irregular mass of soredia is known as *soredia lobules*. These originate along the margins of the lobes, and they are adventitious outgrowths. Lobules are dorsiventral in structure and help in vegetative propagation.

Cephalodia — Generally it develops on lichen thallus as wart or gall like, dark coloured outgrowths of the thallus. They are able to fix atmospheric nitrogen.

Hormocysts— They are found in gelatinous lichens e.g. *Lempholemma.* These are algal structures, soredia or apothecia like appearance.

Cyphellae and Pseudocyphellae — These are circular pores restricted to lower cortex in foliose lichens. Cyphellae are larger pores and pseudocyphellae are smaller pores. They help in gaseous exchange and aeration of the thallus.

Other vegetative structures like tomentum (cottony mat of multicellular rhizoidal chains), rhizines (compact strands of colourless/black hyphae) and cilia are found in different lichen.

REPRODUCTION

Lichens reproduce vegetatively, asexually and sexually in the following manners.

VEGETATIVE REPRODUCTION

It occurs (1) by fragmentation of the vegetative thallus and by the formation of special type of vegetative structures like *soredia, isidia, lobules, cephalodia* etc.

ASEXUAL REPRODUCTION

It occurs by asexual spores like conidia oidia & pycniospores.

SEXUAL REPRODUCTION

In some asco–lichens like *collema*, sexual organs are produced by fungal partner. The male sex organ is spermogonium producing spermatia. Female sex organ is ascogonium or carpogonium developed in the medulla of the thallus. The basal part of filamentous ascogonium is coiled and known as archicarp. The Archicarp continues to form trichogyne. Usually middle cell of the ascogonium directly function as oogonium. A spermatium is lodged at the tip of the trichogyne, the point of contact dossolve and then spermatial contents pass into the trichogyne. The male nucleus is transferred to the middle ascogonium and several ascogenous hyphae develop. Asci are formed either from binucleate penultimate cell or ultimate cell of the ascogenous hyphae. The two nuclei fuse and form 8 ascospores in usual manner. The asci and surrounding sterile hyphae (paraphyses) together form fruit body i.e. ascocarp in the form of an apothecium. On liberation, ascospores germinate to form new lichen on coming in contact with required alga. Some lichen like *Peltigera* has perithecium.

Economic importance — Lichens are used as food and in the form of medicines.

1. *Cladonia rangifera* are eaten by Reindeer found at Polar regions.
2. *Umbllicaria lecanora and certaria islandica* are used as food by human beings.
3. *Parmellia* are also eaten as vegetables by south Indians.
4. *Peltigera caniana* are used in hydrophobia and *Letaria vulpine* are used as antipoisonous.
5. Dyes like orcein are obtained from *Rocella tinctoria.*
6. *Lobaria pulmonaria* are used in perfume industry.
7. Calcium oxalate are obtaibed from *Lecanora esculenta.*
8. *Usnea* causes fire in the forest.
9. It has ecological importance in plant succession.
10. Some lichens iike *Usnea, Everina* etc are responsible for skin disease, respiratory allergy and other such allergic reactions.

CHAPTER 7

SCHIZOMYCETES — BACTERIA

Bacteria were discovered by Anton von Leeuwenhoek (1676) and its was further high lighted by Robert Hooke (1820). Different Scientists also designated the bacteria as contagium vivum. microbes, germs, worms, micro–organisms etc. In the beginning bacteria were believed to be animals. Later on some scientists like Nageli, Cohn and others observed that bacteria are one celled vegetable organisms and subsequently it was classified with the fungi. Anton de Bary (1931) removed the bacteria from fungi and later Alexopoulos (1958) constituted a separate class Schizomycetes.

Bacteria are unicellular, some are aseptate filamentous, devoid of chlorophyll and hence heterophytic. Some bacteria do possess photosynthetic pigments like bacteriochlorophyll. They reproduce vegetatively by fission and sexually by conjugation. Bacteria lack true nucleus, plastids, mitochondria which show resemblance with blue green algae. Only presence/absence of diaminopimelic acid in the cell wall distinguishes them.

HABITAT

They are found everywhere, in soil, water, air, living and dead organic bodies. They are absent in deep strata of rocks & healthy blood stream. They can sustain – 170°C and high temperature upto 80°C Thermophilic Bacteria can survive in absence of free oxygen and hence they are anaerobic, Bacteria living in presence of free oxygen are called aerobic. A hand full of soil contains as many bacteria as there are human beings on the earth.

STRUCTURE OF A BACTERIAL CELL

A typical bacterial cell has a rigid cell wall, below which there is a delicate inner membrane containing mycoprotein and outer rigid layer consists of muramic acid and glucosamine. The other chemical compounds in the cell wall are polysaccharides, lipids and proteins. The cytoplasmic membrane contains permease enzyme which helps in the movement of specific protein.

The cell wall of gram positive bacteria are 20-80 mμ thick and constitutes 85 - 90% mucopeptide and teichoic acids where as the cell wall of gram negative bacteria are 10-30 mμ thick and has 12-20% mucopeptides phospholipids, lipo–polysaccharides and lipo–proteins. It lacks teichoic acids. Some bacterial cell has an envelope outside the cell wall known as capsule which is gelatinous, viscous & transparent. It is made up of polysaccharides (Fig. 47).

CYTOPLASM AND ORGANELLES

After removal of cell wall the bacterial cell has protoplast consisting of cytoplasm and nuclear body. The nuclear body is also termed as nucleoid, chromatic body, genophore or bacterial chromosome. Bacterial cytoplasm contains soluble proteins, enzyme, t-RNA, ribosomes, mesosomes, lamellae in addition to reserve food like starch/glycogen, lipids etc. There is no mitochondria. Stevenson (1970) have shown the presence of respiratory enzymes in the particles of bacterial cytoplasmic membrance.

NUCLEAR BODY

Bacterial cells are prokaryote and they do not have well defined, membrane bound nucleus. It posses genetic material i.e. DNA/RNA which is also known as nucleoid or genophore (Fig. 48).

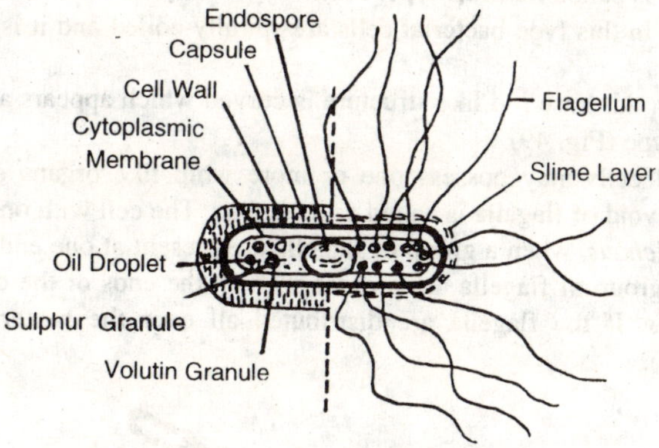

Fig. 47. A capsulated bacterial cell

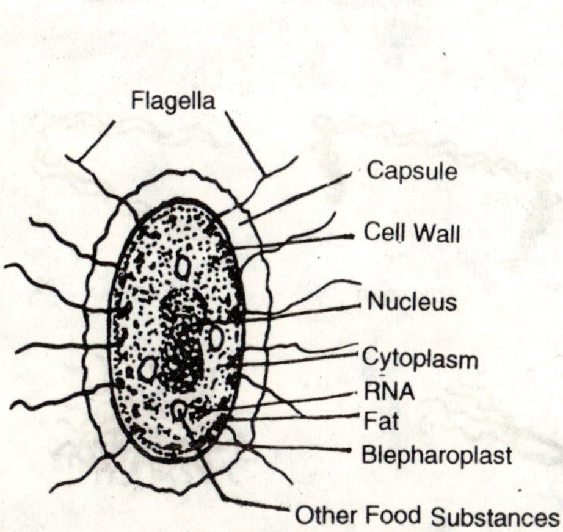

Fig. 48A. Structure of a typical bacterial cell.

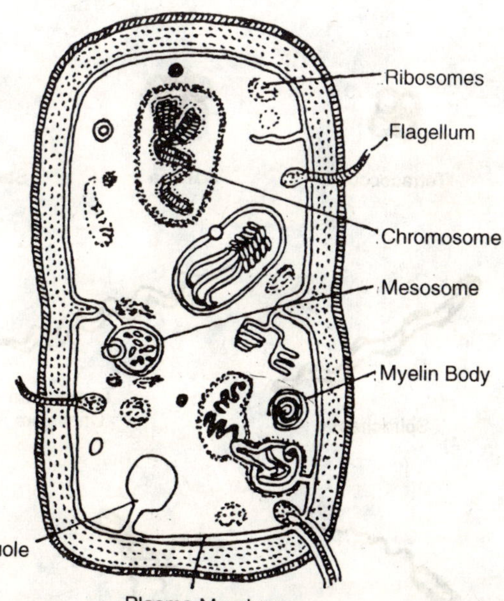

Fig. 48B. A typical bacterial cell showing detailed structure.

SHAPE OF THE TRUE BACTERIA

The shape of the true bacteria are of the following type.

1. *Spherical* — The unicellular bacterial cells are ellipsoidal or spherical. This type is known as *Coccus* (cocci–plural) when the coccus occurs singly – it is called as *monococcus*.
   If coccus is in pairs – it is *diplococcus,* when the cells are in group pf four, it is known as *tetracocci*, if it occurs in chain, it is *streptococcus*; if it occurs in clusters, it is *staphylococcus* and when it occurs like a packet of 8 or more cells, it is known as *Sarcina.* Size of the bacterial cells varies from 0.5 μ to 100 μ μ = microns..
2. *Rod shaped* — It is called *Bacillus* type. In this type bacterial cells are elongated, rod like.
3. *Spiral shaped* — In this type bacterial cells are spirally coiled and it is also known as *Spirillum* type.
4. *Comma like* — In this case rod like structure is curved which appears as comma (,). This is also called as *vibrio* type (Fig. 49).

Flagella — Bacterial cells may possess one or more whip like organs of locomotion known as flagella. Bacterial cell devoid of flagella is called as *atrichous*. The cell with one flagellum at one end of the cell is called *monotrichous*, when a group of flagella are present at one end of the cell – it is termed as *lophotrichous.* If the group of flagella are present on both the ends of the cell – the bacterial cell is termed as *amphitrichous*. If the flagella are distributed all over the bacterial cells it is known as *peritrichous* see (Fig. 49).

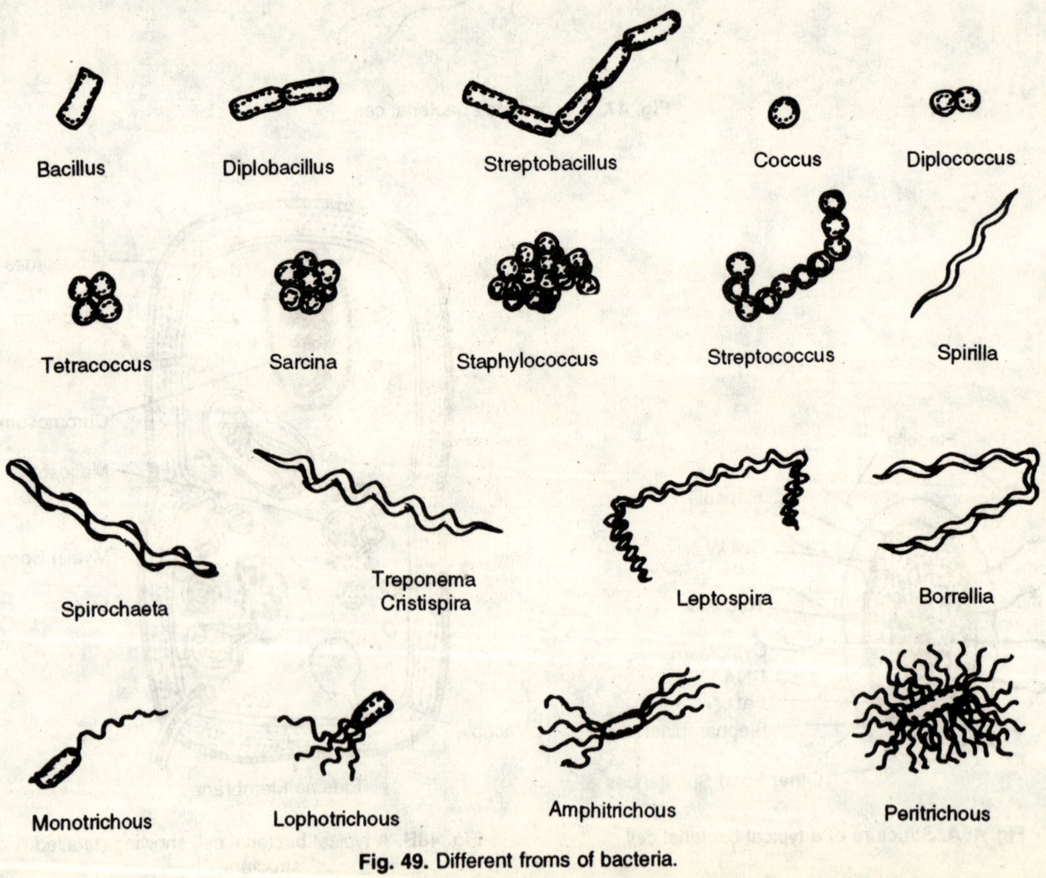

Fig. 49. Different froms of bacteria.

NUTRITION

Most of the bacteria are incapable to synthesise its own food due to absence of chlorophyll in their cells. Therefore, they are either *saprophytes* or *parasites*. Certain bacteria are capable to synthesize food from carbon dioxide and other inorganic substances. These bacteria are called autotrophic bacteria. The autotrophic bacteria are of two types namely (1) *Chemosynthetic bacteria* and (2) *photosynthetic bacteria*. Photosynthetic bacteria like *Chlorobium & Rhodospirillum* obtain energy from light for their food synthesis. *Chemosynthetic bacteria* such as *Acetobacter, Clostridium* etc. obtain the energy needed for their food synthesis from the oxidation of some chemical substances. In the process of chemosynthesis, chemical energy is transformed into another form and water is not used as donor of hydrogen to reduce CO_2 as in photosynthesis. Common chemosynthetic bacteria are as follows:-

IRON BACTERIA

These are filamentous and grow in marshes, lakes containing ferrous iron. Ferrous oxide is oxidised to ferric oxide during which energy is released:

$$\text{(Ferrous) } Fe^{2+} \rightarrow Fe^{3+} \text{ (Ferric)} + e^-$$

SULPHUR BACTERIA

The bacteria grow in sulphur springs and in stagnant water containing hydrogen sulphide (H_2S). H_2S is oxidised by the sulphur bacteria in which energy is released which reduces CO_2 to carbohydrate and other organic compounds.

$$2H_2S + O_2 \rightarrow 2S + 2H_2O + 32.5 \text{ cal.}$$

$$CO_2 + 2H_2O \xrightarrow{\text{Energy}} CH_2O + H_2O + O_2$$

During the reaction some of the sulphur deposits in the bacterial cells are further oxidised to H_2SO_4 (sulphuric acid).

Nitrifying bacteria — These bacteria are found in soil and obtain energy from their oxidative activities e.g. *Nitrobacter & Nitrosomonas*

Protein in the soil decays into NH_3 (ammonia). This ammonia is converted into nitrites by *Nitrosomonas* i.e. nitrite bacteria and then nitrite is transformed into nitrates by *Nitrobacter* i.e. nitrate bacteria. The energy released during the oxidation of ammonia is used in the metabolism with carbon dioxide (CO_2) absorbed from the air.

$$2NH_3 + 3O_2 \rightarrow HNO_2 + 2H_2O + 79 \text{ cal}$$

$$2HNO_2 + O_2 \rightarrow 2HNO_3 + 21.6 \text{ cal.}$$

Photosynthetic bacteria develop photosynthetic pigments. These pigments are bacteriochlorophyll found in purple sulphur bacteria and *bacterioviridin* found in gree sulphur bacteria.

$$\text{Purple sulphur bacterin } 6\,CO_2 + 12\,H_2S \xrightarrow{\text{Light energy}} C_6H_{12}O_6 + 6H_2O + 12S$$

$$\text{Green sulphur bacterins} + H_2S \xrightarrow{\text{Light energy}} 2H + S$$

$$CO_2 + 2H \rightarrow CH_2O + O_2$$

SAPROPHYTIC BACTERIA

These bacteria obtain their food from the dead organic matter. They secrete hydrolytic exo–enzymes into the surrounding medium which converts the food stuffs into diffusible form. The carbohydrates are broken into organic acids, alcohols and hydrogen by fermentation when proteins are decomposed into methane, organic acids, hydrogen sulphide etc. Bad smells come out and the decomposition process is called *putrefaction.*

PARASITIC BACTERIA

Certain bacteria are incapable of producing hydrolytic exoenzymes and hence they live on protoplasm of other living organism. Such bacteria are called parasitic bacteria and some of them cause various types of diseases in plants and animals.

RESPIRATION

There are two different phases in the bacterial respiration. These are :-

i. The reactions in which the substrate is oxidised to CO_2 with the removal of a pair of hydrogen atoms under Kreb's cycle.
ii. The second phase consists of oxidation of hydrogen atoms with the formation of ATP as shown by nitrifying bacteria, sulphur bacteria etc.

Bacterial respiration does not necessarily imply the use of oxygen. On the basis of oxygen requirements during respiration, the bacteria can be classified into the following types.

1. *Obligate anaerobes* — Such type of bacteria respire in absence of oxygen and the respiration is called anaerobic respiration. Here the oxidation is incomplete and a substance other than O_2 serves as hydrogen acceptor.
2. *Facultative anaerobes* — This types of bacteria grow best in presence of oxygen and can also live as anaerobes. In both the types, enormous heat is produced during respiration and stacks of hay may catch a fire. Sometimes, this heat energy is converted into light energy and emits phosphorescent glow. This phenomenon is known as "*Bioluminescence*". "Ghost light" of the forest is caused by bioluminescence.
3. *Obligate aerobes* — This type of bacteria require free molecular oxygen for respiration and this type of respiration is called aerobic respiration in which oxidation is complete.

REPRODUCTION

Reproduction in bacteria occurs by vegetative, asexual and sexual methods.

VEGETATIVE MODE OF REPRODUCTION

It takes place by budding or binary fission or conidia or fragmentation.

Budding — A small outgrowth comes out and DNA migrates into it. A constriction separates the bud which ultimately grows into full sized bacteria e.g. *Bifidibacterium.*

Binary fission — First, the nuclear matter divides into two followed by formation of a constriction across the long axis of the bacterial cell. Cytoplasm divides by centripetal growth of the cell wall. This process is completed within 20-30 minutes. e.g. *Coccibacteria*

Conidia formation — It occurs in filamentous types of bacteria like *Streptomyces.* Conidia are produced in chains in a basipetal succession on the tips of coiled or erect conidiophores.

Fragmentation — In certain bacterium, the protoplast breaks up into two or more fragments. Each fragments containing nuclear material develops into a new–bacteral cell.

ASEXUAL REPRODUCTION

It takes place by cyst or endospore formation.

Cyst formation — It takes place in *Azotobacter.* The whole bacterial cell rounds up and becomes surrounded by a thick wall. The cyst wall is comparatively less resistance to adverse environmental conditions. It germinates to produce a single vegetative bacterial cell.

Endospore formation — In unfavourable condition, the bacterial cell contents shrink into an oval or spherical mass and later, it becomes enclosed in one or two layered protective wall forming an endospore. In suitable medium, the endospore germinates into a new bacterial cell. The endospore formation is a means for survival in extremely adverse physical and chemical environmental conditions.

SEXUAL REPRODUCTION

Sexual reproduction in *E. Coli* was first discovered by J. Lederberg and E.L. Tatum (1946). They noticed in *E. coli* K_{12} strain the genetic material DNA from one bacterial cell passed into the other bacterial cell through a conjugations tube. *E. coli* shows sex differences. One act as donor of genetic material (Male) + and the other as recipient of genetic material (Female) (–). The maleness is due to sex factor or F factor which is labelled as F^+. The female cell is labelled as F^-. The sex factor is a circular DNA, out of bacterial genome and it is autonomous, lies free in the cytoplasm. This phenomenon was termed as "Sexduction" which leads to partial diploidy.

Two another methods of sexual union are known which do not occur in nature but they are experimental methods, as follows —

Transformation — This was discovered by O.F. Griffith (1928) in *Diplococcus pneuminae* or *Pneumococcus.* This involves extraction of DNA from the dead bacterial cells and then it is added to a culture of receipients (female–cells). The extracted DNA moves from cell to cell in the culture medium and transformation is effected. The transformed bacterial cells continue to divide and grow.

Transduction — The transduction was discovered by Lederberg & Zinder (1952). In this method phage particles or viruses infect a male (donor) bacterial cell. These phage particles takes up some of the genetic material of the host (male donor). This is now transferred to a second (female or receipient) cell on infection by the same phage particles. Inside the female bacterium, the DNA brought by the phage particle, pairs with the homologous parts of the female (receipient) chromosome and causes a genetic exchange producing recombinant genotypes. This process of genetic exchange in bacteria is known as transduction.

CLASSIFICATION OF BACTERIA

Among several systems of classification of bacteria, the most widely accepted classification is Bergey's "*Mannual of Determinative Bacteriology*" (1957) as follows. The class schizomycetes (bacteria) has been divided into 10 orders namely, (1) Pseudomonadales, (2) Chlamydobacterials, (3) Hypomicrobiales (4) Eubacteriales (5) Actinomycetales (6) Caryophanales (7) Beggiatoales (8) Myxobacteriales (9) Spirochaetales and (10) Mycoplasmatales.

Order Eubacteriales and Actinomycetales have pathogenic forms of bacteria like *Pseudomonas, Rhizobium, Corynebacterium, Erwinia, Streptomyces* etc.

ECONOMIC IMPORTANCE OF BACTERIA

The bacteria are our friends, due to its beneficial activities, as well as foes because of its harmful activities as mentioned below it:-

BENEFICIAL ACTIVITIES

1. *Nitrogen fixation* — Nitrogen is essential for building of protoplasm and the atmospheric nitrogen is not directly used by the plants. There are nitrogen fixing bacteria which combine molecular nitrogen with oxygen to form nitrates (NO_3) which can easily be absorbed by the plant.

2. *Sanitation* — The dead bodies of plant & animals are decomposed by bacteria. The bacteria also decompose the sewage and kill the pathogens.

3. *Antibiotics* — The powerful antibiotic "Streptomycin" are obtained from *Streptomyces grisens* which are used against tuberculosis. Several other antibiotics like eumycin, colicin, bacillin, subtilin etc. are prepared from bacteria.

4. *Putrefaction* — Proteins are decomposed into amino acids and ammonia by ammonifying bacteria, like *Bacillus vulgaris*. This ammonia combines with inorganic ions present in the soil forming ammonium compounds to be absorbed by the plants.

5. *Vinegar making* — Alcohols are obtained by alcoholic fermentation from sugar with the help of yeast. Then the alcohol is oxidised to acetic acid with the help of *Acetobacter*.

6. *Lactic acid formation* — Sugar is fermented into lactic acid with the help of *Lactobacillus*.

7. *Tanning of leather* — Hairs are removed from hides of the leather and tanning process is done with the help of bacteria.

8. *Retting of flax* — The fibres of flax plant are held together with the help of pactin. The pactin is fermented with the help of *Clostridium*, thus making the fibres loose which are extracted for liner. making.

9. Cheese, butter, chocolate, Silage, Vitamins, Acetone etc are produced with the help of different kinds of specific bacteria.

HARMFUL ACTIVITIES OF BACTERIA

1. *Diseases* — Several disease in man like cholera, diphtheria, dysentry, plague, pneumonia, typoid, tuberculosis, leprosy etc diseases in animals like anthrax, black leg of the cattle etc and diseases in plant like citrus canker, ring rot of potato, black rot of cabbage etc are caused by various bacteria.

2. *Denitrification* — Certain bacteria like *Bacillus denitrificans* convert nitrates into nitrites and finally into free nitrogen, thus reducing the soil fertility.

3. *Spoilage of Penicillin* — Certain bacteria destroy penicillin by an enzyme Penicillinase secreted by them.

4. *Spoilage of food stuffs and domestic articles* — Food stuffs are made unpalatable by the bacterial action. Domestic articles such as leather and woollen goods are destroyed by some bacteria like *Squirochaeta cytophoga*.

Thus, we can say that bacteria are our friends as well as foes.

CHAPTER 8

VIRUSES

The latin word virus means liquid poison. Jenner (1796) was the first to mention the virus to be a causative factor for small pox disease. Viruses are minute, submicroscopic, filterable, disease producing intercellular parasitic organisms. Its genome is either DNA or RNA. Iwanowski (1892) discovered tobacco mosaic virus causing tobacco mosaic disease in tobacco. Stanley (1935) for the first time obtained tobacco mosaic virus (TMV) in crystaline form. Independently, viruses are inert as they are devoid of metabolic system. However, when the virus injects its nucleic acid into the host living cell, it becomes active and takes control over the metabolic activity of the host cell. In host cell, viral nucleic acid replicates new virus particles, in combination with protein synthesized in the host cell. All the viruses are obligate parasites.

NATURE OF VIRUS

There is a puzzle regarding the nature of virus whether it is a chemical molecule or minute living organism. Some consider it as living while others regard them as non – living on the basis of the following features.

Features in favour of virus as living —

1. Viruses exist in particular form and they range from 8 mu to 300 mμ in size.
2. They are of different shapes like rod, spherical, polygonal etc.
3. They are sensitive to heat, ultraviolet rays, X-rays etc.
4. They replicate.

Features in favour of virus as non–*living*.

1. It multiply only in living host.
2. They possess high specific gravity.
3. It can be isolated in crystaline form.
4. They never respire.

Thus, viruses can be considered intermediate between living and non–living and has been said to call them as living molecules. Some consider the virus as wandering self replicating genes.

SHAPE AND SIZE

Generally there are two forms of viruses, namely, rod shaped (TMV) or spherical (influenza or polio viruses). The smallest foot and mouth virus measures 8 to 12 mμ and the largest virus (Potato virus) measures 300 mμ. The different sizes and shapes of the plant and animal viruses are shown in table 1 & Fig. 50.

Name of the plant viruses	size in microns (mμ)	Name of the animal viruses	Size in microns (mμ)
Potato virus 'X'	500 x 12	Foot & Mouth virus	8-12
Tobacco Mosaic virus	300 x 15	Vaccinia variola	250
Turnip yellow mosaic virus	28	Herpes simplex	150
Bacteriophage	60 x 95	Mumps & influenza	100

STRUCTURE AND COMPOSITION

Typically each virus particle consists of a core of nucleic acid surrounded by a protein coat. The protein coat is known as *capsid.* Capsid is made up of one type of protein sub units known as capsomeres. A complete virus particle is called as virion. Some viruses like pox and herpes viruses have host derived lipo–protein envelope around the protein coat. Sometimes, the envelop is covered with projections called spikes e.g. influenza virus (Fig. 50)

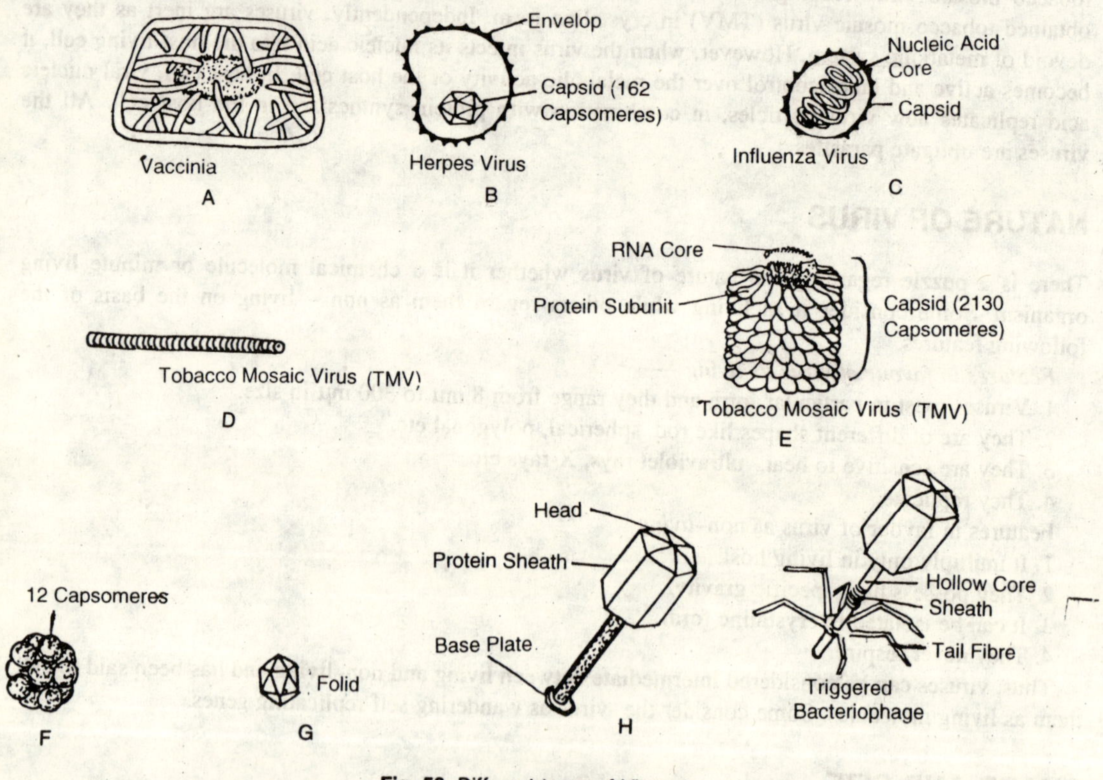

Fig. 50. Different types of Viruses.

The complex vaccinia virus, influenza virus etc. contain lipids. enzymes, vitamin like substances, traces of metals in addition to nucleic acid (RNA/DNA) and protein.

Generally, plant viruses contain RNA, bacterial virus DNA and animal viruses either of the two nucleic acids. Generally RNA is single stranded and DNA is double stranded, but there are some exceptional cases where double stranded RNA (e.g. Reovirus) and single stranded DNA (e.g. QX174 virus) are found. The nucleic acids may be circular or linear in different viruses. The surface projections of the influenza virus contain "hemagglutinin" which agglutinates red blood cells of host.

STRUCTURE OF TMV

It has a helical hollow rod measuring 3000Å in length and 18Å in diameter. Single stranded helical RNA is embeded in the capsomeres of the capsid (protein coat). The capsid has about 2200 capsomeres and each capsomere contain 158 amino acids arranged in a definite sequence. The core RNA is composed of 6400 nucleolides (Fig. 51).

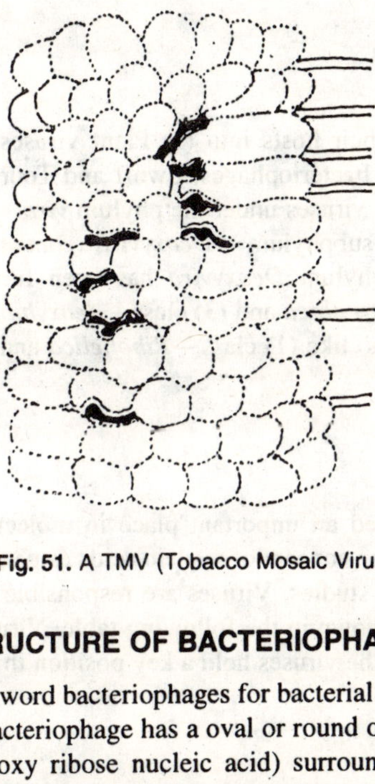

Fig. 51. A TMV (Tobacco Mosaic Virus).

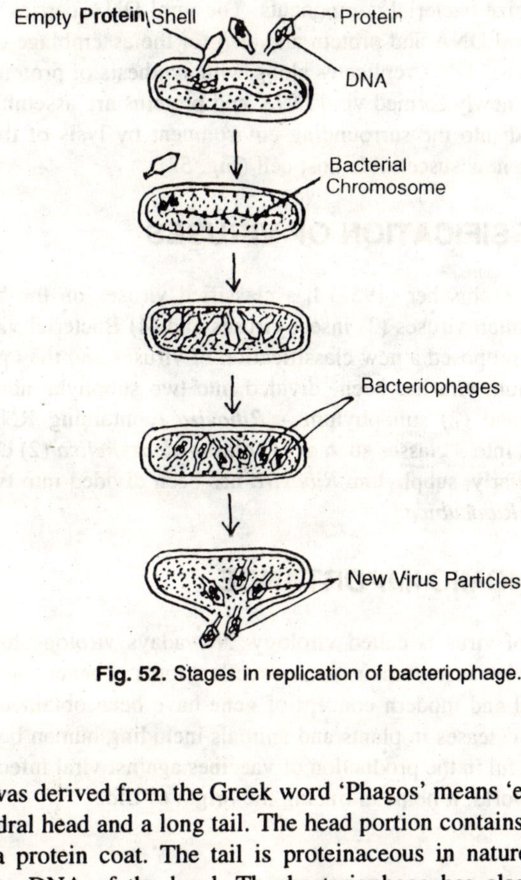

Fig. 52. Stages in replication of bacteriophage.

STRUCTURE OF BACTERIOPHAGE

The word bacteriophages for bacterial viruses was derived from the Greek word 'Phagos' means 'eaters'. A bacteriophage has a oval or round or polyhedral head and a long tail. The head portion contains DNA (deoxy ribose nucleic acid) surrounded by a protein coat. The tail is proteinaceous in nature with different serological contents in comparison to DNA of the head. The bacteriophage has also been reported from Ganges water which has the property of curing many bacterial diseases and hence the water of Ganges is supposed to be sacred. The tail has contractile sheath making it rigid or may not have sheath and hence flexible tail. The *E. coli* phage has a basal plate bearing long tail fibres which is helpful in anchorage of the virus to the wall of the host bacterium (see Fig. 50). The cyanophage (virus attacking blue green algae) was discovered by Safferman and Morris (1963).

REPRODUCTIONS

The viruses have no independent power of self reproduction by budding, fission or similar processes observed in other microorganisms. Multiplication takes place by replication in susceptible host cell. A series of steps are involved in viral replication as follows —

INFECTION

Virus becomes attached to the susceptible surface by its tail fibres. An enzyme lysozyme present in the tail fibres digests the host cell wall and produces a hole. The DNA in the virus head is injected into the host cell (bacterial cell if infected by bacteriophage). The protein coat, which forms the head and tail of the virus, remains outside the bacterial cell.

REPLICATION

Soon after adsorption of the phage DNA, the bacterial nucleus is broken down and cell ceases to synthesize bacterial components. The viral DNA carries the necessary information for the synthesis of new viral DNA and protein and also for the assemblage of these components into mature viral paticles. Thus, viral DNA replicates along with synthesis of protein etc.

The newly formed viral DNA and proteins are assemble into several viral particles which are finally released into the surrounding environment by lysis of the host (bacterial) cell wall which are able to infect a new susceptible host cell (Fig. 52).

CLASSIFICATION OF VIRUSES

Earlier Frobischer (1957) has classified viruses on the basis of their hosts into (1) Plant viruses (2) mammalian viruses (3) insect viruses and (4) Bacterial viruses i.e. bacteriophages. Lwoff and Tourvier (1966) proposed a new classification of viruses and they placed the viruses under the phylum *vira.*

Phylum vira has been divided into two subphyla, namely, (1) subphylum – *Deoxyvira* (containing DNA) and (2) sub–phylum – *Ribovira* (containing RNA). Subphylum *Deoxyvira* has been further divided into 3 classes such as (1) class – *deoxyhelica* (2) class–*deoxycubica* and (3) class – *deoxybinala.*

Similarly, subphylum *Ribovira* has been divided into two classes like (1) class – *Ribohelica* and (2) class – *Ribocubica.*

ECONOMIC IMPORTANCE

Study of virus is called virology. Nowadays virology has occupied an important place in molecular biology because of their use as excellent tools in genetic analysis. The concept of nucleic acids as genetic material and modern concept of gene have been obtained by viral studies. Viruses are responsible for several diseases in plants and animals including human beings as shown in the following table. Viruses are helpful in the production of vaccines against viral infection. As the viruses hold a key position in the living world, it helps in tracing the origin of life.

Table showing diseases caused by viruses in plants.

Name of the disease	*Name of the plants*
1. Tobacco mosaic disease	Tobacco
2. Yellow vein mosaic	Lady's finger
3. Bunchy top	Banana
4. Leaf curl	Tomato
5. Grassy root	Sugar cane

Table showing diseases caused by viruses in human beings.

Name of the disease in men	*Caused by viruses*
1. Small pox	Variola virus
2. Hydrophobia	Rabies virus
3. Infantile paralysis	Poliomycelitis virus
4. Veneral disease	Lympho granuloma
5. Infections pulmonary disease	Priltacoses virus
6. A septic meningitis in man	Echo virus
7. Acquired Immune deficiency Syndrome (AIDS)	Retriovirus of HIV (Human Immuno Deficiency Virus)

SECTION - III

BRYOPHYTA

1. General Features and Classification
2. Hepaticopsida
3. Anthocerotopsida
4. Bryopsida

CHAPTER 1

BRYOPHYTA

GENERAL FEATURES AND CLASSIFICATION

Bryophytes are the simplest and the most primitive land plants after migrating from aquatic environments. Braun (1864) used the term 'Bryophyta' or acotyledonae to a group of Algae, Fungi, Lichens and Mosses. The Bryophytes have aquired terrestrial mode of life partially as all of them require sufficient moisture for vigorous vegetative growth, maturation of sex organs and fertilization. Therefore, bryophytes are found usually on shaded ground, wet rocks, bases of trees and other such humid places and hence they are called as amphibians of the plant kingdom.

SALIENT FEATURES OF BRYOPHYTES

1. The gametophytic plant body is thalloid, green and small in structure generally not more than 5 inches, except *Dawsonia* which attains 1.5 meter in height.
2. The members of Bryophyta depend on water for sexual reproduction.
3. The thalloid plant body grows prostrate on the ground to which it is attached by rhizoids.
4. It lacks vascular tissue.
5. The sex organs are multicellular surrounded by a jacket of cells.
6. The sperms are biflagellate and of whiplash type.
7. Fertilization takes place in presence of water.
8. The fertilized egg (zygote) is retained within the venter of the archegonium and depends on the parent gametophyte.
9. The zygote divides repeatedly into an undifferented mass of cells called embryo.
10. The venter enlarges with the developing embryo and forms a protective, multicellular layer known as calyptra.
11. The embryo produces diploid sporogonium which is sporophyte not differentiated into stem, leaves and roots. Generally, the sporophyte has foot, seta and capsule and there is no root.
12. The sporophyte is dependent on parent gametophyte for its water and minerals requirements.
13. The sporogonium produces haploid spores (meiospores).
14. The spores are alike or dissimilar and hence bryophytes are homosporous. Some are heterosporous, e.g. *Targionia, Cyathodium* (Pant and Singh, 1990).
15. The spore, on germination, gives rise to protonema and ultimately to young new gametophyte. Thus, the alternation of generations in bryophytes is of heterologous or heteromorphic types.

RESEMBLANCE BETWEEN BRYOPHYTES AND ALGAE

The Bryophytes resemble with algae in the following features :-

1. Plant body is gametophyte and thalloid.
2. Absence of vascular tissues.
3. Lack of roots.
4. Presence of autotrophic mode of nutrition.
5. Swimming habit of sperms.
6. Development of gametophyte is from filamentous structure i.e. protonema in bryophytes resembles the filamentous thallus of green algae.
7. Chloroplast in the vegetative cells are identical.
8. Reserve food material i.e. starch is identical in both the bryophytes and the green algae.
9. Cell wall consists of cellulose and pectic substances in both the groups.

Thus, in view of the similarities mentioned above it can be hypothesize that the bryophytes have evolved from algal ancestors specially the green algae.

CLASSIFICATION OF BRYOPHYTA

Schimper (1879) was the first to recognise this group of Plant and treated Bryophyta as a division.

Eichler (1883) divided Bryophyta into two groups; (a) Hepaticopsida and (b) Musci.

Engler (1892) divided Hepaticopsida into three orders; (a) Marchantiales, (b) Jungermanniales and (c) Anthocerotales. Musci was also divided into three orders; (a) Sphagnales, (b) Andreales and (c) Bryales.

Underwood (1894) suggested Anthocerotales to be an isolated group.

Gayet (1897) treated Anthocerotales the rank of a class.

Thus, Bryophyta was divided into three classes namely, Hepaticae, Anthocerotae and Musci as mentioned by Howe (1899), Campbell (1918, 1940), Smith (1955), Takhtajan (1953) etc. Rothmaler (1951) changed the nomenclature of three classes of Bryophyta to Hepaticopsida for Hepaticae, Anthoceropsida for Anthocerotae and Bryopsida for Musci which are also in accordance with the International code of Botanical nomenclature (1956) Utreacht. Later Proskauer (1957) suggested the name Anthocerotopsida for Anthoceropsida.

The modern bryologists like Schuster (1983) and others have classified the Bryophyta into classes, namely, (1) Hepaticopsida, (2) Anthocerotopsida and (3) Bryopsida showing distinct features as described below.

CHAPTER 2

CLASS — HEPATICOPSIDA

The gametophytic plant body is dorsiventrally differentiated. members of this class may be either simple thallose or foliose, internally differentiated into various tissues or histologically homogenous. Sex organs are generally situated on the dorsal side of the plant body and rarely terminal in position. Sporophytes are simple or with foot, seta and capsule. Endothecium of an embryo gives rise to sporogenous tissue. The class Hepaticopsida has been divided into six orders (Smith, 1955) as such :

(a) Sphaerocarpales
(b) Metzgeriales,
(c) Marchantiales
(d) Jungermanniales
(e) Takakiales and
(f) Calobryales.

2.1 RICCIA

It belongs to	Class	—	Hepaticopsida
	Order	—	Marchantiales
	Family	—	Ricciaceae
	Genus	—	*Riccia*

HABITAT

There are more than 130 species in this genus and are widely distributed in tropical and temperate regions of the earth. All the species are terrestrial except *Ricciocarpus natans*, *R. fluitans* which are aquatic.

In India, about 30 species of *Riccia* have been reported. Some of the common species are *R. discolor*, *R. crystallina*, *R. gangetica* etc.

EXTERNAL MORPHOLOGY

The gametophytic plant body is prostrate and dorsiventral thalloid. The thallus is dichotomously branched. Due to occurrence of several dichotomously branched plants together at a place it appears as a rosette. The green thallus has a midrib on the dorsal surface. There are numerous scales and rhizoids on the ventral surface of the thallus. The scales are violet in colour due to presence of violoxanthin, one celled thick. The rhizoids are unicellular and elongated which acts as anchorage organ and absorbs water and mineral nutrients from the soil. Rhizoids are smooth walled and tuberculate. (Fig. 1)

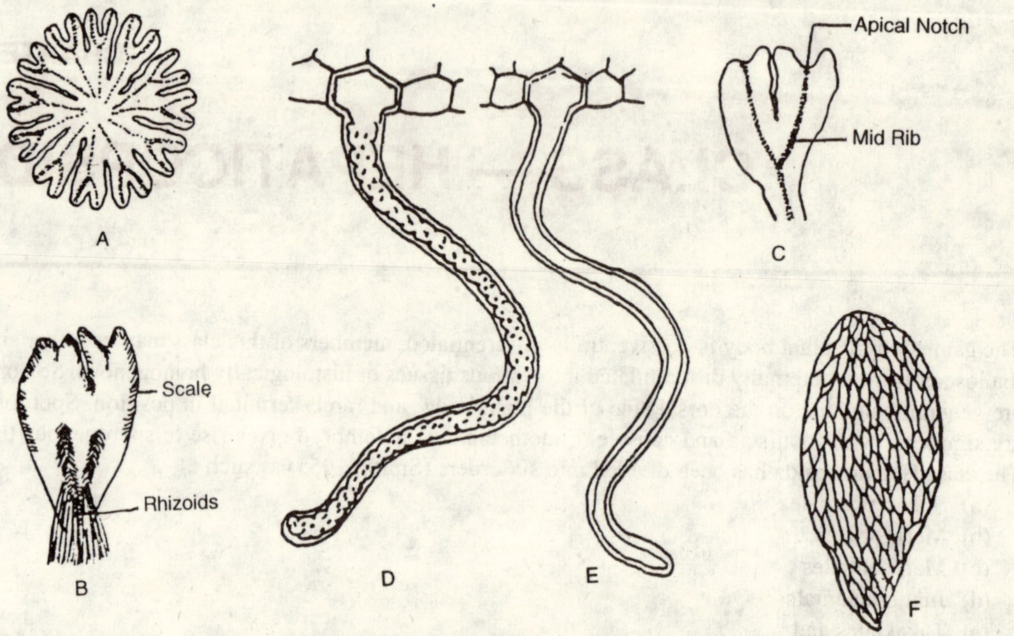

Fig. 1. (A-F) *Riccia* sp. A -rosette of thallus, B-Ventral view of a thallus, C-dorsal view of a thallus, D-tuberculate rhizoid, E-smooth walled rhizoid and F-a scale.

In *R. frostii* and *R. fluitans*, scales and tuberculate rhizoids are absent.

Fig. 1. (A-F) *Riccia* sp. A - rosette of thallus, B - Ventral view of a thallus, C- dorsal view of a thallus, D - tuberculate rhizoid, E - smooth walled rhizoid and F - a scale.

ANATOMY OF THE THALLUS

A vertical cross section of the thallus shows ventral region consists of colourless, compactly arranged parenchymatous cells. The parenchymatous cells are filled with starch. Lower most superficial surface is lower epidermis which gives rise to scales and rhizoids.

The upper or dorsal regioan is made up of chloroplast bearing cells arranged in vertical tiers. These tiers of chlorophyllous cells are separated by alternate vertical air chambers. Each air chamber communicates to the exterior by means of an air pore, which is a simple intercellular space encircled by 4 -8 epidermal cells. The terminal cell of each tier of chlorophyllous cell is colourless which constitutes the discontinous upper epidermal layer (Fig. 2).

VEGETATIVE REPRODUCTION

Vegetative reproduction in *Riccia* occurs by the following methods.

1. By progressive death and decay of the older parts of the thallus upto dichotomay and the two branches after separation develop into two independent plants.
2. By the formation of adventitious branches developing from the central surface. These branches are detached from the parent plant and develops into new plants.
3. By the formation of gemmae like structure at the apices of the rhizoids which develop into new plants.

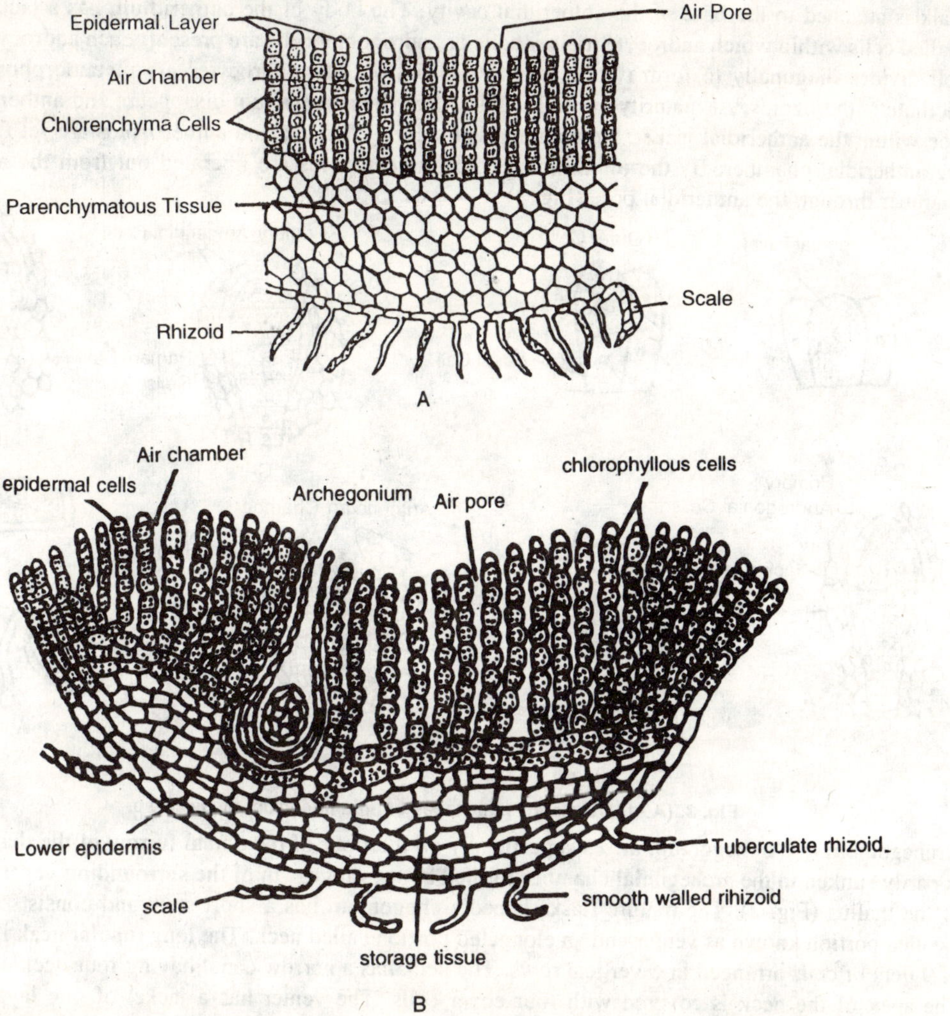

Fig. 2. A—Vertical section (V.S.) of thallus of Riccia discolor. B—V.S. of thallus showing archegonium.

4. By the formation of tuber develop from the thallus at the end of growing season. These tubers tide over the unfavourable condition. In favourable condition these tubers are detached and grow into new plants.

SEXUAL REPRODUCTION

Riccia is monoecious (homothallic) i.e. both male and female sex organs are born on the same plant. *R. personii, R. discolour* are dioecious (heterothallic). Male sex organs (antheridia) and female sex organs (archegonia) are developed alternately alongwith the median longitudinal furrow on the dorsal side of the thallus in monoecious species.

Antheridium — Antheridia occur singly in a discoid area slightly above the general surface of the thallus. A mature antheridium is an elongated structure having an ovoid body born on a short stalk. The stalk is attached to the base of the anthcridial cavity. The body of the antheridium has a jacket of thin walled cells within which androcyte mother cells or androgonial cells are present. Each androcyte mother cell divides diagonally to form two triangular androcytes. The androcytes are metamorphosed into a biciliate antherozoids. At maturity cubical walls within the antheridium disappears and antherozoids lie free within the antheridial jacket. Now antheridial jacket gelatinise and antherozoids are set free within the antheridial chamber. By the imbibitional force, antherozoids are liberated out from the antheridial chamber through the antheridial pore (Fig. 3)

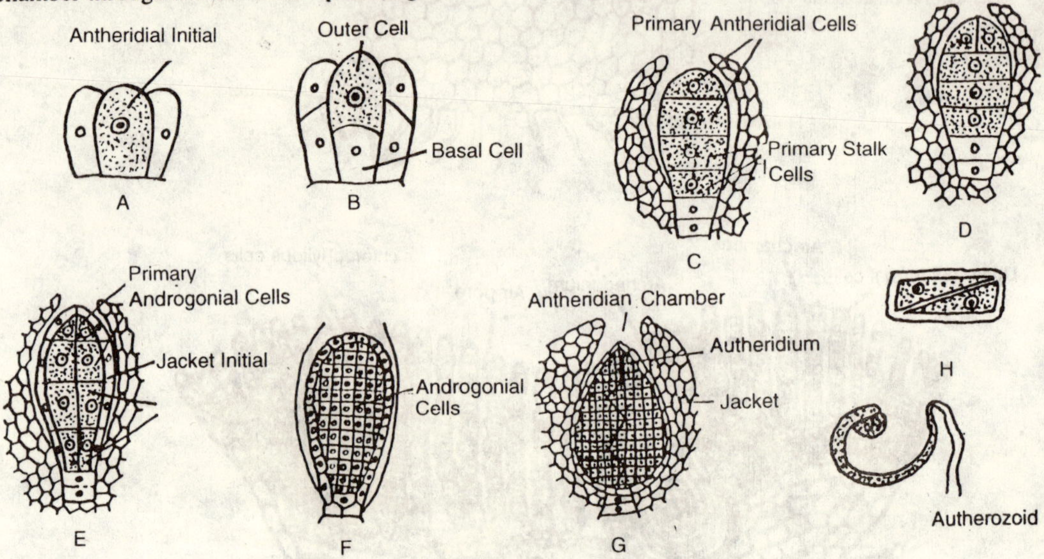

Fig. 3. (A - I) Developmental stages of an antheridium of *Riccia* sp.

Archegonium — Archegonium arises superficially on the floor of the dorsal furrow of the thallus and it is partly sunken in the archegonial chamber formed by the outgrowth of the surrounding vegetative cells of the thallus (Fig. 2). The mature flask shaped archegonium has a short stalk and consists of a basal swollen portion known as venter and an elongated portion called neck. The long tubular neck is made up of 9 tiers of cells arranged in 6 vertical rows. The neck has a narrow canal having four neck canal cells. The apex of the neck is covered with four cover cells. The venter has a jacket of one layer of cells enclosing a ventral canal cell and an egg (Fig. 4).

FERTILIZATION — Just before fertilization, the neck canal cells and the ventral canal cells disintegrate to form a mucilaginous mass which absorbs water, swells and exert pressure which causes in separation of the cover cells and thus leaving an open passage through the neck down to the egg. Water is essential for antherozoids to reach the archegonium through the open neck..Antherozoids are attracted to the mouth of the archegonium under the influence of the secretion of salt of potassium or proteins secreted by the archegonium and finally reaches to the egg. Out of many antherozoids enter the venter only one of them fertilizes the egg and a diploid zygote is formed (Fig. 5).

SPOROPHYTE

The diploid zygote is the first cell of the sporophytic generation. The zygote increases in size and nearly fills the cavity of the venter. The diploid zygote nucleus divides transversly into two cells, each of which again divides vertically as a result of which quadrant i.e. four celled structure is formed. It again divides vertically at right angle to the previous so that eight celled structure-octant-is

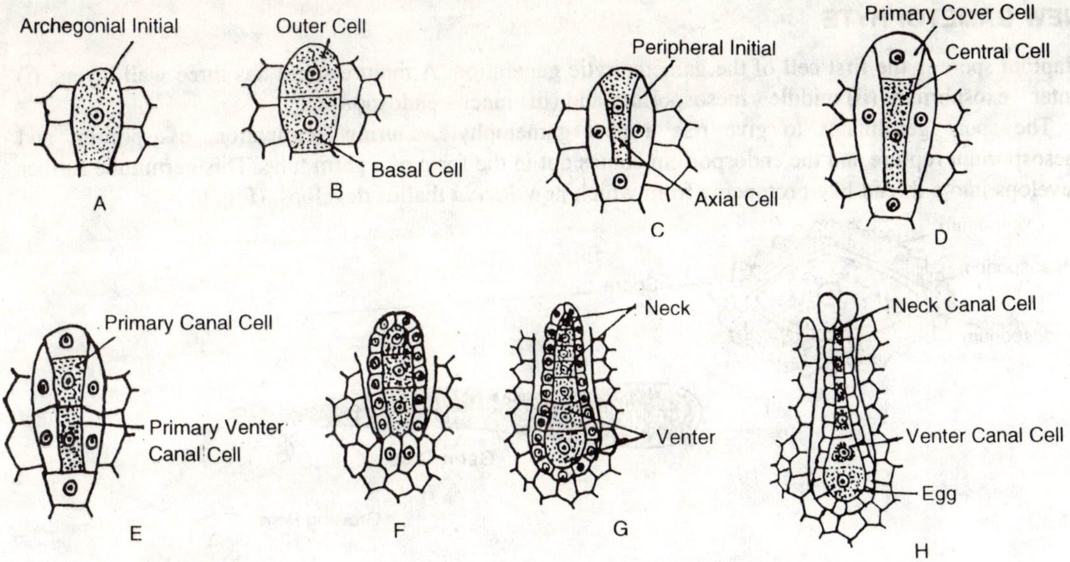

Fig. 4. (A -H) Developmental stages of an archegonium of *Riccia* sp.

formed. The repeated divisions result into 20-40 cells followed by periclinal division (Parallel to the periphery). This leads to formation of an outer layer of cells called amphithecium and an inner mass of cells called endothecium. The venter also divides periclinally into two layers. The outer layer forms the jacket and the inner layer disorganises. The amphithecium also disintegrates and provide nutrition to the developing spores. The endothecium gives rise to sporogenous tissue which differentiates into spore mother cells. The spore mother cells divide meiotically to produce haploid spores. Sometimes some sporogenous tissue remains sterile known as nurse cells which may be considered as forerunners of elaters. The whole structure, thus developed, is mature sporophyte.

The mature sporophyte looks like a globose, capsule like structure without any seta and foot. The capsule has a layer of jacket wall derived from the venter of the archegonium and not from the zygote. Inside the jacket are present spore tetrades and a few sterile cells. As a result of death and decay of the jacket wall of the capsule and adjoining tissue of the thallus, spores are liberated (Fig.5).

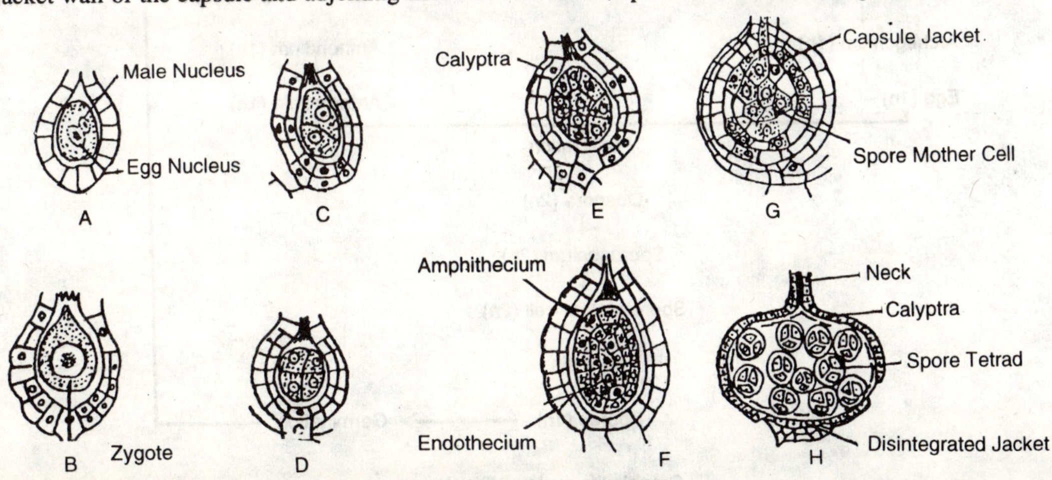

Fig. 5. (A-H) Stages in the development of sporogonium of *Riccia sp.*

NEW GAMETOPHYTE

Haploid spore is the first cell of the gametophytic generation. A mature spore has three wall layers, (i) outer - exosporium, (ii) middle - mesosporium and (iii) inner - endosporium.

The spore germinates to give rise a new gametophyte. During gemination, exosporium and mesosporium rupture and the endosporium comes out in the form of a germ tube. This germ tube further develops into a thread like protonema from which new *Riccia* thallus develops. (Fig. 6)

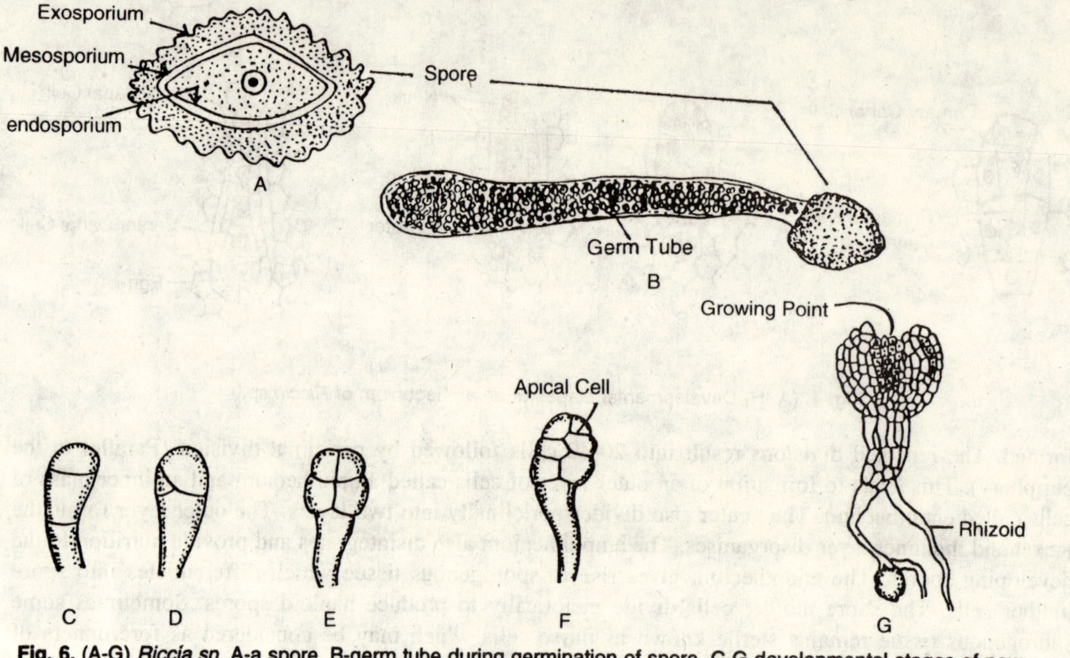

Fig. 6. (A-G) *Riccia sp.* A-a spore, B-germ tube during germination of spore, C-G developmental stages of new thallus.

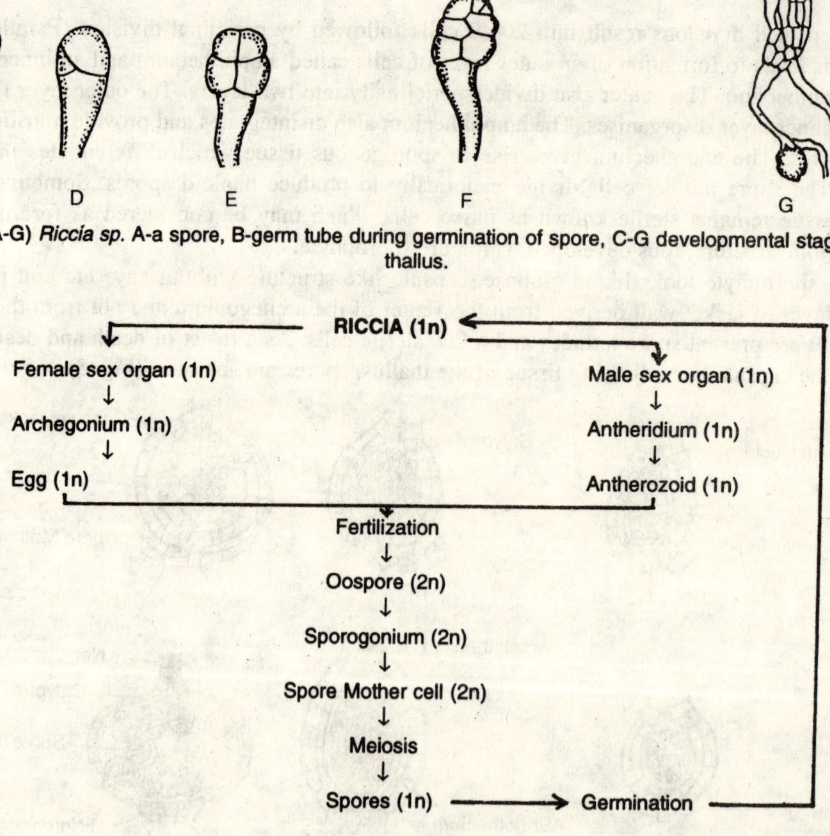

Graphic life cycle of ***Riccia***

3. MARCHANTIA

Marchantia belongs to	Class	—	Hepaticopsida
	Order	—	Marchantiales
	Family	—	Marchantiaceae
	Genus	—	*Marchantia*

HABITAT - There are about 65 species in the genus *Marchantia.* They are cosmopolitan in distribution and grown in moist places mainly in temperate region. In India, about 11 species are reported, mostly from Himalayan region. Some of them are *M. palmata, M. polymorpha* etc.

EXTERNAL MORPHOLOGY - The gametophytic plant body of *Marchantia* is a dichotomously branched, dorsiventral prostrate thallus having a mid rib on the dorsal side. Dorsal surface of the thallus have polygonal areas, each area has a spot in the centre which represents air pore leading to air chamber below the upper epidermis. The apex of the thallus is notched on which growing point is situated near the base of the notch. The dorsal surface of the thallus bears gemma cups or cupules containg gemmae along the midrib (Fig.7).

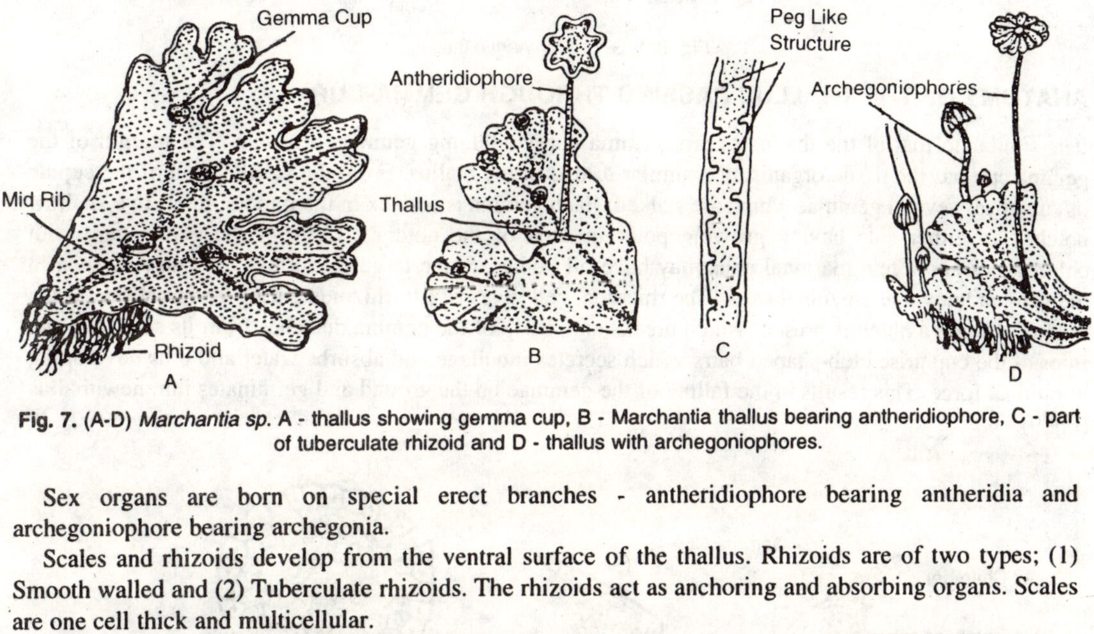

Fig. 7. (A-D) *Marchantia sp.* A - thallus showing gemma cup, B - Marchantia thallus bearing antheridiophore, C - part of tuberculate rhizoid and D - thallus with archegoniophores.

Sex organs are born on special erect branches - antheridiophore bearing antheridia and archegoniophore bearing archegonia.

Scales and rhizoids develop from the ventral surface of the thallus. Rhizoids are of two types; (1) Smooth walled and (2) Tuberculate rhizoids. The rhizoids act as anchoring and absorbing organs. Scales are one cell thick and multicellular.

ANATOMY OF THE THALLUS - Vertical section of the thallus shows tissue differentiation in the thallus. The ventral region of the thallus consists of compactly arranged thin walled parenchymatous cells. Generally, the cells contain starch grains but some cells may have chloroplasts. Some cells may be filled with mucilaginous substance or oil body. The outer most layer of ventral region is of lower epidermis made up of thin walled chlorophyllous cells. Two types of rhizoids and 3 - 4 rows of scales arise from the lower epidermis.

There are many air chambers just below the upper epidermis towards the dorsal region. Each air chamber is separated from each other by a partition of single layered cells containing chloroplasts. Simple or branched chloroplast containing cells in chain are present in the air chamber. Each air chamber opens outside by an air pore. The upper epidermis is interupted by these pores (Fig. 8).

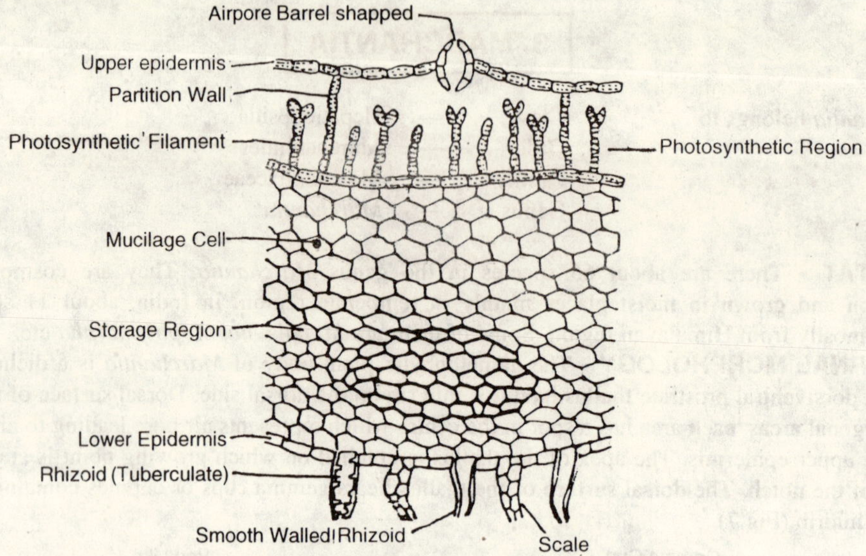

Fig. 8. V.S. of *Marchantia* thallus

ANATOMY OF THE THALLUS PASSING THROUGH GEMMA-CUP

It is similar to that of the thallus except gemma cup containing gemmae are seen. The margin of the gemma cup has the tissue organisation similar to that of the thallus. From the basal region of the cupule or cup arises several gemmae which are stalked. Each gemma is convex in the middle. It has two shallow notches on either side having growing point in each of the notches. Cells of the gemma are with chloroplasts and a few marginal cells may have oil bodies. Some large colourless cells may be seen in the gemma known as rhizoidal cells. The rhizoidal cell gives rise to rhizoids during germination. At the base of gemma a notch is present which breaks and, body of the gemma detaches from its stalk. From a floor of the cup arise club-shaped hairs which secretes mucilage and absorbs water and thus developing imbitional force. This results in the falling of the gemmae on the ground and germinates into new thallus (Fig.9).

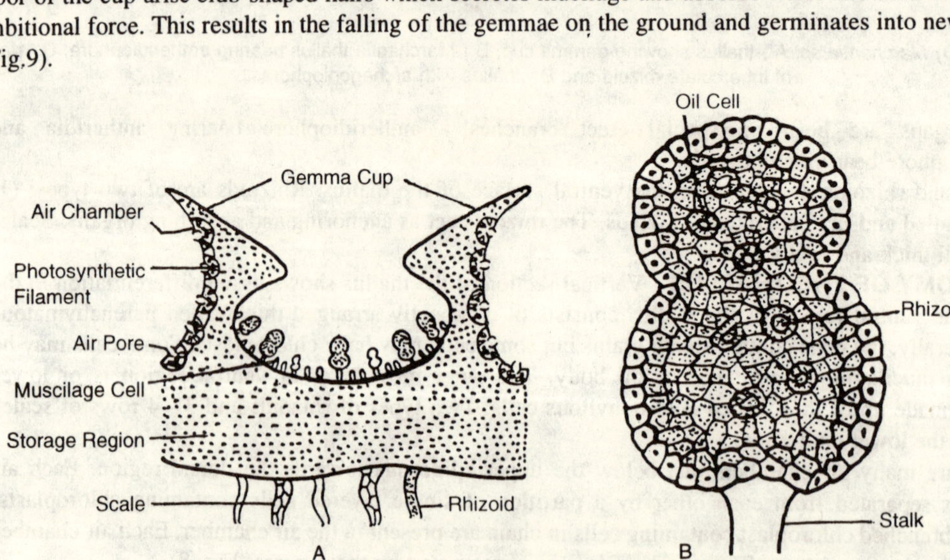

Fig. 9. (A,B) A - *Marchantia sp.* V.S. of thallus through gemma cup, B - a mature gemma.

SEXUAL REPRODUCTION

Marchantia is dioecious. The female sex organs - archegonia are born on special erect stalked branches known as archegoniohores. The male plant bears male sex organ antheridium which is born on erect stalked branch known as antheridiophore. The archegoniophore and the antheridiophore have all thc characteristics of a thallus viz. air pore, air chamber, photosynthetic filaments, scales and rhizoids thereby indicating that antheridiophore and archegoniaphore are modified part of the thallus.

The antheriodiophore - The antheridiophore develops from a region just behind the apex of the thallus. It consists of a 1 - 3 cm long stalk with a disc at its apex. The disc is generally eight lobed. Antheridia are found in flask shaped cavities towards the upper part of the disc. Young antheridia lie towards the periphery of the disc while mature antheridium is pear shaped globular structure having short stalk. The body has a jacket of one layer of thin walled cells. Many androcyte mother cells lie within the antheridial jacket. Each androcyte mother cell divides diagonally into triangular androcytes each of which is metamorphored into a biciliate antherozoid (Fig.10).

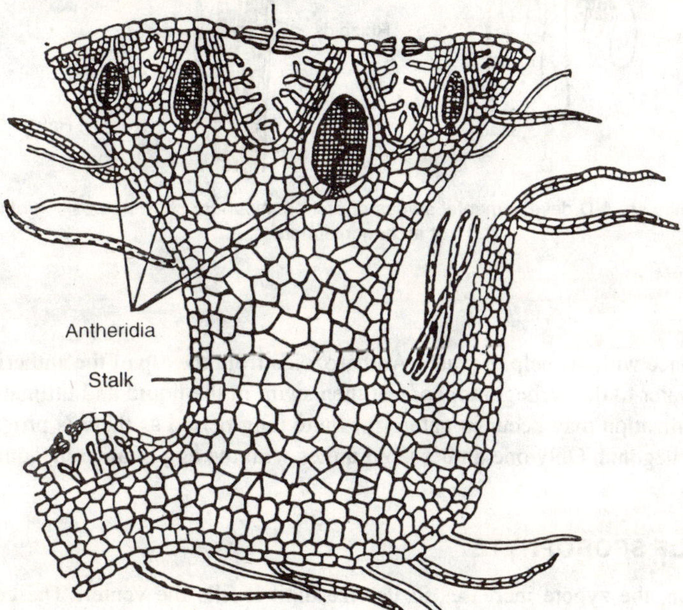

Fig. 10. Longitudinal section (L.S) of antheridiophore of *Marchantia sp.*

The Archegoniophore - Each archegoniophore is similar in position to that of antheridiophore. The mature archegoniophore consists of a long stalk bearing 8 - 9 rayed stellate disc at its apex. The archegonia with their neck downwards, are arranged in radial rows in between the rays. The group of archegonium is protected by a perichaetium. Young archegonia are located towards the centre where as mature archegonia lie superficially towards the periphery of the rayed disc. Each mature archegonium is attached by a short stalk to the lobe of disc. It is flask shaped structure and consists of an elongated neck with four or more neck canal cells and a venter containing a ventral canal cell and an egg. The neck consists of six vertical rows of jacket cell(Fig.11,12A). Haberlandt (1929) reported both archehgonia and antheridia on the same receptacle - termed as ''Androgynous receptacle'' in *Marchantia.* Archegonia are born on the underside of the disc and antheridia are in cavities opening to the outside. Androgynous receptacles have also been reported in *M. palmata* by Srinivasan (1939, 1944), in *M. polymorpha* by Naidu (1973). The occurrence of androgynous receptacles indicate a tendency towards monoecism.

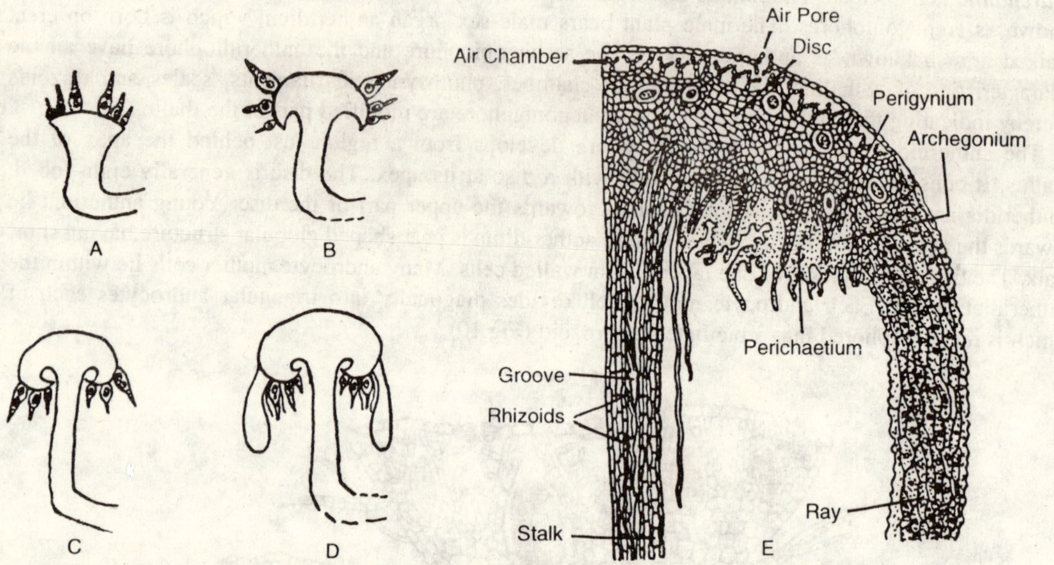

Fig. 11. (a-E) Marchantia sp. A-D developmental stages of archegoniophore showing position of archegonia E - L.S. of archegoniophore.

FERTILIZATION

Fertilization takes place with the help of water. Antherozoids from the top of the antheridiophore disc are splashed by a rain water to the archegoniophore. It then swim in the liquid and ultimately reaches to the egg. Successive fertilization may occur in nature for quite long period as there is progressive formation of antheridia and archegonia. Only one antherozoid unites with the egg of an archegonium and a diploid zygote is formed.

DEVELOPMENT OF SPOROPHYTE

Just after fertilization, the zygote increases in its size until it fills the venter. The cells of the venter divides and redivides to form multilayered calyptra which encircles the developing sporophyte. Some cells at the basal region of the venter divide to form a collar like cylindrical structure, one cell in thickness called perigynium or pseudoperianth.

Zygote nucleus divides transversly into an upper epibasal cell and a lower hypobasal cell. Further vertical divisions result into octant stage. Derivatives of the epibasal cell give rise to capsule and upper part of seta while those of hypobasal cell contribute to the formation of lower part of the seta and foot of the capsule. The periclinal division in the epibasal region gives rise to inner endothecium and outer amphithecium. The amphithecium forms one layered jacket of the capsule and endothecium gives rise to sporogenous cells. About half of the cells produced by endothecium form sterile long, tapering, slender cells with bispiral thickening on the wall known as elaters and remaining cells form spore mother cells. The spore mother cell divides meiotically to form haploid spores (Fig. 12).

Mature sporophyte - The mature sporophyte is more or less elongated structure and is differentiated into (a) foot, (b) seta and (c) capsule. The foot is bulbous directed towards the base of archegonium. The

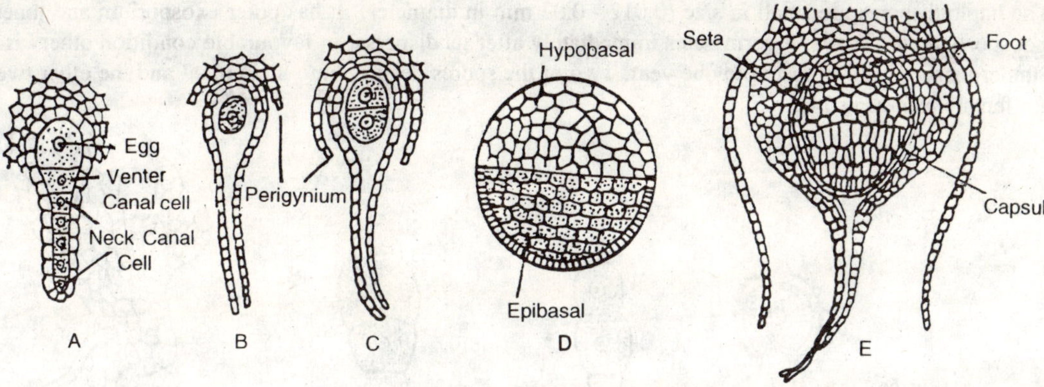

Fig. 12. (A-E) *Merchantia* sp A-An archegonium, B-zygote in the venter, C-division in the zygote, D-hypobasal and epibasal region and E-differentiation in sporophyte.

seta is thick and short in between foot and capsule. The capsule is oval or spherical having a single layered jacket. The capsule contains elaters and spores. The elaters help in scattering of the spores. The mature capsule depends on the gametophyte for its water and mineral requirements. The seta elongates suddenly which causes rupturing of the calyptra. The capsule is exposed from the calyptra, perigynium and perichaetium. Soon after exposure, the wall of the capsule splits longitudinally from the apex to the middle into several segments. The spores are liberated. The elaters are hygroscopic and due to hygroscopic movement, it helps to loosen the spore mass and thus spores are dispersed in the air(Fig.13).

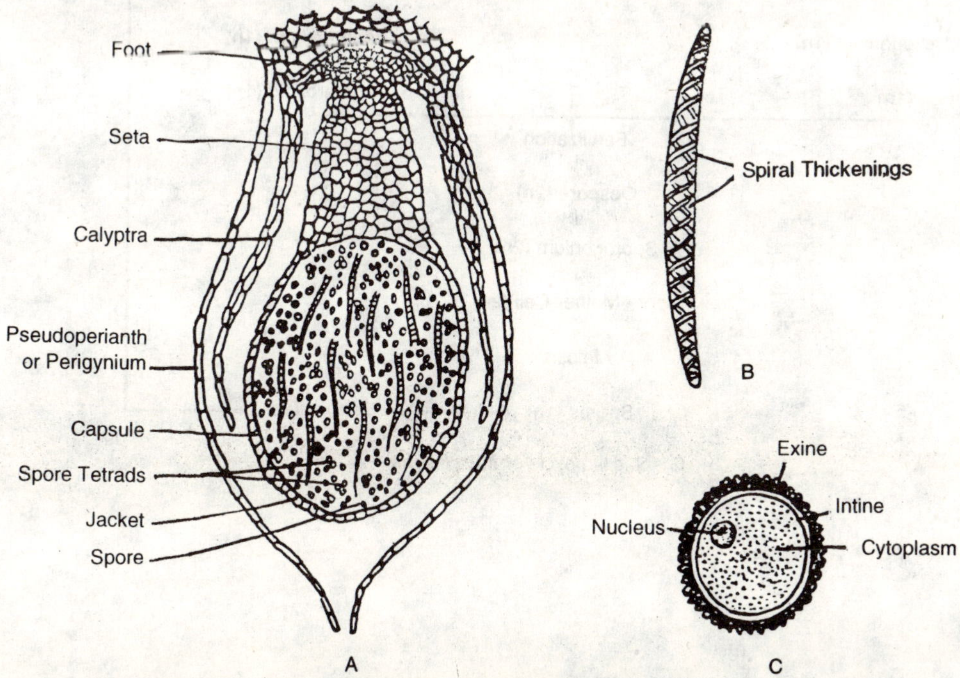

Fig. 13. (A-C) *Marchantia sp.* A - L.S. of sporogonium B - an elater and C - a spore.

FORMATION OF YOUNG GAMETOPHYTE

The haploid spores are small in size (0.012 - 0.03 mm in diameter). It has outer exosporium and inner endosporium wall layers. It germinates immediately after its dispersal in favourable condition otherwise it undergoes a period of rest upto one year. Two of the spores develop into male plant and the other two into female plant (Fig.14).

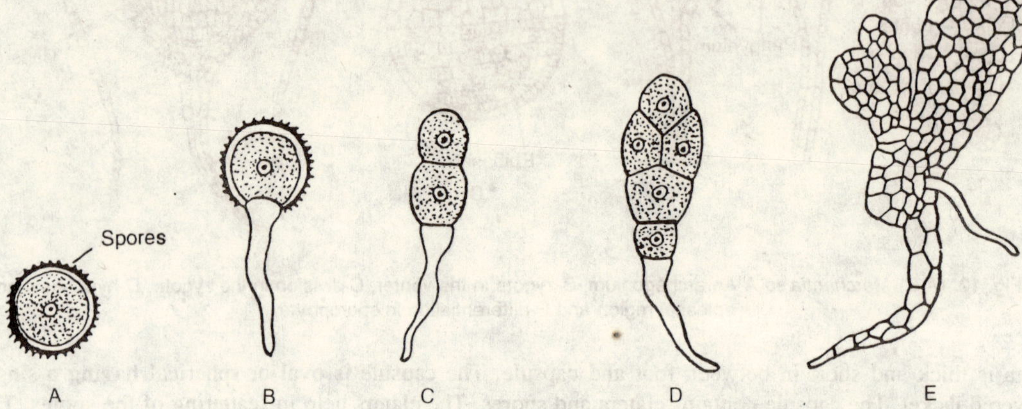

Fig. 14. (A-E) *Marchantia sp.* Germination of spore and stages of thallus formation.

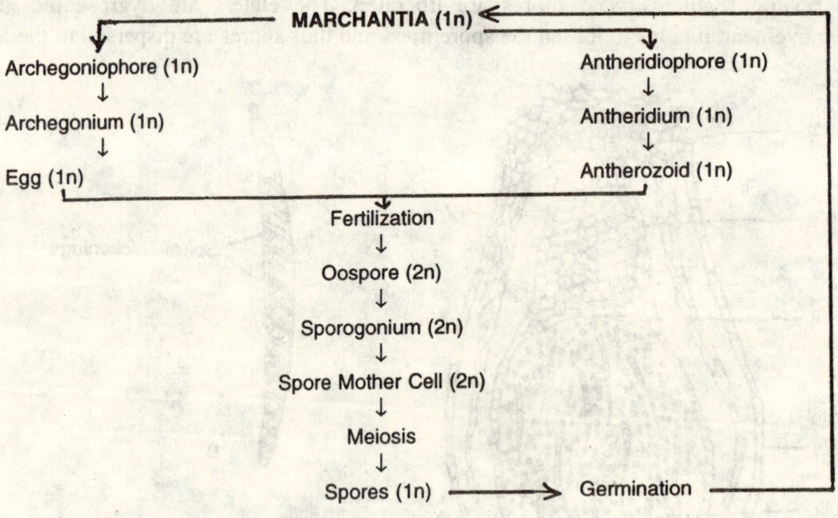

Graphic life cycle of ***Marchantia***

2.3. CYATHODIUM

It belongs to	Division	—	Bryophyta
	Class	—	Hepaticopsida
	Order	—	Marchantiales
	Family	—	Targioniaceae
	Genus	—	*Cyathodium*

The genus *Cyathodium* was placed under the family Targioniaceae by Lang (1905) which was supported by Cavers (1911) and Campbell (1911), but on the other hand Kashyap (1914) consider it to be under the family Marchantiaceae as it has directly descended from a *Marchantia* like form. Some of the important species of *Cyathodium* are *C. cavernatum* reported by Lang (1905), *C.tuberosum* (Kashyap, 1914) and *C. Kashyapi* (Khanna, 1929)

HABIT AND HABITAT

Cyathodium is hygrophilous, Growing in moist and shady places and therefore it differs anatomically from *Targionia.* Gametophytic plants may be monoecious or dioecious (*C. tuberosum*), thalloid, thin, small in size and grow on rocks or ground. The colour of the thallus depends on the habitat, those that grow in open places are bright green in colour, while those grow in shady places are yellowish green. Thallus is differentiated into dorsal and ventral surfaces, dichotomously divided. Male plants are branched with linear or oblong lobes Female plants are fan–shaped due to repeated dichotomy (Fig. 15). Breadth of the plant varies from 2 mm to 2 cm and the length is generally 1 cm. Smooth and thick walled, but not tuberculate, rhizoids develop. Scales are minute in two rows or wholly absent. Air pores are present on both the dorsal and ventral surfaces. Dorsal pores are well developed in female plant. Pores are encircled by concentric rings of cells (Fig. 15).

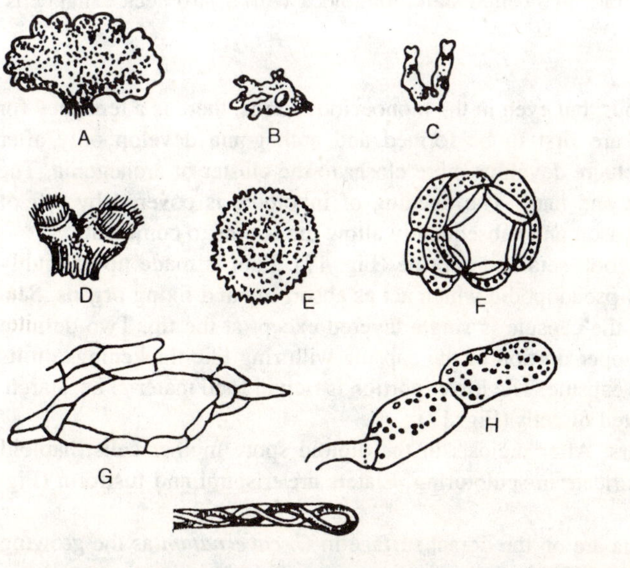

Fig. 15. (A-I) *Cyathodium sp.* A - Fan shaped female thallus, B.C. - male thalli, D - thallus with apical buds, E - a spore, F - a pore on dorsal surface, G - a pore on ventral surface, H - a scale and I - an elater.

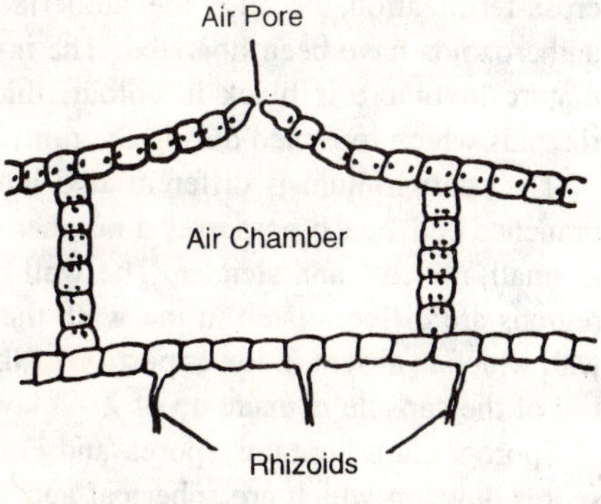

Fig. 16. *Cyathodium sp.* V.S. of thallus.

ANATOMY OF THE THALLUS

Plants are very simple internally, composed of ventral and dorsal layers separated by air chambers (Fig. 16). Air chambers are devoid of assimilatory filaments. Chloroplasts are present in the cells forming the upper layer as well as the partition wall of the air chamber. The outer wall of the cells or the thallus is convex thus the diffuse light is reflected back by the inner wall giving the plant a phosphorescent appearance. Some of the cells of the partition wall also contain oil drops. Colonies of some blue green algae and or eggs of some insects are found within the air chambers. These colonies or eggs might have entered through the ventral pores (Fig. 16).

REPRODUCTION

A. Vegetative propagation takes place (1) by progressive growth and decay of the thallus and (2) by means of perenating tubers developed at the marginal end of the thallus.

B. Sexual Reproduction — On the male plant, the antheridia are grouped into receptacles. The male receptacle is very interesting. The position of the receptacle in the thallus in different plants may vary. It may be terminal, central or in between the fork of the two lobes. Plant may develop more than one receptacle and on the same plant the position of the receptacles may differ. The receptacle represents a branching system and the varying position of the receptacles may be due to different way of the division of the growing region.

The male receptacle stands on a stalk which may be one or two layers. The receptacle proper consists of a number of chambers, each containing a single antheridium. Mature antheridium consists of two celled stalk and a body having single layered jacket enclosing a mass of androcytes. The antheridial chamber communicates to out side through one opening at the top of the receptacle called ostiole.

The mode of development of sex organs are typical of marchantiales.

The archegonia donot develop on special branches. They grow on the main thallus, in the apical region, two to three cells behind the growing point. When more than one receptacle is formed, they grow in acropetal succession. A plant may have a number of receptacle. Each receptacle consists of 4 -6 archegonia. A mature archegonium has a short, two celled stalk, long neck with 8 - 10 neck canal cells.

FERTILIZATION

Cyathodium may be monoecious or dioecious, but even in the monoecious forms, there is a tendency for cross-fertilization, because the antheridia are first to be formed and archegonia develop only after antherozoids have been liberated. The involucre develops more closer to the cluster of archegonia. The mature involucre is black in colour, thick and hard. The opening of involucre is·covered by tuft of rhizoids which loosened during the rainy season and subsequently allow the spores to come out.

The sporogonium is differentiated into foot. seta and capsule (Fig. 17). Foot is made up of highly branched cells, each possesses a number of pseudopodia which act as absorbing and fixing organs. Seta is small, delicate and slender. The wall of the capsule is single layered except at the tip. Two definite regions are differentiated in the wall, the upper portion of the capsule with ring like thickenings on its wall which is absent in lower portion of the capsule. The lower portion is rich in food material i.e. starch. Lid of the capsule is made up of 2 - 3 layered of cells (Fig. 17).

Sporogonium contains spores and elaters. After meiosis in the diploid spore mother cells, haploid spores develop which are spherical and muricate in sculpturing. Elaters are trispiral and fusiform (Fig. 15).

According to Lang (1905) the archegonia are on the dorsal surface in *C. cavernatum* as the growing point is not pushed downward. There is slight difference in the sporogonum of this species showing large foot and seta indicating more of sterilization.

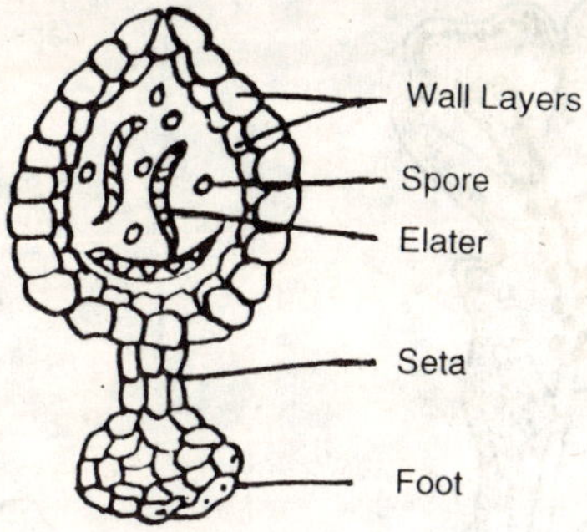

Fig. 17. *Cyathodium* sp. L.S of sporogonium.

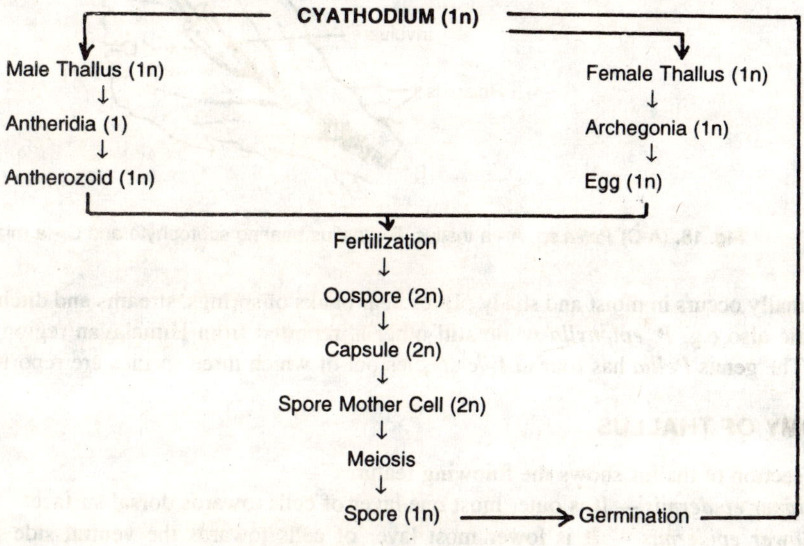

Graphic life cycle of ***Cyathodium***

2.4. PELLIA

Pellia belongs to

Class	—	Hepaticopsida
Order	—	Jungermanniales
Family	—	Pelliaceae
Genus	—	*Pellia*

HABIT AND HABITAT

The plant body is thalloid and gametophyte. The dorsiventral and prostrate thallus is green and smooth without any air pores. A distinct mid rib is present. The thallus is dichotomously branched. Only smooth walled rhizoids are present on the ventral surface (Fig. 18).

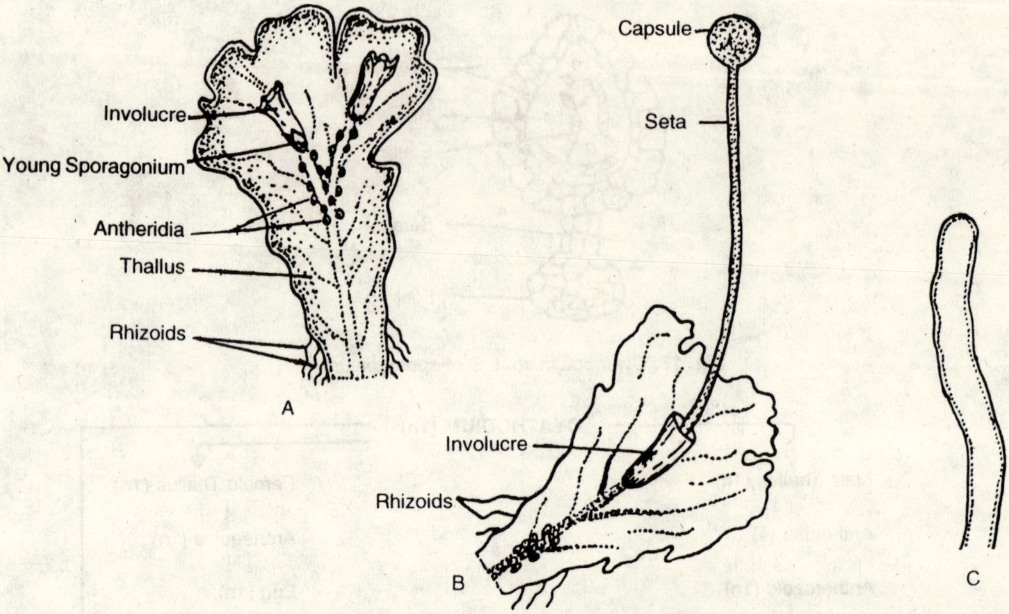

Fig. 18. (A-C) *Pellia* sp. A - a thallus, B - thallus bearing sporophyte and C - a rhizoid.

It normally occurs in moist and shady places near banks of springs, streams and ditches. Some species are aquatic also e.g. *P. epiphylla* while still other is reported from Himalayan region at an altitude of 8000 ft. The genus *Pellia* has four or five species out of which three species are reported from India.

ANATOMY OF THALLUS

Vertical section of thallus shows the folowing features —

1. *Upper epidermis* — It is outer most one layer of cells towards dorsal surface.
2. *Lower epidermis* — It is lower most layer of cells towards the ventral side from where only smooth walled rhizoids develop.
3. In between upper & lower epidermis polyhedral parenchymatous cells are found which are uniform. Chloroplasts are restricted to upper epidermal cells. Rest of the cells have starch and oil drops (Fig. 19).

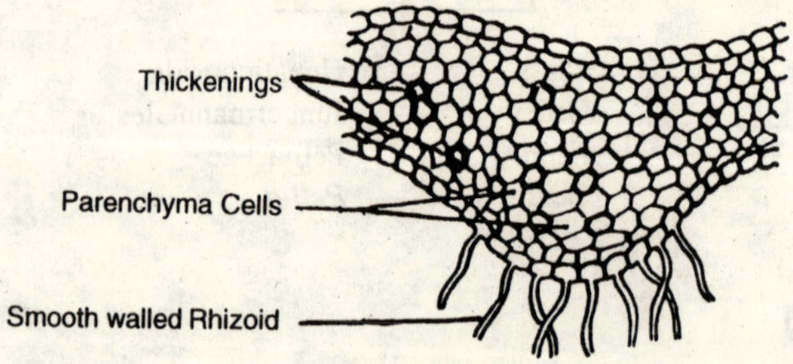

Fig. 19. V.S. of thallus of *Pellia* sp.

REPRODUCTION

It is of two types (1) vegetative and (2) sexual.

Vegtative reproduction — It takes place by means of adventitious buds develop on the dorsal surface of the thallus. On detachment, these buds give rise to new thalli. Vegetative propogation also occurs by death and decay of the posterior region of the thallus. Growth and branching takes place in the interior region which results into formation of many new thalli and eventually separated out.

Sexual reproduction — It is oogamous type and takes place by male and female sex organs known as antheridium and archegonium respectively. The sex organs are born on thallus. The thallus may be monoecious (*P. epiphylla*) or dioecious (*P. neesiana*)

Antheridium — Antheridia are developed on the dorsal surface along the midrib region of the thallus. The antheridium is sunk in the antheridial cavity (Fig. 20).

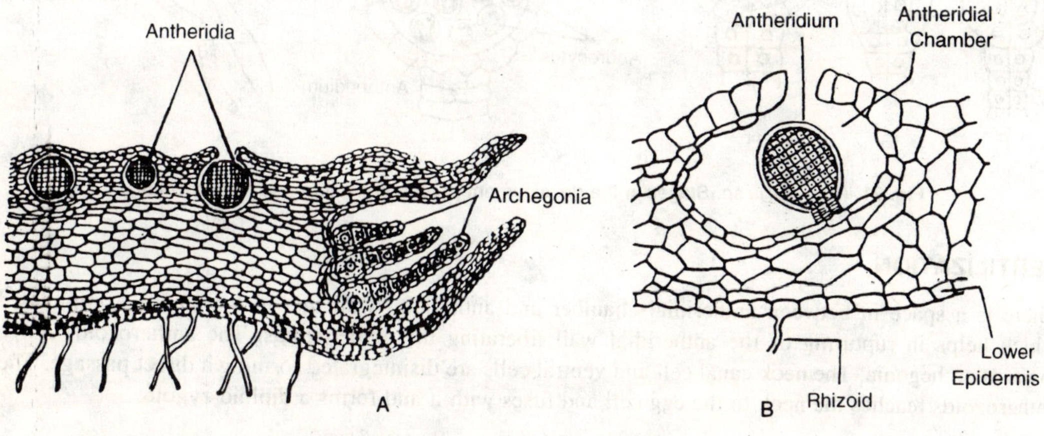

Fig. 20. A - V.S. of monoecious thallus of *Pellia* sp

Fig. 20. B - V.S. of thallus showing an antheridium in antheridial chamber.

The antheridium develops from superficial cell of the thallus which behave as antheridial initial. It divides transversely into two cells, an outer upper and an inner basal cell. The outer cell again divides to form primary antheridial cell and a primary stalk cell which forms the stalk of the antheridium. The antheridial cell forms the jacket of the antheridium and primary androgonial cells. The primary androgonial cell divides to form androcytes which get metamorphosed into biciliate coiled antherozoids (Fig. 21).

Thus, the mature antheridium is stalked and globular structure having one layered wall enclosing many antherozoids.

Archegonium — Archegonia are formed in cluster on dorsal surface near the growing apex. Each cluster has 4 - 12 archegonia and are protected by involucre which is formed by the surrounding tissue of the thallus.

Some apical cells of the apex of the thallus act as archegonial cell. It divides transversely into outer and basal cell. The outer cell divides by three vertical division forming two peripheral cells and a central cell. The peripheral cells divide to form jacket of the archegonium and the central cell forms the primary cover cell and the lid cell and the central cell divides to form 6 - 8 neck canal cells, one ventral canal cell and an egg cell (Fig. 22).

A mature archegonium is flask shaped consisting of a neck with 6 - 8 neck canal cells and a swollen venter having a ventral canal cell and an egg cell.

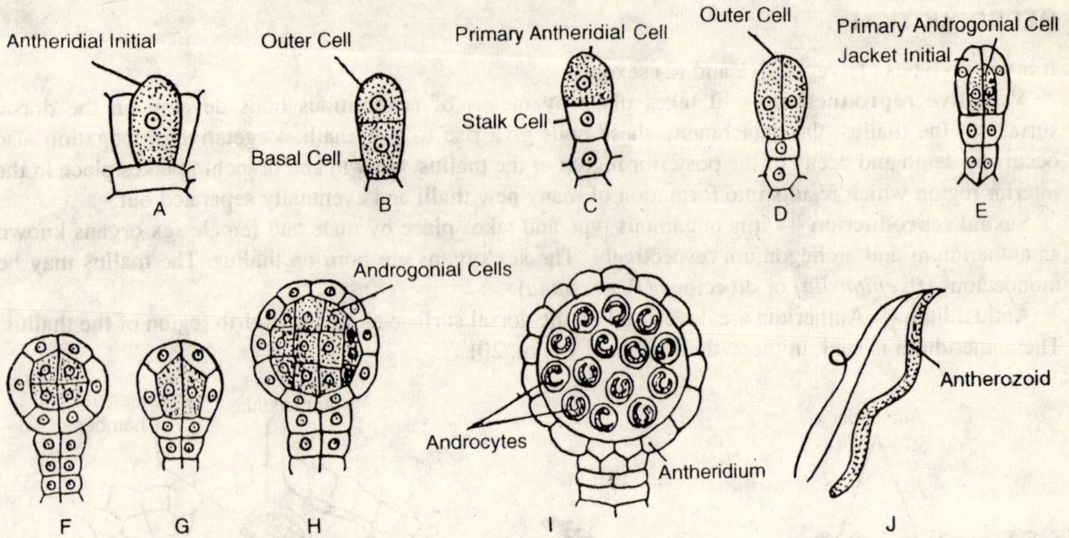

Fig. 21. (A-J) *Pellia* sp. Stages in the development of an antheridium and antherozoids.

FERTILIZATION

There is a space in between antheridial chamber and antheridial wall in which water is accumulated which helps in rupturing of the antheridial wall liberating the antherozoids. The antherozoids move towards archegonia. The neck canal cell and ventral cells are disintegrated forming a direct passage. The antherozoids reaches the neck to the egg cell and fuses with it and forms a diploid zygote.

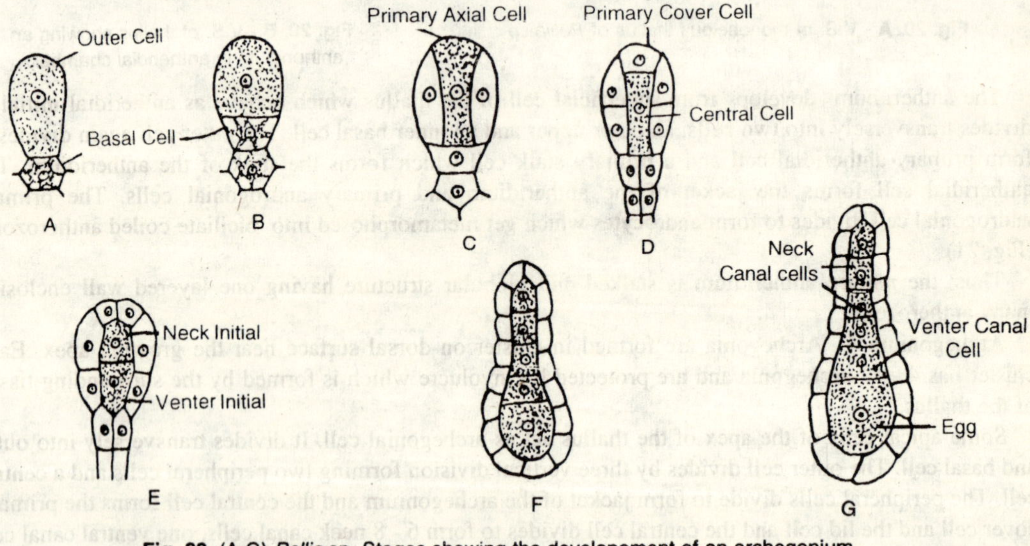

Fig. 22. (A-G) *Pellia* sp. Stages showing the developoment of an archegonium.

SPOROPHYTIC GENERATION

The diploid zygote is the first cell of the sporophytic generation. The zygote divides transversely into a lower hypobasal cell and upper epibasal cell. The hypobasal cell gives rise suspensor or haustorium. The epibasal cell further divides into eight cells, out of which four upper cells form the capsule and four lower cells form foot and Seta. The four upper cells of capsule divides periclinally to form inner endothecium and outer amphithecium. The endothecium forms archesporium while amphithecium gives rise single layered wall of capsule. The archesporium or sporogenous tissue further divides to give rise spore mother cells, elaters and elaterophores. The spore mother cell divides meiotically to form haploid spores (Fig. 23).

A mature sporophyte consists of foot, seta and capsule. The capsule contains spores, elaters and

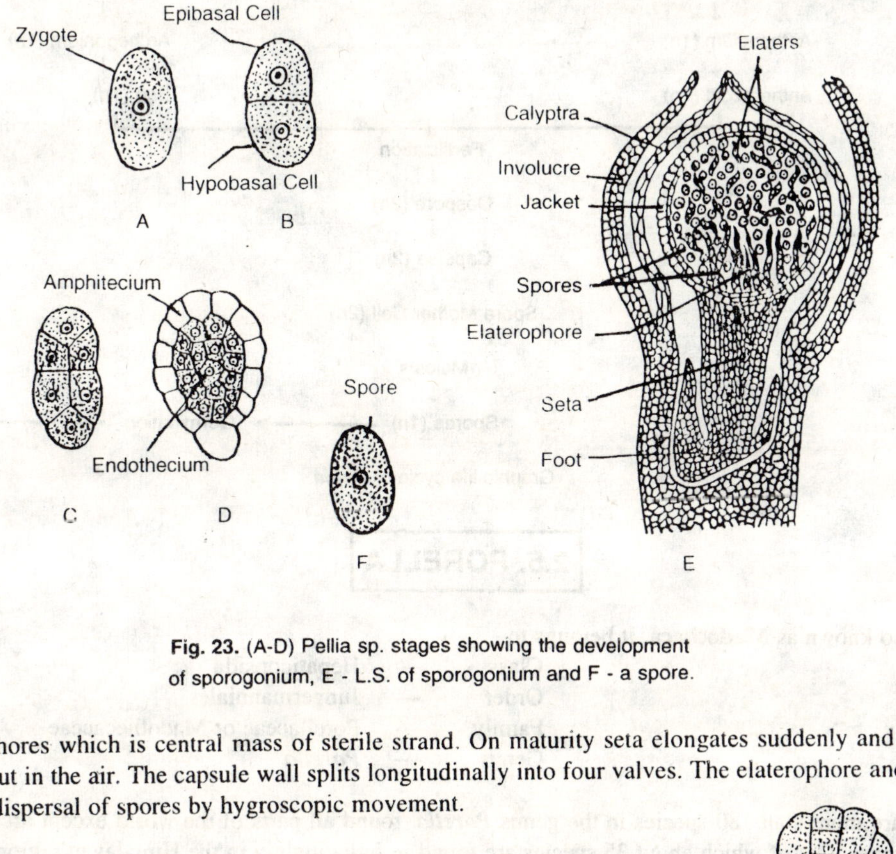

Fig. 23. (A-D) Pellia sp. stages showing the development of sporogonium, E - L.S. of sporogonium and F - a spore.

elaterophores which is central mass of sterile strand. On maturity seta elongates suddenly and capsule comes out in the air. The capsule wall splits longitudinally into four valves. The elaterophore and elaters help in dispersal of spores by hygroscopic movement.

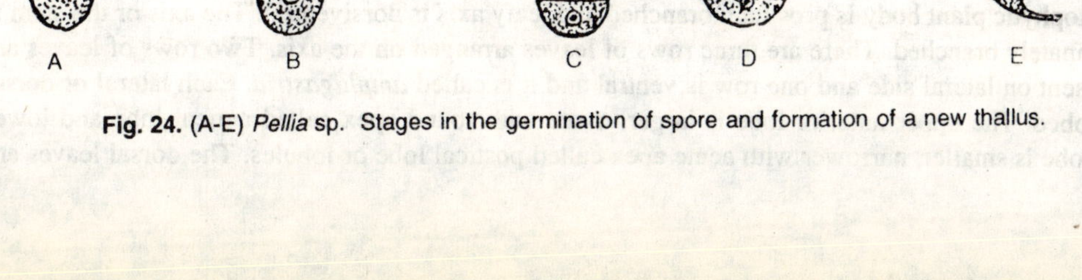

Fig. 24. (A-E) *Pellia* sp. Stages in the germination of spore and formation of a new thallus.

GAMETOPHYTIC GENERATION

The haploid spore is the first cell of gametophytic generation. The spores start to germinate while still within the capsule. The uninucleate haploid spore divides transversely into a row of four cells. The central two cells divides vertically and thus six celled structure is formed. Now this is liberated out of capsule and further divides outside the capsule. The lower cell gives rise rhizoidal cell and the upper cell further divides to form the new gametophytic plant body (Fig. 24).

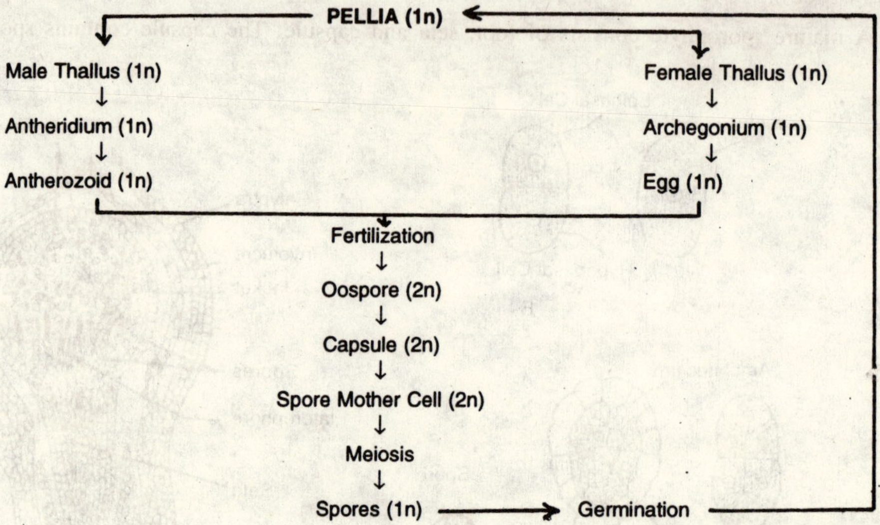

Graphic life cycle of ***Pellia***

2.5. PORELLA

It is also known as **Madotheca**. It belongs to

Class	—	Hepaticopsida
Order	—	Jungermanniales
Family	—	Porellaceae or Madothecaceae
Genus	—	*Porella*

There are more than 180 species in the genus *Porella*. found all parts of the world except arctic and antarctic zones. Out of which about 35 species are found in India mainly in the Himalayan region and a few have been reported from South India. The common Indian species are *P. obtusifolia*, *P. decurrents*, *P. platyphylla*, *P. pulmosa*, *P. densifolia*, *P. ovalis*, *P. trigonifolia* etc.

HABIT AND HABITAT

The gametophytic plant body is prostrate, branched and leafy axis is dorsiventral. The axis or the stem is bi or tripinnately branched. There are three rows of leaves arranged on the axis. Two rows of leaves are dorsal present on lateral side and one row is ventral and it is called *amphigastria*. Each lateral or dorsal leaf is bilobed. The upper anterior lobe is larger, ovate with round apex called antical lobe and lower posterior lobe is smaller, narrower with acute apex called postical lobe or lobules. The dorsal leaves are arranged in *incubous* manner i.e. hind (lower) edge of each leaf is covered by the forward (upper) edge of the next leaf below. The leaves of the ventral row are small and resemble the postical lobes of dorsal leaves except that they are broader with decurrent bases. The margin of the leaves may be dentate as in *P. denticulata* or entire as in *P. acutifolia* (Fig. 25, 26)

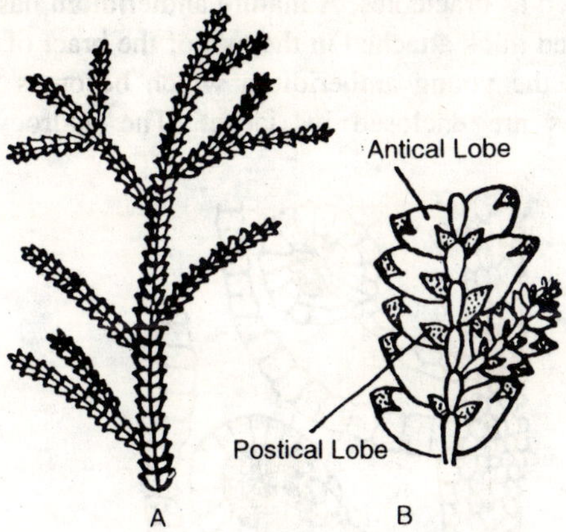

Fig. 25. *Porella* sp. Leafy shoot, B. Fertile branch

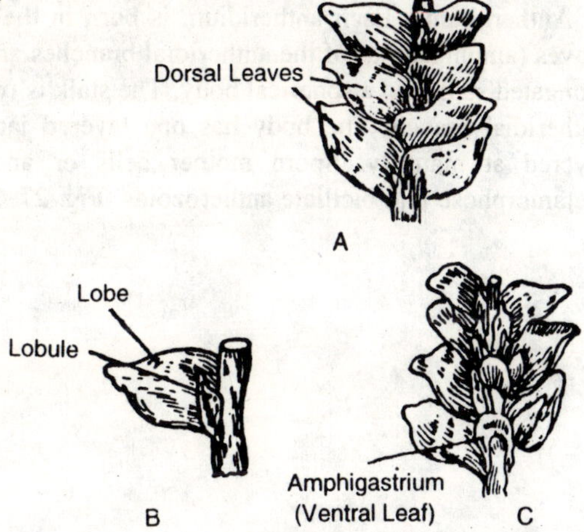

Fig. 26. *Porella* sp. A. Dorsal view of a part of branch, B. Dorsal leaf, C. Ventral view of a part of branch.

Several unicellular smooth walled rhizoids develop from the ventral surface of the stem. It acts as anchorage organ.

Porella plants usually form green patches on shady moist rocks, tree trunks and sometimes on soil also.

Anatomy (Internal structure) of the stem —

Transverse section of the stem (axis) shows little tissue differentiation. The small cortex is made up of 2-5 layers of thick walled parenchymatous cells and the cells of central medulla are thin walled and elongated. Leaves shows internally a single layer of isodiometric, parenchymatous cells containing many chloroplasts. There is neither mid rib nor vascular tissue. Some oil cells are found in the leaf.

GROWTH

It is apical and thallus grows by the activity of pyramidal or tetrahedral apical cell with three cutting faces.

REPRODUCTION

Porella has two methods of reproduction, (i) vegetative and (ii) sexual.

Vegetative reproduction : It occurs by two methods (1) By progressive death and decay of the thallus. The apical growth takes place from the point of dichotomy of the foliose axis resulting in the development of two branches, each of the branches grow into a new plant.

(2) By the formation of gemmae or adventitious buds : In *P. rotundifolia* adventitious buds are formed on the lower surface of leaves which grow into new gametophytic plant. These buds have been considered to be gemmae by some bryologists.

Some species growing in humid conditions multiply by fragmentation also.

Sexual reproduction : It is of oogamous type. *Porella* is dioecious and the male plants are smaller in size than the female plants. The male sex organs are antheridia and the female sex organs are archegonia. Male *porella* plant bears lateral antheridial branches which are projected at right angles from the main axis. The female *Porella* plant bears archegonial branches which are smaller than the vegetative and antheridial branches.

Antheridium : Each antheridium is born in the axil of a concave leaf known as bract. The ventral leaves (amphigastria) of the antheridial branches are termed as bracteoles. A mature antheridium has an elongated stalk and a spherical body. The stalk is two celled thick attached in the axil of the bract of the antheridial branch. The body has one layered jacket in the young antheridium which becomes 2-3 layered at maturity. Spore mother cells or androcytes are enclosed by jacket. The androcytes metamorphose into biciliate antherozoids (Fig. 27, 28).

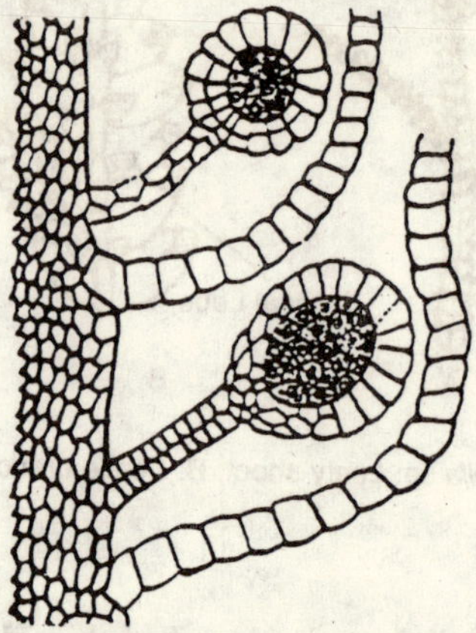

Fig. 27. *Porella sp.* A. Longitudinal section (L.S.) of an antheridial branch.

Dispersal of antherozoid : The distal part of the antheridial jacket is made up of thin walled cells and it is single layered. When it come in contact with water it breakes into several irregular lobes followed by liberation of mass of antheriozoids in water.

Development of antheridium : Antheridium develops from an antheridial initial differentiated at the base of the young bract. It divides transversely into an outer and a basal cell. The outer cell acts as antheridial mother cell. The basal cell forms the embeded part of the stalk.

The antheridial mother cell divides transversely into an upper primary antheridial cell and a lower primary stalk cell. The primary stalk cell divides transversely and vertically to form two celled thick long stalk of the antheridium. The primary antheridial cells divides vertically to form two equal antheridial cells. Each of them divides periclinally into an outer first jacket initial and an inner primary androgonial cell. The primary androgonial cell divides to form a second jacket initial. Both the jacket initials (first and second) divides anticlinally to form a single layered jacket of the antheridium. Further the cells of lower part of the jacket divide periclinally to give rise 2-4 layered lower part of the antheridium. The primary androgonial cell divides in all planes to produce a large number of rectangular androgonial cells. The last generation of androgonial cells is termed as androcyte mother cells which divides diagonally to form two androcytes. The androcytes metamorphose into biciliate, rod shaped antherozoids (Fig. 28).

Archegonium : The archegonium develops in group of the apex of archegonial branch on female plant. The archegonial branch is smaller with 2 - 5 leaves only. The lower bracts form an involucre and the two upper most bracts unite to form a perianth. the perianth encloses a group of 10- 15 archegonia.

A mature archegonium has a venter and a neck. The venter is two layered containing a ventral canal cell and an egg. The neck is made up of 5 vertical rows of neck cells having 6- 8 neck canal cells (Fig. 29).

Development of archegonium : The archegonium develops in acropetal succession i.e. the youngest

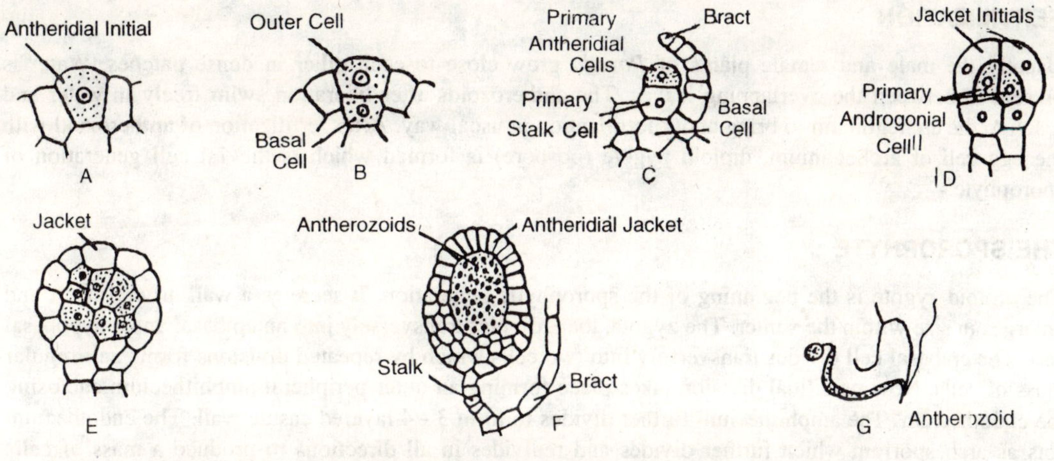

Fig. 28. *Porella* sp. A -E. Successive stages in the development of an antheridium, F. A mature antheridium, G. An antherozoid.

archegonia are at the top and the mature archegonia are at the base of the archegonial head. The apical cell of the archegonial branch fisrt develop into bracts and then the derivative of the apical cell functions as archegonial initial which increases in size and forms a papillate structure. The papillate outgrowth divides transversely to form a *basal* (pedicel) cell and a *distal* cell. The basal or pedicel cell divides repeatedly to form a stalk of the archegonium. The distal cell acts as archegonial mother cell. It divides vertically into surrounding peripheral cells and a primary axial cell. The peripheral cells give rise to neck and the primary axial cell divides into primary cover cell and central cell. Primary cover cell forms 4 cover cells of the neck and the central cell divides into primary neck canal cell and primary venter cell. The primary neck canal cell divides to form 6 - 8 neck canal cells and the primary venter cell divides to form a venter canal cell and an egg cell (Fig. 29). The jacket of venter and basal part of neck is two layered.

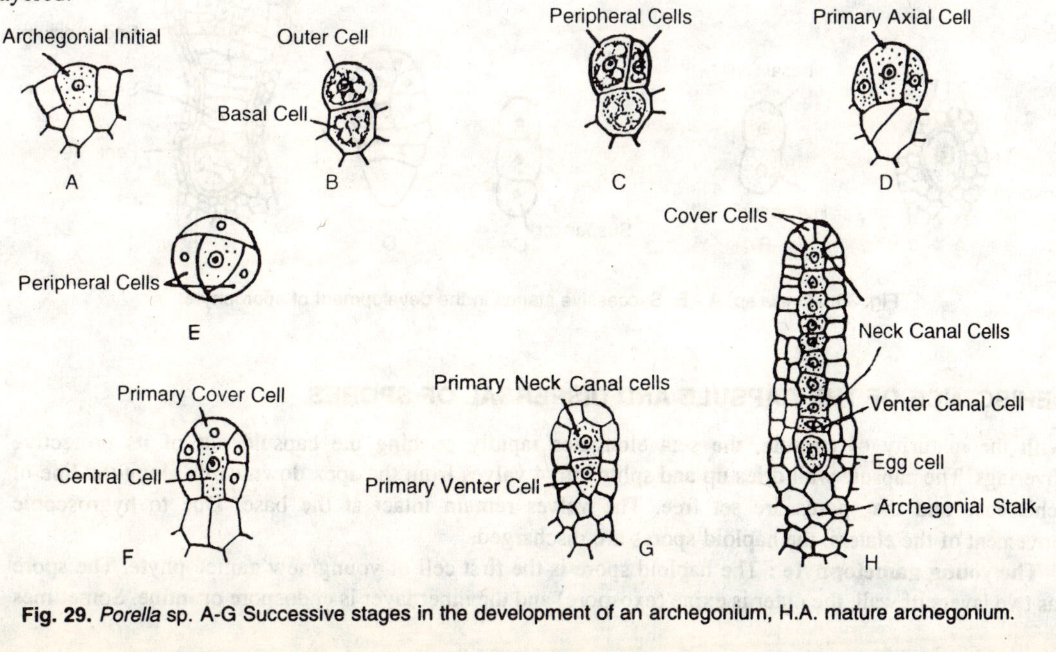

Fig. 29. *Porella* sp. A-G Successive stages in the development of an archegonium, H.A. mature archegonium.

FERTILIZATION

Usually the male and female plants of *Porella* grow close to each other in dense patches. Water is present in between the overlapping leaves. The antherozoids after liberation swim freely in water and reach to the archegonium to bring about fertilization in usual way. After fertilization of antherozoid with the egg cell of archegonium, diploid zygote (oospore) is formed which is the 1st cell generation of sporophyte.

THE SPOROPHYTE

The diploid zygote is the beginning of the sporophytic generation. It secretes a wall around itself and enlarges in size within the venter. The zygote, then, divides transversely into an epibasal and a hypobasal cell. The epibasal cell divides transversely into two cells which by repeated divisions forms an irregular mass of cells. Now periclinal division takes place forming an outer peripheral amphithecium enclosing the endothecium. The amphithecium further divides to form 3 - 4 layered casule wall. The endothecium acts as archesporium which further divides and redivides in all directions to produce a mass of cells called sporogenous tissue. The sporogenous tissue later differentiates into elater mother cells and spore mother cells. The spore mother cells divides meiotically to give rise haploid spores. The elater mother cells directly develop into elongated elaters with tapering ends and spiral bands. The foot and seta originate from the lower part of the embryo or endothecium.

Thus, a sporophyte has a globose capsule, a short indistinct seta and a less conspicuous bulbous foot. The young sporophyte is protected by three coverings viz. (1) the multilayered calyptra formed from the venter of the archegonium, (2) the perianth formed by the union of the bracts of the archegonium and (3) the involucre formed by fertile bracts of the archegonail branch. (Fig. 30).

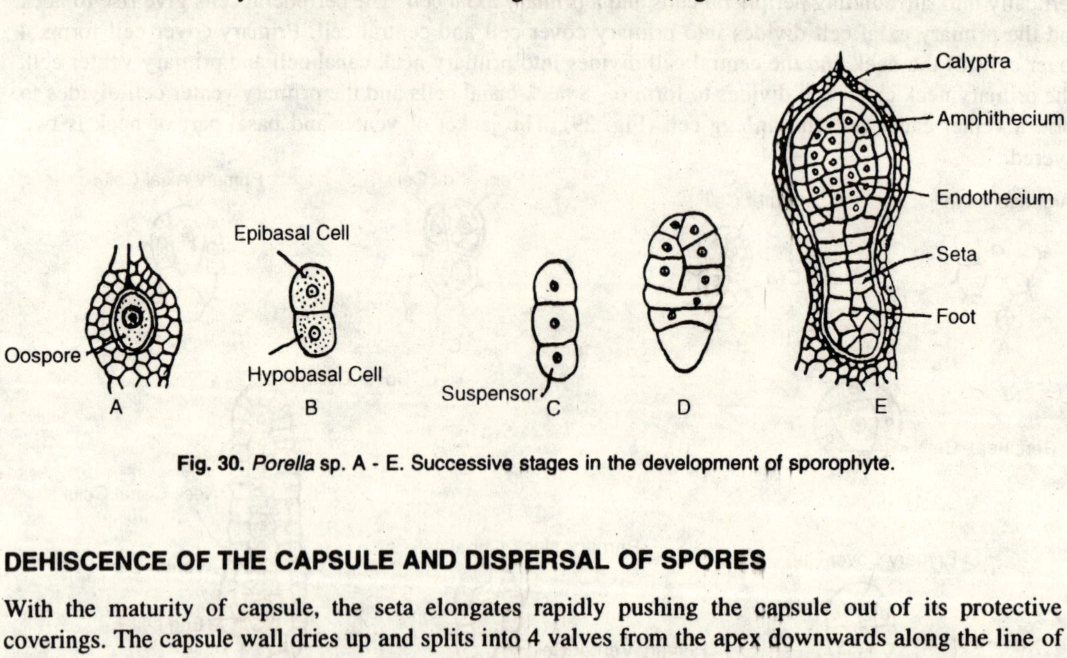

Fig. 30. *Porella* **sp. A - E. Successive stages in the development of sporophyte.**

DEHISCENCE OF THE CAPSULE AND DISPERSAL OF SPORES

With the maturity of capsule, the seta elongates rapidly pushing the capsule out of its protective coverings. The capsule wall dries up and splits into 4 valves from the apex downwards along the line of dehiscence and the spores are set free. The valves remain intact at the base. Due to hygroscopic movement of the elaters, the haploid spores are discharged.

The young gametophyte : The haploid spore is the first cell of young/new gametophyte. The spore has two layers of wall, the outer is exine (exospore) and the inner layer is endospore or intine. Sometimes an additional layer - Perigynium is found outside the exine.

Spore germinates while within the capsule and hence the spores are multicellular at the time of its dispersal. Soon after falling the spore on a suitable substratum it germinates into leafy gametophyte through a thalloid protonemal stage (Fig. 31, 32).

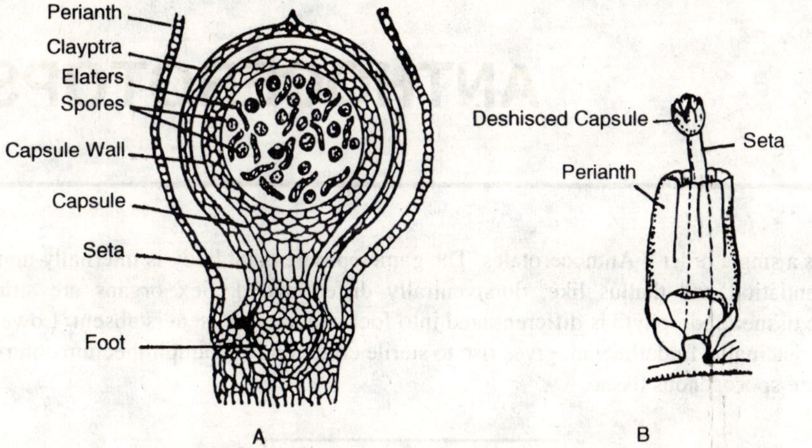

Fig. 31. ***Porella*** **sp. A mature sporophyte in L.S., B. Mature capsule after dehiscence.**

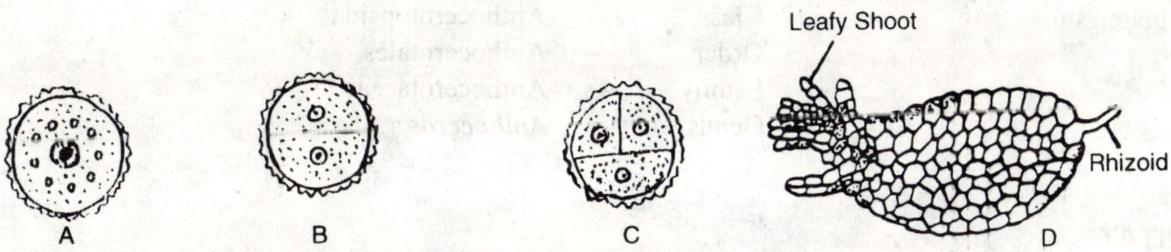

Fig. 32. ***Porella*** **sp. A - C stages of spore germination, D. Young gametophyte.**

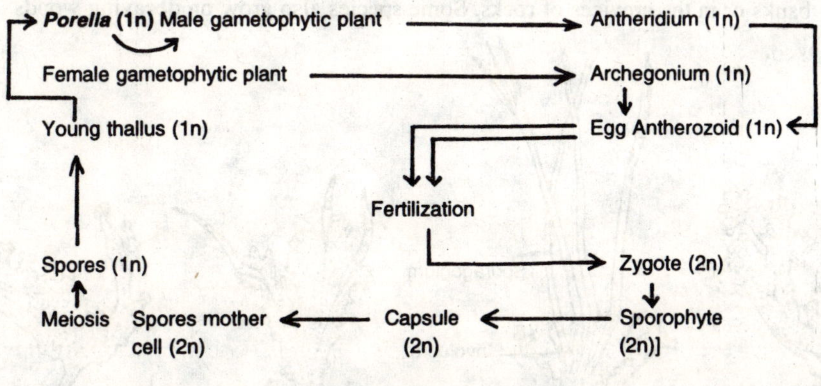

Graphic life cycle of *Porella*

CHAPTER 3

ANTHOCEROTOPSIDA

This class has a single order – Anthocerotales. The gametophytic plant body is internally homogenous in tissue differentiation and thallus like, dorsiventrally differentiated. Sex organs are situated in the gametophytic tissue. Sporophyte is differentiated into foot and capsule, seta is absent. Lower part of the capsule is meristematic. Endothecium gives rise to sterile columella and amphithecium contributes in the development of sporogenous tissue.

3.1. ANTHOCEROS

It belongs to

Class	—	Anthocerotopsida
Order	—	Anthocerotales
Family	—	Anthocerotaceae
Genus	—	*Anthoceros*

HABITAT

There are about 200 species in the genus *Anthoceros* confined to temperate and tropical regions of both the hemisphere. From India, about 25 species have been reported. Some common species of them are *A. erectus*, *A. himalayensis*, *A. crispulus* etc. Anthoceros grows in shady and very moist places near ditches, clay banks or in the crevices of rocks. Some species also grow on decaying woods.

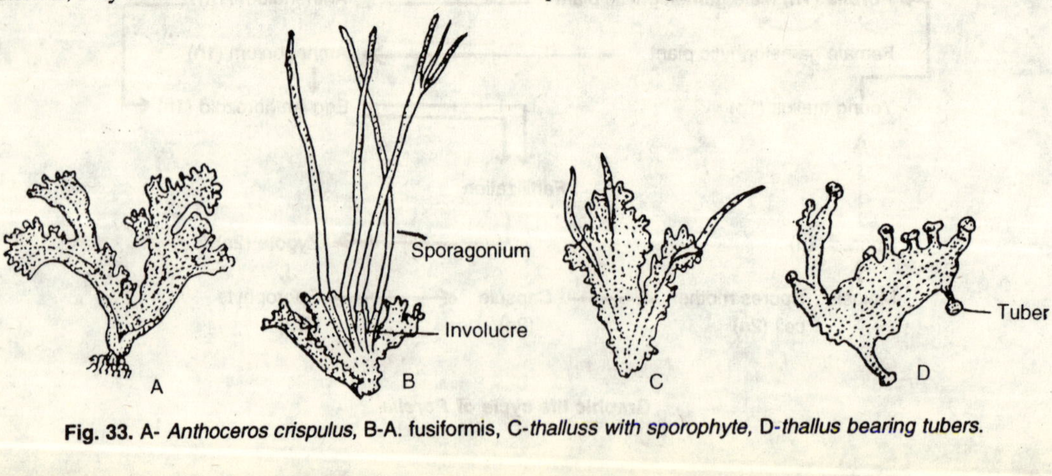

Fig. 33. A- *Anthoceros crispulus*, B-A. fusiformis, C-*thalluss with sporophyte*, D-*thallus bearing tubers.*

EXTERNAL MORPHOLOGY

The gametophytic plant body is small, dorsiventral, dark green and prostrate thallus like. the thallus is variously lobed, thicker in the region of midrib. From the ventral surface only smooth walled rhizoids are attached. Scales are absent (Fig. 33)

ANATOMY OF THALLUS

Vertical section of the thallus shows no tissue differentiation. The thallus is made up of soft parenchymatous cells. Each cell has chloroplast in which pyrenoid is centrally located a characteristics of green algae, but the pyrenoids of *Anthoceros* are not homologus to those of green algae. In the ventral

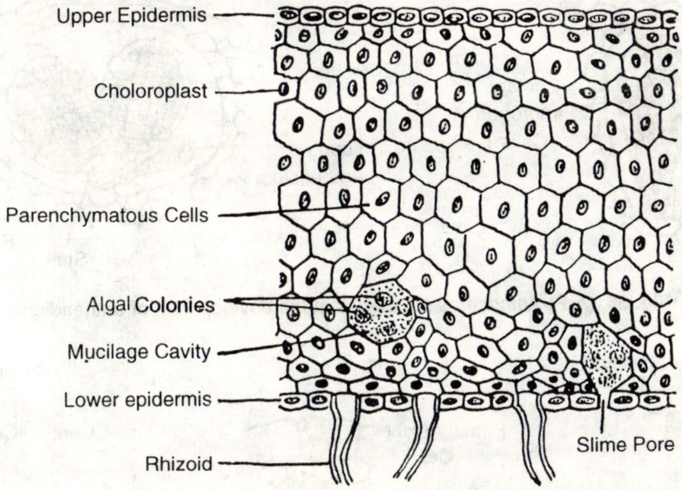

Fig. 34. V.S. of thallus of *Anthoceros sp.*

side intercellular cavities filled with mucilage are present which open to the ventral surface as slime pores. The slime pores are generally inhabited by endophytic *Nostoc* Fig. 34).

VEGETATIVE REPRODUCTION

Vegetative reproduction in *Anthoceros* takes place by progressive death of the older parts followed by growth of the apical region. Some tubers are formed on the margin of the thallus. These tubers have outer corky layer. In favourable condition it germinates into new plants.

SEXUAL REPRODUCTION

Anthoceros is homothallic (*A. himalayensis*) as well as heterothallic (*A. erectus*). The homothallic species are protandrous i.e. antheridia mature earlier.

Antheridia — It develops in clusters from the hypodermal cell of the thallus. They are enclosed within antheridial chamber. Mature antheridium is a club shaped, stalked and has a jacket of one layer ofcells containing many androcytes which form linear and biflagellate antherozoids (Fig. 35).

Archegonia —It develop singly from superficial cell of the thallus and are produced in acropetal succession. It has no stalk and embeded in the thallus, in direct contact with vegetative cells. The archegonia are formed later in the monoecious species. The archegonium has surrounding mound of mucilage looks like a funnel (Fig. 36).

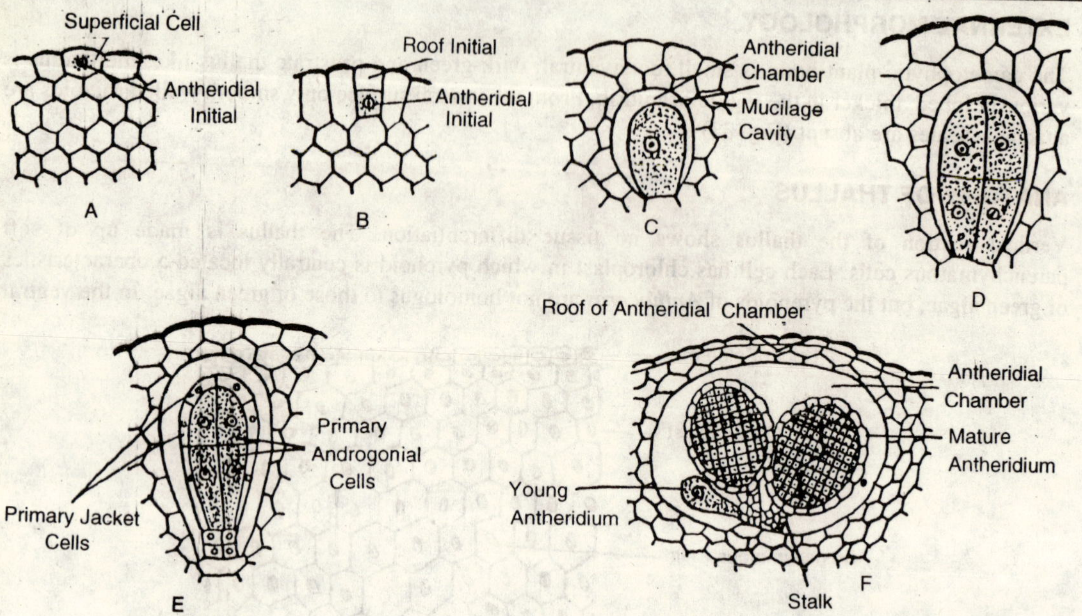

Fig. 35. (A-F) *Anthoceros sp.* Stages in the development of antheridium.

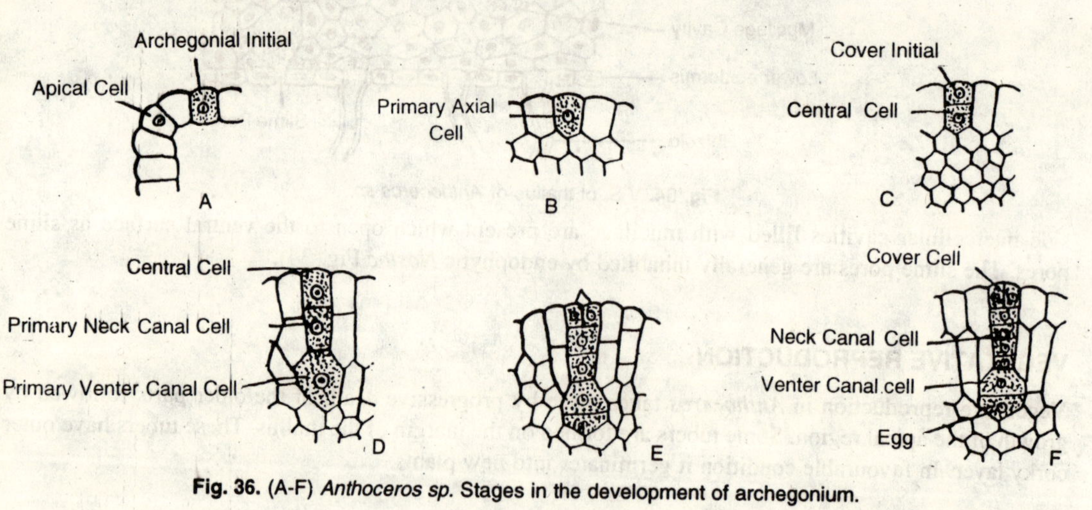

Fig. 36. (A-F) *Anthoceros sp.* Stages in the development of archegonium.

The mature archegonium consists of a vertical row of 4-6 neck canal cells, a ventral canal cell and an egg. The four cover cells at the neck protrude slightly above the general surface of the thallus.

Before fertilization occurs, the neck canal cells and ventral cell disorganise and gelatinise and the cover cells separate forming a direct passage to the egg.

FERTILIZATION

Only one of the antherozoids enter through the neck and fertilises the egg, resulting in the formation of a diploid zygote. The diploid zygote is the beginning of the sporophytic generation.

SPOROPHYTE

After fertilization the diploid zygote increases in its size to fill the venter and secretes a wall around itself. The zygoe divides vertically into two daughter cells. These two cells again divide transversely into four celled structure i.e. quadrant. The quadrant again divides vertically at right angle to the previous vertical division forming octant or proembryo of two tiers of four cells each. The lower tier of four cells give rise to foot and the upper tier of four cells develop into capsule. The upper four cells divide transversely and then periclinally into an outer amphithecium and inner endothecium. The endothecium gives rise to columelle i.e. central sterile axis and the amphithecium further divides periclinally into an outer initial of jacket layer and an inner sporogenous layer called archesporium. The jacker initial divides to form wall of the capsule, 4 - 6 layers in thickness. The archesporium breaks up into alternate layers of sterile pseudoelaters and spore mother cells. Pseudoelaters are rod shaped devoid of spiral thickenings unlike elaters. Each spore mother cell divides meiotically to form four haploid spores. The mature sporophyte contains bulbous foot and smooth, slender capsule. The capsule shows all the stages of sporogenesis. The basal part is meristematic and the apical has mature spores and in between the two extremities are intermediate stages. Seta is absent but a meristematic zone is present which helps in

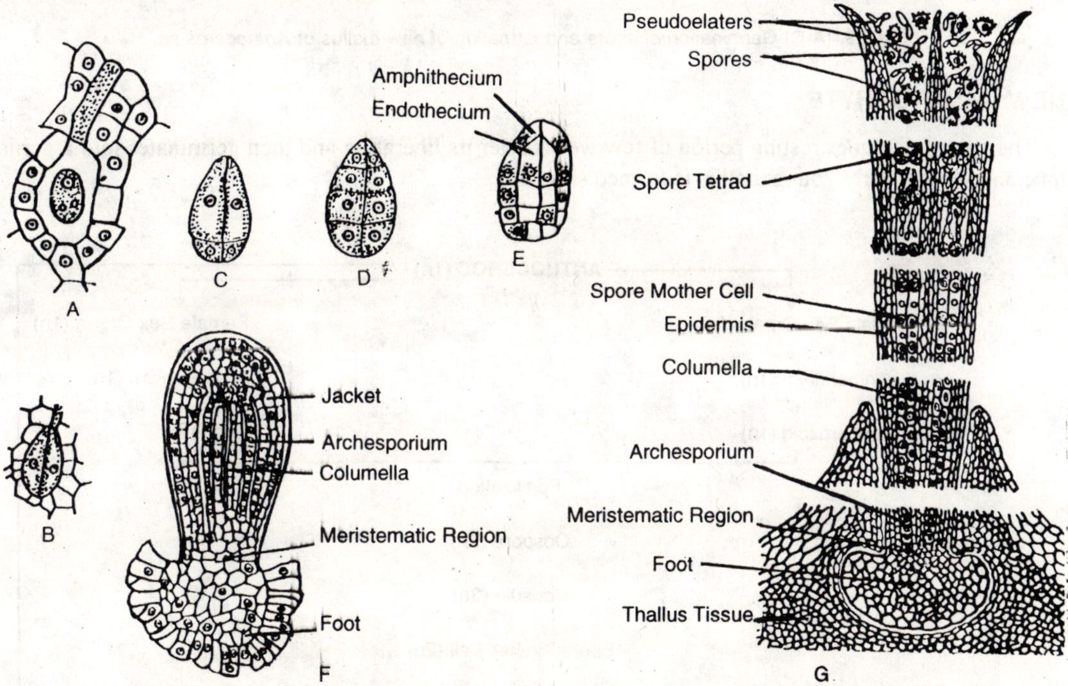

Fig. 37. (A-F) Stages in the development of sporophyte of *Anthoceros sp.*

growth of the capsule. The capsule has a central sterile axis columella, which is 16 celled structure as seen in transverse section. The capsule wall is 4 - 6 layers of cells. The outer wall is epidermis having stomata (Fig. 37).

SPORE DISPERSAL

In dry condition, capsule loses water and the tip of capsule gets shriveled and dehiscence of the capsule takes place by spliting into two valves and thus spores are exposed upon the columella. With the help of hygroscopic movement of valves, pseudoelaters and columella, spores are liberated and taken away by air current.

The haploid spores are the beginning of gametophytic generation.

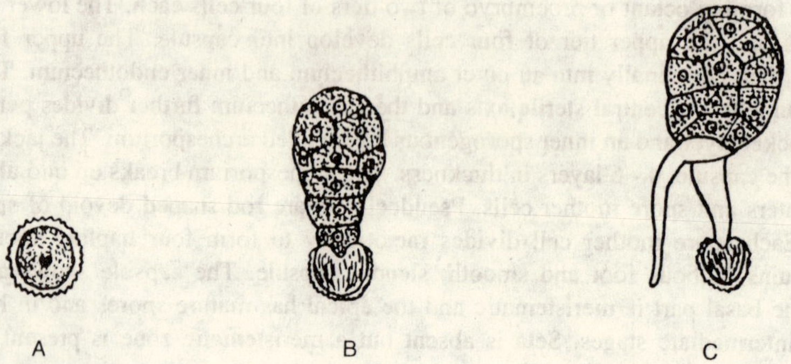

Fig. 38. (A-C) Germination of spore and formation of new thallus of *Anthoceros sp.*

NEW GAMETOPHYTE

The spore undergoes resting period of few weeks after its liberation and then germinates into a germ tube and subsequently young thallus is formed (Fig. 38)

ANTHOCEROS (1n)

Male Sex Organ (1n) → Antheridium (1n) → Antherozoid (1n)

Female Sex Organ (1n) → Archegonium (1n) → Egg (1n)

Fertilization → Oospore (2n) → Capsule (2n) → Spore Mother Cell (2n) → Meiosis → Spores (1n) → Germination → ANTHOCEROS (1n)

Graphic life cycle in ***Anthoceros***

AFFINITIES OF *ANTHOCEROS*

Anthoceros shows some features which are common with Algae, Bryophyta and Pteridophyta as follows:-

Features common with Chlorophyceae :-

1. Presence of pyrenoid in the chloroplast.
2. Simple, green, flattened thallus like gametophytic plant body resembles with green algae.
3. Occurrence of biflagellate antherozoids.

Features common with Hepaticopsida :-

1. Absence of tuberculate rhizoids and similarity in the form and structure of gametophyte like *Pellia*.
2. Occurrence of apical growth of the thallus lobes.
3. Presence of biflagellate antherozoids.
4. Differentiation of archesporium into spore mother cells and sterile cells.

Features common with Bryopsida.

1. Presence of columella, endothelial in origin resembles *Sphagnum*
2. Reduction in the archesporium sporogenous tissue.
3. Presence of stomata in sporophyte as in *Funaria*
4. Origin of archesporium from inner amphithecium.

Features common with Pteridophyta :-

1. Similarity in the structure of thallus of *Anthoceros* with the prothallus of Pteridophyta (Ferns).
2. Position of sunken sex organs.
3. Similarity in the structure of archegonium.
4. Semiparasite sporophyte of *Anthoceros* resembles with fossil Psilophytales.

All these resemblances of *Anthoceros* with other groups of plant kingdom suggest that the *Anthoceros* is a synthetic type.

3.2. NOTOTHYLAS

It belongs to

Class	—	Anthocerotopsida
Order	—	Anthocerotales
Family	—	Notothylaceae
Genus	—	*Notothylas.*

HABITAT

The genus *Notothylas* has a number of species (about 11 species) distributed in tropics and temperate regions. Out of these only four species namely *N. indica*, *N. chaudhurii*, *N. javanicus* and *N. levieri* are reported from India. They are found in humid, shady, areas on moist rocks and damp soil.

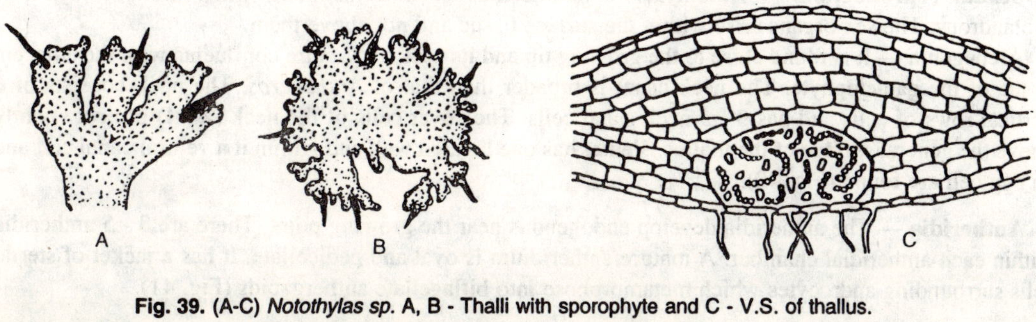

Fig. 39. (A-C) *Notothylas sp.* A, B - Thalli with sporophyte and C - V.S. of thallus.

EXTERNAL MORPHOLOGY

The thallus in thin and delicate, dorsiventrally differentiated. The plant body is gametophyte and it is orbicular or suborbicular in appearance. It is lobed and yellowish or light green in colour. From the ventral surface, smooth walled unicellular rhizoids arise, scales and tuberculated rhizoids are absent. Fig. 39).

ANATOMY OF THALLUS

Vertical section of the thallus shows 6 - 8 layers of cells in the middle portion forming midrib. Gradually it becomes thinner in the expanded portion of the thallus to single layer of cells at the margin. The cells of the limiting layer at the upper and lower surface are smaller in size than the cells in the interior. Soft parenchymatous cells are present in between the two limiting layers. Some cavities containg *Nostoc* and mucilage are also found. The mucilage cavities open by narrow slit at the ventral surface. The cell has chloroplast with a single pyrenod in each chloroplast (Fig. 39).

REPRODUCTION

It is of two types, (1) vegetative and (2) sexual.

Vegetative reproduction — It occurs by gemmae or ventral tubers. It also multiplies vegetatively by death and decay of older parts and the remaing younger part of the thallus develop into new gametophyte.

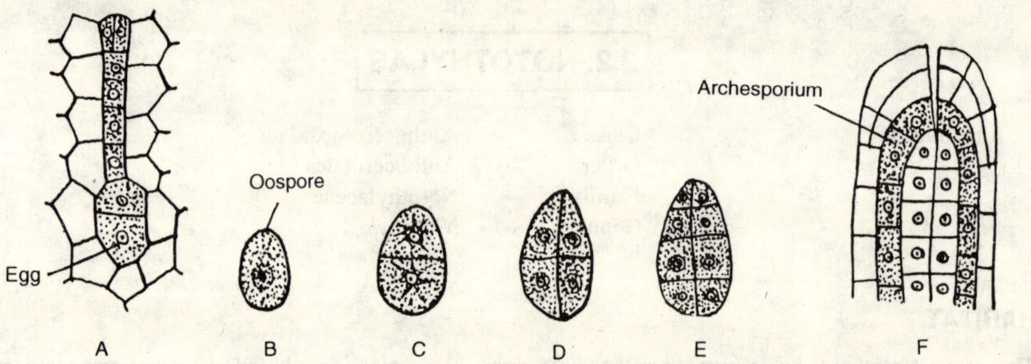

Fig. 40. (A-F) *Notothylas sp.* A - An archegonium, B - F development of capsule from oospore.

Sexual reproduction — *Notothylas* is monoecious or dioecius both, when monoecious, it is protandrous. The sex organs arise within the surface tissue and not above them.

Archegonia — It is found close to the growing tip and its neck and ventre confluents with the adjacent tissue of the gametophyte. The neck canal is broader than that of *Anthoceros.* The neck consists of 6 vertical rows of cells and has 3 - 5 neck canal cells. The cover cells of the neck (2 - 4) project slightly above the general surface of the thallus. Venter has one layered wall and within it a ventral canal cell and an egg cell are found (Fig. 40).

Antheridia — The antheridia develop endogenous near the growing point. There are 3 - 5 antheridia within each antheridial chamber. A mature antheridium is oval and pedicellate. It has a jacket of sterile cells surrounding androcytes which metamorphose into biflagellate antherozoids (Fig. 41).

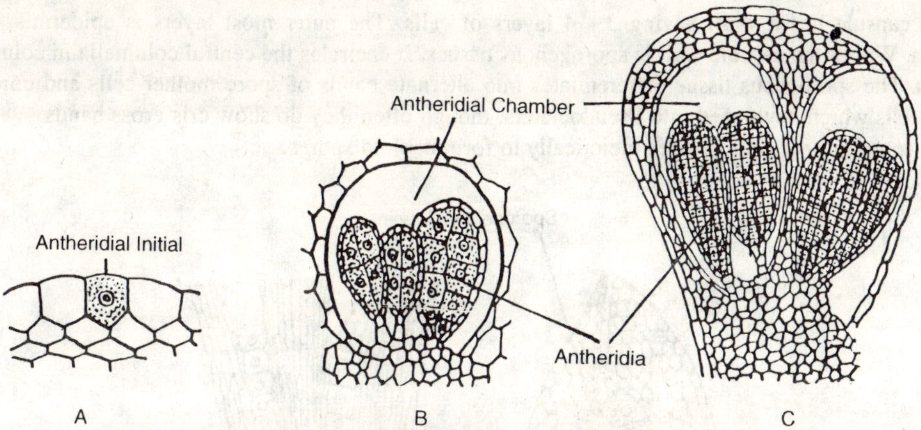

Fig. 41. (A-C) Stages in the development of antheridium of *Notothylas sp.*

FERTILIZATION

At maturity the neck canal cell and the ventral cell of the archegonium disintegrate and the canal widens into a cavity where the egg is situated. Cover cells are thrown off. A biflagellate antherozoid swimes down the canal and fuses with the egg to form a diploid zygote.

SPOROPHYTE

The zygote is the first cell of sporophytic generation. It swells to fill the venter cavity and secretes a wall around itself.

The zygote divides transversely followed by vertical division or vice-versa. Thus, an embryo of quadrate stage is formed. It again divides vertically into octant arranged in two tiers of four cells each. The cells of upper tier again divide transversely and thus there are 3 tier of 4 cells each. The cells of the upper tier form the capsule and the intermediate narrow zone. Foot is formed from the lower two tiers.

The periclinal division in the upper tier of 4 cells results into central endothecium and peripheral amphithecium. On the basis of the role of endothecium the *Notothylas* has been divided into two categories. (1) columellate species and (2) non-columellate species. In columellate species entire endothecium contribute in the formation of columella as in *N. indica.* In non–columellate type the entire endothecium forms the archesporium as in *N. chaudhurii.* Columella is entirely absent. Amphithecium forms the capsule wall. The archesporium is differentiated into alternate bands of spore mother cells and sterile cells. The spore mother cells divide meiotically into haploid spores.

Mature sporophyte

The mature sporophyte (sporogonium) is marginal in position and are born horizontally between the lobes usually in pairs (Fig. 42). The sporophyte is short, compact, about 3 mm in length and 0.5 mm in diameter. It is cylindrical but tapers towards both the ends. The sporogonium is surrounded by a thin envelop called involucre. The sporogonium can be divided into three parts, namely; the foot, the narrow intermediate zone and the capsule.

The foot absorbs water and nutrient from the parent thallus. The narrow intermediate zone shows little meristematic activity.

The capsule has a wall, having 3 - 4 layers of cells. The outer most layers is epidermis without stomata. Within the capsule wall is sporogenous tissues. It encircles the central columella in columellate species. The sporogeous tissue differentiates into alternate bands of spore mother cells and unicellular sterile cells which developed into Pseudoelaters, though often they do show cris-cross bands.

The spore mother cells divides meiotically to form haploid spores.

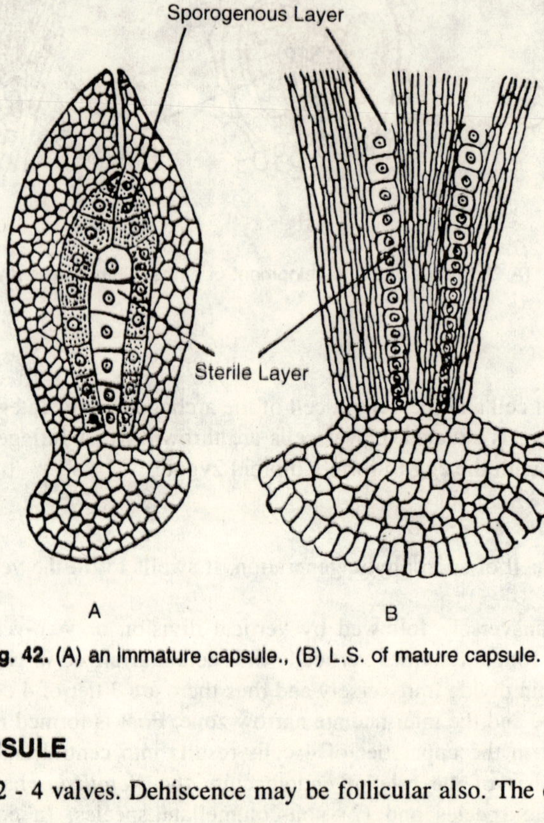

Fig. 42. (A) an immature capsule., (B) L.S. of mature capsule.

DEHISCENCE OF CAPSULE

The Capsule dehisces by 2 - 4 valves. Dehiscence may be follicular also. The capsule opens by one or two sutures.

NEW GAMETOPHYTE

Spore on dispersal, absorbs moisture and germinates. The exospore (outer wall) ruptures and the endospore (inner wall) bulges out in the form of a short papilla. The papilla divides transversely and vertically resulting into octant stage and finally it develops into new *Notothylas* plant.

AFFINITIES AND EVOLUTIONARY HISTORY OF *NOTOTHYLAS* :-

The gametophyte of *Notothylas* resembles with that of *Anthoceros* and liverworts. The sporophyte of *Notothylas* is different from that of *Anthoceros*. It grows horizontally from the thallose lobe in *Notothylas*. The *Notothylas* capsule is short and compact like liverworts. Endothecial origin of sporogenous tissue, absence of columella in some species of *Notothylas,* absence of stomata, photosynthetic tissue in the capsule wall and inactive basal meristem are common in Notothylas and liverworts. Thus, *Notothylas* can be considered as a link between liverworts and *Anthocerotales* (Horn worts).

The evolutionary position of *Notothylas* is debatable. According to Lang (1907) *Notothylas* is reduced member of Anthocerotales. It has evolved from a thallus like *Anthoceros* or some species of Anthoceros by a process of simplification like loss of columella as in the *Notothylas*. According to Cavers (1941) *Notothylas* is primitive. Absence of stomata and photosynthetic tissue in the capsule wall and presence of inactive basal meristem are all primitive characters in the *Notothylas*. Hence, *Notothylas* is primitive genus and *Anthoceros* is advanced genus which has evolved from *Notothylas* by progressive evolution.

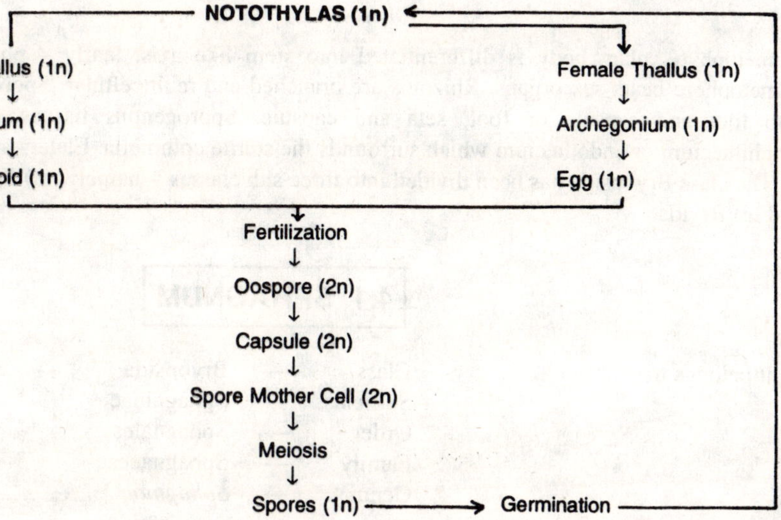

Graphic life cycle of ***Notothylas***

CHAPTER 4

BRYOPSIDA

Gametophytic plant body is differentiated into stem like axis, leafly – phylloid and rhizoids. The gametophore bears sex organs. Rhizoids are branched and multicellular. Sporophytes are differentiated into foot and capsule or foot, seta and capsule. Sporogenous tissues are derived from either amphithecium or endothecium which surrounds the sterile columella. Elaters are not present.

The class Bryopsida has been divided into three sub classes :- namely, (a) Sphagnidae, (b) Andreadae and (c) Bryidae.

4.1. SPHAGNUM

It belongs to

Class	—	Bryopsida
Sub-class	—	Sphagnidae
Order	—	Sphagnales
Family	—	Sphagnaceae
Genus	—	*Sphagnum*

HABITAT

It is commonly known as "Peat moss" or "Turf moss" or "Bog moss". *Sphagnum* has about 342 species distributed in temperate, tropic, sub arctic and sub antarctic zones in both the hemispheres. It grows in dense masses in ponds, swamps, margins of the lakes, moist hill sides etc. Sharma (1949) has reported 17 species of *Sphagnum* from India. Some common Indian species are *S. ovatum*, *S. robustrum*, *S. khasianum*, *S. squarrosum* etc. Generally, the gemetophytic plant of *Sphagnum* is perennial. The upper part of the gemetophyte continues to grow from year to year while the lower parts die.

During the metabolism of *Sphagnum*, certain acids are liberated. Owing to presence of acidic environment there is little decay of dead basal portions of the gemetophyte (gametophore). In this way there is a constant increase in the mass of dead but partially decomposed gametophytic tissue along with other plant remains from year to year. These tissues are slowly compressed by increasing weight of the fresh layers of dead tissues above it and consequently it hardens into a compact, dark substances rich in carbon known as peat and therefore the name peat moss has been assigned to the genus *Sphagnum*. The peat is converted into peat coal after longer duration.

EXTERNAL MORPHOLOGY

The gemetophyte shows two distinct stages (1) juvenile stage of simple thallose, one cell thick protonema and (2) mature, leafly shoot - the gametophore. The gametophore has an upright stem bearing leaves and leafy branches. The weak stem bear lateral branches. Branches are of two types (1) Long and pendent branches in tufts of 3 arising from the axils of leaves on the stem. (2) Short branches of limited

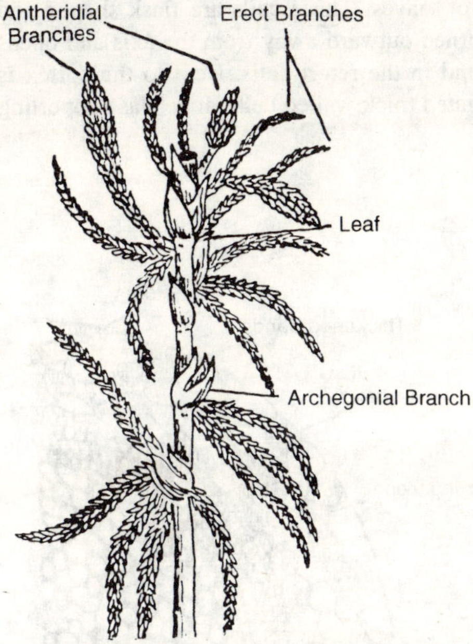

Fig. 43. Gametophore bearing archegonial and antheridial branch of *Sphagnum sp.*

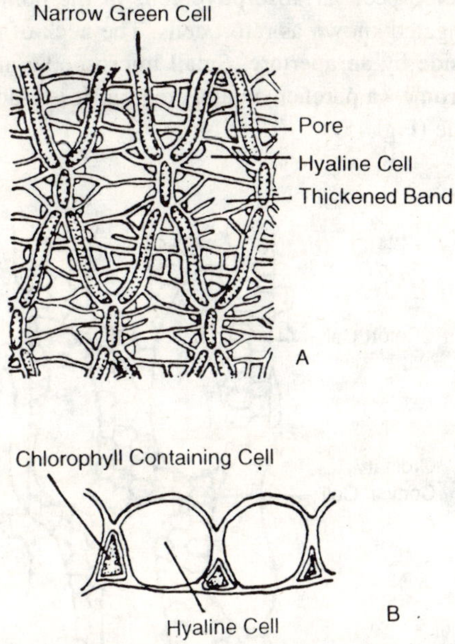

Fig. 44. (A,B) *Sphagnum sp.* A - arrangement of cells in a leaf, B - T.S. of leaf showing green and hyaline cell.

growth near the apex of the stem forming coma or head or comal tufts (Fig 43).

Leaves — Leaves occur on the main stem and the branches. The leaves are sessile small and are arranged spirally in three vertical rows on the axis. The midrib is absent. The apex is acute and the margin is entire. The leaves show two different types of cells in surface view. namely (1) narrow, living and chlorophyll containing cells and (2) dead, rhomboidal, hyaline cells with pores and spiral thickening. The pores cause the leaf to absorb and retain water like a sponge. Therefore, the hyaline cells are also known as capillary cells. The *Sphagnum* leaves play an important role in the absorption and retention of water due to the presence of dead capillary cells. This fact is made use of utilizing the *Shpagnum* as packing material to pack live plants or its parts like bulbs, cuttings, seedlings and other aquatic animals which otherwise would die in absence of water. It is also used in seed beds and green houses to root cuttings and as stable litter and bedding.

ANTOMY OF LEAVES

Transverse section of young leaf shows square or rectangular cells but it is wedges shaped in mature leaf. It alternates with small living chlorophyllous cells. The leaves are one cell in thickness (Fig. 44)

ANATOMY OF STEM

Transverse section of the stem shows well differentiation of tissue into three zones. These are (1) cortex or hyalodermis (2) parenchymatous zone or hadrome and (3) axial cylinder or medulla.

The outer cortex is one cell thick in young stem but many cells thick in mature stem. The cortical cells in older stem becomes spongy and store water like velamen in orchid roots. It (the cortical cells) absorb water by capillary action and compensate for the absence of rhizoids in the adult gemetophyte.

The cortex of the side branches are one cell thick. In *S. molluscum* and others the cortical cells develop peculiar absorptive cells at the point of insertion of leaves. These cells are flask shaped and elongated known as retort cells. The neck of retort cell is turned outward away from the axis and opens outside by an aperture. Small microscopic animals are found in the retort cells. Next to the cortex is hadrome - a parenchymatous region. It is made up of elongated thick walled cells. It acts as supporting tissue (Fig. 45).

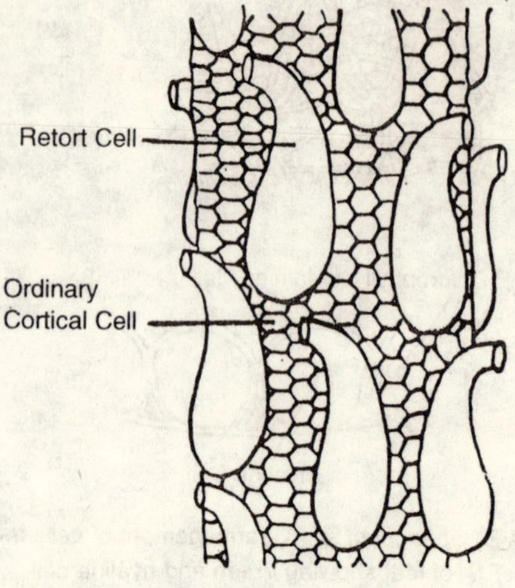

Fig. 45. Retort cells in the stem cortex of *Sphagnum sp.*

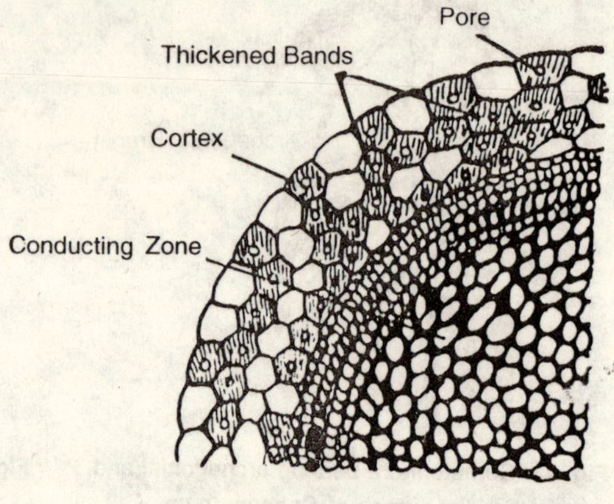

Fig. 46. T.S. of stem of *Sphagnum squarrosum* (A sector).

The medulla or axial cylinder forms the core of the stem. It is made up of colourless collenchymatous cells. The medulla is equivalent to the pith of the higher plants and act as storage region (Fig. 46).

VEGETATIVE REPRODUCTION

There is no special structure for vegetative propagation. There is progressive disintegration of the stem from the basal older parts to upwards causing the branches to cut off and developing into new independent gemetophyte plants.

Sphagnum also propagate by means of innovation. Sometimes one of the branches in the axillary cluster turn upward and grows upward. This long upright branch acquires all the characteristics of main axis. It is known as innovation. The basal older part of the innovation die and is separated from the main stem and finally establishes itself as an independent plant.

Woester (1934) observed in *S. palustre* that the buds and plates of cells from the young growing apices of stems and young leaves develop into new leafly gametophyte.

Vegetative reproduction also occurs by multiplication of protonemal stage. Primary protonema may become meristematic and forms a green cellular filament. The apical part of this green filament develops into thallus like flat, green, secondary protonema. From marginal cells of the secondary protonema arises the leafy gametophyte. Redhead (1981) discovered gemmae on *S. capillaceum* which are double walled and globose in appearance. They occur in cluster or double even singly. It gives rise a small uniseriate filamentous protonema followed by prothallus.

SEXUAL REPRODUCTION

Sphagnum may be dioecious or monoecious. In monoecious species, sex organs are born on different branches of the same plant. Sex organs are born on modified short branches (Fig. 47).

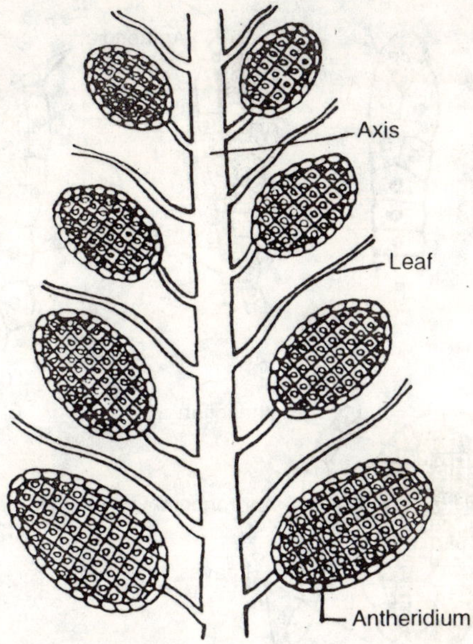

Fig. 47. L.S. of an antheridial branch of *Sphagnum* showing arrangement of leaves and antheridia on the axis.

Antheridia — In monoecious from the anthridia i.e. male sex organs are found on special leafy branches like catkins. Solitary, globular and long stalked antheridium develops in the axil of the leaf. Mature antheridium has a long stalk made up of 2 - 4 rows of cells. The globular body is covered by a jacket of single layer of cells. Within the jacket are many sperm mother cells which is metamorphosed into sperms. Each sperm or antherozoid is biflagellate and spirally coiled on maturity. The jacket wall near the apex of the antheridium is ruptured and the sperms are liberated (Fig. 48).

Archegonia — The archegonia are born on the apex of short and green archegonial branches. archegonial leaves are larger and there are usually three archegonia on each branch. (Fig. 49).

Mature archegonium has a long stalk, a long twisted neck and a venter. The venter and the neck are not very distinct. The venter is two to three celled thick. The upper part of the neck is one cell in thickness. The primary cover cell constitutes the terminal part of the neck. The neck consists of six vertical rows of neck cells. Usually 8 or 9 neck canal cells are in the neck. The venter has a ventral canal cell and an egg (Fig. 50).

FERTILIZATION

Fertilization takes place in presence of water. A film of water is essential for the sperms to reach the neck of the archegonium. The sperm or antherozoid fuses with the egg and zygote is formed. Zygote of one archegonium in a group develops into sporogonium (sporophyte) while zygotes of other archegonia degenerate. The zygote enlarges in size and secretes a wall around itself.

SPOROPHYTE OR SPOROGONIUM

The zygote divides transversely into two cells. These further divide transversely resulting in the formation of a short filament or 6 - 12 cells. The upper 3 - 4 cells develop into capsule while foot and seta develop from the rest of the cells. Each cell in the upper region divides by two successive vertical

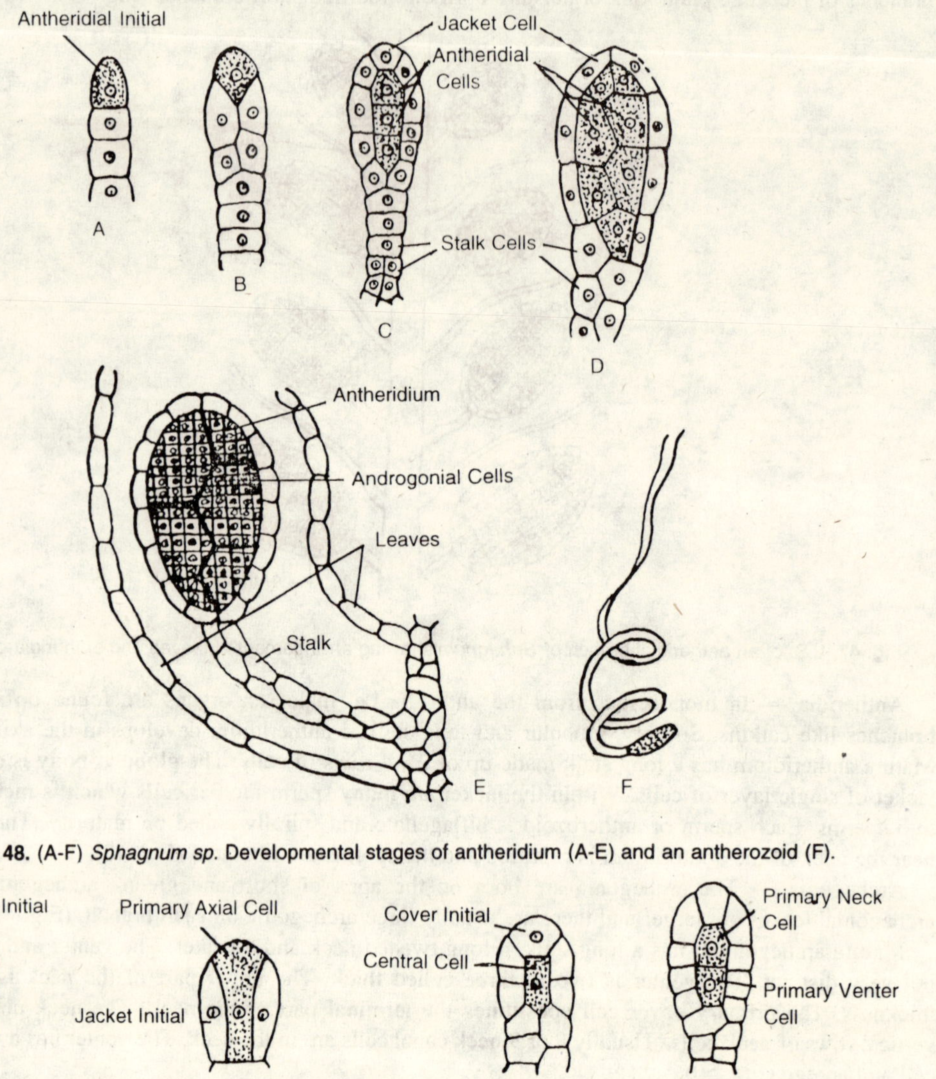

Fig. 48. (A-F) *Sphagnum sp.* Developmental stages of antheridium (A-E) and an antherozoid (F).

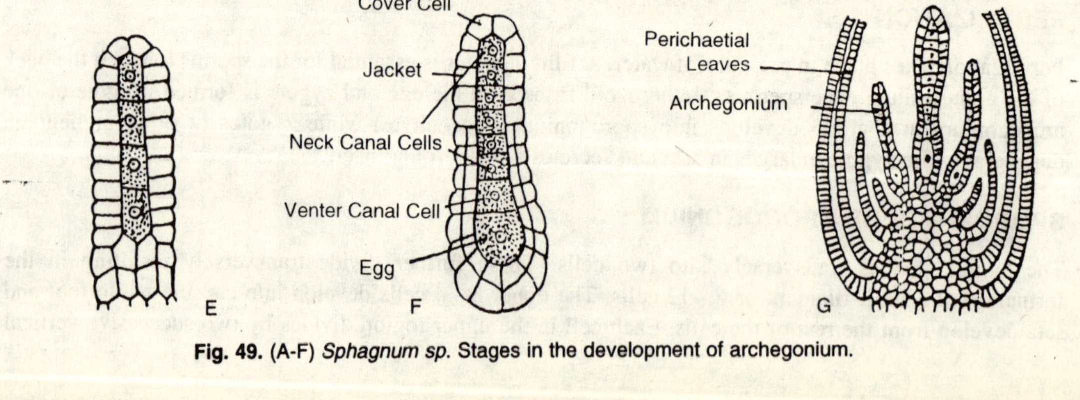

Fig. 49. (A-F) *Sphagnum sp.* Stages in the development of archegonium.

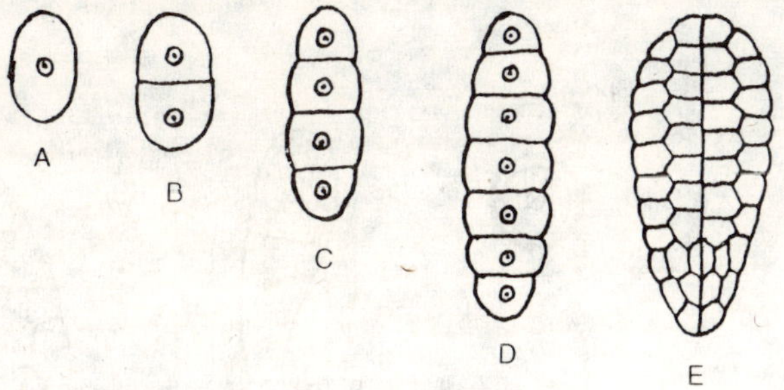

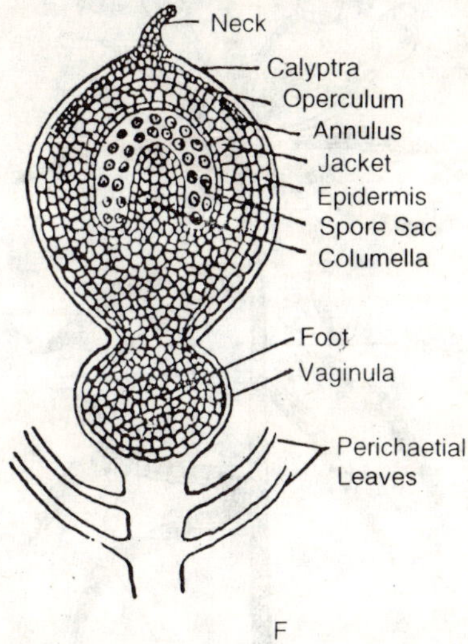

Fig. 51. (A-F) Stages in the development of sporogonium of *Sphagnum sp.*

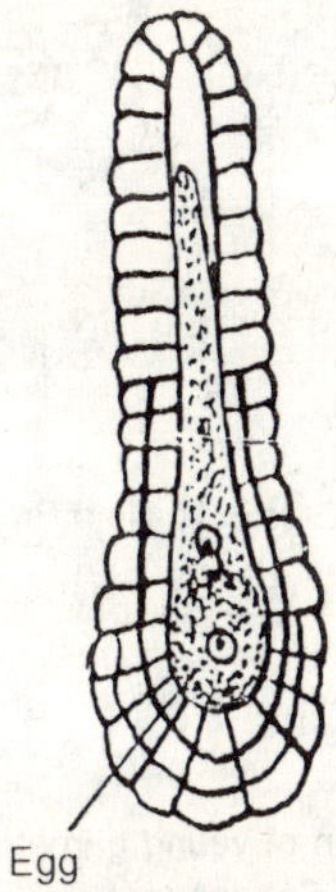

Fig. 50. A mature archegonium of Sphagnum sp.

division into a quadrant followed by periclinal divisions leading to the formation of central endothecium surrounded by amphithecium. Endothecium develops into mass of central sterile tissue known as columella. The amphithecium again divides periclinally into inner sporogenous tissue or archesporium and outer jacket layer (Fig. 51). The mature sporogonium or sporophyte consists of a bulbous foot or haustorium and a small spherical capsule. A short narrow, neck like seta connects the capsule and foot. The capsule has a central columella overarched by a dome shaped spore sac having haploid spores. The outer layer of capsule wall is of epidermis with non–functional stomata. A disc like circular operculum is present at the apex of the capsule. The operculum is separated from the rest of the capsule by annulus which is a circular groove of thin cells. The mature sporogonium or sporophyte is situated on an elongated axis called pseudopodium and the sporogonium is protected by calyptra. The basal part of the calyptra and the distal end of the pseudopodium together form a sac like structure known as vaginula. The foot of the sporophyte is embeded within the vaginula (Fig. 52).

DEHISCENCE OF CAPSULE AND FORMATION OF NEW GAMETOPHYTE

Dehiscence of capsule in *Sphagnum* occurs in sunny days. The columella of the capsule dries and shrivels and is replaced by air. Air creats a pressure in the columella as a result of which the capsule becomes almost spherical. In the meantime, air in the capsule below the spore sac is compressed and the operculum is forcibly hurled off and coloured, dry, powdery spores are ejected.

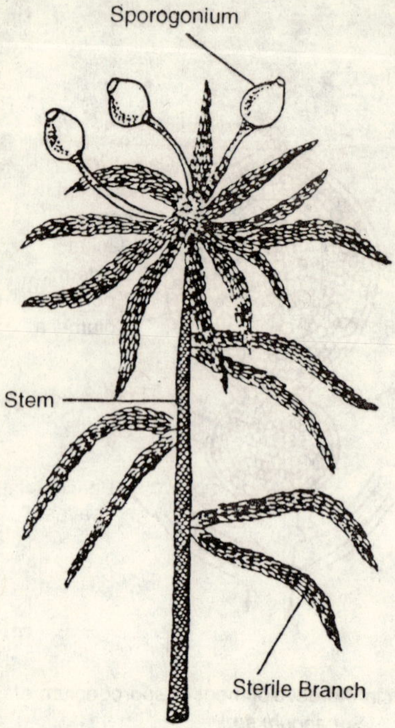

Fig. 52. *Sphagnum* plant with sporogonium.

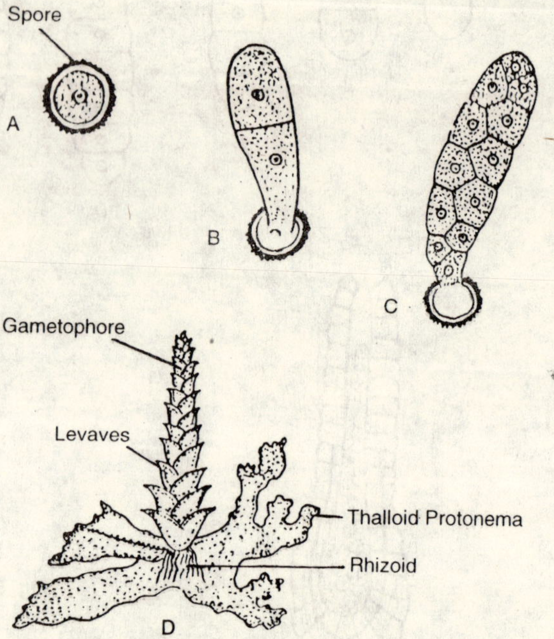

Fig. 53. (A-D) Stages in the formation of young gametophyte (D), from spore (A) in *Sphagnum*.

SPHAGNUM (1n)

Male branch (1n) ↓ Antheridium (1n) ↓ Antherozoid (1n)

Female branch (1n) ↓ Archegonium (1n) ↓ Egg (1n)

↓ Fertilization ↓ Oospore (2n) ↓ Capsule (2n) ↓ Spore Mother Cell (2n) ↓ Meiosis ↓ Spores (1n) → Germination → SPHAGNUM (1n)

Graphic life cycle of ***Sphagnum***

Under favourable conditions the haploid spores germinates into a filamentous primary protonemal structure. This again gives rise to flat thallose secondary protonema with rhizoids. The secondary protonema bears leaf, bud i.e gametophore and ultimately gives rise to adult *Sphagnum* (Fig. 53).

RELATIONSHIP OF SPHAGNUM WITH MOSSES

Sphagnum resembles mosses in the following characters —

1. Leafy upright gametophore.
2. Multicellular rhizoids with oblique septa,
3. Structure of archegonium with a massive venter and long stalk,
4. Absence of elaters,
5. Dehiscence of capsule by the separation of operculum,
6. Presence of pseudopodium as in Andreales.

Characters common with Anthocerotales – *Sphagnum* resembles Anthocerotae in the following features :-

1. Absence of apical growth in the sporophyte,
2. Origin of archesporium from amphithecium,
3. Dome shaped archesporium overarching the columella,
4. Columella formation from endothecium,
5. Presence of constriction like seta and massive foot.

RELATIONSHIP OF SPHAGNUM WITH JUNGERMANNIALES

Sphagnum resemble with Jungermanniales in the following characters :-

1. Flat disc shaped protonema,
2. Axillary antheridia,
3. Position and development of archegonia,
4. Presence of non–functional stomata on the capsule wall.

CHARACTERISTIC FEATURES OF *SPHAGNUM*

1. Absence of rhizoids in the adult gametophore.
2. Origin of branches in tufts in the axil of every fourth leaf.
3. Absence of midrib in the leaves,
4. Spongy cortex with retort cells,
5. Leaves with hyaline cells and assimilatory cells,
6. Unique physiology of water absorption, retension and conduction,
7. Presence of certain organic substances of colloidal nature in cell wall. It absorbs bases and releases acid and hence water is acidic in which *Sphagnum* grows.

Thus, *Sphagnum* links the three classes of Bryophyta and has its own peculiar characters. Thus, *Sphagnum* may be treated as synthetic type.

ECONOMIC IMPORTANCE OF *SPHAGNUM*

1. The peat deposits of *Sphagnum* are used as fuel,
2. Dried, cleaned and sterilized *Sphagnum* is used as guaze to dress wounds and surgical dressing in hospitals,
3. Dried *Sphagnum* is remoistened and used for packing live plants and cut flowers,
4. It acts as soil builder.

ECOLOGICAL IMPORTANCE

Sphagnum is of great ecological importance. Due to extensive growth it covers the surface of water in the lake. The plants are interwined so as to give the appearance of solid soil. Such areas are called quacking bogs. Hydrophytes, grow on the bog. The moss plants gradually die and settle on the bottom. In the course of long period these ponds, lakes, swamps become filled with partially decomposed old parts of this moss and other hydrophytic plant bodies. Ultimately these are converted into solid soil. Later, the hydrophytic plants are replaced by mesophytic plants. Thus, *Sphagnum* modifies the landscape.

4.2. POGONATUM

It belongs to	Class	—	Bryopsida
	Order	—	Polytrichales
	Family	—	Polytrichaceae
	Genus	—	*Pogonatum*

HABIT AND HABITAT

It has about 200 species distributed in cool, temperate and tropical regions of the world. About 34 species are reported from India. Some of these are *P. microstonum*, *P. junghunianum*, *P. aloides* etc.

The adult gamietophytic plant body is differentiated into basal rhizoids and erect upright stem covered with leaves. Lower leaves are scale like, smaller and pale in colour. The upper leaves are spirally arranged on the stem. Leaf base is sheathing. Each leaf has mid rib which is covered with parallel longitudinal vertical plate like structures known as lamellas. (Fig. 54).

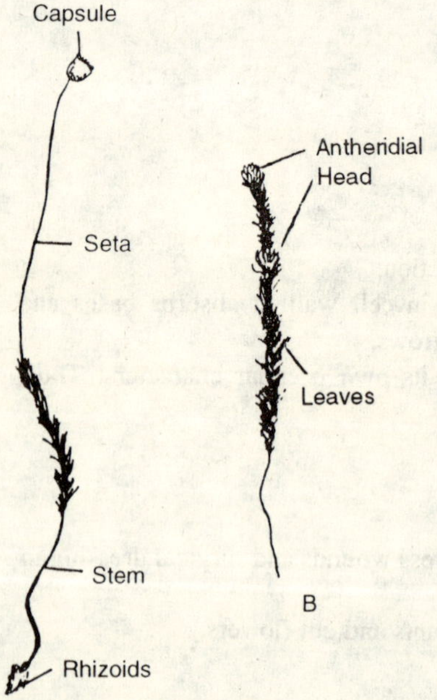

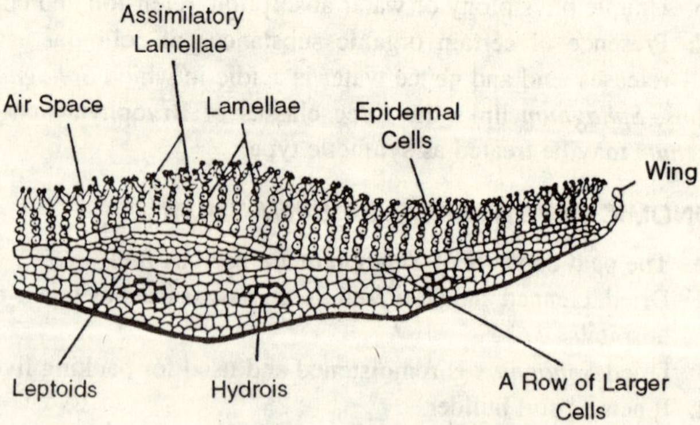

Fig. 54. (A,B) *Pogonatum* sp. A - female plant, B - male plant.

Fig. 55. T.S. of rhizome of *Pogonatum* sp.

The rhizoids absorb water and act as anchorage organs. It may bear buds which are meant for vegetative propagation.

The *Pogonatum* grow in damp soil, on moist rocks, in swampy places and under shade of trees. They are found at an altitude of 3000 - 8000 feet in the Himalayan region and South Indian hills.

ANATOMY OF LEAF

Transverse section of the leaf shows the following organisations. It has upper and lower epidermis. From the upper epidermis arise numerous filamentous structure, each of 3-4 cells in a single row. The terminal cell is in the form of a paired bottle shaped structure. In between the upper and lower epidermis - curved plate of deuter cells, begleiter cells, scleroids and hydroid cells are found as shown in (Fig 55).

ANATOMY OF RHIZOME

Transverse section of rhizome shows the following characters.

1. It is circular in outline.
2. Epidermis of one cell thick. Some epidermal cell gives rise to rhizoids.
3. Cortex — It is multicellular having 3 hypodermal radial strands which have thickened wall and deep coloured cells.
4. Endodermis — It forms 3 arc, alternate with radial strands. Endodermal cells are elongated.
5. Leptoid tissue — It is composed of small cells. It is below the radial strands.
6. Pericycle — It has thin walled cells. Central strand is known as steroid tissue.

In the middle of the steroid cells, thin walled hydroid tissue are found. Both steroid and hydroid cells are meant for conduction (Fig. 56)

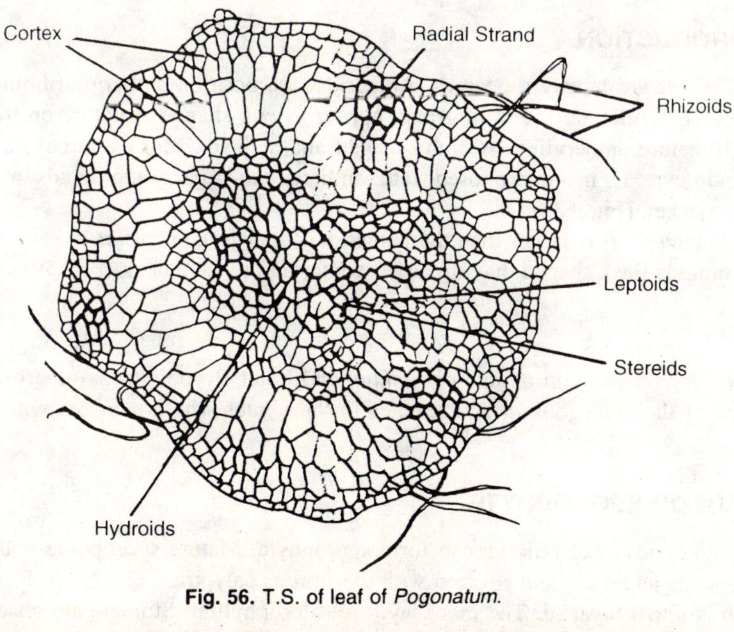

Fig. 56. T.S. of leaf of *Pogonatum.*

ANATOMY OF AERIAL STEM

Transverse section of the stem has the following structure :—

Epidermis — It is outermost layer of cells.

Cortex — Inside the epidermis lies cortex. It consists of living cells filled with starch. Outer cells of cortex are thick walled inner cells of cortex are parenchymatous. Leaf traces are also seen in the cortex.

Endodermis — It is not clear.

Pericycle — It is rudimentary.

Leptome cells — It is zone of elongated cells without starch. Some leptoid cells with starch are also present. These cells are known as leptoid mantle.

Hydrome cylinder — It is central region of the stem. It has two types of cells (a) sclereides having thick walled elongated cells with living content and (b) hydroids, smaller cells devoid of living contents. (Fig. 57).

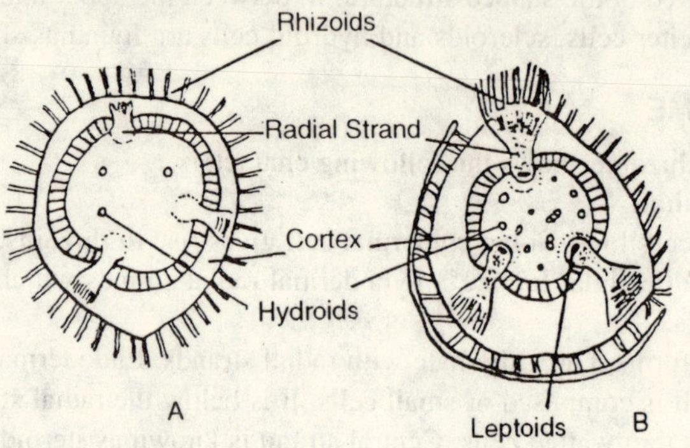

Fig. 57. (A,B) T.S. of aerial stem of *Pogonatum sp.* (diagramatic).

SEXUAL REPRODUCTION

The Pogonatum plants are mostly dioecious. Antheridia are born on antheridial branch. In the axil of perigonial leaves, antheridia are found in group, appear as cup shaped structure on the apex known as male head. Each mature antheridium is club shaped and stalked., Many androcytes lie within jacket layers. Each androcyte is metamorphosed into antherozoid. The antherozoids are liberated after dehiscence of the jacket. (Fig. 58).

Archegonial branch — It is larger than the antheridial branch. Upper part is known as female head. Mature archegonium is flask shaped, having larger venter and twisted neck (Fig. 59).

FERTILIZATION

Water is required for fertilization as in *Polytrichum* and other Bryophytes. Antherozoids come to the apex of the neck of the archegonium and reaches to the venter where it unites with the egg forming diploid zygot.

SPOROGONIUM OR SPOROPHYTE

The diploid zygote divides and redivides to form sporophyte. Mature sporophyte is differentiated into foot, long slender seta and a capsule covered with the fibrous calyptra.

Capsule wall is multi layered. The inner layer is chlorophyllous.Stomata are absent in the capsule wall. Next to the wall there is a layer of cylindrical air space (outer). This outer air space is connected by filaments of green cells. Internal to air space, there is spore sac. Mature spore sac contains haploid spores. There is another air space (inner) next to the spore sac which is also traversed by green filaments.

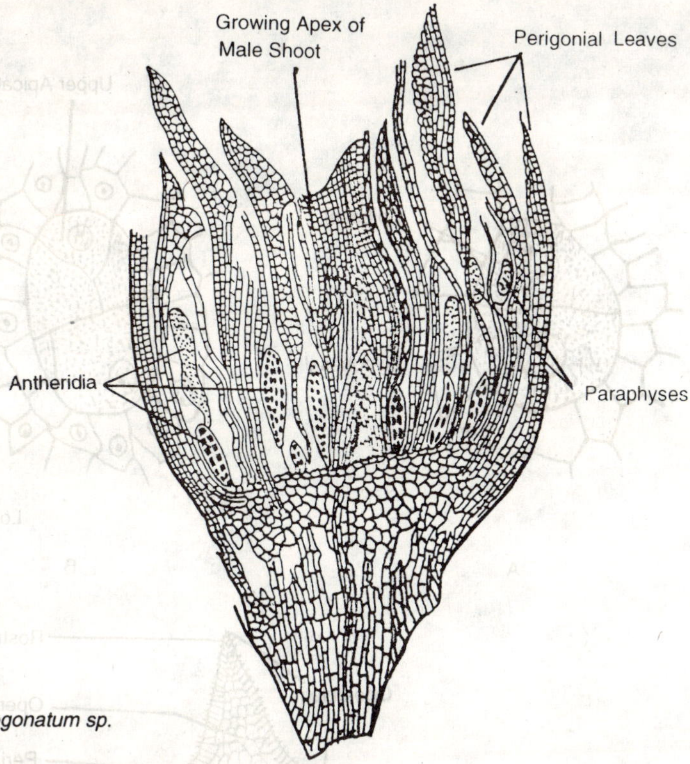

Fig. 58. L.S. of antheridial branch of *Pogonatum sp.*

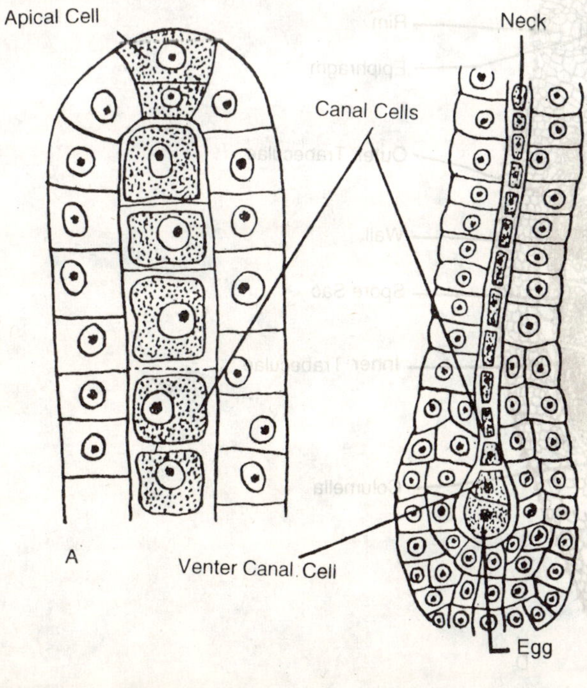

Fig. 59. (A,B) Developmental stages of an archegonium of *Pogonatum sp.*

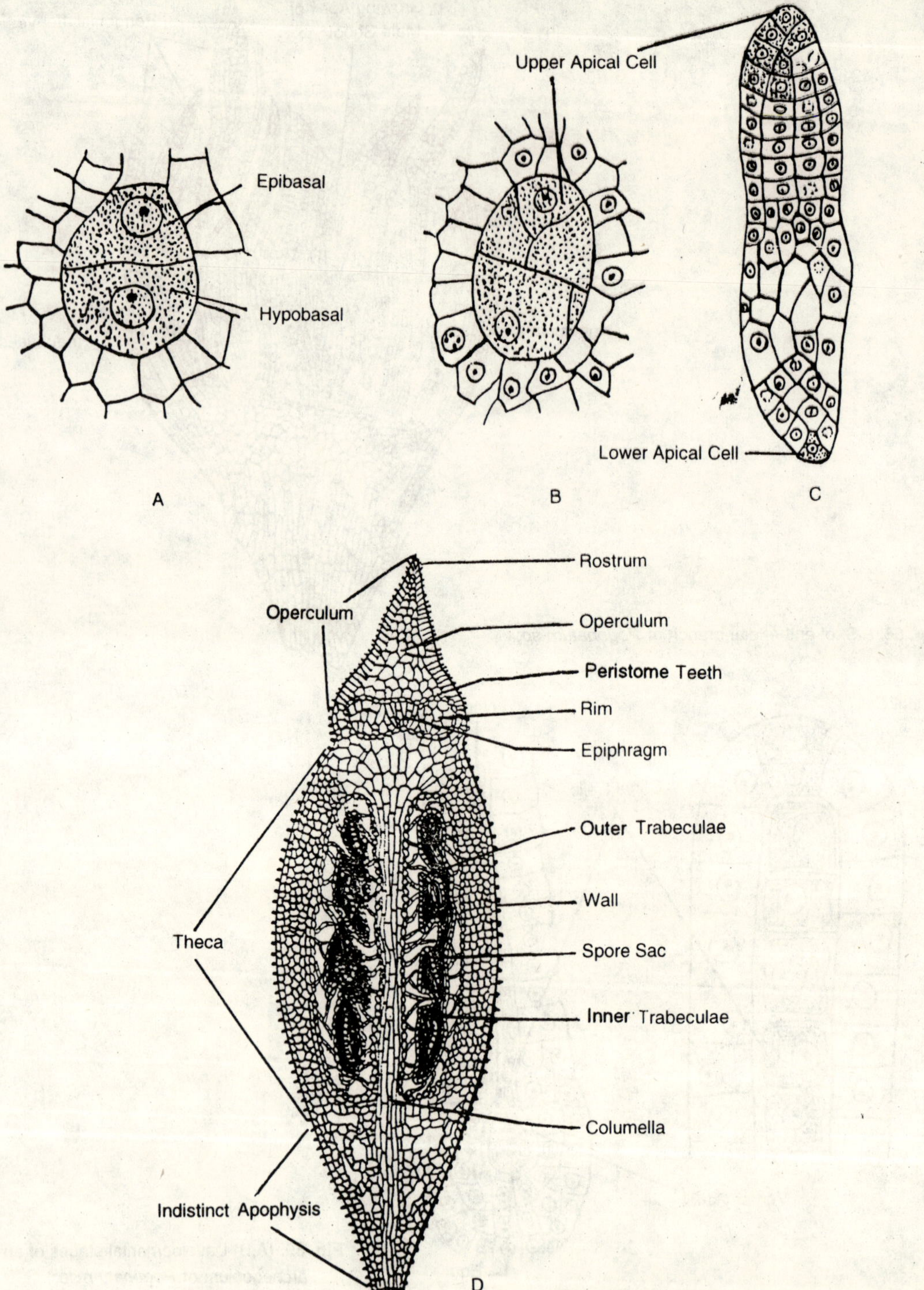

Fig. 60. (A-D) *Pogonatum sp.* (A-C) Stages in the development of sporogonium and (D) L.S. of capsule.

The central portion of the capsule is of columella, made up of colourless elongated cells. The columella extends upwards forming drum like roof of the capsule called epiphragm or tympanum. A beaked operculum is present above the epiphragm. The operculum is connected with the capsule by a ring like diaphragm. There is no organised annulus. The peristome of the ring of 32 short teeth is present just above the diaphragm. Peristome teeth are solid consists of bundles of fibrous cells. (Fig. 60).

On maturity capsule dries up, the operculum falls off and the cells between epiphragm and peristome break forming a slit through which haploid spores come out. The spores germinate to give rise new *Pogonatum* plants (Fig. 61)

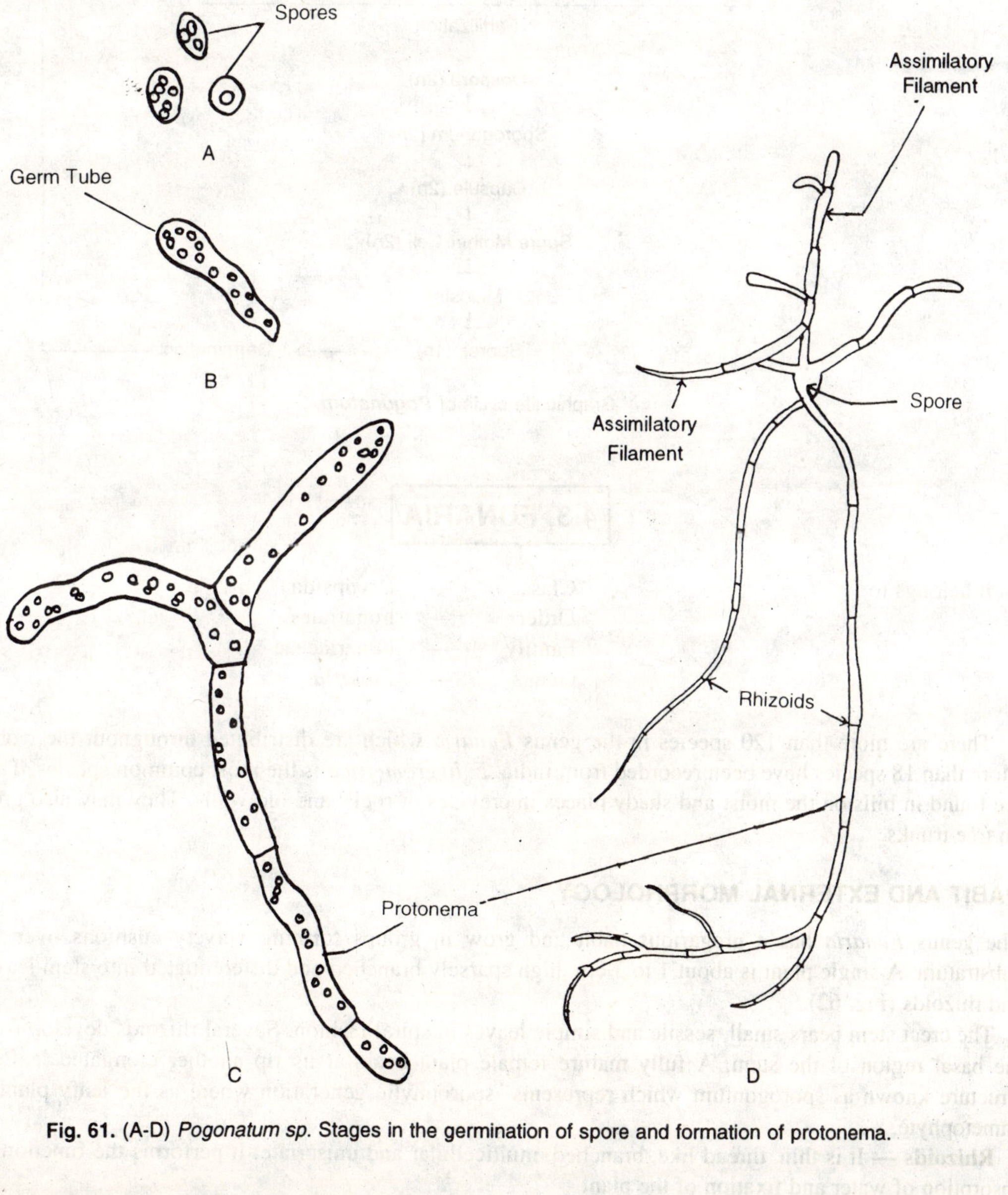

Fig. 61. (A-D) *Pogonatum sp.* Stages in the germination of spore and formation of protonema.

POGONATUM (1n)

Male Plant (1n) → Male Head (1n) → Antheridium (1n) → Antherozoid (1n)

Female Plant (1n) → Female Head (1n) → Archegonium (1n) → Egg (1n

↓

Fertilization
↓
Oospore (2n)
↓
Sporogonum (2n)
↓
Capsule (2n)
↓
Spore Mother Cell (2n)
↓
Meiosis
↓
Spores (1n) → Germination → POGONATUM (1n)

Graphic life cycle of ***Pogonatum***

4.3. FUNARIA

It belongs to			
	Class	—	Bryopsida
	Order	—	Funariales
	Family	—	Funariaceae
	Genus	—	*Funaria*

There are more than 120 species in the genus *Funaria* which are distributed throughout the world. More than 18 species have been recorded from India. *F. hygrometrica* is the most common species. They are found in hills on the moist and shady places in crevices of rocks and old walls. They may also grow on tree trunks.

HABIT AND EXTERNAL MORPHOLOGY

The genus *Funaria* has a gregarious habit and grow in groups forming velvety cushions over the substratum. A single plant is about 1 to 3 cm. high sparsely branched and differentiated into stem leaves and rhizoids (Fig. 62).

The erect stem bears small, sessile and simple leaves in spiral fashion. Several rhizoids develop from the basal region of the stem. A fully mature female plant bears at its tip another elongated leafless structure known as sporogonium which represents sporophytic generation where as the leafy plant is gametophyte.

Rhizoids — It is thin, thread like, branched, multicellular and uniseriate. It performs the function of absorption of water and fixation of the plant.

Leaf — It is ovate in outline, serrate, sessile, simple with one midrib. It is composed of one cell thick plate except at mid region where it is a few cell thick. The cells possess chloroplast and hence photosynthetic in nature (Fig. 63).

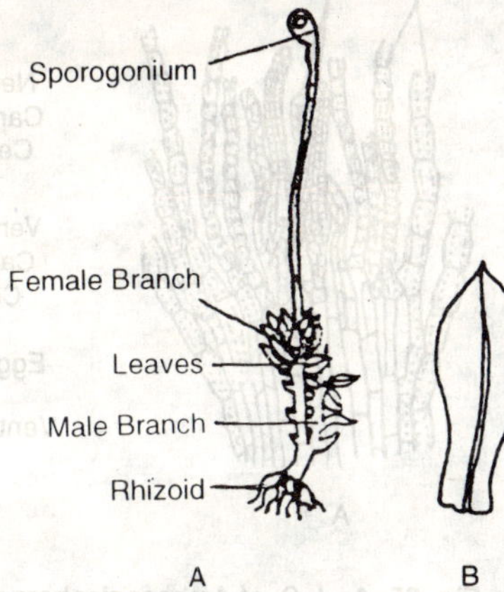

Fig. 62. A - A gametophyte Plant with a mature sporophyte of *Funaria*. B - A leaf

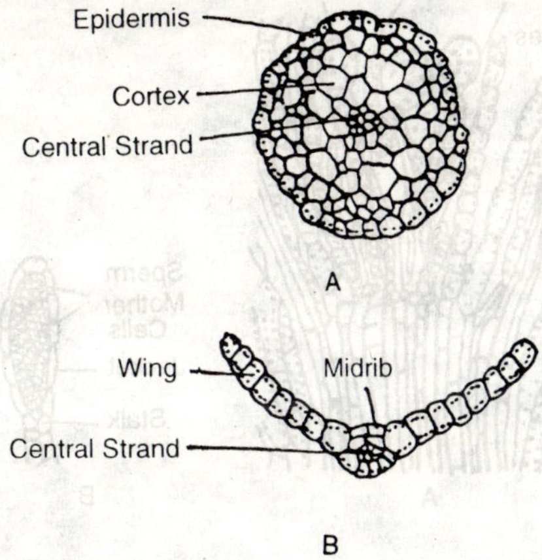

Fig. 63. A - T.S. of stem of *Funaria*. B - T.S. of leaf *Funaria*.

Stem — The stem is branched and branches arise from below the leaves. The transverse section of the stem shows an outer epidermal layer followed by multilayered parenchymatous cortex. The central strand is of thin walled, elongated colourless cell (Fig. 63).

REPRODUCTION

Funaria reproduces both vegetatively and sexually.

Vegetative reproduction — It occurs by the following structure

1. *Bulbils* — It develops on rhizoids or protonema. It is small resting buds. It grow to form new protonemal structures which bear leafy shoots.
2. *Protonema* — The spore germinates into a multicellular filamentous structure called protonema. Each cell of the protonema is capable to give rise to leafy plant.
3. *Secondary protonema* — Sometimes any detached part of the plant gives rise to filamentous structure known as secondary protonema which is turn will bear leafy shoots.

Sexual reproduction — It takes place with the help of antheridium and archegonium, the male and female sex organs respectively. These sex organs are born on the apices of the leafy shoots. surrounded by leaves known as *involucoral leaves*.

Funaria is monoecious but antheridia and archegonia are born on separate branches. The male branch is usually main axis and the female branch appears as lateral branch.

Male Branch — It is smaller in size. The leaves on the upper part of the male branch are broader crowded to form a rosette enclosing in the centre a group of antheridia. The leaves encircling the antheridia are termed as perigonial leaves. A longitudinal section of the male shoot shows several club shaped antheridia surrounded by paraphyses and perigonial leaves (Fig. 64).

Each antheridium has a short multicellular stalk and a long cylindrical body. The body has one cell thick jacket and a central cavity containing androgonial cells which forms androcytes or sperm mother cells. Each androcyte metamorphoses into an antherozoid or male gamete. On maturity the antheridial wall breaks open at the top through which the antherozoids come out. Antherozoids are biflagellate (Fig. 64).

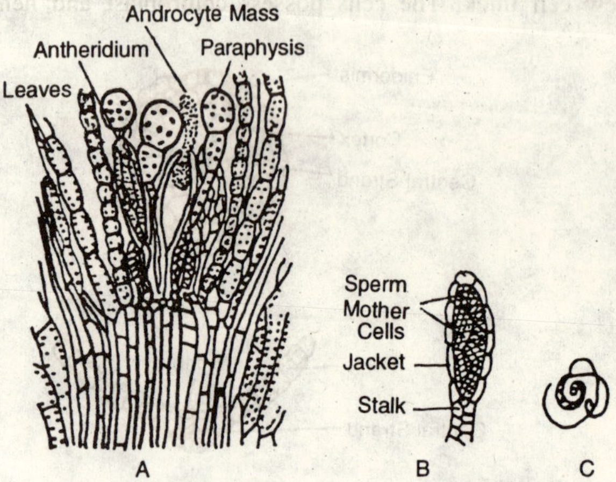

Fig. 64. A—L.S. of Antheridiophore of *Funaria* showing antheridia and paraphysis. —An antheridium, C—A biciliate antherozoid.

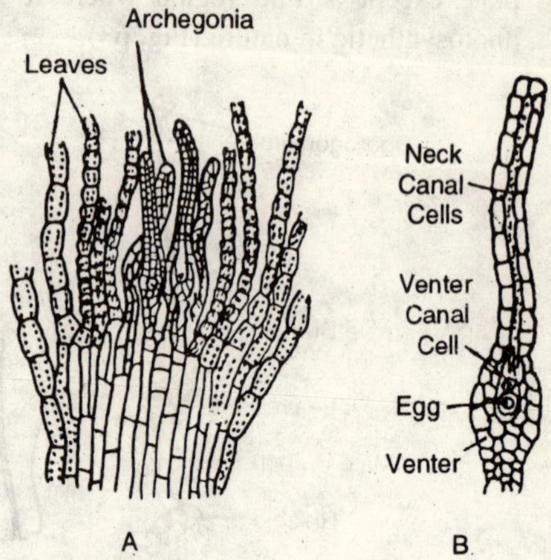

Fig. 65. A—L.S. of Archegoniophore of *Funaria*. B—A mature archegonium.

Female branch — A longitudinal section of a female branch shows archegonia at the flattened tip. Paraphyses are found in between the archegonia – the female sex organs. The invoiucoral leaves surrounding the archegonia are termed as perichaetial leaves. An archegonium is flask shaped body having a short, multicellular stalk, a swollen base called venter and a long narrow, tubular neck. It has a sterile jacket enclosing a canal. The jacket is one cell thick having six vertical rows of cells. The venter is 2 - 3 cells thick and many cells in perimeter. The cavity of the venter has an egg cell and a small venter canal cell above the egg. Generally 6 - 8 or more neck canal cells are present in the neck. The tip of the neck has lid or cover cells (Fig. 65).

FERTILIZATION

On maturity the neck canal cell and venter canal cell disintegrate to form a mucilaginous substance. It absorbs moisture, swells up and exerts pressure to open the cover cells. The mucilage oozes out and attracts the antherozoids. One of the antherozoids move into the archegonium and fuses with the egg nucleus and fertilization is effected. After fertilization the egg becomes diploid oospore or zygote which is the 1st cell of sporophytic generation.

THE SPOROPHYTE AND SPOROGONIUM

The diploid zygote starts segmentation and forms a young embryo with two growing regions. The cells of the jacket divide to form a protective covering called calyptra. The embryo further grow into sporogonium. The mature sporogonium is 2 - 4 cm long and is divisible into foot, seta and capsule.

Foot is short, slender and embeded in the stem tip from where is draws nourishment for the developing sporogonium.

Seta — It is thin, slender bearing capsule at the tip. Seta has epidermis, cortex and central strand. Seta keeps the capsule upright and helps in dispersal of spores.

Capsule is pear shaped, obliquely born at the tip of seta. The capsule contains (1) apophysis (11) theca or body and (III) operculum.

Apophysis is basal part of the capsule. Theca is spore containing region of the capsule. It has central sterile cells called columella surrounded by cylindrical spore sac bounded by walls. On the outside of spore sac, air space is transversed by multicellular filaments called trabeculae. Outside the air space there are capsule wall of 4 - 6 layered cells. Outer layer is of epidermis. Below the epidermis one layered hypodermis is present which is followed by chlorenchymatous cells. The spore sac has archesporial cells which divide to form spore mother cells. The spore mother cells divides meiotically to give rise haploid spores.

Operculum or lid is the caplike terminal part of the capsule. It has 4 - 5 layers of cells. Outer layer is epidermis. Inner layers are of thin walled cells. Peristome and annulus are present in between the operculum and the theca (Fig. 66).

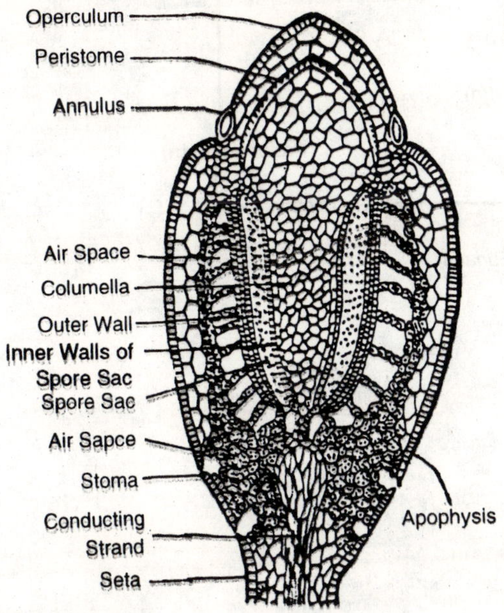

Fig. 66. L.S. of capsule of *Funaria* showing detailed structure.

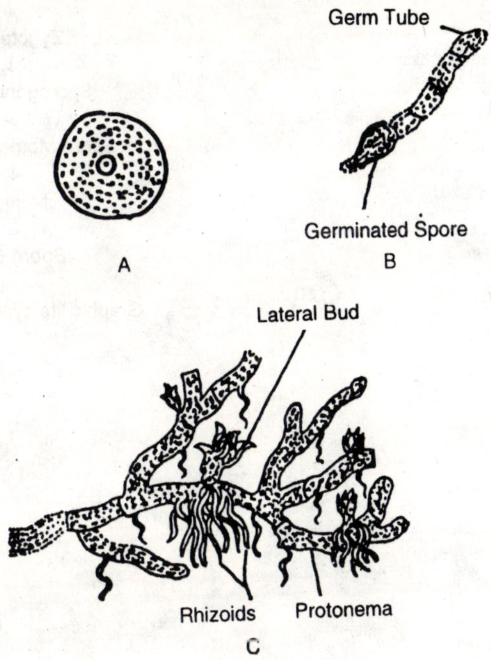

Fig. 67. A - A spore of *Funaria*, B - Spore with germ-tube. C - Protonema with lateral bud and rhizoids.

Peristome is made up of 32 triangular teeth like processes in two rows of 16 each. The peristome teeth are hygroscopic and regulate the dispersal of spores. In dry condition the peristome teeth loose water and curved backward leaving the mouth of the theca open. The spores come out and carried away by wind.

Annulus has a ring of 4 - 6 superimposed layers of epidermal cells. It causes loosening and fall of operculum.

The spores and gametophytic generation — The spores are 12 - 20 μ in diameter. It has outer thick layer - exospore and inner thin layer - endospore. On falling it germinates to give rise germ tube which further divides to form a multicellular filamentous, branched structure called protonema. Every cell of protonema is capable to give rise new leafy gametophyte (Fig. 67).

ALTERNATION OF GENERATION

There is alternation of gametophytic and sporophytic generation in the life cycle of *Funaria* as has been shown in the graphic life cycle.

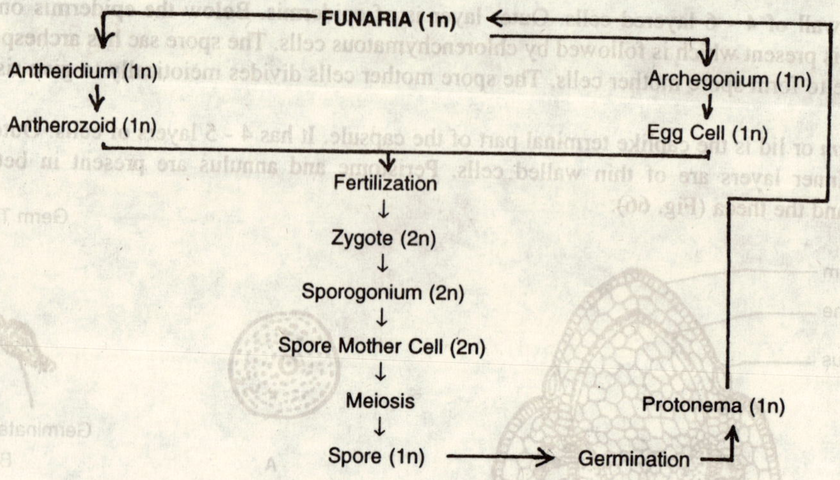

Graphic life cycle of *Funaria*

SECTION - IV

PTERIDOPHYTA

1. General Features and Classification
2. Psilotopsida
3. Lycopsida
4. Sphenopsida
5. Pteropsida

CHAPTER 1

PTERIDOPHYTA

GENERAL FEATURES AND CLASSIFICATION

Haeckel (1866) was the first to introduce the name Pteridophyta for a group of plants having vascular tissues and invisible sex organs externally. It is a group of Cryptogam — a term suggested by Linnaues (1754) — for non–flowering plants in which sexual reproduction was not known at one time. On the basic of presence of vascular tissue i.e. xylem and phloem, Pteridophytean plants are also called Vascular Cryptogams. According to Parihar (1977) Pteridophytes are the most primitive fossil and living vascular plants. The fossil records show that the Pteridophytes were dominant vegetation of the earth's flora about 35, 000, 000 years back in Paleozoic age.

SALIENT FEATURES

1. Plant body is sporophyte.
2. Stem with apical growth in the sporophyte.
3. Occurrence of sporangia in the sporophyte.
4. The roots are generally adventitious. The primary roots are of ephemeral nature.
5. Stomata are present on aerial parts of plants.
6. The sporangia bearing leaves are termed as sporophylls.
7. The cambium is absent, though a well developed vascular system is present.
8. Different types of steles are met in different plants.
9. Members of Pteridophyta are both heterosporous (having two different types of spores i.e. micro and macro/mega spores, e.g. *Selaginella)* and homosporous (with only one type of spores, e.g. *Lycopodium*) forms.
10. The sporangia are present in the either specialised bodies known as sporocarps, e.g. *Marsilea* or in organised groups called sori, e.g. Ferns, or in the form of compact structures known as strobilii or cones, e.g. *Lycopodium, Equisetum.*
11. Occurrence of antheridia and archegonia in the gametophyte.
12. Sex organs are concealed.
13. Presence of alternation of generations of small haploid gametophyte and a large diploid sporophyte.
14. Young sporophyte is completely or partially dependent on gametophyte for some time.

There are other characteristics of the Pteridophytes which show differences and resemblances to the Bryophytes as such.

DIFFERENCES FROM BRYOPHYTES

1. Plant body in Bryophytes is gametophytic (1n) whereas it is sporophytic (2n) in Pteridophytes.
2. Plant body in Bryophytes is thalloid whereas it is differentiated into root, stem and leaves in Pteridophytes.
3. Vascular elements are present in Pteridophytes whereas in Bryophytes it is absent.
4. Roots are present in Pteridophytes while it is absent in Bryophytes.
5. Pteridophytes, in general, are much larger in size than Bryophytes.
6. In Pteridophytes, vegetative reproduction is less prevalent than Bryophytes.
7. Pteridophytes are both homo and heterosporous while majority of the Bryophytes are homosporous.

RESEMBLANCES TO THE BRYOPHYTES

1. Members of both bryophytes and pteridophytes show heteromorphic alternation of generations.
2. Both the groups have antheridia and archegonia.
3. Sex organs are multicellular in both the groups.
4. Presence of motile male gametes and non–motile female gametes are shown by both the groups.
5. Formation of sexual spore by mitosis is absent in both of them.
6. Presence of oogamous type of sexual reproduction is shown by both the groups.
7. Rhizoids are present in all the bryophytes where as it is present in some pteridophytes, e.g. *Rhynia* and *Psilotum*.
8. Majority of pteridophytes and bryophytes show homosporous condition.
9. Fertilization takes place in presence of water in both pteridophytes and bryophytes.

Besides, there are differences as well as resemblances to the gymnosperms as follows.

DIFFERECNES FROM GYMNOSPERMS

1. Roots are adventitious in pteridophytes whereas tap roots are present in gymnosperms.
2. Pteridophytes grow in humid and shady places, i.e. they are hydrophytes whereas gymnosperms exhibit xerophytic features.
3. In gymnosperm, cambium is present while it is absent in pteridophytes.
4. There is absence of neck canal cells and ventral canal cells in gymnosperms whereas it is present in pteridophytes.
5. Megaspore is permanently retained within the megasporangium in gymnosperms whereas it develops independently after being shed from megasporangium in pteridophytes.
6. In gymnosperms seeds are formed while seed formation has not been observed in pteridophytes.
7. There is no pollen tube formation in pteridophytes whereas pollen tube formation occurs in gymnosperms.

RESEMBLANCES TO THE GYMNOSPERMS

1. Plant body is sporophyte (2*n*) in both pteridophytes and gymnosperms.
2. There is regular alternation of sporophytic and gametophytic generations in both the groups.
3. Circinate vernation in young leaves are seen in both the groups.
4. Phloem has no companion cells in both of them,

5. Vessels are exceptionally present in pteridophytes (e.g. *Seleginella*) sp.) as well as in gymnosperms (e.g. *Gnetum*).
6. In both the groups, gametophytic generation is dependent upon the sporophytic generation.
7. Both the groups are characterized by permanent retention of megaspores within the megasporangium.
8. Pteridosperms (i.e. ferns with seeds) was the common name given to the Cycadofilicales due to its resemblances with ferns.

CLASSIFICATION OF PTERIDOPHYTA

The classification of Pteridophyta is some what complicated mainly because of many discoveries in the field of fossil plants. As early as in 1876, Prantle classified Pteridophyta into three classes; namely Lycopodinae, Equisetinae and Filicinae.

Eames (1936) divided Tracheophyta (vascular Plants) of Sinnott (1935) into four groups, namely (1) Psilopsida, (2) Lycopsida, (3) Sphenopsida and (4) Pteropsida. Further, each group was divided into order and families as follows:-

(1) Psilopsida : Orders
    1. Psilophytales : Families : Rhyniaceae, Psilophytaceae etc.
    2. Psilotales : Family : Psilotaceae.

(2) Lycopsida : Orders
    1. Lycopodiales : Family : Lycopodiaceae
    2. Selaginellales : Family : Selaginellaceae
    3. Lepidodendrales : Family : Lepidodendraceae, Sigillariaceae
    4. Pleuromeiales : Family : Pleuromeiaceae
    5. Isoetales : Family : Isoetaceae

(3) Sphenopsida : Orders
    1. Hyeniales :- Family :- Hyeniaceae
    2. Sphenophyllales :- Family :- Sphenophyllaceae
    3. Equisetales :- Family :- Equisetaceae.

(4) Pteropsida : subgroups
    1. Filicinae, 2. Gymonspermae, 3. Angiospermae.
    Subgroup Filicinae — Orders —1.Coenopteridales. Family—Botryopteridaceaea
    2. Ophioglossales :- Family :- Ophioglossaceae
    3. Marattiales :- Family :- Marattiaceae
    4. Filicales :- Families :- Osmundaceae, Polypodiaceae, Salviniaceae, Marsileaceae etc.

Psilopsida, Lycopeida, Sphenopsida and Pteropsida have been considered as divisions rather than groups by Zimmermann (1930) and Arnold (1947). However, Wardlaw (1955) considered them as subdivisions of Pteridophyta. Tippo (1942) gave these four, ranks of sub–phyllum under the Phyllum Traceophyta.

Riemers (1954) proposed a classification of Pteridophyta as publised in Engler's *Syllabus der Pflanzen familien*.

Division — Pteridophyta

A. Sub–division : Psilophytopsida

Order — Psilophytales

Family — Rhyniaceae, Zosterophyllaceae, Psilophytaceae, Asteroxylaceae.

B. Sub–division : Psilopsida

Order — Psilotales
Family — Psilotaceae, *Tmesipteridaceae*

C. Sub-division : Lycopsida
Order — 1. Protolepidodendrales
Family — Drepanophycaceae, Protolepidodendraceae
Order — 2. Lycopodiales
Family — Lycopidiaceae
Order — 3. Lepidodendrales
Families — Lepidodendraceae, Bothrodendraceae, Sigillariaceae and pleuromeiaceae
Order — 4. Isoetales
Family — Isoetaceae
Order — 5. Selaginellales
Family — Selaginellaceae

D. Sub– division : Sphenopsida
Order 1. Hyeniales
Families — Protohyeniaceae, Hyeniaceae
Order 2.— Sphenophyllales
Families — Sphenophyllaceae, Cheirostrobaceae
Order — 3 — Calamitales
Families — Asterocalamitaceae, Calamitaceae
Order — 4 — Equisetales
Family — Equisetaceae

E. Sub–division — Pteropsida
A– Class — Primofilices
Order — 1 Cladoxylales
Families — Cladoxylaceae, Pseudosporochnaceae
Order — 2 — Caenopteridales
Families — Zygopteridaceae, Stauropteridaceae, Botryopteridaceae
B–Class — Eusporangiatae
Order —1 — Marattiales
Families — Asterothecaceae, Angiopteridaceae, Marattiaceae, Dauaeaceae, Christenseniaceae
Order — 2 — Ophioglossales
Family — Ophioglossaceae
C–Class — Osmundidae
Order — Osmundales
Family — Osmundaceae
D–Class — Leptosporangiatae.
Order —1 — Filicales
Families — Schizaceae, Gleicheniaoeae, Hymenophyllaceae, Dicksoniaceae, Matoniaceae, Dipteridaceae, Cyatheaceae, Dennstaedtiaceae, Adiantaceae, Polypodiaceae
Order—2 — Marsileales
Families — Marsileaceae, Pilulariaceae
Order—3 — Salviniales
Familes — Salviniaceae, Azollaceae

Smith (1955) has proposed the classification of Pteridophyta as follows :

Division 1. Psilophyta
Class — Psilophytinae
Division 2. Lepidophyta
Class — Lycopodinae
Division 3. Calamophyta
Class — Equisetinae
Division 4. Pterophyta
Class — Filicinae

Cronquist, Takhtajan and Zimmermann (1966) have another classification of Pteridophyta as such :

Sub kingdom — 1. Thallobionta
2. Embryobionta

Division— 1. Rhyniophyta
2. Bryophyta
3. Psilotophyta
4. Lycopodiophyta
5. Equisetophyta
6. Polypodiophyta
7. Pinophyta (Gymnosperms)
8. Magnoliophyta (Angiosperms)

Bold (1967), Bierhorst (1971), Parihar (1977) and Kato (1983) are other botanists who have also proposed classifications of Pteridophyta.

It has been suggested that the Pteridophyta is not a phylogenetic taxon but a combination of four independent taxa. hence, the question arises whether the term Pteridophyta be retained as a divisional name or each of the higher taxa of the Pteridophyta should be considered a division. According to international rules of Botanical Nomenclature there is no taxon called phyllum and the suffix for division is phyta, for subdivision — Phytina, for class — opsida and four sub–class — idae. Against the deletion of the name Pteridophyta, it may be suggested that Pteridophyta as a group, possess certain common peculiarities. They are all embryophyta, archegoniatae and show a life history in sporophytic and gametophytic generations. They have not acquired the seed habit. Therefore, Pteridophyta should be considered as a division of the Embryophytae and higher Pteridophytic taxa as classes ending in–opsida, e.g. sub kingdom — Embryophytae

Division — Pteridophyta
Class — 1. Psilophytopsida
2. Psilotopsida
3. Lycopsida
4. Sphenopsida
5. Noeggerathiopsida
6. Filicopsida

However, Riemer;s (1954) classification has been followed in the proceeding text.

CHAPTER 2

PSILOTOPSIDA

The members of the Class — Psilotopsida shows a close similarity with the Silurian and Devonian members of Psilophytopsida. Psilotopsida has only one order Psilotales which contain two families; (1) Psilotaceae and (2) Tmesipteridaceae, each with one living genus i.e. *Psilotum* in the former and *Tmesipteris* in the latter.

2.1 PSILOTUM

In belongs to —	Class	—	Psilotopsida
	Order	—	Psilotales
	Family	—	Psilotaceae
	Genus	—	*Psilotum*

HABITAT AND HABIT

There are only two species in the genus *Psilotum* and they are (1) *P. nudum* and (2) *P. flaccidum.* They are found in tropics and subtropics. In India, *P. nudum* is reported from Assam, Bengal, Kulu, (H.P) and Panchmarhi (M.P) Hills. *P. flaccidum* is reported from some pacific islands, Mexico and Jamaica.

P. nudum is a shruby plant. Plant body is erect and slender found in the crevices of rocks. Sometimes it occurs as an epiphyte on trees ferns, on coconut trees etc. *P. nudum* attains a height of upto 25 cm where as *P. flaccidum,* a pendulous epiphyte reaches upto 90 cm in length.

EXTERNAL MORPHOLOGY

The plant body is sporophyte consisting of an aerial erect shoot and a subterranean rhizome. The rhizome is profusely branched, brown in colour with numerous rhizoidal hairs. The plants are devoid of roots and rhizoids perform the function of absorption. Rhizome is dichotomously branched and associated with intracellular fungal hyphae.

The aerial shoot is slender, dichotomously branched and green. The basal part of the aerial shoot is cylindrical whereas upper parts have three longitudinal ridges. It bears small and scale like appendages and sporangia (Fig. 1).

ANATOMY

Appendages (Leaves) : They are small and simple. It has a cutinised epidernal layer without stomata.

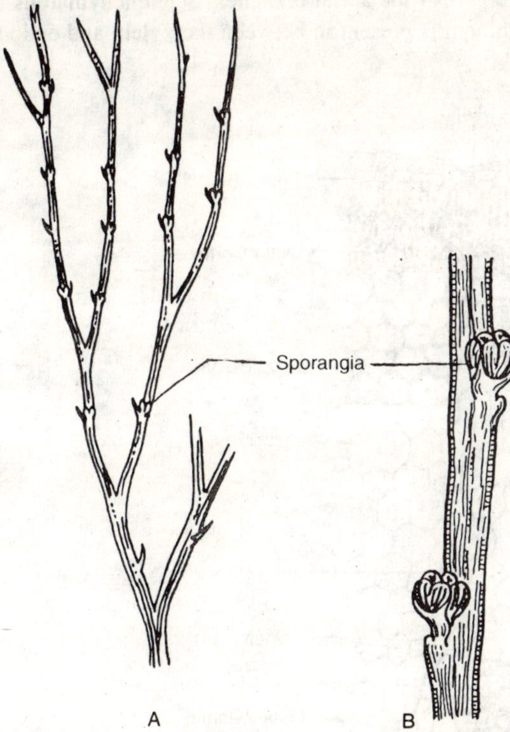

(A) Habit Sketch (B) Sporangia on Axis

Fig. 1. *Psilotum nudum.*

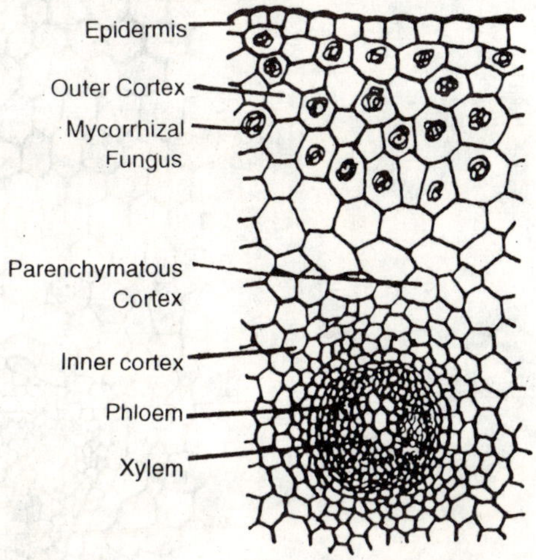

Fig. 2. T.S. of Rhizome of *Psilotum* sp.

Interior region of the leaves consists of chlorophyll containing parenchyma cells. The leaves have no veins. Leaf trace is found in *P. flaccidum*. These leaves or appendages are replaced by fertile appendages in the upper part of shoots.

Rhizome — Transverse section of rhizome of *P. nudum* consists of (1) outer most one larger epidermis followed by (2) Cortex which is differentiated into (a) outer cortex containing endophytic mycorrhizal fungus (b) middle cortex consisting of parenchyma filled with starch and (c) inner cortex of 2- 4 layers of cells. (3) One layered endodermis is present just outside the stele. (4) Below the endodermis one layered parenchymatous pericycle is present (5) Finally central core of axis i.e. stele is present which is protostelic. Centrally placed xylem is surrounded by phloem. (Fig. 2)

Stem — Transvers section of the aerial shoot-stem shows the following structure.

(1) Epidermis — One layered, well developed epidermis. It is covered with a thick cuticle. Stomata are also present.

(2) Cortex — It is differentiated into three regions ; (a) Outer cortex — It is 2 - 5 layered, made up of chlorophyll containing parenchyma cells. Intercellular spaces are present; (b) middle cortex consisting of 4 - 5 layers of sclerenchymatous cells and (c) the inner cortex is made up of thick walled parenchyma cells. There is no intercellular spaces in this region.

(3) One layered endodermis is present outside the stele.

(4) The stele is actinostelic. The xylem is exarch and the number of actionstelic xylem rays may be

3 - 10 depending upon the species and the part of the aerial branches. Sclerenchymatous fibres are also seen in the centre of the xylem. Phloem is present in between the xylem and endodermi

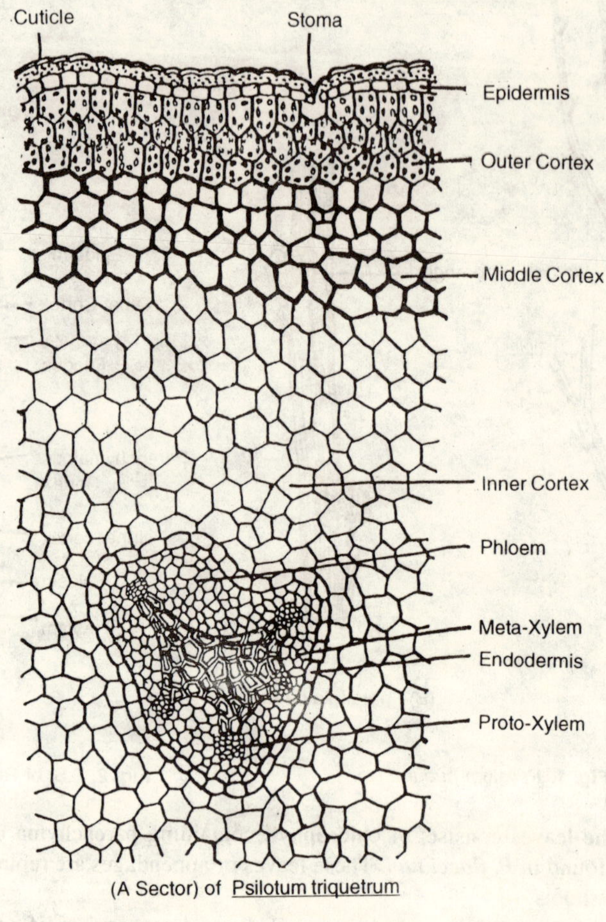

Fig. 3. T.S. of stem of *Psilotum* sp. (A sector).

VEGETATIVE PROPAGATION

Holloway (1939) has mentioned the occurrence of vegetative buds on the gametophyte performing the function of vegetative propagation. Bierhorst (1954) reported the presence of gemmae on the gametophytes or prothalii and on the rhizome of *P. nudum*. Gemmae are ovoid, minute, multicellular outgrowth.

SPORE BEARING ORGANS

Spores are produced in sporangia. Sporangia are produced in a group of 2 - 4 and hence this group of fused sporangia is known as synangium. The morphological nature of fertile appendages has been controversial. The concept that the fertile axis — appendage as well as synangium is a condensed branch system is being favoured. Unlike foliar structures, the fertile axis is vascularized. A vascular bundle extends into a synangium and subdivides into three parts, corresponding to three sporangia (Bierhorst, 1971). Synangia are born on minute appendages subtended by a bract. Transverse section of a synangium shows the presence of 4 - 5 celled thick jacket. The cell wall of upper jacket layer becomes thickened except in a small vertical row, from where longitudinal dehiscence of the sporangium takes place.

Within the jacket, spore mother cells divide meiotically to give rise haploid, kidney–shaped spores. Some of the sporogenous cells divide into plasmodial mass of spores which serve as nourishment to the developing spores. (Fig. 4).

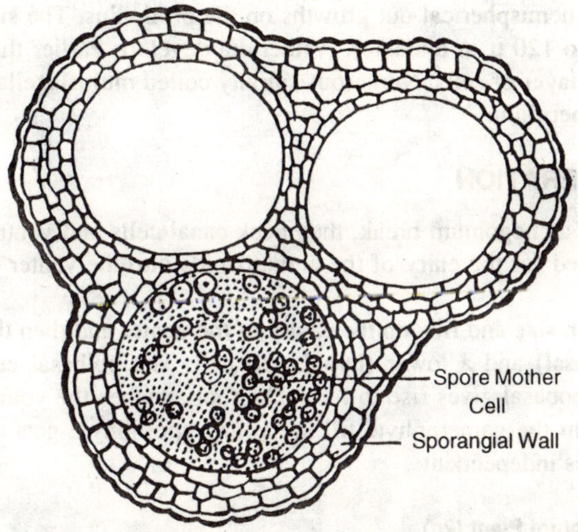

Fig. 4. T.S. of a synangium of *Psilotum nudum*.

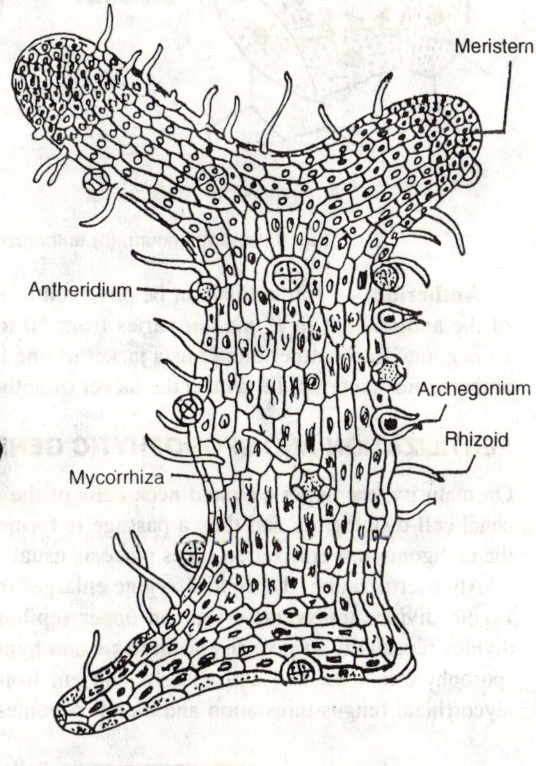

Fig. 5. A prothallus bearing sex organs of *Psilotum nudum*.

GAMETOPHYTIC GENERATION

The haploid spore represents the first cell of the gemetophytic generation. *Psilotum* is homosporous and hence spores are alike and kidney shaped and the average size is 0.065 x 0.032 mm. A median slit is present on the spore wall. it has outer reticulate exine and the inner intine. Spore starts to germinate after 4 months of its dehiscence. Median slit splits and the inner content comes out in the form of a conical mouth. It divides transversely into a basal large cell and a upper small cell. Upper cell again divides further into a mass of multicellular structure called prothallus. The prothalli are colourless, cylindrical structure covered with rhizoids. Endophytic fungus makes its entry into the developing prothalli. Prothallus is monoecious i.e. homothallic. Both antheridia and archegonia develop on the same prothallus. (Fig. 5).

Archegonium — The archegonia are sunken with short projecting neck. The neck is 4 - 5 cells in height having two canal cells, the venter has one ventral canal cell and an egg. (Fig. 6).

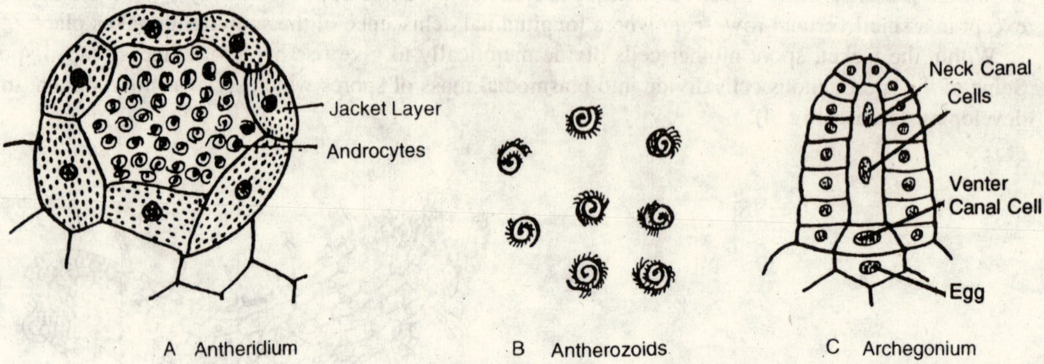

Fig. 6. (a) Antheridum, (b) antherozoids and (c) archegonium of *Psilotum* sp.

Antheridia — Antheridia can be observed as hemispherical out growths on the prothallus. The size of the antheridium in *P. nudum* varies from 50 to 120 μ in diameter. Antheridia develops earlier than archegonia. Each antheridium has a jacket of one layer of cells. Numerous spirally coiled multiflagellate antherozoids (sperms) lie within the jacket of antheridium.

FERTILIZATION AND SPOROPHYTIC GENERATION

On maturity, the upper elevated neck cells of the archegonium break, then neck canal cells and ventral canal cell disintegrate and thus a passage is formed for the entry of the antherozoids into the venter of the archgonium. Fertilization takes place as usual.

After fertilization, the diploid zygote enlarges in size and fills up the cavity of the venter and then the zygote divides transversely into an upper (epibasal) and a lower (hypobasal) cell. The epibasal cell divides repeatedly to give rise to the axis and hypobasal gives rise to foot. The foot attaches the young sporophyte into the soil and absorbs nutrient from the gametophyte till the young sporophyte gets an mycorrhizal fungus infestation and then it becomes independent.

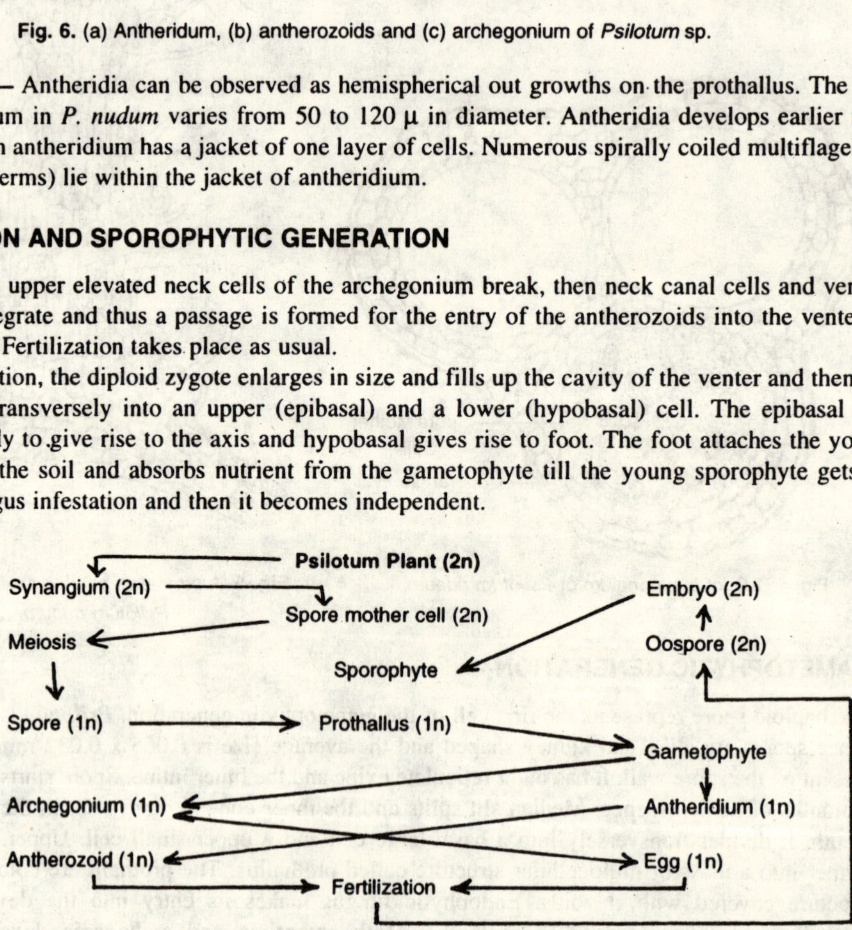

Graphic Life cycle of *Psilotum*

CHAPTER 3

LYCOPSIDA

HISTORICAL DESCRIPTION

The class Lycopsida is represented by fossils as well as living vascular cryptogams and this group is extended from the Palaeozoic era to the present days.

SALIENT FEATURES

1. The sporophytic plant body is differentiated into roots, stem and leaves.
2. The leaves are microphyllous having a single vein in each of them.
3. The arrangement of leaves are opposite spiral or whorled.
4. The leaves are ligulate also, e.g. *Selaginella.*
5. The steles may be protostelic, siphonostelic or polystelic.
6. Leaf gaps are present.
7. Sporangia are found on the dorsal side of the leaves (sporophylls) and are on the terminal part of the branches.
8. Sporangia bearing leaves i.e. sporophylls are loosely arranged into a strobilus.
9. The sporangia may be heterosporous; i.e. *Selaginella* or homosporous, e.g. *Lycopodium.*
10. Antherozoids may be biflagellate, e.g. *Lycopodium* or multiflagellate, e.g. *Phylloglossum.*

The class Lycopsida has been divided into 5 orders (Sporne, 1970) and 9 families. Some of the living as well as fossil representative are described in this book.

3.1 LYCOPODIUM (Club Moss)

The genus Lycopodium belongs to —	Class	—	Lycopsida
	Order	—	Lycopdiales
	Family	—	Lycopodiaceae
	Genus	—	*Lycopodium*

HABITAT AND HABIT

There are about 400 species (Bierhorst, 1971) of the genus *Lycopodium* growing mainly in tropical and sub–tropical forests. Some species are reported from temperate and arctic regions also. About 33 species of *Lycopodium* from India mainly from the hills of South India and Eastern Himalayas have been reported by Chowdhury (1937). Common species are *L. cernuum L. clavatum, L. selago, L. sikkimenseis and L. phlegmaria* etc.

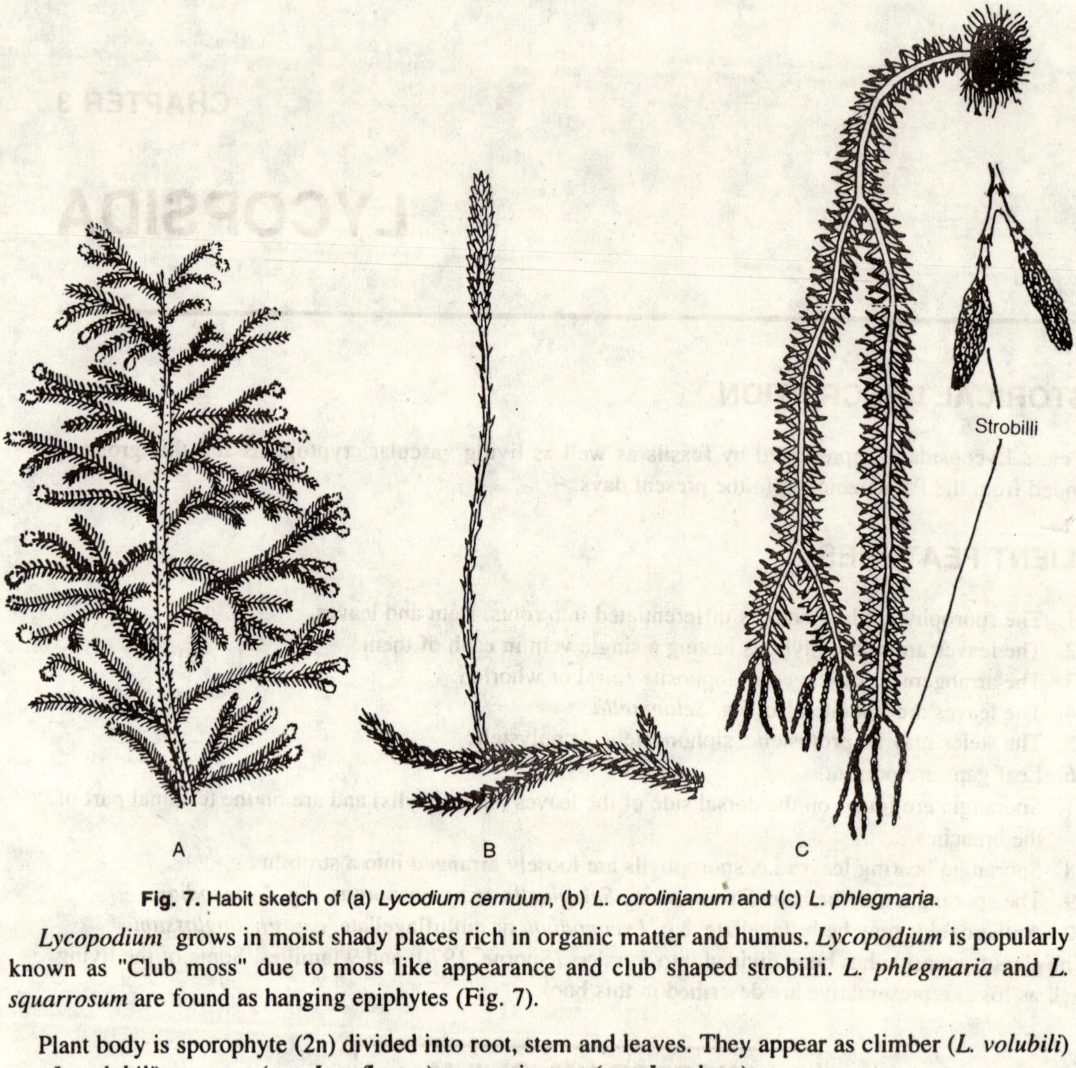

Fig. 7. Habit sketch of (a) *Lycodium cernuum*, (b) *L. corolinianum* and (c) *L. phlegmaria.*

Lycopodium grows in moist shady places rich in organic matter and humus. *Lycopodium* is popularly known as "Club moss" due to moss like appearance and club shaped strobilii. *L. phlegmaria* and *L. squarrosum* are found as hanging epiphytes (Fig. 7).

Plant body is sporophyte (2n) divided into root, stem and leaves. They appear as climber (*L. volubili*) e.g. *L. volubili*); as erect (e.g. *L. reflexum*); as semi–erect (e.g. *L. selago*).

EXTERNAL MORPHOLOGY

Stem is weak, slender and rhizomatous, Prostrate herbaceous type bears erect dichotomous branches followed by monopodial branches as in *L. clavatum.* Stem and branches are covered with many small leaves.

Roots — It develops mainly from the basal part of the axis. Roots are adventitious, small and generally dichotomously branched. Primary root is ephemeral.

Leaves — They are sessile, small, simple and lanceolate with an unbranched mid vein. The arrangement of leaves may be opposite (e.g. *L. alpinum*) or spiral (e.g. *L. clavatum*) or whorled (e.g. *L. cernuum*). Generally, the foliage leaves are heterophyllous

INTERNAL STRUCTURE : ANATOMY OF ROOTS

Transverse section of root shows the following features.

1. One layered epidermis of thin walled cells. Many root hairs are given out from the epidermal cells.
2. Several cells thick cortex made up of outer thick walled cells and inner parenchymatous cells.
3. A stele (protostele) which is monarch, diarch or triarch with one, two or three protoxylem groups respectively. The xylem is "U" or "C" shaped with protoxylem at the tip of "U" or "C". The phloem lies in between the arms of "U" or "C". (Fig. 8).

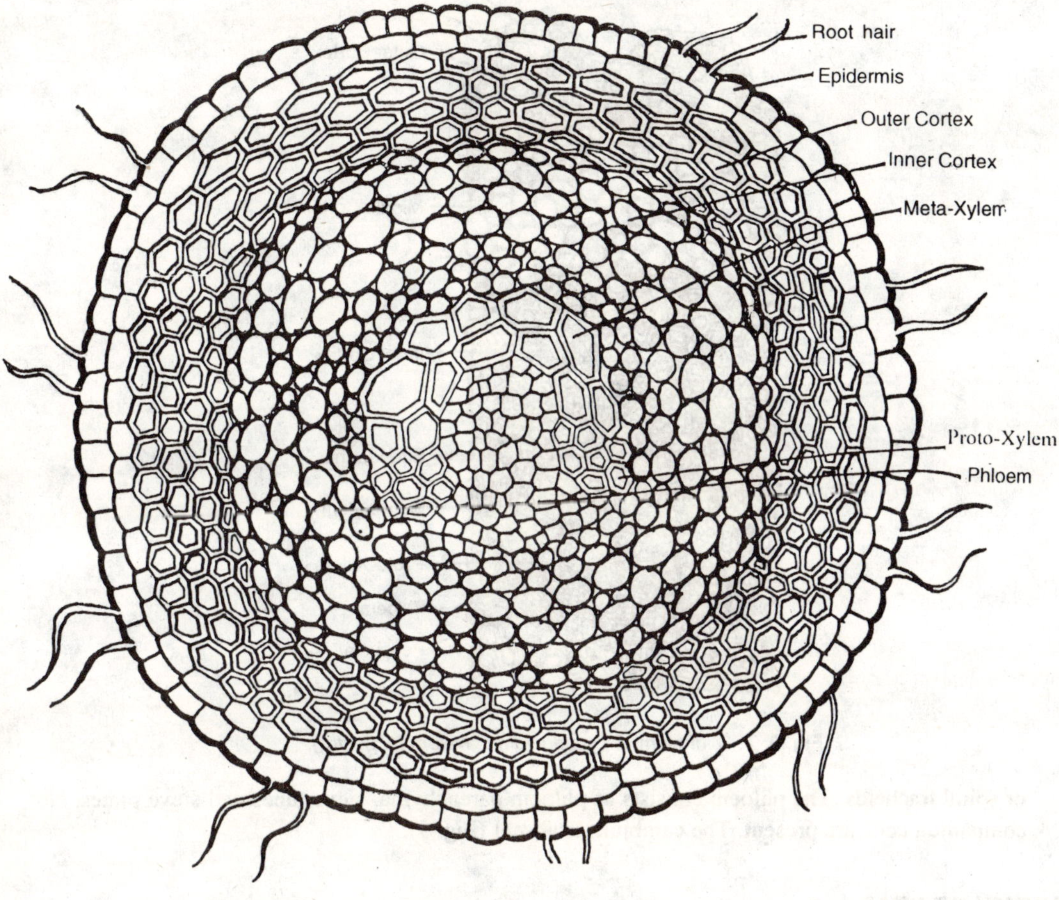

Fig. 8. T.S. of root of *Lycopodium* sp.

ANATOMY OF STEM

Transverse section of the stem shows the following structure :

1. *Epidermis* — One layered superficial epidermis with cutinised outer cell wall. Stomata are present in the epidermis.
2. *Cortex* : The cortex is broad and may be homogenous i.e. either parenchymatous cells or sclerenchymatous cells throughout or may be divided into three zones, (a) outer cortex consisting

of sclerenchyma (b) midde cortex of parenchyma and (c) inner cortex of sclerenchyma.

3. Endodermis — It is one cell in thickness, made up of thick walled cells with conspicuous casparian strips.
4. *Stele* — Internal to the endodermis, pericycle is present which is made up of 3 - 6 layers of thin walled cells. Next to the pericycle, the stele is present. It is protostele and cylindrical with exarch xylem. Xylem may be in star like form (actinostelic) or may be in the form of isolated transverse bands (plectostelic). Phloem lies in between xylem rays or strands. The xylem consists of annular

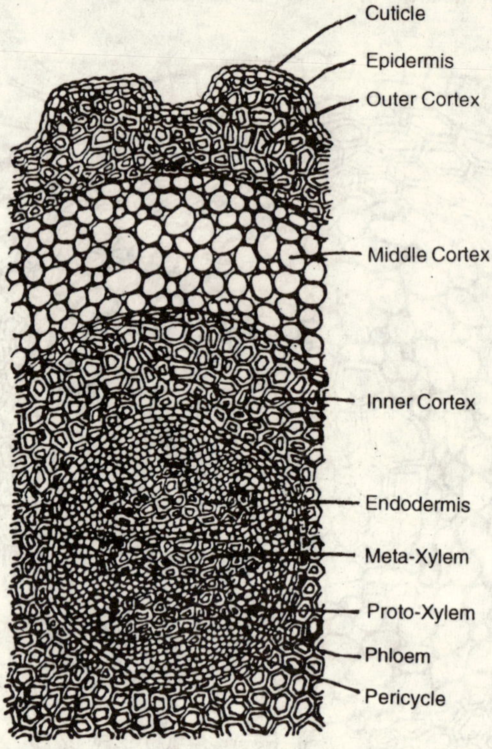

Fig. 9. T. S. of stem of *Lycopodium clavatum* (A Sector).

or spiral tracheids. The phloem consists of phloem parenchyma, sieve tubes and sieve plates. No companion cells are present. The cambium is absent (Fig. 9).

ANATOMY OF LEAF

Internally, leaf shows epidermis with cuticle, mesophyll composed of either angular or rounded parenchyma and a central vascular strand which is concentric in structure i.e. xylem is surrounded by phloem. (Fig. 10).

VEGETATIVE PROPAGATION OF THE SPOROPHYTE

Vegetative propagation takes place by the following methods.

1. *Gemmae or Bulbils* : These are modified buds of lateral branches which develop into form of out-

growths near the stem apices or in the axil of leaves. On falling off on the ground, it forms new plant.

2. *Root tuberacles* — These are bud like structure produced by parenchymatous cells of cortex of root. On germination it gives rise to new plants.
3. *Fragmentation* — Plant fragments in epiphytic species and may give rise to new individual.

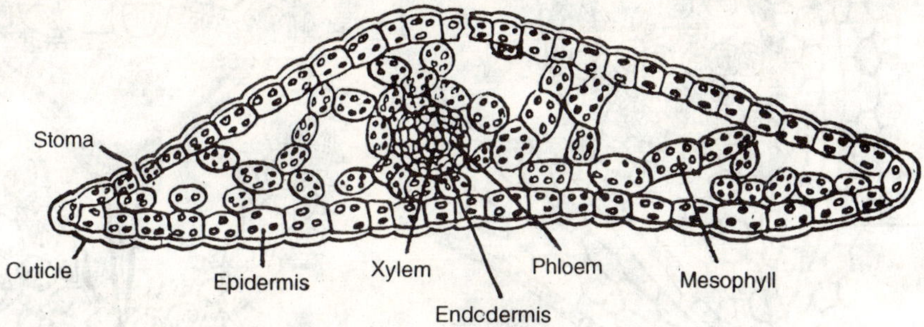

Fig. 10. T. S of leaf of *Lycopodium* sp.

SPORE BEARING ORGANS (REPRODUCTIVE STRUCTURES).

The spore are produced in sporangium. The sporangia are produced singly on ventral (upper and adaxial) surface of the leaves. Sporangia bearing leaves are called sporophylls.

In species like *L. clavatum*, sporophylls are grouped together forming a compact body called cone or strobilus. In some species like *L. selago*, sporophylls alternate with sterile foliage leaves. (Fig. 11, 12)

Strobilus — It is simple or dichotomously branched, cylindrical, 2.5 cm. to 6 cm in length, sessile or stalked having a centrally situated axis upon which sporophylls are spirally arranged.

Each sporophyll has a sporangium either in the axil of sporophyll or on the upper surface of the sporophyll. Mature sporangium is kidney shaped, orange or yellow in colour with outer jacket of sterile cells. Within the jacket sporogenous tissues are present which differentiates into spore mother cells. The spore mother cells divide meiotically into haploid spores. *Lycopodium* is homosporous. Haploid spore is the beginning of the gametophytic generation.

GAMETOPHYTE

Spore is the first cell of the gametophyte. Spores are very small, light, having smoothed or pitted walls. It is 0.03 mm in diameter. It has triradiate ridge over its surface. The spores have a little of chlorophyll.

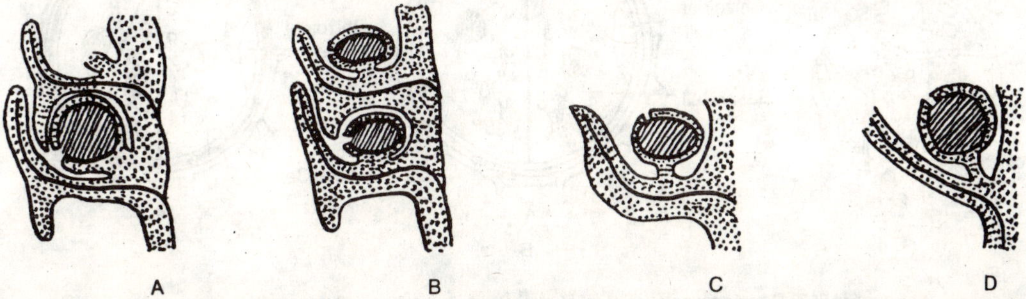

Fig. 11. Part of strobilus showing position of sporangia of (a) *Lycopodium inundatum*, (b) *L. cemuum*, (c) *L. squarrosum* and (d) *L. lucidulum*.

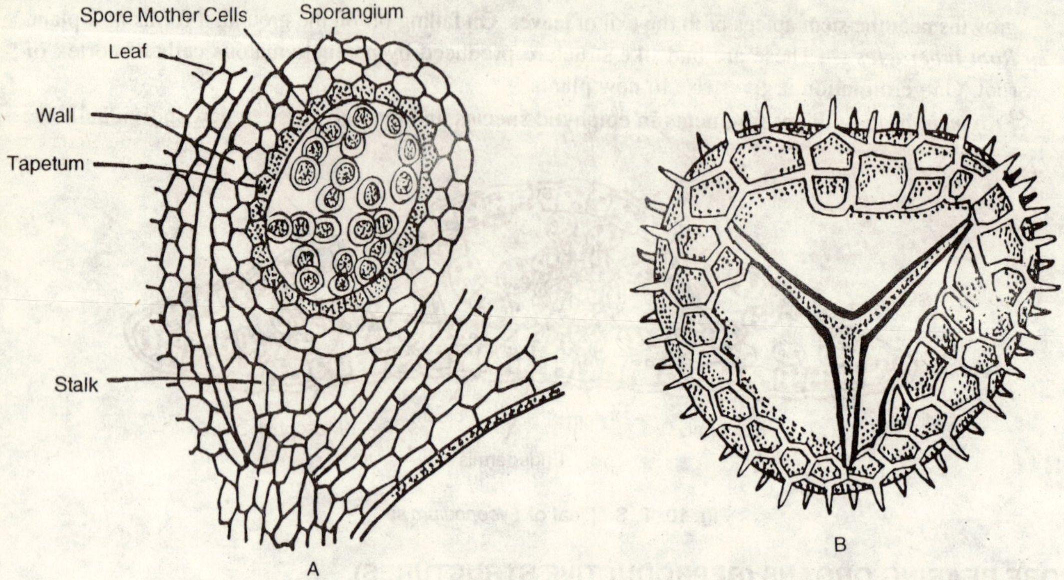

Fig. 12. (a) L.S. of sporangium of *Lycopodium* sp. and (b) A spore

Upon germination spores give rise to multicellular gametophytes or prothalli. Spores may germinate within a few days after they are shed (Treub, 1898) but in several other species germination starts after 3 - 8 years (Bruchmann, 1910) and the formation of sex organs may occur within 8 months to 6 - 15 years.

Spore divides into small biconvex lens shaped rhizoidal cell and a longer cell. The larger cell divides vertically into a basal cell near the rhizoidal cell and an outer cell. The outer cell divides by two successive divisions forming an apical cell with two cutting faces and thus a five celled stage of young gametophyte is attained. It goes under resting period for about a year and during this period infection of mycorrhizal fungus takes place.

If there is no mycorrhizal infection, further development of the gametophyte stops (Fig. 13). Prottalli are monoecious.

Structure of mature Prothalli — Three main types of prothalli in *Lycopodium* may be distinguished.

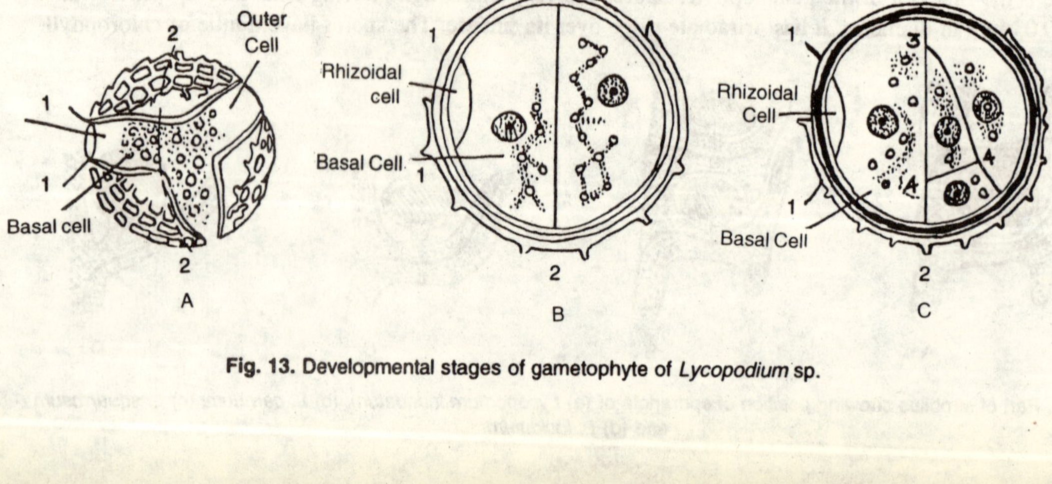

Fig. 13. Developmental stages of gametophyte of *Lycopodium* sp.

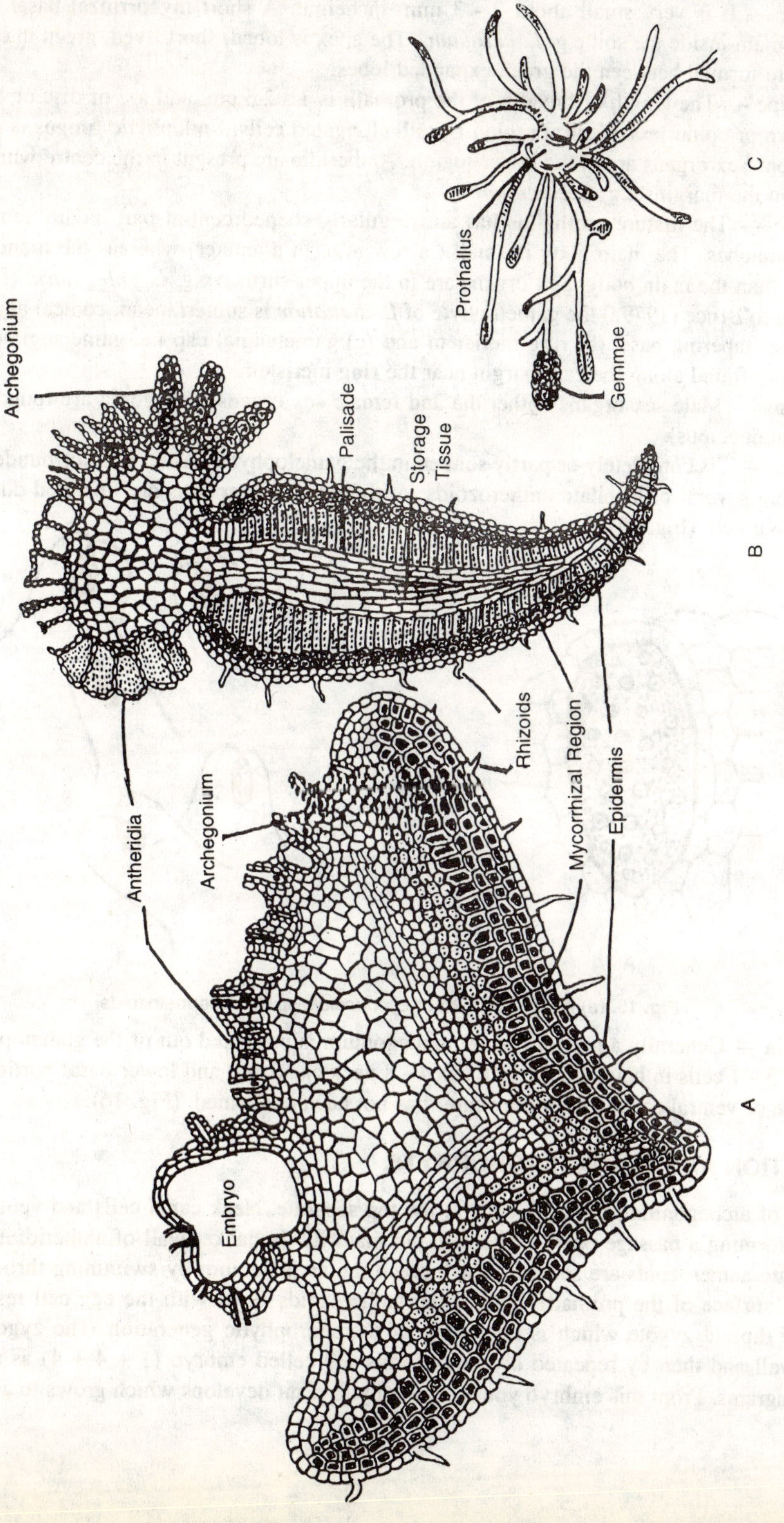

Fig. 14. Gametophytes of (a) *L. clavatum* (b) *L. complanatum* and (c) *L. phlegmaria.*

First type — It is very small about 2 - 3 mm. in height. A short mycorrhizal basal region of the prothallus remain inside the soil e.g. *L. cernuum.* The apex is lobed, short lived, green in colour and the sex organs are formed between the green expanded lobes.

Second type — The length or breadth of the prothalli is 1 - 2.5 cm. and are of disc or carrot shaped, yellow, brown or colourless. Central region is with elongated cells. Endophytic fungus is present in the cortical region. Sex organs are in the upper region. Antheridia are present in the centre while archegonia are located on the margins e.g. *L. clavatum.*

Third type — The mature prothallus has an irregularly shaped central part having many colourless cylindrical branches. The main body is small (a few mm. in diameter) whereas the branches are 2 - 5 times longer than the main body. Sex organs are in the upper surface e.g. *L. phlegmaria* (Fig. 14).

According to Bruce (1979a) the gametophyte of *L. digitatum* is subterranean, conical and divided into three parts; (a) tapering base, (b) ring meristem and (c) gametangial cap i.e. gametangia (antheridia & archegonia) are found along the cap margin near the ring meristem.

Sex organs — Male sex organs antheridia and female sex organs archegonia are found on the same prothallus (monoecious).

Antheridia — It is completely or partly sunken in the gametophytic tissue. It is surrounded by a jacket layer enclosing several biflagellate antherozoids. Antherozoids i.e sperms are liberated due to breaking of the opercular cell. (Fig. 15).

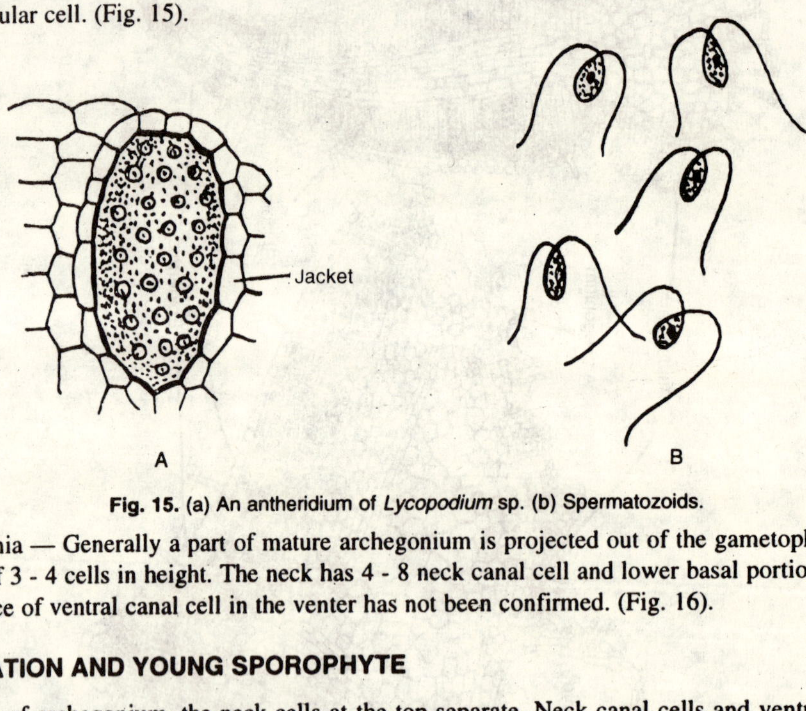

Fig. 15. (a) An antheridium of *Lycopodium* sp. (b) Spermatozoids.

Archegonia — Generally a part of mature archegonium is projected out of the gametophyte. It has a long neck of 3 - 4 cells in height. The neck has 4 - 8 neck canal cell and lower basal portion has an egg cell. Presence of ventral canal cell in the venter has not been confirmed. (Fig. 16).

FERTILIZATION AND YOUNG SPOROPHYTE

On maturity of archegonium, the neck cells at the top separate. Neck canal cells and ventral canal cell disintegrate forming a passage open to the egg. On maturity the jacket wall of antheridium breaks and the biflagellate antherozoids are set free which reach the archegonium by swimming through a film of water on the surface of the prothalli. One of the antherozoids fuses with the egg cell resulting in the formation of diploid zygote which is beginning of the sporophytic generation. The zygote surrounds itself by a wall and then by repeated divisions forms a 9 celled embryo (1 + 4 + 4) as shown in the following diagrams. From this embryo young sporophytic plant develops which grows to a mature plant (Fig. 17).

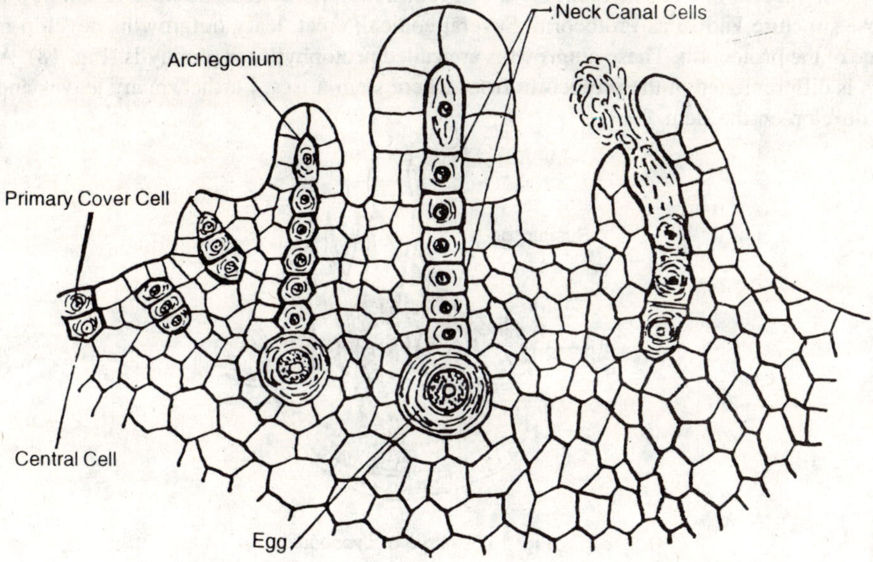

Fig. 16. Developing archegonia of *Lycopodium* sp.

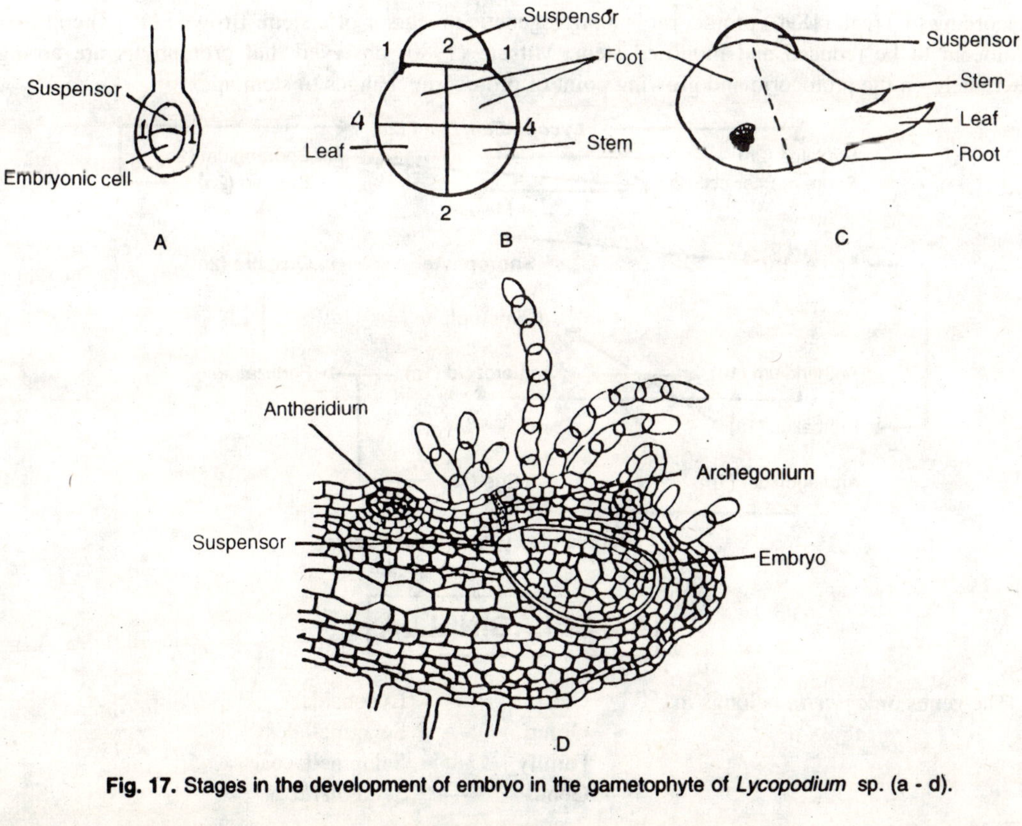

Fig. 17. Stages in the development of embryo in the gametophyte of *Lycopodium* sp. (a - d).

In other species like *L. clavatum* the distal four cells of 9 celled structure of embryo develop into a globose structure known as Protocorm. Several conical, erect, leafy outgrowths develop from the upper surface of the protocorm. These outgrowths are called protophylls, or prophylls (Fig. 18). A meristematic region is differentiated in the protocorm from where stem arises. Further, many leaves and adventicious roots develop on the stem.

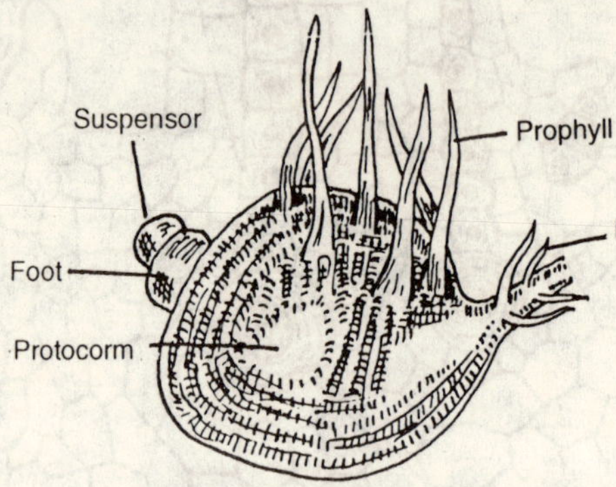

Fig. 18. Embryo of *Lycopodium sp.*

MORPHOLOGICAL NATURE OF PROTOCORM

According to Treub (1890) protocorm is a phylogenetic precursor of a stem. Browne (1913) considered protocom to be reduced and modified stem. Mitsuta (1980) observed that protophylls are arranged alternately on the protocorm and growing point of protocorm changes to stem apex.

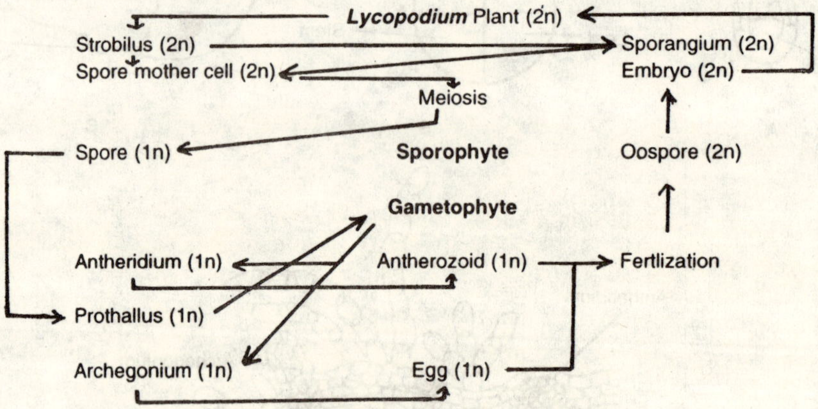

Graphic life cycle of *Lycopodium*

3.2 SELAGINELLA

The genus *Selaginella* belongs to

Class	—	Lycopsida
Order	—	Selaginellales
Family	—	Selaginellaceae
Genus	—	*Selaginella*

HABIT AND HABITAT

Panigrahi & Choudhury (1961) have reported about 65 species of *Selaginella* from India. According to Sporne (1970) there are about 700 species in the genus *Selanginella.* It is commonly known as 'Small club moss'. Plant body is sporophyte, generally perennial or rarely annual prostrate herbs creeping on soil surface. Some species are erect (*S. erythropus*) or suberect (*S. trachyphylla*). The size of the sporophytic plant body varies from few centimeters (*S. Selaginoides*) to about 20 meters (*S. willdenowii*). The genus *Selaginella* is worldwide in distribution. Majority of the species occur in rain forest of tropical countries in damp, shaded and humid conditions. Some species are xerophytes (*S. rupestris*) some are epiphytes (*S. oregana*). *S. bryopteris* are grown as ornamental plants under the name of Sanjivani (Dixit, 1982).

EXTERNAL MORPHOLOGY OF SPOROPHYTE

The genus *Selaginella* has been divided into two subgenera, viz, Homeophyllum and Heterophyllum on the basis of types of leaves. The sporophytic plant body is differentiated into stem, leaves, rhizophore and roots. (Fig. 19).

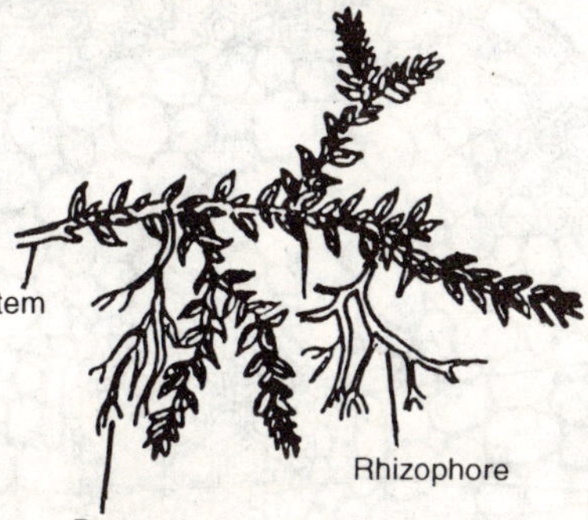

Fig. 19. A twig of *Selaginella kraussiana.*

Stem — Stem is prostrate, suberect in the subgenus heterophyllum, while stem in the subgenus homeophyllum is erect showing dichotomous branching, usually dorsiventral and prostrate. Near the place of branching, a long, unbranched, leafless structure towards the lowerside arises in the stem. This structure is called rhizophore. It becomes branched at its top and develops many adventitious roots.

MORPHOLOGICAL NATURE OF THE RHIZOPHORE

There are several views regarding the morphological nature of the rhizophore as follows —

1. Van Tieghem and Harvey Gibson (1902) considered rhizophore as capless root due to root like anatomy and leafless and positively geotropic nature. Webster & Steeves (1960, 1964) found rootcap in *S. dene.*
2. Pfeffer (1871), Bruchmann (1909) and Worsdell (1910) regarded rhizophore as leafless shoot due to its exogenous origin, lack of root caps and root hairs, development from 'angle meristems' and totipotency to grow into leafy shoots under experimental conditions.
3. Goebel (1905) and Bower (1908, 1935) observed that the rhizophore is neither shoot nor root but organs '*sui generis*'

   However, on the basis of the work done by Wochok and Sussex (1974) and considering the anatomical features, it has been suggested by Rashid (1976) that the term rhizophore should be of historical importance only and it is nothing but a root.

ANATOMY OF RHIZOPHORE

Transverse section of rhizophore shows the following features —

Epidermis — It is made up of thick walled cells.

Hypodermis — Below the epidermis, multilayered, thick walled hypodermis.

Cortex — Below the hypodermis are present few layers of parenchymatous cortex.

Endodermis — Cortex is limited by one layer of endodermis towards centre.

Pericycle — Below the endodermis one layered pericycle is present.

Stele — The stele of rhizophore is typically a protostele. Some variations in its form and arrangement of protoxylem are found in different species. In *S. kraussiana* centroxylic condition is found in which protoxylem is surrounded by metaxylem. In *S. martensii* stele is monarch and exarch (Fig. 20).

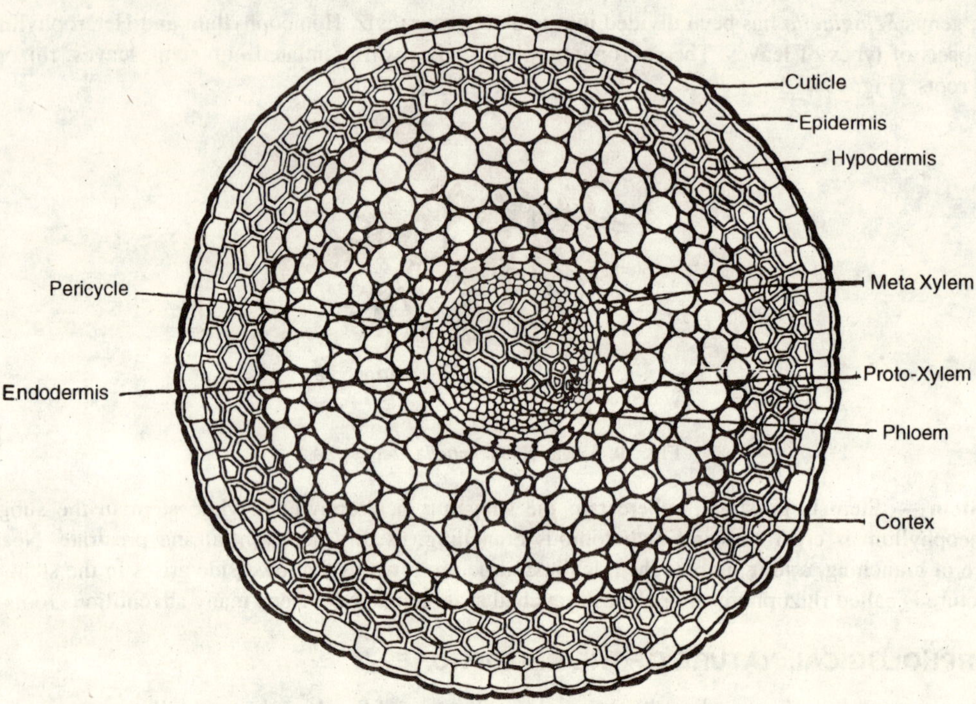

Fig. 20. T. S. of Rhizophore of *Selaginella martensii.*

Leaves — The leaves are small, simple, lanceolate to ovate, with a mid rib. A ligule is present at the base of upper (adaxial) surface of each leaf. Each ligule has a basal hemispherical structure known as glossopodium. Ligule is associated with water conservation. It may help in upward movement of inorganic solutes. Phyllotaxy of leaves may be spiral or decussate or in four longitudinal rows out of which two rows are present in ventral surface and two rows on dorsal surface (Fig. 21).

Roots — It is adventitious and dichotomously branched. It develops from the place of bifurcation of stem as in *S. laevigata*, on the stem as in *S. lepidophylla*.

ANATOMY OF STEM

Transverse section of stem shows the following structures.

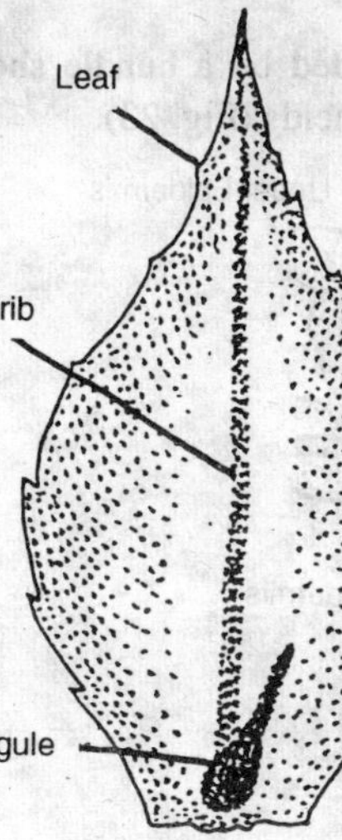

Fig. 21. A leaf of *Selaginella* sp. showing ligule on adaxial surface.

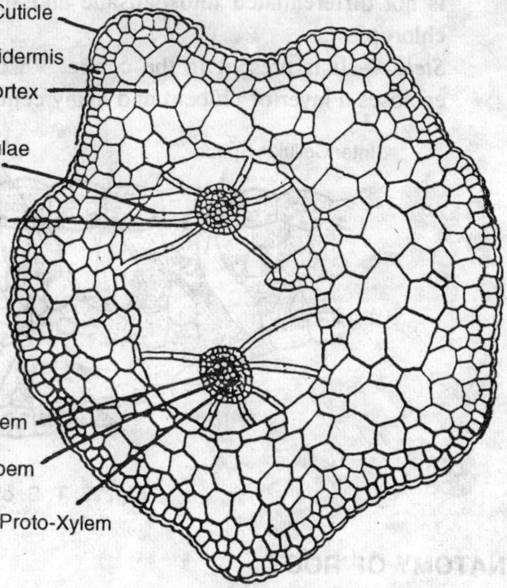

Fig. 22. T. S. of stem of *Selaginella kraussiana*.

Epidermis — It is outermost layer, one cell thick made up of prosenchymatous cutinized cells without stoma.

Hypodermis — it may be present or may not be. If it is present, it is made up of 2 - 3 layers of sclerenchyma.

Cortex — It is made up of thin walled parenchymatous cells. In xerophytic stem, cortex is sclerenchymatous, e.g. *S. rupestris*.

Stele — Central core of axis is stele. It is connected with trabeculae, made up of long radially elongated cells. Large lacunae or intercellular spaces are present in between the trabeculae. In *S. rupestris* and other xerophytic species trabeculae are absent.

Trabeculae is endodermal in origin as evidenced by the presence of casparian strips on the radial walls of trabeculae. The number of stele varies from 1 to 16 depending upon the species. The organization of stele also varies from a simple protostele to polyxylic siphonostele. Each stele has pericycle, phloem and Xylem. Pericyle is made up of parenhymatous cells. Phloem consists of phloem parenchyma and sieve cells. Xylem has one or two groups of protoxylem facing in opposite direction. Xylem is exarch. Metaxylem has tracheids with scalariform thickening and protoxylem tracheids are spirally thickened.

There is no secondary growth in *Selaginella*. However, Bruchmann (1897) has reported secondary growth in *S. selagenoides*. (Fig. 22).

ANATOMY OF LEAF

Vertical section of leaf shows the following features

Epidermis — Upper and lower epidermis of one cell thickness. Stomata may be found on upper or lower or on both the epidermis.

Epidermal cells have chloroplast.

Mesophyll — Mesophyll cells are present in between the upper and lower epidermis. Mesophyll is not differentiated into palisade and spongy parenchyma. Mesophyll cells have cup shaped chloroplast.

Stele — It is present in the centre. Vascular bundle is surrounded by a bundle sheath which encloses a layer of phloem and many centrally placed xylem tracheids (Fig. 23).

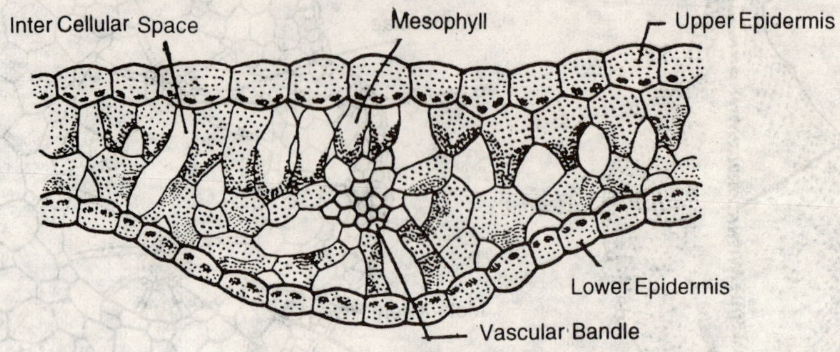

Fig. 23. T. S. of leaf of *Selaginella* sp.

ANATOMY OF ROOT

Internal structure of root shows the following organization.

Epidermis — It is outermost layer of cells. Root hairs may arise from epidermal cells.

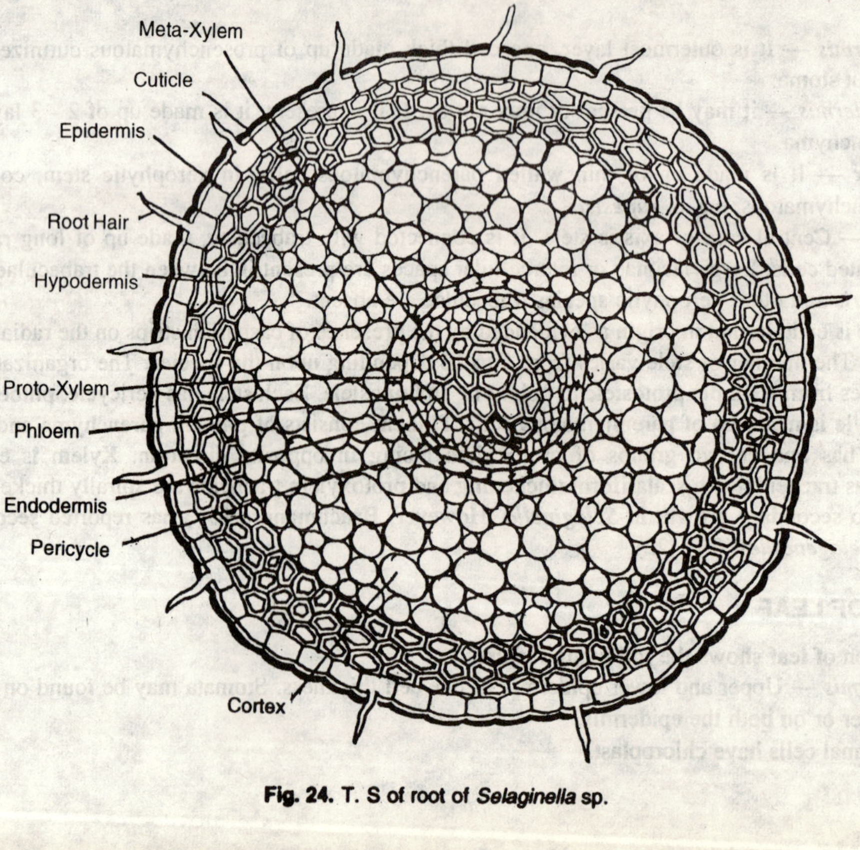

Fig. 24. T. S of root of *Selaginella* sp.

Cortex — Below the epidermis, multilayered parenchymatous cortex is present. In old roots, the outer cortex becomes sclerenchymatous.

In some species like *S. densa* trabeculae is present which resemble that of stem.

Stele — Endodermis may be found or may not be well developed. Pericycle is 1 - 3 layered in different species. Stele may show monarch to tetrarch condition and exarch in nature. The phloem surrounds the xylem (Fig. 24).

VEGETATIVE PROPOGATION

Selaginella propagates vegetatively by fragmentation, bulbil formation, tuber formation and resting bud formation.

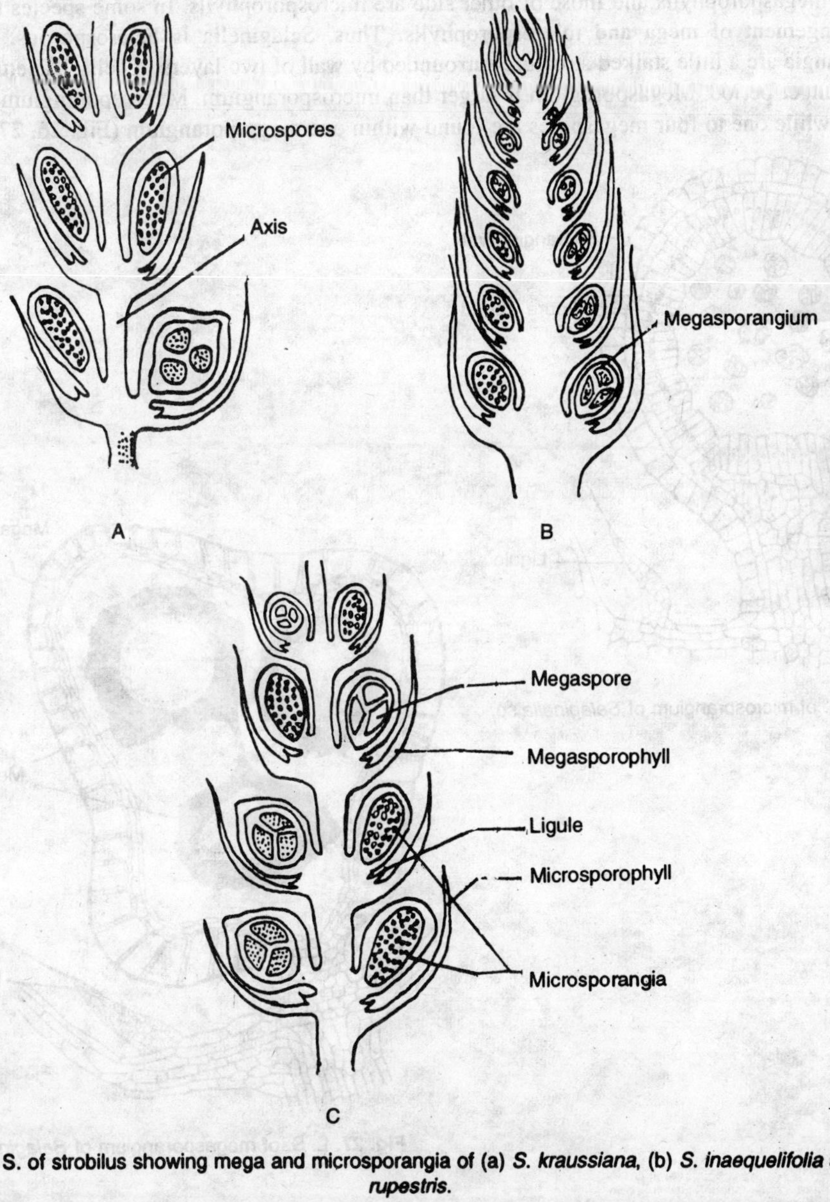

Fig. 25. L. S. of strobilus showing mega and microsporangia of (a) *S. kraussiana*, (b) *S. inaequelifolia* and (c) *S. rupestris*.

SPORE PRODUCING ORGANS

Spore producing organs are called sporangia which are present on the apex of main axis and on the lateral branches. The sporangia are found in the axil of leafy structures called sporophylls. Each sporophyll has a ligule and a stalked sporangium. Sporophylls are loosely or spirally arranged on the axis forming a loose cone like structure called strobilus. The length of the strobilus ranges from few millimeter to 4 - 5 cm in different species.

Generally, two types of sporophylls i.e. megasporophylls and microsporophylls are present on the same strobilus. In *S. atroviridis* and *S. gracilis* strobilus has either microsporophylls or megasporophylls only. In *S. kraussiana* basal sporophyll is megasporophyll bearing megasporangia and remaining sporophylls are microsporophylls bearing microsporangia. In *S. oregana* sporophylls of one side of strobilus are megasporophylls and those of other side are microsporophylls. In some species there is no definite arrangement of mega and microsporophylls. Thus, Selaginella is heterosporous. (Fig. 25). Mature sporangia are a little stalked structure surrounded by wall of two layers of cells. Tapetum may be present for longer period. Megasporogium is larger than microsporangium. Mecrosporangium has many microspores while one to four megaspores are found within one megasporangium (Fig. 26, 27).

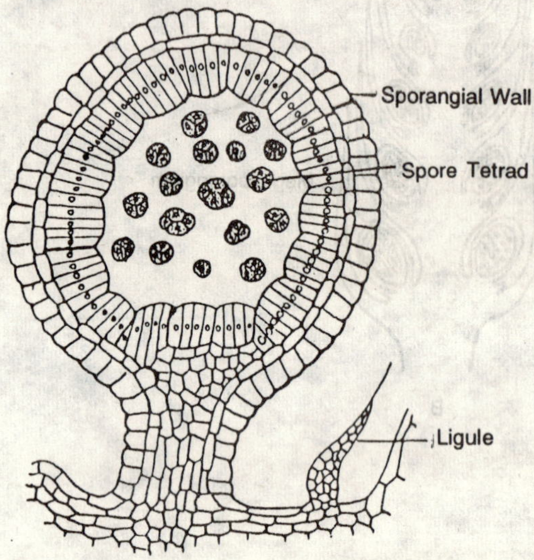

Fig. 26. L. S. of microsprangium of *Selaginella* sp.

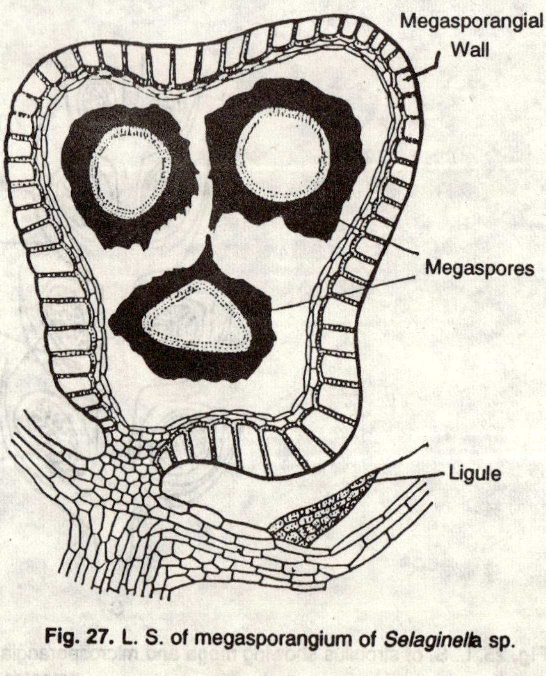

Fig. 27. L. S. of megasporangium of *Selaginella* sp.

SPORE AND DEVELOPMENT OF GAMETOPHYTA

Microspores are spherical or rounded structure. Its diameter varies from 0.015 to 0.06 mm surrounded by an outer thick and ornamented exine and an inner thin and smooth intine. Megaspores are tetrahedral and its diameter varies from 0.5 mm to 1.5 mm. The wall is of threc layers i.e. outer thick exospore, middle mesospore and the innermost thin endospore.

Microgametophyte — The microspore start to germinate within microsporangium. It is dehisced when it attains 13 celled stage (1 prothallial cell + 4 primary spermatogenous cell + 8 jacket cells). After dehiscing each of the four primary spermatogenous cells may undergo six successive divisions forming 256 androcytes or sperm mother cells which later metamorphoses into biflagellate antherozoids. Jacket cells and prothallial cell are disorganised at later stage and mass of uninucleate, biflagellate antherozoids remains swimming for some time (Fig. 28, 29).

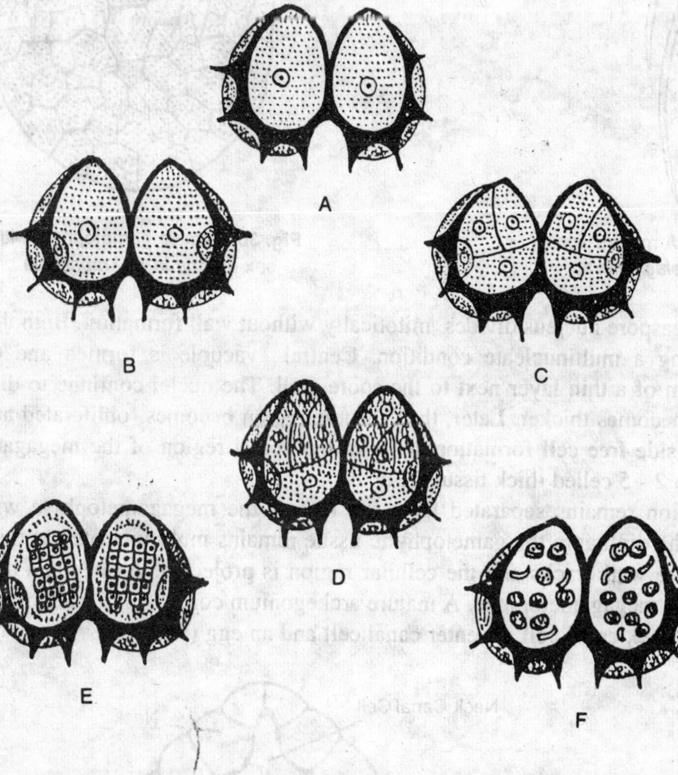

Fig. 28. Diagramatic representation of developmental stages of male gametophyte in vertically splitted position in *Selaginella* sp.

Megagametophyte — The megaspore begins to develop into megagametophyte in situ, i.e. while it is still within the megasporangium. In some species, megaspores are shed after first division has taken place, but in others after the formation of archegonail initial. According to Lyon (1901) megaspores remain indefinitely within the megasporangium of *S. rupestris* till fertilization and embryo development occurs. Young roots and leaves may develop within young sporophyte while it is still attached to the megagametophyte and ultimately upon parent sporophyte. This feature is observed mainly in angiosperms.

Development of megagametophyte starts with a conspicous enlargement of the germinating

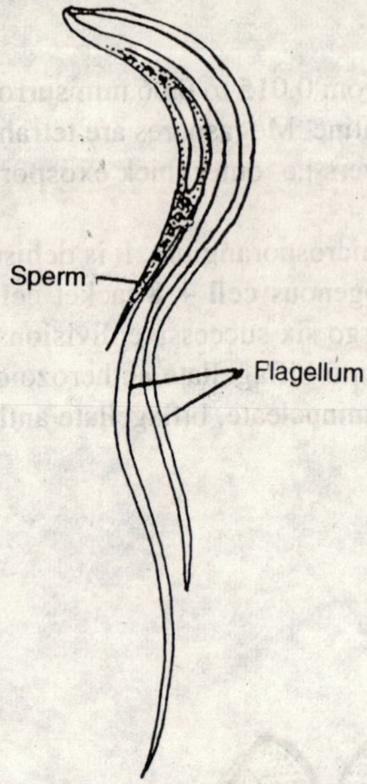

Fig. 29. A mature sperm of *Selaginella* sp.

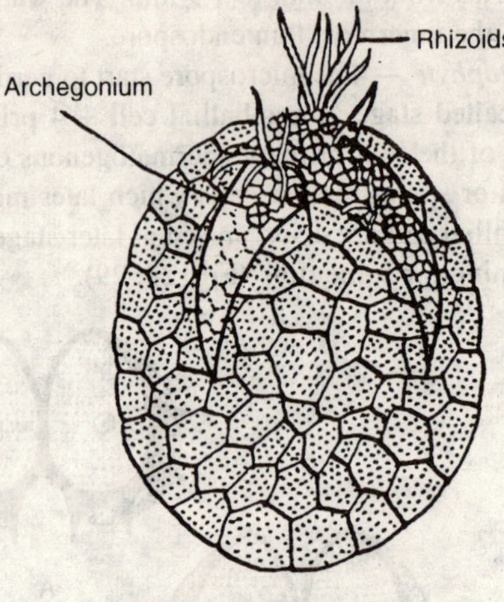

Fig. 30. Female gametophyte with sex organs in *S. kraussiana*.

megaspore. The megaspore nucleus divides mitotically without wall formation. Both these nuclei divide and redivide forming a multinucleate condition. Central vacuole is formed and the cytoplasm is restricted in the form of a thin layer next to the spore wall. The nuclei continue to divide and the thin layer of cytoplasm becomes thicker. Later, the vacuole region becomes obliterated and filled with the cytoplasm. Side by side free cell formation starts in the apical region of the megagametophyte which finally develops into 2 - 5 celled thick tissue. (Fig. 30).

This cellular region remains separated from the rest of the megagametophyte with the help of a diaphragm. Below the diphragm the gametophytic tissue remains multinucleate. At this stage the upper part of the megaspore wall cracks and the cellular region is projected. Archegonia develops from this cellular portion of the megagametophyte. A mature archegonium consists of a neck made up of two tiers of four cells each, a neck canal cell, a venter canal cell and an egg (Fig. 31).

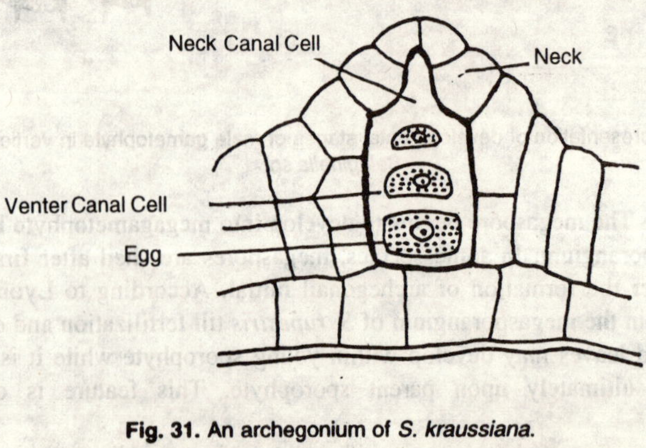

Fig. 31. An archegonium of *S. kraussiana*.

FERTILIZATION & EMBRYO DEVELOPMENT

Fertilization may take place while the complete megagametophyte is still within the megasporangium. In some other species the fertilization takes place after the megagemetophyte falls on the ground. At the time of fertilization the neck cells are spread apart, the neck canal cells and venter canal cells are disintegrated, leaving free passage for the antherozoid to enter and unite with the egg. Rain drops or dew

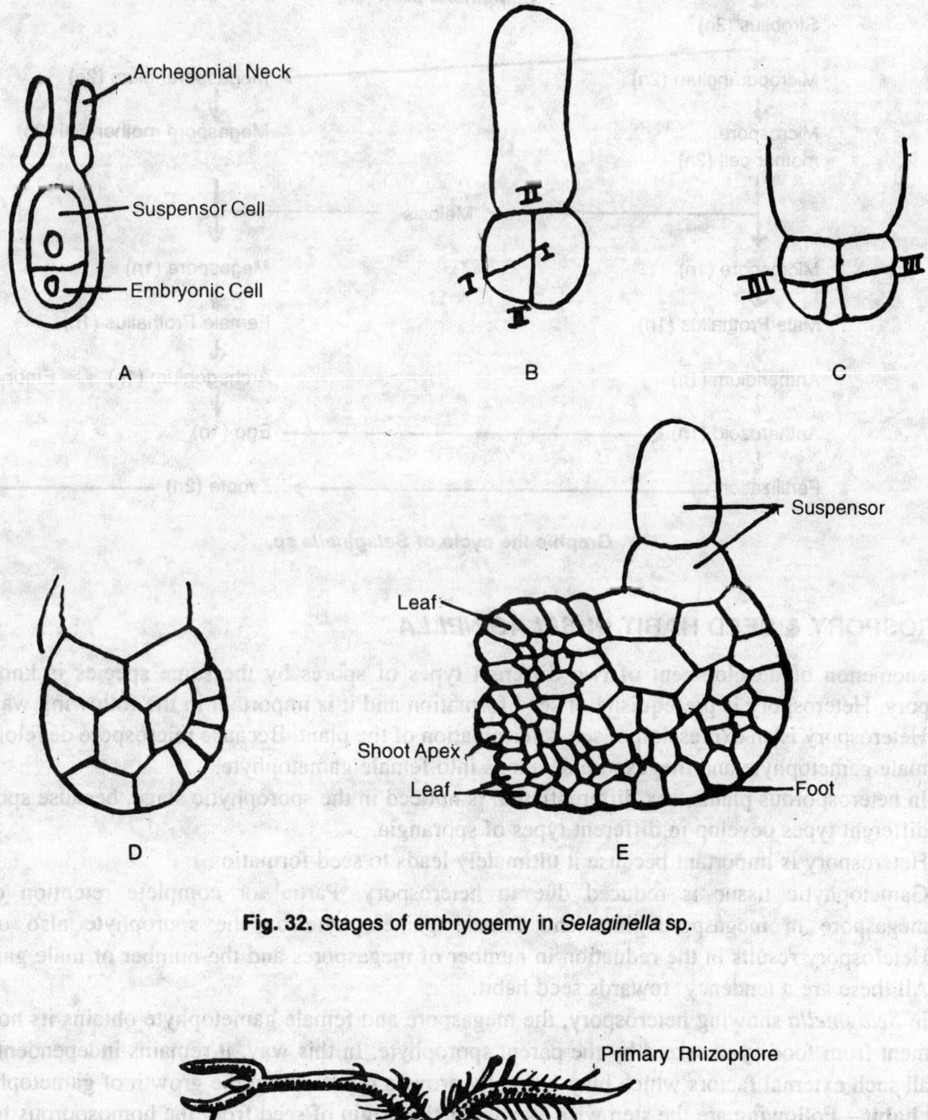

Fig. 32. Stages of embryogemy in *Selaginella* sp.

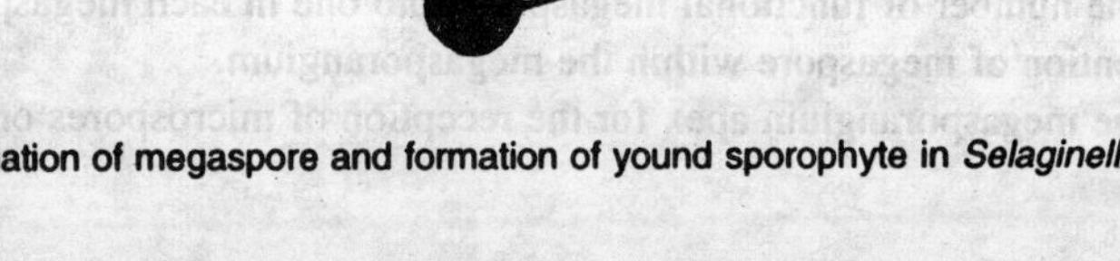

Fig. 33. Germination of megaspore and formation of yound sporophyte in ***Selaginella kraussiana.***

helps in the transfer of antherozoid upto the neck of the archegonium. After fertilization, zygote is formed which is beginning of the new sporophytic (diploid) generation. The zygote develops into an embryo. First of all, the zygote divides transversely into two cells, (1) the upper epibasal or suspenser cell towards the neck of archegonium and (2) the lower hypobasal or embryonic cell. The suspensor cell forms the suspensor and the embryonic cell forms the remainder of the embryo. The embryo is endosporic (Fig. 32, 33).

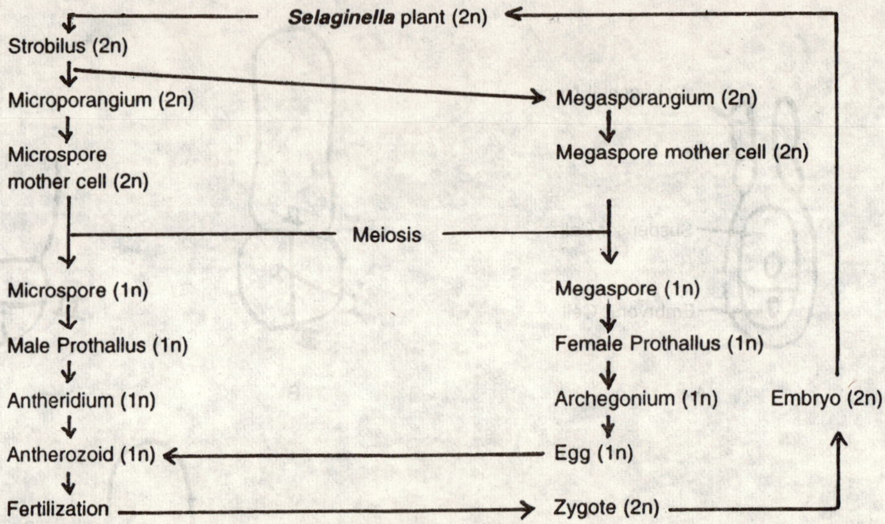

Graphic life cycle of *Selaginella* sp.

HETEROSPORY & SEED HABIT IN *SELAGINELLA*

The phenomenon of development of two different types of spores by the same species is known as heterospory. Heterospory is prerequisite of seed formation and it is important in the following ways :

1. Heterospory is an expression of sex determination of the plant. Because microspore develops into male gametophyte and megaspore develops into female gametophyte.
2. In heterosporous plants, sex differentiation is noticed in the sporophytic stage, because spores of different types develop in different types of sporangia.
3. Heterospory is important because it ultimately leads to seed formation.
4. Gametophytic tissue is reduced due to heterospory. Partial or complete retention of the megaspore in megasporangium and female gametophyte on the sporophyte also occurs. Heterospory results in the reduction in number of megaspores and the number of male gametes. All these are a tendency towards seed habit.
5. In *Selaginella* showing heterospory, the megaspore and female gametophyte obtains its nourishment from food synthesized by the parent sporophyte. In this way, it remains independent from all such external factors which may normally prove a hindrance in the growth of gametophyte.

Seed habit—Following are the step wise events for the origin of seed from the homosporous form :-

1. Development of two types of spores i.e. heterospory.
2. Reduction in the number of functional megaspore upto one in each megasporangium.
3. Permanent retention of megaspore within the megasporangium.
4. Widening of the megasporangium apex for the reception of microspores or pollen grains.

5. Fertilization and embryo development also takes place in situ.
6. Formation of integuments outside the megasporangium by the union of megaspore and megasporangium.

HOW FAR *SELAGINELLA* ATTAINS SEED HABIT

In the light of the above noted events, *Selaginella* attains the seed habit as follows:

1. It is heterosporous
2. In certain species like *S. rupestris* and *S. monospora*, the number of megaspore is reduced to one.
3. Germination of megaspore takes place within the megasporangium and it is retained within the megasporangium depending upon the species.
4. Archegonia develop in situ in *S. rupestris.*
5. The fertilization and the development of embryo up to the formation of cotyledons and roots also occur in situ i.e within the megasporangium.

In spite of all these factors favourable for seed formation, well developed seeds are not found in Selaginella because of (1) the absence of integuments around the megasporangium, (2) the absence of permanent retention of megaspore within megasporangium except a few species and (3) the absence of complete historical fusion between the megaspore and the megasporangium wall.

Above all Parihar (1977) rightly said the Selaginella should be regarded as progenitor of seed plants.

CHAPTER 4

SPHENOPSIDA

HISTORICAL DESCRIPTION

The existence of sphenopsida can be traced back from the lower Devonian period attaining their maximum development in the carboniferous period and at present it is represented by only a single living genus *Equisetum.* The class sphenopsida has also been named as Articulatae, Arthrophyta or Equisetophyta.

SALIENT FEATURES

1. According to sporne (1970) Sphenopsida is represented by one living taxon *Equisetum* and about 18 fossil taxa.
2. The plant body is sporophyte devided into root, stem and leaves.
3. The stem is ribbed, articulated, longitudinally furrowed and well branched.
4. The leaves are small, scaly and whorled.
5. The stele is medullated protostele.
6. The sporangia are born on sporangiophore.
7. Mostly they are homosporous but fossil forms were heterosporous.
8. Antherozoids are multiflagellate.
9. Embryo is without suspensor.
10. Secondary thickening was noticed in some extinct forms.

4.1 EQUISETUM

It belongs to	Class	—	Sphenopsida
	Order	—	Equisetales
	Family	—	Equisetaceae
	Genus	—	*Equisetum*

HABIT AND HABITAT

Equisetum is commonly known as Horsetail or 'Scouring rushes'. It has 20 - 30 species, cosmopolitan in distribution. However, *Equisetum* has not been recorded from Australia and New Zealand. Some common Indian species are *E. arvense, E. debile* etc, Equisetum grow in a variety of habitats. Some species are found in marshy land (E. palustre), some grow in damp shady places (E. pratense). *E. arvense* grow in open grass fields. *Equisetum* are used as ecological indicators to indicate the mineral contents of the soil in which they grow. Some *Equisetum* species accumulate minerals including gold and hence can be used to know the presence of new ore deposits. The plant body is sporophyte differentiated into rhizomes, stems, roots and leaves. The height of plant varies from 15 cm to 10 meters. The maximum thickness of stem is 2 cm only (Fig. 34).

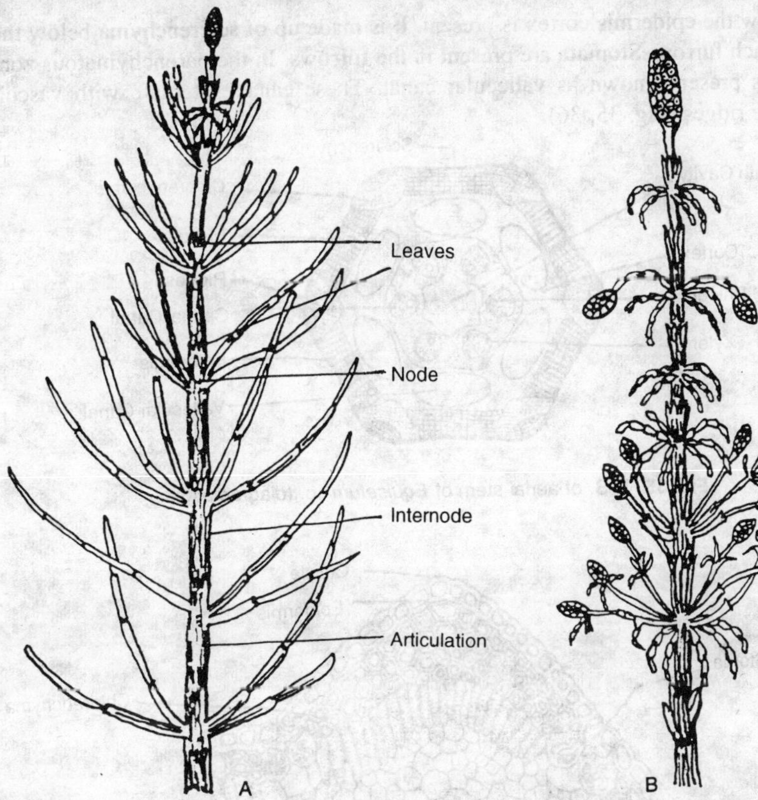

Fig. 34. Twig of (a) *Equisetum pratense* and (b) *E. sylvaticum.*

EXTERNAL MORPHOLOGY OF SPOROPHYTE

It is branched, perennial herb having horizontal underground rhizome from which erect aerial shoot arise. Rhizome bears adventitious roots at the nodes. Stem is unbranched in *E. hyemale*.

Stem — Rhizome is long, creeping, branched, differentiated into nodes and internodes. Many scaly leaves are present on its nodes. Scaly leaves are small, slender and laterally united with each other to form a sheath on the node. Branch primordium is present on the node. Branch primordium may develop into tubers also e.g. *E. arvense*. Aerial shoot develops from rhizome which may be branched or unbranched. Aerial shoots may be either fertile or sterile. Sterile shoots are branched, green & photosynthetic in nature while fertile shoots are unbranched, colourless, bearing cover at their apices.

The rhizome and aerial shoots are articulated (jointed) and ribbed longitudinally differentiated into nodes and internodes. Number of ridges corresponds to the number of leaves.

Leaves — Leaves are scaly, minute, thin, uninerved and arranged in whorl.

Roots — Roots arise from the node of the rhizome or from the base of the stem. They are adventitious, long, branched and slender.

ANATOMY OF AERIAL SHOOT

The transverse section of the internode of aerial shoot (sterile) has the following features :

Epidermis — It is outer most layer of cells. The cells of this layer has deposit of silica. Stomata are present in this layer.

Cortex — Below the epidermis cortex is present. It is made up of sclerenchyma below the ridge and chlorenchyma in each furrow. Stomata are present in the furrows. In the parenchymatous zone of cortex a large air canal is present known as vallecular canal. These canals alternate with vascular bundles situated beneath the ridges (Fig. 35, 36).

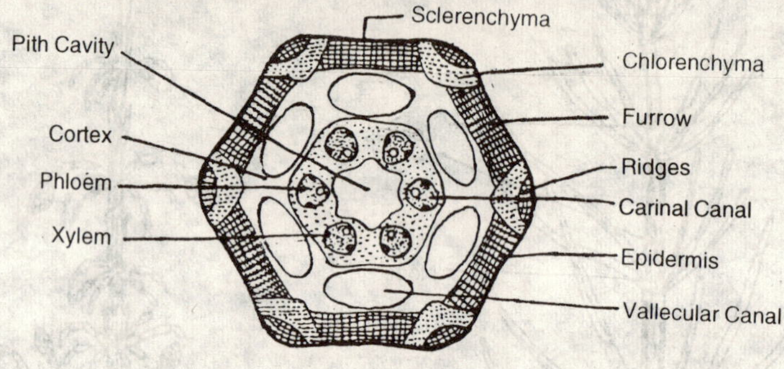

Fig. 35. T. S. of aerial stem of *Equisetum* sp. (diagramatic).

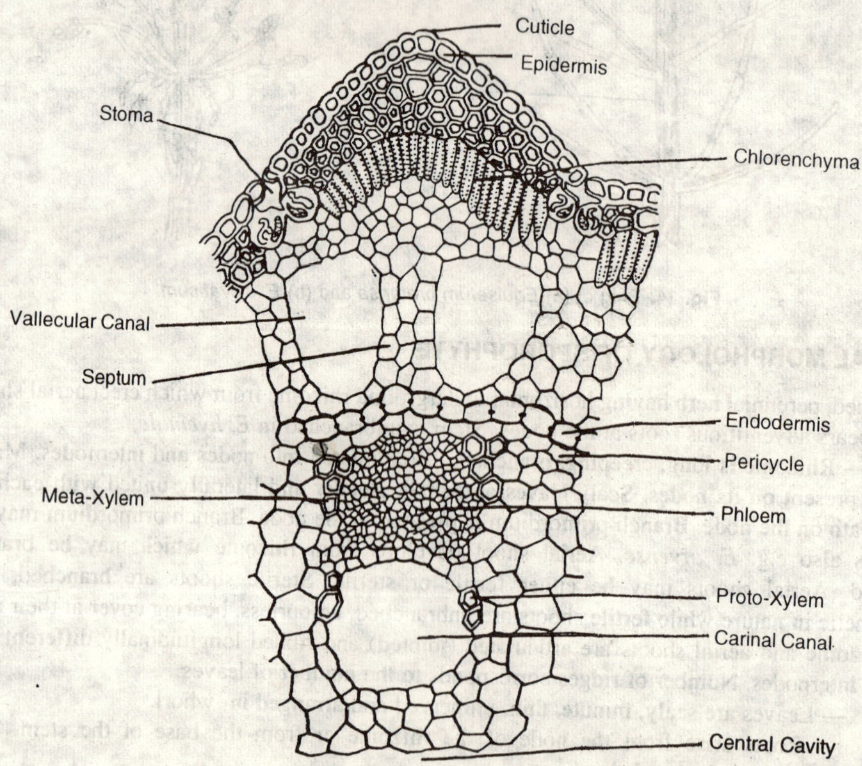

Fig. 36. T. S. of internode of aerial stem of *Equisetum* sp.

Endodermis — In *E. palustre*, endodermis forms a sheath surrounding the entire stele. In *E. sylvaticum* an inner endodermis is present besides the general outer endodermis. In *E. litorale* each vascular bundle is surrounded by special endodermis.

Pericycle — One layered pericycle is present below the endodermis. In some species it is not well marked.

Vascular cylinder — The vascular cylinder is siphonostelic. Vascular bundles are arranged in a ring. Each V.B. is conjoint, collateral and closed. It consists of xylem, phloem and some parenchyma. In each V.B. a water canal or cavity is present known as carinal canal. Xylem is endarch made up of protoxylem and metaxylem. Pholem consists of sieve tubes and phoem parenchyma.

Pith — The centre of the aerial shoot is of pith in the form of cavity. There is no pith cavity in *E. scirpoides.*

Aerial shoot has xerophytic as well as hydrophytic characters. Presence of ridge and furrows, thick cuticle, sunken stomata, well developed sclerenchyma and vascular bundles are xerophytic characters. Presence of carinal canals, vallecular canals and well developed pith cavity are hydrophytic characters.

Anatomy of internode of rhizome — Antomically rhizomes are similar to aerial shoot. However, it differs from aerial shoot in the following features :

1. Ridges and furrows, not prominent.
2. Absence of stomata and chlorenchymatous region.
3. Poorly developed sclerenchyma.
4. Ill developed pith cavity or absence of pith cavity (Fig. 37).

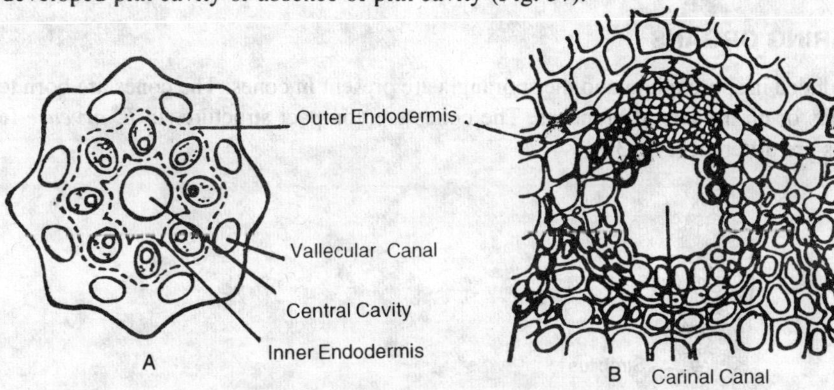

Fig. 37. T. S. of rhizome of *Equisetum* sp. (a) diagramatic and (b) (A sector).

Anatomy of internode of aerial fertile shoot —
there are similarity in fertile and sterile shoot except the followings:

1. Absence of stomata in some species.
2. Poorly developed sclerenchymatous and chlorenchymatous regions.

ANATOMY OF ADVENTITIOUS ROOT

T. S. of adventitious root shows the following anatomical features.

1. *Epidermis* — It is outermost layer from which root hair may or may not develop.

   Cortex — It is below the epidermis and many layered. Cortex may be divided into outer thick walled exodermis and inner parenchymatous cortex with intercellular spaces.

   Endodermis — It is two layered thick. But outer may be of endodermis and inner layer of pericycle as the secondary root develops from inner endodermis which is also devoid of casparian strips.

Stele — The stele is protostele and triarch to hexarch. Phloem is present in between the space of protoxylem (Fig. 38).

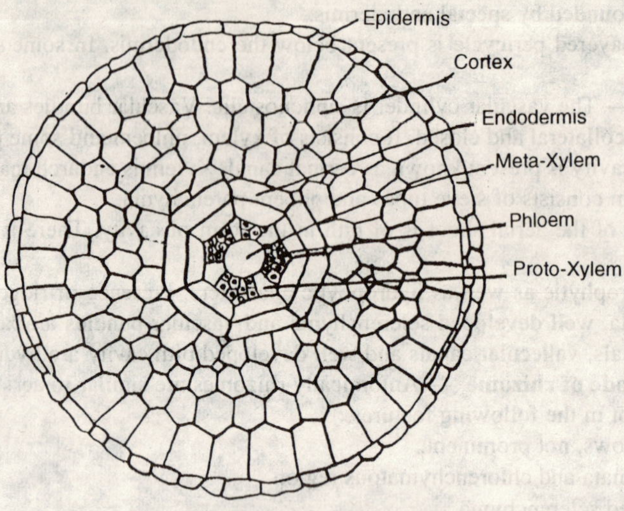

Fig. 38. T.S. of root of Equisetum sp.

SPORE BEARING ORGANS

Spores are produced in sporangium and the sporangia are present in cones. The cones are born terminally on the main axis or on the lateral branches. The cones are compact structure. In *E. arvense* fertile and sterile branches are different (Fig. 39).

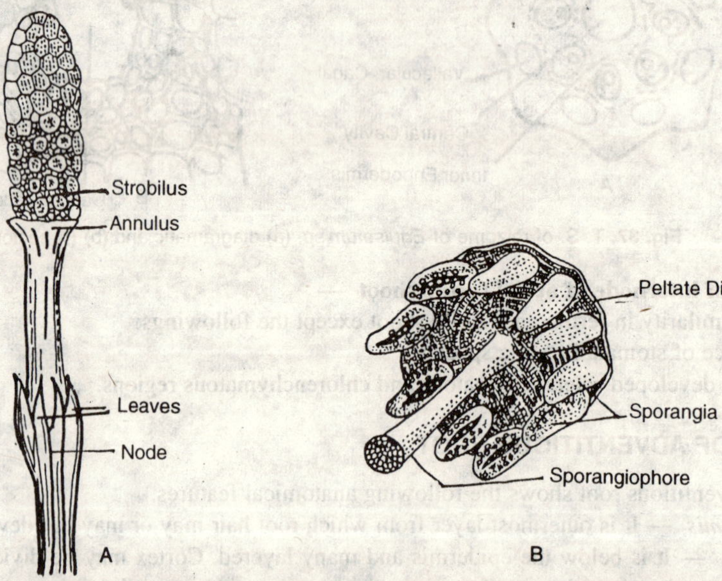

Fig. 39. (a) Tip of fertile shoot and (b) ventral view of sporangiophore of *Equisetum* sp.

Each cone or strobilus has a central axis known as strobilus axis to which many umbrella like sporangiophores are attached. Each sporangiophore is a stalked structure bearing sporangia. The free end of the sporangiophore is flattened like a peltate disc. The disc is hexagonal in appearance developing at right angle from the axis. Many sporangia (5 - 10) are found on the under surface of the disc. A calyx like whorl below the strobilus may be found in some species.

A mature sporangium is sac like elongated structure, surrounded by two layers of jacket wall. Many haploid spores are enclosed inside the jacket. Spores are of only one type and hence *Equisetum* is homosporous (Fig. 40).

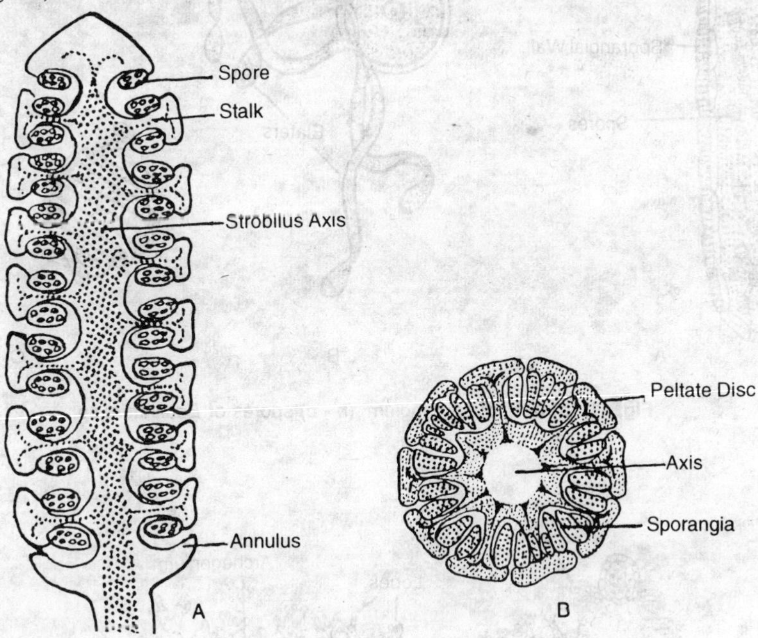

Fig. 40. (a) T. S. of strobilus and (b) L.S. of strobilus of *Equisetum* sp.

Each spore is surrounded by a wall of four layers; innermost is intine or endospore. Outside intine is exine or exospore. The exospore is further surrounded by middle layer which is again covered by perispore or epispore. The Perispore is differentiated into four narrow, spirally coiled with spoon like tips known as elaters attached to the common point on the spore. The elaters are hygroscopic in nature.

McClean and Cook (1951), Duckett and Pang (1984) have observed some signs of heterospory in *E. giganteum.*

GERMINATION OF SPORE AND GAMETOPHYTE

Spore germinates readily after shedding As it remains viable only for a few days. On germination, it develops into elongated, well branched prothallus (Gametophyte). The gametophyte is several cells thick, cushion like, small, developing many rhizoids towards lowerside. Chloroplast is found on the upper side of the cushion. The margin of the prothallus is meristematic. The mature prothallus is 1 mm to 10 mm in diameter and it is upto 3 cm. in diameter in *E. debile* (Fig. 41)

It is a controversial question whether *Equisetum* is monoecious (homothallic) or dioecious (heterothallic). *E. arvense* is monoecious but under unfavourable condition some of the prothalli develop either antheridia or archegonia only. According to Campbell (1940) *E. maximum* are dioecious. The Dioecism is generally due to environmental condition.

Sex organs : Antheridium — Many antheridia develop on the marginal parts of prothallus after the

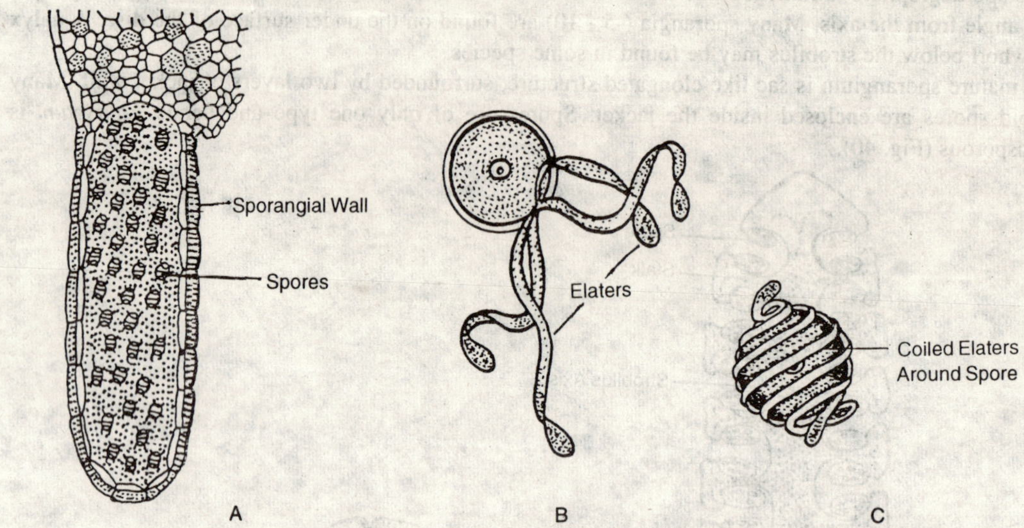

Fig. 41. (a) L. S. of sporangium, (b - c) spores of *Equisetum* sp.

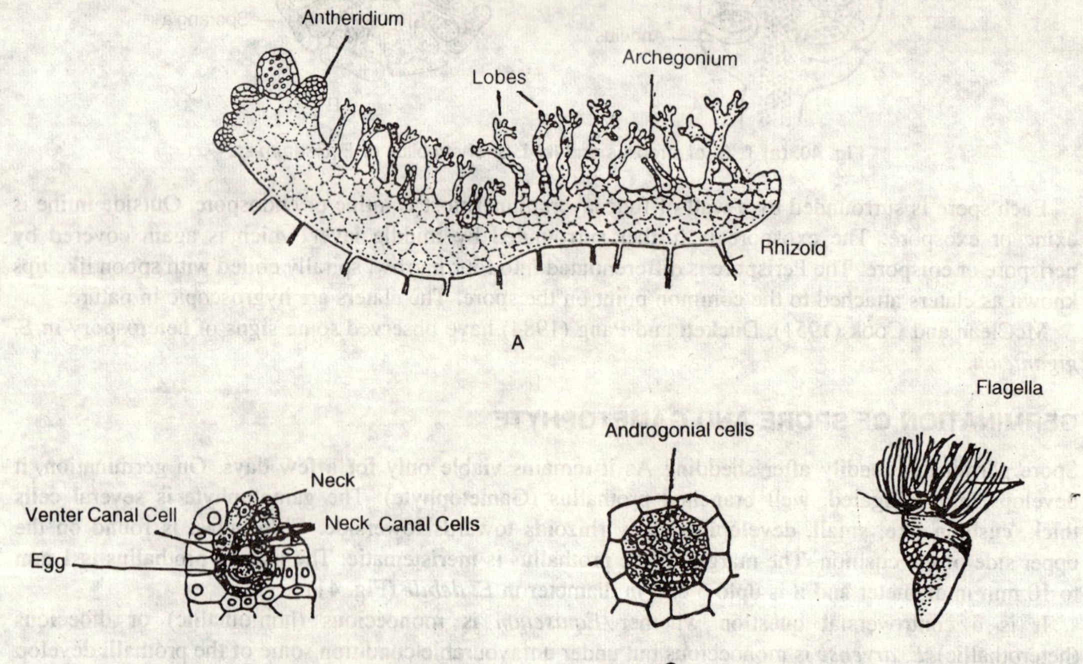

Fig. 42. (a) Gametophyte of *Equisetum arvense*, (b) an archegonium, (c) an antheridium and (d) an antherozoid of *Equisetum* sp.

development of archegonia. On the basis of the development of antheridium on the margin of the delicate lobes of the gametophyte (prothallus) or along the meristematic margin i.e. rim of the gametophyte, the antheridia have been called as projecting type or embedded type respectively.

The antheridium is more or less spherical structure, consisting of an outer jacket layer, one cell in thickness and inner sporogenous cells which give rise to sperm mother cells. The sperm mother cells divide meiotically forming spore tetrad which is further transformed into haploid, large spirally coiled and multiflagellate antherozoids.

Archegonium — The mature archegonium has a projecting neck and a venter embedded in the gametophyte. The neck is short made up of four tiers of cells with three cells in each tier. One or two neck canal cells are present. Venter has a ventral canal cell and an egg (Fig. 42).

FERTILIZATION AND EMBRYO DEVELOPMENT

This is done by the disorganization of the neck canal cells and the ventral canal cell. Muny antherozoids make entry through the neck canal reaching the venter. Only one antherozoid penetrate the egg. Fertilization takes place resulting into a diploid zygote which is the first cell generation of sporophyte.

The first division of zygote is transverse resulting into an epibasal (upper) and a hypobasal (lower) cell. There is no suspensor. Subsequent division is longitudinal forming quardrant stage. The hypobasal region develops into foot and epibasal develops into stem and root. Root and stem elongate at a very fast rate and finally a new sporophyte is produced (Fig. 43, 44).

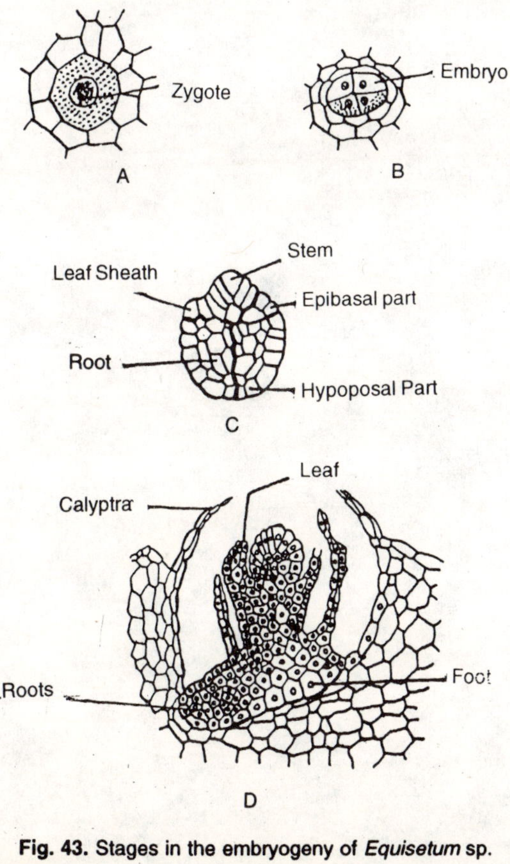

Fig. 43. Stages in the embryogeny of *Equisetum* sp.

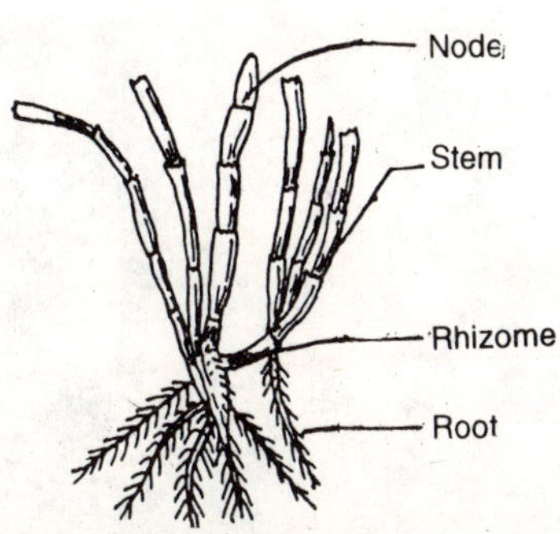

Fig. 44. Young sporophyte of *Equisetum* sp.

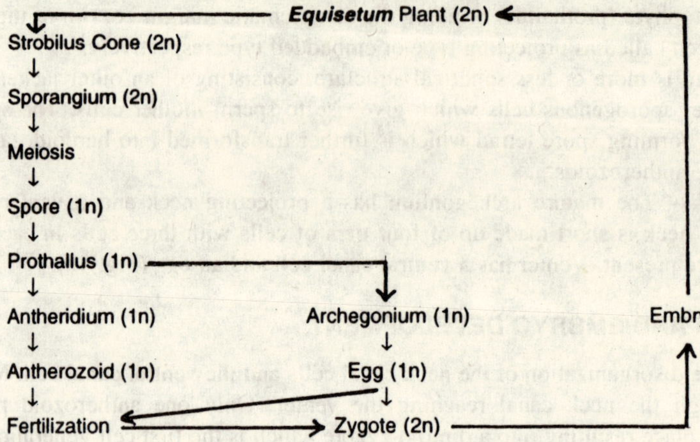

Graphic life cycle of *Equisetum* sp.

CHAPTER 5

PTEROPSIDA

HISTORICAL DESCRIPTION

The class Pteropsida includes ferns and some fossil plants and are cosmopolitan. They are known from Devonian period became extinct during the Permian period. Smith (1955) suggested that in the Triassic, Jurassic and Cretaceous many new families evolved and are still surviving.

SALIENT FEATURES

1. The sporophytic plant body is differentiated into root, stem and spirally arranged leaves.
2. Majority of the taxa grow in moist and shady habitats. Most of them are terrestrials, some are epiphytes (*Ophioglossum pendulum*) and a few are aquatic, (*Salvinia, Azolla* and *Marsilea*).
3. Generally, the leaves are compound, but in *Ophioglossum* they are simple.
4. Leaves may be exstipulate (e.g. *Filicales*) or stipulate.
5. The stele varies from protostele to siphonostele, solenostele, dictyostele or polystele.
6. Czeczuga (1985) has reported β - cryptoxanthin, lutein, epoxide, violaxanthin and rhodoxanthin types of carotenoids.
7. The spores are produced in sporangia which occur in groups called sori.
8. The sori are on leaves.
9. The development of sporangia may be eusporangiate (developing from more than one initial) or leptosporangiate (developing from a single initial).

5.1 OPHIOGLOSSUM (Adder's tongue fern)

It belongs to

	Class	—	Pteropsida
	Sub-class	—	Eusporangiatae
	Order	—	Ophioglossales
	Family	—	Ophioglossaceae
	Genus	—	*Ophioglossum*

HABIT AND HABITAT

Ophioglossum is worldwide in distribution and it is represented by over 45 species. In India more than a dozen species are found. Some of them are *Ophioglossum pendulum, O. vulgatum, O. costatum* etc. It is also known as 'Adder's tongue fern. Almost all the species are perennial herbs. Some species are epiphytes (e.g. *O. pendulum*) while others grow on damp soil.

PLANT BODY AND ITS EXTERNAL FEATURES

The sporophytic plant body is differentiated into rhizome, adventitions roots and a single mature leaf i.e. frond (Fig. 45).

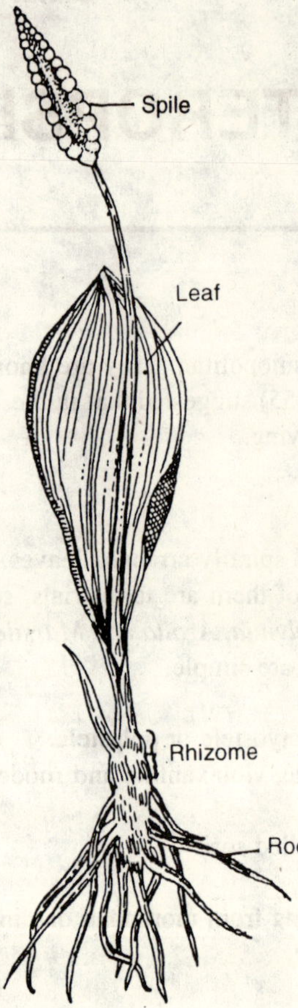

Fig. 45. A plant of *Ophioglossum* sp.

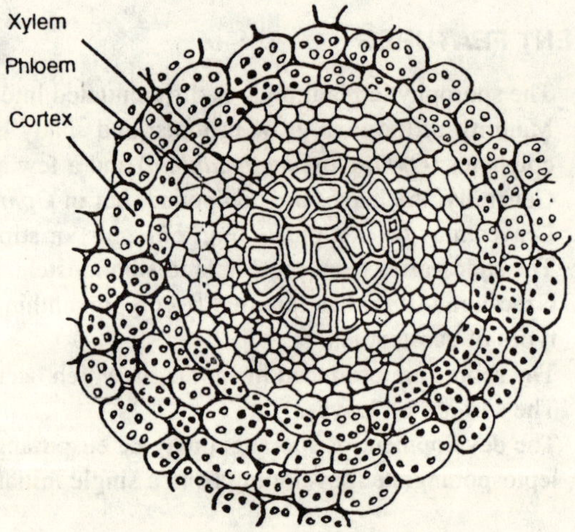

Fig. 46. T. S. of rhizome of *Ophioglossum* sp. showing starch grains in xylem and absence of endodermis.

Roots — Many thick adventitious roots are present on the rhizome. Roots are mycorrhizal in nature without root hair. Roots may be branched or unbranched.

Leaves — Most of the species produce only one leaf in one growing season. A leaf remains in the bud for about 3 years and in the fourth year it comes out. The leaves are simple or dichotomously forked. The leaf is differentiated into blade and petiole. The blade or lamina may be entire or palmately cut into many segments (e.g. *O. palmatum*). The leaf of *O. pendulum* is about 2 m in length. There is no midrib in the leaf and venation is reticulate. Stomata are found on both the surfaces of the leaves. At the juncture of petiole and the blade a single unbranched fertile spike is found. *O. palmatum* has several fertile spikes. The spikes are simple and linear.

Anatomy of Rhizome — Transverse section of rhizome shows the following organizations.

Epidermis — It is outermost layer of cells.

Cortex — Below the epidermis, cortex is present made up of thin walled oval or ellipsoidal cells. In mature rhizome endodermis is not differentiated.

Stele — Different type of stele are found in different species ranging from protostelic condition at the basal region of rhizome to ectophloic siphonostelic condition. Leaf gaps are also present and hence it becomes ectophloic solenostele. Sometimes leaf gaps overlap one another and the ectoploic siphonostelic condition changes to dictyostelic condition.

Meristele — The xylem is endarch in each meristele. The phloem is external, 4 - 5 cells thick and hence collateral bundle.

Pith — The pith is centrally iocated. It consists of large, thin walled parenchymatous cell (Fig. 46, 47).

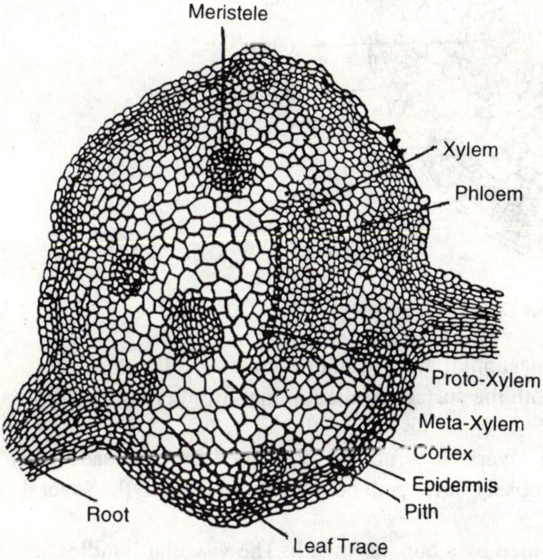

Fig. 47. T.S. of rhizome of *Ophioglossum vulgatum.*

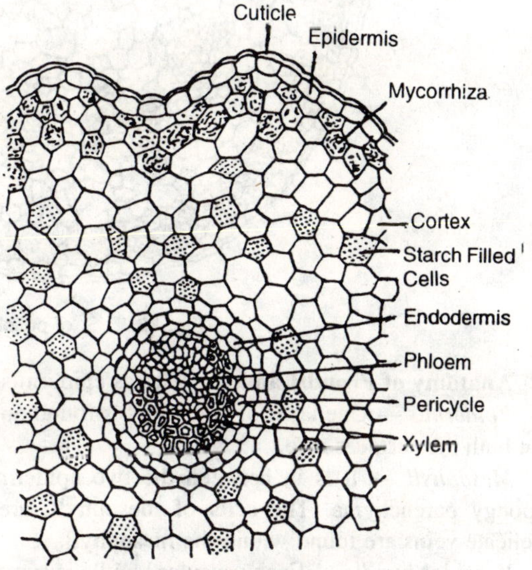

Fig. 48. T.S. of *Ophioglossum* sp.

Anatomy of root — Anatomically the root has epidermis, cortex and stele.

Epidermis — It is outermost single layer of cells. The outer wall of cells are suberized. Root hairs are absent. In older roots, epidermal layer is replaced by exodermis derived from outer cortical cells.

Cortex — The cortex is divisible into outer cortex and inner cortex. The outer cortex is made up of 4 - 7 layer of parenchymatous ceils occupied by mycorrhizal phycomycetous fungus. The inner cortex has round cells filled with starch.

Endodermis — It is the inner most cortical layer showing casparian strips.

Stele — The stele varies from monarch to tetrarch. In diarch type of roots, the xylem is in the form of a plate having protoxylem at both the ends of the plate. Phloem is present on either side of the xylem.

Phloem group is separated from the xylem by 2 - 3 cells thick parenchymatous tissue (Fig. 48).

Anatomy of Petiole — T. S. of petiole shows the following structure :

Epidermis — It is outermost layer of thick walled cells.

Ground tissue — Just below the epidermis, 2 - 3 layers of chlorenchymatous cells are present which are the part of ground tissue. The rest of the ground tissue consists of parenchymatous cells.

Stele — Many vascular bundles are found in 'C' manner within the ground tissue. Each vascular bundle is almost circular in outline, collateral and endarch. No bundle–sheath is present. The phloem is found on the outer side of the bundle (Fig. 49).

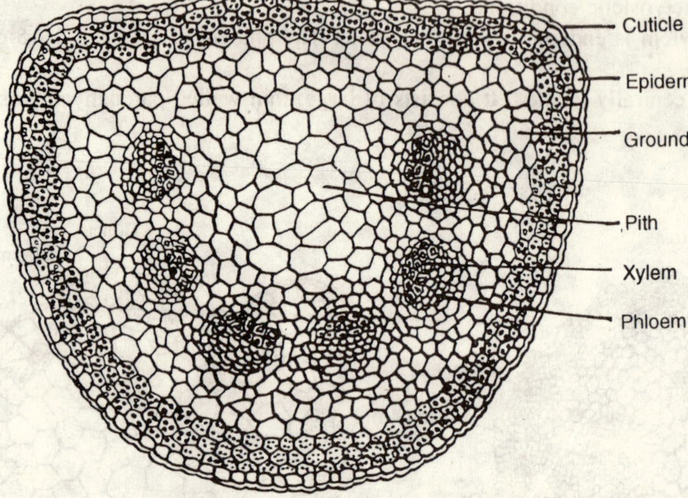

Fig. 49. T. S. of petiole of *Ophioglossum* sp.

Anatomy of Frond/Lamina — It has epidermis, mesophyll and vascular bundle as follows :

Epidermis — One layer of epidermis is found on both the surface of the lamina. Stoma may be found on both the surfaces also.

Mesophyll — It is in between the two epidermal layers. It is not differentiated into palisade and spongy parenchyma. The cells of mesophyll; are loosely arranged containing chlorophyll. Several delicate veins are found within the mesophyll.

Vascular bundle — Each vascular bundle is surrounded by a bundle–sheath. The vascular bundles are endarch and collateral (Fig. 50).

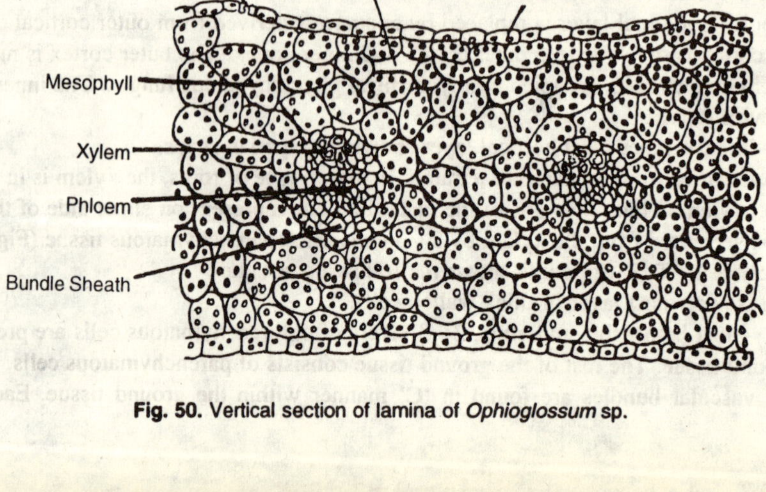

Fig. 50. Vertical section of lamina of *Ophioglossum* sp.

Spore producing organs — The spores are produced in sporangia born on a fertile spike. The mature spike has a stalk or peduncle. Two rows of sporangia are arranged on either side of the spike. The apex of the spike is devoid of sporangia. The number of sporangia in a fertile spike varies between 6 - 20. Each sporangium is subspherical, fused with the leaf and its diameter ranges between 0.5 and 3 mm. It is surrounded by a wall of several layers of cells. Stomata are present on the epidermal layer of the sporangial wall. The innermost layer acts as tapetum. The sporangial cavity is filled with sporogenous cell or spore mother cells which divides meiotically giving rise haploid spores. *Ophioglossum* is homosporous (Fig. 51).

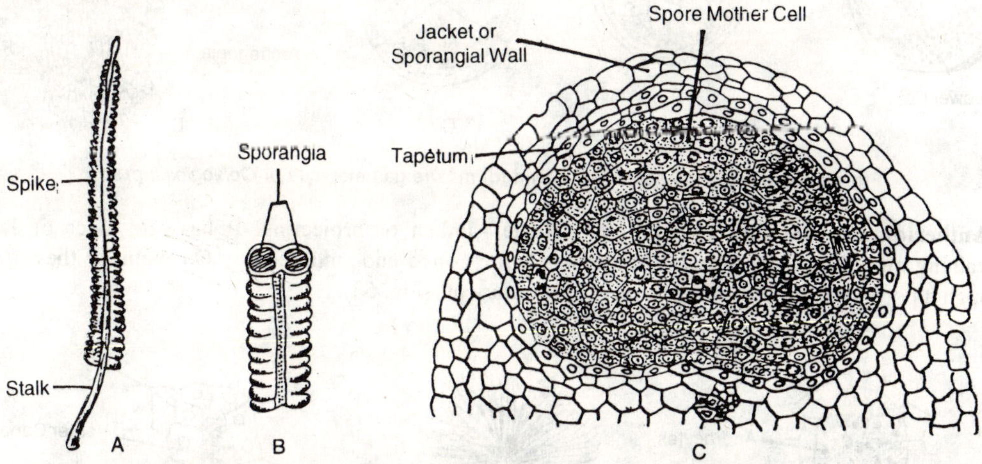

Fig. 51. (a) Spike, (b) part of spike and (c) T. S. of spike of *Ophioglossum* sp.

MORPHOLOGICAL NATURE OF THE FERTILE SPIKE

According to Bower (1896, 1908)) fertile spike of *Ophioglossum* is a single septate sporangium. Chrysler (1910) suggested that the fertile spike is the result of the fusion of two basal pinnae of a leaf. But Goebel (1915) said that the fertile spike is equivalent to a single pinna. Zimmermann (1930) mentioned that sterile lamina and fertile spike are the two dichotomies of a shoot. The sterile lamina is photosynthetic in function while fertile spike is responsible for reproduction. This view was accepted by Chrysler (1945) and Nishida (1952). Smith (1955) said that fertile spike in pinna like in nature. Khandelwal (1986) holds the view that the fertile spike is derived from the modified pinnae of a compound leaf. This view is based on the observation of vegetative compound leaves possessed by related genera of Ophioglossaceae i.e. *Botrychium* and *Helminthostachys.*

GAMETOPHYTIC GENERATION

The haploid spores are the first cell generation of gametophyte. The spores are small, yellow tetrahedral surrounded by outer thick exosporium and inner thin endosporium. During germination the spore absorbs water and becomes enlarged resulting in the bursting of spore wall along the tritradiate ridge. It divides transversely into two equal cells followed by vertical division in the lower cell only and thus a three celled stage is formed. Further development occurs only after the infection of mycorrhizal fungus leading to the formation of prothallus. Prothalli are linear, ovoid, cylindrical, branched or unbranched structure. It may survive upto 20 years. Vegetative buds may be seen on the prothallus of *Ophioglossum* meant for vegetative propagation. The prothallus is monoecious. The two sex organs are distributed on the surface of the prothallus. (Fig. 52)

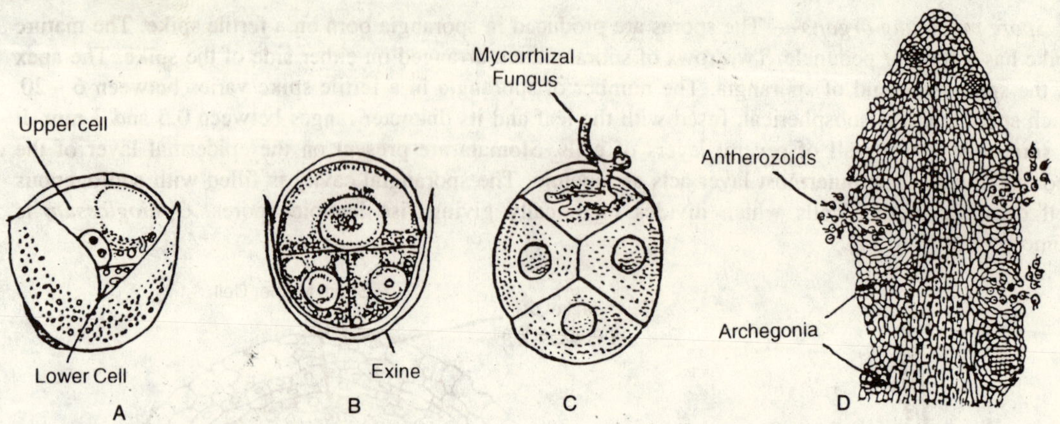

Fig. 52. Germination of spore (a - c) and (d) mature gametophyte of *Ophioglossum* sp.

Antheridium — Mature antheridium is large, sunken or projecting. It has one layer of Jacket containing numerous antherozoids. Antherozoids are coiled and multiciliate. On maturity they escape through a pore formed by disintegration of opercular cell (Fig. 53).

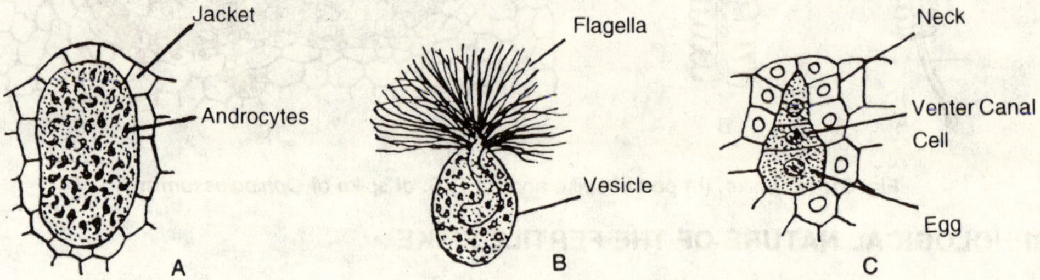

Fig. 53. (a) An antheridium, (b) an anteherozoid and (c) an archegonium of *Ophioglossum* sp.

Archegonium — The archegonia are some what sunken in the gametophyte. It has a neck made up of four vertical rows of cells. It has a single binucleate neck canal cell. Sometimes two neck canal cell may be seen. The venter has ventral canal cell and an egg. (Fig. 54).

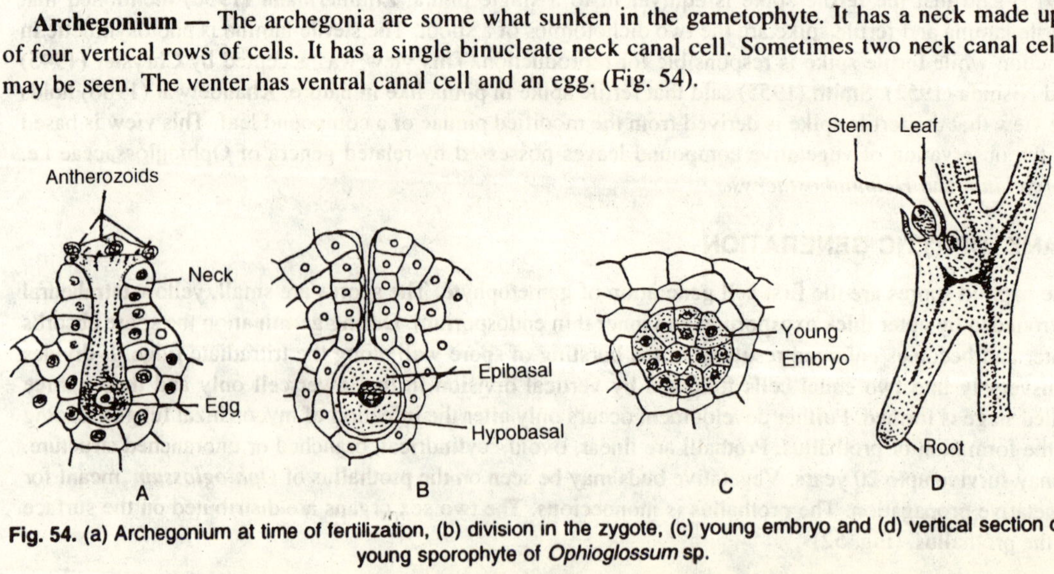

Fig. 54. (a) Archegonium at time of fertilization, (b) division in the zygote, (c) young embryo and (d) vertical section of young sporophyte of *Ophioglossum* sp.

FERTILIZATION AND YOUNG SPOROPHYTE

When the archegonium matures, the neck canal cell and ventral canal cell disintegrate leading to a passage to the egg for the entry of antherozoids. Fertilization is effected by the antherozoids swimming down the canal of archegonium and fertilizes the egg resulting in the formation of a diploid zygote.

The zygote is the first cell of young sporophyte. The zygote divides transversely into an upper epibasal and lower hypobasal cells. Further divisions are irregular leading to a multicellular body. The suspensor is absent and embryogeny is exoscopic. The cells of hypobasal region give rise to first formed root and foot. The epibasal region gives rise to stem apex and the cotyledon. The first cotyledon remains underground and second leaf comes out of the soil. Thus young sporophyte of *Ophioglossum* develops.

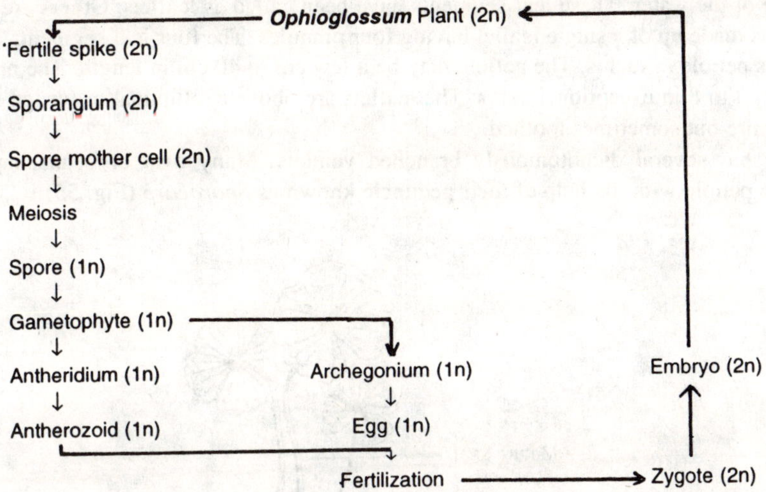

Graphic life cycle of *Ophioglossum*

5.2 MARSILEA

Marsilea belongs to	Class	—	Pteropsida
	Sub-class	—	Leptosporangitae
	Order	—	Marsileales
	Family	—	Marsileaceae
	Genus	—	*Marsilea*

HABIT AND HABITAT

The genus *Marsilea* was established by Carl Linnaeus (1753) after the Italian Count Luigi Fernando Margigli. It is represented by 531 living species and 10 fossil species. It is widely distributed in northern hemisphere, tropical Africa and Australia. They are aquatic as well as amphibious, rooted in mud, occurring in marshy and shallow pools and ponds. *M. hirsuta* occur in soil which remains dry throughout the year. In India 9 living species of *Marsilea* are reported by Gupta (1962). Some of them are *M. condensa, M. minuta, M quadrifolia, M. rajasthanesis* etc.

PLANT BODY

The sporophytic plant body possess rhizome bearing roots towards the lowerside and leaves towards the upper side. In young condition, the plants are covered with numerous unbranched, multicellular hairs.

Rhizome or Stem — It is long, slender, branched, growing below or on the soil surface. *M. minuta* has a creeping dichotomously branched rhizome with nodes and internodes.

Roots — the primary root is short lived i.e. ephemeral. The adventitious roots arise from the lowerside of the rhizome and fix the plants in the soil. The roots in *M. minuta* may be 13 cm in length.

Leaves — The leaves are compound, petiolate and long developing from the nodes of the rhizome in two rows. It shows circinate vernation. *Marsilea* can be easily recognized by four leaf segments floating on the surface of the water. These leaf segments have been called as leaflets. Others are of opinion that Marsilea leaf is made up of a single leaflet having four pinnules. The four leaf segments are on a slender stalk known as petiole or rachis. The petiole may be a few cm to 40 cm in length. The number of leaflet may vary from 3 to 8 in exceptional cases. The leaflets are obovate, elliptical or wedge shaped. Margin is generally entire but sometimes toothed.

The leaflet has several dichotomously branched veinlets. Many oval or bean shaped bodies are attached to the petiole with the help of their peduncle known as *Sporocarp* (Fig. 55)

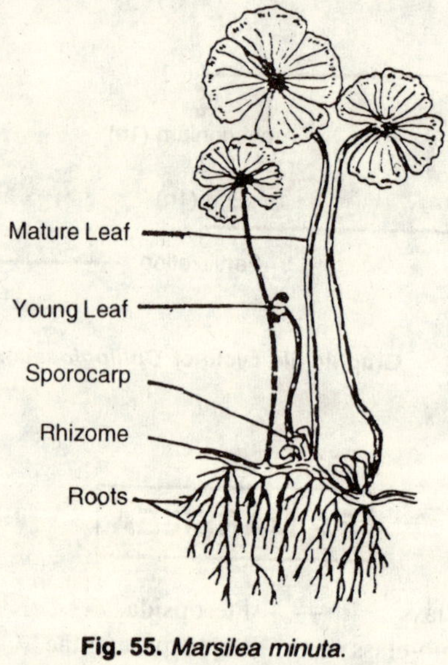

Fig. 55. *Marsilea minuta.*

Anatomy of rhizome — In transverse section of the rhizome, following structures are seen.

Epidermis — It is the outermost continuous layer of cells. No stomata are present. The epidermal cells are thick walled and compactly arranged.

Cortex — Below the epidermis, cortex is found which is differentiated into four regions. The outer cortex is made up of several layers of parenchyma cells. Below this parenchymatous zone is the air chamber separated by parenchymatous septa. Below the acrenchyma is the zone of sclerenchymatous cortex. The inner most zone of cortex contains compact parenchymatous cells.

Stele — It is amphiphloic siphonostele. Xylem is surrounded by phloem on both of the sides of xylem. Pith is present in the centre.

Just outside the pith is a layer of inner endodermis surrounded by a layer of inner pericycle. Inner phloem is present outside the inner pericycle. Then there is a zone of xylem ring. Outside the xylem is present outer phloem covered by outer pericycle and outer endodermis (Fig. 56).

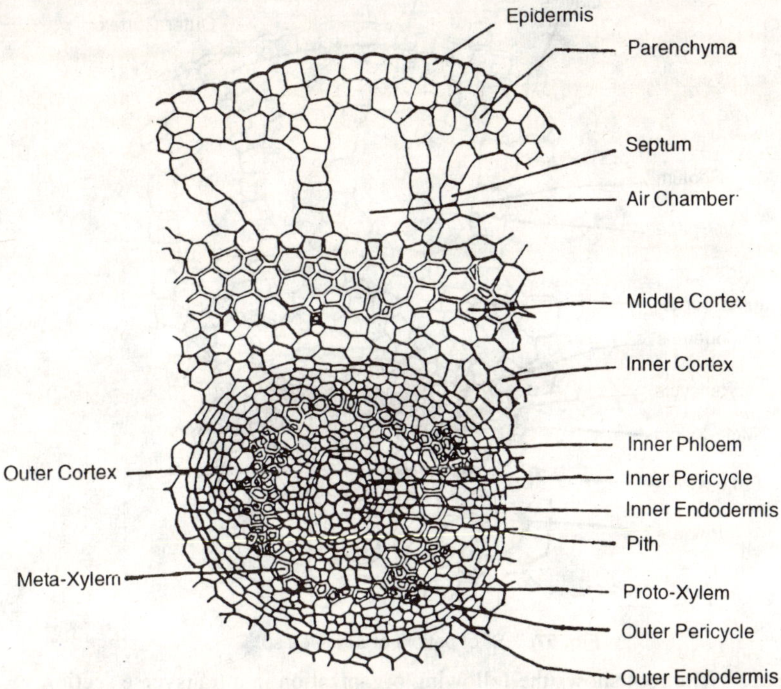

Fig. 56. T. S. of rhizome of *Marsilea minula.*

Anatomy of petiole — Anatomically the petiole consists of epidermis, hypodermis, cortex and stele.

Epidermis — It is single outer layer of cells.

Hypodermis — Below the epidermis is the hypodermis of few cells thick.

Cortex — Hypodermis is followed by cortex which is differentiated into outer and inner cortex. The outer cortex has aerenchyma (air cavities) separated by one celled thick septa or trabeculae. The inner cortex consists of parenchymatous cells filled with starch and tannin.

Stele — The stele is irregular in outline present in the centre showing protostelic nature. The inner cortex is delimited by a layer of endodermis whose cells are with casparian strips. One layered pericycle is present just below the endodermis. Xylem is 'V' or 'U' shaped having a metaxylem in the centre of 'V' and 'U'. Protoxylem is at the ends. The xylem is surrounded by phloem (Fig. 57).

Anatomy of leaflet — Vertical section of leaflet shows upper and lower epidermis. Stomata are present on both the epidermal layers. Stomata are somewhat sunken. In aquatic species stomata are on upper epidermal layer only.

Mesophyll is differentiated into palisade and spongy parenchyma situated in between the epidermal layers. The palisade is found just below the upper epidermis and the spongy parenchyma cells face the lower epidermis. Large intercellular air spaces are found in the spongy parenchyma. In submerged species there is no differentiation of mesophyll tissue.

The vascular bundles are concentric with xylem in the centre surrounded by phloem and a layer of endodermis (Fig. 58).

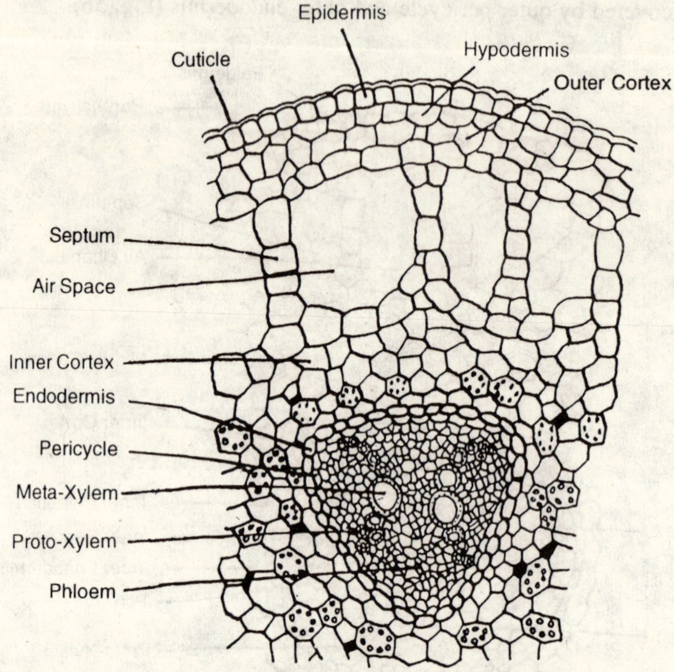

Fig. 57. T.S. of petiole of *Marsilea* sp.

Anatomy of root — The root shows the following organization in a transverse section.

Epidermis — The outermost layer is of epidermis whose outer walls are thick.

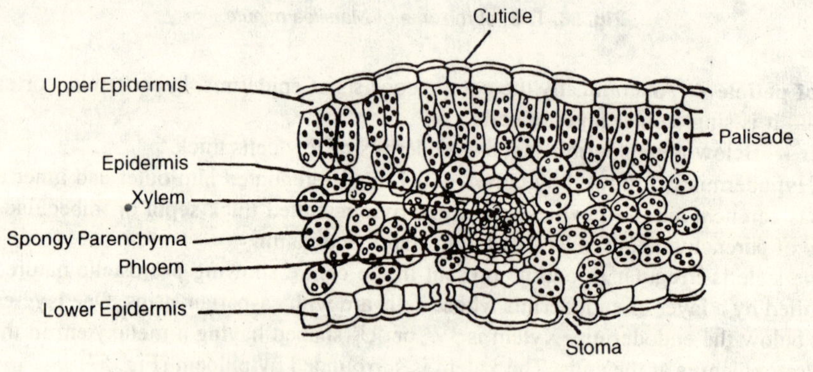

Fig. 58. V .S. of leaflet of *Marsilea* sp.

Cortex — It has two regions namely, outer cortex and inner cortex. The outer cortex contains many air chambers separated by trabeculae. The inner cortex is compact and of parenchyma cells or sclerenchyma if the roots are in dry condition.

Stele — The stele is surrounded by a layer of endodermis and layer of pericycle. The xylem may be monarch or diarch. Two groups of protoxylem are present towards the periphery. The phloem is present in the form of two bands. There is no pith. White (1961) has mentioned the presence of vessels in the roots of *M. hirsuta* (Fig. 59)

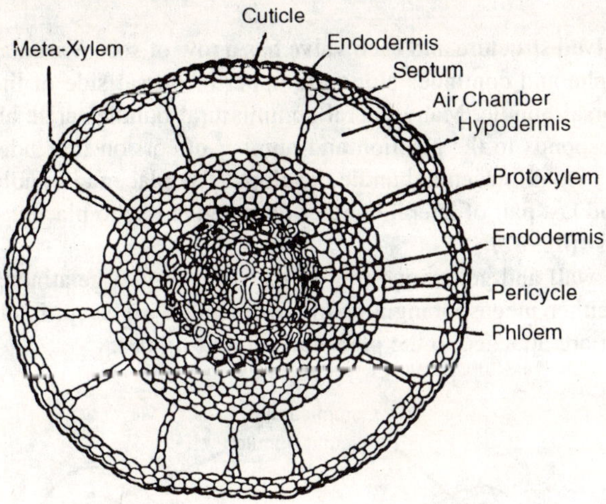

Fig. 59. T. S. of root of *Marsilea* sp.

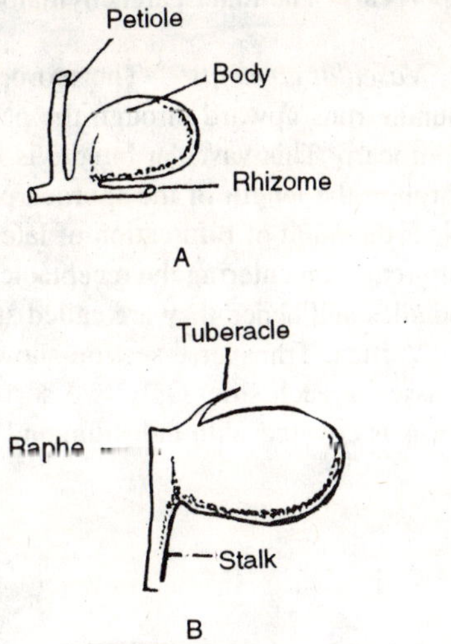

Fig. 60. Sporocarp of (a) *Marsilea pubescens* and (b) *M. uncinata.*

SPORE PRODUCING STRUCTURES

Marsilea is heterosporous and spores are produced in sporangia (megasporangia and microsporangia). Many such sporangia are found in bean shaped bodies known as *sporocarps.* Each sporocarp is ovoid, bean shaped or capsule like structure. They may be green in young condition or black and hard at maturity. Sporocarps are born on a short lateral branch of petiole known as pedicel or peduncle. The point of attachment of the pedicel or peduncle with sporocarp body is called raphe. Just above the raphe are present two protuberances known as tuberacles (Fig. 60).

The internal anatomy of the sporocarp reveals the following structures as seen in vertical transverse section and vertical longitudinal section.

Wall of sporocarp has three zones (a) outermost of epidermis (b) two hypodermal palisade layers of cells and (c) parenchymatous zone of 2 - 3 cells in thickness.

Epidermis — It is one cell in thickness covered by cuticle. Multicellular hairs and stomata are present. The stomata have two guard cells and are sunken in nature.

Hypodermis — It consists of two layers of elongated cells.

Parenchymatous zone — Below the second hypodermal layer palisade is present made of 2 - 3 layers

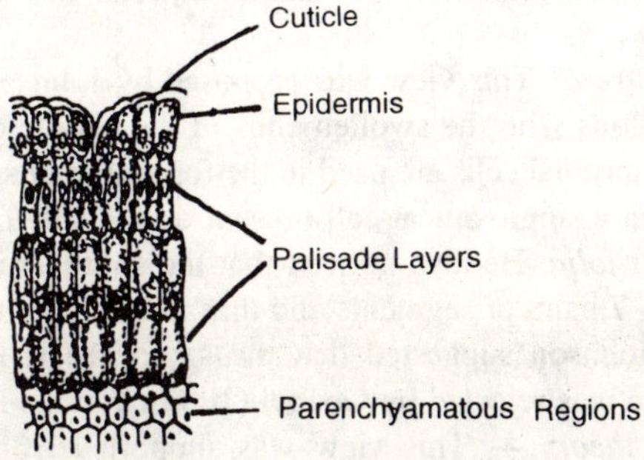

Fig. 61. Showing structure of sporocarp wall of *Marsilea* sp.

of parenchyma cells. The cells of this zone near raphe gelatinise and help in the opening of the sporocarp. The inner parenchymatous layer forms gelatinous tissue (Fig. 61).

Vascular elements — The sporocarp is a bivalved structure and each valve has a row of sori. Vascular bundle runs upward through the pedicel and raphe and continues along the upper or dorsal side of the sporocarp. This vascular bundle is known as dorsal bundle. Many lateral commissural bundles arise all through the length of the sporocarp which corresponds to the position and number of sori on that side. Near the point of bifurcation of lateral bundles, a small placental bundle develops. The placental bundle bifurcates on entering the receptacle. The first and last pair of lateral bundles do not give rise to placental bundles and hence they are called sterile bundles (Fig. 62).

Vertical Transverse section shows sporocarp wall and gelatinous ring in the form of two gelatinous masses at each side. Only two sori containing either megasporangia or microsporangia are seen. Each sorus is covered with indusium and both the sori are attached to the placental ridge (Fig. 63).

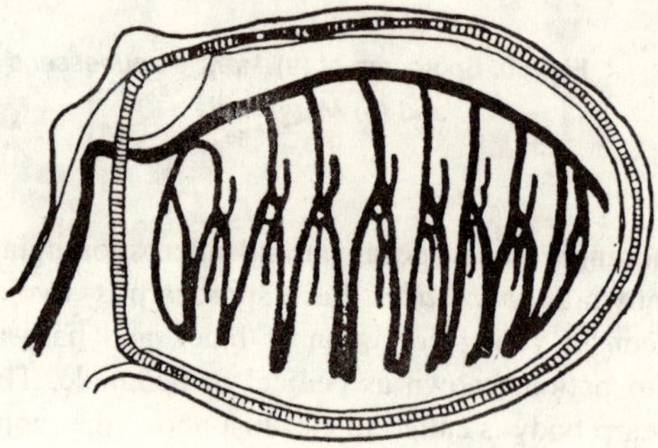

Fig. 62. Showing vascular supply to one half of sporocarp of *Marsilea* sp.

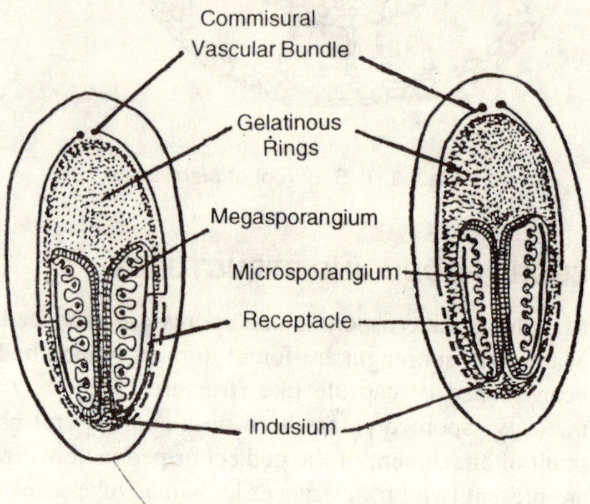

Fig. 63. Vertical transverse section of sporocarp of *Marsilea* sp. (diagramatic).

Horizontal longitudinal section reveals all the sori and number of sori and sporangia can be determined. Each sorus is protected by two layered indusium and the sori of two sides are alternate. In each sorus two microsporangia on the sides and one megasporangium at the apex are present. The dorsal bundle, lateral bundle, placental bundle and stalk bundle can be seen (Fig. 64).

Morphological nature of sporocarp — The morphological nature of sporocarp of *Marsilea* has been a much controversial and debated question. Two main interpretations regarding morphological nature of the sporocarp are given below.

Petiolar or whole leaf nature — This view was proposed by Johnson (1898, 1953) and according to him the sporocarp is homologous with the swollen ends of the petiole of only "the sterile branch of the leaf" of *M. quadrifolia*. The marginal cells are used in the formation of sporangia and not the lamina. The sporocarp also originates from a single apical cell present on the side of the leaf primordium similar to the origin of leaf in *M. quadrifolia*. He also noticed that the sporocarp appears when the young fertile leaf consists of only about 6 - 7 pairs of segments and thus long before the emergence of the lamina. On the basis of these findings Johnson suggested that the sporocarp is homologous to the petiole. The petiolar hypothesis of Johnson was rejected by Goebel (1905), Pande (1923) and Puri and Garg (1953).

Laminar or leaf segment theory — This view was supported by Russow (1872) Busgen (1890),

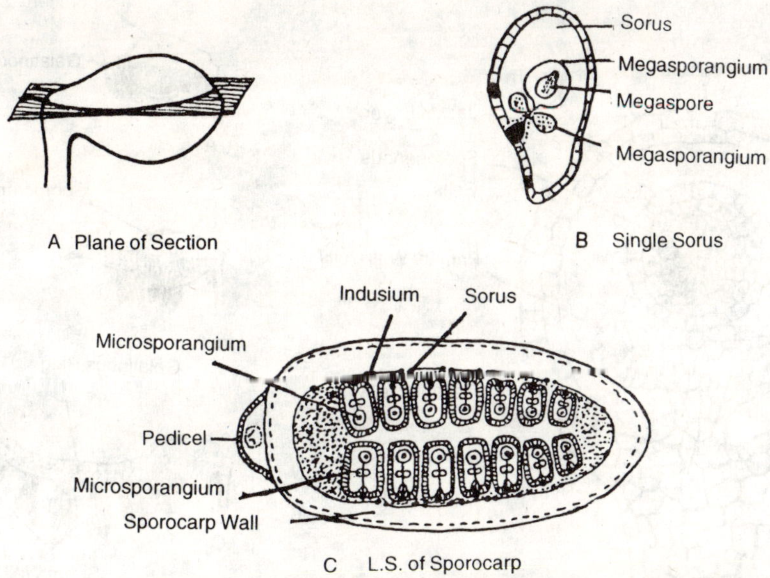

Fig. 64. (a) Plane of section, (b) single sorus and (c) L.S. of sporocarp of *Marsilea* sp.

Campbel (1918), Bower (1926) Goebel (1905), Eames (1936) Puri and Garg (1953), Smith (1955) and Gupta (1962). According to them sporocarp of *Marsilea* is a modified lateral fertile segment of the leaf or frond which is comparable with the fertile part of the sporophyll. This theory was accepted by all on account of the following.

1. Sporocarp consists of two leaflets with their ventral surfaces facing each other.
2. Marsileal sporocarp is equivalent to a single leaflet with two rows of fertile pinnules on either side.
3. Sporocarp is modified pinna developing on the rachis of a fertile leaf.
4. Sporocarp is equivalent to the tip of the leaf with its four leaflets and that the body of the capsule represents the two distal leaflets.
5. Sporocarp may be compared with modified pinna with a single midrib bundle and on either side 15 - 20 lateral veins are present. Presence of a single bundle in the peduncle and single mid vein in the sporocarp indicate clearly that sporocarp is derived from a single pinna.
6. Each sporocarp is equivalent to a single leaflet which contains as many pinnules as number of the commissural bundles.

Thus, laminar interpretation gives a more satisfactory explanation than the petiolar interpretation.

Sporangium — *Marsilea* is heterosporous. Microsporangium has as many as 32 microspores and megasporangium has only one megaspore. Megasporangium arise at the top while microsporangia develop on the sides of the receptacle. The development of both the types of sporangia are identical upto the spore formation stage. All the 32 or 64 haploid spores survive in case of the microsporangium while in megasporangium, all these haploid spores degenerate except one which acts as megaspore (Fig. 65).

Micro and megasporangia are globose, long and short stalked respectively having single layer of jacket cells without annulus. Tapetum of 2 - 3 layers of cells are present within the jacket. Below the tapetum, sporangenous tissues are present. Within each microsporangium 8 - 16 microspore mother cells are produced. All of them divides meiotically to give 32 - 64 haploid microspores. In case of

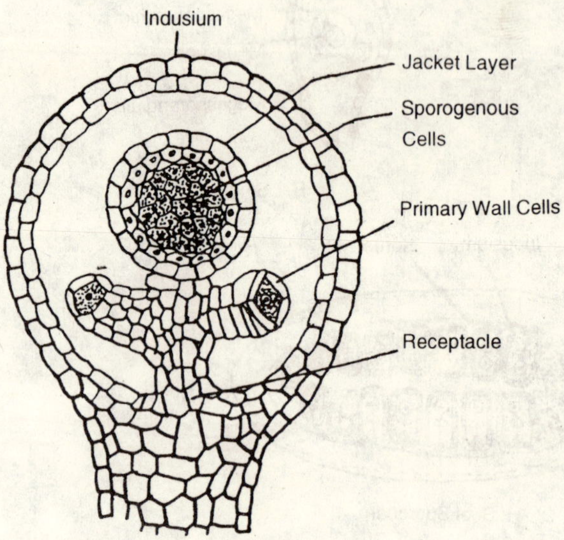

Fig. 65. Developed sporangium in a sorus of *Marsilea* sp.

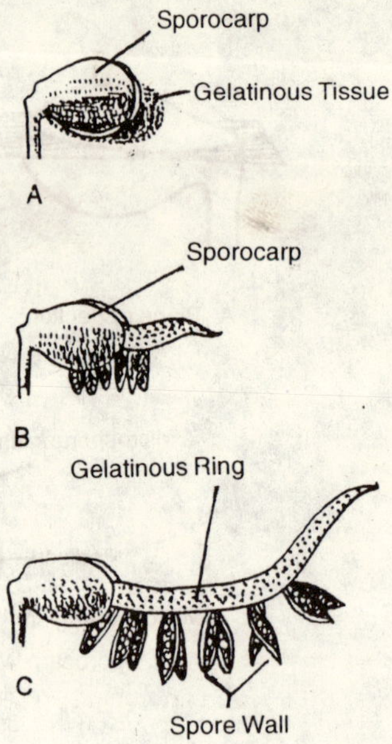

Fig. 66. Dehiscing stages of sporocarp of *Marsilea sp.*

megasporangium all the megaspore mother cells except one disintegrate, The remaining one divides meiotically. to give 4 megaspores but only one megaspore survives which becomes larger and develops a thick wall.

Mature sporocarps are detached from the plant and remain in water or muddy soil. Sporocarp opens into two valves along the ventral side from base to apex. The coiled gelatinous ring absorbs water, swells, comes out of the ruptured sporocarp and thus pulled out of the sori still attached to the gelatinous ring. (Fig. 66). The delicate sporangial wall breaks and spores are liberated which germinate at once.

GAMETOPHYTIC GENERATION

Microspores are yellow in colour and its size varies from 45 μ to 60 μ in diameter. Microspores develop into male gametophyte within 12 - 20 hrs. Microspore divides by an unequal division forming a small prothalial cell and a large apical cell. The prothalial cell further divides to form two antheridial initials. Each antheridial initial divides and redivides giving rise to jacket of three cells and one primary androgonial cell which further divides to produce 16 androcytes or sperm mother cells. At this stage jacket and prothallial cell disintegrate due to which two masses of androcytes representing two antheridia float freely within the original spore wall. Further, each androcyte metamorphoses into a multiflagellate screw like coiled sperm. On bursting of spore wall, sperms are set free (Fig. 67).

Each megaspore has a short apical papilla. Megaspore nucleus divides into two unequal nuclei and subsequently a small apical cell and a large basal cell is formed. Female gametophyte develops from the small apical cell. The basal cell functions as nutritive cells only. Mature female gametophyte is a reduced structure containing a single archegonium embedded in a cap of tissue attached over the apex of basal nutritive cell. Mature archegonium contains a neck made up of two tiers of four cells each, one neck canal cell, a ventral canal cell and an egg. (Fig. 68).

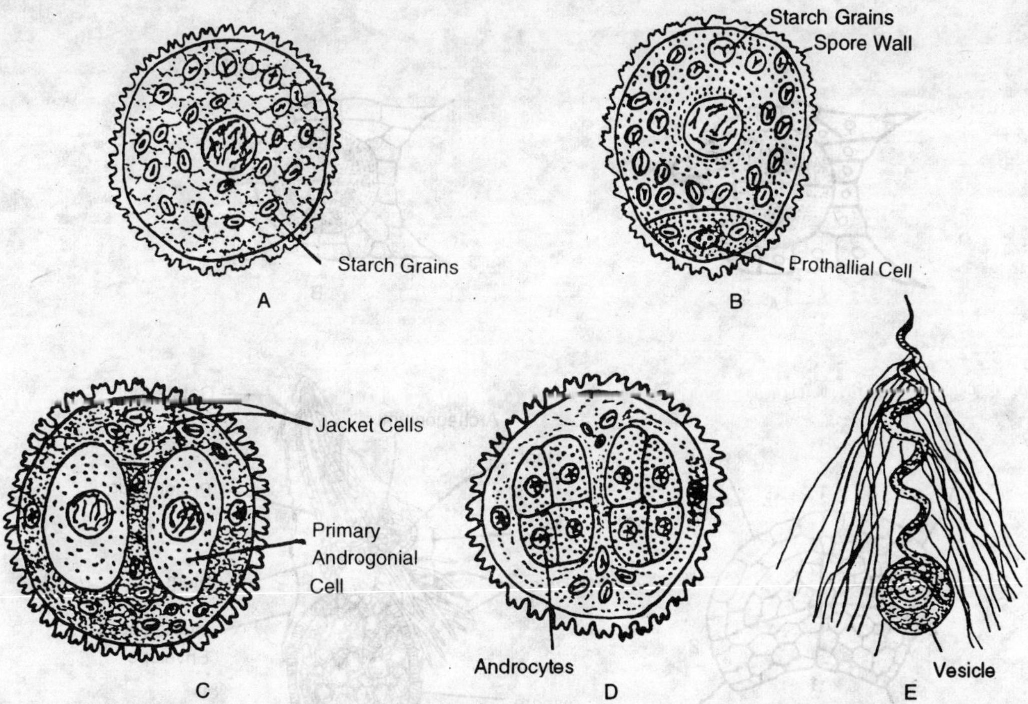

Fig. 67. Developmental stages of male gametophyte (a - d) and (e) an antherozoid of *Marsilea sp.*

FERTILIZATION AND YOUNG SPOROPHYTE

Antherozoids swim towards an archegonium and only one enters through the neck to the egg and fuses with the egg and the structure becomes diploid (2n) which represents a zygote. Zygote is the beginning of sporophytic generation.

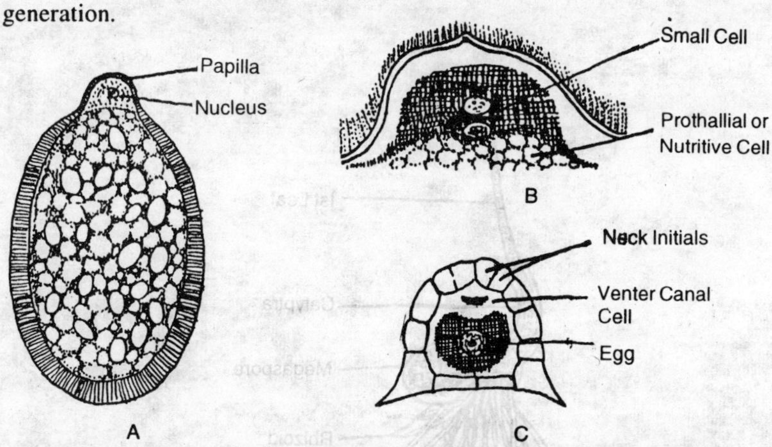

Fig. 68. Stages in the development of female gametophyte of *Marsilea sp.*

Soon after the formation, zygote divides and redivides resulting into the formation of an embryo which contains four segments, each representing a leaf, root, stem and a foot which in course of time develops into a mature. *Marsilea* sporophyte plant (Fig. 69, 70).

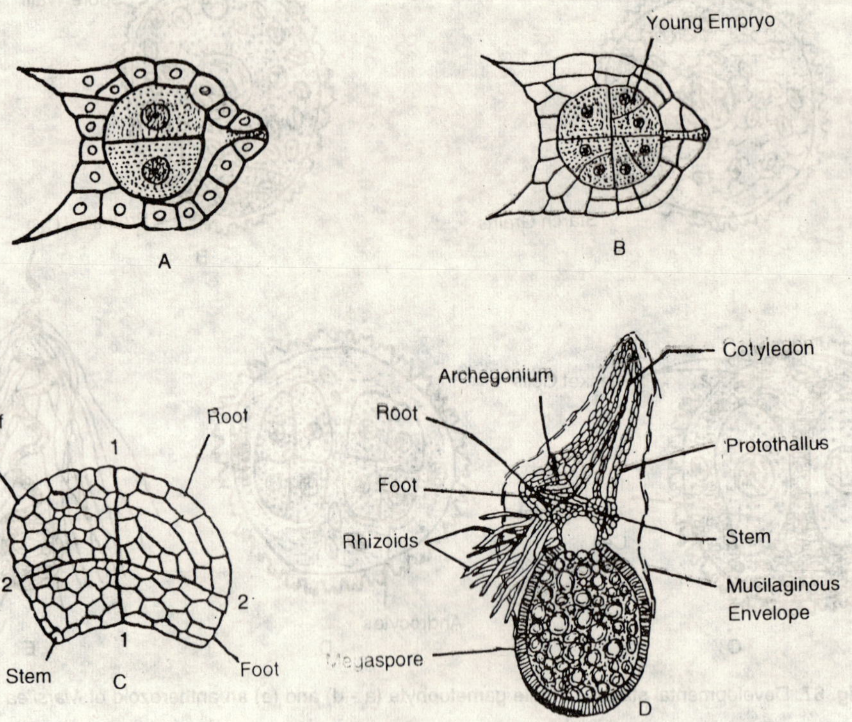

Fig. 69. Stages in the development of embryo (a - c) and (d) developing embryo within the gametophytic tissue of *Marsilea* sp.

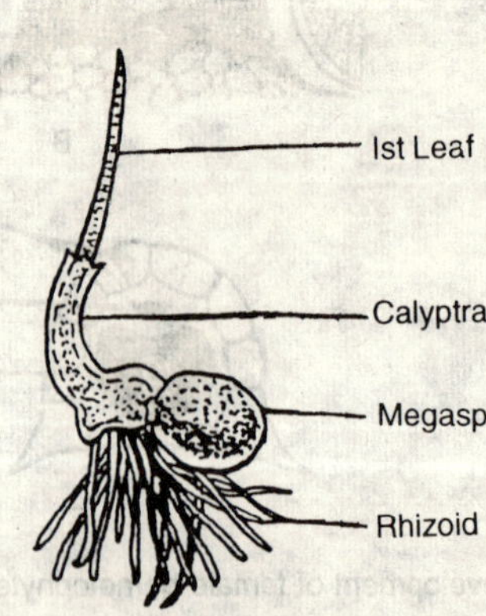

Fig. 70. Young sporophyte of *Marsilea* sp.

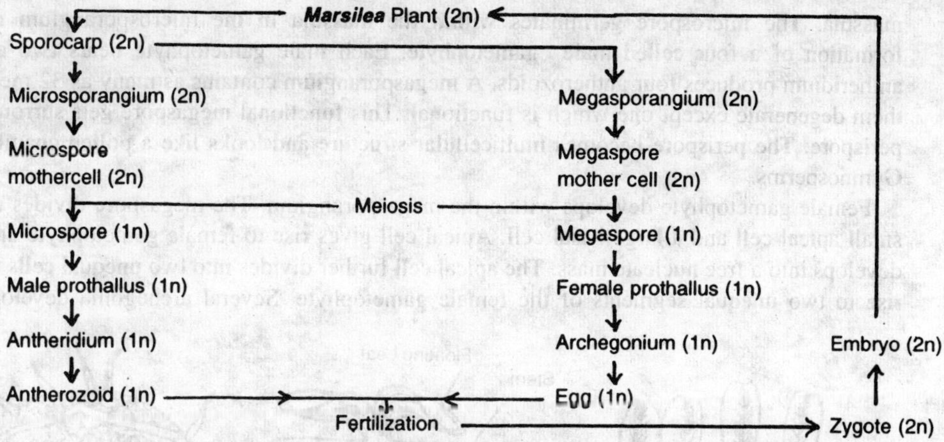

Graphic life cycle of *Marsilea*

5.3 SALVINIA

It belongs to

	Class	—	Pteropsida
	Sub-class	—	Leptosporangiatae
	Order	—	Salviniales
	Family	—	Salviniaceae
	Genus	—	*Salvinia*

HABIT AND HABITAT

The genus *Salvinia* is represented by 13 species and most of them occur in tropical and warm temperate regions of the world. The common Indian species are *S. natans*, *S. molesta* etc.

The sporophytic plant body is differentiated into well branched horizontal rhizome bearing leaves in the whorls of three. No roots are present. Out of three leaves present on rhizomes, two lateral leaves are floating while the third leaf is submerged. The submerged leaves are highly branched and covered with hairs and seems to function as roots. The two lateral leaves born at each node are about 2 cm long, laminate with reticulate venation. They appear like cup shaped and its upper convex surface bear large number of hairs. These hairs remain dry inspite of being on the surface of water. The reproductive structure — sporocarps are born on the submerged leaves.

Anatomical structure of rhizome is very simple. It has a poorly developed vascular system. A central pith is surrounded by only a few tracheidal cells. The leaf trace is simple.

SPORE PRODUCING ORGANS

The sporocarp develop on the branches of the submerged leaves. Morphologically all sporocarps are similar but proximal one or two sporocarps contain only megasporangia while others contain only microsporangia. The sporocarp has wall of two layers. The wall is covered with hairs. Each sporocarp bears an elevated receptacle bearing mega or microsporangia. One layered tapetum is present in the sporangia. Sporangial wall is unilayered and without annulus. A microsporangium contains four microspores which remain covered by tapetal cytoplasm. It gets hardened in a single frothy unit called massula. The microspore germinates within the massula in the microsporangium resulting in the formation of a four celled male gametophyte. Each male gametophyte bears two antheridia. Each antheridium produces four antherozoids. A megasporangium contains as many as 32 megaspores. All of them degenerate except one which is functional. This functional megaspore gets surrounded by a thick perispore. The perispore becomes multicellular structure and looks like a pollen chamber of a seed of Gymnosperms.

Female gametophyte develops within the megasporangium. The megaspore divides unequally into a small apical cell and a large basal cell. Apical cell gives rise to female gametophyte and the basal cell develops into a free nucleate mass. The apical cell further divides into two unequal cells which later give rise to two unequal segments of the female gametophyte. Several archegonia develops in the upper

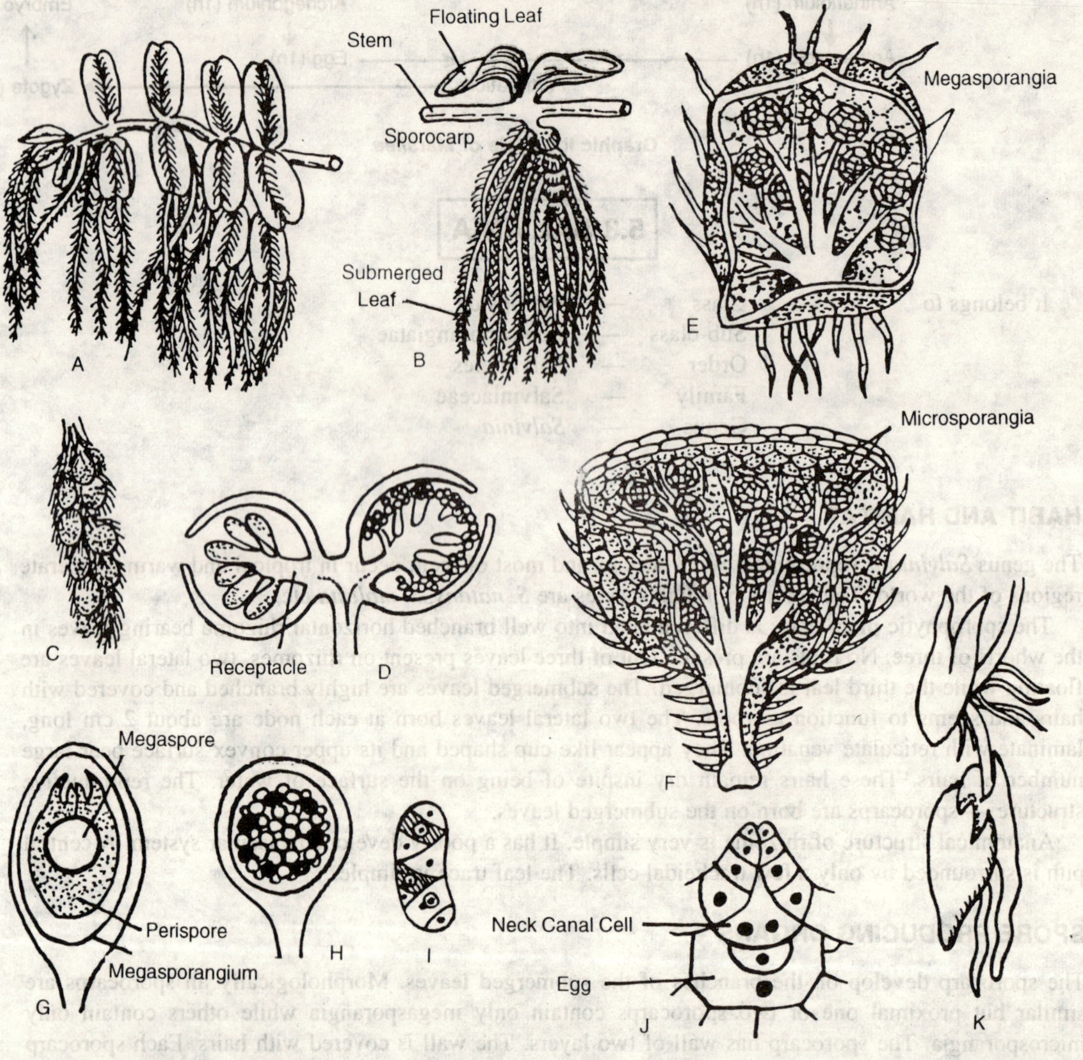

Fig. 71. (a) Part of *Salvinia natans* plant, (b) a node showing sporocarp, (c) sporocarp with submerged leaf, (d) V.S. of sporocarp showing mega and microsporangia, (e) V.S. of sporocarp showing megasporangia, (f) V.S. of sporocarp showing microsporangia (g) a megasporangium (h) a microsporangium (i) male prothallus (j) an archegonium (k) young sporophyte attached with female gametophyte.

segments of the gametophyte. An archegonium has a short neck, a binucleate neck canal cell, a ventral canal cell and an egg. After fertilization a diploid zygote divides longitudinally into two cells. Repeated divisions result into octant stage. The outer four cells give rise to the stem and leaf. Four basal cells give rise to the foot. Root primordia are not developed at any stage. Fig. 71).

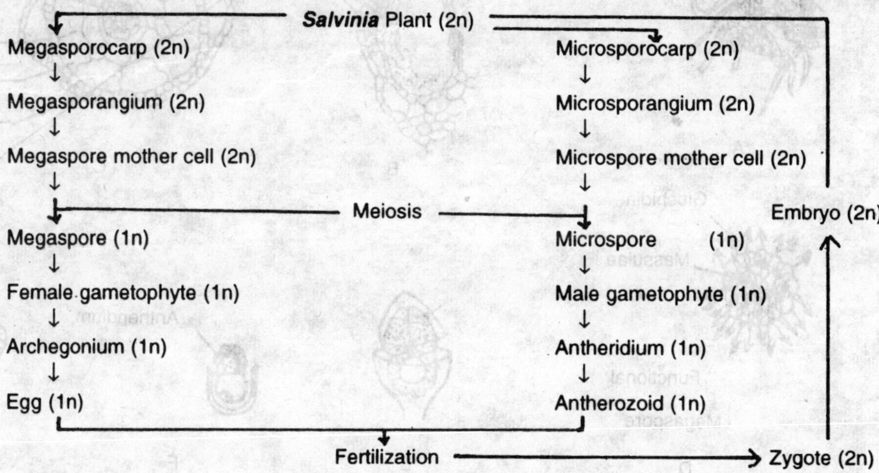

Graphic life cycle of *Salvinia*

5.4 AZOLLA

It belongs to	Class	—	Pteropsida
	Sub-class	—	Filicinae
	Order	—	Salviniales
	Family	—	Salviniaceae/Azollaceae
	Genus	—	*Azolla*

HABIT AND HABITAT

The genus *Azolla* has five species. Some of them are *A. caroliniana* and *A. filiculoides*. The plant body is sporophyte and exhibits free floating habit on the surface of permanent pools and backwaters of sluggish streams. *Azolla* can be recognised from a considerable distance due to its reddish colour. Vegetative reproduction occurs by progressive death and growth by abscision of lateral branches which results in a carpet of plantlets sufficient to conceal the water. Plant body is differentiated into pinnately branched, horizontally floating stem. A long adventitious root develops from the underside of the brancch. The stem and its branches are densely covered with small, overlapping, alternately arranged leaves. Each leaf has two lobes of equal size. The green and thick dorsal (upper) lobe is aerial and the thin ventral (lower) lobe is submerged and colourless. Live colonies of a blue green alga, *Anabaena azollae* are present in the space enclosed by an overarching of young leaves. There is a true symbiosis in which the *Anabaena* fixes atmospheric nitrogen for the host. Anatomically the stem shows a cortex of 5 - 8 cells in thickness made up of parenchymatous cells, followed by endodermis and pericycle of one cell in thickness and nine cells in perimeter. There are about six xylem elements and about twelve phloem elements internal to the pericycle. hence, the central cylinder is protostelic (Fig. 72).

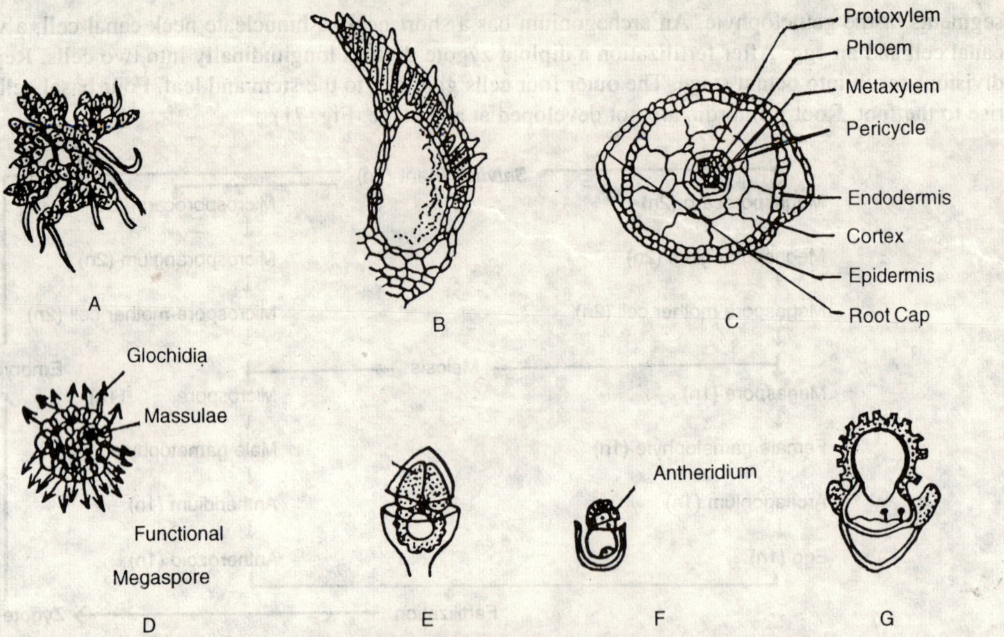

Fig. 72. (a) Azolla filiculoides plant (b) L.S of dorsal lobe of leaf (c) T.S. of root (d) a massula from microsporangium (e) Megasporangium with massula (f) male prothallus (g) female prothallus.

Anatomy of adventitious root — Transverse section of adventitious root shows the following organization—

Epidermis — It is outermost single layer of cells.

Cortex — Below the epidermis is cortex of two layers. Outer layer is of nine cells and inner layer of six cells in mature roots.

Endodermis — It is one cell thick consists of 6 cells.

Pericycle — It is also of 6 cells in one layer.

Stele — In mature roots, the stele has four protoxylem elements and two metaxylem in the centre. Xylem is surrounded by four phloem elements. Root hairs are not present in the mature leaf. However, the embryonic epidermal layer has root hair.

Anatomy of leaf — The distal half of a mature ventral lobe is made up of cells, one cell in thickness where as the proximal half is of more than one cell in thickness enclosing a large chamber. There is a cavity on the adaxial face near the leaf base in the dorsal lobe. The cavity opens outside by a circular pore through which *Anabaena* migrates into this cavity. Later, an outgrowth from the margin of the pore makes the *Anabaena* imprisoned within the cavity. The mature dorsal lobe consists of an upper and a lower epidermis. The upper epidermal layer has many, one or two celled hairs. In between the epidermal layers, palisade tissue with intercellular spaces is present. A small vein is also present.

SPORE PRODUCING ORGAN

Spores are produced in sporangia. *Azolla* is heterosporous. Only the lower most leaf of a branch is fertile. Two or four sporocarps are formed in the axil of the dorsal lobe. Indisium overarches sporangium and contains one or two hormogones of *Anabaena*. By an approximation of the free margins of the indisium closes the opening of an indusial cap.

At first macrosporangium starts to develop. A mature macroporangium has an outer layer of protective layer followed by one layer of tapetal cells enclosing eight macrospore mother cells. After meiosis 32 haploid macrospores are produced. In the meantime tapetal cells break down forming a multinucleate plasmodium. All sporocarps show such type of ontogeny upto this stage. One microspore within a macrosporangium begins to enlarge to form a functional macrospore. In such a situation, there is further development of microsporangia below the macrosporangium. As the functional macrospore enlarges four quadrately arranged alveolar bodies called massulae are formed by the tapetal plasmodium. When the macrospore attains maturity, a transverse rupturing of the surrounding macrosporangium and indusium takes place. The functional macrospore lies in the large massula and the three massulae with non–functional spores, macrosporangium and distal part of indusium remain attached to the massula having functional macrospore. This is known as swimming apparatus. When all the haploid macrospores disintegrate within the macrosporangium, the microsporangial initials situated on macrosporangial stalk begin to develop microsporangia in basipetal succession. In this way all sporocarps on a leaf may be macrosporocarps or microsporocarps or both of them depending on the fate of the macrospores and macrosporangium. A mature microsporangium are similar in structure to that of macrosporangium in having a protective layer, a tapetal layer enclosing eight microspore mother cells. The microspore mother cells divide meiotically to form 32 haploid microspores, all of them are functional. They move to the periphery of the plasmodium followed by formation of four or more alveolar massulae containing microspores. Each massula develops many elongate hooked processes called glochidia on its surface on maturity of microsporocarp. Indisium breaks and sporangial wall ruptures. Massulae are liberated which float away. Several microsporic massulae may become attached to the macrosporic massula with the help of glochidia.

Male gametophyte - The microspore remains embedded within the massula utill it develops into a gametophyte. During germination of microspore outer spore wall bursts and inner wall protrude out enclosing cytoplasm and nucleus. The protuberant part becomes antheridial initial by forming a cross wall near the apex of the spore cavity which contains a vegetative cell. The vegetative cell cuts off a small lenticular cell. The antheridial initial develops into an antheridium having a jacket of few cells enclosing eight androcytes which metamorphose into antherozoids.

Female gemetophyte - It is producted from macrospore. The macrospore increases in its size before germination. Its nucleus divides into two forming a small lenticular cell at the upper end of the macrospore and a large sister cell which does not divide further but becomes multinucleate. The lenticular cell divides vertically into two unequal cells. The larger cell further divides and forms a young macrogametophyte or female gemtophyte like a lenticular disc and two cells in thickness. One of the median cells in the upper layer acts as archegonial initial. Now the microspore wall ruptures and developing gemtophyte is projected through the opening. One archegonium develops from the first archegonial initial. If fertilization is not effective, then another archegoinum is formed form the additonal archegonial initial differentiated laterally to the first archegonium and this process is continued untill a dozen or more have been formed.

A mature archegonium has a short neck of 3 - 4 cells in height. The neck has one or two neck canal cells. The venter has a ventral canal cell and a large egg. (Fig. 72).

Fertilization and young sporophyte - The antherozoids reach to the neck of the archegonium and only one is able to fertilize with the egg forming a diploid zygote. The zygote elongates and then divides transversely which further divides at right angles to the first resulting in four cells. The two cells near the neck give rise to cotyledon and stem, the remaining two cells produce the foot and primary root. Further development leads to the formation of young sporophyte plant.

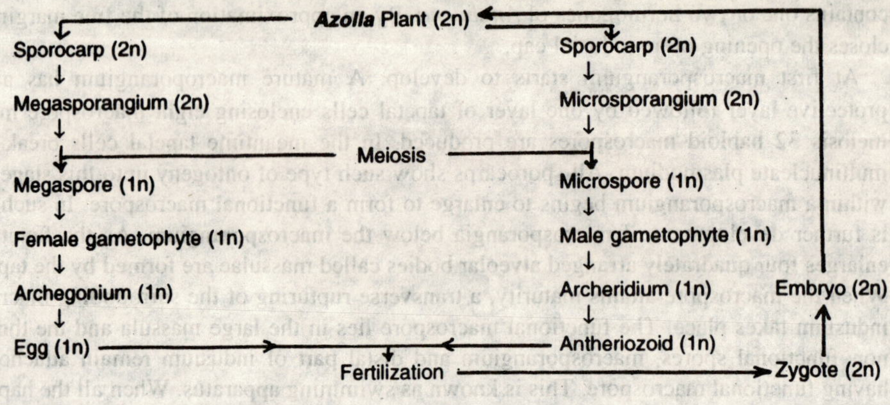

Graphic life-cycle of *Azolla* sp.

SECTION - V

GYMNOSPERMS

1. General Features and Classification
2. Cycas
3. Pinus and Taxus
4. Gnetum

CHAPTER 1

GYMNOSPERMS

GENERAL FEATURES AND CLASSIFICATION

Theophrastus (300 B.C) used the word "Gymnosperms" in his book entitled "*Enquiry into Plants*" for all those plants bearing unprotected seeds (Gymons = naked, Sperma = seed).

The gymonsperms are the most ancient seed bearing plants which originated during the late Palaeozoic era (Devonian Period) about 265 million years ago and flourished during the Mesozoic. The distinguishing characters of the gymnospermous plant can be summarised as follows —

1. Gymnospermous plants lack vegetative means of reproduction and are slow growers. However, *Cycas* propagates vegetatively by means of bulbils developed on the stem.
2. It has limited means of dispersal and are unable to grow under varied habitats.
3. Vessels are absent (except in *Gnetum*) in the xylem and phloem has no companion cells.
4. Bisexuality is absent resulting in reduction of self pollination.
5. Ovule and seeds are uncovered.
6. Plant body is sporophyte, differentiated into root, stem and leaves.

CLASSIFICATION

There are many systems of classification of gymnosperms. Some of them are given below —

1. **Coulter and Chamberlain (1910) classified gymnosperms into seven orders, namely; Cycadofiicales, Bennettitales, Cycadales, Cordaitales, Ginkgoales, Coniferales and Gnetales.**

2. **Sahni (1920) divided the gymnosperms into two major groups. These are :-**

   I. Stachyospermae including orders (1) Cordaitales, (2) Ginkgoales, (3) Coniferales, (4) Taxales.
   II. Phyllospermae which includes orders — (1) Cycadofilicales (2) Cycadales (3) Bennettitales.
   His classification is based on foliar or axial origin of the ovule. Gnetales has not been covered under his classification.

3. **Arnold (1948) divided the gymnosperms into 3 phyla as such : (i) Cycadophyta (ii) Coniferophyta and (iii) Chlamydospermophyta**

   Arnold's classification of gymnosperms can be summarised as follows :

Phylum : *Tracheophyta*

Sub–*phylum* :

(1) Psilopsida
(2) Lycopsida
(3) Sphenopsida
(4) Pteropsida (includes all the members of gymnosperms)

Classes of Pteropsida :

(1) Cycadophyta	:	Orders :	1. Cycadales	2. Pteridospermae	3. Cycadeoidales
(2) Ginkgophyta	:	Orders :	1. Ginkgoales	2. Cordaitales	
(3) Coniferophyta	:	Orders :	1. Coniferales	2. Taxales	
(4) Chlamydospermophyta	:	Orders :	1. Gnetales	2. Ephedrales	

4. Pant (1957) classified the gymnosperms into three divisions which are further divided into classes and orders. His classification is as follows :

Gymnosperm

Division : 1. Cycadophyta.	Class :	1. Pteridospermopsida 2. Cycadopsida 3. Pentoxylopsida 4. Cycadeoideopsida (Bennettitopsida)
Division : 2. Chlamydospermophyta.	Class :	1. Gnetopsida
Division : 3. Coniferophyta :	Class :	1. Coniferopsida 2. Ephedropsida 3. Cxekanowskiopsida 4. Taxopsida

5. Andrews (1961) has divided the gymnosperms into six divisions as follows :

1. Pteridospoermophyta having 4 families under one order Pteridospermales.
2. Cycadophyta includes two orders namely, (1) Cycadales and (2) Bennettitales.
3. Ginkgophyta including one order Ginkgoales.
4. Coniferophyta having two orders namely (1) Coniferales and (2) Cordaitales.
5. Gnetophyta includes order Gnetales.
6. Gymnosperms of uncertain position having Pentoxyleae and Vojnouskyales orders.

6. Delevoryas (1963) supported the classification of Chamberlain (1934) and recognized Taxales as a separate order under coniferophyta.

7. Takhtajan, Cronquist and Zimmermann (1966) proposed a classification of gymnosperms in the following way and called division Pinophyta for gymnosperms. It was divided into three subdivisions.

Classes under each subdivision as follows :-

Sub-division — Cycadicae   Class :   1. Lyginopteridatae (= Cycadofilicales)
2. Cycadatae (= Cycadales)
3. Bennettitatae (= Bennettitales)

Sub division : Pinicae   Class :   1. Ginkgoatae (= Ginkgoales)
2. Pinatae : Sub-class : 1. Cordaitidae
2. Pinidae (= Coniferales)

Sub division : Gneticae (= Gnetales)   Class :   1. Gnetitae
Sub-Class   1. Ephedridae
2. Welwitschiidae
3. Gnetidae.

8. Bierhorst (1971) divided the gymnosperms into three classes and each class into several orders as follows:-

Classes under Gymonsperms:

(1) Cycadopsida : Orders :
1. Pteridospermales
2. Caytoniales
3. Cycadeoidales
4. Cycadales
5. Pentoxylales
6. Glossopteridales

(2) Coniferopsida : Orders :
1. Cordaitales
2. Protopityales
3. Ginkgoales
4. Coniferales
5. Taxales

(3) Gnetopsida : Orders :
1. Ephedrales
2. Gnetales
3. Welwiitschiales

Classification of Bierhorst (1971) has been followed in this text.

AFFINITIES OF THE GYMNOSPERMS

From the phylogenetic point of view the Gymnosperms occupy a position in between Pteridophytes and Angiosperms. Hence, Gymnosperms have well marked affinities with both these groups.

RESEMBLANCES OF GYMNOSPERMS WITH PTERIDOPHYTES

The gymnosperms show resemblances with pteridophytes in the following ways :-

1. Both have sporophytic plant body differentiated into roots, stem and leaves.
2. In both the groups phloem lacks companion cells and xylem lacks vessels.
3. Many cycads resemble ferns in the circinate ptyxis of the leaves and large compound leaves.
4. Female sex organs in both the groups are archegonia.
5. The male gametes in Cycads and *Ginkgo* are motile like that of pteridophytes.
6. Many pteridophytes like *Selaginella, Marsilea* etc. are heterosporous like that of gymnosperms.
7. The gametophyte of heterosporous pteridophytes and that of gymnosperms are endosporic.

8. The embryo formation is endoscopic in all gymnosperms and majority of pteridophytes.

DIFFERENCES BETWEEN GYMNOSPERMS AND PTERIDOPHYTES

1. All the gymnosperms are heterosporous whereas majority of the pteridophytes are homosporous.
2. In most of the gymnosperms, the roots are tap root where as they are adventitious in pteridophytes.
3. In all the gymnospermous plants, stems are aerial while they are rhizome in most of the pteridophytes.
4. Gymnosperm is seed bearing where as pteridophytes do not produce seeds.
5. Secondary growth is present in gymnosperms but it is absent in pteridophytes.
6. Development of pollen tube from pollen grains is absent in pteridophytes whereas it takes place in gymnosperms.
7. In gymnosperms, the megasporangium is protected by integuments which are absent in pteridophytes.
8. There is no neck and neck canal cells in gymnosperms whereas it is present in pteridophytes.
9. There is no ovule in pteridophytes which is present in gymnosperms.

RESEMBLANCES OF GYMNOSPERMS WITH ANGIOSPERMS

1. Root has secondary growth and xylem is exarch in roots.
2. Stele is eustelic. There is secondary growth in the stem of both gymnosperms and angiosperms.
3. Seeds are produced by both the groups.
4. In the ovule, the nucellus is surrounded by integuments.
5. Pollen grains grow into pollen tubes in both the groups.
6. Male gametes are non–motile in all angiosperms and in majority of gymnosperms.
7. The embryo formation is endoscopic.

DIFFERENCES BETWEEN GYMNOSPERMS AND ANGIOSPERMS

1. The gymnosperms are not herbaceous while many of angiosperms are herbaceous.
2. The gymnosperms are unisexual, monoecious or dioecious whereas angiosperms are bisexual, unisexual, monoecious or dioecious.
3. The gymnosperms are perennial (except a few), but angiosperms are annual, biennial or perennial.
4. Generally no vegetative means of reproduction in gymnosperms while this method is common in the angiosperms.
5. Among gymnosperms pollination and dispersal of seeds are by wind, in angiosperms it is anemophily, entomophily, hydrophily or zoophily.
6. Gymnosperms lack petals and sepals.
7. Ovule is naked in gymnosperms, but it is protected by carpel in angiosperms.

CHAPTER 2

CYCAS

Cycas belong to	Class	—	Cycadopsida
	Order	—	Cycadales
	Family	—	Cycadaceae
	Genus	—	*Cycas*

HABIT AND HABITAT

The genus *Cycas* has 15 - 20 species distributed mainly in the eastern hemisphere. In India only four species of the genus *Cycas* are found. These are *C. beddomei* found in Tamil Nadu and Andhra; *C. rumphii* found in Andmann and Nicobar Islands; *C. pectinata* found in Khasia Hills of Assam, Champaran district of Bihar and Sikkim and *C. circinalis* found in Andhra, Tamil Nadu and Orissa. Besides, *C. revolutea* are grown as an ornamental garden plant in India and has been called a "living fossil" due to its primitive characters. It is also known as Sago Palm in Japan and China (Fig. 1).

The sporophytic plant body of *Cycas* looks like an ever green palm and is differentiated into root,

Fig. 1. *Cycas revoluta*, A female plant.

stem and leaves. The height of the plant ranges from 8 - 50 feet.

Root — The primary root is tap root which is very long. Sometimes the root becomes short, thick and tuberous. Some of the lateral roots give rise branches which grow vertically upward i.e. negatively geotropic just below the ground level. These roots are dichotomously branched, coral like masses. They are called the coralloid roots or corallorhiza. The coralloid roots are inhabited by *Anabaena* and *Nostoc*. The surface of the coralloid root is beset with lentical like openings suggesting thereby that they are respiratory in function.

Stem — The stem is columnar but in young stage it is tuberous. Normally, the stem is unbranched and is covered with thick peristent leaf bases. A crown of large compound leaves are present at the apex.

Leaves — The leaves are of two types (a) scale leaves and (b) foliage leaves. They are spirally arranged alternating with each other. The alternating clusters of peristent leaf bases of foliage and scale leaves give the stem a rugged look. The scale leaves are brown in colour and are persistent and protective in function. The foliage leaves are large and pinnate compound. Pinnae are closely set on the rachis and are sessile and paripinnate. The pinnae are narrow, linear and leathery in texture showing xerophytic nature. The margin is curved downward and inwards. Each leaflet has a single mid vein. The ptyxis of the leaflet is circinate. The new cluster of leaves is born every year or every alternate year.

ANATOMY OF STEM

Transverse section of the stem shows the following features. (Fig. 2).

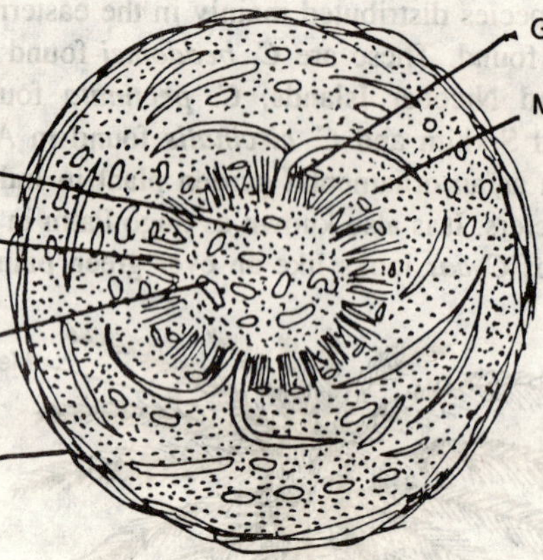

Fig. 2. Transverse section (t.S) of stem of *Cycas* (diagramatic).

Epidermis — It is the outermost single layer of stem which is heavy in outline due to persistent leaf bases and woody scales.

Cortex — It is massive and made up of parenchyma cells, densely filled with starch grains. Many mucilage canals are present in the cortical region. The occurrence of the girdles i.e. peculiar curved leaftraces, is the significant characters of stem anatomy of *Cycas*. The leaf trace does not take a direct path from stem to petiole but form a girdle system. Each leaf is supplied by two main trace bundles which are formed by the branching of one trace that arises from the primary vascular cylinder on the side of the stem opposite to the insertion of the leaf. It is originated from the inner edge of the primary xylem. It runs obliquely outwards through the cortex and divides into two leaf trace bundles. These leaf trace bundles diverge and run in opposite direction in the outer cortex. These covering leaf traces are known as girdle bundles or girdles. The girdles meet at the leaf base and enter the petiole on opposite side from the point of departure from the stele. It divides repeatedly to form a large number of bundles arranged in the omega (horse shoe) pattern in the petiole. The girdle bundles are collateral and endarch. Later, the bundle structure is modified, consisting of centripetal xylem and a remnant of centrifugal xylem separated by parenchyma. Such bundles are mesarch, a characteristic of ferns. It is primitive character. Presence of two xylem type is called diploxylic bundles.

SECONDARY GROWTH

It is like that of dicotyledonous stem. The primary vascular bundles are open having an intrafascicular cambium. The interfascicular cambium develops as in normal dicot stem. The ring of vascular bundles slowly increases in size radially due to the formation of secondary xylem and secondary phloem by cambium. The medullary rays are also formed. The primary cambium is of short duration and later a secondary cambium is formed outside the secondary region. It is formed in the cortex or pericycle. It cuts off the second ring of concentric wood. The secondary cambium also dies and is superseded by the development of a third. It arises outside the secondary vascular ring. In this way several rings of accessory cambium arise in the cortex forming corresponding rings of secondary vascular tissues. These rings are growth rings different from the annual rings of dicot stems (Fig. 3).

Fig. 3. T. S. of stem of *Cycas* showing secondary growth.

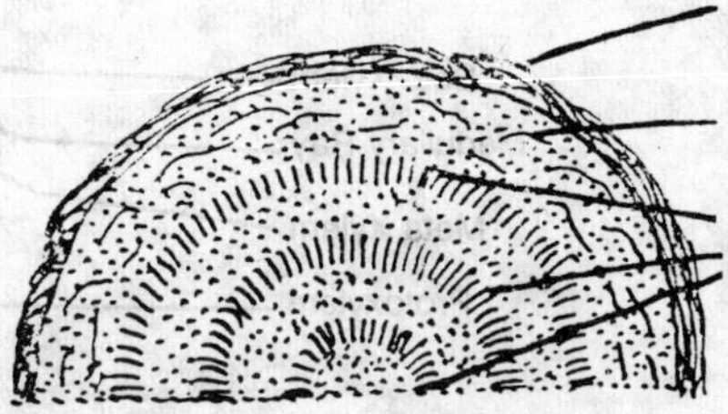

Fig. 4. T. S. of stem of *Cycas* showing armour of leaf bases.

Due to the formation of secondary vascular tissues, the outer tissues of the stem gets tangential pressure leading to its rupture. Prior to this, a special protective tissue known as periderm is formed outside the cortex by the activity of a special type of cambium i.e. cork cambium or phellogen developed in the outer cortex. (Fig. 4).

ANATOMY OF ROOT

Cycas has two types of roots ;

(a) Positively geotropic normal root and (b) Negatively geotropic coralloid root.

Transverse section of the *normal root* shows the following organisations —

Exodermis or Epiblema — It is outermost single layer of cells.

Cortex — Cortex is large, made up of parenchymatous cells. Cortical cells may have tannin cells and mucilage canals.

Endodermis — The cortex is delimited by a single layer of endodermis.

Pericycle — Below the endodermis is present pericycle made up of single layer of cells.

Stele — Younger roots shows diarch condition but in mature root, the stele is tetrarch. Protoxylem is towards periphery and metaxylem towards the centre. Number of phloem bundles are equal to the number of xylem bundles and alternate with the protoxylem elements. Pith is present in the centre.

Secondary growth takes place in the same manner as in dicotyledonous root but several irregular concentric rings of vascular bundles and periderm are formed in old roots. The root is protected by root cap developed from periblema (Fig. 5).

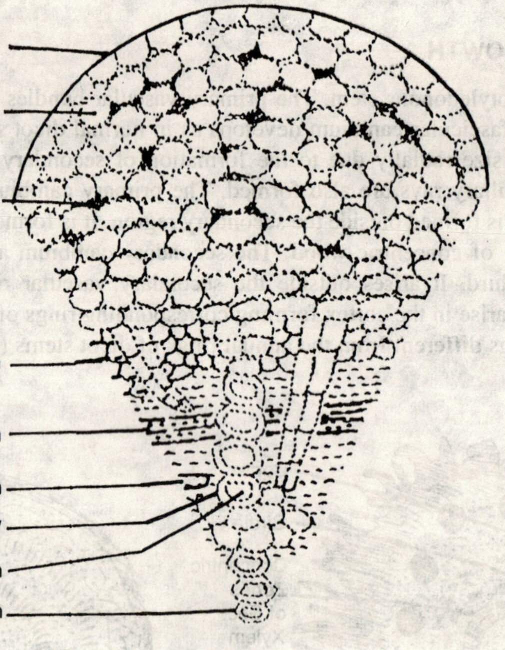

Fig. 5. T.S. of root of *Cycas* (A sector).

CORALLOID ROOT

Transverse section of coralloid root shows the following features. However, it shows the similar structure to that of the primary positively geotropic root.

Outer zone — Cortex made of several layers of cells constitute the outer zone.

Cork cambium — The outer cortical zone is delimited by a layer of cork cambium.

Middle cortex — Below cork cambium lies the parenchymatous middle cortex which includes 'Algal zone'. The algae are present as symbioant. The Algal zone is formed of large disintegrated cells containing *Nostoc* and *Anabaena* species.

Inner cortex — It is below the algal zone consisting of several layers of parenchyma cells.

Endodermis — Inner cortex is followed by single layered endodermis.

Pericycle — Single layer of pericycle is present below the endodermis.

Stele — The stele is diarch or triarch. Phloem is alternately situated on different radii. Coralloid root also show the secondary growth (Fig. 6).

ANATOMY OF PETIOLE OR RACHIS

Rachis of *Cycas* is stout and woody with midrib bearing paired rows of leaflets. The transverse section of the petiole or rachis shows the following features.

Epidermis — It is the outermost layer of cells covered with thick article.

Hypodermis — Below the epidermis are two layers of sclerenchymatous cells forming hypodermis.

Ground tissue — It is below hypodermis made up of parenchyma cells with pitted walls.

Vascular bundles — Many vascular bundles are arranged in the form of inverted omega (ω a Greek letter). Each vascular bundle is surrounded by an outer thick walled bundle sheath. One to several layers

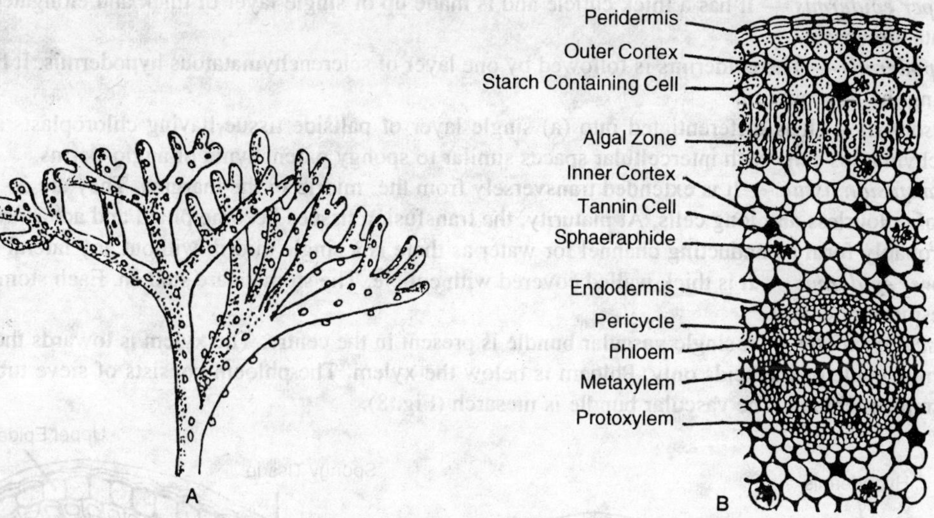

Fig. 6. *Cycas* (A Coralloid root; (B) Transeverse section (A sector).

of pericycle is present below the bundle–sheath. Xylem and phloem follow the bundle sheath. The bundles are open. Cambium is present on the upper surface of the centrifugal metaxylem. Bundles are endarch near the base of the rachis. At the apex of the rachis, the bundles are exarch. It has been noticed that the centrifugal metaxylem gradually disappears as the rachis grows upwards. The gradual disappearance of centrifugal xylem and simultaneous appearance of centripetal xylem is a condition known as *diploxylic* (Fig. 7 A, B & C).

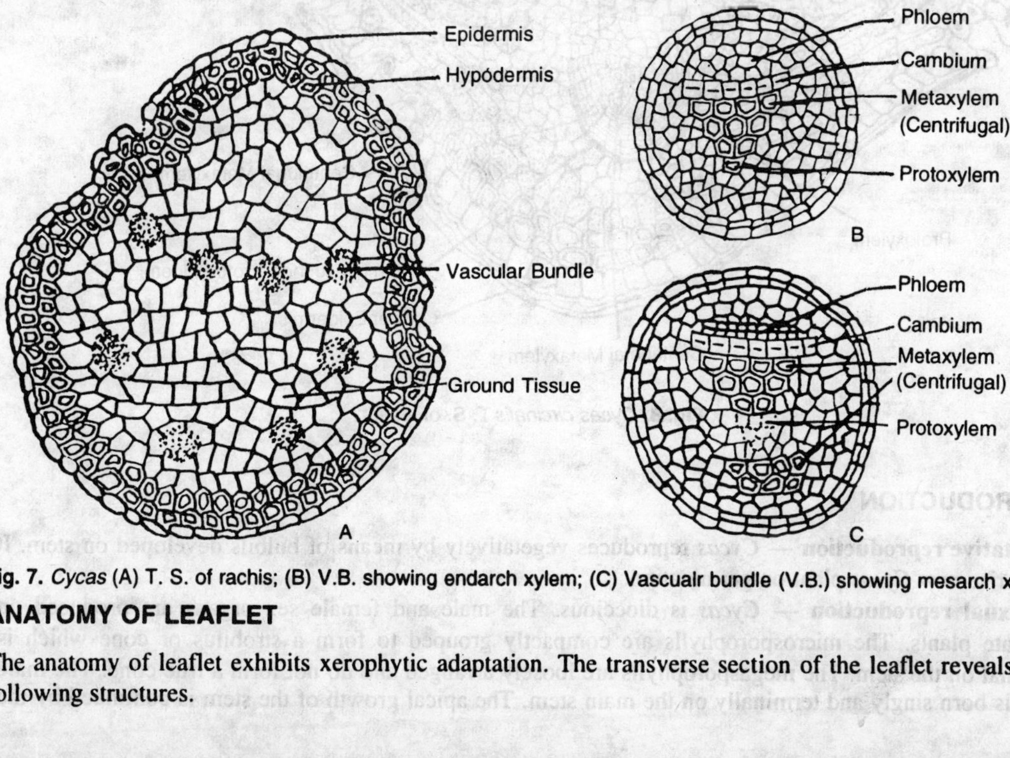

Fig. 7. *Cycas* (A) T. S. of rachis; (B) V.B. showing endarch xylem; (C) Vascualr bundle (V.B.) showing mesarch xylem.

ANATOMY OF LEAFLET

The anatomy of leaflet exhibits xerophytic adaptation. The transverse section of the leaflet reveals the following structures.

Upper epidermis — It has a thick cuticle and is made up of single layer of thick and elongated cells. Stomata are absent.

Hypodermis — The epidermis is followed by one layer of sclerenchymatatous hypodermis. It helps in reducing the transpiration.

Mesophyll — It is differentiated into (a) single layer of paliside tissue having chloroplasts and (b) parenchymatous cells with intercellular spaces similar to spongy parenchyma of angiosperms.

Transfusion tissue — It is extended transversely from the midrib to the margins. They are 3 - 4 cells thick of colourless and long cells. At maturity, the transfusion tissues become pitted and act as tracheids and probably form a conducting channel for water as there is a single midrib without any lateral veins.

Lower epidermis — It is thick walled covered with cuticle. The stomata are sunken. Each stoma leads to a respiratory cavity.

Vascular bundle — A single vascular bundle is present in the centre. The xylem is towards the upper epidermis made of tracheids only. Phloem is below the xylem. The phloem consists of sieve tubes and phloem parenchyma. The vascular bundle is mesarch (Fig. 8).

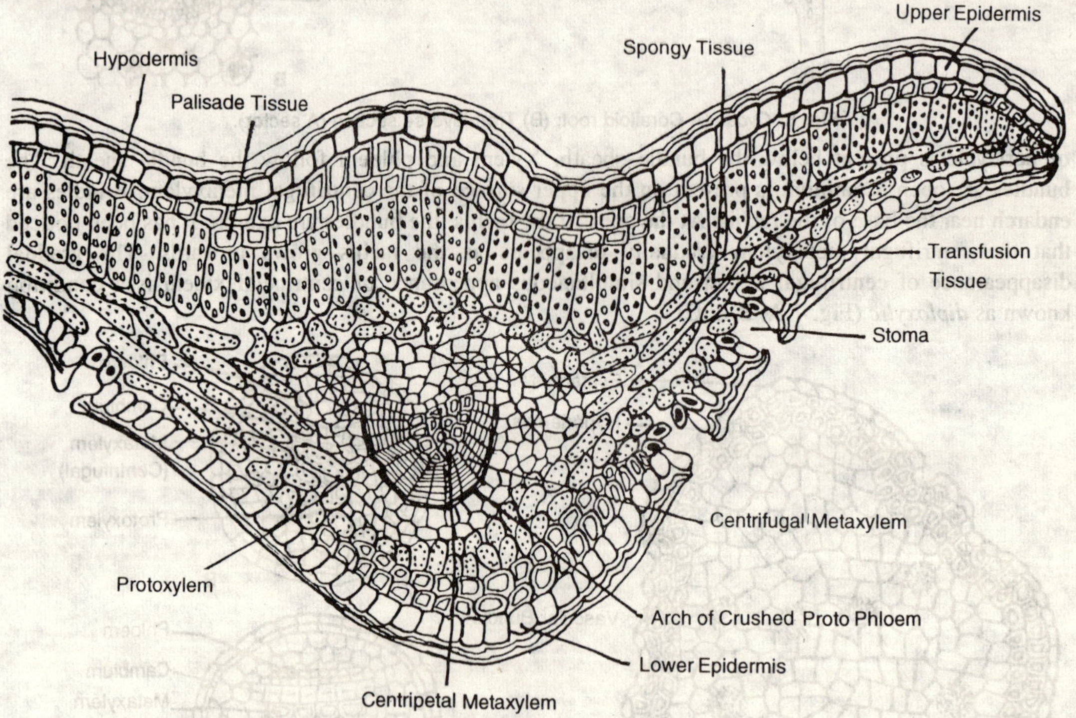

Fig. 8. *Cycas circinalis* T. S. of leaflet.

REPRODUCTION

Vegetative reproduction — *Cycas* reproduces vegetatively by means of bulbils developed on stem. It gives rise new *Cycas* plant on germination.

Sexual reproduction — *Cycas* is dioecious. The male and female sex organs are produced on separate plants. The microsporophylls are compactly grouped to form a strobilus or cone which is terminal on the stem. The megasporophylls are loosely arranged and do not form a true cone. The male cone is born singly and terminally on the main stem. The apical growth of the stem is continued by the

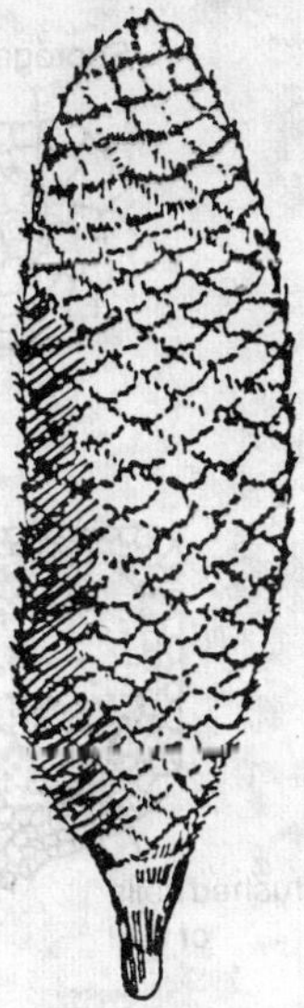

Fig. 9. *Cycas revoluta.* A male cone.

Fig. 10. *Cycas* Microsporophylls (Ventral view)

development of an axillary bud near the base of the cone. It acts as new stem apex. As it grows, the male cone is displaced to one side.

The male cone — It is woody, compact, long (about 50 cm.) and spindle shaped. It is the largest reproductive structure in gymnosperms. The male cone has an axis on which microporophylls or stamens are arranged spirally. The microsporophyll is flattened and narrow below and expanded above into a sterile disc called apophysis (Fig. 9). The basal and terminal microsporophylls are sterile and rest of the microsporophylls bear microsporangia or pollen sacs on its lower side in a group of 3 - 5 (called sorus) separated by a median sterile line. The microsporangia are present on the entire lower surface. The microsporangium has a wall of many layers of cells covered by the epidermis. The sporogenous cells or microspore mother cells divide meiotically to produce haploid microspores or pollen grains. The tapetum derived from cell wall or from the sporogenous tissue, disintegrates and forms a liquid mass which provides nourishment to the developing spores (Fig. 10).

Dehiscence of microsporangium — The outer thick layer of wall shrinks due to the loss of water which causes splitting open of the wall along the abaxial side. The cells at this point is smaller and thinner. Thus, the open sporangium looks like boat shaped. Microsporophylls get separated from the male cone and microspores fall out of the dehisced microsporangium (Fig. 11). Microspores are simple in structure and without wings.

Female cone or ovulate strobilus — It forms a rosette of megasporophylls developed in acropetal succession, loosely arranged in spiral fashion. Megasporophylls are born each year between successive whorls of foliage leaves. Below the whorls of foliage leaves are whorls of scale leaves suggesting thereby that the megasporophylls replace scale leaves and are equivalent to them.

The megasporophylls of *Cycas* are large (6 - 8 inches long) and leafy in nature. Upper part of megasporophyll is broadly pinnate like a leaf and taper to a point. The upper expanded portion and the lower stalk like axis are densely covered with brownish hairs. Two lateral rows of orange coloured megasporangia (ovules) are present in the notches on either side of the lower half of megasporophyll. The ovules of cycads are the largest in the plant kingdom. They are dark green colour in *C. circinalis* and red in *C. revoluta* (Fig. 12).

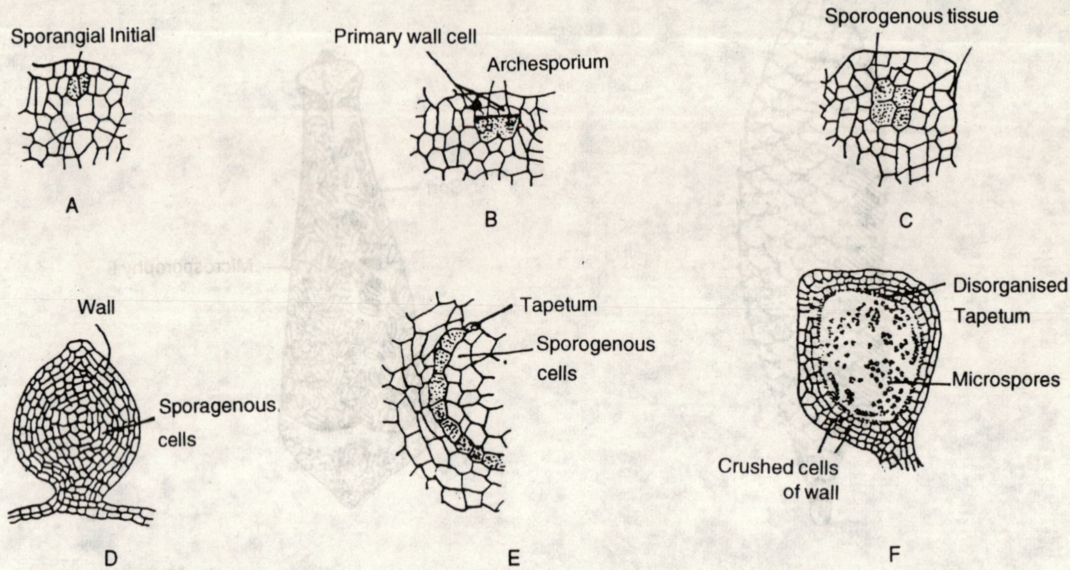

Fig. 11. Stage in the development of microspores within microsporangium as studied by Land (A to F)

Structure of the mature ovule — The ovule is orthotropous in position. It has a single massive integument enclosing the nucellus except at the upper end which forms micropyle. The integument consists of three layers. Outer and inner layers are fleshy and the middle layer is stony. The vascular supply to the ovule is uniform. At the apex of the nucellus, a nucellar beak is present formed owing to the vigrous growth of the tissue at the apical nucellar region. The centre of the beak is hollow enclosing the pollen chamber in which pollen grains come after pollination. The pollen chamber is in continuity with the micropyle. A large megaspore embryosac is seen within the nucellar mass of tissue. Haploid megaspore develops after meiosis in megaspore mother cells. Out of 4 linear haploid megaspores produced due to meiosis, only the lower most haploid megaspore is functional and the remaining three degenerate. (Fig. 13).

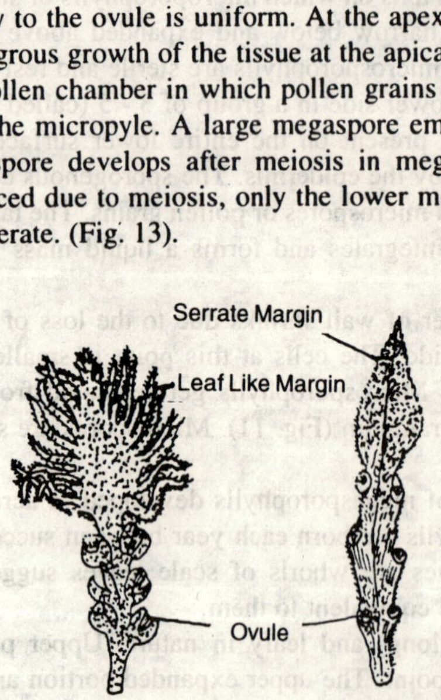

Fig. 12. (A) megasporophyll of *Cycas revoluta*; (B) megasporophyll of *C. circilalis*

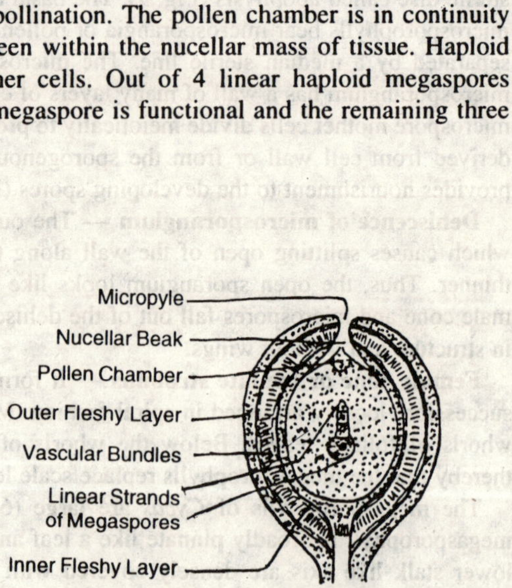

Fig. 13. Longitudinal section (L.S) of ovule of *Cycas*.

FEMALE GAMETOPHYTE

Megaspore is the 1st cell generation of female gametophyte. Megaspore germinates *in situ* and begins to enlarge in its size and its nucleus divides mitotically forming 1000 or more small nuclei by free nuclear divisions. All the megaspore nuclei lie in the cytoplasm of the megaspore. A central vacuole appears in the megaspore. As the vacuole grows in size, the free nuclei form a peripheral layer within the megaspore wall by wall formation around the free nuclei. The cells of the peripheral tissue grow towards the centre and finally the central vacuole is filled up. The tissue thus formed within the meagspore wall is the prothalus or female gametophyte. The mature female prothallus is enclosed in the nucellus surrounded by the integument. It is devoid of chlorophyll and rhizoids.

Development of Archegonium — Shortly after pollination, some cells of the periphery of the female prothallus near the micropylar end begin to differentiate into archegonial initials. The functional archegonial initials divide transversely into an outer primary neck cell and an inner central cell. The primary neck cell divides vertically to form short neck of the archegonium. There are no neck canal cells. The central cell prior to fertilization further divides into a small ventral canal cell and a large egg cell (Fig. 14.)

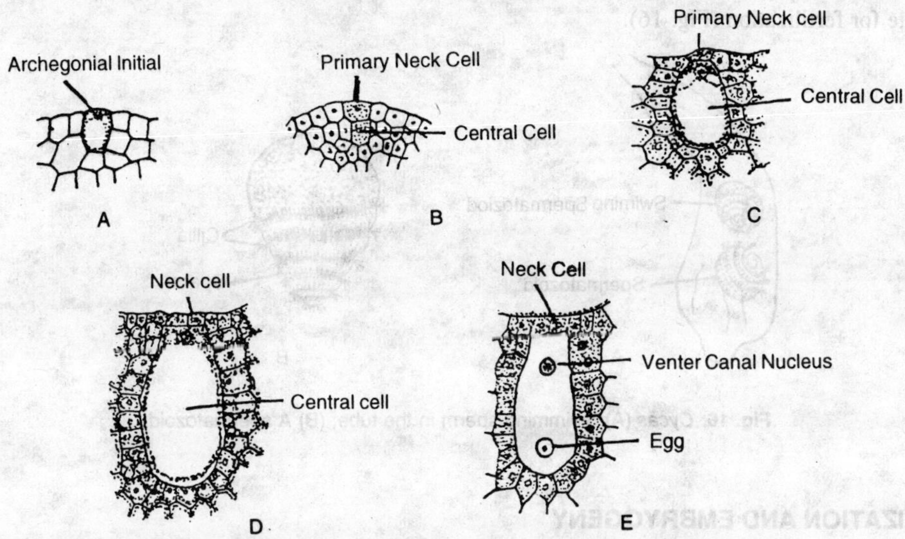

Fig. 14. (A to E) Developmental stages of archegonium of *Cycas.*

MALE GAMETOPHYTE

Haploid microspore is the first cell generation of the male gametophyte. The microspore has two layers of wall, outer layer called exine and inner thin layer called intine. The microspore begins to germinate while still in the microsporangium. It divides into two unequal cells; a small persistent prothallial cell and a large antheridial cell. The antheridial cell further divides into a small generative cell and a large tube cell. It is the three celled structure when the pollen grains are shed from the pollen sac and carried away by wind. At the time of pollination, cells near the apex of the nucellar beak break down and form a mucilaginous drop which oozes out through the micropyle. Some of the pollen grains are caught in this drop. The droplets get dried and the pollen grains reaches into the chamber.

The pollen grain germinates in a weak after pollination and further development takes place in the pollen chamber. The exine bursts and the intine comes out in the form of a pollen tube. The pollen tube moves down carrying the prothalial and generative cells with it. The generative cell divides into two cells, the stalk cell and the body cell. After about four months when fertilization time approaches, the body cell enlarges and two star shaped structure called blepharoplasts appear in it. The body cell divides longitudinally producing two multiflagellate antherozoids. (Fig. 15).

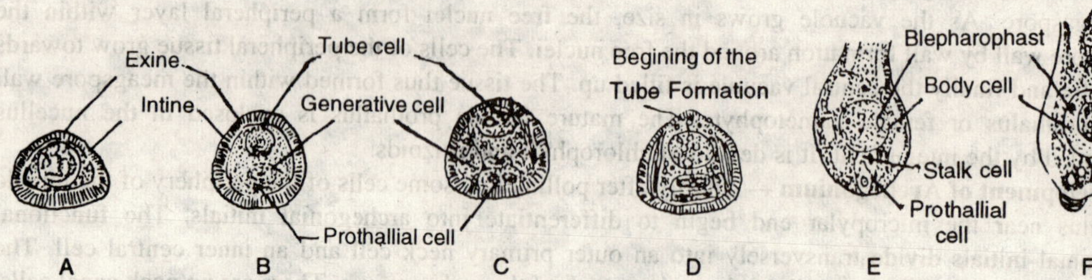

Fig. 15. Development of male gametophyte in *Cycas* (A - F)

The sperm mother cell breaks and sperms come to lie freely in the cavity of the body cell. The sperms then pass on to the pollen tube and starts swimming, ultimately reaches to the tip of the pollen tube ready to liberate for fertilization (Fig. 16).

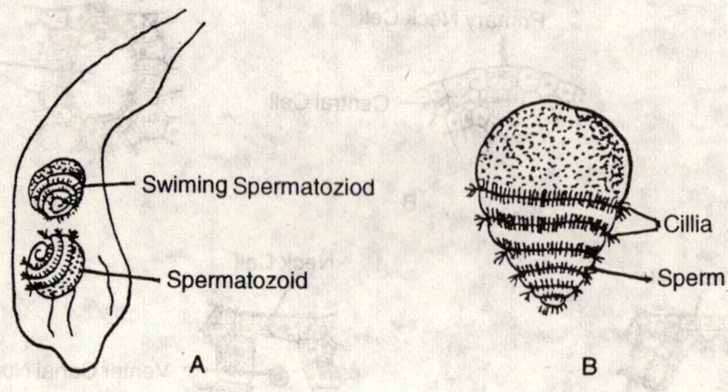

Fig. 16. *Cycas* (A) Swimming sperm in the tube; (B) A spermatozoid.

FERTILIZATION AND EMBRYOGENY

By this time the pollen chamber breaks, portion of nucellus covering archegonail chamber also breaks and hence a continuous cavity is formed. The archegonial chamber is moist. The turgid end of the tube bursts and discharges the fluid it contains in which the sperms swim and enter the neck of the archegonium. The entire spermatozoid enters the egg but its nucleus slips out of its cytoplasmic sheath and ciliated band and moves towards the egg nucleus and ultimately fuses to form diploid zygote or oospore.

After fertilization the zygote nucleus divides by free nuclear divisions. A large central vacuole is formed due to the migration of all the free nuclei to the periphery which form a parietal layer. Wall formation starts after sometime. This is called pro–embryo. The pro–embryo gets differentiated into three regions. (a) an upper haustorical part in contact with nutritive substance (b) middle portion of suspensor and (c) lower group of cells forming the embryo cells.

More than one archegonia may be fertilized but ultimately only one embryo matures. The embryo cells form an embryo which invades and absorbs the endosperm (female gametophyte). The mature embryo consists of radicle, plumule and two cotyledons. Root appears later.

SEED

Integument forms the testa and the ovule is metameophosed into seed. A mature seed has a fleshy outer layer and an inner stony layer. The embryo is straight and remains embedded in the gametophyte (endosperm). The seed of *Cycas* represents three generation and they are (a) the sporophytic represented by testa (b) gametophytic represented by endosperm and (c) newly formed sporophyte rcpresented by the embryo (Fig.17).

Seed germinates immediately without undergoing a period of rest. The mode of germination is hypogeal. The root rapidly grows into the soil and forms a tap root. The plumule forms an inconspicuous stem. The cotyledons remain inside the seed coat (Fig. 18).

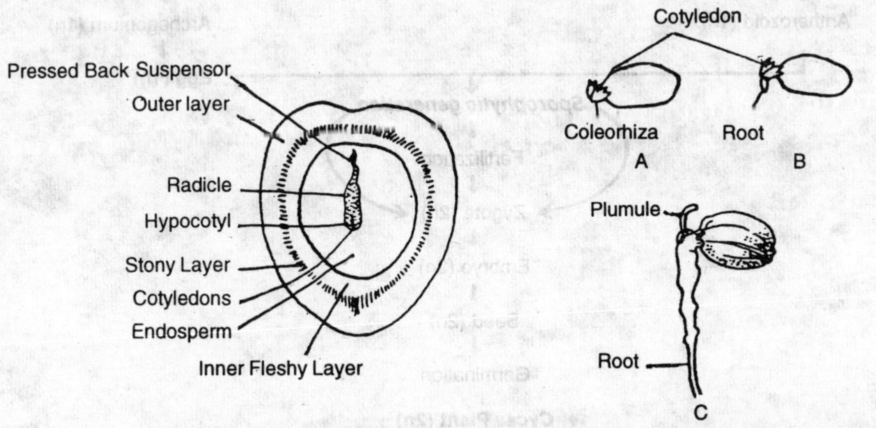

Fig. 17. L. S. of seed of *Cycas.* **Fig. 18.** Germination of *Cycas* seed (A - C)

CYCAS AS A LIVING FOSSIL

Cycas revoluta is a most common species grown in India. This is known as living fossil because it resembles with *C. fujiana* a fossil from Japan (Yokoyana), 1911). The members of cycadales including *Cycas* are decreasing rapidly due to natural decline and extended cultivation of land in tropics. Consequently, time may come when all or many of the species would disappear. Hence, cycas is known as 'living fossil'.

FERN LIKE CHARACTERS OF *CYCAS*

Cycas resembles fern in having the following characters :-

1. Circinate vernation of leaves.
2. Motile sperm with many cilia.
3. Microsporangia are born on abaxial surface of the microsporophyll in sori like fern.
4. Presence of archegonia in the female gametophyte.
5. Crown of pinnate compound leaves as in tree fern.
6. Presence of ramenta.

ECONOMIC IMPORTANCE OF *CYCAS*

The leaves of cycas are used to prepare mats, baskets and hats. Pollen of C. circi*nalis* is narcotic. The juice of tender leaves is used in vomiting. Sago is obtained from *C. revoluta* The resin obtained from *C.*

rumphin is used in malignant ulcers.

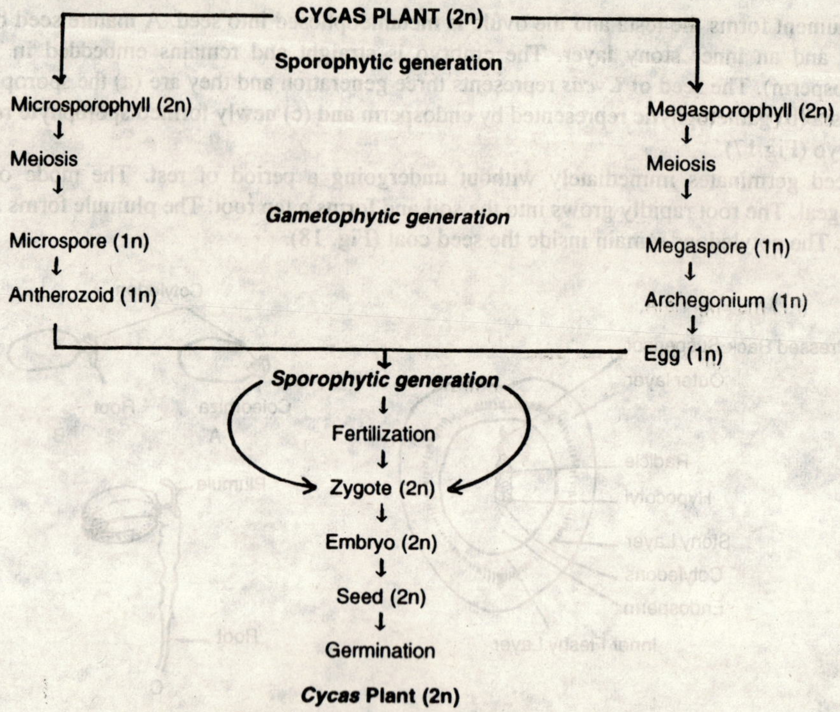

Graphic life cycle of *Cycas* sp.

CHAPTER 3

PINUS AND TAXUS

3.1 PINUS

Pinus belongs to	Class	—	Coniferopsida
	Order	—	Coniferales
	Family	—	Pinaceae
	Genus	—	*Pinus*

HABIT AND HABITAT

The genus *Pinus* is represented by about one hundred species in the world. They grow on slope of the hills and forms dense vegetation in the north temperate zones of the world. They are also reported from sub–arctic zones and tropical hills. Some of the common Indian species are *Pinus roxburghii* Sarg. It is also known as *Pinus longifolia* Roxb or chir pine. It grows at a height of 1500 to 7500 feet above the sea level on the hill slopes of western and eastern Himalayas. It is a tall tree reaching a height of 50 - 60 meters and varies in diameter from 1.5 to 3 meters. The branches are of two types, long and dwarf shoot. The leaves, commonly known as needles are confined only to the dwarf shoot in a group of 3 needles. The scaly leaves are found on the main stem, long shoot and also on dwarf shoot. The winged seeds are edible. *Pinus* is also cultivated as ornamental. *Pinus excelsa* are found at a height of 6000 - to - 11,000 feet above sea level reported from Garhwal, Simla Hills, Kulu, Chamba and Kashmir in the Western Himalaya and from Meghalaya, Nagaland in the eastern Himalayan regions. Its height is from 100 - 150 feet and diameter is 8 - 10 feet. The stem shows excurrent habit bearing whorled branches. The dwarf shoot bears group of 5 needles. The dwarf shoot arise in the axil of a scale leaf and is covered with 10 - 12 spirally arranged cataphylls. The first formed two cataphylls are known as prophylls. The male cones develop in the axils of lower scale leaves on the long shoot and are longer in size than those of *P. longifolia. P. gerardiana* grows in northwest Himalayas at a height of 5000 - 12,000 feet above the sea level. It is commonly called Chilgoza pine. Its dwarf shoots bear three needles. Billings (1957) reported *Pinus aristata* from California which is about 4000 years old. The plant body is sporophyte differentiated into root, stem and leaves (Fig. 19)

The primary root is tap root. The tip of root is covered with root cap. Root hairs are poorly developed The new young branches developing from tap root remain short. There are mycorrhizal roots.

ANATOMY OF STEM

Transverse section of stem shows the following features.

Epidermis — It is outermost single layer of cells which are highly cutinized.

Cortex — Below the epidermis, cortical cells are found. Inner cortex is made up of thin walled

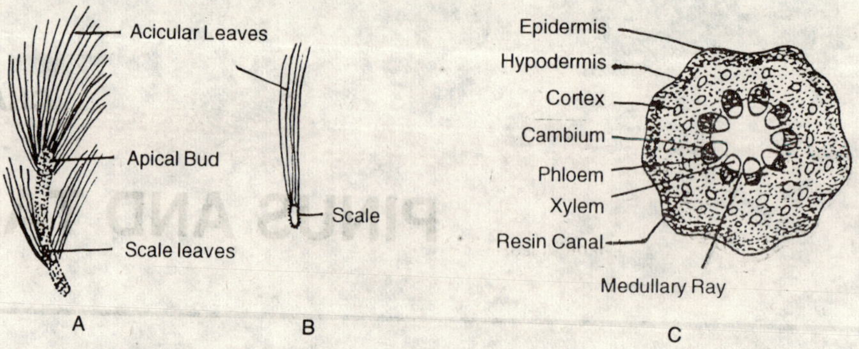

Fig. 19. *Pinus* shoot, (A) of unlimited growth; (B) dwarf shoot; (C) T. S. of young stem of *Pinus*

parenchymatous cells while the outer cortex is of the thick walled cells forming hypodermis. Inner cortex contains resin canals or ducts lined by parenchymatous glandular secretory cells which forms the epithelium. The epithelial cells secrete resin into the canal. Resin is a major source of natural turpentine an antiseptic reagent. No such resin canals are found in angiosperms. Endodermis and pericycle are not distinguished.

Primary vascular elements — A ring of five to six separate primary vascular bundles are found. The bundles are collateral and open. Each vascular bundle has a primary xylem on the inner side, primary phloem on the outerside and cambium in between these two. Primary medulary rays lie between the primary vascular bundles and connect the pith with cortex. It is narrow consisting of parenchymatous tissue.

Secondary tissues — The secondary structures are formed in the same manner as in dicotyledons. The primary vascular cambium extends tangentially resulting in the formation of a complete ring of cambium. It divides to form secondary xylem towards inside and secondary phloem towards outside. The cambium remains as a permanent meristematic tissue in between secondary xylem and phloem. Each year a band of secondary xylem and secondary phloem is formed by the cambium which appears as a series of concentric layers in a transverse section. Each band or layer represents growth of a year and is called an annual ring. Resin canals are present in the secondary and primary wood. The tracheids become functionless due to development of tyloses into the cavity of tracheideal cells. Bars of sanio are also found around the bordered pits.

Cambium also forms secondary medullary rays. They traverse the secondary xylem and secondary phloem at some places. They are one cell broad and 2 - 12 cells in height. The rays consist of thick walled rectangular parenchymatous cells with starch grains. They have simple pits. Marginal ray tracheids are elongated horizontally and have bordered pits on their lateral end walls and thus radial diffusion of watery fluids takes place. The ray tracheids are absent in the secondary xylem, phloem and cambium regions. They are replaced by albuminous cells having proteins.

As the secondary vascular structures develop, the outermost layer of stem eventually ruptures and are peeled off as thin scaly bark. Prior to this, a special protective layer of periderm or cork is formed. A layer of outer cortical cells become meristematic which is known as phellogen or cork cambium. It divides by two parallel walls. The inner cells form secondary cortex and the outer constitute the cork or periderm (Fig. 20, 21)

ANATOMY OF ROOT

Transverse section of root reveals the following structure.

Epidermis or Piliferous layer — It is outer most layer of cells.

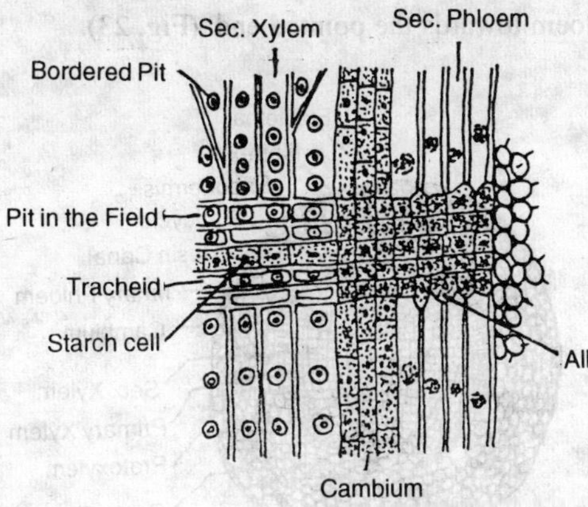

Fig. 20. *Pinus.* Tangential longitudinal section (T.L.S) of an old stem showing the structure of secondary xylem and secondary phloem.

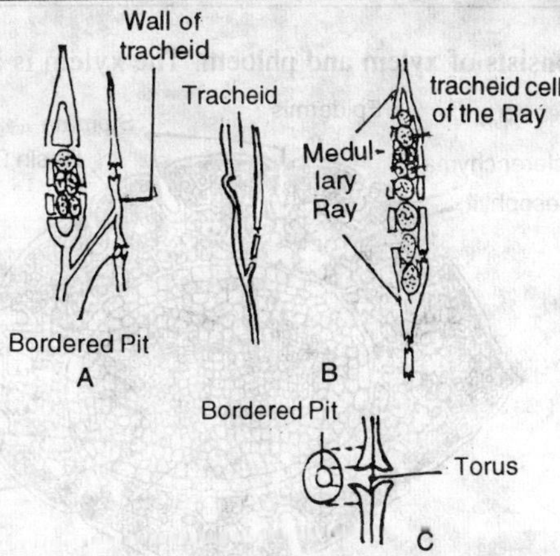

Fig. 21. *Pinus.* Radial longitudinal (R.L.S.) of section stem showing Bordered pits (A.C.); and medullary ray (B).

Cortex —Below the epidermal layer is the cortex of parenchymatous cells. It is bounded by endodermis.

Endodermis — It is one layer thick of suberised cells.

Pericycle — It is multilayered containing starch.

Stele — The stele may be diarch to hexarch. Phloem bundle alternates with the xylem bundle. Each protoxylem group is forked resulting Y shaped xylem bundle. A resin canal is present in between the arrows of the Y.

In transverse section of mycorrhizal root, fungal hyphae are seen in between the cortical cells.

Secondary growth in roots takes place by the development of a cambial strip in the parenchyamatous cells in between metaxylem and phloem. These cambial strips unite to form a complete ring. Now this meristematic cambial ring divides to form secondary xylem towards the centre and secondary phloem towards the periphery. The annual rings are also present.

The cork cambium or phellogen develops in the pericycle. It produces periderm towards the outside (Fig. 22).

ANATOMY OF LEAF

The cross section of the leaf (needle) shows the following structure—

Epidermis — It is outermost layer of cells. Epidermal cells are covered with cuticle. Sunken stomata are present on the epidermis.

Hypodermis — It is below the epidermis and it is made up of one or two layers of sclerenchyma. Air spaces beneath the stomata are present in the hypodermis.

Mesophyll — Below the hypodermis, parenchymatous mesophylls are present. Several small infoldings are present into the cavities of mesophyll cells. Mesophyll also contains resin canals just below the hypodermis.

Endodermis — It delimits the mesophyll. It encloses central vascular tissue of the leaf.

Pericycle — Many layered pericycle is present below the endodermis. It possess parenchymatous cells, tracheidal cells and albuminous cells rich in protein. The tracheidal cells are adjaent to the xylem which serve to carry watery fluids from the xylem to the mesophyll. These special types of cells collectively constitute the transfusion tissue. In addition to these, pericycle also include sclerenchymatous cells between the bundles.

Vascular bundle — Two vascular bundles are embedded in the pericycle separated by a band of sclerenchymatous fibre. In some species only one vascular bundle is present. Each vascular bundle consists of xylem and phloem. The xylem is above the phloem towards the pointed end. (Fig. 23).

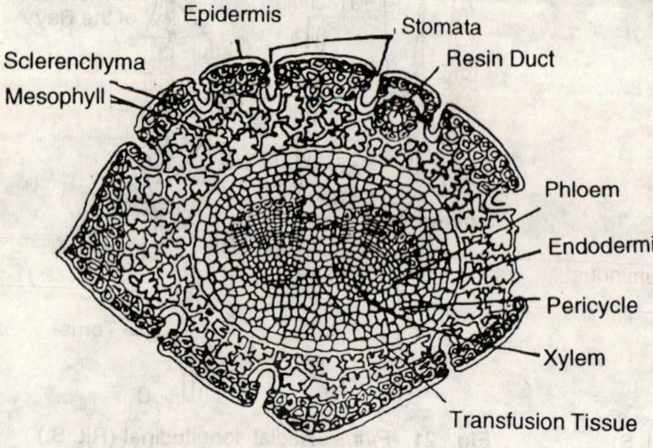

Fig. 22. *Pinus*. T. S. of root showing diarch condition.

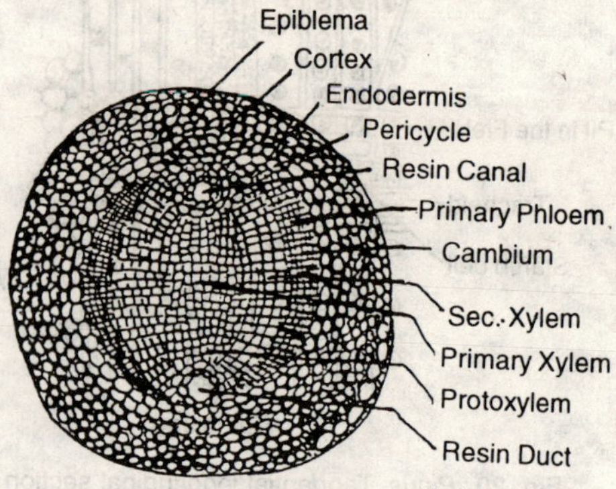

Fig. 23. *Pinus longifolia* T. S. of needle showing detailed anatomy.

REPRODUCTION

Pinus reproduces by means of seeds. Vegetative reproduction has not been reported in Pinus.

Spore producing organs— All seed plants are heterosporous. It produces two types of spores. (1) microspores and (2) megaspores produced in microsporangium and megasporangium respectively. Sporangia are produced on sporophylls which are organised into cones or strobili. Cones are of two types; namely, male cone or microsporangiate strobilus and female cone or megasporangiate strobilus. *Pinus* in monoecious and bears both types of cones on the same plant but on different branches.

Male cone — Bisporangiate cones occur occasionally as in *Pinus montana*, *Pinus maritima* and *Pinus roxburghii*. (= Staminate strobilus). It is found in clusters, each in the axil of a scale leaf. The male cone replaces the dwarf shoot during its development. Male cones appear in March on hills and in January - February on the plain. Pollen grains are shed during April to June. The male cone has a short stalk and an elongated central axis bearing spirally arranged microsporophylls. The microsporophylls are similar to the stamens of angiosperms. Each misrosporophyll originates from the central axis, placed horizontally. Its ends are sterile, flattened head which turns up in such a manner to fit over the microsporophyll above it. It bears two pollen sacs or microsporangia. The sporangia are filled with numerous winged pollen grains (microspores). A mature cone is yellow or dark brown in colour (Fig.24, 25).

Development of microsporangium is eusporangiate as in Cycas. A mature microsporangium has a sporangial wall, tapetum and microspore mother cells in the centre. The microspore mother cells divide meiotically to form numerous haploid microspores (pollen grains). The pollen grains are yellow in colour and winged. On maturity the microsporangium dehisces through a longitudinal slit along the long axis. A large number of pollen grains are shed forming a cloud, generally called "shower of sulphur" because of their pale yellow colour. The male cone withers and falls from the tree after the Pollens are shed. It is compound in nature and forms a true cone like structure (= Ovulate strobilus) It appears in February in the plains and in May in the hills. It develops in a cluster of 3 - 4 in the axils of scale leaves on the long shoot taking the place of dwarf shoot. In the beginning it is green in colour which turns brown at maturity.

Female Cone — The female cone is hard, woody and dry. It has a central axis on which numerous spirally arranged megasporaphylls are found. The megasporophyll has a short stalk and a large ovuliferous scale. A bract scale is attached on the lower side of the ovuliferous scale. Each ovuliferous scale bears two anatropous ovules or megasporangia near the base on the upper surface. The ovuliferous scale is wedge shaped whose broader end is sterile and called apophysis. There are about 80-90 megasporophylls in one female cone. The famale cone becomes compact and close after pollination. When cone becomes 22 months old, the seeds are shed (Fig. 26, 27).

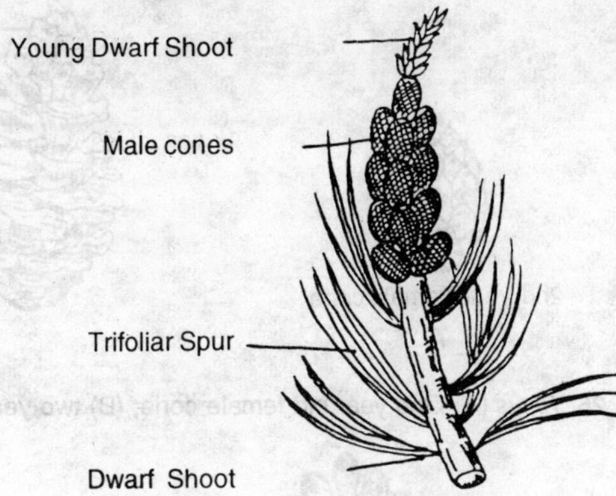

Fig. 24. *Pinus* shoot of unlimited growth with male cones.

MORPHOLOGICAL NATURE OF THE OVULIFEROUS SCALE

Several views have been put forward regarding the morphological nature of ovuliferous scale in *Pinus* as follows:-

1. Robert Brown (1827) suggested that ovuliferous scale of *Pinus* is an open carpel which was not accepted by others. Sachs and Eichler (1868) said that the female cone of *Pinus* is a simple flower bearing open carpel. Ovuliferous scale has been considered to be a ligule situated above the bract. The branch was said to be a sporophylls and ovule as *sui generis*.

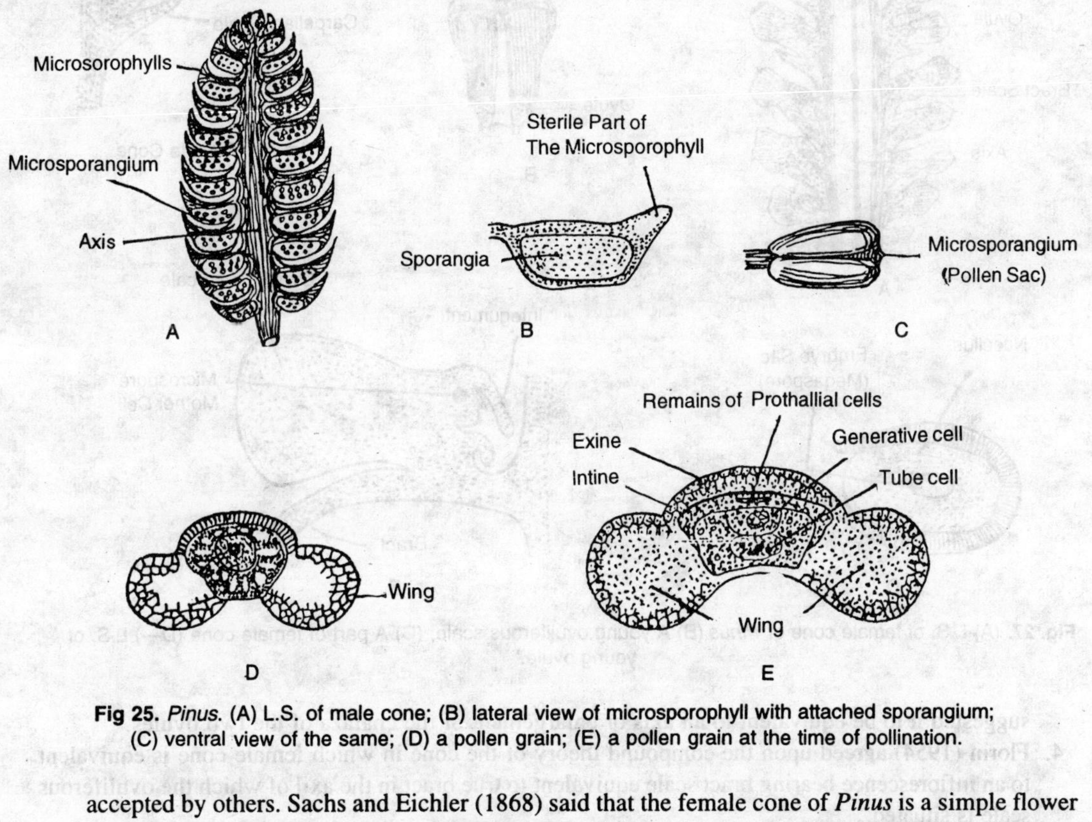

Fig 25. *Pinus.* (A) L.S. of male cone; (B) lateral view of microsporophyll with attached sporangium; (C) ventral view of the same; (D) a pollen grain; (E) a pollen grain at the time of pollination.

2. Schleiden (1829) regarded the ovuliferous scale as an axial placenta which develops in the axil of the leaf bearing two ovules. The bract scale represents true carpel.
3. A. Brown (1842) considered ovuliferous scale as axillary shoot on which two or three fertile leaves are present. These fertile leaves bear two ovules on its dorsal surface. Kubart and Bessey

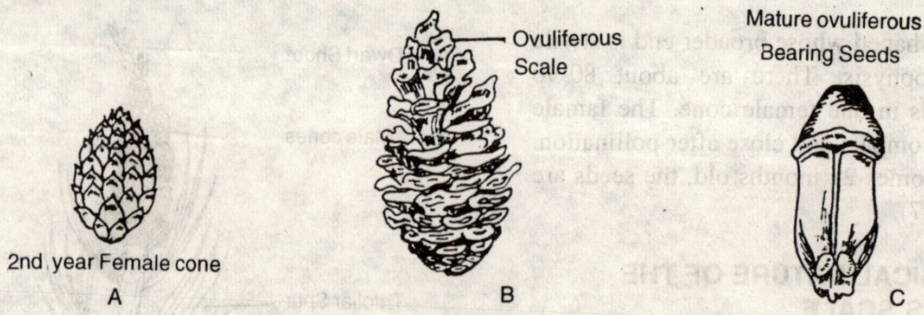

Fig. 26. *Pinus* (A) One year old female cone; (B) two years old female cone (C) mature ovuliferous scale with seeds.

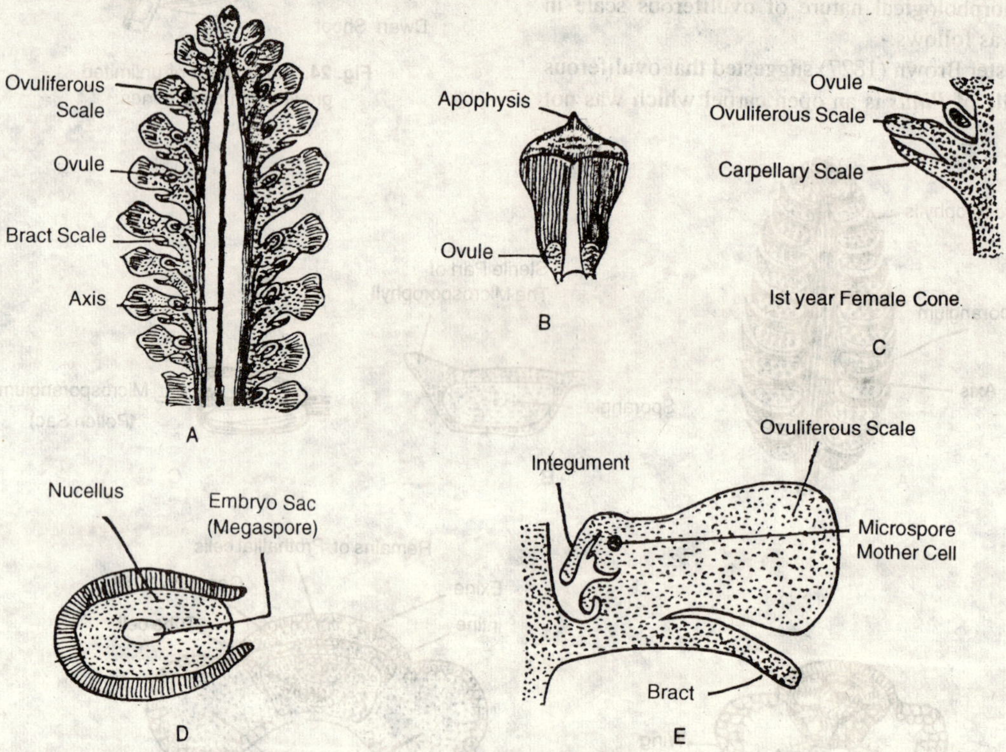

Fig. 27. (A) L.S. of female cone of *Pinus* (B) A young ovuliferous scale; (C) A part of female cone (D—) L.S. of young ovule.'

suggested it to be equivalent to an axis or enlargement of the chalaza of the two ovules.

4. Florin (1954) agreed upon the compound theory of the cone in which female cone is equivalent to an inflorescence bearing bract scale equivalent to true bract in the axil of which the ovuliferous scale is situated.
5. Baillon (1863) interpreted the ovuliferous scale as axillary shoot bearing two bicarpellary ovaries.
6. Van Tieghem (1869) regarded ovuliferous scale as the first and only leaf of an axillary branch.
7. Von Mohl (1871) suggested that the ovuliferous scale is the first two leaves of an axillary shoot.
8. Bessey (1892) interpreted the ovuliferous scale as a chalazal development of the ovules.

9. Chamberlain (1935) regarded the ovuliferous scale as a modified shoot with or without leaves bearing the ovules.

As ovule has a nucellus surrounded by an integument except near the apex to form a micropyle. The integument contains three layers e.g. an outer fleshy, a middle stony and an inner fleshy. All are fused together. Only one megaspore mother cell is differentiated within the nucellar mass of tissue. Megaspore mother cell divides meiotically to give rise four haploid megaspores. All the upper three megaspores degenerate and the lower most remains functional.

MALE GAMETOPHYTE

Pollen grain or microspore is the first cell generation of male gametophyte. It has an outer exine and an inner intine layer. The exine becomes inflated into two wings. The microspore starts to germinate inside the microsporangium prior to shedding of microspores.

Microspore nucleus divides to form two small prothallial cells and a large antheridial cell. Prothalial cells are ephemeral in nature. Antheridial cell divides to form a large tube cell and a small generative cell. At this four celled structure, the microspores are shed and further development occurs after pollination when they reach the ovule (Fig. 28).

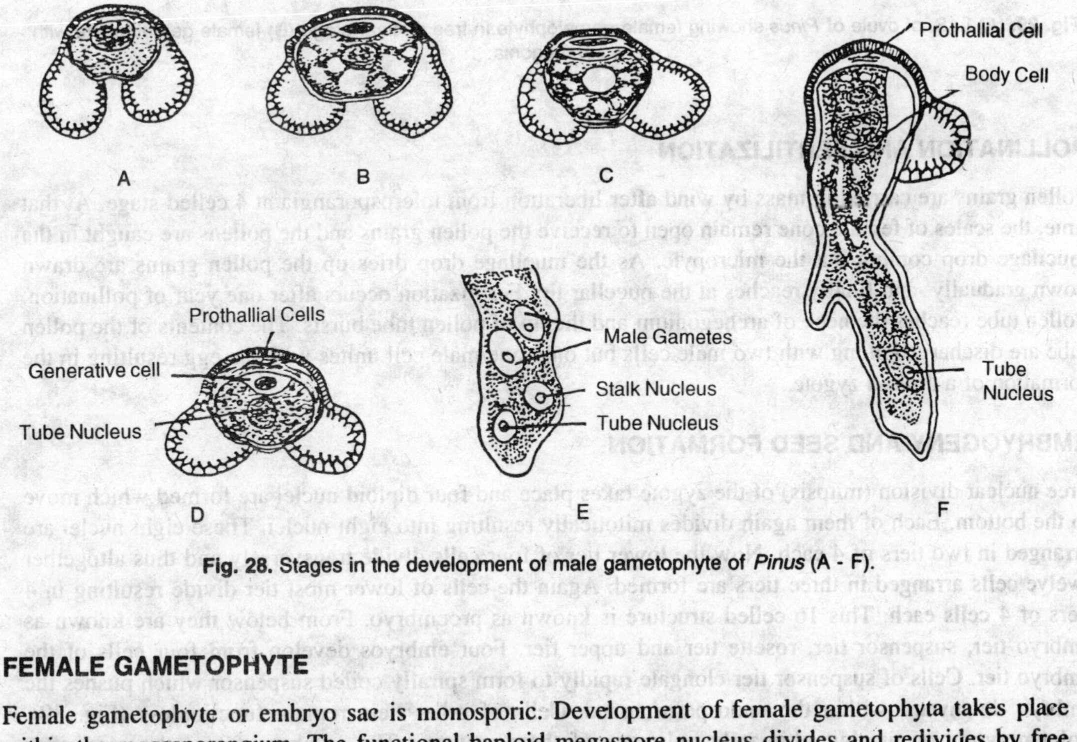

Fig. 28. Stages in the development of male gametophyte of *Pinus* (A - F).

FEMALE GAMETOPHYTE

Female gametophyte or embryo sac is monosporic. Development of female gametophyta takes place within the megasporangium. The functional haploid megaspore nucleus divides and redivides by free nuclear divisions forming many (about 1200) small nuclei and are distributed in the cytoplasm of embryo sac i.e. megaspore. Protoplasm is pushed towards the periphery and a large central vacuole is formed. The wall formation starts around the free nuclei. This results into a solid mass of gametophytic tissue i.e. endosperm tissue. This is haploid and has only one type of cells. Near the micropylar end of the female gametophyte, two to three archegonia are formed from the superficial archegonial initials. The archegonial initial divides to form an upper primary neck initial and a lower large central cell. The neck initial further divides and redivides to form a neck of eight cells. Neck canal cell is absent. The lower central cell divides to form a ventral canal cell and a large egg (Fig. 29).

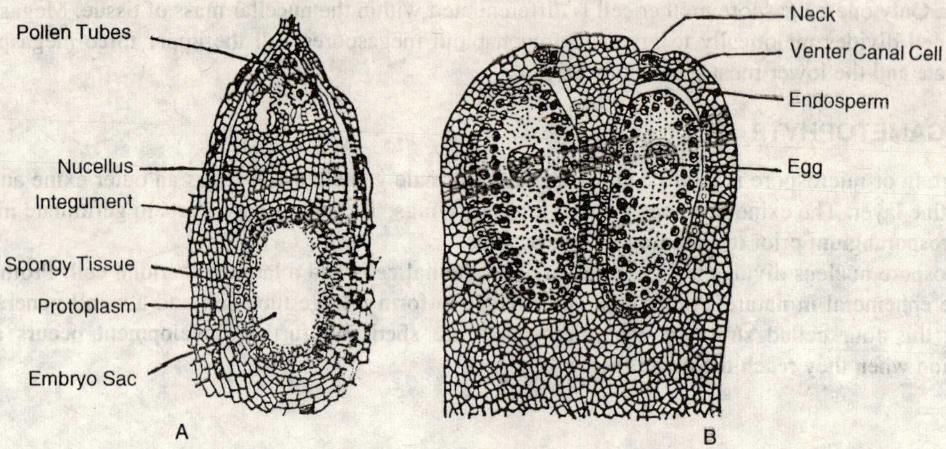

Fig. 29. (A) L. S. of ovule of *Pinus* showing female gametophyte in free nuclear stage (B) female gametophyte with two archegonia.

POLLINATION AND FERTILIZATION

Pollen grains are carried in mass by wind after liberation from microsporangia at 4 celled stage. At that time, the scales of female cone remain open to receive the pollen grains and the pollens are caught in the mucilage drop coming out the micropyle. As the mucilage drop dries up the pollen grains are drawn down gradually and finally reaches at the nucellar tip. Fertilization occurs after one year of pollination. Pollen tube reaches the neck of archegonium and the tip of pollen tube bursts. The contents of the pollen tube are discharged along with two male cells but only one male cell unites with the egg resulting in the formation of a diploid zygote.

EMBRYOGENY AND SEED FORMATION

Free nuclear division (mitosis) of the zygote takes place and four diploid nuclei are formed which move to the bottom. Each of them again divides mitotically resulting into eight nuclei. These eight nuclei are arranged in two tiers of 4 each. Now the lower tier of four cells divide transversely and thus altogether twelve cells arranged in three tiers are formed. Again the cells of lower most tier divide resulting in 4 tiers of 4 cells each. This 16 celled structure is known as proembryo. From below they are known as embryo tier, suspensor tier, rosette tier and upper tier. Four embryos develop from four cells of the embryo tier. Cells of suspensor tier elongate rapidly to form spirally coiled suspensor which pushes the embryo downward within the endosperm tissue. Cells of other tiers remain functionless (Fig. 30). Polyembryony occurs but ultimately only one of them matures. The embryo forms the seed after maturity. The integuments of the megasporangium is transformed into seed coat. Middle stony layer of integument forms the testa. The outer fleshy layer of integument gets dried. The inner most layer of integument remains present as a thin membrane. The mature seed contains perisperm and kernel (Fig 31). Perisperm is nutritive tissue and diploid. Kernel surrounds the embryo and is nutritive tissue which is haploid.

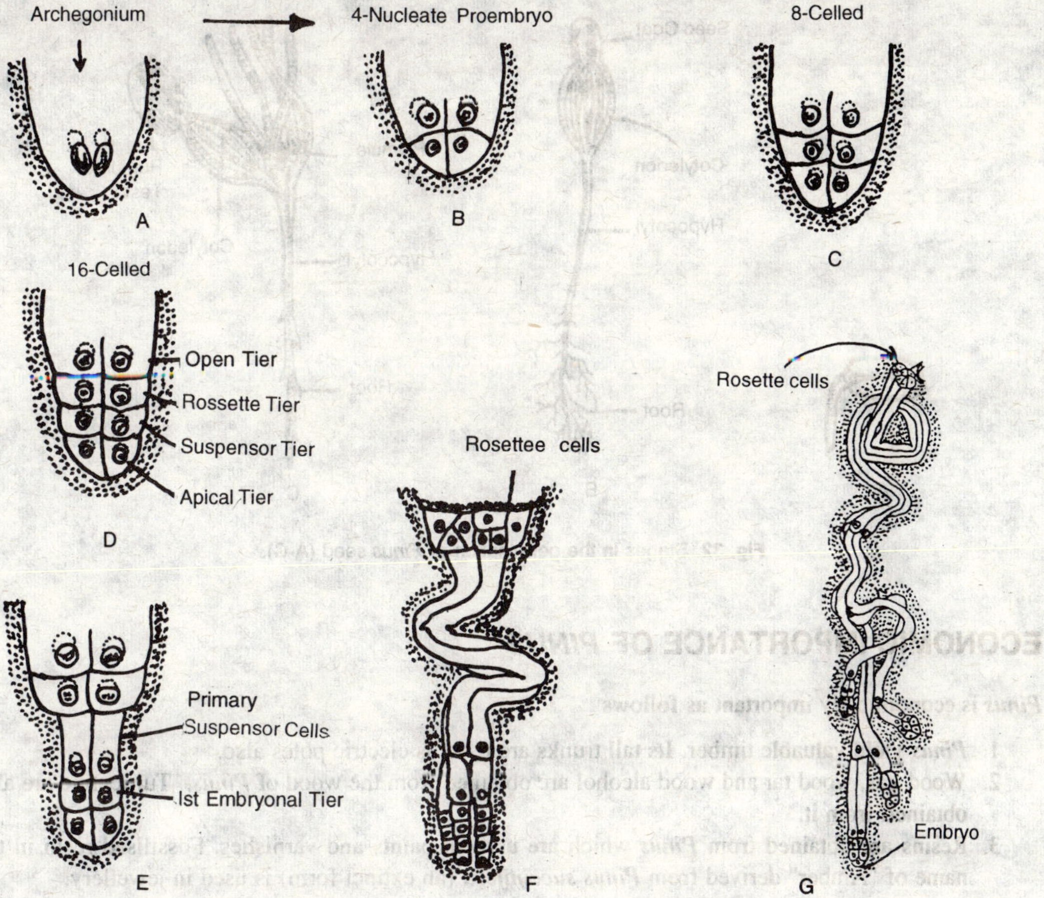

Fig. 30. Stages in the development of embryo in *Pinus* (A-G)

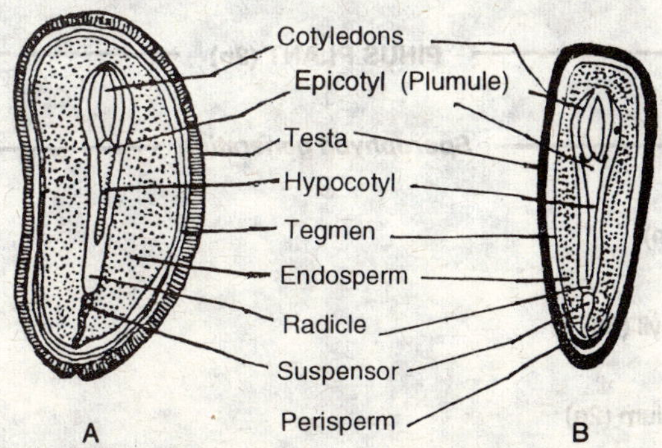

Fig. 31. L. S. of seed of *Pinus* (A, B).

The embryo contains a radicle, hypocotyl, 3 or more cotyledons and a plumule. After some resting period, the seed germinates in epigeal fashion into a new sporophytic *Pinus* plant (Fig. 32).

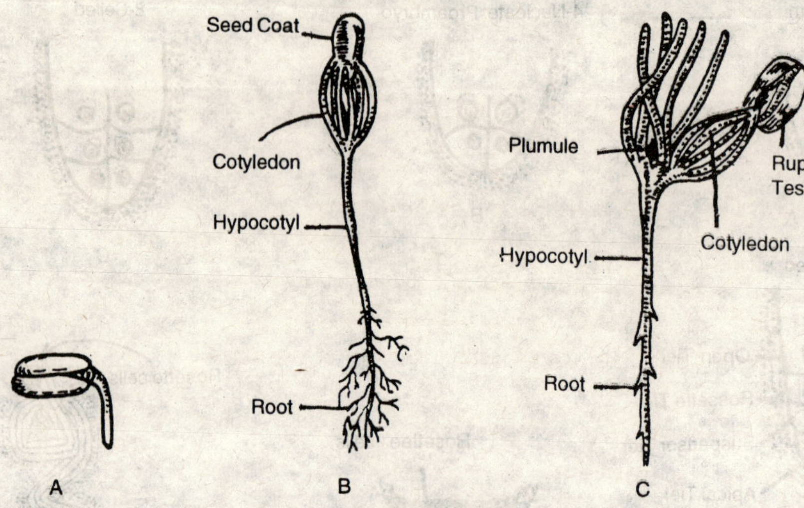

Fig. 32. Stages in the germination of *Pinus* seed (A-C).

ECONOMIC IMPORTANCE OF *PINUS*

Pinus is economically important as follows :

1. *Pinus* yield valuable timber. Its tall trunks are used as electric poles also.
2. Wood gas, wood tar and wood alcohol are obtained from the wood of *Pinus*. Turpentine are also obtained from it.
3. Resins are obtained from *Pinus* which are used in paints and varnishes. Fossilised resin in the name of "Amber" derived from *Pinus succinifera* (an extinct form) is used in jewellery.
4. The seeds of *Pinus gerardiana* are edible and known as Chilgoza.
5. The wood of Pinus is also used as fuel.
6. The vast pine forests along with other conifers are effective in checking the soil erosion.

PINUS PLANT (2n)
↓
Sporophytic generation
↓

Male cone (2n)	**Female cone (2n)**
↓	↓
Microsporophyll (2n)	**Megasporophyll (2n)**
↓	↓
Microsporangium (2n)	**Megasporangium (2n)**
↓	↓
Microspore mother cell (2n)	**Megaspore mother cell (2n)**
↓	↓
Meiosis	**Meiosis**

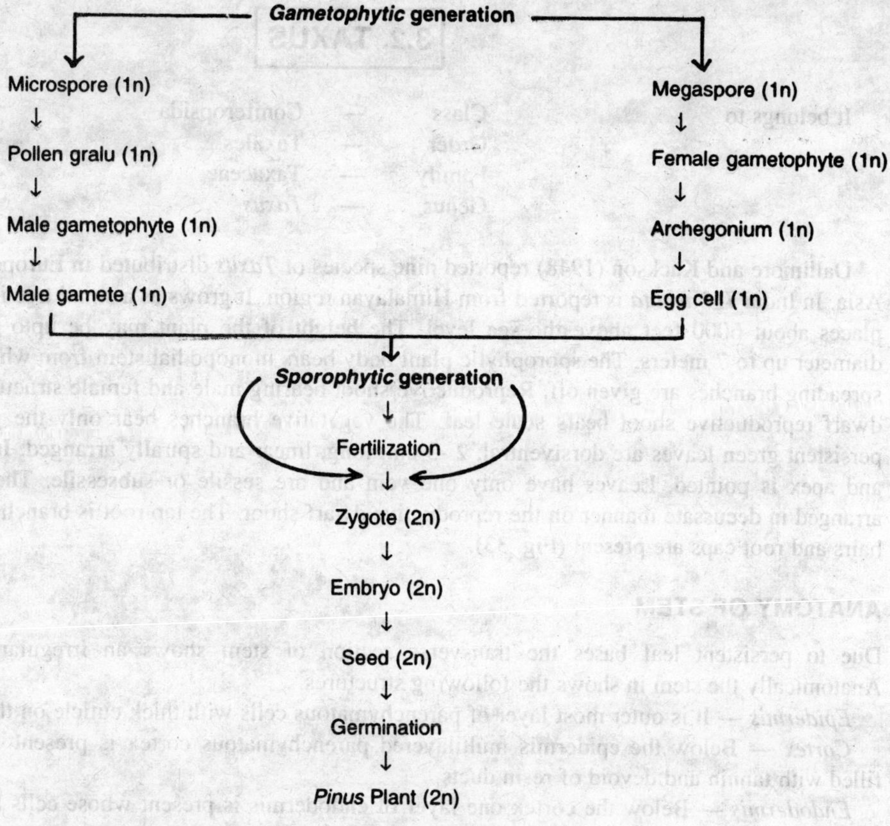

Graphic life cycle of *Pinus*

DISTRIBUTION OF PINUS IN INDIA

Following species of *Pinus* are found in different parts of India as follows :

P. insularis : It is commonly known as Khasi pine or *P. Khasya*, widely distributed in Khasya region of Assam at an altitude of 2200 feet to 6000 feet. The foliar spurs are trifoliate as specific feature.

P. longifolia : This species is found at an altitude of 1500 - 7000 feet in Kashmir, Himachal Pradesh, Uttar Pradesh and Punjab. Each foliar spur has three needles. It is commonly known as chir pine or *P. roxburghii*.

P. gerardiana : It is commonly called as Chilgoza pine. It is also found at an altitude of 6000 - 10000 feet in Himachal Pradesh and Kashmir. It bears trifoliate spurs.

P. armandi : This species is located at an altitude of 5000 feet in north east part of India. It bears pentafoliate spurs.

P. excelsa : It is also known as blue pine or *P. wallichiana*. It is also found in northern India at an altitude of 5000 - 10000 feet. Each foliar spur has five needles.

P. merkusii : It is about 10' to 15' tall and found at an altitude of 500 - 2000 feet in Bengal. Each foliar spur has two needles. It is also known as Merkus pine.

In addition to the above species, several other species like *P. sylvestris*, *P. montana*, *P. lancio* etc. are also found in India.

3.2. TAXUS

It belongs to

Class	—	Coniferopsida
Order	—	Taxales
Family	—	Taxaceae
Genus	—	*Taxus*

Dallimore and Kackson (1948) reported nine species of *Taxus* distributed in Europe, N. America and Asia. In India *T. baccata* is reported from Himalayan region. It grows as a small tree in moist and shady places about 6000 feet above the sea level. The height of the plant may be upto 20 meters and its diameter up to 7 meters. The sporophytic plant body bears monopodial stem from which horizontal and spreading branches are given off. Reproductive shoot bearing male and female structure are dwarf. The dwarf reproductive shoot bears scale leaf. The vegetative branches bear only the green leaves. The persistent green leaves are dorsiventral, 2 -3 cm. long, linear and spirally arranged. Its margin is entire and apex is pointed. Leaves have only one vein and are sessile or subsessile. The scale leaves are arranged in decussate manner on the reproductive dwarf shoot. The tap root is branched and deep. Root hairs and root caps are present (Fig. 33).

ANATOMY OF STEM

Due to persistent leaf bases the transverse section of stem shows an irregular circular outline. Anatomically the stem in shows the following structures.

Epidermis — It is outer most layer of parenchymatous cells with thick cuticle on the outer walls.

Cortex — Below the epidermis multilayered parenchymatous cortex is present. Cortical cells are filled with tannin and devoid of resin ducts.

Endodermis — Below the cortex one layer of endodermis is present whose cells have no casparian strips.

Fig. 33. *Taxus.* A twig with fruits.

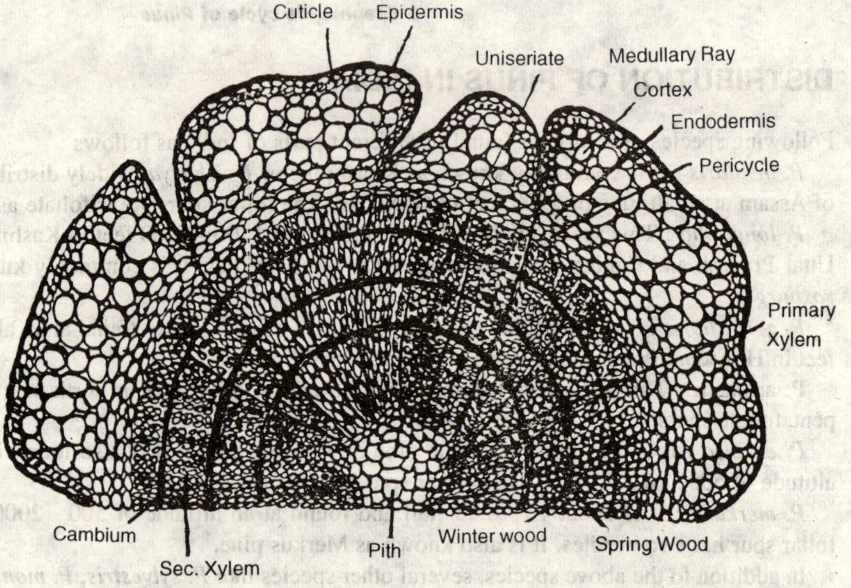

Fig. 34. *Taxus baccata.* T. S. of stem showing secondary growth.

Pericycle — The pericycle is present below the endodermis and it is sclerenchymatous in nature.

Vascular bundle — In young stem vascular bundles are arranged in an interupted ring. The vascular bundles are conjoint, collateral, open and endarch.

Pith — A distinct parenchymatous pith is seen in the centre. Secondary growth takes place by a single persistent cambium which cuts off secondary xylem and secondary phloem towards centre and cortex respectively. Tertiary spiral thickenings in secondary wood of *Taxus* is found. The medullary rays are present. Annual rings are also distinct. No resin canal is present in secondary wood (Fig. 34).

ANATOMY OF ROOT

Transverse section of root shows the following structures-

Epiblema or piliferous layer — It is the outer most layer bearing long unicellular root hairs.

Cortex — Next to the epiblema is the cortex made up of several layers of parenchymatous cells. No resin canal is present.

Endodermis — It is single layered and distinct.

Pericycle — It is multilayered. Resin cells are not present in the pericycle.

Stele — It is exarch and diarch. Two phloem bundles alternate with the xylem.

Pith — It is absent.

Secondary growth in the root is similar to that of *Pinus*.

ANATOMY OF LEAF

Vertical section of leaf shows the following.

Epidermis — Upper and lower epidermis of one layer of parenchyma cells are found. The upper epidermis is covered with cuticle. Lower epidermis has thin cuticle and sunken stomata.

Palisada — Two layered palisada is present below the upper epidermis. Spongy parenchyma are loosely arranged and found in between the palisada and lower epidermis.

Vascular bundle — In the midrib region a single vascular bundle is present. Vascular bundle is encircled by bundle sheath or endodermis which is made up of barrel shaped parenchyma cells. Vascular bundle is collateral. Phloem faces lower epidermis and xylem is towards upper epidermis. A patch of lignified cells are present on either side of the xylem which represents transfusion tissue. One layer of pericycle and one layer of endodermis are also present. Fig. 35).

Xerophytic characters of the leaf

(i) Thick cuticle to minimise transpiration.

(ii) Sunken stomata.

(iii) Presence of transfusion tissue.

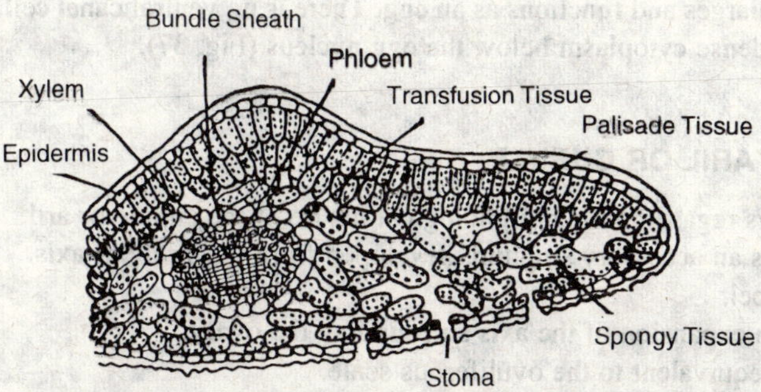

Fig. 35. T. S. of *Taxus* leaf.

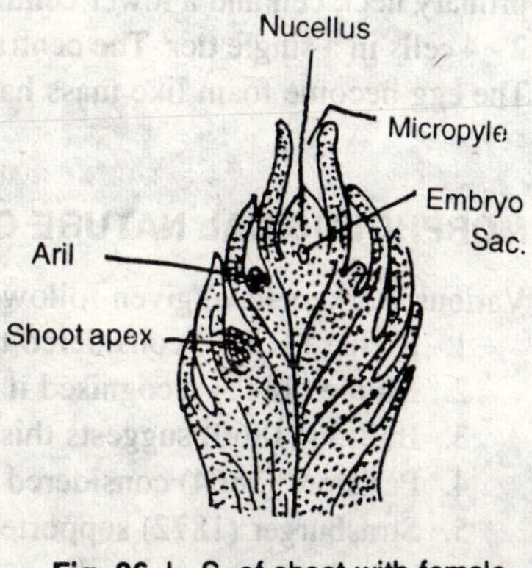

Fig. 36. L. S. of shoot with female flower in *Taxus*.

REPRODUCTIVE ORGANS

There is no vegetatively propagating structure in *Taxus*. *Taxus* plant is dioecious i.e. male and female plants are separate but are morphologically similar. *Taxus* bears male and female flowers which appear in the month of February and March. The male reproductive organs are organised into strobili or cones and the female reproductive organs are generally termed as female flowers.

Female flowers — There is a bud in the axil of one of the foliage leaves on a vegetative shoot. The bud is covered with several imbricate scales. This constitute the primary axis. The bud does not grow much. A secondary bud develops in the axil of the upper most scale of the primary bud. The secondary bud is protected by three pairs of scale leaves which are decussate. This secondary bud grows into secondary axis. The apex of the secondary axis form an apical ovule which is orthotropous. Another bud may arise in the axil of the penultimate bract which develops into another axis bearing another ovule (Fig. 36). This constitutes the female flower. Thus the female flower of *Taxus* is not a cone.

The ovule is sessile and orthotropous. It has a large nucellus covered with a single thick integument which remains free from the nucellus from the micropyle to the base of the nucellus. The integument can be differentiated into outer and inner fleshy layers separated by middle stony layer. A ring like outgrowth arises from the base of the integument which grows slowly and ultimately covers the entire ovule after the embryo formation takes place. This outgrowth in the form of an envelope is called "cupule" or "aril" It is juicy and of red colour observed in the mature seed. The nucellus does not possess nucellar beak and pollen chamber.

At the time of fertilization the ovule consists of a well developed female gametophyte whose apical region is flask shaped and called the "tent pole". There is no tapetum around the embryosac. The female gametophyte generally bears 3 - 17 archegonia.

A hypodermal cell in the nucellus divides transversely into an outer parietal cell and an inner archesporial cell. The archesporial cell further divides into several sporogenous cells. One or more sporogenous cells function as megaspore mother cells. The megaspore mother cell divides meiotically into 4 haploid megaspores. All of them may grow into female gametophytes.

FEMALE GAMETOPHYTE

The haploid megaspore is the first cell generation of female gametophyte. The megaspore enlarges in size and its nucleus undergoes repeated free nuclear divisions to from 128 - 256 free nuclei. The tent pole appears as a flask shaped cellular structure from the apical part of the gametophyte. A big central vaccule develops in the megaspore and the free nuclei lie towards periphery. Later, wall formation starts out of the free nuclei and a mass of tissue is formed enveloped within the megaspore membrane. Archegonium develops from a superficial initial in the gametophytic tissue and divides transversely into an upper primary neck cell and a lower central cell. The primary neck cell divides and redivides to form a neck of 2 - 4 cells in a single tier. The central cell enlarges and functions as an egg. There is no ventral canal cell. The egg become foam like mass having a dense cytoplasm below the egg nucleus (Fig. 37).

MORPHOLOGICAL NATURE OF THE ARIL OR CUPULE

Various workers have given following views regarding the morphological nature of the cupule or aril.

1. Richard (1826) considered the aril as an accessory structure developed from the strobilar axis.
2. Blume (1847) recognised it as a carpel.
3. Baillon (1860) suggests this to be an expansion of the axis surrounding the ovary.
4. Parlstore (1864) considered it as an equivalent to the ovuliferous scale.
5. Strasburger (1872) supported the view of Baillon.

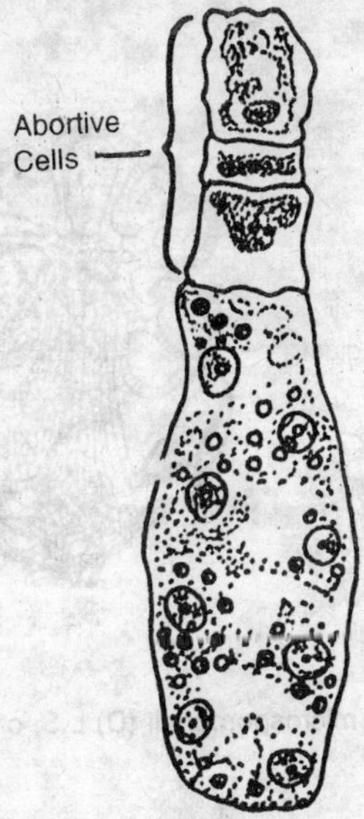

Fig. 37. *Taxus.* Female gametophyte showing eight nuclear stage.

6. Bertrans (1878) and Schumann (1902) claimed the aril a special structure.
7. Celakovsky (1890) and Worsdell (1899) regarded the aril of *Taxus* equivalent to ovuliferous scale of conifers.
8. Sinnot (1913) considered the aril of *Taxus* as equivalent to the epimatium of *P. odocarpus.*
9. Coulter and Chamerlain (1917) suggested that the aril in *Taxus* is outer fleshy layer free from hard layer of integument right from the base. This view was also shared by Dupler (1920).

MALE CONE OR MALE STROBILUS

It is found at the apex of a lateral short branch devloped in the axil of a foliage leaf. This short branch bears ten sterile leaves arranged in decussate manner forming a cone bearing 6 - 14 asymmetrical microsporophylls or sporangiophores. Each microsporophyll bear 6 - 8 microsporangia. In young condition microsporophylls are yellowish green and are compactly arranged. their peltate heads are fitted tightly. The microsporophylls are protected by sterile scales in the beginning.

A microsporophyll appears like sporangiophore of *Equisetum.* It has a short stalk attached to the centre of a disc like polygonal head, and hence peltate. 6 - 8 microsporangia arise from the underside of the peripheral disc. The sporangia are sessile having yellow microspores or pollen grains (Fig. 38).

Each microsporangium has a wall of two layers cells and encloses many sporogenous cells. The outer sporogenous cells are differentiated into tapetum. The other sporogenous cells function as microspore mother cells which divide meiotically to form haploid microspores.

The microsporangium dehisces along a longitudinal slit developed towards the stalk. The microspores are shed and carried by wind to the micropyle of the ovule. At the time of pollination during March the microspores are uninucleate. The ovule secretes a pollination drop which traps the pollen grain, where the pollen grains start to germinate without passing through resting period.

MALE GAMETOPHYTE

Microspore is the 1st cell generation of male gametophyte. The diameter of the pollen grain is 26 μ. It is surrounded by an outer exine and an inner intine. The pollen grain germinate on the nucellus. Its nucleus divides to form a tube cell and a generattive cell. No prothallial cells are produced. The intine grows out through the germ pore into a short pollen tube which penetrates the nucellus. The tube nucelus moves

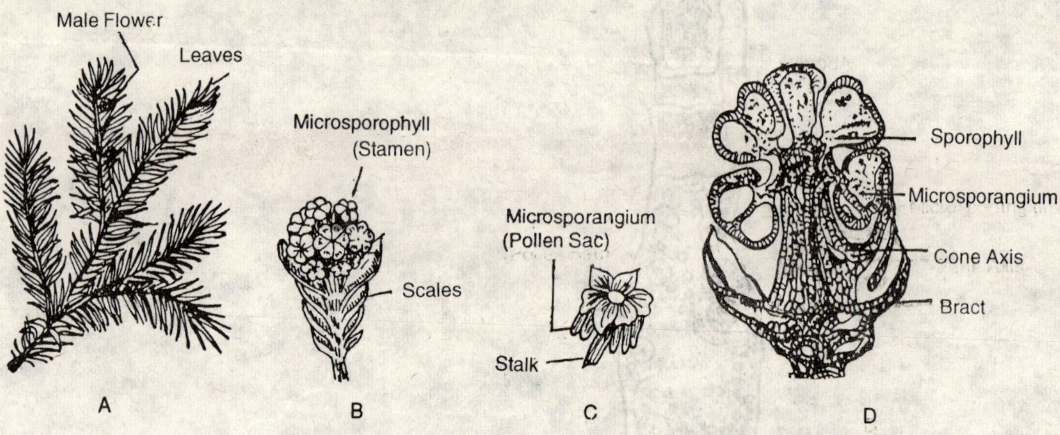

Fig. 38. *Taxus*. (A) male twig (B) male cone (C) A mature microsporophyll (D) L.S. of male sone.

into the pollen tube. The generative cells divides into a stalk cell and a body cell. The stalk nucleus also moves into the pollen tube. The body cell divides into two unqeual male gamete or male nuclei. The pollen tube ultimately reaches the archegonial neck, having the tube nucleus the stalk nucleus and two male nuclei at its tip. (Fig. 39).

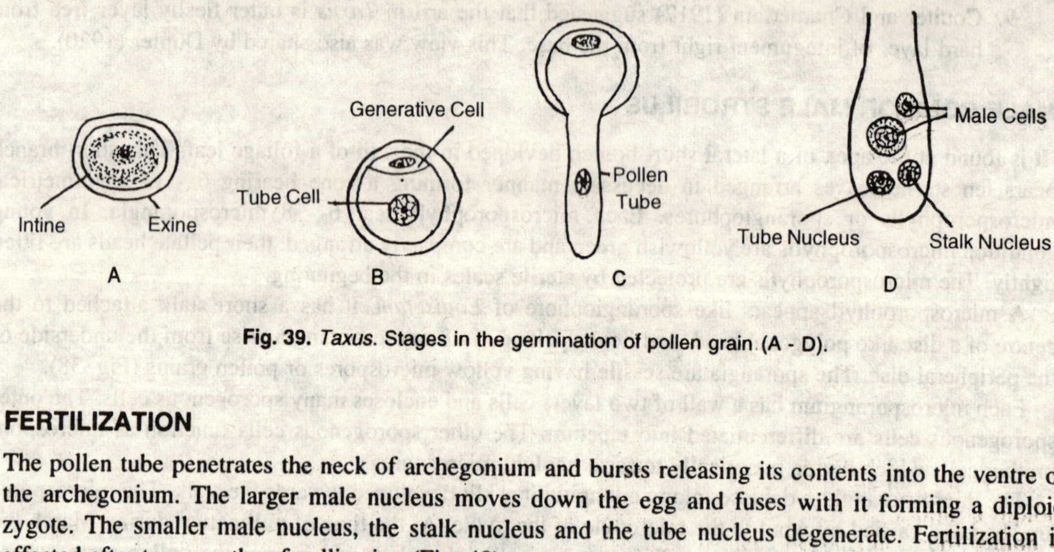

Fig. 39. *Taxus*. Stages in the germination of pollen grain (A - D).

FERTILIZATION

The pollen tube penetrates the neck of archegonium and bursts releasing its contents into the ventre of the archegonium. The larger male nucleus moves down the egg and fuses with it forming a diploid zygote. The smaller male nucleus, the stalk nucleus and the tube nucleus degenerate. Fertilization is effected after two months of pollination (Fig. 40)

DEVELOPMENT OF EMBRYO AND SEED

The zygote nucleus divides and redivides into 16 free nuclei followed by wall formation. Now it is proembryo having upper tier of 9 - 13 cells and lower tier of 3 - 7 cells. Another division in upper tier results in the formation of lower embryonal tier, middle suspensor tier and upper open tier. The

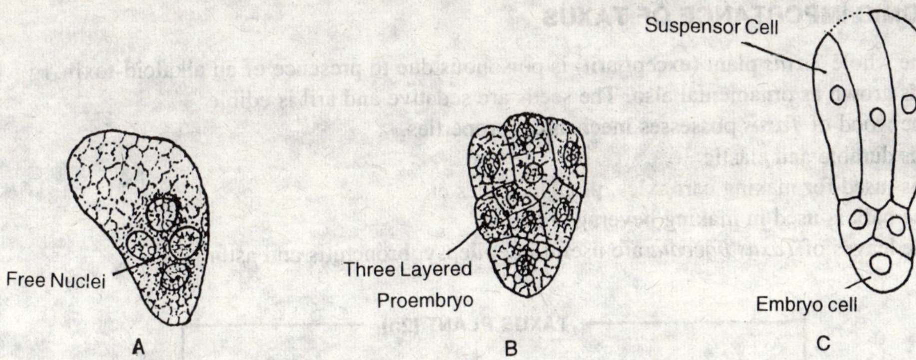

Fig. 40. *Taxus.* Developmental stages of embryo

suspensor elongates pushing the embryonal tier out of the archegonium into the female prothallus. Sterling (1948) reported cleavage of the embryo into many embryos in *Taxus cuspidata*. The embryo is dicotyledonous. The mature embryo has a radicle towards the micropyle, then a hypocotyle came next and then plumule hidden in between the two cotyledons. One ovule has only one mature embryo. The developing embryo consumes the entire female prothallus and hence the seed is non–endospermic.

SEED

During seed development, the stony layer becomes testa and the outer integument becomes brown and papery. The inner integument shrivels up. The nucellus is completely consumed by the female gametophyte. The young embryo remains surrounded by the endosperms but the developing embryo consumes the entire endosperm. The aril becomes fleshy, scarlet in colour and becomes edible, eaten by birds which help in dispersal of the seeds. The seed represents three generations (1) the testa is of parent sporophytic generation (2) the endosperm represents gametophytic generations and (3) the young embryo is the future sporophytic generation. The seed germinates into young seedling having cotyledonous leaves. The plumule grows into shoot which bear spirally arranged foliage leaves. The mode of germination is epigeal (Fig. 41).

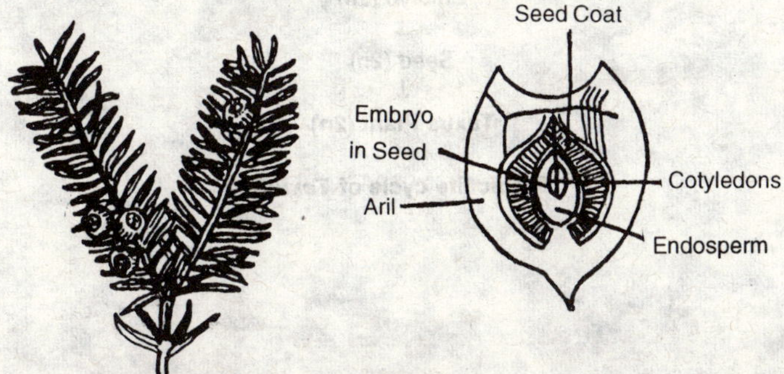

Fig. 41. *Taxus.* (A) A Twig with seeds (B) L. S. of seed.

ECONOMIC IMPORTANCE OF TAXUS

1. The whole *Taxus* plant (except aril) is poisonous due to presence of an alkaloid-toxin.
2. It is grown as ornamental also. The seeds are sedative and aril is edible
3. The wood of *Taxus* possesses mechanical properties.
4. It is durable and elastic
5. It is used for making cart axles, ploughs, poles etc.
6. The bark is used in making beverage like tea.
7. The leaves of *Taxus baccata* are useful in epilepsy, bronchitis and asthma

TAXUS PLANT (2n)
↓
Sporophytic Generation

Staminate strobilus (2n)	Ovulate strobilus (2n)
↓	↓
Microsporophyll (2n)	Megasporophyll (2n)
↓	↓
Microsporangium (2n)	Megasporangium (2*n*)
↓	↓
Microspore mother cell (2n)	Megaspore mother cell (2n)
↓	↓
Meiosis	Meiosis
↓ ***Gametophytic*** **generation**	↓
Microspore (1n)	Megaspore (1n)
↓	↓
Male Gametophyte (1n)	Female Gametophyte (1n)
↓	↓
Sperm nucleus (1n)	Egg nucleus (1n)

↓
Fertilization
↓
Sporophytic Generation
↓
Zygote (2n)
↓
Proembryo (2n)
↓
Embryo (2n)
↓
Seed (2n)
↓
Taxus Plant (2n)

Grapic life cycle of *Taxus*

CHAPTER 4

GNETUM

Gnetum belongs to	Class	—	Gnetopsida
	Order	—	Gnetales
	Family	—	Gnetaceae
	Genus	—	*Gnetum*

There are 30 - 35 species under the genus *Gnetum* occuring mostly in tropical rain forests. Five species of *Gnetum* are reported from India. These are G. *gnemon* reported from Naga Hills of Assam, *G. montanum* from Assam and Sikkim, *G. latifolium* from Andman and Nicobar Islands. *G. ula* from Western ghats, Orissa and Keral, *G. contractum* from Keral, Madras and Nilgiri Hills.

HABIT

The sporophytic plant body is differentiated into root, stem and leaves. They are climbers e.g. *G. ula*, *G. montanum* etc. tree e.g. *G. gnemon* and shrubs also e.g. *G. contractum*, *G. trinerve* is a parasite. The stem is woody and branched. The branches are of two types (a) dwarf shoot and (b) long shoot (Fig. 42).

Fig. 42. *Gnetum.* A twig with strobili.

Dwarf shoots have distinct nodes and internodes bearing foliage leaves arranged in decussate manner. Long shoot bear cup shaped pairs of scale leaves. The nodes are swollen. The leaves are of two types foliage leaves found on dwarf shoot and scale leaves present on long shoot. The shape of lamina may be oblong, lanceolate or elliptical depending on the species. The leaves are shortly petiolate. Lamina shows reticulate venatin, apex is acute and margin is entire. Due to reticulate venation and shape of lamina, *Gnetum* resembles to a dicotyledonous angiosperm

ANATOMY OF STEM

Transverse section of stem of *Gnetum* shows the following structures.

Epidermis — It is outer most continuous single layer of rectangular cells interrupted by sunken stomata. Papillate growths are seen from the epidermal cells. It has a thick cuticle.

Cortex — Below the epidermis, large cortex is present. The cortex is divisible into three distinct zones: (a) outer chlorenchymatous zone of 5 - 7 layers, (b) middle parenchymatous cortex and (3) the inner sclerenchymatous zone of 2 - 5 layers.

Endodermis — It is not very distinct.

Pericycle — It is also not very clear.

Vascular bundles — The vascular bundles are arranged in a ring. The vascular bundles consists of xylem, phloem and cambium i.e. they are conjoint, collateral and open. The xylem consists of vessels and tracheids and the pholem contains sieve cells and phloem parenchyma. Medullary rays are also present in between vascular bundles.

Pith — It is the central parenchymatous region (Fig. 43).

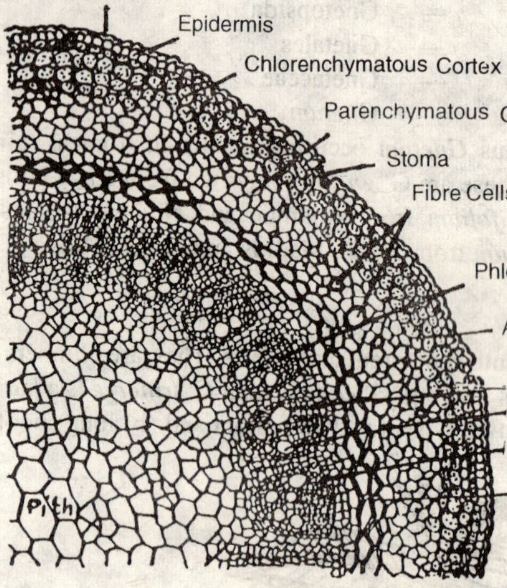

Fig. 43. *Gnetum ula*. T. S. of stem showing primary structure.

SECONDARY GROWTH IN STEM

It is of normal type. The cambium forms a complete ring which cuts off cells of secondary xylem towards centre and secondary phloem towards periphery. The amount of secondary xylem is more than that of secondary phloem.

Secondary xylem is made up of three types of cells. These are :- (a) Tracheids (b) Xylem parenchyma and (c) Vessels. The phellogen or cork cambium arises in the epidermis and may not form a complete layer of cells which results in irregular layers of cork (Fig. 44).

ANATOMY OF ROOT

Transverse section of young root shows a conspicuous cortex made up of parenchymatous cells. Sclerenchymatous patches are seen among the cortical cells. The endodermis of one layer is also distinct. Pericycle is made up of 4 - 6 layers of parenchymatous cells.

The vascular elements are diarch and exarch. Secondary growth takes place by the activity of cambium ring formed internal to phloem and external to xylem. Secondary xylem consists of vessels,

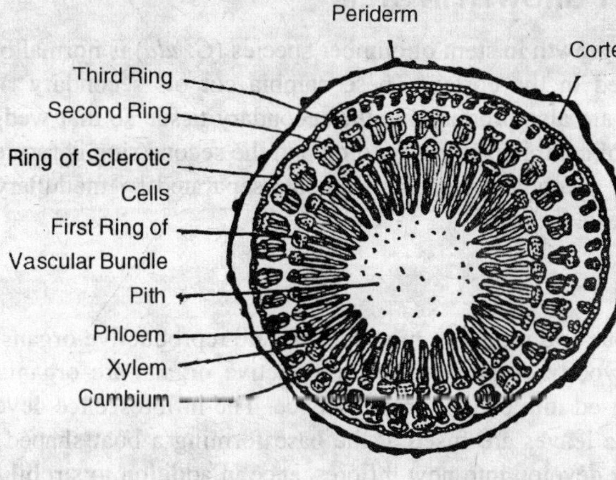

Fig. 44. *Gnetum ula.* T.S. of stem showing secondary growth.

tracheids and xylem parenchyma. The phloem contains sieve cells and phloem parenchyma. The secondary medullary rays are multiseriate. Outer layer of cortex gives rise to cork cambium which forms periderm (Fig. 45).

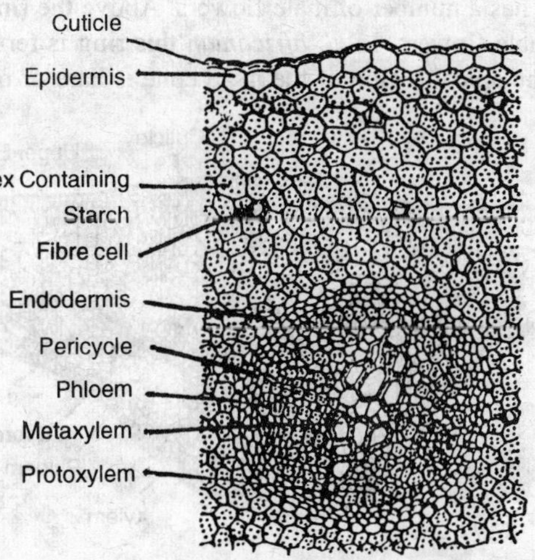

Fig. 45. *Gnetum.* T. S. of root showing diarch condition.

ANATOMY OF LEAF

Vertical section of leaf shows distinct upper and lower epidermis of one layer cells covered with cuticle. Stomata are found on the lower epidermis.

Mesophyll is differentiated into palisade and spongy parenchyma. The palisade is of one layer and towards upper epidermis. The spongy parenchyma has loosely arranged chlorenchymatous cells, stellate sclereids near the lower epidermis, scattered fibres in groups around the mid rib zone and latex tubes around the mid rib region. An arc of vascular bundles are present in the mid rib region. Xylem lies towards the upper epidermis while phloem faces the lower epidermis. The vascular bundles are conjoint, collateral and endarch.

ANOMALOUS SECONDARY GROWTH IN STEM

In the beginning the secondary growth in stem of climber species (*G. ula*) is normal but later, successive rings of cambium are produced in the cortex. These cambia cut off secondary rings of xylem and phloem. Broad medullary rays are also produced in the secondary tissue so that wedge shaped vascular bundle are seen. The first ring of cambium stops dividing and the second ring is formed out side the first ring and forms another ring of secondary vascular elements separated by medullary rays into distinct bundles and this process is repeated.

REPRODUCTIVE ORGANS

The plant of *Gnetum* is dioecious and produces male and female reproductive organs on separate plants which may be tree, shrub or woody climbers. The reproductive organs are organised into strobili or cones. These strobili are organised into panicle inflorescence. The inflorescence develops in the axil of paired decussate scale leaf. The leaves are fused at the base forming a boat shaped bracts. The bracts bear accessory buds which may develop into new inflorescence in addition to strobilus.

Male strobilus and Male flowers: The male strobilus has a long axis showing distinct nodes and internodes. The internodes are very short. The nodes of the axis bear scaly bracts arranged in whorls. These Nodal bracts fuse together to form a cup like structure called collar or cupule. Thus each node of the axis bears a collar. The number of collar varies from 10 - 25. Above each collar there are 3 - 6 rings of male flowers and each ring has a number of male flowers. Above the ring of male flower there is one ring of ovules or abortive female flowers. In *G. africanum* this ring is fertile with female flowers, thus the cone becomes bisexual. The apical region of the male cone is bare or naked or sterile. (Fig, 46).

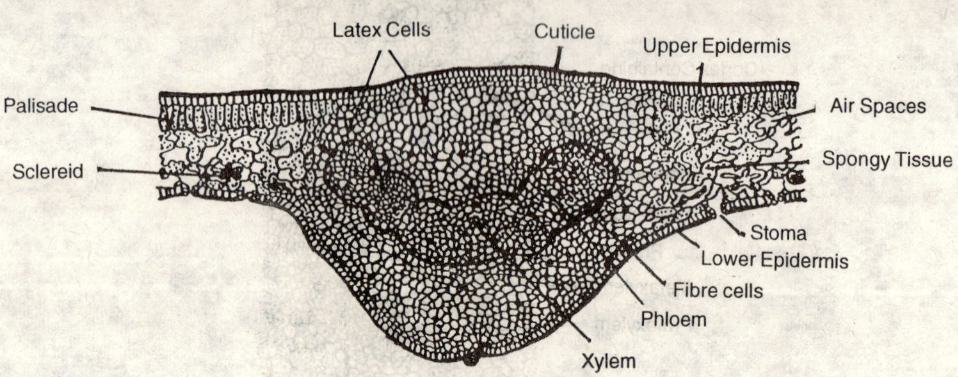

Fig. 46. *Gnetum* sp. T. S. of leaf

Each male flower is covered by a sheath like perianth. The male flower has a stalk bearing two anthers at the apex. Each anther has a single chamber of microsporangium. The stalk elongates and project beyond the perianth at maturity. The number of anthers on one stalk varies from 1 - 4 (Fig. 47).

FEMALE STROBILUS

The organisation of the female strobilus is similar to that of the male strobilus except that in female strobilus there is a single ring of 4 - 10 ovules above each collar. In the early stage of development female strobilus cannot be distinguished from the male strobilus. All the ovules never develop into seeds. Only a few of them attain maturity. The upper most collar may not bear ovule. (Fig. 48).

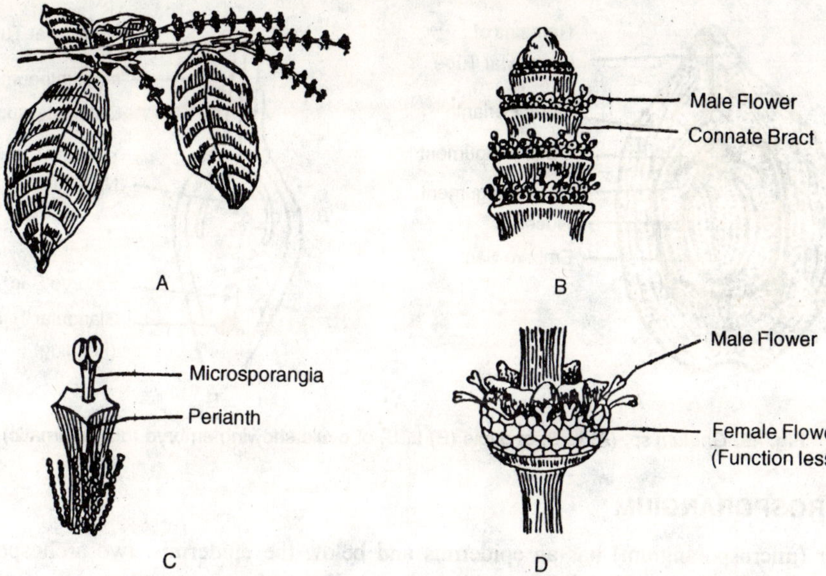

Fig. 47. *Gnetum* sp. (A) twig with male strobili (B) Staminate strobilus (C) A male flower (D) A part of staminate strobilus with functionless female flowers.

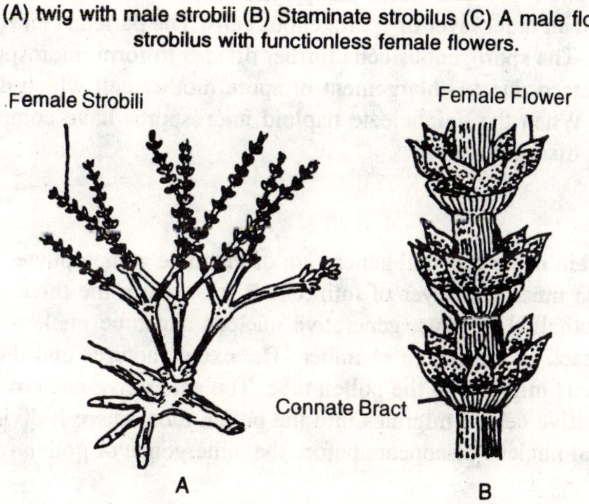

Fig. 48. *Gnetum* sp. (A) twig with female strobili (B) A part of female strobilus

STRUCTURE OF OVULE (megasporangium)

Each ovule has a central mass of cell known as nucellus. The nucellus is surrounded by three layers (envelops) The outer most envelope is the perianth, the middle and inner envelops are called outer and inner integument. The inner envelope grows beyond the middle envelope and forms a narrow, cylindrical tube known as micropylar canal or the style. A rudimentary pollen chamber is found at the nucellar apex. The nucellus contains the female gametophyte. There is no nucellar beak. The inner integument is fused with the nucellus in the lower region and is free above. Stomata are present in the epidermal layer of outer two envelops. The perianth of the outer envelope becomes thick and fleshy in the seed. The middle envelope forms the stony layer. The ovules are stalked in *G. ula* and in other species they are sessile or subsessile (Fig. 49).

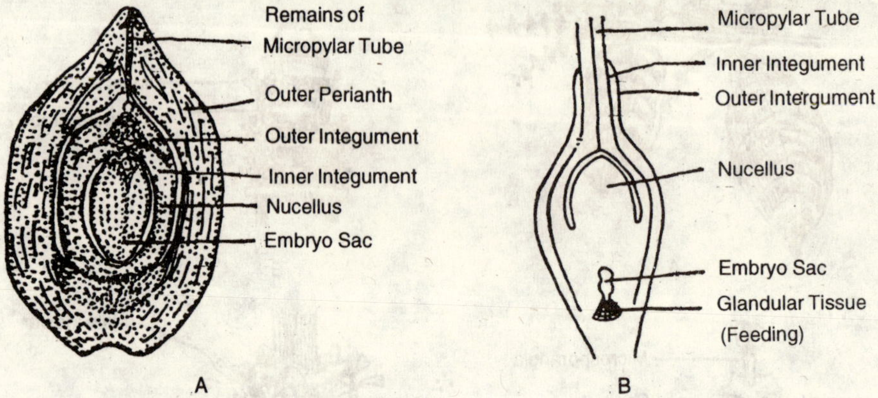

Fig. 49. *Gnetum* sp. (A) L. S. of ovule (B) L. S. of ovule showing embryo (diagrammatic).

THE MICROSPORANGIUM

The anther (microsporangium) has an epidermis and below the epidermis, two archesporial cells are differentiated. They divide and redivide to form many celled archesporium. The cells in the outer most layer are of parietal cells and an inner layer of sporogenous cells. The parietal cell further divides to form wall layer and tapetal layer. The sporogenous cells further divides to form microspore mother cells. The wall layer becomes compressed due to enlargement of spore mother cell which divides meiotically to form haploid microspores. When the uninucleate haploid microspores have completely developed the tapetum and wall layers get disorganised.

MALE GAMETOPHYTE

MIcrospore or the pollen grain is the first cell generation of the male gametophyte. It has outer thick and spiny layer of exine and the inner thin layer of intine. It is released in the three nucleate stage. These three nuclei are called prothallial nucleus, generative nucleus and tube nucleus. At this stage pollen grains are dehisced and reach to the pollen chamber. The exine ruptures and the intine grows into a pollen tube. The tube nucleus migrates to the pollen tube. The generative nucleus gets surrounded by a membrane forming a generative cell. It migrates into the pollen tube where it divides into two unequal male gametes. The prothalial nucleus disappears before the emergence of pollen tube (Fig. 50).

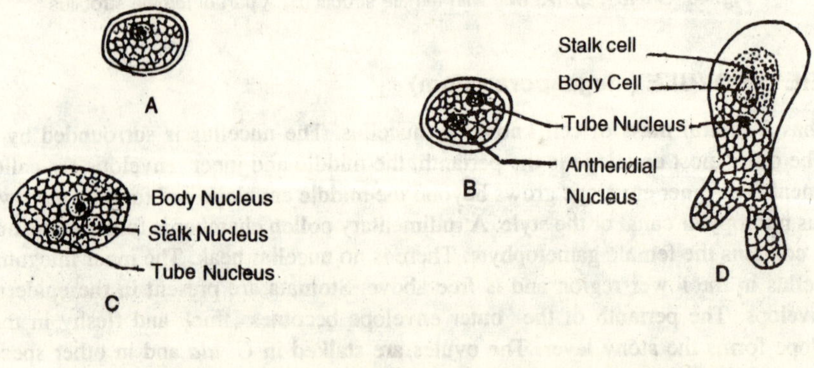

Fig. 50. Developmental stages of male gametophyte in *Gnetum gnemon*.

FEMALE GAMETOPHYTE

Embryo sac of female gametophyte is tetrasporic and about 8 - 16 megaspore mother cells start developing within the nucellus of the ovule. Each of the megaspore mother cell divides meiotically to form 4 haploid megaspore nuclei. The free haploid megaspore nuclei divide further to form 16 free nuclei. At this stage most of the developing gametophytes degenerate and two or three undergo free nuclear divisions to form 256 - 1500 free nuclei depending on the species. The female gametophyte at this stage elongates towards the chalazal end and looks like a spatulate in outline. The free nuclei are arranged on periphery forming a central vacuole. Further development takes place in one female gametophyte while the others degenerate. The nuclei at the chalazal end develop wall around them to form a cellular tissue while those near micropylar end remain free. Thus, the gametophyte is partly cellular and partly nuclear. There are no archegonia in the *Gnetum*. One or more nuclei become larger in the micropylar region of the female gametophyte and act as egg nuclei (Fig. 51).

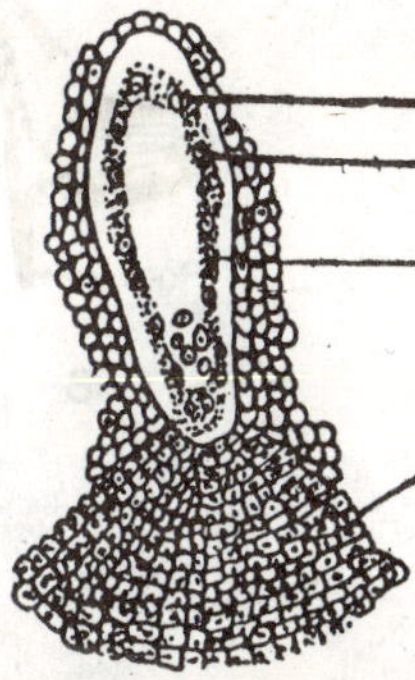

Fig. 51. Female gametophyte of *Gnetum* sp.

The cells of the nucellus lying below the female gametophyte divide to form a fan shaped structure made of many rows of cells. This was called as pavement tissue by coulter (1908). This tissue is absorbed later. Nucellus is also completely absorbed by the growing female gametophyte except a small part in the micropylar region which persists in the seed as a nucellar cap.

FERTILIZATION

The pollen tube enters through the membrane of the female gametophyte near the group of cells at the micropylar region. The tip of pollen tube bursts and male gametes are released. Both the male gametes are functional and can fertilize two eggs lying side by side. Many zygotes have been noticed in one female gametophyte.

ENDOSPERM DEVELOPMENT

Before fertilization, the lower part of the gametophyte becomes cellular and the upper part also becomes cellular after fertilization as a result of which whole of the gametophyte contain nucleated cells. The cells of endosperm are multinucleate and later these nuclei fuse to form polyploid cells. In some cells two nuclei fuse and in others three or four nuclei fuse together and thus from 1n to 12n cells are found in the gametophyte. This is termed as gradate ploidy.

EMBRYOGENY

Vasil (1959) has studied the embryogeny in *G. ula* as follows –

The zygote divides into two cells and these become tube like structure. One of the two tubes divides to form two to three cells and thus this tube is called as primary suspensor tube. The primary suspensor tube becomes coiled. The nucleus at the tip of the tube divides into two unequal nuclei. The smaller nucleus forms a cell known as peculiar cell. The larger nucleus may degenerate or form a secondary suspensor. At this stage the seed is shed from the plant and further development of embryo occurs on the soil (Fig. 52).

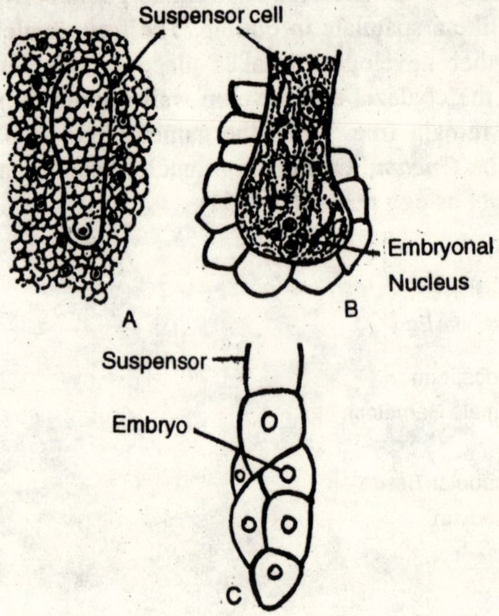

Fig. 52. Stages in the development of embryo in *Gnetum* sp. (A - C).

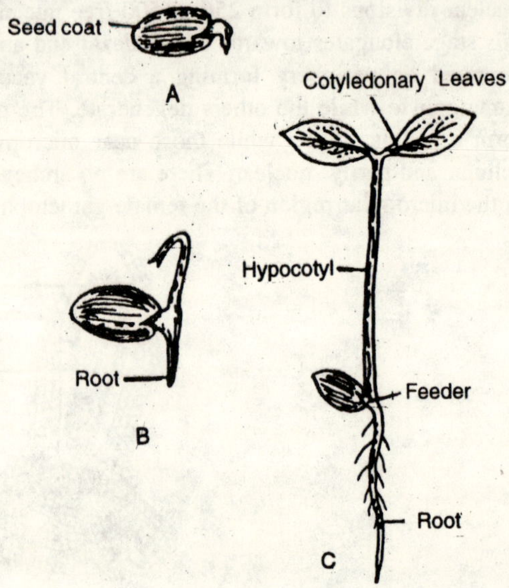

Fig. 53. Stages in the germination of seed of *Gnetum* sp. (A - C).

The peculiar cell becomes spherical and divides anticlinally or periclinally to form two cells side by side or one above the other. Further division results into four cells. Third transverse division results in an octant. Further divisions lead to the formation of mass of cells at the tip of other tube. The cells at the tip of the tube develop into embryo where as other cells form secondary suspensor. The stem tip is differentiated at the end of the embryonal mass. It is surrounded by two cotyledons. The root tip is differentiated at the other end of the embryonal mass. A small hump develops in between the stem tip and root tip, which becomes "feeder" at later stage. The feeder has its own epidermis, cortex and vascular elements. Hypocotyl is distinct. The suspensor shrivels up.

Gnetum shows polyembryony as the zygote produces many tubes and the tip of each tube develops into an embryo. But only one attains maturity.

THE SEED

The seed has three envelops. The outer envelope is succulent and green in colour and is free from other envelops. Its epidermis has stomata. The middle envelope is protective and stony. Its epidermal layer has stomata. The inner envelope is parenchymatous. It forms the micropylar tube.

All these envelops enclose the endosperm in which dicotyledonous embryo is embedded. The endosperm grows into a protuberance at its apex known as tent pole.

The mode of germination of seed is epigeal (Fig. 53).

RESEMBLANCE WITH OTHER GYMNOSPERMS

Gnetum resembles gymnosperms in the following features —

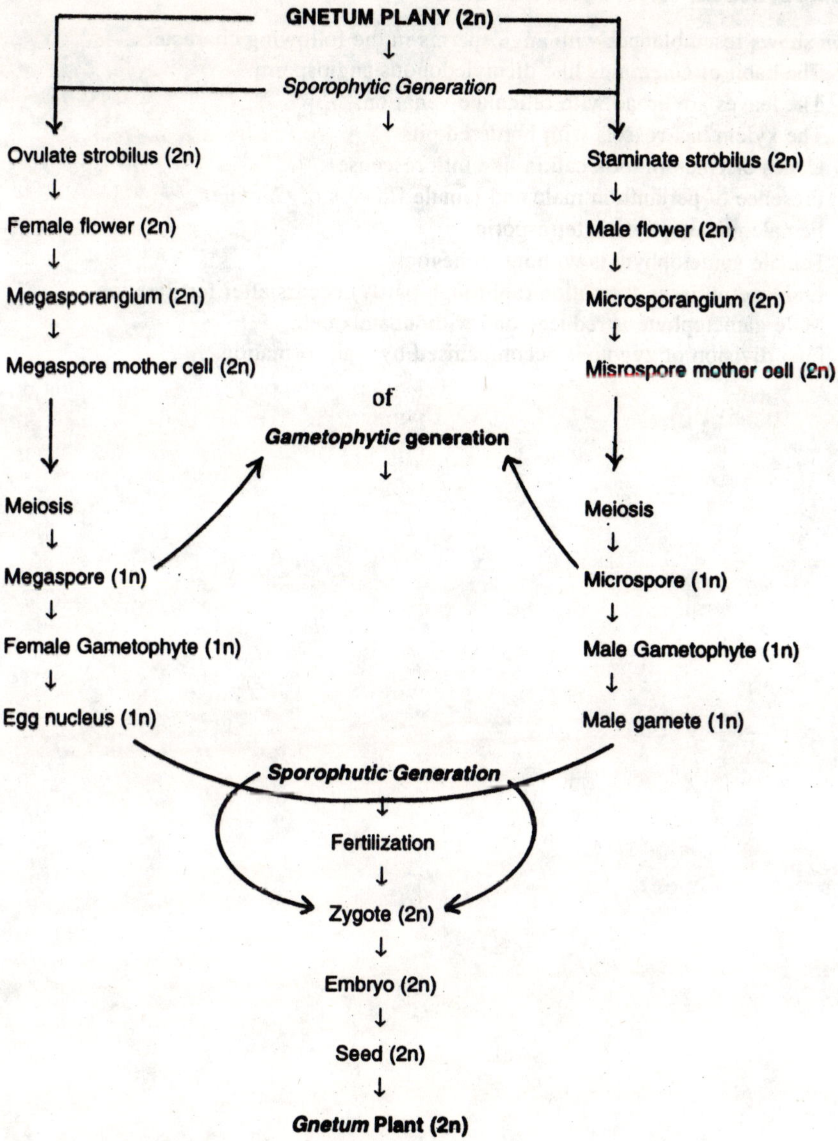

Graphic life cycle of *Gnetum*

1. The phloem is like that of typical gymnosperms.
2. Presence of one prothallial cell in the male gametophyte.
3. Occurrence of free nuclear divisions in the female gametophyte.
4. Presence of rudimentary pollen chamber at the tip of the nucellus.
5. The development of incipient type of endosperm tissue at the chalazal region before fertilization.
6. Presence of naked seeded condition.

RESEMBLANCES WITH ANGIOSPERMS

Gnetum shows resemblances with angiosperms in the following characters —

1. The habit of *Gnetum* is like dicotyledonous angiosperm.
2. The leaves are broad with reticulate venation.
3. The xylem has vessels with bordered pits.
4. Cones of Gnetum look catkin like inflorescense.
5. Presence of perianth in male and female flowers of *Gnetum.*
6. Female gametophyte is tetrasporic.
7. Female gametophyte is without archegonia.
8. Endosperm tissue formation (althrough partly) occurs after fertilization.
9. Male gametophyte is reduced and without stalk cell.
10. First division of zygote is accompanised by wall formation.

SECTION - VI

FOSSILS AND PALEOBOTANY

1. General Features and Classification
2. Rhynia
3. Lepidodendron
4. Calamites
5. Bennettites (Cycadeoidea)
6. Lyginodendron
7. Williamsonia

CHAPTER 1

FOSSILS & PALEOBOTANY

GENERAL FEATURES AND CLASSIFICATION

FOSSIL **may be defined as remains or trace of a once living organism that has been preserved in rocks or in ice. The word fossil has been derived from a latin verb *fodere* (= to dig).**

PALAEOBOTANY **is the branch of science which deals with the plants of past geological ages through the analyses of fossils.**

GEOLOGICAL TIME SCALE

It has been estimated by radioisotope (radionuclide) method of dating that the earth was formed about 4600 million years ago and the oldest fossils are only 3200 millions years old. The first 1400 million years of the earth's history are thus something of a mistery. Barghoorn and Tylet (1950) reported the presence of fossil micro–organism termed *Stromatolites* over 3000 million years old, from Pre–Cambrian rocks, near Lake Superior, Ontario. The Geologists have divided the geological history of earth into 5 geological eras viz; Archaeozoic, Proterozoic, Palaeozoic, Mesozoic and Cenozoic, Each era is further divided into periods and each period into epochs are follows:

SUMMARY OF THE GEOLOGICAL TIME SCALE

Ere	Periods	Epoch	Beginning of period in years from the present time
1. Cenozoic	1. Recent	1. Recent	1,000,000
	2. Quaternary	1. Pleistocene	2,000,000
	3. Teriary	1. Pliocene	7,000,000
		2. Miocene	26,000,000
		3. Oligocene	38,000,000
		4. Eocene	54,000,000
		5. Palaeocene	65,000,000
2. Mesozoic	1. Cretaceous		1,36,000,000
	2. Jurassci		1,95,000,000
	3. Triassic		2,25,000,000
3. Palaeozoic	1. Permian		2,80,000,000
	2. Carboniferous		3,45,000,000
	3. Devonian		3,95,000.000
	4. Silurian		4,35,000,000
	5. Ordovician		5,00,000,000
	6. Cambrian		5,70,000,000

4. Proterozoic	36,00,000,000
5. Archaeozoic	50,00,000,000

IMPORTANCE AND TYPES OF FOSSILS

The importance of fossils are as such :

1. Graphite is a fossil of organic origin which is used in lead pencil.
2. Amber is fossilised forms of gums/resins of conifers which encloses fossils of insects and flowers. Amber is used in Jewellery.
3. Coal is highly compressed fossil.
4. Diatomite is fossil of (algae) diatoms. It is of great industrial importance.
5. Limestone are also considered to be fossils of earlier ages.
6. Petroleum are of algal origin and may be considered as a fossil.
7. Study of fossil plants helps in the study of evolution and interrelationship between the different plant groups.
8. It helps in the determination of age of earth's strata.
9. Fossils also indicate the existence of once united land which is now scattered apart.

Types of fossils :

On the basis of process of fossilisation, fossils are classified as follows

1. *Petrifactions* — In this petrification process of fossilisation, the organic tissue of normal cells are replaced with silica and other minerals forming a hard stone. Coal balls containing preserved fragments of coal forming plants are its example.
2. *Compressions* — Here the fossilisation takes place by vertical pressure of the sediments under which buried parts become flat. If the compressed organic is flat like leaf, it does not show much change. It helps in the study of external morphology of the plants or its parts.
3. Incrustation or cast — In this type of fossil, external form of the organism is preserved, but the internal structure is decayed. Sediments deposit around the plants and its part in the form of a hard coal. Plant tissues are removed and a cavity is formed which becomes filled up with mud or sand and finally becomes hard to form a cast. This fossil does not show cellular details of the plant/or its parts.
4. *Compactions* — It is formed due to vertical pressure against one another plants or plant parts. There is no intervening matrix in between them. Hard fruits, seeds and leathery leaves are preserved in compaction.
5. *Impressions* — In this type of fossil, the leaves or any other organic parts after falling on a clay, forms an imprint over its surface - known as impressions. When the clay becomes solid like a stone, the impression becomes permanent. It helps in the study of external features of root, stem, leaves, flowers etc.
6. *Amber* — It is a fossil form of resinous substances of conifers which after falling on the forest floor becomes hard. Sometimes, it encloses fossils of insects or flowers.

PROCESS OF FOSSILISATION

The process of fossilisation or preservation of organisms or its parts in the form of fossil, is a spontaneous process. However, following two theories have been proposed to explain the process of fossilisation.

1. *Infiltration theory* — After burial, the plant or its part undergoes partial disintegration and then infiltration of minerals like silica, $CaCO_3$, $MgCO_3$ etc. takes place. It is followed by precipitation due to interaction between minerals and free carbon released from the plant cell walls. In other words there is precipitation of minerals which infiltrate the cell wall.
2. *Replacement theory* — Here the molecules of the original substance of plant or its parts are replaced by the molecules of minerals in soil solution. It is due to hydrolysis or weathering of the organic compound present in the organism.

Rules for nomenclature of fossils — The remains of dead plant rarely get preserved as they are liable to get decomposed and fossil of only fragments of plants like stem, root, leaf, flower, etc. are found. Softer plants or tissues have greater chance of disintegration while harder plants have better chance of fossilisation. An entire plant cannot get fossilised and therefore fossils of parts of plants are found. The generic names are applied only to such plant parts without indication to which plant it belongs. Each part represents a form genus or artificial genus. A complete plant is reconstructed by bringing together these form genera on the basis of their similarity and period to which they belong. *Calymatotheca haeninghausi* a fossil plant has root — called *Kaloxylon hookeri, stem* — called *Lyginopeteris oldhamium (Lyginodendron oldhamium)*, petiole — known as *Sphenopteris haeninghausi*, rachis — called as *Rhaciopteris aspera* and seeds — known as *Lagenostoma lomaxi.*

Following suffixes are applied to different parts while naming it.

For stem — *dendron*; e.g. *Lyginodendron*

For leaf — *Phyllum* ; e.g. *Lepidophyllum*

For woody part — Xylon ; e.g. *Kaloxylon, Dadoxylon*

For seed — *Stoma, carpon, spermum* or *carpus*; e.g. *Lagenostoma, Lepidocarpon, corytospermum, sterocarpus* etc.

For microsporangia — *Theca* ; e.g. *Crossotheca.*

For cone — *Strobus* ; e.g. *Lepidostrobus*

For Inflorescence — *Thus* ; e.g. *Cordainthus*

CHAPTER 2

FOSSIL PTERIDOPHYTES : *Rhynia*

Rhynia belongs to	Class	—	Psilophytopsida
	Order	—	Psilophytales
	Family	—	Rhyniaceae
	Genus	—	*Rhynia*

HABIT AND HABITAT

Rhynia was discovered by Mackie (1913) and fully described by Kidston and Lang (1917) from Middle Devonian rocks (about 38 crore year old) of Rhynie Chert in Scotland. They are found in petrified form and thus

1. The sporophytic plant body grew near volcanoes in swampy marshes 20 to 50 cm in height with a diameter of 1 mm to 6 mm.
2. There are two species in this genus namely (i) *R. major* and (ii) *R. Gwynne — Vaughani.* The former attained a height of about 50 cm with a diameter of aerial stem ranging from 1.5 mm to 6 mm and the latter species showed a height of 20 cm with a diameter ranging from 1 to 3 mm.
3. The plant had a dichotomously branched rhizome bearing erect, aerial shoots with unicellular rhizoids towards lower side.
4. Roots were absent.
5. Adventitious branches were found on the aerial shoots and rhizome of *R. Gwynne-Vaughani.*
6. No lateral appendage was seen in *R. major.*
7. Aerial shoots had stomata and were photosynthetic in nature.
8. Pear-shaped terminal sporangia were found on the aerial shoots of both the species (Fig. 1).

ANATOMY OF AERIAL SHOOT AND RHIZOME

1. Anatomically the aerial shoot and rhizome were similar in having one celled thick epidermis, cortex and stele.
2. Epidermis was covered by a layer of cuticle. Stomata were present in aerial shoot only.
3. Below the epidermis was a region of cortex differentiated into 1 - 4 cells thick outer cortex and inner cortex having intercellular spaces (Fig. 2).
4. The stele had a central xylem surrounded by phloem (protostele). Xylem was made up of tracheids having annular and spiral thickenings.

REPRODUCTIVE ORGANS

1. Aerial shoots wore sporangia – oval to cylindrical in shape.
2. The length of sporangium of *R. Gwynne–Vaughani* was about 12 mm and the diameter measured 4 mm.

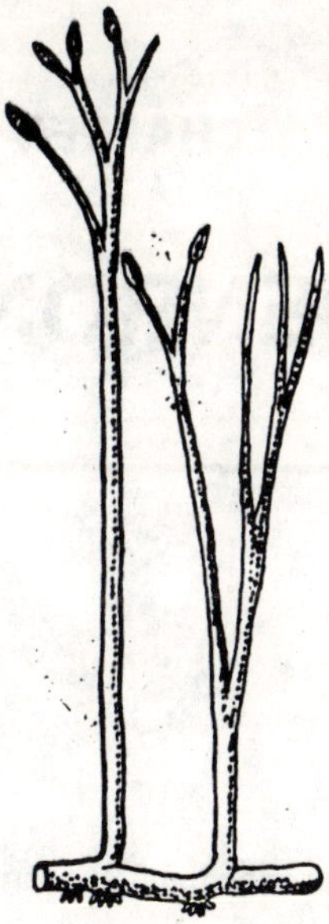

Fig. 1. Plant of *Rhynia major* with sporangia.

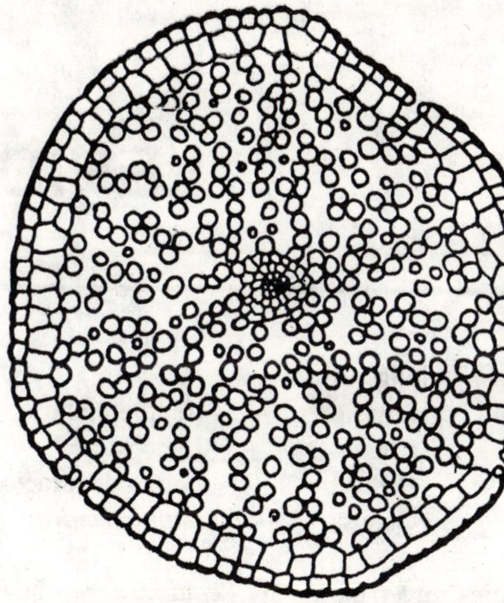

Fig. 2. T. S. of stem of *R. major.* of *R. major.*

Fig. 3. L. S. of sporangium

3. Sporangial wall was 5 cells thick.
4. Inner most wall layer was of tapetum.
5. Many spores were present inside the tapetal layer.
6. The spores were arranged in tetrads and were homosporous.
7. The diameter of the spores was about 65 μ (Fig. 3).
8. Due to tetrahedral arrangement of the spores it is presumed that the spores would have been produced by meiosis and the structure bearing them belonged to sporophytic generation.

GAMETOPHYTE

Some rhizomatous structures were suspected to be gametophyte of *Rhynia* by Merker (1958, 59) but it was rejected by Sporne (1966) on the plea that no antherdia or archegonia were seen in such structures. Pant (1962) and Lemoigne (1968, 1969) have suggested some of rhizomatous structure of *Rhynia major* as gametophytes. Rashid (1976) observed *R. Gwynne–Vaughani* a gametophytic generation of *R. major.* But no valid information are available regarding gametophyte of *Rhynia.*

CHAPTER 3

LEPIDODENRON

The form genus *Lepidodendron* belongs to

Division	—	Lepidophyta
Class	—	Lycopsida
Order	—	Lepidodendraceae
Genus	—	*Lepidodendron*

More than one hundred species under the genus *Lepidodendron* have been described. It appeared during upper devonian, flourished in carboniferous and disappeared in permian.

PLANT BODY

It is tree and reaches up to a height of 40 meters and the diameter of the trunk was approximately 50 centimeters. The trunk was straight and columnar, unbranched upto certain distance above the ground. Dichotomous branches were clothed with spiral or whorls of leaves. Leaves (*Lepidophyllum*) were deciduous, simple, ligulate, linear to acicular in shape and 2 to 18 cm in length. Leaves were shed by abscission leaving the base attached to the branches called leaf cushion which appeared as projecting truncated cone or pyramid like. The trunk at the base was attached to stigmarian root system which appeared as dichotomously forked thick and spreaded (Fig. 4)

ANATOMY OF THE TRUNK

The trunk was differentiated into central stele surrounded by cortex. The cortical zone was very thick and can be differentiated into (a) inner cortex, (b) secretary zone, (c) middle cortex and (d) outer cortex.

The inner cortex was made up of parenchyma cells. The Secretary zone was composed of large and small cells, some of them were filled with dark coloured substance. The middle cortex was similar to inner cortex in structure and appearance and the outer cortex was composed of alternating patches of thin and thick walled tissue.

The outer cortex was encircled by hard periderm layer formed by phellogen. In many of the species the stem showed secondary thickening. The secondary woods were thick on one side and thin on the opposite side.

The stele was either siphonostelic or protostelic. The protoxylem was exarch and showed polyarch condition. The metaxylem of tracheids was with scalarifom thickening and the protoxylem was with spiral thickenings. The secondary wood has scalariform tracheids and small wood rays. (Fig. 5A).

LEAVES

It is known as *Lepidophyllum*. They were born spirally on the stem and were triangular in shape. Stomata

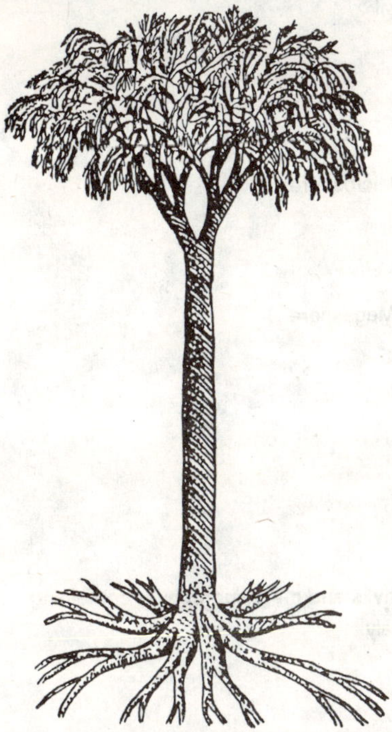

Fig. 4. Reconstructed plant *Lepidodendron*.

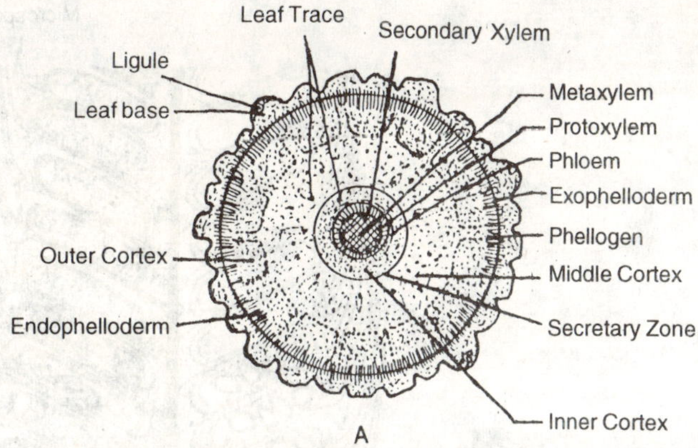

Fig. 5A. Transverse section of a stem *Lepidodendron vascular* Benney.

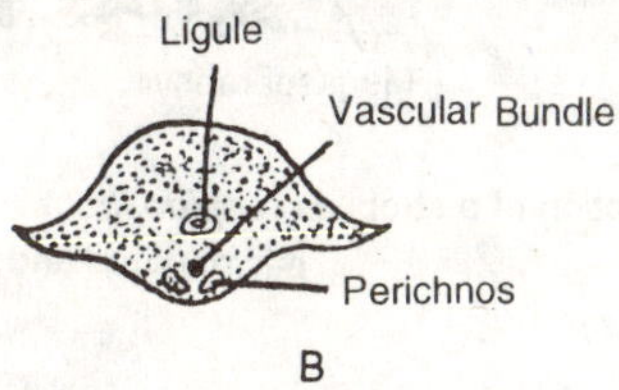

Fig. 5B. Transverse section of leaf base of *Lepidodendron aculeatum* sternb.

were present on the abaxial side in two longitudinal grooves. In cross section, the leaf base was seen with a small, single vascular strand. This vascular strand was flanked by two triangular or rounded areas or scars - one on each side. These scares were termed as *perichnos.* The perichnos represented secretory or aerating parenchyma cells extending from stem cortex into the leaf. A ligular scar or pit was present in the centre of the cushion, above the perichnos. The ligule was shunken and small. The mesophylls were present in the central region of the leaf (Fig. 5B).

REPRODUCTIVE ORGAN

Many strobili of Lepidodendraceae were discovered from carboniferous rocks and were named as form genus *Lepidostrobus.* These strobili *(lepidostrobus)* were ellipticle born terminally on the lateral branches of the crown. They were 2.5 to 30 cm long and 1 to 7.5 cm in diameter. The strobili were heterosporous having microsporophylls and megasporophylls arranged spirally or verticillately on the axis of the strobilus. The sporophylls were ligulate. Both the sporangia were sessile, elongated and of same size born on ventral (adaxial) surface near the base of the respective sporophylls. The sporangia may be septate or aseptate. The wall of the sporangia were made up of one layer of prism shaped cells. The microsporangium had many small microspores and the megasporangium had 5 - 16 megaspores. The size of the microspores ranged from 0.02 to 0.03 mm in diameter and that of megaspores ranged from 0.5 to 2.0 mm in diameter (Fig. 6).

Structure of Gametophyte

The male gametphyte has not yet been reported. Female gametophyte with archegonia has been reported. The megaspore developed into female gametophyte while still within the megasporangium (Fig. 7).

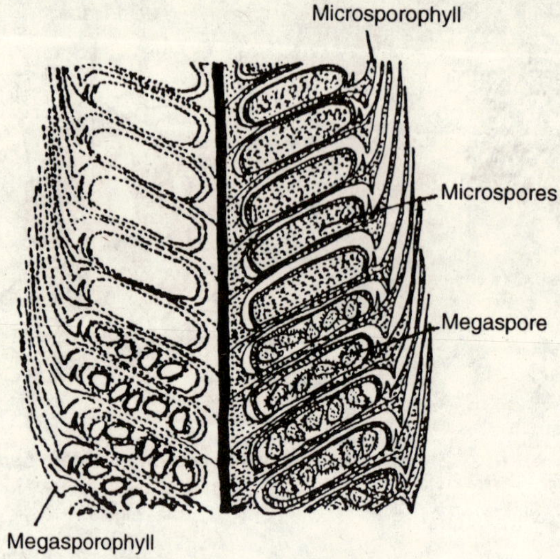

Fig. 6. Vertical Section of a strobilus (*Lepidostrobus*) showing microsporophylls and megasporophylls containing microspores and megaspores respectively.

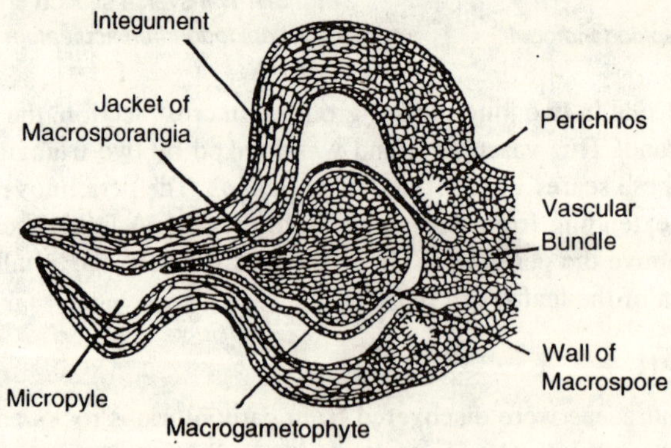

Fig. 7. Longitudinal section of seed (Llepidocarpon lomaxi Scott.

CHAPTER 4

CALAMITES (Ancient scouring rushes)

It belongs to — Arthophyta or Sphenophyta or Calamophyta (Tippo 1942; Benson 1977; Smith 1955)

Division	—	Calamophyta
Class	—	Calamopsida
Order	—	Calamitales
Family	—	Calamitaceae
Genus	—	*Calamites*

IMPORTANT FEATURES

1. The *Calamites* were over 60 feet tall.
2. They apparently originated in Devonian and then, due to unable to adopt the changing climatic conditions, disappeared in the Triassic.
3. The name *Calamites* was originally used for the pith cast in 1784 by Suckow. Separate generic names have been given to all parts of the plant including the pith casts, leaf whorls and strobili.

Subgenera of Calamites on the basis of mode of branching:

1. *Stylocalamites* — branches are few and irregularly scattered.
2. *Calamitina* — branches in whorls only at certain nodes.
3. *Eucalamites* branches are born at every node.

Types — (a) *Calamites cruciatus* — many branches per whorl.

(b) *C. carinatus* — pair of opposite branches at node.

Calamites is a large and diversified genus. The plants were bamboo like, gregarious in habit and the diameter of the stem ranges from 15 - 30 cm. and the height of the plant varies from 15 - 60 feet. Stems are upright and adventitious roots arise from the lower most node and grew in muddy soil. (Fig. 8a).

Anatomy

1. Large pith cavity enclosed by parenchymatous tissue in which a ring of vascular bundle (V.B) is found.
2. V. B. are next to the pith but due to development and disrupted by carinal canal they are disrupted and fragments are found adhering to the sides of the canal.
3. Protoxylem has annular and spiral thickening and it is succeeded by centrifugal metaxylem.

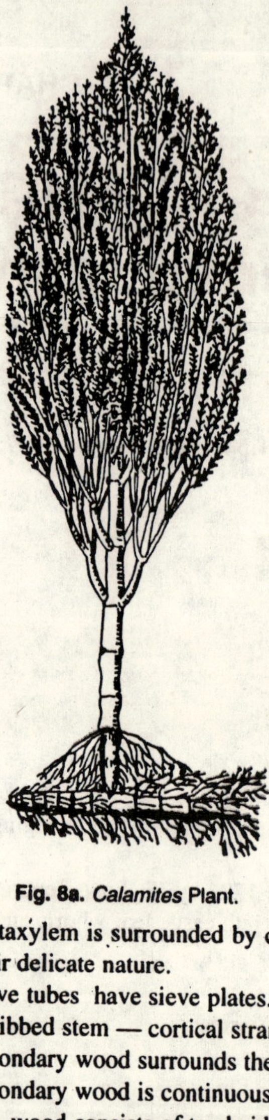

Fig. 8a. *Calamites* Plant.

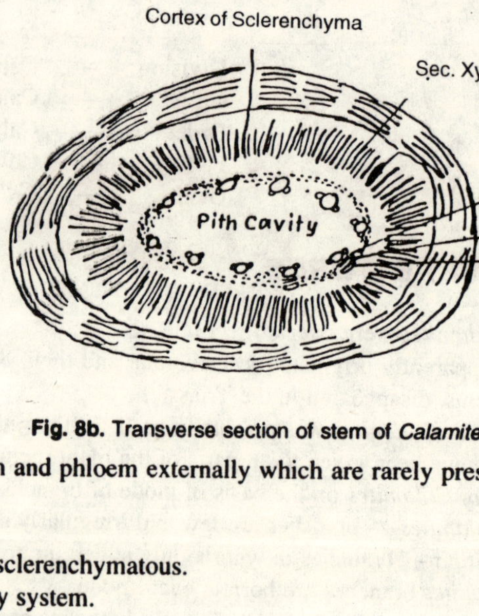

Fig. 8b. Transverse section of stem of *Calamites*.

4. Metaxylem is surrounded by cambium and phloem externally which are rarely preserved due to their delicate nature.
5. Sieve tubes have sieve plates.
6. In ribbed stem — cortical strands are sclerenchymatous.
7. Secondary wood surrounds the primary system.
8. Secondary wood is continuous and cylindrical.
9. Sec. wood consists of tracheids and rays.
10. Tracheids bear bordered pits on the radial walls.
11. *Arthrodendran, Calamodendron* and *Arthropytis* are the common type of stem.
12. Insertion of the leaf trace is found.
13. Traces depart at nodes.
14. No leaf gaps (Fig. 8b).

RHIZOME

Horizontal rhizomes had aerial branches. Nodes and internodes were present, whorls of adventitious roots were present at every node.

ROOT

1. It is variable in size and structure.
2. Smaller roots have diarch to triarch actinostele.
3. Secondary wood surrounds the primary wood.
4. Carinal canal absent.
5. Endodermis two layered.
6. Pith is small.
7. Parenchymatous/cortex is with air space.
8. Outside the cortex, Periderm is present.
9. When petrified, it is described as *Astromyelon* and
10. When compressed, it is termed as *Pinnularia*

LEAVES

Born on main stem and are simple, linear and in whorls. The leaf types most commonly found are —

1. *Annularia* and (2) *Asterophyllites* (3) *Lobatanularia.*

Annularia

1. Arranged in whorls around the stem.
2. Linear, lanceolate or spathulate with single vein.
3. Size varry from 5 to many centimeters.

Asterophyllites — Leaves more slender, softer, curved upward, free at the base.

Lobatanularia — Leaf whorl centric with a gap toward the base of the branch.

Petrified Asterophyllites has following structure —

1. One layer epidermis
2. Stomata present
3. Guard cell of stomata has cuticular ridge as in *Equisetum.*
4. Mesophyll tissue of radiating palisade (Fig. 9).
5. A small vascular strand surrounded by bundle sheath in the centre which in turn are circled by mesophyll.

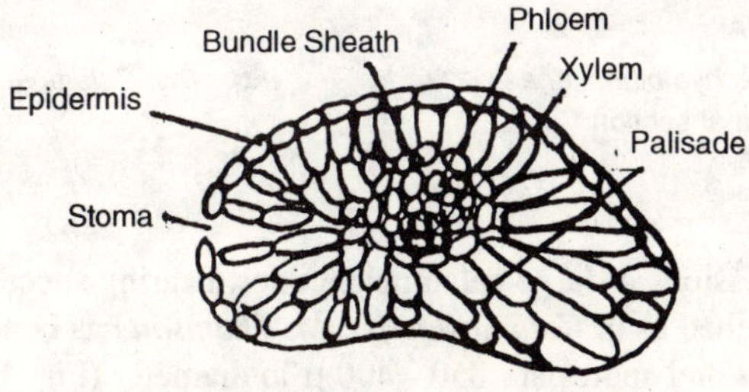

Fig. 9. T. S. of leaf of *Calamites.*

FRUCTIFICATION

The fructifications of *Calamites* are of interest not only on anatomical and morphological ground but also on the problem of origin and evolution of the Sphenopsida.

The cones or strobili or fructifications of Calamites are of at least five types as described below - (1) *Calamostachys* (2) *Palaeostachya* (3) *Macrostachya* (4) *Cingularia* and (5) *Calamocarpon.*

CALAMOSTACHYS

It is a large and widely distributed organ genus. The cone axis of *C. Binneyana* contains a central pith surrounded by 3 or more separate V . B. (The number is one-half of the sporangiophores in a whorl.) Cone bundles do not alternate at the nodes but passed continuously along the long axis) The axis supports successive whorls of sterile bracts and sporangiophores. The sporangiophores are cruciate organs born at right angles to the axis. The sporangial wall is usually one cell thick. The spores of *C. Binneyana* are numerous homosporous, measuring about 90 μ diamter, *C. casgeaba* is *heterosporous* (Fig. 10B).

PALAEOSTACHYA

It is similar to *Calamostachys* except that the peltate sporangiophores are situated in the axils of the sterile bracts. Vascular bundle supplying the sporangiophore passes vertically upward to about middle of the inter node and then it bends downward and enters the sporangiophore at the base (Fig. 10A).

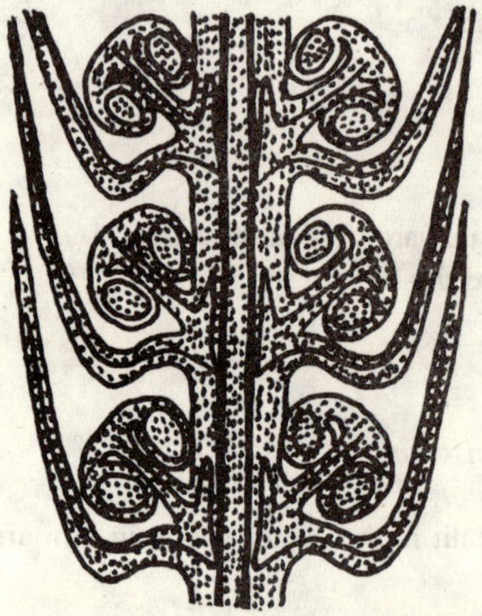

A

Fig. 10A. *Palaecstachya binneyana* in Longitudinal section.

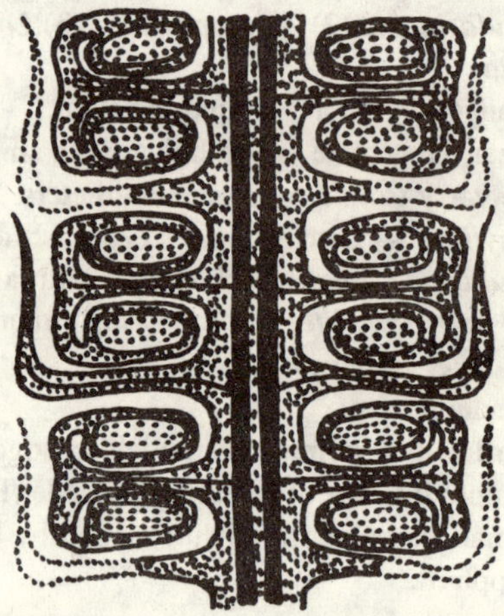

B

Fig. 10B. *Calamostachys binneyana* in L.S.

MACROSTACHYA

It is the name given to compressions of large calamitean cones, bearing successive whorls of bracts and sporangiophores probably attached as in *Calamostachys. M. Thomson* has cone, 21 cm long and 2.5 cm. in diameter. It is homosporous and spores are 350 - 400 μ in diameter (Fig. 11).

CINGULARIA

It is a lax cone in which sporangiophore is horizontally extended and divided into an upper and a lower lobe. In *C. typica* the upper lobe is a sterile bract. The lower portion is split apically into two short lobes and each bear two interior sporangia. In *C. cantrilli*, both upper and lower lobe bear sporangia and no sterile bracts are present. It is also found as compressions (Fig. 12).

CALAMOCARPON

It is the fifth type of cone of *Calamites* found as petrifactions.

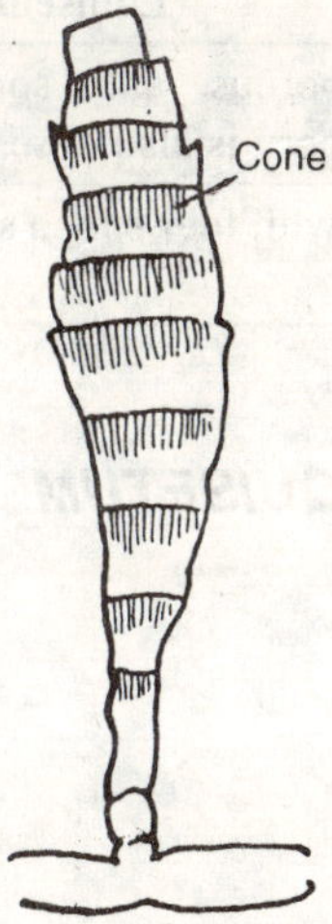

Fig. 11. *Macrostachya infundibuliformis*, a *strobilus* of *Calamites*.

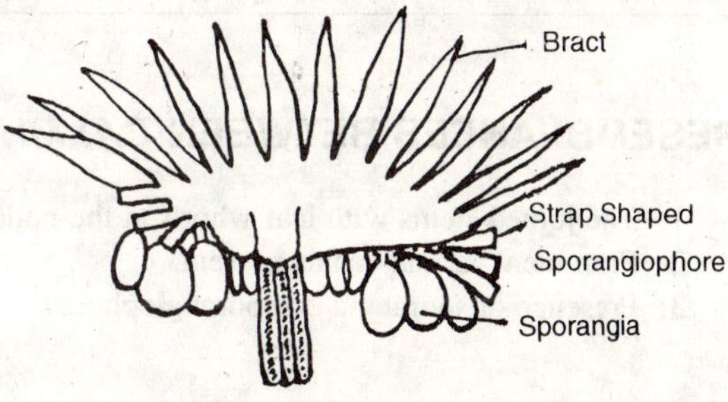

Fig. 12. Part of *Cingularia*, a strobilus of *Calamites*.

DIFFERENCES BETWEEN *CALAMITES* AND *EQUISETUM*

	Calamites		*Equisetum*
1.	Preserved in corboniferous period and world wide in distribution	1.	Living form and found all over the world except Australia and New Zealand
2.	Large leaves containing Chlorophyll and function as photosynthetic organ	2.	Scaly leaves, non-green, deciduous not acting as photosynthetic organ.
3.	Ribs of stem one above another in stead of alternating with each other.	3.	Ribs of stem alternate with each other at node.
4.	Absence of Vallecular canal in the cortex of stem.	4.	Vallecular canal present in the stem cortex.
5.	Stem has neither stoma nor chlorenchyma-thus-nonphotosynthetic	5.	Stem has stomata and chlorenchyma and thus photosynthetic.
6.	Cambium present in vascular bundle (V.B.)	6.	No cambium in V.B.
7.	Secondary growth takes place.	7.	No secondary growth
8.	Periderm present	8.	Absence of Periderm.
9.	Secondary xylem with pitted tracheids and vascular rays.	9.	Absence of secondary xylem.
10.	Root cortex has large air space.	10.	No air space in root cortex.
11.	Different forms of strobili present.	11.	Only one type of strobili present.
12.	Strobili with bracts and sporangiophores alternately arranged.	12.	Absence of bracts between whorls of sporangiophores.

(*Contd.*)

	Calamites		Equisetum
13.	Generally homosporous but heterospory is also observed.	13.	Homosporous and sometimes incipient heterospory is also observed.
14.	Spores without elaters	14.	Spores with four spoon shaped hygroscopic elaters.

RESEMBLANCES BETWEEN *CALMITES* AND *EQUISETUM*

1. The joined stems with leaf whorls at the nodes.
2. Prominent carinal canals present.
3. Presence of sporangia on sporangiophores.

CHAPTER 5

FOSSIL GYMNOSPERMS : *Bennettites* (*Cycadeoidea*)

It belongs to	Division	—	Cycadophyta
	Sub-Division	—	Pteridospermae
	Order	—	Bennettitales (Cycadeoidales)
	Family	—	Bennettitaceae (Cycadeoidacease)
	Genus	—	*Bennettites* (*Cycadeoidea*)

The fossils of the order Cycadeoidales were discovered from triassic to lower cretaceous period of mesozoic era in Mexico, Europe, South Africa, Australia, North and South America and India, (Rajmahal Hills in Bihar, Talchir and Orrissa) and other places of southern hermisphere. The members of bennettitales resembled modern cycads but has different habit. It occurred as petrifications.

The generic name *Cycadeoide*a was given to the petrified trunks discovered from the Isle of whight in 1860. *Bennettities gibsonianus* was discovered by Williamson (1868) from lower carboniferous as silicified petrifactions from the port land off the South coast of England. Later, studies indicated that *Bennettites* and *Cycadeoidea* belong to the same genus and it was prefer to call *Cycadeoidea* as *Bennettites*. Following are the chief features of *Bennettites* :-

1. The genus *Cycadeoidea* (*Bennettites*) has a short unbranched or branched, spherical, conical or irregular trunk with a diameter of about 50 cm (Fig. 13).
2. The surface of the petrified trunk was marked by many rhomboidal leaf bases with multicellular hairs in between them.
3. The height of the trunk varies from less than one meter to several meters. (*C. jenneyyana*).
4. Trunks are low growing and profuse branching give the appearance of a bunch of pine apples.
5. Pinnate–compound leaves, about 10 feet in length forms a crown at the apex of the trunk.
6. Transverse section of the stem shows a wide parenchymatous cortex traversed by many leaf bases and mucilage canals.
7. The epidermis is not well preserved.
8. Primary vascular elements consist of a ring of endarch, collateral, conjoint and open V. B.
9. Parenchymatous pith is present in the centre.
10. Parenchymatous rays are observed in between vascular bundles (V. B.)
11. Secondary wood encircles the primary xylem and consists of tracheids with scalariform thickenings and bordered pits.
12. Secondary medullary rays are found in between the secondary xylem and phloem.
13. Cambium is seen in between secondary xylem and phloem.

14. Leaf traces develop singly from the primary vascular strand and divides into many mesarch strands in the cortex and look as horse–shoe shaped.
15. The leaf trace is C shaped at the time of its origin. (Fig. 14).

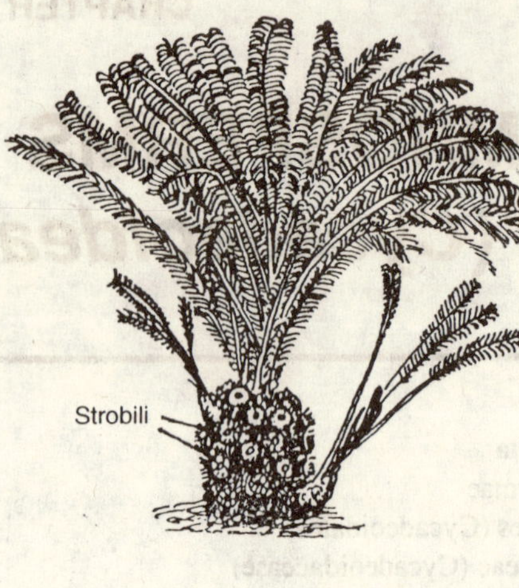

Fig. 13. *Cycadeoidea* Plant.

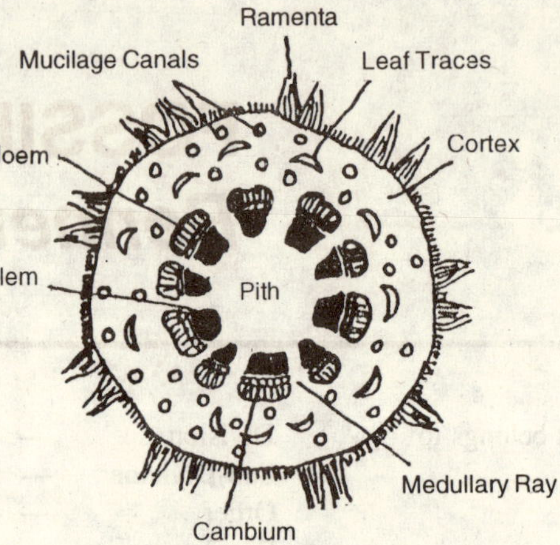

Fig. 14. Transverse section of stem of *Bennettites* (*Cycadeoidea*)

LEAF

1. Vertical section of the pinnule shows a distinct upper and lower epidermis.
2. Mesophylls are differentiated into palisade and spongy parenchyma.
3. Phloem faces the lower epidermis and Xylem is towards upper epidermis.
4. V. B. is surrounded by bundle sheath.
5. Stomata are present on the lower epidermis.

REPRODUCTIVE ORGANS

These are called flowers.

1. The flowers are bisexual.
2. They are axillary and solitary.
3. Plant flowers only once in its life time.
4. *Cycadeoidea wielendii* is unisexual.
5. The stalk of a bisexual flower is 5 - 10 cm in diameter and about 6 cm long.
6. Microsporangia and megasporangia are protected by 100 - 150 hairy, elongated bracts.
7. Microsporophylls or androecium consists of 19 - 20 unipinnate appendages developing in whorls from the base of the conical receptacle (Fig. 15).
8. The microsporophylls are united at their base to form a disc.
9. Megasporangium or gynoecium consisted of several stalked ovules originating around the whole convex protuberance of the receptacle.
10. Short stalk of ovules of *C. dacotensis* arose horizontally while it arose vertically in *C. gibsoniana*.

11. Interseminal scales with expanded tips were present interspersed among the ovules.
12. On maturity the sterile hairy bracts expanded to form a cup shaped structure resembling a perianth (Fig. 16).

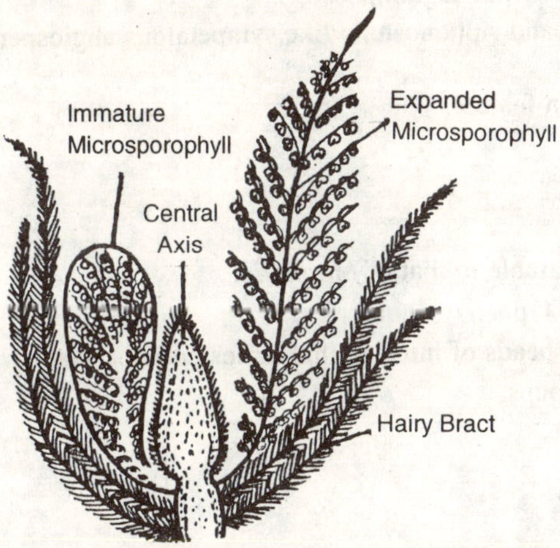

Fig. 15. Strobilus of *Cycadeoidea* showing an unfolded stamen (*Microsporophyll*).

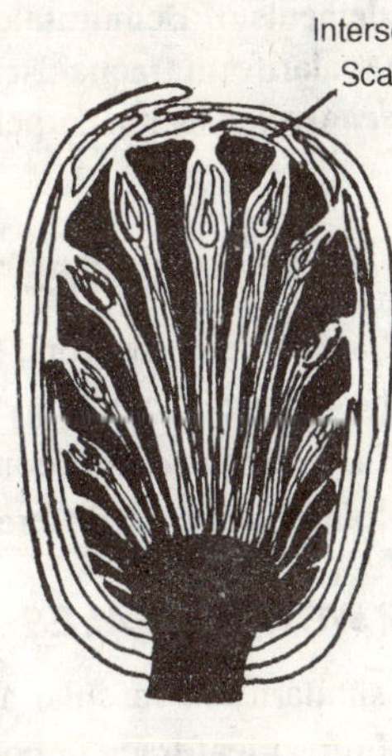

Fig. 16. Strobilus of *Cycadeoidea* showing seeds and interseminal scales.

***Microsporophyll* (Androecium)**

1. Each microsporophyll has a central axis bearing many pinnae alternating with each other.
2. The pinnae have two rows of bean shaped short stalked pollen capsule (Synangia).
3. The tip of the microsporophyll was fused to its base.
4. The line of dehiscence is seen around the base of each microsporophyll.
5. Synangium or pollen capsule measures 2.5 x 3.5 mm having many (20-30) microsporangia (pollen sacs).
6. Synangium wall has outer palidase layer followed by thin walled cells.
7. A ring of microsporangia are arranged around the periphery.
8. Microspores are released into the synangial cavity.
9. The synangia opened by an apical slit into two halves.
10. Multicellular microspores represented male gametophyte.

***Megasporophyll* (Gynoecium)**

1. It consists of a conical or spherical receptacle bearing many stalked ovules and interseminal scales.
2. Each ovule has a single integument and 1 mm long.
3. Integument fuses with the nucellus except at its apex.
4. Each ovule has a pollen chamber and an external nucellar beak.
5. The ovules are orthotropous having long micropylar beaks.
6. The fused tips of interseminal scales forms a protective covering which surrounds the seeds (Fig. 16)
7. Crepet and Delevoryas (1972) have discovered bisporangiate cones of *Cycadeoidea*.

AFFINITIES OF *BENNETTITES* (*CYCADEOIDEA*) WITH ANGIOSPERMS:

According to Wieland the Bennettitales are the ancestor of flowering plants. This view is based on the following features |-

1. Bennettitelian strobili closely resemble the flower of Magnoliaceae.
2. Vascular elements of Bennittitales are endarch and siphonostelic like sympetalous angiosperms.
3. Both have scalariform tracheids.
4. *Cycadeoidea* ovules lack a carpel - a magnolian feature.

DIFFERENCES FROM ANGIOSPERMS

1. Bennettitalian stamens are frond like not comparable to that of *Magnolia.*
2. Ovule of the *Cycaeoidea* is of gymnospermous type.
3. Pericarp of *Cycadeoidea* fruit consists of fused heads of interseminal scales and not ovary wall.
4. Habit and foliar nature are different in these groups.

RELATIONSHIP WITH GNETALES

1. Both have similarity in vascular anatomy.
2. Presence of direct leaf trace in both of them.
3. Absence of suspensor in the embryo.

RELATIONSHIP WITH GRINKGOALES

1. Pycnoxylic nature of secondary wood in both the groups.
2. Presence of narrow medullary rays.
3. Tree like habit of the plants of both of groups.

RESEMBLANCE WITH FERN

1. Presence of direct leaf trace.
2. Microsporangia in the form of synangia.
3. Presence of ramental hairs.
4. Morphology of leaves are the same.
5. Microsporophylls are pinnae like.
6. Strobilus is axillary - a peculiar fern character.

RESEMBLACE WITH CYCADOFILICALES

1. Presence of ramenta.
2. Presence of lateral branching.
3. Vascular anatomy identical in both of them.
4. Presence of direct leaf trace.
5. Seed structure of similar nature.
6. Presence of cupule in both the groups.

RESEMBLANCES WITH CYCADALES

1. General habit of the plant.

2. Repeated dichotomy of stem of *Wielandiella* can be compared to the sympodial habit of *Cycas* and *Zamia*.
3. Similarity in the anatomy of stem and leaf.
4. Presence of mucilage canals.
5. Presence of ramenta.
6. Restriction of lateral branching to the apical region.
7. Abaxial microsporangia.
8. General structure of the ovule.
9. Dicotyledonous embryo.

Thus, with the present day knowledge of the subject, we may conclude that there are two branches, namely (1) plants bearing bisporangiate strobili and (2) plants bearing monosporangate strobili. The bisporangiate strobili form (Bennettitales) gave off an off shoot, the angiosperms which continued directly into the present day angiosperms.

The monosporangiate strobili form continued into the Cycads of the present time.

CHAPTER 6

LYGINODENDRON

It belongs to —	Division	—	Cycadophyta
	Subdivision	—	Pteridospermae
	Order	—	Cycadofilicales
	Family	—	Lyginopteridaceae
	Form genus	—	*Lyginopteris* (*Lyginodendron*)

The plant was first described by *Binney* (1866) under the name of ''*Dadoxylon oldhamium*'' Williamson (1873, 95) gave its name *Lyginodendron oldhaunium*'' and gave thorough knowledge of its vegetative structure.

Potonie (1898-99) renamed the genus as "*Lyginopteris*"

THE STEM

It is long, slender and branched. *Lyginodendron oldhamium* or *Lyginopteris oldhamium* bore spirally arranged fronds. Stem is 2 mm to 4 cm in diameter.

Transverse section (T.S) of stem shows the following features-

1. Monostelic structure.
2. Middle of the stele occupied by a large parenchymatous pith, containing irregular groups of dark sclerotic tissue.
3. Primary xylem of collateral vascular bundles (V.B), which are 5 - 9 in number and surround the pith.
4. Around the primary xylem, secondary xylem with pitted tracheids and medullary rays are found.
5. Opposite the primary xylem, group of primary phloem is recognised.
6. Bast formed of cambium is present.
7. Beyond the phloem zone, pericycle is present.
8. Collateral leaf trace bundle, embedded in pericycle are found.
9. Few layers of periderm are found outside the pericycle.
10. Beyond the periderm, thin walled inner cortex and outer cortex of sclerchyma is present which appear as dark radial bands.
11. First cases of branching were discovered by Mr. James Lomax in 1902 (Fig. 17)

THE LEAVES

1. The main petioles of the leaves associated with stem reaches a centimeter in diameter.
2. The petioles were named *Rachiopteris aspera.*
3. Phloem completely surrounds the xylem.
4. Inner cortex contains bands of sclerotic cells.

5. Leaflet has epidermis, hypodermis and palisade parenchyma towards upper surface.
6. Towards the lower surface, mesophyll is of spongy parenchyma.
7. Traces of stomata on lower surface.
8. V.B. enclosed in sheaths.
9. V. B. collateral.
10. It is compound and like fern leaflets with xerophytic structures.
11. *Sphenopteris* is the name for leaflet.

THE ROOTS

It has a distinct name — *Kaloxylon Hookeri*

Features: Diameter is about 5 mm. T. S. shows the following features:

1. Secondary tissues at all stages of development.
2. Triarch or diarch vascular bundles.
3. 4 - 8 xylem groups — alternating with phloem.
4. Pericycle one or more layer surrounds the vascular tissue.
5. Endodermis beyond the pericycle.
6. Inner cortex of lax parenchyma.
7. Double peripheral layers of exodermis.
8. Secondary growth like gymnosperms and dicotyledons.
9. No distinct formation of periderm (Fig. 18).

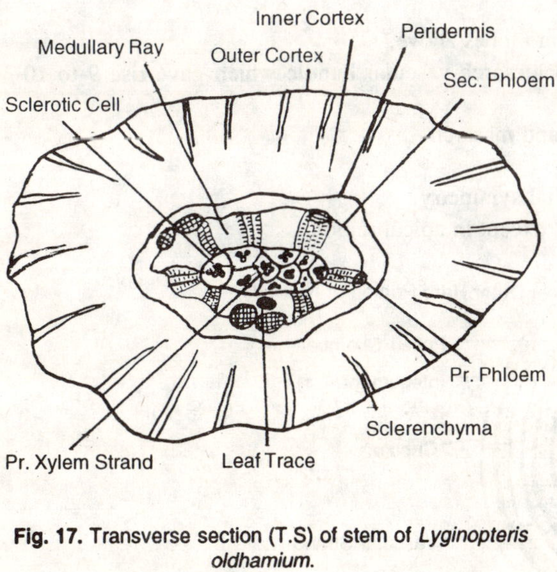

Fig. 17. Transverse section (T.S) of stem of *Lyginopteris oldhamium.*

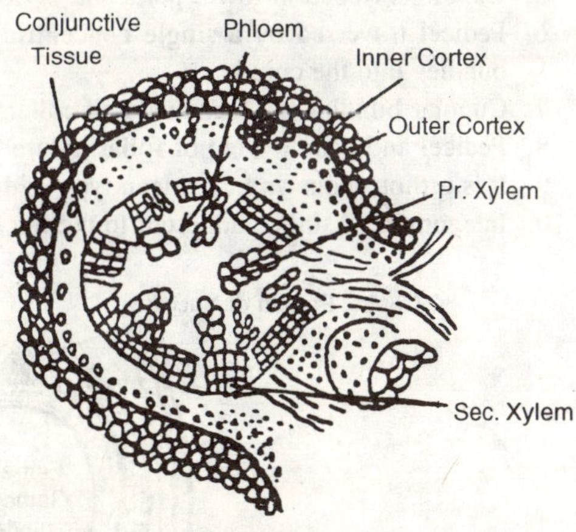

Fig 18. Transverse section of root of *Lyginopteris oldhamium.*

THE SEED

F. W. Oliver (1903) identified the seeds of *Lyginodendron* (*Lyginopteris*) by presence of glands on its enveloping husk.

Williamson named the seeds as "*Lagenostoma Lomaxi*".

It possess the following features:

1. Seed is barrel shaped, 5.5 mm in length, 4.25 mm in diameter.
2. Enclosed in an outer husk or cupule.
3. Attached with pedicel, pedicel and cupule studded with capitate glands. (Fig. 19).

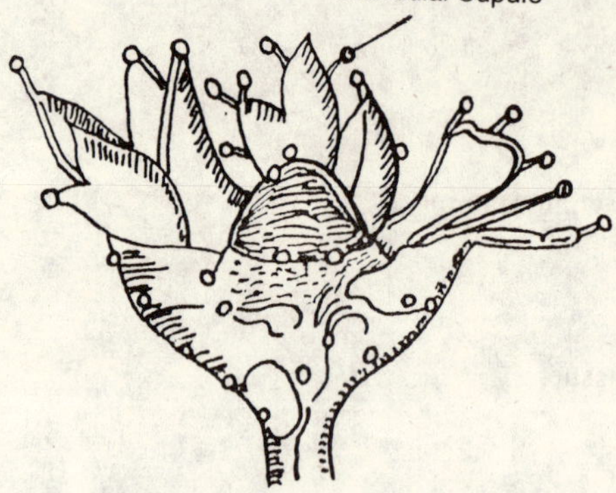

Fig. 19. Seed (*Lagenostoma lomaxi*) surrounded by cupule of *Lyginopteris oldhamium*.

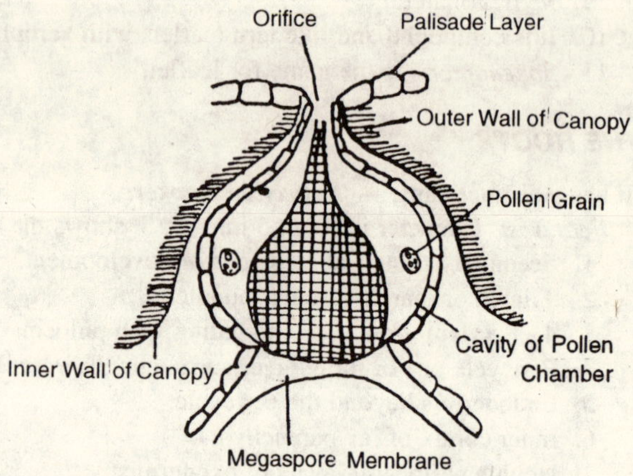

Fig. 20. Upper portion of *L. lomaxi* in Longitudinal section.

4. Cavity of the head is empty.
5. Cupule is ribbed in lower parts and divided into lobes above.
6. Pedicel traversed by a single concentric and mesarch vascular bundle which gave rise 9 to 10 bundles into the cupule.
7. Cupular bundles are branched and collateral and mesarch.
8. Pedicel and cupule were of foliar nature.
9. It is orthotropous and cycadean type with radial symmetry.
10. Integument is single, adherent to the nucellus except in apical region.

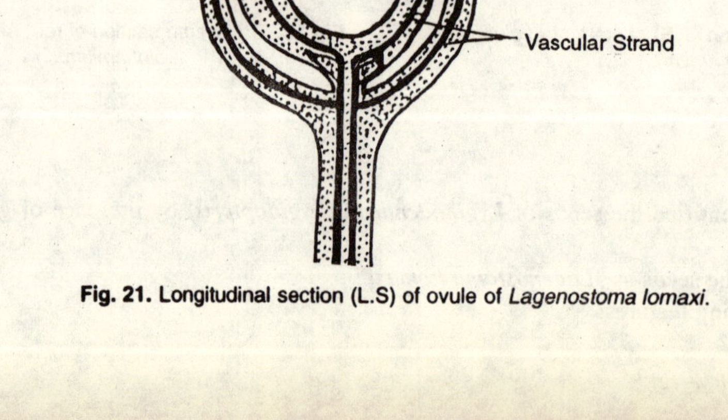

Fig. 21. Longitudinal section (L.S) of ovule of *Lagenostoma lomaxi*.

11. Central strand of pedicel, after giving of cupular bundles, passes straight up and becomes the chalazal strand which is surrounded by mass of thick walled strengthening tissue.
12. The integument expands towards the micropyle which forms 9 chambered canopy. In each locule, one of the nine V. B. entered.
13. Canopy may represent water storage for pollination by drop mechanism.
14. Outer layer of integument has columner structure.
15. Free apex of the nucellus forms the pollen–chamber (Fig. 20).
16. Pollen grains are multicellular.
17. Outline of megaspore or embryo sac can be traced.
18. Absence of trace of embryo (Fig. 21).

CHAPTER 7

WILLIAMSONIA

It belongs to	Class	—	Cycadopsida
	Order	—	Cycadeoideales (Bennettitales)
	Family	—	Williamsoniaceae
	Form Genus	—	*Williamsonia*

Many Species of *Williamsonia* have been discovered from Triassic, Jurassic and Cretaceous periods of Mesozoic era from India, Europe and N. America. Williamson (1870) discovered its fossil remains from the Jurassic period of Yorkshire and named it as *Zamia gigas*. Later Carruthers named it as *Willaimsonia.* More than five species of *Williamsonia* have been reported from Raj Mahal Hills of Bihar. Some of these are *W. Sahni*, *W. Sewardiana*, *W. Indica W. Santalensis* etc. Sahni (1932) reconstructed *W. Sewardiana* from Jurassic beds of Raj Mahal Hills. Three organs like leaves, stem and fructification were found from different localities in Raj Mahal Hills (Amrapara, Brindaban etc.) and then the complete plant was reconstructed and named *Williamsonia Sewardiana.* It can be described as follows—

STEM

1. The stem of small tree is columner which terminates in a crown of pinnate leaves.
2. It is armoured with alternate area of scaly (small) and foliage (large) leaf bases.
3. The stem is branched and slender about two meters in height (Fig. 22).

LEAVES

1. Pinnate leaves were described under the name *Ptilophyllum cutchense.*
2. Leaflets were linear and parallel veined.
3. Leaves were mixed with printed scales (leaves).
4. Thus, leaves are of two types viz. (1) Simple. scale like and (2) pointed Pinnately compound foliage leaves.

FLOWERING BRANCH

1. It arose through the leaf bases as lateral branches.
2. They were covered with bracts.
3. It beared only a few foliage leaves.
4. The fertile branch terminates in a female flower.

ANATOMY OF STEM

1. It appears as a rough circular in outline in cross section.
2. Cortex was parenchymatous with secretory sacs.

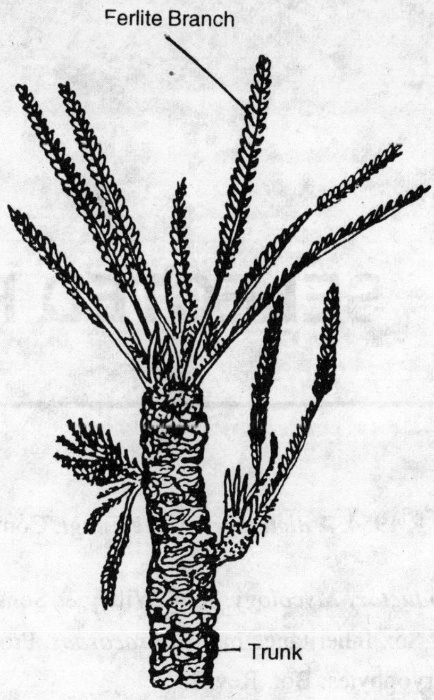

Fig. 22. ***Williamsonia*** **Plant**

3. **Pith was also parenchymatous, narrow and possessed secretory sacs.**
4. **Vascular bundles were endarch and collateral arranged in a ring.**
5. **Secondary wood formed an extensive cylinder around the primary xylem.**

SELECTED REFERENCES

1. Ainsworth, G. C. and Bisby, G. R 1954. *A dictionery of the Fungi*. Common wealth mycological institute Kew Survey.
2. Alexo-poulos, C. J. 1952. *Introductory Mycology*, John Wilwy & Sons Inc. New York.
3. Allen, C. E. 1919. The basis of Sex Inheritance in *Sphaerocarpos*. Proc. Amer. Phil. Soc. 58.
4. Allen, 1935. The genetics of Bryophytes. Bot. Rev. I.
5. Andrews, H. N. 1961. *Studies in Palaeobotany*. McGraw Hill Book Co. New York.
6. Allen, C. E. 1919. The basis of Sex Inheritance in *Sphaerocarpos*. Proc. Amer. Phil. Soc. 58.
7. Bierhorst D. W. 1971. *Morphology of Vascular plants*. The McMillan Company, New York.
8. Billings, W. D. and Thompson I. H. 1957 **38.**
9. Bold, H. C. and Wynne, M. J. 1985 ***Introduction to the Algae. Structure and Reproduction 2nd ed.*** Printice Hall, Englewood Cliffs, New Jersey 720 pp.
10. Bold, H. C. 1957. *Morphology of plants*. Harpers Brothers, New York.
11. Bold, H.C. 1963. *The Plant Kingdom*. Prentice Hall of India Ltd. New Delhi.
12. Boodle, L. A. 1901. Comparative anatomy of the Hymenophyllaceae. Schizeaceae and Gleicheniaceae. Ann. Bot. 15.
13. Bower, F. O. 1908. *The Origin and Land flora*. McMillan.
14. Bower 1896. Studies in the Morphology of Spore producing members II. Ophioglossaceae. London.
15. Bower, 1926. *The Ferns*. Vol. II Cambridge Univ. Press.
16. Bower, F.O. 1935. *Primitive Land plants*. London.
17. Bower, 1913 Medullation in the Pteridophyte. Ann. Bot. 25.
18. Browne, I. M. 1913. A Colonial distribution of our knowledge of *Lycopodium* New Phytol 12.
19. Bruce J. G. 1979a. Gametophytes of *Lycopodium digitatum* Am. J. Bot. 66(10)
20. Brener, G. 1902. On the anatomy of *Danaea* and other marattiaceae. Ann. Bot. 16.
21. Butler, E. J. 1907. An account of the genus *Phythium* and some Chytridiaceae. Mem. Dept. Agrica India Bot. Ser. I.
22. Vacers, F. 1903 New Phytol. 2, 9.
23. Cavers 1910. New Phytol. 9.

24. Campbell, D. H. 1918. *The structure & development of Mosses & Ferns*. New York.

25. Campbell, D.H. 1940. *The Evolution of Land Plants. California*

26. Chapmann V. J. and Chapmann. D. J. 1973. *The Algae* 2nd ed. MacMillan, New York.

27. Champmann. V. J. and Chapmann D. J. 1980. *Seaweeds and their uses*. 3rd ed. Champmann & Hall, London.

28. Chamberlain, C. J. 1935. *Gymnosperms : Structure & Evolution*. University of Chicago Press.

29. Chrysler, M. A. and D. S. Johnson 1939. Spore production in *Regnellidium* Bull. Torrey. Bot. Club. 66.

30. Christensen, T. 1962. Algae *Systematisk Botanik*. Vol. 2. (Boeher, T. W., Lauge, M. and Sorensen, T. eds) Munksgaard, Copenhagen.

31. Coulter J. M. & Chamberlain C. J. 1955. *Morphology of Gymnosperms* Ind. Ed. Central Book Depot. Allahabad.

32. Coulter, J. M. Barnes C. R. and Cowles, H.C. 1956. *A Text Book of Botany* Vol. I (Morphology) Ind. Ed. The World Press, Calcutta.

33. Coulter J.M. 1908. Bot. Gaz. 46. ·

34. Cronquiat, A. Takhtanjan, A. and Zimmermann, W. 1966. On the higher taxa and Embryonta. *Taxon* 15(4): 129-134.

35. Cronquist, A. 1968. *The Evolution and Classification of flowering plants*. Thomas Nelson and Sons Lt. London.

36. Davoson, J. W. 1859. On the Fossil plants from the Devonian rocks of Canada. Quar. Jour Geo. Soc. London 15.

37. Delevoryas, T. 1963. *Morphology and Evolution of Fossil Plants*. Rinehart & Winston Inc. U. S. A.

38. Dodge J. D. 1974. *Fine structure and Phylogeny in the algae* Sci. Prog. Oxford.

39. Duckett J. G. and W. C. Pang 1984. The Origin of heteospory Bot. J. Linn. Soc. 88.

40. Dupler, A. W. 1920. Bot. Gaz. 9.

41. Eames, A. J. 1936. *Morphology of vascular plants* McGraw Hill Book Co. New York.

42. Eames, A. J. and Mac Daniels, L. H. 1947. An *Introduction to plant Anatomy* Mc Graw Hill Book Co. N. Y.

43. Esau, K. 1953. *Plant Anatomy*, John Wiley & Sons. New York.

44. Florin, R. 1954. Biol. Rev. 19.

45. Fogg G. E. 1951. Ann. Bot. Lon. N. S. 15 : 23-36.

46. Foster J. W. 1949. *Chemical activities of Fungi*. Academic Press, New York.

47. Fritsch F. E. 1945. Ann. Bot. N. S. 9 (Origin of Bryophyta).

48. Fritsch, F. E. 1935: *The structure and Reproduction of the algae* Vol. I. Cambridge University Press.

49. Ibid 1945, Ibid Vol. II Ibid.

50. Frobischer M 1957 *Fundamentals of microbiology* W-B. Sounders Co. Philadelphia.

51. Goebel K. 1915. Apogamy in *Selaginella*. Flora 108

52. Goebel, K. 1881. Sporangial development in Pteridophytes. Bot. Zeit. 39.

53. Grambast, L. J. 1974. *Phylogeny of Charophyta*. Taxon 23

54. Gupta, K. M. 1962. *Marsilea*. Botanical monograph C. S. I. R. New Delhi.

55. Gwynne-Vaughan, D. T. 1903. Stelar theory Ann. Bot. 17.

56. Gwynne Vaughan, H. C. I. and Barnes, B. 1951. *The structure and development of the Fungi* 2nd ed. Cambridge University Press.

57. Haberlandt. G. 1914. *Physiological Plant Anatomy* Mac Millan & Co. London.

58. Harper, R. A. 1909. Sexual reproduction in *Pyronema confluens* and the morphology of the ascocarp. Ann. Bot. 14

59. Hollowwy J. E. 1939. The gametophyte, embryo and young rhizome of *Psilotum triquetrum* Ann. Bot. N. S. 3.

60. Home, M. A. 1899. Mem. Torrey Bot. Club 7

61. Jeffrey E. C. 1898. Stelar theory. British Assn. Adv. Sci. Tept. Toronto 7.

62. Jeffrey E. C. 1902. The structure and development of the stem in the pteridophyta & Gymnosperms. Phil. Trans, Rey. Soc. London 195.

63. Johnson, D. S. 1898 On the leaf and sporocarp of *Marsilea quadrifolia* Ann. Bot. 12.

64. 1933. The curvature symmetry and homologies of the sporocarps of *Marsilea & Pilularia* Bull. Torrey Bot. Club. 60.

65. Kashyap, S. R. 1914. Structure and Deyelopment of the prothallus of *Equisetum debile*. Ann. Bot. 28.

66. Ibid 1919. Proc Asiatic Soc. Bengal N. S. 15.

67. Kidston, R. and W. H. Lang, 1917-1920 & 21. On Old Red Sand stone plants showing structure from the Rhynie chert bed, Aberdeenshire, Plt. I-V. Trans. Roy. Soc. Edin. 51, 52 & 54.

68. Kylin, H. 1933. Lunds Univ. Arssker. N. F. 29 : (2)

69. Lewin, R. A. 1977. *Prochloron* Type genus of Prochlorophyta, Physiologia. 16 : 217.

70. Linnaeus C. 1754. *Genera Platarum* Ed. Holmiae.

71. Ibid 1953. *Species Platarum* 2.

72. Lomax, J. 1902. Some new features in relation to *Lyginodendron Oldhamium* Annals of Botany. 16.

73. Lyon, F. M. 1901. A study of the sporangia & gametophytes of *Selaginella apus* and *S. rupestris*. Bot. Gaz. 32.

74. Martin G. W. 1950. *Outline of the fungi*, Dubuge, Iowa.

75. --- 1940. The Myxomycetes Bot. Rev. 6.

76. --- 1932. Systematic Position of slime molds and its bearing on classification of fungi. Bot. Gaz. 93.

77. McLean H. M. C. and Ivimey–cook W. R. 1960. *Text Book of Theoretica Botany*. 3rd Impression. Longmans London.

78. Mehta, K. C. 1940. *Further studies on cereal rust in India*. I. C. A. R., New Delhi.

79. Mehta, K. C. and Pal, B. P. 1954. Rust resistant wheat to India, Nature 146 : 98.

80. Metcafe, C. R. and Chalk L. 1950. *Anatomy of the Dicotyledons* Oxford.

81. Metcafe, C. R. 1960 *Anatomy of Monocotyledons* I. Graminae, Oxford.

82. Mitsuta, S. 1980. Branching patterns of *Lycopodium cernuum* Mem. Rac. Kyto. Univ. Ser. Biol. 8(1).

83. Nawaschin, S. 1897. Flora 83.

84. Oliver, F. W. 1902. On some points of apparent resemblance in certain fossil and recent gymnospermous seeds. New phytologist. 1.

85. Pandey, S. K. 1932. Jour. Indian Bot. Soc. 11.

86. Pandey, S. S. 1932. Some observations on the biology of *Marsilea* Proc. Lahore Phil Soc. 41.

87. Pant, D. D. 1957. *The Classification of Gymnospermous plants*. Palaeobotanist 6(2) : 65-69.

88. Potonie, H. 1899. Lehrbuch der pflanzenpalaeontologie Berlin.

89. Parihar, N. S. 1957. *Biology & Morphology of pteridophyta.* Central Book Depot. Allahabad.

90. Porter C. L. 1959. *Taxonomy of Flowering Plants* W. H. Freeman & Co. San Francisco.

91. Prescot, G. W. 1969. *The Algae, A Review.* Thomas Nelson & Sons Lts. London.

92. Puri V. and M. L. Garg 1953. A contribution to the anatomy of sporocarp of *Marsilea* minuta with a discussion of the nature of sporocarp in Marsileaceae. Phytomotphology 3.

93. Rashid, A. 1976. *An Introduction to Pteridophyta : Diversity and Differentiation.* Vikas New Delhi.

94. Reimer, H. 1954. In Engler, H. H. Melchior and E. Werdermann Syllabus der pflanzeufamilien, Vol. I Bacteria - Gymnosperms, Berlin.

95. Roberts, K. Gurney-Smith, M and Hills, G. J. 1972, Structure position and morphogenesis of the cell wall of *Chlamydomonas reinhardii* I Ultrastructure and Preliminary analyses J. Ultrastr Res. 40 : 599.

96. Sahni, B, 1920. Ann. Bot. 34.

97. Scott, D. H. 1908, 1909. *Studies in Fossil Botany* Vol. I & II London.

98. Seward, A. E. 1933. *Plant life through the ages* Cambridge University Press.

98. (ii) Simpkins, J and Williams, J. I. 1990. *Advanced Biology* (3rd Ed.). Unwin Hyman Ltd., 15-17 Broadwick Street, London, WIVIFP.

99. Sinnoott, E. W. 1946. *Botany, Principles & Problems.* 4th ed. Mc Graw Hill Book Co. New York.

100. Smith, G. M. 1955. *Cryptogamic Botany Vol* I & II Mc Graw Hill Book Co. N. Y.

101. Smith G. M. 1950. *Fresh Water Algae of the United States.* 2nd Ed. McGraw Hill Book Co. New York

102. Sparrow, F. K. 1943. *Aquatic phycomycetes,* University of Michigan Press.

103. Sporne. K. R. 1971. *The Morphology of Gymnosperms* Hutchinson University Press Library, London.

104. Sporne, K. R. 1966. *The Morphology of Pteridophytes.* The structure of Ferns and Allied plants. Hutchinson Univ. Lib. London.

105. South, G. R. and Whittick A. 1987 *Introduction to phycology.* Black well Scientific publications.

106. Sterling, C. 1948. Bull. Torrey Bot. Club 75.

107. Stanley, W. M. 1936. Chemical studies on Virus of Tobacco mosaic. Phytopathol. 25.

108. Strasburger, E. 1872. Die Coniferen and die Gnetacean Zen. Jeitsch.

109. Strasburger, E. 1967. *Text Book of Botany.* Longmans Green & Co. Ltd. London.

110. Stevenson, G. B. 1970. *The Biology of Fungi Bacteria and Viruses.* 2nd ed. Edward Arnold Ltd. London.

111. Stewart, W. 1983. *Paleobotany & the Evolution of Plants.*

112. Tippo, O. 1942. A modern Classification of the plant Kingdom. Chron. Bot. 7: 2-3 - 206.

113. Treub, M. 1888. Edudes sur Less Lycopodiacees. Ann. Jard Bot. Buitenzong. 7.

114. Ibid 1890. Embryo of *Lycopodium* Ibid 8.

115. Udar, R. 1966. *An Introduction to Bryophytes. Shashidhar Malviya Prakashan, Lucknow.*

116. Van Tieghem, P. and H. Douliot. 1886. Surla Polystelie Ann. Sc. Nat. Bot. Ser. 7 . 3.

117. Verdoorn, F. 1932. *Manual of Bryology* Chronica Botanica. Waltham Mass.

118. Verdoorn, F. 1938. *Mannual of pteridology.* Martinus Nighoff. The Haque.

119. Vasil, Vimla 1959. Phytomorphology. 9.

120. Von Mohl, Hugo 1845 Veber den Bau des Cycadeenstammes. Abh. K. Acd. Munchen I. Vermischte Schriften.

121. Walker J. C. 1957. *Plant pathology* Mc Graw Hill Book Co. N. Y.

122. Wardlaw C. W. 1955. *Embryogenesis in plants*. London.

123 Wardlaw, C. W. 1950 A discussion on Morphogenesis in Ferns Proc. Linn. Soc. London.

124. Webster T. R. and Steeves 1963. Morphological nature of *Selaginella* rhizophore. Phytomorphology 13.

125. Ibid 1964. Developmental morphology of *Selaginella root*. Can. J. Bot. 42.

126. Webster, J. 1970. *Introduction to fungi*. Cambridge University Press, London.

127. Williamson, W. C. 1873. On the organisation of the fossil plants of coal-measures IV *Dictyoxylon, Lyginodendron* and *heterangium* Phil. Rans. Roy, Soc. London 163.

128. Wieland, G. R. 1899. A study of some American fossil cycads. Ame. Jour. Coc. II

129. Worsdell, W. C. 1902. Stelar Theory Bot. Gaz. 34.

130. White, R. A. 1961. Vessels in the roots of *Marsilea* Science 133.

131. Woorsdell W. C. 1910. The rhizophores of *Selaginella* New Phytol 9.

132. Wolf, F. A. & Wolf F. T. 1947. *The Fungi* Vol. I & II Hohn Wiley & Sons Ine N. Y.

133. Zimmermann, W. 1930. Die Phylogenie der pflanzen I. Auflage, Jena.

APPENDIX

ALGAE

1. Economic importance of algae
2. Ecological importance of algae and other cryptogams
3. Range of thallus organization in algae
4. Origin and evolution of sex in algae
5. Life cycle in algae

FUNGI

6. Heterothallism, parasexuality and degeneration of sex
7. Economic importance of fungi
8. Differences between algae and fungi

BRYOPHYTA

9. Economic importance of bryophytes
10. Methods of spore dispersal in bryophytes
11. Bryophytes withstand long period of drought
12. Small and inconspicuous nature of bryophytes
13. Bryophytes have adapted land habit
14. Phylogeny of bryophytes
15. Vegetative reproduction in bryophytes
16. Sterilization of sporogenous tissue in bryophytes

PTERIDOPHYTA

17. Stelar system and its evolution
18. Economic importance of pteridophytes
19. Apogamy, apospory and parthenogenesis in pteridophytes
20. Origin of pteridophytes

ALGAE

1. ECONOMIC IMPORTANCE OF ALGAE

Economically algae are of great economic importance as all organism are directly or indirectly benefited from it. Following are the positive and negative importance of algae.

POSITIVE IMPORTANCE

Following are the Positive importances of Algae.

1. As food : Sea–weeds and some other algae are used by the people of coastal countries as food *Ulva, Chlorella Porphyra, Caulerpa, Codium, Laminaria* etc. are a great source of vitamins, proteins, minerals and starch.
2. Some of the brown algae contain soda, potash, alginic acid, iodine etc. which are used as supplement to fodders and fertilizers. Majority of marine algae are rich in zinc, copper, manganese, iron, boron, molybdenum, cobalt, vanadium etc.
3. Alginates obtained from cell wall of brown algae are used in paints, polishing materials, flame proof fabrics, plastic articles etc.
4. Agar-agar a gelatinous substance is obtained from *Gelidium* and *Gracilaria* which is used in making jelly, ice-cream, soup, cosmetics. Agar agar is also used in preparing culture media.
5. As fodder : *Laminaria, Ascophyllum, Fucus* etc. are used as fodder for goats, sheep, cattle etc.
6. As fertilizers — Blue green algae and sea-weeds are rich in various elements and nitrogenous compounds and hence they are used as fertilizers. Soil fertility is increased due to nitrogen fixing ability of blue green algae.
7. In antibiotic production — Chlorellin — type of antibiotic and others are obtained from *chlorella, Lyngbya* etc.
8. Diatomite is obtained from Bacillarariophyceae, found in marine and fresh water basins of the world. It is used in tooth paste, fireproof layers and insulation. It is also used in the manufacture of paints, varnishes etc.
9. *Chlorella* and *Synechococcus* are used in space vehicles and nuclear submarines to generate oxygen and water recycling.
10. Decomposition of sewage — *Scendesmus, Euglena, Chlorella* etc. help in decomposition of sewage by providing oxygen. After decomposition of sewage several inorganic nutrients are obtained.

NEGATIVE IMPORTANCE

There are some negative importance of algae as follows.

1. Toxicity — Several blue–green in the reservoirs cause death of fish and other domestic animals. Several toxic planktonic algae like *chlorella, Lynbya* etc. cause various disease syndrom of respiratory, gastric and skin infection.
2. Sometimes profound algal growth forms algal nets in which fishes are entangled and killed by chocking of mouth or gills.
3. Some kelps (sea-weeds) are attached to hulls and wood work of vessels and ships which retard the speed and shortened the life of the ships and vessels.

2. ECOLOGICAL IMPORTANCE OF ALGAE AND OTHER CRYPTOGAMES

There is a growing awareness towards the necessity of mass education about the fundamentals of interrelationship between man and his environment. With this view ecological importance of various groups of plants are discussed below :

It is well known that environmental pollution brings out changes in the biological system. Presence of algal bloom in the reservoirs cause unpleasant smell and taste to drinking water besides producing toxins and other such chemical compounds harmful to aquatic flora and fishes.

The green plants are the primary producers of the ecosystem. The planktonic algae serve as primary food for fishes and other aquatic animals. Algae like *Euglena, Spirogyra, Cladophora* etc. absorbs radioactive elements and heavy metals and thus minimises the pollution. Specific trophic condition can be assessed by the presence and dominance of a particular set of alga. Some silica scaled algal species like *Synura, Sphagnicola, Diatoms* etc. indicate the presence of acids and hence algae may be called as pollution indicators. Sometimes in small ponds, tanks or banks of streches of fresh water, free moving megaphytes like *Salvinia, Azolla, Riccia* and other hydrophytic angiosperms constitute Pleuston or Macroplankton or Hydrocharid formation. Various group of algae indicates various types of industrial wastes.

Lichens helps in plant succession on bare land and it prepares a base for the growth of advance group of plants. In xerosere the early developmental stages like crustose lichen stage, Foliose lichen stage and Moss stage are invaded by lichen and Mosses and it prepares a ground for the invasion of the land by higher angiospermic plants leading to climax forest stage.

Mosses are ecologically important. It helps in soil conservation and soil development during plant sucession either on bare lands or in ponds, lakes etc. After death and decay of these (Mosses and *Sphagnum*) plants, it form humus. The humus containing soil is favourable for growth of higher plants and in turn forests grow well on such soils. Mosses also check soil erosion. Thus, the members of cryptogames like algae, lichens, mosses, *Sphagnum* etc. have their ecological significance as soil binders, pollution indicators, primary producers and play a great role in plant succession on bare land, marshy land or watery land and so on.

3. RANGE OF THALLUS ORGANIZATION IN ALGAE

The algal bodies vary from unicellular to giant kelps. However, they lack vascular tissues. Following are the different forms of algal thalli.

Motile form — They may be (a) Unicellular : e.g. *Chlamydomonas*, (b) Coenobial : *Gonium* and (c) Colonial : e.g. *Volvox*.

Non–motile form — They may be (a) Unicellular : e.g. *Chlorococcum* and (b) Coenobial : e.g. *Hydrodictyon.*

Filamentous form — It develops from cell division in one plane with linear arrangement of daughter cells. They may be (a) Unbranched : e.g. *Zygnema*, (b) Branched : e.g. *Cladophora* and Pseudobranched : e.g. *Scytonema*

Thalloid form — It results after cell division in several planes. They may be (a) Tubular parenchymatous form : e.g. *Enteromorpha* and (b) Foliose parenchymatous form : e.g. *Ulva*

Heterotrichous form — In this form thallus has two parts : (1) prostrate system growing along the substratum and (2) erect system with branched filaments e.g. *Coleochaete*

Siphonaceous form — Here thallus is coenocytic i.e., nonseptate, multinucleate. It may be branched

(Vaucheria) or may be differentiated into rhizoidal system, rhizomatic system and erect system (*Caulerpa*)

Complex form — Thallus may have root, stem and leaf like organs as in *Laminaria.* In many red algae like *Polysiphonia* multiseriate thallus with cytoplasmic connections are found.

4. ORIGIN AND EVOLUTION OF SEX IN ALGAE

A review of reproductive processes of different divisions of algae is a pre-requisite to trace out the origin and evolution of sex in them. The simplest and primitive plants belong to the division Cyanophyta which lacks sexual reproduction.

In higher members of algae viz. Chlorophyta asexual reproduction occurs by means of motile zoospores and sexual reproduction is done by the fusion of two gametes. In *Chlamydomonas* and *Ulothrix* it was presumed that the asexual zoospores were produced earlier than the gametes for sexual reproduction. Therefore, the origin of sex is related with the origin of gametes. The gametes might have originated from zoospores which had become too small and weak to produce new individuals by themselves.

The methods of formation of zoospores and gametes in *Chlamydomonas* and *Ulothrix* are similar, except the size. The (+) and (-) gametes in isogamous algae resemble the zoospores. But in anisogamous forms male gametes are similar to zoospores. Zoospores give rise new individuals directly on germination where as gametes fuse in pair to produce diploid zygote whose nucleus divides meiotically and develops into new plant.

In *Ulothrix* two types of zoospores (Macro and Micro) are formed. The macrozoospore contains some factor responsible for the development of new plants. The microzoospores do not possess this factor and fails to develop into new plant. The accidental fusion of such microzoospores is presumed to restore the amount of factor for further development into new plants. This factor may be hormonal, electrical components or chemical. The difference in size in between macro and microzoospores is due to number of divisions of the parent protoplast. If this number or less, the products are larger (macrozoospores) and if this number is more, the products are smaller (microzoospores). The microzoospores behave either as asexual zoospores or gametes. Thus, sex in algae has originated as a result of accidental fusion between weaker microzoospores.

The next step of evolution of sexuality is from isogamy through anisogamy which are observed in *Chlamydomanas.* Formation of active (male) and passive (female) gametes are seen in *Spirogyra* during conjugation. Here the gametes are morphologically similar but physiologically different and hence anisogamy. In *Volvox* two anisogametes, one motile (smaller and male) and another non–motile (larger and female) unites during sexual reproduction. This is evolution of sexuality towards oogamy.

In *Chara, Dictyota* and others, there is highest step of sexual reproduction i.e. oogamous. Male gametes are produced in antheridium and female gametes are produced in oogonia. Oogonium contains a single female gamete i.e. egg whereas antheridium contains a large number of male gametes i.e. sperms.

In some species of *Ectocarpus* some larger gametes act as female gametes produced by withdrawing the cilia with which motile male gamete unites. It may be termed as heterogamy.

In *Fucus* and *Dictyota* the egg produced by oogonium is liberated out in water which unites with ciliated sperms in water. Fertilization is external i.e. outside the oogonium.

The members of Rhodophyceae show oogamous type of sexual reproduction. The male and female gametes are not sharply differentiated rather they are represented by protoplast without any differences from vegetative protoplast. Finally, the oospore is produced within the oogonium in oogamous mode of sexual reproduction. In *Coleochaete* the oospore is encircled by pseudoparenchymatous layer.

Thus, the evolution of sex in algae has taken place from simple to high (complex) type.

5. LIFE CYCLE IN ALGAE

Life cycle is the sequence of changes in cytological and/or morphological phases during the growth and development of the organism.

Drew (1955) has mentioned three types of life cycles in algae viz. (1) monomorphic or monophasic, (2) dimorphic or diphasic and (3) trimorphic or triphasic based on distinct morphological phases. On the basis of occurrence of haploid and diploid phases alternating with each other 5 types of life cycles can be visualized in algae. They are as such -

Haplontic — In this type of life cycle, the vegetative plant body is haploid ($1n$) or gametophyte. During sexual reproduction haploid gametes coming from two different parents (male and female or (+) and (-) strain) unite to produce diploid ($2n$) or sporophyte zygote. The nucleus of the zygote divides meiotically resulting in 4 haploid nuclei and further develop into 4 spores. These haploid spores give rise to haploid/gametophyte plant. Thus, there is alternation of haploid phase and single cell diploid phase (only $2n$ zygote). The majority of chlorophyceae like *Chlamydomonas*, *Ulothrix*, *Oedogonium* etc. show this type of life cycle.

Diplontic — In this type of life cycle the vegetative plant body is sporophyte i.e. diploid ($2n$). Sex organs produced on the sporophytic plant body give rise to gametes after reduction division (meiosis). Two haploid gametes fuse to form a diploid ($2n$) zygote. The diploid zygote divides and redivides in different planes to produce sporophytic plant. Here, gametophytic phase is represented by only gametes. Such type of life cycle is found in *Fucus*, diatoms etc.

Diplohaplontic — Here both the gametophytic and sporophytic phases are represented by two distinct vegetative individuals alternating each other. The gametophytic plant ($1n$) body produces sexually and the sporophytic plant ($2n$) produces haploid spores ($1n$) after meiotic division in spore mother cell which ultimately give rise to new haploid vegetative plant body. This type of life cycle is found in *Cladophora*, *Ectocarpus* etc.

Haplobiontic — In this type of life cycle haploid phase occurs twice. During sexual reproduction zygote ($2n$) is formed which divides meiotically to produce haploid cells. These haploid cells do not act as haploid spores, rather they divide to produce small vegetative individual known as carposporophyte as in *Batrachospermum*. The haploid carposporophyte obtains its nourishment from the parent gametophytic plant. The terminal cell of the carposporophyte act as carposporangium which produces haploid carpospore. The carpospore on liberation gives rise new haploid plant. Here the sporophytic ($2n$) phase is represented by only zygote.

Diplobiontic — Here diploid ($2n$) phase occurs twice in the life cycle. In *Polysiphonia* diploid zygote divides mitotically and not meiotically as in Batrachospermum to form diploid carposporophyte which are small and compact plantlet and lives on parent plant. The diploid carposporophyte produces diploid carposporangia which in turn give rise to diploid carpospore. The carpospore germinates to form free living tetrasporophyte. The $2n$ tetrasporophyte bears tetrasporangia which in turn produces haploid tetraspores after meiosis. These haploid tetraspores germinate to form gametophytic plant.

Here, there are two diploid free living phases (parent gametophyte and tetrasporophyte) and one haploid phase represented by tetraspores.

All these types of life cycles found in algae are represented in the following graphic sketches :

1.

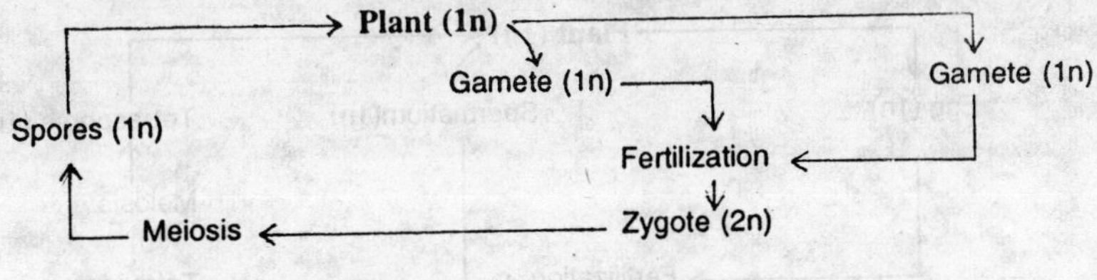

Haplontic life cycle as in *Ulothrix*.

2.

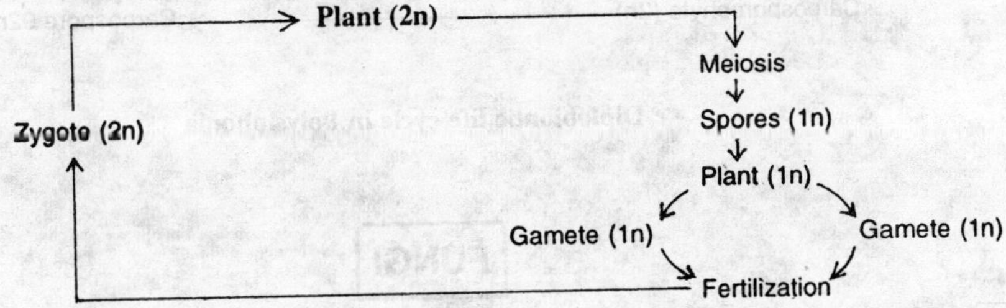

Diplohaplontic life cycle as in *Cladophora*.

3.

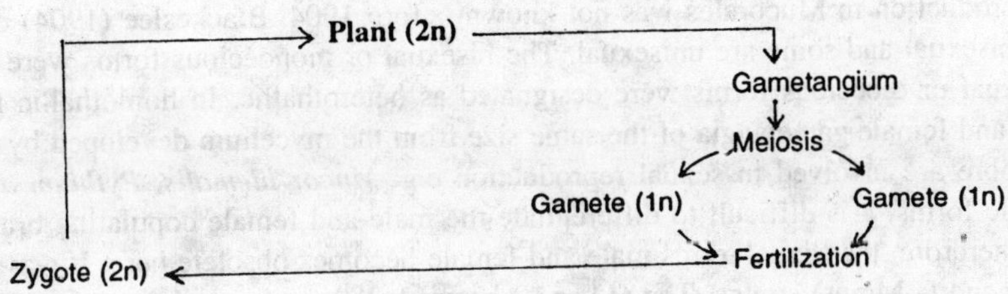

Diplontic life cycle as in *Fucus*.

4.

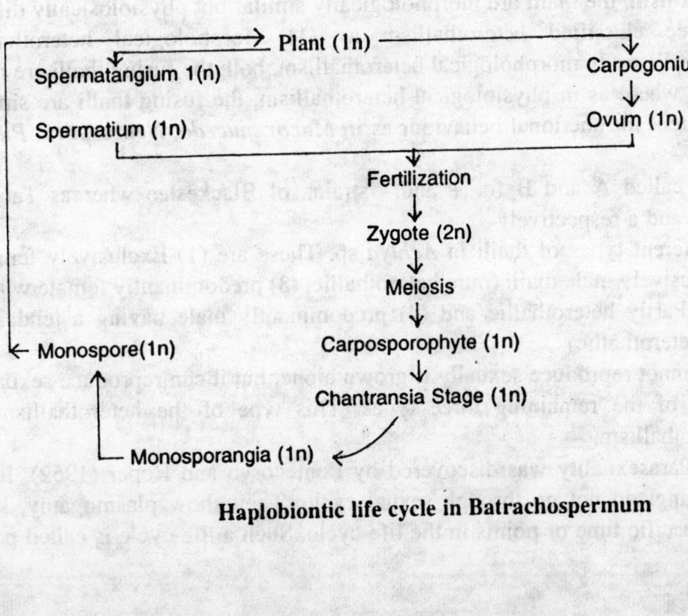

Haplobiontic life cycle in Batrachospermum

5.

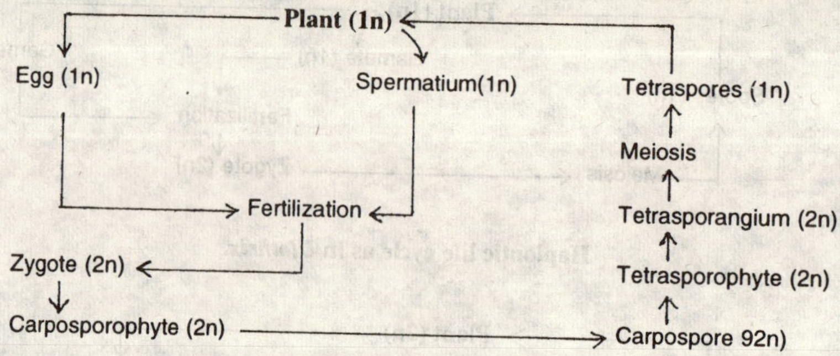

Diplobiontic life cycle in Polysiphonia

FUNGI

6. HETEROTHALLISM, PARASEXUALITY AND DEGENERATION OF SEX

Sexual reproduction in Mucorales was not known before 1904. Blackeslee (1904) observed that some fungi are bisexual and some are unisexual. The bisexual or monoecious forms were called homothallic and unisexual or dioecious forms were designated as heterothallic. In homothallic forms, two hyphae with male and female gametangia of the same size from the mycelium developed by the germination of a single spore are involved in sexual reproduction e.g. *Mucor hiemalis*, *Pythium debaryanum* etc. In heterothallic forms, it is difficult to differentiate the male and female copulating branches as in *Mucor mucedo*. Therefore, the sexual terms male and female becomes obsolete here. It was termed as mycelia of (+ Plus) and (- Minus) strains. The (+) or (-) heterothallic forms produce only sporangia and did not show sexual reproduction. The sexual reproduction occurs only when two different heterothallic forms (+ and -) intermixes with each other e.g. *Mucor mucedo*.

Thus, in **heterothallism**, the thalli are morphologically similar but physiolosically different.

Further, Blackeslee classified heterothallism as (1) Morphological heterothallism and (2) physiological heterothallism. In morphological heterothallism, both the fusing thalli are morphologically similar (*Saprolegnia*) where as in physiological heterothallism, the fusing thalli are similar in external morphology but different in functional behaviour as in *Mucor mucedo*, *Neurospora*, *Puccina graminis*, *Ustilago violacea* etc.

Shear and Dodge called A and B for + and - strains of Blackeslee whereas Tatum and Beadle designated these as A and a respectively

There are four different types of thalli in *Achlya* sp. These are (1) Exclusively female thalli (pure heterothallic) (2) exclusively male thalli (pure heterothallic, (3) predominantly female with a tendency to produce male thalli (Partly heterothallic and (4) predominantly male having a tendency to produce female thalli (Partly heterothallic)

These four types cannot reproduce sexually if grown alone, but it can reproduce sexually if grown in association with any of the remaining three types. This type of the heterothallism is known as Gynandromictic heterothallism.

Parasexuality — Parasexuality was discovered by Pontecorvo and Roper (1952). It has also been observed that some fungi do not go through sexual cycle. They show plasmogamy, karyogamy and meiosis but not at a specific time or points in the life cycle. Such a life cycle is called parasexual cycle and the phenomenon is known as parasexuality e.g. *Aspergillus midulans*. Following are the sequence of events in parasexual cycle.

Heterokaryosis — It is a process in which genetically different nuclei are associated in the same protoplast, and the resulting individual is known as heterokaryotic. Somatic hyphae of different genetic constituents are fused by anastomosis leading to dikaryotic mycelium as occurs in mushrooms and other basidiomycetes.

Karyogamy — Haploid nuclei of different genetic constituents as well as of same genetic constituents unite in heterokaryotic mycelium resulting in the formation of heterozygous diploid nucleus respectively.

Mitotic crossing over — During the multiplication of diploid nucleus, mitotic crossing over takes place. It forms mitotic recombinations. Such recombinations are important phase of parasexual cycle as it provides advantages of sexuality.

Formation of diploid strains — Diploid nuclei are incorporated into conidia which in turn germinate to produce diploid mycelia.

Haplodization — Some of the diploid nuclei undergo haplodization in the mycelium which in turn produces haploid conidia and subsequently germinate into haploid colonies.

Degeneration of sex — In Phycomycetes group of fungi, the sexual reproduction is oogamous, anisogamous and isogamous. In higher forms of Phycomycetes, Ascomycetes and Basidiomycetes, the sexual processes proceed with the progressive simplification of processes. It is generally termed as "degeneration of sex". The degeneration of sex means structural or functional degeneration of sex organs leading to simplification of the phenomenon and not the degeneration of sexuality. hence, this phenomenon may be termed as " simplification of sexual reproduction" in place of degeneration of sex". The members of Basidiomycetes do not possess sex organs but exhibit highest degree of sexuality.

In oomycetes, there is advanced type of sexual reproduction i.e. oogamy (oogonia and antheridia are well developed). In zygomycetes, the sexual reproduction involves gametangial copulation. In mucorales, the sexual reproduction occurs by means of conjugation of two similar coenogametangia of different physiological (+) and (–) strains.

There is a gradual and progressive deterioration of sexual phenomenon in different members of ascomycetes resulting in simplification of sexual reproduction. There is functional degeneration of anthridium followed by structural degeneration in *Aspergillus herbariorum*, *Collema pulposum* (a lichen) etc.

In Basidiomycetes, there is no trace of sex organs, but union takes place between hyphae of sexually distinct strains (+, -) leading to plasmogamy. Karyogamy takes place in young basidium.

The causative factor of such degeneration seems to be nutritional pattern of fungi. The heterophytic mode of nutrition in fungi necessisated the sexual process to be simple by degenerating the sex organs and only the karyogamy was maintained.

7. ECONOMIC IMPORTANCE OF FUNGI

Fungi show great economic importance. These may be beneficial or harmful as follows —

Beneficial economic importance — 1. *Destruction of organic waste*. Plant debris contain cellulose, lignin, cutin, suberin, starch, pectin, hemicellulose etc which are destroyed and digested by several members of fungi and bacteria.

2. *Fungi as food* — Mushrooms, yeasts and morels are eaten.

3. *Fungi and Industry* — Metabolic products of fungi like ethanol, penicillin, amylase etc. are manufactured at commercial level for the use of mankind.

4. *Bread making* — *Sacchromyces cerevisiae* are used by bakers in Bread making. It causes alcoholic fermentation producing CO_2 which makes bread spongy.

5. Fungi in medicine — Several medicines including penicillin and other antibiotics are manufactured from different genera of fungi.

6. *Fungi and enzymes, vitamines* — Several enzymes like invertase, amylase, protease, pectinase, oxidase etc. and vitamin B and D are obtained from fungi.

7. *Fungi and insecticide* — Entomogenous fungi viz. *Isaria farinosa, Empusa sipulchralis* help in elimiation of moth pupa.

Harmful activities of fungi — 1. Many fungi causes disease in plants, animals and human beings as shown in the following tables 1 & 2.

Table - 1. *Some of the diseases in plants caused by fungi.*

Causal organism	*Disease*	*Host*
1. *Cystopus candidus*	White rust	Crucifers
2. *Ustilago tritici*	Loose smut	Wheat
3. *Puccinia graminis*	Stem rust	Wheat
4. *Colletotrichum falcatum*	Red rot	Sugarcane
5. *Phytophthora infestans*	Late blight	Potato
6. *Peronospora pisi*	Downy mildew	Pea

Table-2. Some of the diseases in animals caused by fungi

Causal organism	*Diseases*
1. Hemophilous influenzae	Influenza
2. *Mycobacterium tuberculosae*	Tuberculosis
3. *Aspergillus*	Apergillosis of human being ear–drums
4. *Diplococcus pneumoniae*	Pneumonia
5. *Eberthella*	Typhoid
6. *Cornybacterium diphtheriae*	Diphtheria
7. *Microsporum andoouini*	Dhobitch of man

2. Decaying of fallen timber and standing trees — *Polyporus scheweimitzil* causes rot in the fallen timber. Similarly, several basidiomycetes fungi cause heart rot in the standing tree.
3. *Spoilage of textile products — Alternaria, Penicillium* etc spoil woolen garments, *Fusarium, Rhizopus* destroy cotton garments.
4. *Spoilage of paper, leather, rubber, paint* etc.— These are also spoiled by *Cladosporium herbarium, Aspergillus niger, Rhizopus nigricans* respectively.
5. *Spoilage of food* — Dairy products are destroyed by *Mucor, Penicillium* etc. *Penicillium digitatum* spoils orange. Mucor spoils bread, *Neurospora, Aspergillus* spoil meat and so on.
6. *Damage to electrical/optical instruments* — Certain molds spoil the insulated cables, radio sets etc. Camera lenses are damaged by actinomycetous fungus.

8. DIFFERENCES BETWEEN ALGAE AND FUNGI

Though both the groups i.e. algae and fungi belong to division thallophyta of the plant kingdom, they differ in the following features :—

	ALGAE		FUNGI
1.	It possess Photosynthetic pigments	1.	They are devoid of such pigments.
2.	They are autotrophs	2.	They are heterotrophs and may live as either parasites or saprophytes.
3.	Algae are photophilic	3.	Fungi are either Photophilic or Photophobic.
4.	Algal bodies are made up of true parenchymatous tissue	4.	Fungal bodies are made up of fine thread like structure called mycellium or plectenchyma— an interwoven mass of mycelium or pseudoparenchyma.
5.	They are prokaryotic as well as eukaryotic	5.	Fungi are eukaryotic
6.	Cell wall is made up of true cellulose	6.	Cell wall is made up of nitrogenous compound, chitin and rarely of fungus-cellulose.
7.	In majority of them reserve food is carbohydrate (Starch).	7.	They possess glycogen as reserve food.

BRYOPHYTA

9. ECONOMIC IMPORTANCE OF BRYOPHYTES

Bryophytes have the following economic importance —

1. *Marchantia polymorpha* can be used to cure pulmonary tuberculosis as suggested by Roig Y, Mesa (1945)
2. Antitumor properties of *Marchantia polymorpha* & *Polytrichum commune* have been suggested by Hartwell (1971)
3. Banerjee and Sen (1979) reported antibiotic activity of 40 genera of Bryophyta.
4. Roque (1941) has mentioned the use of *Polytrichum commune* to dissolve stones of kidney and gall blader.
5. Walkinton (1966) mentioned the antibiotic activities of several species of Mosses.
6. Mechanism of sex determination in plants was reported firstly in *Sphaerocarpus* by Allen (1935, 45).
7. Because of great absorbent power and slight antiseptic properties of *Sphagnum*, it is used in surgical dressing.
8. Peat contains partially decomposed and carbonised dead plants deposits of *Sphagnum* and other mosses. Peat is used as fuel.
9. Cellulose in the peat is converted into alcohol.

10. Ammonium sulphate can be obtained as a bi–product during the production of gas from peat.
11. Tanning materials, nitrates etc. have been produced from peat.
12. *Sphagnum* is used as a packing material for shipment of live plants, cut flowers, vegetable and other perishable fruits, as it retains enough moisture for a long time.
13. The accumulation of heavy metal in mosses is used as pollution indicators.
14. The luxuriant growth of moss as thick carpet helps in soil conservation.
15. Mosses play an important role in the formation of soil and subsequent development of vegetation.
16. Weaver and Clements (1938) mentioned that mosses play a significant role in bog succession from open water to climax forest.
17. Certain mosses like *Bryum*, *Hypnum* etc. growing in association with other aquatic plants like *Chara* and other algae play an important role as rock builders. These plants growing in various water bodies having huge amount of calcium carbonate, bring about decomposition of bicarbonic ions. As a result of which insoluble calcium carbonate precipitates and harden to form calcarious or lime rock like deposits. These deposits are used as a building stone.

10. METHODS OF SPORE DISPERSAL IN BRYOPHYTES

The spores are produced within the sporogonium (Sporophyte) from the spore mother cell. They are haploid, minute uninucleate and spherical in out line. It represents the first cell generation of gametophytic or haploid generation. The methods of spore dispersal greatly varies in different genera of Bryophytes depending upon the structure and position of sporophyte as follows.

In Riccia :- It has no special mechanism for spore dispersal. The sporogonium/sporophyte is globular in appearance embeded in the gametophytic tissue. Just before the maturation of spore, wall of capsule disintegrates. Outer layer of calyptra and adjacent tissue decays and spores are left in the soil which are later dispersed to longer distance by the wind.

In Marchantia :- The dispersal of spores in *Marchantia* takes place with the help of hygroscopic movement of elaters. Sterile elaters are with annular thickenings. Wall of capsule splits longitudinaly into several lobes exposing spores and elaters. Hygroscopic elaters loosen the spores which are then carried by wind.

In Pellia :- The method of spore dispersal in *Pellia* is same as that of *Marchantia.* Separation of spores is assisted by hygroscopic movement of elaters. The flicking to and fro of elaterophores helps in the gradual shedding of spores. After dispersal of spores, the elaterophores stands like a column in the centre of four spreading valves.

In Porella :- Here the spores are dispersed by splitting of capsule wall into four longitudinal valves. Elaters help in the dispersal of spores.

Ingold (1939) has mentioned three mechanism of spore dispersal in Hepaticopsida viz. (1) Water rupturing mechanism seen in leafy jungermanniaceae, (2) hygroscopic mechanism as in *Marchantia* and Metzgerineae and (3) spiral spring mechanism observed in Frullaniaceae and Lejeuneaceae.

In Anthoceros :- The spores are discharged and dispersed with the help of pseudoelaters. Ripe capsule of *Anthoceros* dehisces basipetally along two longitudinal splits which extends downward from near the apex. On drying, the valves become spirally twisted owing to reversible hygroscopic reaction of pseudoelaters. This results in shedding of spores which may be scattered by air currents. Similar mechanism are also seen in *Notothylas.* However, Pandey (1932) has reported follicullar dehiscence of spores by one suture in *Notothylas.*

In Sphagnum :- Spore dispersal in *Sphagnum* takes place by air pressure developed in the spore sac during dry condition. The capsule dehisces by an explosive mechanism on sunny day. According to Nawaschin (1897) the capsule ruptures violently with audiable sound. As the capsule wall dries and shrinks in sunny day, the spherical capsule becomes cylindrical. On shrinkage of capsule wall, the thickened lid cell resists the shrinkage, annulus gets strain the ruptures under the pressure of air within. This loosen the convex lid which is then blown off. The imprisoned air is released with the spores as a cloud of spores which is taken away by the wind causing dispersal of spores. This mechanism is known as "Air gun" mechanism.

In Mosses :- In mosses like *Funaria, Polytricum, Pogonatum* etc. the sporophytes are of advance type. In *Funaria* at the apex of capsule there is a cup like operculum around the base of which is ring of cells known as annulus. Inner most layer of operculum contains rows of teeth forming peristome which is hygroscopic. During dehiscence annulus ruptures, operculum is thrown off exposing the peristome. The spores are dispersed gradually by the activity of peristomial teeth which are hygroscopic in nature. Seta helps in dispersal of spores which are ultimately disseminated by air.

In Polytricum :- Spores are dispersed by censor mechanism. There are pore capsule in *Polytrichum* in which the teeth of peristome are united with the epiphragm. There is a small opening at the margin of the epiphragm between the teeth through which the spores are escaped out as the capsule sways by the force of the wind.

In Pogonatum :- When mature capsule dries up the operculum falls off and the cells between teeth and the tympanum break forming a cylindrical slit though which spores come out.

11. SMALL AND INCONSPICUOUS NATURE OF BRYOPHYTES

Due to the following features Bryophytes remain small and inconspicuous.

1. Haploid plant body.
2. Absence of root and vascular tissue required for large growth.
3. Vascular elements essential for water and food conduction were never formed.
4. Mechanical tissue with thick walled, long fibrous cells are never differentiated.
5. Secondary meristems to give thickness and additional cortication were not formed.
6. Presence of thin walled porous thallus.
7. Depends on water for fertilization.

12. BRYOPHYTES WITHSTAND LONG PERIOD OF DROUGHT.

Majority of Bryophytes can withstand long period of drought due to some adaptive characters met with them as follows.

1. The thalloid plant bodies of Bryophytes are covered with epidermis containing air pores which helps to protect descication.
2. The concealed position of ovum in the archegonum and its retention in situ, after fertilization provides protection against the drying influence of air.
3. Thick walled spores and
4. Primitive vascular system in the form of conducting strands are other adaptations to withstand long period of drought.

13. BRYOPHYTES HAVE ADAPTED LAND HABIT

Bryophytes are regarded as amphibians of plant kingdom i.e. neither aquatic nor terrestrial. They are originated from algal stock as evidenced by the retention of swimming habit of male gametes. Following are the adaptive features of Bryophytes acquired for land habit.

1. Development of organs (rhizoids) for attachment and absorption of water.

2. Epidermis, with air pores and coated with waxy substance.
3. Gaseous exchange through air pores.
4. Sex organs protected by multicellular jacket layer. It protects reproductive cells from drying and mechanical injury.
5. Retention of zygote within the archegonium serves double purpose namely, (a) ensures water and food supply from the parent plant body during the development of multicellular embryo and (b) affords protection from drying out.
6. Formation of thick walled wind spores.

14. PHYLOGENY OF BRYOPHYTES

Phylogeny of Bryophytes or the origin and evolution of Bryophytes includes the study of historical development of evolutionary lines in Bryophytes. Nothing definite is known about the phylogeny of Bryophytes. No fossil forms more primitive than the present day Bryophytes are known. The views on its phylogeny must be based on the following evidences.

1. Evidences from the comparative morphology of the living taxa.
2. Evidences from the ontogeny (anatomy of phylogeny) of the living plants.
3. Evidences based on analogies of the living plants of other groups.

There are two main views regarding the origin of Bryophytes.

A. *Pteridophytean hypothesis* — Supported by Lang, (1917), Scott, (1924), Kashyap (1919), Haskel (1949), Christenson (1954) and Proskaur (1960).

B. *Algal hypthesis* — Supported by Bower, (1900), Cavers (1911), Smith (1955), Campbell (1936), and Fritsch (1916).

Pteridophytean hypothesis — According to this view, Bryophytes have originated from Pteridophytes on the basis of the following features —

1. Close similarity between sex organs of the two groups.
2. Resemblance between the sporogonioum of *Anthoceros* and terminal sporangium of *Horneophyton.*

Besides, similarities in the pigments, structure of cell wall, reserve food, reproductive methods and life cycle support the view that Bryophytes have evolved from Pteridophytes by progressive reduction or simplification.

But due to complete absence of relics of vascular tissue in the sporophytes of Bryophytes, this theory has been cancelled by many others.

Algal hypothesis — According to this hypothesis, Bryophytes have evolved from Algae having aquatic mode of life as follows —

1. Occurrence of flagellated sperms in Bryophtes which requires the free water for fertilization is a clear sign of aquatic ancestry.
2. The development of filamentous algae like protonema in the life cycle shows the algal origin of Bryophytes. It is a biological principle that the juvenile stage of an organism resembles its ancestral form.
3. On the basis of identical photosynthetic pigments (chlorophyll & xanthophyll) essentially thallus like plant body without vascular tissue, starch as reserve food, cell wall of cellulose, type and number of flagella in the male gamets — *Chlorophycean* hypothesis of the origin of Bryophytes has been favoured.

Smith (1955) has suggested " Fritschiella" member of chaetophoraceae — as the probable primitive ancestral form from which Bryophytes have evolved.

Systematic Position of Bryophytes — The Bryophytes resembles with Algae on one hand and

Pteridophytes on the other hand, hence it should be placed in between Algae (Thallophyta) and Pteridophtes.

15. VEGETATIVE REPRODUCTION IN BRYOPHYTES

Correns (1899) and Cavers (1903) have described the various means of vegetative reproduction in Bryophytes as follows —

1. *By death and decay of the older parts of the thallus* : As soon as the plant becomes mature, the older parts start to degenerate up to the point of dichotomy. The living branches separated out and develop into new plants as in *Riccia, Marchantia, Pellia, Anthoceros* etc.
2. *By growing apices* — In dry condition the thalli of *Riccia, Anthoceros* and others die excepting its growing apices. The growing apical parts remain burried in the soil till the adverse condition. On return of favourable season it develop into new thalli.
3. *By the formation of adventitious branches* — The adventitious branches are produced on the ventral sides of the thalli which separate out and give rise new plants. For example *Riccia, Marchantia* etc.
4. *By tubers* — Such tubers are formed in *Riccia, Anthoceros* and *Notothylas*. It gives rise to new thalli.
5. By gemmae — Gemmae are formed within the gemma cup. It may be multicellular, stalked and discoid as in *Marchantia* and *Lunularia*. On detachment from gemma cup, the rhizoidal cell of gemmae develops into rhizoid and new thalli originate from the marginal notches of the gemmae. In *Porella rotundifolia* gemmae are produced on the leaves. In *Funaria* gemmae are produced on protonemal branches.
6. *By death and decay of rhizoids* — In *Funaria* the prostrate rhizoids give rise to erect branches which develops into new independent plants.
7. *By Protonema* — Protonema are formed after germination of spores in Mosses.
   The primary protonema bears buds which give rise new plants. Any parts of moss plant may develop secondary protonema and subsequently new plants.
8. *By resting buds* — Sometimes in Mosses, buds are formed on the protonema or rhizoids. On favourable condition it develops into new plants.
9. *By creeping shoot* — In *Funaria* sp. long axis gives rise to creeping shoot with reduced leaves which becomes separated and develops into new plant.

16. STERILIZATION OF SPOROGENOUS TISSUE IN BRYOPHYTES

There is progressive evolution of sporophytes in Bryophytes which is associated with sterilization of sporogenous tissue. This theory of Bower (1890) was supported by Cavers (1910) and Campbell (1918). According to this view the sporophyte of *Riccia* is the most primitive and simple while that of *Funaria* is the most advance and complex as follows.

In Riccia — After fertilization, the zygote divides and redivides to form multicellular globular structure (embryo). Periclinal division takes place in the 30 celled embryo which differentiates into outer amphithecium and inner endothecium. Endothecium gives rise to sporogenous tissue. Amphithecium forms only one layered jacket of the sporogonium which are negligible in comparison to sporogenous tissue. The sporogenous tissue gives rise to spores and nurse cells. Thus, the sporophyte of *Riccia* is the simplest sporophyte among Bryophytes. There is no foot or seta and no sterilization of sporogenous tissue.

In Marchantia — The endothecium gives rise archesporium and subsequently mass of sporogenous tissue. The sporogenous cells elongate to form elaters and 32 spore mother cells which divides meiotically to form haploid spores. Thus each sporogenous cell gives rise either one elater or 32 x 4 = 128 spores (1n).

The mature sporogenium is elognated structure differentiated into foot, seta and capsule. Capsule has a sterile jacket within which long, narrow and spirally coiled sterile elaters and spherical spores are found. It shows a step towards progressive sterilization of sporogenous tissue.

In Pellia — The archesporium in *Pellia* develops from andothecium. The sporogenous cells in the centre produce elaters, elaterophores and spore mother cells. The mature sporophyte consists of foot, seta and capsule. In this case more sterilization of sporogenous tissue.

In Anthoceros — In this case, the entire endothecium remains sterile and forms a central sterile region called columella. The archesporium develops from amphithecium and overarches the apex of the columella. The sporogenous cells form spore mother cells and pseudoelaters. The mature sporophyte or sporogonium is a cylindrical structure, consists of bulbous foot, slender and erect capsules, (2 - 3 cm) above the gametophytic thallus. The seta is reduced or absent. The columella is surrounded by sporogenous tissue which produces spores and pseudoelaters. The capsule wall is of 2 - 6 layers of cell, having stomata on the epidermal layer.

In sphagnum — In *sphagnum* endothecium divides to form columella. The amphithecium divides to produce inner fertile region and outer jacket layer of capsule. The columella is surrounded by arch shaped sporogenous tissue developed from inner layer of amphithecium.

In Funaria — There is more sterilization of sporogenous tissue in *Funaria*. Here the zygote divides transversely into epibasal and hypobasal cells. One apical cell is cut off by the hypobasal cell which gives rise to capsule with few fertile tissue. The sterile tissue is represented by operculum, peristome, epidermis, central columella and apophysis. The fertile region is hardly 1%. Thus, it is clear that Bower's theory of sterilization offer a possible explanation in upward direction.

Reduction theory — It was thought by Kashyap (1919), Church, Goebel and Evans (1939) and held that the evolution of sporophyte in Bryophyte is retrogressive i.e. downward and it is accompanied by simplification of the sporophytic structure in series. According to this view the simplest sporophyte of *Riccia* is highly evolved or advanced but reduced due to progressive simplification. The significant serial reduction in sporophyte is as follows:

1. Presence of simple dehiscense apparatus or mechanism.
2. No photosynthetic tissue in capsule wall.
3. Disappearance of stomata and intercellular spaces in capsule wall.
4. Decrease in thickness of capsule wall.
5. Elimination of foot and seta.
6. Elimination of elaters.
7. Increase in fertility of sporogenous cells.

PTERIDOPHYTA

17. STELAR SYSTEM AND ITS EVOLUTION

Central core of axis is known as stele. Van Tieghem and Douliot (1886) proposed stelar theory. According to them stele includes xylem, phloem, pericycle, vascular rays and pith, if present. Stele is a real entity and present in all axis of plants. Endodermis is in between cortex and stele. Jeffrey was the first to interpret the stelar theory from phylogenetic point of view. According to him protostele is the most primitive type of stele consisting of central xylem surrounded by phloem and all other types of stele have been derived from the protostele during the course of evolution.

DIFFERENT TYPES OF STELE FOUND IN PTERIDOPHYTES

Protostele — Solid mass of xylem surrounded by phloem e.g. *Lycopodium.*

Haplostele — Central xylem, smooth in outline, sourrounded by concentric layers of phloem, Brebner (1902) introduced the term Haplostele e.g. *Lygodium, Rhynia* etc.

Actinostele — A term actinostele used by Brebner (1902) has central xylem with radiating ribs. Phloem is present in separate groups which alternate with the distant ends of the star shaped or stellate xylem.

Plectostele — Xylem is broken into several parallel plates. Such parallel xylem plate alternate with phloem plates. Zimmermann (1930) called such a stele as plectostele.

Mixed plectostele with pith — In this type central protostele is occupied by the parenchymatous cells among the tracheids e.g. *Hymenophyllum dilatum.*

Mixed protostele — When xylem groups are uniformly scattered in the ground mass of phloem it is called mixed protostele e.g. *Lycopodium cernuum.*

Siphonostele — In this type of stele, centrally placed xylem is replaced by parenchymatous cells known as pith. The pith is surrounded by xylem and hence siphonostele is medullated protostele. In Transverse section at different levels from base upwards in genera like *Gleichenia, Botrydium, Anemia* etc. different stages of changing of protostele into siphonostele are seen (Fig. 73)

PHYLOGENY AND ORIGIN OF SIPHONOSTELE

Two views have been proposed regarding the origin of siphonostele from protostele and they are as follows:

(1) **Extrasteler origin of pith** : Jeffrey (1902) suggested that parenchymatous tissue internal to the phloem and xylem is cortical in origin by invasion of cortical parenchymatous cells into the stele. The invasion takes place through the leaf and branch gaps. Presence of an inner endodermis proves that the parenchymatous cells encircled by this endodermis are cortical in origin. But such cortical invasion is practically impossible which would produce polycylic siphonostele.

(2) **Intrastelar origin of pith** : The another view proposed by Boodle (1901) and Gwynne-Vanghan (1903). A siphonostele originated from a protostele by a metamorphosis of the inner vascular elements into parenchyma and the origin of pith is intraxylic. The mixed pith in the protostele may be considered as a transitional stage between true protostele and true siphonostele. Eames (1936) and Eames and MacDaniels (1947) put forwarded a third view that the pith is interstelar in origin in some of the pteridophytes like some Lycopods and in others like higher ferns, where the pith is extrastelar in origin.

Types of siphonostele — According to Jeffrey (1898) siphonosteles are of two types (a) Ectophloic siphonostele and (b) Amphiphloic siphonostele.

Ectophloic siphonostele — In this type phloem is restricted to the external face of xylem.

Amphiphloic siphonostele — It is siphonostele with phloem both internal and external to the xylem. The origin of internal phloem is by intrusion and hence amphiphloic siphonostle is more primitive than an ectophloic siphonostele.

Modification of siphonostele — Jeffrey (1910) coined the term cladosiphonic siphonostele to such siphonostele which is without leaf gap e.g. *Selaginella.*

Phyllosiphonic siphonostele — It is siphonostele perforated with small or large leaf gaps as in members of Filicophyta.

Solenostele — It is siphonostele perforated at one or more places corresponding to the origin of leaf trace. It may be of following types.

Ectophloic solenostele — In this perforated solenostele phloem is present on the outer side only.

Amphiphloic solenostele — It is perforated solenostele in which phloem is present on both the sides

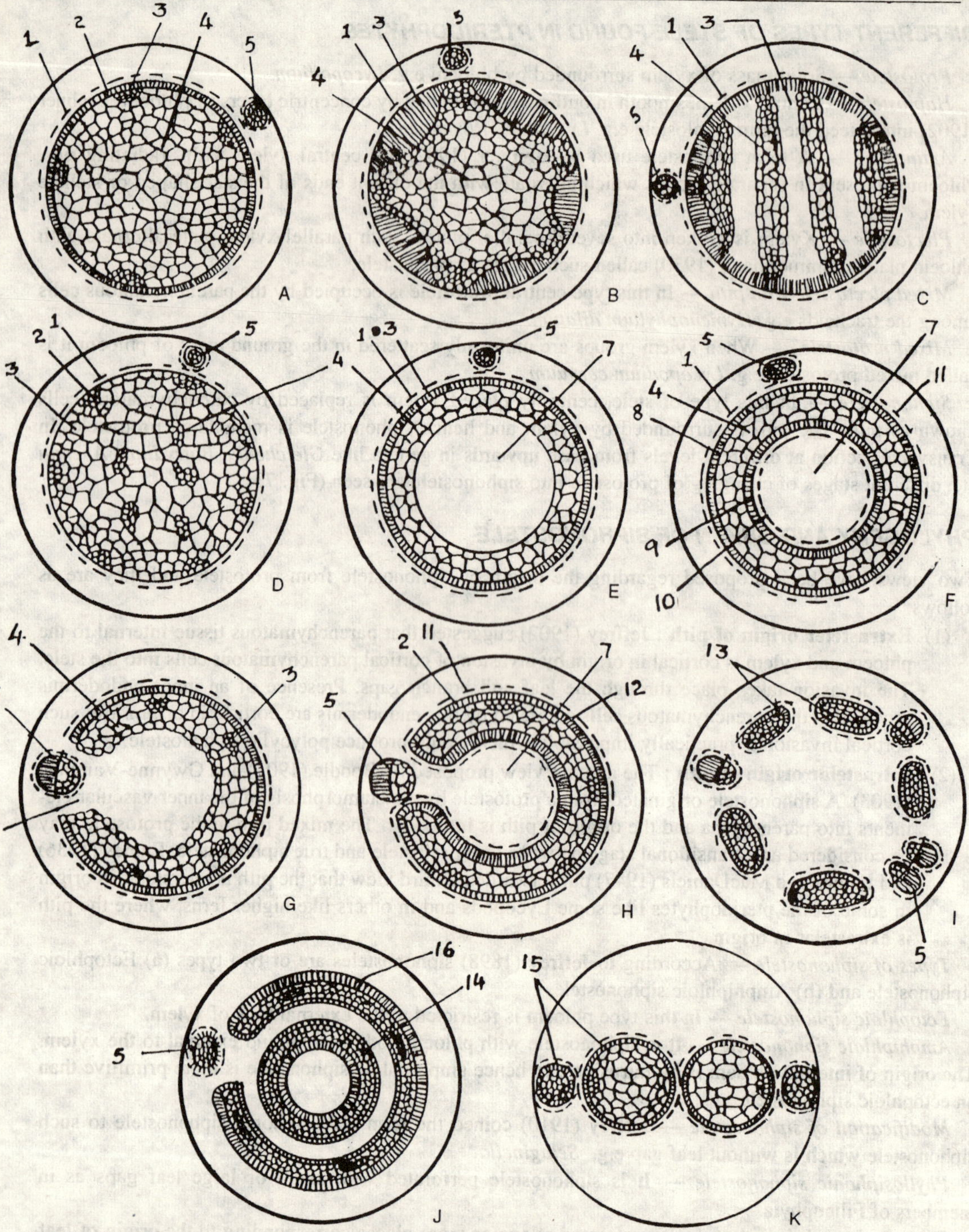

Fig. 73. Various types of stele found in Pteridophytes (diagrammatic view) (a) Haplostele (b) Actinostele (c) Plectostele (d) Mixed protostele (e) Ectophloic siphonostele (f) Amphiphioic siponostele (g) Ectophloic solenostele (h) Amphiphloic solenostele (i) Dictyostele (j) Polycyclic solenostele and (k) Polystele.
In each figure 1 = Endodermis, 2 = Pericycle, 3 = Phloem, 4 = Xylem, 5 = leaf trace, 6 = leaf gap, 7 = pith, 8 = Outer phloem, 9 = Inner phloem, 10 = Inner endodermis, 11 = Outer endodermis, 12 = Outer pericycle 13 = Meristeles, 14 = Siphonostelic cylinder, 15 = st

of xylem e.g. *Adiantum pedatum.*

Dictyostele — In this type of solenostele, leaf gaps are more than one and overlapping. The part of vascular tissue lying in between two gaps is known as meristele. Each meristele is protostelic in nature as in *Dryopteris.*

Eustele — It is modified form of ectophloic siphonostele. In eustele, the stele is split into distinct collateral vascular bundle. The splitting occurs due to overlapping of leaf gaps e.g. dicot stem.

Atactostele — According to Esaue (1953) it is another condition of eustele in which vascular strands are scattered e.g. monocot stem.

Polycyclic stele — It is always siphonostelic having an internal vascular system connected with an outer siphonostele. Generally, it has two or more concentric vascular cylinders e.g. *Pteridium aquilinum.* It may be polycyclic solenostele or polycyclic dictyostele.

Polycyclic dictyostele — It is polycyclic stele having an outer cylinder of dictyostele.

Polycyclic solenostele — In this type outer cylinder is of solenostele.

Polystele — In some axis more than one stele are present. This condition is called polystelic. Each stele is protostele and hence it might have originated from protostele e.g. *Selaginella* (Fig. 74).

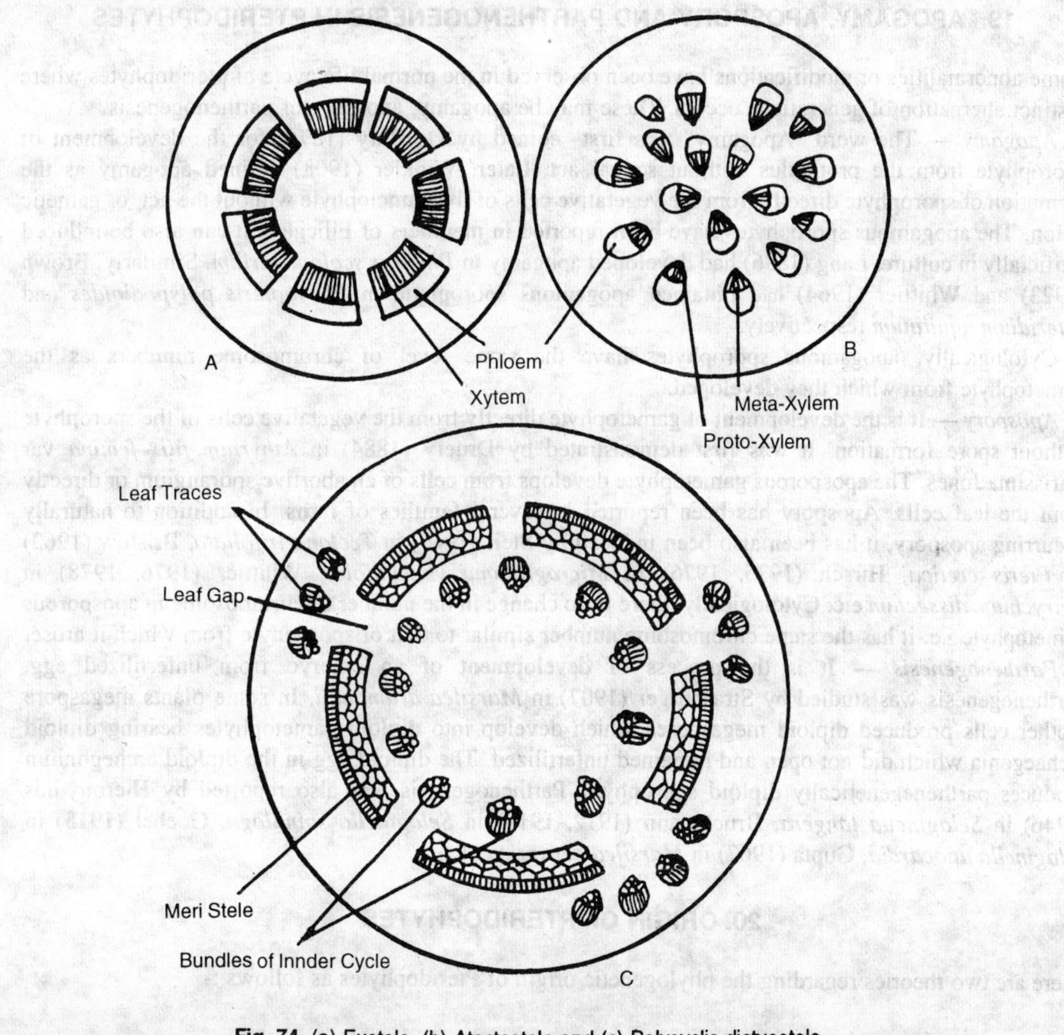

Fig. 74. (a) Eustele, (b) Atactostele and (c) Polysyclic dictyostele.

18. ECONOMIC IMPORTANCE OF PTERIDOPHYTES

Members of Pteridophytes are important in several ways as follows :

During Christmas festival *Lycopodium* and *Selaginella* are used as garland and for various kinds of table decoration. The spores of *Lycopodium* are highly inflammable and are used for producing stage lighting under the name of "vegetable Brimstone". *Lycopodium* is of medicinal value and is used as a stimulant for kidney. *Selaginella pilifera* and *S. lepidophylla* are famous for the periodic changes in the colour of their leaves and are sold under the name "resurrection plants". The corm of *Isoetes* are eaten by ducks and other aquatic animals. The stem of *Equisetum* is used for polishing alloy dishes, floor and furniture. *Equisetum* species are used as indicators of mineral content in the soil in which they grow. It is also used in promoting the discharge of urine. Ferns are of ornamental value too and enhances the beauty of glass houses and the gardens. Tree ferns are used in the building of houses. The stalk and leaves of *Marsilea* are used as vegetables. The natives of Australia prepares cakes from the starchy paste of sporocarps of *Marsilea drumondii*. *Pteris* and *Dryopteris* are of medicinal value. All most all Pteridophytes take part in coal formation.

19. APOGAMY, APOSPORY AND PARTHENOGENESIS IN PTERIDOPHYTES

Some abnormalities or modifications have been observed in the normal life cycle of pteridophytes where distinct alternation of generations occurs. These may be apogamy, apospory or parthenogenesis.

Apogamy — The word "Apogamy" was first coined by De Bary (1878) for the development of sporophyte from the prothallus without sexual act. Later, Winkler (1908) defined apogamy as the formation of sporophyte directly from the vegetative cells of the gametophyte without the act of gametic union. The apogamous sporophytes have been reported in members of Filicales. It can also be induced artificially in culture. Lang (1896) had developed apogamy in *Phyllitis scolopendrium*. Similarly, Brown (1923) and Whittier (1964) had obtained apogamous sporophyte in *Pheyopteris polypodioides* and *Pteridium aquilinum* respectively.

Cytologically, apogamous sporophytes have the same level of chromosome numbers as the gametophyte from which they developed.

Apospory — It is the development of gametophyte directly from the vegetative cells of the sporophyte without spore formation. It was first demonstrated by Druery (1884) in *Athyrium filix–femina* var clarissima Jones. The aposporous gametophyte develops from cells of an abortive sporangium or directly from the leaf cells. Apospory has been reported in several families of ferns. In addition to naturally occurring apospory, it has been also been induced by Steil (1944) in *Tectona trifoliata*, Bristow (1962) in *Pteris cretica*, Hirsch (1975, 1976) in *Microgramma vaccinifolia*, Whittier (1976, 1978) in *Botrychium dissectum* etc. Cytologically, there is no change in the number of chromosome in aposporous gametophyte i.e. it has the same chromosome number similar to that of sporophyte from which it arose.

Parthenogenesis — It is the process of development of an embryo from unfertilized egg. Parthenogenesis was studied by Strasburger (1907) in *Marsilea drumondii*. In some plants megaspore mother cells produced diploid megaspores which develop into diploid gametophytes bearing diploid archaegonia which did not open and remained unfertilized. The diploid egg in the diploid archegonium produces parthenegenetically diploid sporophyte. Parthenogenesis was also reported by Hieronymus (1946) in *Selaginella langera*, Bruchmann (1912, 1919) in *Selaginella spinnloga*, Goebel (1915) in *Selaginella anocardia*, Gupta (1962) in *Marsilea aegyptica* etc.

20. ORIGIN OF PTERIDOPHYTES

There are two theories regarding the phylogenetic origin of Pteridophytes as follows :-

THEORY OF ALGAL ORIGIN

According to this theory Pteridophytes originated from Algae on the basis of existence of similarities in between Pteridophytes and some part of Algae. According to Fritsch (1945) Pteridophytes originated from chaetophoraceous type of filamentous algae having alternation of generation and erect vegetative body like Pteridophytes.

Arnold *et al.*, (1947) suggested the origin of Pteridophytes either from brown algae or from green algae.

THEORY OF BRYOPHYTIC ORIGIN

This theory was supported by Campbell (1899, 1924) Bower (1935), Zimmermann (1938) and others on the basis of similarities found in some bryophytes and pteridophytes as mentioned below.

1. General similarities in between the gametophytic structure of *Riccia*, *Anthoceros* etc. and prothallus of *Equisetum,* ferns etc.
2. Similarities in the structure of sex organs in both bryophytes and pteridophytes.
3. Retention of embryo in the venter of the archegonium and partial dependence of young sporophyte upon the gametophyte in both the groups.
4. Occurrence of heteromorphic alternation of generation. Campbell believed that pteridophytes originated from *Anthoceros* on the following features.
   (a) Presence of indefinite growth of sporophyte with chlorophyllous tissue of *Anthoceros* may develop into fern like sporophyte of pteridophytes.
   (b) The sporophyte of *Anthoceros* may exist independently if it is allowed to grow.

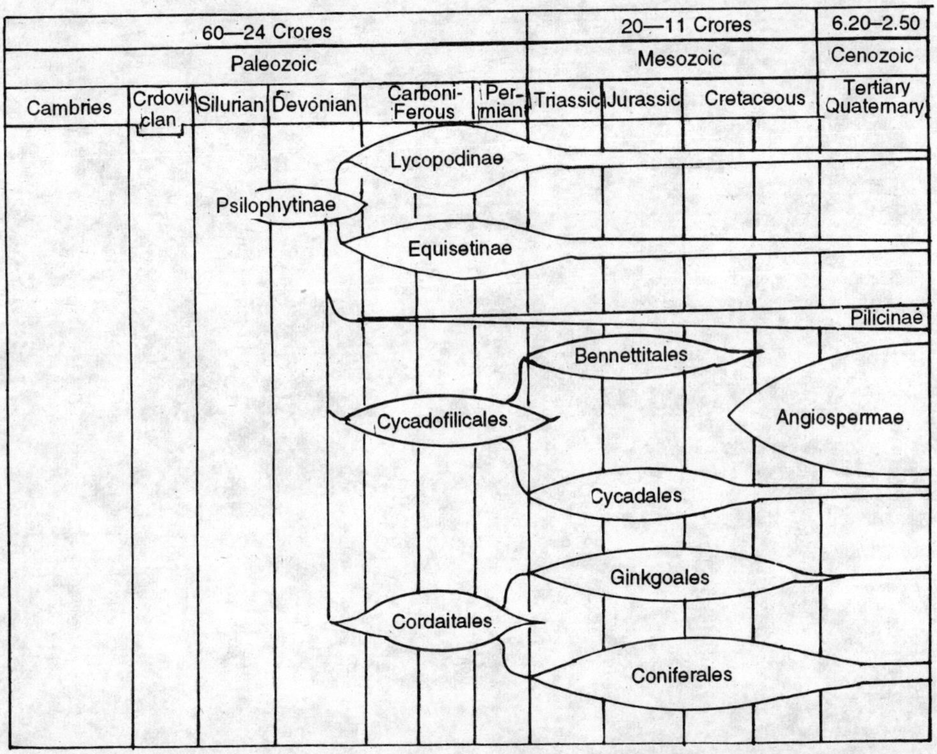

Fig. 75. Chart showing Geological history of vascular plants and their apparent relationships.

(c) The primitive psilophytean plants with rootless and leafless shoot indicates the anthocerotean origin of pteridophytes.

(d) If the meristematic zone of sporophyta of *Anthoceros* is shifted from base to apex, development of dichotomous branch may take place and sporangia may develop terminally on the branch which would resemble closely with the sporophyte of *Psilotum* or *Rhynia*. In this way *Anthoceros* exhibits beginning of condition towards the origin of Pteridophytes in which columella of *Anthoceros* sporophyte may become differentiated into conducting strands.

(e) The exoscopic pattern of embryogeny in *Psilotum* has more in common with *Anthoceros* than the rest of pteridophytes.

GEOLOGICAL AND FOSSIL HISTORY OF PTERIDOPHYTES

The geologists have divided the earth's history into five geological eras namely, 1. Archeozoic, 2. Proterozoid, 3. Paleozoic, 4. Mesozoic and 5. Cenozoic. The eras have been further divided into periods and period into epochs. The archeozoic is the oldest era and its duration was 550,000,000 ears. Similarly the durations of proterozoic, paleozoic, mesozoic and cenozoic were 900,000,000; 368,000,000; 125,000,000 and 60,000,000 years respectively. Ihe oldest rocks of the earth's crust are about 2003 million years old.

The pteridophytes first appeared in the Silurian period. They flourished well in between Devonian and Upper carboniferous period of the Paleozoic era. Members of Lycopsida and Sphenopsida constituted the dominant flora during carboniferous period (Fig. 75). Thus, late Paleozoic era can be considered as the "Age of *Pteridophytes*".

SELECTED QUESTIONS

ALGAE

Cyanophyceae

1. Write the salient features of cyanophyceae. Describe its phylogeny and interrelationship with other algae.
2. Describe the cell structure of Myxophyceae.
3. Describe the structure and reproduction in *Nostoc*, *Scytonema* and *Oscillatoria.*
4. What are heterocysts ? How do they originate. Discuss its role in nitrogen fixation.

Chlorophyceae

1. Write the range of vegetative body in Chlorophyceae.
2. Write a note on the classification of chlorophyceae and their important characters.
3. Give an account of *Volvox.* Compare it with *Chlamydomonas.*
4. Describe the life history of *Oedogonium* with special reference to the alternation of generation.
5. Give an account of *Chara* and its relationship with other members of algae.
6. Describe the vegetative structure and mode of reproduction in *Vaucheria.*
7. Write short notes on the following (a) Globule (b) Nucule (c) dwarf male (d) Macrandrous (e) Synzoospores (f) Androspores.
8. What do you mean by isogamy, anisogamy and oogamy. Discuss it with the help of *Chlamydomonas.*
9. Describe different types of asexual and sexual modes of reproduction in Chlorophyceae.

Chrysophyceae — Bacillariophyceae

1. Describe the general features and cell division of diátoms.
2. Give an account of the modes of reproduction in diatoms.
3. Write structure and reproduction in *Botrydium.* Discuss its relationship.

Phaeophyceae

1. Write the salient features of Phaeophyceae and its classification.
2. What do you understand by isomorphic alternation of generation ? Give an account of various types of life cycle
3. Describe the life history of *Ectocarpus* or *Sargassum.*
4. Give an illustrated account of vegetative structure of *Sargassum* and post fertilization changes in it.
5. Describe the life history of *Laminaria* or *Fucus.*
6. Write a comparative account of life cycle in *Laminaria* and *Fucus.*

Rhodophyceae

1. Describe briefly the general characters of class Rhodophyceae. Give an account of its classification.
2. Discuss the life history of *Batrachospermum.*
3. Give an comparative account of sexual reproduction in *Batrachospermum* and *Polysiphonia.*
4. Describe the structure and reproduction in *Polysiphonia.*
5. Write notes on the following (a) Tetraspores (b) Cystocarp (c) Chantransia stage (d) Carposporophyte (e) Gonimoblast filaments (f) Trichogyne.

Algae — General

1. Describe various types of sexual and asexual reproduction in algae studied by you.
2. Write the economic importance of algae.
3. What do you mean by thallophyta. Characterise the division thallophyta.
4. Describe classification of Algae.
5. Write the modes of reproduction in algae studied by you.
6. Describe in brief about the ecological importance of Algae.
7. Give an illustrated account of thallus organization in Algae.
8. Discuss the evolution of sex in algae.
9. Describe the types of life cycles found in algae
10. Give an account of characteristic features of different classes of algae.

FUNGI

Phycomycetes

1. Describe in brief the recent views on the classification of fungi studied by you and mention diagnostic features of various classes.
2. With the help of lebelled sketches describe the life cycle of *Synchytrium endobiotium.* What disease is caused by it ?
3. What is diplanetism ? Describe the structure and reproduction in *Saprolegnia.*
4. With the help of suitable diagrams describe the life history of *Pythium.*
5. Give the name and symptom of disease caused by *Albugo*. Describe the life cycle of it.
6. Describe the structure and reproduction in *Phytophthora*. Give the symptom of the disease caused by it.

Ascomycetes

7. Give an account of structure and reproduction in *Aspergillus*. What light does it throw on the degeneration of sex organs in Ascomycetes.
8. What is ascus ? Describe the process of ascospore formation in *Penicillium.*
9. Describe the structure and reproduction in Penicillium.
10. What do you mean by Powdery mildews ? Describe the structure and reproduction in *Erysiphe.*
11. Describe the formation of Sclerotium in *Claviceps* and also comment upon reproduction and Sphacelial stage in this fungus.
12. Give an illustrated account of morphology and reproduction in *Peziza.*

Basidiomycetes

13. What is 'Smut' ? How "loose smut" can be distinguished from "covered smut" ?

14. With the help of suitable sketches give an account of life history of *Ustilago.*
15. What do you mean by heteroecious and macrocyclic rust ? Describe the formation of aecidium in *Puccinia.*
16. Describe various types of spores formation in *Puccinia graminis*. Mention its significance in its life cycle.
17. Which part of the life cycle of *Puccinia graminis* occurs on Berbery. Describe the spores found on this host.

Deuteromycetes

18. What are fungi imperfectii. Mention their salient features and classification.

Lichens

19. What are lichens? Describe their structure and modes of reproduction.
20. Describe the classification of lichens. Also mention its economic importance.

Baceteria

21. Write in detail the structure of a typical bacterial cell.
22. Bacteria are our friends as well as foes. Discuss it.
23. Describe the role of bacteria in nitrogen fixation.

Viruses

24. Describe the nature of virus. Write the mode of its multiplication.
25. What are viruses? Give the structure of TMV (Tobaco Mosaic Virus). What role does it play in modern genetics.

General

26. What do you mean by heterothalism ? How would you differentiate between homothallic and heterothallic fungi.
27. What do you understand by parasexuality ? How does it differ from the sexual cycle ?
28. Describe in brief the economic importance of fungi.

BRYOPHYTA

Riccia

1. Describe the development and structure of sporophyte of *Riccia.*
2. Describe the mode of vegetative and sexual reproduction in *Riccia.*
3. Write an illustrated account of thallus of *Riccia.* How does it differs from that of *Marchantia.*

Marchantia

1. Give an illustrated account of male and female receptacles of *Marchantia.*
2. How will you differentiate between antheridiophore and archegoniophore of *Marchantia.*
3. With the help of labelled diagramme describe the structure of gemma and gemma cup. What is its significance.
4. Describe the sporophyte of *Marchantia* and role of elaters.

Cyathodium

1. Write the salient features of Cyathodium. How does it differs from *Marchantia* ?
2. Give an illustrated account of anatomy of thallus of *Cyathodium*. Describe the mode of reproduction in it.

Pellia/Porella

1. Give an illustrated account of life history of *Pellia/Porella.*
2. Describe the sporophyte of *Pellia* and compare it with that of *Marchantia.*
3. Write vegetative structures of *Pellia* and compare it with that of *Marchantia* and *Riccia.*

Anthoceros

1. Write in brief the diagnostic characters and affinites of *Anthoceros.*
2. Discuss the inter relationship of *Anthoceros* with Algae, Pteridophytes and other members of Bryophytes studied by you.
3. What are horn worts ? Describe the life cycle of *Anthoceros.*
4. Describe the structure of sporophyte of *Anthoceros* and mode of dispersal of spores.
5. "*Anthoceros* examplifies remarkable association of a simple gametophyte with highly specialised advanced sporophyte''. Discuss it.

Notothylas

1. Give an illustrated account of thallus of *Notothylas* and compare it with that of *Anthoceros.*
2. Write a comparative account of sporophyte of *Notothylas* and *Anthoceros.*
3. Describe the structure of sex organs in *Notothylas* and mode of reproduction in it.
4. Write in brief the systematic position, distribution and diagnostic characters of *Notothylas.*

Sphagnum

1. Write the systematic position, salient features and economic importance of *Sphagnum.*
2. Give an account of the structure of sporophyte of *Sphagnum.* On what ground *Sphagnum* is regarded as a synthetic type ?
3. Discuss the relationship of *Sphagnum* with other members of Bryophytes.
4. Describe the vegetative structure and reproduction in *Sphagnum.*

Pogonatum

1. Give in brief the systematic position, distribution and diagnostic characters of *Pogonatum.*
2. With the help of suitable diagrammes give an account of the structure of Sporophyte of *Pogonatum* and explain the mechanism of dispersal of spores.
3. Describe the structure of gametophyte of *Pogonatum.*
4. Discuss the life cycle in *Pogonatum.*

General

1. Describe briefly the general characters & economic importance of Bryophytes.
2. Write the different views regarding the origin, ev tion and relationship of Bryophytes.
3. Discuss the interrelationship of Bryophytes with Pteridophytes and Algae.
4. Describe in brief the general features of different classes of Bryophytes.
5. What is an archesporium? How does it originate and what does it give rise in the Bryophytes

studied by you?

6. What is an endothecium? How does it originate and what does it give rise in different members of Bryophytes studied by you?
7. Discuss the progressive sterilization of sporogenous tissue in Bryophytes studied by you.
8. Describe the biological and economic importance of Bryophytes.
9. Give an account of vegetative methods of reproduction in Bryophytes.
10. Describe the different modes of spore dispersal in Bryophytes.
11. How Bryophytes have adapted to land habit?
12. How Bryophytes are able to withstand long period of drought?
13. Why mosses remained small and inconspicuous?
14. Describe the photosynthetic tissue in Bryophytes.

PTERIDOPHYTA

Psilotum

1. Describe the salient features of *Psilotum.* Where are they found in India ? How does it help in evolutionary studies.
2. Write the anatomical structure of stem of *Psilotum.*
3. What is synangium ? Write the structure of synangium.
4. Describe the gametophyte of *Psilotum.*
5. Discuss the primitive features of *Psilotum.*

Lycopodium

1. What do you mean by Club mosses ? Describe in brief the systematic position distinguishing characters and economic importance of *Lycopodium.*
2. Write anatomical structures found in stem of *Lycopodium.*
3. Describe the various types of gametophyte found in different species of *Lycopodium.*
4. Describe the prothalli of *Lycopodium*'.
5. How sporangia are born upon the *Lycopodium* plant ?
6. Describe the structure of the strobilus of *Lycopodium.*

Selaginella

1. Describe the structure of ligule of *Selaginella.*
   What evidences are there that the Rhizophores in *Selaginella* are stem like organs.
2. With the help of labelled diagrams, describe the chief peculiarities of the stelar structure in stems of *Selaginella.*
3. What is heterospory ? Explain its significance.
4. How *Selaginella* approaches the seed habit except that there is no formation of seed.
5. Describe the female gametophytes, process of fertilization and formation of embryo in *Selaginella.*
6. Discuss briefly the distribution, systematic position distinguishing features and economic importance of *Selaginella.*

Equisetum

1. What do you mean by Horse tail ? Describe in brief the systematic position, distribution, distin-

guising characters and economic importance of *Equisetum*.
2. Give an illustrated acount of anatomy of internode of aerial shoot of *Equisetum* and discuss the features of ecological interest.
3. Describe the structure of cone of *Equisetum* and write the development of spores produced in it.
4. Give an acount of structure and development of prothallus of *Equisetum*.
5. Describe the structure and development of gametophyte in *Equisetum*.

Ophioglossum

1. What do you mean by "Adder's tongue fern" ? Give in brief the systematic position, distribution and salient features of *Ophioglossum*.
2. Discuss the morphological nature of spike of *Ophioglossum*.
3. Write the anatomy of stem and root of Ophioglossum.
4. Describe the gametophyte of *Ophioglossum*.

Marsilea

1. Describe the systematic position, distribution and external morphology of *Marsilea* plant.
2. Give an illustrated acount of sporocarp of *Marsilea* and discuss in the brief its morphological nature.
3. Describe the internal structure of rhizome of *Marsilea* and compare it with that of petiole.
4. Why the sporocarp of *Marsilea* cannot be considered as seed ?
5. Describe male and female gametophyte of *Marsilea*.
6. Describe the germination of megaspore of *Marsilea* and changes after fertilization, leading to embryo formation.

Salvinia & Azolla

1. Describe the systematic position, distribution and salient features of *Salvinia/Azolla*.
2. Give an illustrated acount of spore producing organs (sporocarp) of *Salvinia/Azolla*.
3. Describe the root anatomy of *Salvinia / Azolla* and compare it with that of rhizome.
4. Write the structure of glochidia and massulae.

General

1. Describe the salient features and affinity of Pteridophytes.
2. Give a brief acount of classification of Pteridophytes.
3. What is stele ? Describe the different types of stele found in Pteridophytes.
4. Describe different views on the evolution of steles in Pteridophytes.

GYMNOSPERMS

Cycas

1. Discuss the anatomy of leaflet of *Cycas* and describe the features of special interest found in it.
2. Write in brief the anatomical structure of stem and root of *Cycas*.
3. Give an account of the megasporophyll and the ovule of *Cycas*.
4. Describe the structure of male and female gametophyte of *Cycas* and the changes brought about in it after fertilization.
5. Discuss "*Cycas* is a living fossil".

6. Describe the development of embryo in *Cycas*. Why in most gardens of your locality *Cycas* do not bear seeds.

Pinus

1. Describe in brief the systematic position, geographical distribution, external morphology and economic importance of *Pinus*.
2. Write the anatomical features of *Pinus* needle and discuss the significance of the transfusion tissue.
3. Give an illustrated account of the internal structure of *Pinus* stem.
4. Discuss in brief the morphological nature of the ovuliferous scale in *Pinus*.
6. Give an account of the development of embryo and seed of *Pinus*.

Taxus

1. Describe the anatomy of stem of *Taxus* and comapre it with what of *Pinus*.
2. Write in brief the morphological nature of aril or cupule of *Taxus*.
3. Describe the structure of male and female gametophyte in *Taxus*.
4. Discuss the process of embryogeny in *Taxus*.
5. Write the systematic position, external features and economic importance of *Taxus*.
7. Describe the primitive features of seed of *Taxus*.

Gnetum

1. Write a brief monograph on *Gnetum* and its affinities with other groups.
2. Describe the wood structure found in the stem of *Gnetum*.
3. Give a brief account of leaf and root anatomy of *Gnetum*.
4. Describe the morphological features found in the flowers of *Gnetum*.
5. How far *Gnetum* resembles with angiosperm ? Discuss it.
6. Describe the process of embryo and seed formation in *Gnetum*.

General

1. Describe in brief the salient features of Gymnosperms and its classification.
2. How Gymnosperms differs from Pteridophytes ? Also add a brief note on its economic importance.

FOSSILS AND PALEOBOTANY

1. What do you mean by fossils ? How it is formed.
2. Describe the importance of fossils and its time–scale.
3. Discuss the sporophyte of *Rhynia*.
4. What are ancient Souring rushes. Describe anatomical structure of *Calamites* stem.
5. Describe the fructifications of *Calamites* and its relationship with *Equisetum*.
6. What is pteridosperms ? Describe the stem of *Bennettites*.
7. Write the reproductive structures of Bennettites.
8. Give the internal structure of stem of *Lyginodendron*.
9. Write the seed structure of *Lygenopteris lomaxi*.
10. Describe *Willaiamsonia*.

INDEX

ALGAE

'A'

Air bladder 67
Akinetes 6
Amylase stars 42
Anabaena 21
Androspore 35
Anisogamy 28
Antheridium 35
Antheridial filament 43
Antherozoid 31
Aplanospore 40
Autogamy 6
Autospore 6
Auxospore 51

'B'

Bacillariophyceae 50
Bangiales 69
Bangioidae 69
Batrachospermum 69, 88
Benthos 3
Biflagellate 26
Biadulphia 50
Blepheroplast 26
Botrydium 47
Botrydiaceae 47

'C'

Calyptra 18
Cap 35
Cap cells 35
Carpogonium 69, 73, 90
Carposporangia 73
Carpospore 73, 87
Carposporophyte 76
Central nodules 50
Centric 50
Centrales51
Centroplasm 13, 14
Ceramiales 69
Chaetophorales 25
Chantransia 72
Chara 42
Chareles 33, 42, 53
Charophyceae 24, 33, 42
Charophyte 42
Chlamydomonas 26
Chlamydomonaceae 26
Chlorococcales 25
Chlorophyceae 24
Chlorophyta 24
Chromatic adaptation 14
Chromatophore 54
Chromoplasm 2, 14
Chrysophyta 47
Cladophora 32
Cladophoraceae 32
Cladophorales 32
Clump formation 66
Coenobium 30
Coenocyst 48
Coenocytic 39
Coenozoospores 39
Colonial 4
Colony 30
Conceptacles 68, 85
Corona 43
Conjugales 25
Cortical threads 70
Corticating cells 42
Crown 43
Crytoblast 67
Cryptogamia 3
Cryptonemiales 69
Cryptophytes 3
Cutlerials 54
Cyanophyceae 13
Cyanophyta 13
Cyclosporae 54
Cystocarp 75
Cysts 40

'D'

Dasycladiales 25
Dendroid 4
Desmarestiales 54
Diatomaceous earth 53
Diatomin 4.
Diatoms 50,, 51, 53
Diatomite 53
Dictyotales 54
Dioecious 36
Diplobiontic 354
Dwarf male 37

'E'

Ectocarpaceae 63
Ectocarpales 54, 63
Ectocarpus 63, 64
E. siliculosus 65
Endophytes 3
Endospores 6, 22
Endozoids 3
Epilethic 3
Epipelic 3
Epiphytic 3
Epitheca 50
Epizoic 3, 80
Eukaryotic 4, 33
Exospores 6, 22
Eye spot 26

'F'

Felty mass 21
Filament 2, 14
Flagella 4
Flavacene 5
Florideae 69
Floridean starch 2, 69
Frog spawn 70
Frond 60, 67

Frustule 58, 65
Fucales 59, 84
Fucoxanthin 54
Fucus 59
Fuller earth 53

'G'

Gelidiales 69
Germling 34
Gigartinales 69
Girdle 50
Gloecocapsa 17
G. atrata 18
Glomerule 70
Gonidia 30
Gonimoblast initial 72
Gulf weed 67
Gynandrosporous 37

'H'

Haplobiontic 69, 354
Haplodiplobiontic 69
Heterocyst 6, 21, 22
Heterogamy 6
Heterogeneratae 54
Hetermorphic 54, 56
Hetersiphonales 47
Heterothallic 28
Heterotrichous 54.
Hold fast 3, 47
Hologamy 7
Homothallic 28
Hormospore 15, 32
Hormogonium 15
Hypnospore 6, 37, 52
Hypotheca 50

'I'

Idiondrosporous 37
Incipient nucleus 14
Isogeneratae 54
Isomorphic 44, 54, 56

'L'

Lamella 14
Laminaria 54
Laminariales 56
Laminarin 54
Leucosin 47
Licmophore 50
Lithophytes 54
Littoral 54

'M'

Mannitol 54
Macrandrous 37
Macrogametes 6
Manubrium 43
Medulla 57, 67
Melosira 52
Microgametes 6
Monoecious 36
Monosiphonous 64
Monospore 69
Myxophyceae 13

'N'

Nanandrium 37
Nanandrous 37, 46
Nannocysts 15
Nemalionales 69
Neuromotor 26
Nitella 46
Nodules 6
Nostoc 19, 28

'O'

Oedogoniales 35
Oedogonium 35
Oogamy 6, 38
Oogonium 38
Oscillatoria 18
Ostiole 67

'P'

Palmella stage 27
Palmelloid 4
Paradesmose 26
Paramylum 4
Parasites 3
Parthenogenesis 29
Pennales 51
Phaeophyceae 54
Phaeophyta 54
Phialopore 30
Phycocyanin 5
Phycoerythrin 5
Pinnate 50
Plakea 30
Pleurocladia 54
Plurilocular 65
Polar nodules 22, 50
Polysiphonia 73
Polysiphonous 64
Primary capitulam 43
Primordial utricle 54
Prokaryotic 14
Propagule 55
Protonema 6
Pyrenoids 4

'R'

Raphe 50
Receptacle 67
Receptive spot 36
Rejuvenscent cell 51
Rhizocysts 48
Rhizoplast 26
Rhizopodial 4
Rhodomeniales 69
Rhodophyceae 69
Rhodophyta 69
Rivularia 22
Rivulariaceae 22
Rivulariales 22

'S'

Saprophytes 3
Sargassum 68
Scytonema 20
Scytonemataceae 20
Schizogoniales 24
Secondary capitulum 43
Setae 70
Shield cell 43
Siphonales 24
Siphonocladiales 25
Sirenine 65
Spermatia 76
Spermatangium 76
Sphacelaria 55
Sphacelariales 54
Sporochnales 54
Statospore 52
Stigma 4, 36
Stipe 67
Stolon 6
Stratified sheath 17
Suffultory cell 37
Swarmer 48, 61
Symbionts 3
Synzoospore 40

'T'

Tetraporales 24
Tetraspore 69
Thallophyta 3
Thallus 3

Thermophytes 4
Tilopteridales 54
Tinsel 4
Trichogyne 14
Trichome 71
Trichothallic growth 64
Trichotomous 33
Tubers 6

'U'

Ulotrichales 25
Ulvales 24
Unilocular 64, 69

'V'

Vaucheria 39
Vaucheriaceae 39
Volvocales 30, 33
Volvox 30

'W'

Water bloom 16

'X'

Xanthophyceae 47

'Z'

Zoospores 6, 37

FUNGI

'A'

Actinomycetous fungus 358
Acervulus 129
Aecial stage 126
Aecidiospore 127
Aecidium 127
Aerobic 136
Aflatoxin 108
Agaricales 121
Agaricus 80
AIDS (Acqutred Immune Deficiency Syndrome) 147
Albugo 97
Allomyces 83
Alternaria 130
Amphigynous 96
Amphitrichous 138
Anastomosis 4, 357
Anaerobic 136
Ancysistales 85
Androgynous 92
Anisogamy 5
Antheridium 88
Anthrax 142
Apiam Spore 6
Aplanospore 80
Apothecium 104
Appresorium 132
Aquatic 6
Archicarp 116
Archimycetes 81
Arthrospores 120
Asci 26
Ascobolus 102
Ascocarp 104
Ascogenous hyphae 102
Ascogonium 102
Ascolichens 133
Ascomycetes 81
Ascospore 80
Ascus mother cell 103
Aspergillosis 56, 358
Aspergillus 105, 358
Athlet's foot 130
Atrichous 138
Autobasidiomycetes 81
Autotrophic 46

'B'

Bacillus 138
Bacteria 136
Bacteriochlorophyll 136
Bacteriophage 145
Bacterioviridin 139
Barbery 125
Basidial stage 125
Basidiolichens 133
Basidiocarp 119
Basidiomycetes 81
Basidiospore 80
Basidium 40, 125
Basipetal 112
Beverage 108
Bioluminescence 140
Biplanetic 83
Bipolar 122
Bird's nest fungi 119
Bisby 83
Black leg of cattle 142
Black rot 142
Black wart 85
Blastocladiales 84
Blastospore 129
Blue mould 109
Botrytis 79
Brachet fungi 119
Brachymeiosis 104
Brown rust 128
Budding 80
Bullers's phenomenon 120
Bunchy top 147

'C'

Carpogonium 135
Capsid 144
Capsomere 144
Capsule 136
Cephalodia 134
Chlamydospore 80
Chitin 79
Chytridiales 84
Citric acid 108
Citrus canker 142
Clamp connection 119
Claviceps 114
Cleistothecium 104
Coccus 138
Coenocentrum 100
Coenocytic hypha 79
Coenogametangia 43
Collar root 91
Colletotrichum 77
Conidiophore 99
Conidium 80
Contagium vivum 136
Covered smut 121
Crook cell 103
Crozier 103
Crustose lichen 133
Cyanophage 145
Cyphellae 134
Cystidia 120
Cystopus 97

'D'

Damping off 91
Degeneration of sex 356, 357
Dematiaceae 130
Deuteromycetes 129
Deoxyvira 146
Dhobi itch 358
Diaminopimellic acid 136
Dicaryotic 81
Diclinous 92
Dictyospore 129
Dikaryon 102

Dikaryotisation 120
Diplanetism 88
Diplodization 120
Diplophase 120
Diptheria 358
Discomycetes 81
Disease of Pigeon Pea 52
Displacement cell 126
Disjunctor cell 99

'E'

Ear drums 358
Early blight 130
Ellipsoidal 116
Endoparasite 85
Epibasidium 125
Epispore 89
Ergot 114
Ergotism 115
Erysiphae 111
Euascomycetes 105
Eurotium 105
Exobasidiales 121
Exospore 89

'F'

Facultative parasite 79
Fertilization tube 100
Fission 80
Flavicin 108
Flexus hyphae 126
Foliose lichens 133
Foot cell 106
Foot rot 91
Fragmentation 80
Fruticose lichens 133
Fungi 79
Fungi imperfecti 81
Fungus 79

'G'

Gallic acid 110
Gametangial contact 80
Gametangial copulation 80
Gangerine 115
Gelly fungi 119
Gentisyl alcohol 110
Genophore 137
Ghost light 140
Glucosamine 79
Glutamic acid 108
Gonidial layer 134
Gram negative 136
Gram positive 136
Grassy root 147
Green mould 109
Gynandromictic 356

'H'

Haplophase 120
Haplodization 357
Haustoria 125
Heart rot 56
Helicospore 129
Hemiascomycetes 105
Heterobasidiomycetes 121
Heteroecious 124
Heterophyte 98
Hetero karyosis 357
Hettero karyotic 357
Heterothallism 356
Holocarpic 85
Hologamy 102
Homobasidiomycetes 121
Homothallic 84
Honeydew stage 114
Hook 103
Hormocysts 134
Hydrophobia 147
Hymenium 104
Hyperplasia 85
Hypertrophy 124
Hypha 79
Hypocreaceae 114
Hypocreales 114

'I'

Influenza 358
Intercalary cell 127
Isidia 134
Isogamy 81

'K'

Karyogamy 97, 357

'L'

Late blight 94
Leaf curl 147
Leptomiales 85
Lichens 82
Lipopolysaccharides 136
Lipoprotein 136
Lobules 134
Loose smut 121
Lophotrichous 138
Lycoperdales 121
Lysozome 146

'M'

Macroconidia 129
Macrocyclic 124
Medulla 134
Melampsora 127
Melanconiaceae 131
Melanconiales 130
Mesosome 137
Mesosynchytrium 85
Metulae 109
Microbes 136
Microconidia 129
Mitotic crossing over 357
Moniliales 129
Monoblepharidales 85
Monokaryotic 119
Monoplanetic 83
Monotrichous 138
Mucopeptide 136
Mucor 80
Muramic acid 136
Mushrooms 115
Mycelia sterilla 130
Mycelium 79
Mycology 81
Mycophycophyta 133
Mycoprotein 136
Mycorhiza 79
Mycorrhizative 83
Mycoses 105

'N'

Nematodes 130
Nidulariales 121
Nucleoid 136

'O'

Obligate ectoparasite 111
Obligate parasite 79
Oidia 40, 129
Oidium 80
Oogamous 92
Oogamy 357
Oomycetes 81
Ooplasm 92
Oosphere 89
Oospore 89
Orcein 135
Ostiole 125

'P'

Papilla 91

Parmellia 135
Paralysis 116
Paraphyses 115
Parasexuality 129, 356
Parasites 79
Peltigera 135
Penicillin 110
Penicillium 109
Penicillosis 110
Penultimate cell 103
Perforated septa 129
Peronosporales 85
Peridium 108
Periplasm 97
Perithecium 104
Peritrichous 138
Permease 136
Pestalsia 79
Peziza 116
Phallales 121
Phialids 107
Phialospore 129
Phospholipid 136
Phycomycetes 81
Phytophthora 94
Planozygote 84
Plasmogamy 84
Plectomycetes 81
Pneumonia 358
Polyplanetic 83
Polymorphic 124
Polyporales 121
Polysaccharides 136
Polyspore 129
Powdery mildews 111
Primary mycelium 119
Primary zoospores 79
Prokaryote 137
Promycelium 123
Prosorus 85
Protobasidiomycetes 81
Protomycetales 85
Pseudocyphallae 134
Puccinia 123
Pucciniaceae 123
Pulvic acid 134
Pustules 125
Putrefaction 140
Pycnial stage 126
Pycniospores 126
Pycnium 125
Pycnosynchytrium 85
Pyrenomucetes 81
Pythium 91

'R'

Receptive hyphae 126
Red rot 131
Resting sporangium 86
Rhizophidium 81
*Rhizopus*79
Riboflavin 108
Ribovira 146
Rind 134
Ring rot 142
Ringworm 130
Rocella tinctoria 135
Retting of flex 142
Rusts 119
Rust fungi 124

'S'

Sac fungi 102
Saprolegnia 87
Saprophytes 91
Sarcina 138
Schizomycetes 136
Sclerodermatales 121
Sclerotium 80
Scoleospores 129
Secondary basidiospore 123
Secondary mycelium 119
Secondary zoospore 88
Sexduction 141
Sexual gametangia 10
Small pox 147
Smuts 119
Somatogamy 81
Soredia 134
Sorus 87
Spermatium 104
Spermatization 81
Spermatiophore 104
Spermogonia 125
Spheropsidales 129
Spikes 144
Spirillum 138
Sporangiophore 83
Spores 80
Sporidium 123
Sporulation 122
Sprout cell 45
Stalk cell 34
Stautospores 129
Sterigmata 107
Stink horns 119
Streaks 125
Stroma 112
Subterminal cell 34
Summer sporangium 85
Summer spore 85
Symbiosis 79
Synchytrium 85

'T'

Tanning of leather 142
Teichoic acid 136
Teleutospore 122
Teleutosori 125
Telia 125
Telial stage 125
Thallospore 129
Thermophilic 136
Tikka disease 130
Tinsel 83
Tobacco Mosaic Virus 143
Toxin 108
Transformation 141
Transduction 141
Tremellales 121
Trichogyne 102
Trinomial nomenclature 124
Tuber rot 91, 94
Typhoid 358

'U'

Uredial stage 124
Uredinales 123
Uredinium 124
Uredosorus 124
Uredospores 124
Ustilaginales 121
Ustilago 358

'V'

Vaccines 147
Vesicle 85
Vibrio 138
Vira 146
Virion 144
Viruses 143

'W'

Wart disease 85
Water droplet method 120
Water mould 87
Whiplash 83
White rust 98
Woroninella 85

'Y'

Yeast 79
Yellow stain 110
Yellow vein mosaic 147

'Z'

Zoospores 80
Zygospore 80
Zygomycetes 81

BRYOPHYTA

'A'

Acotyledonae 151
Acropetal succession 175
Adventitious buds 1169
Air chamber 1154
Air gun mechanism 361
Amphithecium 156
Amphigastria 172
Andreales 152
Androcyte 156
Androgonial cell 169
Androgynous receptacle 161
Annulus 193
Antheridia 156
Antheridial 156
Antheridiophore 161
Antherozoid 156
Anthoceros 178
Anthocerotales 178
Anthocerotopsida 178
Antical-lobe 172
Archegonia 156
Archegonial cell 169
Archegoniophore 161
Archesporium 171
Assimilatory filaments 166

'B'

Basal 196
Begleiter cells 197
Bog moss 188
Bryales 152
Bryophyta 151
Bryopsida 188
Bulbil 203

'C'

Calyptra 162
Calobryales 153
Capillary cells 189
Capsule 162
Censor menclanism 361
Chlorenchymatous 204
Colloidal 195
Columella 181
Coma 189
cupules 159
Cyathodium 165

'D'

Deuter cells 197
Dichotomously 153
Dioecious 155
Dorsiventral 153

'E'

Egg 169
Elaterophores 171
Elaters 163
Endophytic 179
Endosporium 158
Endothecium 157
Endothelial 183
Epibasal 162
Epiphragm 361
Exosporium 158
Explosive mechanism, 360

'F'

Follicular 186
Follicular dehiscence 360
Foot 151
Funaria 202
Funariaceae 202
Funariales 202
Fusiform 166

'G'

Gametophore 188
Gametophyte 158
Gemma cup 159
Gemmae 159

'H'

Hadrome 189
Haustorium 193
Hepaticopsida 153
Heterologous 155
Heteromorphic 151
Heterothallic 156
Homosporous 151
Homothallic 155
Horn worts 186
Hyaline cells 189
Hyalodermis 189
Hydroid cells 197
Hygrophillous 165
Hygroscopic 163
Hypobasal 162

'I'

Incubous 173
Innovation 190
Involucoral leaf 204
Involucre 166

'J'

Jacket 157
Jungermanniales 152
Juvenile stage 188

'L'

Lamellae 196
Land scape 196
Leptoid tissue 127
Leptome 198
Lobules 172

'M'

Madotheca 172
Marchantia 159
Marchantiaceae 159
Marchantiales 159
Medulla 190
Meiospore 151
Meristematic 178
Meristematic zone 181
Mesoporium 158
Metzgeriales 153
Monoecious 155
Muricate 166
Musci 152
Monoecism 162

'N'

Neck 156
Neck canal cell 156
Non-columellate 185
Notothylaceae 183
Notothylas 183
Nurse cell 157

'O'

Octant 162

Oogamous 173
Operculum 193

'P'

Parenchymatous 179
Peat moss 188
Pellia 167
Pelliaceae 167
Perichaetium 161
Periclinal 157
Perigonial leaves 203
Perigynium 162
Peristome 201
Phosphorescent 166
Photosynthetic filament 161
Phyllogeny 362
Phylloid 188
Pogonatum 196
Polyhedral parenchyma 168
Polytrichaceae 196
Polytrichales 196
Porella 172
Postical-lobe 172
Proembryo 181
Protandrous 184
Protonema 203
Pseudoperianth 162
Pseudopodium 166
Pseudoelaters 181
Pyrenoid 179

'Q'

Quacking bogs 196
Quadrant 181

'R'

Receptacle 166
Retort 190
Rhizoidal cell 160
Rhizoids 153
Riccia 153

'S'

Scales 153
Sclereids 198
Scleroids 197
Seta 157
Soil conservation 360
Sphaerocarpales 153
Sphagnales 188
Sphagnidae 188
Sphagnum 188
Spong 189
Sporogenous 157
Sporogonium 191
Sporophyte 156
Stellate disc 161
Sterile strand 171
Sterilisation 363
Stomata 181
Suspensor 170
Synthetic type 183

'T'

Takakiales 153
Targionaceae 165
Trispiral 166
Tuberculate 154
Tubers 155
Turf moss 188
Twisted neck 191
Tympanum 201

'V'

Vaginula 193
Vegetative reproduction 154
Velamen 189
Venter 156
Venter canal cell 156

'W'

Whiplash 151

'Z'

Zygote 156

PTERIDOPHYTA

'A'

Actinostele 365
Actinostelic 215
Adder's tongue fern 249
Aerenchyma 257
Alveolar bodies 266
Amphiphloic siphonostele 365
Amphiphloic solenostele 237, 365
Androcytes 234, 262
Androgonial cell 262
Annular tracheids 222
Antheridia 218
Apogamy 368
Apospory 368
Archegonia 218, 2326
Archeozoic 370
Arthrophyta 240
Articulatae 240
Atactostele 367
Àzolla 267

'B'

Bulbil 222
Botrychium 253
Bundle sheath 252

'C'

Carboinferous 240, 340
Carinal canal 243
Casparian strips 222
Cenozoic 370
Centroxylic 230
Circinnate vernatian 210
Club moss 220
Collateral 252
Cummussural bundle 260
Cones 209
Cotyledons 239
Cretaceous 249
Cycadofilicales 211

'D'

Devonian 240, 370
Diarch 221
Dictyostele 367
Diphragm 236

'E'

Ectophloic solenostele 365
Elaters 245
Endarch 243, 252
Endophytic fungus 217
Endospore 235
Endosporic 238
Endosporium 253
Epibasal 247
Epiphytes 214, 220, 229
Epoxide 249
Equisetales 240, 341
Equisetophyta 240
Equisetum 241
Eusporangiate 249
Eustele 367
Exarch 215
Exodermis 243
Exoscopic 255
Exospore 235
Exosporium 253

Extrastelar origin 265

'F'

Fertile appendages 215
Fertile spike 250
Filicinae 267
Fossils 219
Frond 252
Furrows 243

'G'

Gelatinous ring 260
Gelantinous tissue 225, 260
Gemmae 216, 222
Glochidia 269

'H'

Haplostele 365
Helminthostachys 253
Heterophyllum 229
Heterosporous 209
Heterothallic 245
Heterospory 238
Homeophyllum 229
Homologus 260
Homosporous 217
Homothallic 217, 245
Hormogones 268
Horsetail 240
Hydrophytes 210
Hypobasal 247

'I'

Indusium 260
Integuments 239
Intraslelar origin 235

'J'

Jurassic 249

'L'

Lamina 252
Leaf gaps 219
Leaflets 256
Leptosporangiate 249, 265
Lenticular cell 269
Leutin 249
Ligulate 221
Ligule 230
Lycopodiaceae 219
Lycopodiales 219
Lycopodium 220
Lycopsida 219

'M'

Marsilea 255
Marsileaceae 255
Marsileales 255
Massula 266
Medulated protostele 240
Megagametophyte 235
Megasporangium 235
Megaspores 235
Megasporophylls 234
Meristele 251
Mesozoic 370
Microgametophyte 235
Microphyllous 219
Microsporangium 235
Microsporophylls 234
Microspores 234
Mixed plectoslele 265
Mixed protostele 365
Monarch 221
Monoecious 217
Mycorrhizal fungus 215
Mycorrhizal root 250

'N'

Neck canal cell 226
Nutritive cell 262

'O'

Opercular cell 218
Ophiolossum 249
Organ sui generis 229

'P'

Palaeozoic era 219, 370
Palisade 252
Papilla 262
Parthenogenesis 368
Pedicel 259
Peduncle 259
Peltate disc 245
Perispore 245
Petiole 256
Placental bundle 260
Plasmodial mass 217
Plasmodium 269
Plectosteleic 222
Polycyclic stele 367
Polystelic 367
Prophylls 228
Proterozoic 370
Prothallus 217, 245
Prothallial cells 235
Protocorm 228
Protophylls 228
Protostele 221
Psilotopsida 211
Psilotum 2
Pteridophyta 209
Pteridosperms 211
Pteropsida 249

'R'

Rachis 256
Raphe 260
Resurrection plants 368
Rhizome 241
Rhizophore 229
Rhodoxanthin 249
Ridge 243
Root tuberacles 222

'S'

Salvinia 265
Salviniaceae 265
Salviniales 265
Scouring rushes 240
Selaginella 228
Selaginellaceae 228
Selaginellales 228
Siphonostele 243
Siphonostelic 365, 219
Solenostele 365, 247
Sori 249
Spermatogenous cell 235
Sphenopsida 240
Spiral tracheids 222
Spongy parenchyma 252
Sporangium 216, 223
Sporocarp 259
Sporophylls 218, 223
Stelar system 365
Stelar theory 365
Strobilus 223
Synangium 216

'T'

Tapetal plasmodium 269
Trabeculae 231, 257
Triarch 221
Triassic 249
Tuberacle 259

'V'

Vallecular canal 242

Vascular cryptogams 209
Vegetable brimstone 368
Vegetative buds 216
Venter 218
Ventral canal cell 218
Violaxanthin 245

'X'

Xerophytes 229

GYMNOSPERMS

'A'

Accessory cambium 247, 279
Accessory structure 302
Albumiuous cells 290
Algal zone 248, 280
Amber 298
Anabaena 280
Annual ring 247, 279
Antheridial cell 285
Antherozoids 286
Antiseptic reagent 290
Anatropous ovule 293
Apophysis 293
Archegonia 285
Archegonial chamber 286
Archegonial initial 285
Aril 302
Axial placenta 293
Axillary shoot 293

'B'

Bark 290
Bars of sanio 290
Bennettiales 273
Bicarpellary ovaries 294
Blepharoplast 286
Body cell 286
Bordered pits 290
Bundle sheath 249

'C'

Carpel 302
Cataphylls 289
Caytoniales 275
Central cell 285
Cetrifugal metaxylem 281
Centripetal xylem 247, 279
Circinnate 287
Chilgoza Pine 289
Chlamydospermophyta 274
Collateral 278
Concentric wood 279
Cone 282
Coniferales 289
Coniferophyta 274
Coniferopsida 289
Conjoint 272
Coralloid root 278, 280
Corallorhiza 278
Cordaitales 273
Cork combium 279
Cotyledons 254
Cycadales 273, 274, 277
Cycadeoidales 274
Cycas 277

'D'

Decussate 302
Diarch 280
Dioecious 282
Diploxylic 279, 281
Dwarf shoot 289

'E'

Egg cell 285
Elliptical 304, 307
Embryo 313
Embryo cells 286
Embryogeny 286
Embryosac 284
Endarch 281
Endosperm 314
Ephedrales 274
Ephimeral 295
Epiblema 279
Epigeal 297
Epithelial cells 290
Eusporangiate 292
Excurrent 289
Exine 295
Exodermis 279

'F'

Feeder 313
Female cone 283
Female flower 302
Female gametophyte 295
Foliage leaves 278, 283

'G'

Generative cell 295
Geotropic 280
Ginkgoales 274
Girdle 278
Glossopteridales 275
Gnetaceae 307
Gnetales 307
Gnetopsida 3307
Gnetum 307
Gradate ploidy 313
Gymnosperms 273

'H'

Haustorial part 286
Heterosporous 292
Hypocotyl 313
Hypogeal 287

'I'

Inflorescence 294
Integument 284
Interfascicular cambium 279
Intine 285
Intrafascicular cambium 279

'K'

Kernel 296

'L'

Lanceolate 307
Leathery 278
Living fossil 277
Long shoot 289

'M'

Male cone 283
Male gametophyte 285
Medullary rays 279
Megasporophylls 282
Mesarch 279
Metaxylem 279
Micropyle 284
Microsporangia 283
Microspore mother cell 292
Microsprophylls 282
Monosporic 295
Mucilage canal cell 279
Mucilaginous drop 285
Multifeagillate 286
Multiseriate 309
Mycorrhizal roots 289

'N'

Neck canal cell 285

Needles 289
Non endospermic 304
Nostoc 278
Nucellar beak 284
Nucellus 284

'O'

Oblong 307
Omega 280
Oospore 286
Orthotropous 284
Ovulate strobilus 283
Ovule 284
Ovuliferous scale 302

'P'

Palisade 309
Paripinnate 278
Pavement tissue 312
Peculiar cell 313
Peltate heads 303
Pentoxyleae 274
Pentoxylopsida 274
Penultimate bract 302
Perianth 310
Pericycle 279
Periderm 279
Peripheral disc 303
Perisperm 296
Phellogen 279
Piliferous layer 290
Pinaceae 289
Pinophyta 274
Pinnae 278
Pinus 289
Plumule 287
Pollen chamber 284
Pollen grains 284
Pollen sacs 284
Pollination drops 303
Polyembrony 313
Primary neck cell 285
Proembryo 286
Prophylls 256
Prothallial cell1 286
Prothallus 285
Protopityales 275
Protoxylem 279
Pteridopermae 274

'R'

Rachis 280
Radicle 286
Remnant 279
Resin 290, 298
Resin canals 256, 290
Root caps 300
Rudimentary pollen chamber 314

'S'

Sago 277
Scale leaf 278
Secondary growth 279
Seed 287
Shower of sulphur 293
Sorus 283
Spatulate 312
Spongy parenchyma 309
Sporogenous cell 283
Sporogenous tissue 283
Sporangiophore 303
Stachyosper mac 273
Staminate strobilus 292
Strobilus 282
Sui generis 293
Sunken 282
Suspensor 254
Symbiont 280

'T'

Tangential pressure 279
Tannin cells 279
Tap root 289
Tapetum 283
Taxaceae 300
Taxales 300
Taxopsida 274
Taxus 300
Tent pole 302
Turpentine 290
Testa 287
Tetrarch 279
Tetrasporic 312
Tracheids 282
Transfusion tissue 282
Tube cell 285
Tuberous 278
Tyloses 290

'U'

Ulcers 288

'V'

Vacuole 285
Ventral canal cell 285
Vojnouskyales 274

'W'

Welwitschidae 275
Winged seeds 289
Wings 295

'Z'

Zygote 286

FOSSILS & PALEOBOTANY

'A'

Amber 320
Angiosperms 336
Annularia 329
Archeożoic 319
Arthrodendron 328
Arthropytis 328
Artificial genus 321
Astromyelon 329
Astero[phyllites 329

'B'

Bennettitaceae 333
Bennettitales 333
Bennettites 333

'C'

Calamites 327
Calamitina 327
Calamocarpon 329
Calalodendron 328
Calamostachys 329
Calymatotheca 321
Cambrian 319
Carboniferous 319
Carpon 321
Carpus 321
Cast 320
Cigularia 329
Coenozoic 319
Compaction 320
Compressions 320
Cordaianthus 321
Corytospermum 321
Cretaceous 319
Crossotheca 321
Cupule 340
Cycadeodea 333

Cycadeoidales 342, 333
Cycadeoidaceae 333
Cycadophyta 333, 338
Cycadofilicales 338
Cycas 337

'D'

Dadoxylon 321, 338
Devonian 319
Diatomite 3201

'E'

Eocene 319
Elaters 332
Equisetum 329
Eucalamites 327

'F'

Fern 336
Flowers 334
Fossils 319
Fossilisation 319
Fructifications 329

'G'

Gametophyte 323
Geological time scale 319
Ginkgoales 336
Gnetales 336
Graphite 320

'H'

Heterosporous 332
Homosporous 332

'I'

Impressions 320
Incrustation 320
Infiltration theory 321
Interseminal scales 335

'J'

Jewellery 320
Jurassic 319

'K'

Kaloxylon 329, 339

'L'

Lagenostoma 321
Lepidocarpon 321
Lepidodendron 324
Lepidophyllum 321
Lepidostrobus 321
Lime stones 320
Lobat annulatia 329
Lygenopteridaceae 338
Lygenodendron 321, 338
Lyginopteris 321, 338

'M'

Macrostachya 329
Mesozoic 319
Metaxylem 328
Miocene 319
Mucilage canal 337

'N'

Nomenclature 321

'O'

Oligocene 319
Ordovician 319
Orthotropous 335

'P'

Paleobotany 319
Paleocene 319
Paleostachya 329
Pleistocene 319
Permian 319
Petrifaction 320
Petroleum 320
Pinnularia 329
Pliocene 319
Proterozoic 319
Protoxylem 327
Pteridospermae 333
Ptilophyllum 342
Psilophytopsida 322
Psilophytales 322

'Q'

Quarternary 319

'R'

Recent 319
Replacement theory 321
Rachiopteris 321, 338
Rhizome 322,
Rhynia 322
Rhyniaceae 322
Rhynie chert 322

'S'

Sieve tube 329
Silurian 319
Spermum 321
Sphenopteris 338, 321
Sterocarpus 321
Stoma 321
Stylocalamites 327
Synangia 335

'T'

Tertiary 319

'V'

Vallecular canal 331

'W'

Wielandiella 337
Williamsonia 342
Williamsoniaceae 342

'Z'

Zamia 337